The Psychology of
Human Differences

THE CENTURY PSYCHOLOGY SERIES

Richard M. Elliott, *Editor*

Kenneth MacCorquodale, *Assistant Editor*

LEONA E. TYLER

University of Oregon

The Psychology of
Human Differences

SECOND EDITION

New York

APPLETON-CENTURY-CROFTS, INC.

Preface to the Second Edition

I HAVE HAD the revision of this book on my conscience as well as on my mind for several years. The tremendous amount of new information that has accumulated in the decade since World War II made it a challenging but forbidding job. Because so much needed to be added, changes in organization and emphasis were required; one could not simply add the new wine to the old bottles.

The time seemed to be ripe for a rather thoroughgoing reformulation of what our efforts to study individual differences of all sorts have taught us. What general concepts and principles are beginning to emerge? In what directions is current research moving?

Because there was so much to be covered, the problem of keeping the whole work within reasonable limits gave me some concern. The decisions I made are different in some respects from the ones the earlier edition represents. In the first place, I decided to confine myself to quantitative studies, although the distinction here is an arbitrary one, especially in the personality areas. Secondly, I decided to omit or curtail the sections on statistical methods and assume that the reader was already familiar with the elementary ideas, such as mean, standard deviation, and correlation. I have tried to emphasize only the aspects of these statistical concepts which are essential to the interpretation of research findings. The more complex methods, such as factor analysis, multiple regression, and analysis of variance, have been explained in a more detailed way. The one concept which I have emphasized most strongly is *statistical significance*. The student who grasps the meaning of this explanation can understand most of the research results without knowing much about the methods used in obtaining and analyzing the data.

It was necessary to select from the very large number of published studies on each topic rather than to cite them all. Where several of them point in the same direction I have chosen the most adequate one of the set.

But in instances where some new approach or conclusion has been suggested, sometimes even poorly planned or very tentative studies have been included. Thus I have tried not to omit anything which might throw light on any aspect of a problem.

I have envisaged my readers as intelligent upper-division or graduate students with at least a basic course in general psychology. I hope that not only prospective psychologists but workers in other human-relations fields, such as education, social work, and business administration, may find some of this material useful.

As before, I am indebted to a large number of persons who have helped make this book possible. Acknowledgments to authors and publishers who have granted me permission to use various quotations and illustrations will be found at appropriate places in the text. I should like also to express my gratitude to Mrs. Betty Crosley and Mrs. Helen Talbot, who did much to put the manuscript and bibliography in order. Finally I wish once more to voice my appreciation to my colleagues and students, whose ideas have been a constant source of stimulation to me.

L. E. T.

Contents

CONTENTS

Part Four

FACTORS PRODUCING DIFFERENCES

The Psychology of
Human Differences

PART ONE

The Field of Differential Psychology

CHAPTER 1

Historical Introduction

WAYS OF LOOKING AT HUMAN DIFFERENCES

THOUGHTFUL PERSONS in all periods of history have been confronted with the facts of individual differences. The philosopher in ancient Athens, like the philosopher in twentieth-century America, was sure to see among his neighbors persons ranging all the way from stupidity to genius, from meanness to magnanimity, from emotional stability to psychotic disintegration. The schoolmaster in Rome, like the schoolmaster in Chicago, noted that some children found it difficult or impossible to master the tasks assigned to them, whereas a few forged far ahead of the rest. The church fathers were continually baffled by the problem of heretics. The builders of democracy found it necessary to give considerable thought to the creation of institutions that would prevent the strong from taking advantage of the weak. Planners of coöperative societies found that motivation differed so widely in members of the group that the same situation brought out very diverse reactions from different individuals.

There are two kinds of ideal for mankind which may grow out of the contemplation of these facts. Both are represented not only in the writings of eminent men of all historical periods, but in the accepted opinions of persons whom we know. For one kind of person the important thing, to be stressed above all others, is the equality of men. Such persons prefer to think that in every human being lie the potentialities for almost unlimited development. They hold that the reason for the great differences in individual traits which we observe is that opportunities for the development of full human potentialities have always been anything but equal. The task before us, as they see it, is to hold high the ideal of equality and to work unceasingly at the task of making the *opportunities* for all men truly equal. This way of thinking fits in very well with our American democratic philosophy. Back of the delight we all take in stories of the poor boy's rise to fame and fortune lies the tacit belief that any one of us could, if he wished, achieve the same success. Our great faith in the power of education to overcome all handicaps and inequalities is related to this belief. The statement, "All men are created equal," accepted without qualification, satisfies a basic emotional need for many people, even if their own achievements have clearly been mediocre.

The line of approach taken by the other group of persons starts with the assumption that the differences between men are basic and ineradicable, biological facts which cannot be ignored. The ideal that such a belief generates is of a society fully utilizing these varied gifts for the enrichment of the common life. The caste system of India, in its ideal aspect, is based on such a philosophy. Plato, in the *Republic*, discusses the problem of variation in individual endowments and even proposes a sort of aptitude test to select persons who are particularly well qualified for military careers. The philosophy back of the educational systems in most European countries is based on this type of thinking. After their elementary schooling in the basic skills, only those individuals who show special intellectual gifts are selected for secondary and higher education along academic lines. Even in democratic Britain, the unlimited educability of every individual has never been assumed.

It is well to admit at the beginning that neither of these theories with regard to human individuality can be either proved or disproved. It is not necessary that we adopt one or the other consistently. Many workers in social-science fields do, in fact, look at their data now from one point of view, now from the other. Until we have equal opportunity for all, we can never know with certainty that inequalities would persist in spite of it. It is also true that each view carries with it the possibility that some one may draw from it unwarranted conclusions. The philosophy that differences are basic and ineradicable lends itself very conveniently to those who need a rationalization for the existence of the privileged classes. Hindu upper-caste leaders, pre-Civil War slave owners, modern industrialists and business leaders—all have found it easy to adopt this system of thinking without scrutinizing it too carefully to make sure that it fits all the facts. The equalitarian philosophy, while it avoids this type of warped reasoning, may lead to another difficulty. If one believes that all normal human beings are creatures of unlimited possibilities, then one is almost certain to be greatly disappointed in the achievements of many of them who have failed to measure up to the opportunities they have had. The result of this disappointment is that wives nag their husbands, teachers prod their slower students, and many men and women live out their lives in the shadow of a haunting feeling of failure. Both tolerance toward others and a frank admission of one's own limitations are encouraged by an acceptance of human differences at their face value.

Sometime, generations hence, it may be possible to form a definitive judgment as to the relative merits of the two general philosophical positions. The viewpoint to be adopted in this book is that while all individuals may be considered to have equal *value*, they are not alike in how they think and feel and act. We assume that for all practical purposes of individual placement and group planning the fact that there are differences between people must be taken into consideration. Our first need is to understand what the differences are.

THE DEVELOPMENT OF QUANTITATIVE METHODS

The one factor that gives modern thinkers an advantage over Plato and the ancients in analyzing differences between people is that we have recently made great strides toward the *quantitative* measurement and appraisal of the basic human traits. What this means in a practical situation can be illustrated by recent work in the field of aviation. Any one of us, if pressed, could probably develop a fairly adequate description of the qualities a pilot needs. He must be intelligent, we would say, because he must be able to learn a considerable amount of difficult material. He must be emotionally stable, the sort of person who will not go to pieces in a crisis. He must be skillful and quick in his movements and in his perception of a whole situation. He must have the qualities of leadership that will fit him for taking responsibility and eliciting the best efforts of the members of his crew. Such descriptions, however, though complete and logical enough, were of very little value to the army officers who were required to select young men for pilot training. Boys who seemed to possess all these desirable traits "washed out" in great numbers during their training, causing frustration and disappointment to themselves, and an enormous waste of time and money to the army. Psychologists went to work and produced a battery of tests with scores weighted according to the relationship they actually showed to success in aviation training. They worked out a system of derived scores on the combined test battery ranging from 1 to 9. In order to check the efficiency of the battery, they allowed one group of applicants to enter training regardless of their scores. All of them, low and high together, were given the same opportunity to make good. Instructors did not know how well any of the men had done on the tests. This procedure made it possible to compare the failure rate for the different score groups. The psychologists found that had they selected only men whose scores were 6 or higher, 70 per cent of the failures could have been eliminated before they started. From then on, of course, selection was made on this basis (AAF, 1945). This is the sort of undertaking with which differential psychologists are increasingly concerned in many areas of human endeavor.

Until about a century ago, the whole idea of *measuring* any aspect of human mental life was unthinkable. Mind was generally held to be an order of reality to which figures were just not applicable. The discovery of the possibility of numerical description of the way an individual's nervous system functions was made by accident, and by an astronomer, not a psychologist. Bessel, looking over a history of the Greenwich Astronomical Observatory in 1816, was struck by an incident recorded there. A young assistant had been dismissed in 1796 for continually re-porting the time of the apparent transit of stars across a hair line in the telescope nearly a second later than his master did. Bessel asked himself why the young man should have been so slow, even when his job was at stake. He began to try out his fellow-astronomers, and discovered that there was considerable variation among individuals in the speed with which they reacted to a visual stimulus. He called this the personal equation. Its importance to psychology was its demonstration that at least one mental characteristic could be measured.

At about the same time, work was in progress on the development of methods of dealing with the numerical quantities obtained in the measure-ment of any human trait, physical or mental. Quetelet, the Belgian mathe-matician, was the first to discover the application of the mathematical theory of probability to human measurements. Sir Francis Galton, ex-plorer, meteorologist, biologist, one of the most brilliant and versatile men of the nineteenth century, made great contributions to the science of handling such data. He was interested primarily in the problem of heredity, but found that he needed to measure human characteristics in order to get evidence. He set up an anthropometric laboratory in London and made physical measurements of thousands of persons who volunteered to serve as subjects. In order to get at their mental charac-teristics, he developed some ingenious methods of his own such as the Galton whistle for determining degree of sensitivity to high pitches and the famous breakfast-table test for determining the strength of an indi-vidual's imagery (Galton, 1883). Many of the methods we shall take up in later chapters are based on Galton's pioneer activities.

The rise of psychology as a science in the latter half of the nineteenth century and the founding of the great psychological laboratories brought about a tremendous increase in the number of measurable human traits. Much research was done on sensation, and exact measurements were made of various aspects of vision, hearing, and the skin senses. Some workers were concerned with discrimination processes and measured the accuracy with which subjects could judge differences in weights and brightnesses and lengths of lines. Others worked on memory and developed methods for measuring how quickly the individual learned and how much he remembered. Processes of attention, observation, aesthetic judgment, and even thinking itself came under the scrutiny of these indefatigable workers.

Most of the early psychologists were far more interested in discovering general laws of human nature which would hold for everybody than in exploring differences between people. For each experiment, they would use enough subjects so that they could feel that the average of the group was a dependable index of the trait they were considering. But one of the early students in the laboratory of the great German psychologist, Wundt, became interested in the *differences between* the subjects and in the possible significance of these differences. He was James McKeen Cattell, an American. By thus changing the emphasis, he initiated the mental-test movement, which has become increasingly important from 1890 on to the present time. Though Cattell seems to have been the first to use the term *mental test*, others at about the same time were initiating the same project. In Germany, Oehrn (1889) published the results he had obtained using a series of tests of perception, memory, association, and motor functions. Kraepelin (1895) was also attempting to work out a set of tests for several traits. Ebbinghaus (1897) whose research on memory has made him famous, developed some tests at the request of the Breslau school authorities, among them the completion test which has become a permanent part of our test repertory. In America, J. McK. Cattell (1890, 1896), Jastrow (1891), Munsterberg (1891), Bolton (1891-2), J. A. Gilbert (1897), Sharp (1898-9), Woodworth (1910), and a number of others were all attacking the problem in various ways. Most of this early work, however, failed to produce any significant results. Later research has shown that this was because it was based on a false premise. The aim of these early test-makers was to measure intelligence. They were assuming that if you could measure all aspects of sensation, perception, attention, discrimination, and speed of reaction in the individual, the total efficiency index would be an index to his general intelligence. This seemed a reasonable inference, because the accepted psychological theory of the time held that all of mental life was built up of units of sensory experience, just as all the physical world is made up of atoms. Unfortunately, when the early mental testers checked up on the measurements they had made, they found that there was something wrong with the idea. Persons who were quick, accurate, and skillful at simple tasks did not necessarily turn out to be highly intelligent.

The most famous name in mental testing is that of Alfred Binet, who in 1905, with the collaboration of Simon, published the first mental test that really worked. In the course of his work he developed assumptions quite different from those of his orthodox colleagues. He held that the complex mental abilities we classify under the term *intelligence* are not made up of simple abilities. If we are to measure them at all, we must do it directly. If judgment in a complex situation is what we wish to evalu-- ate, we must give the individual a complex situation to work on and see how he handles it. If his ability to solve problems of various sorts is in question, we must give him those problems to grapple with. It seemed to many psychologists at the turn of the century that this approach to mental measurement could never be practical because of the simple fact that you could never *measure* such complex traits in seconds or millimeters or any other meaningful numerical unit. Binet got around this difficulty when, in the 1908 revision of the scale first published in 1905, he arranged the tests in groups according to difficulty and introduced the concept of *mental age*. Although this is not the same kind of measuring unit as inches or seconds, it has proved to be a very satisfactory method for treating different performance levels quantitatively. It has been the standard method of scoring intelligence tests for children from then on to the present time. Stern in Germany and Terman in this country supplemented the mental-age concept with the additional idea of dividing the obtained mental age by the actual chronological age in order to get an index of the *rate* at which mental growth occurs in a given individual. Terman called this the *intelligence quotient* and used it in the 1916 Stanford-Binet scale. The term immediately became popular both with psychologists and with the general public until, at present, there is scarcely a person who does not know something about IQ tests—whether or not what he knows is correct.

For the student of individual differences, perhaps the most significant aspect of all this early research on mental tests is the indication it gives us of the great *demand* for such tools. As school attendance became more universal, the problem of the slow-learning child became acute. Both Ebbinghaus and Binet, it is to be remembered, were working on definite assignments from the school authorities to develop some technique by which the children who *could* not master the work of their grade might be distinguished from those who *would* not. With the professionalization of social services, the need arose for instruments by means of which the dependent individual's capacity for adjustment could be measured. The earliest work on Binet tests in the United States was done by Goddard, one of whose chief interests was the relationship of feeble-mindedness to delinquency. With all their flaws, mental tests made it possible to handle the problems created by individual differences more intelligently than they had ever been handled before. It is this plain fact that has kept research alive and flourishing.

THE SHAPING OF THE NEW SCIENCE

At about the turn of the century when all this activity centering around the attempt to measure individual differences was going on, two comprehensive statements about the aims and methods of the new science were published. Binet and Henri (1895) began their article, "We broach here a new subject, difficult and as yet very meagerly explored." They then proposed as the two chief aims of this undertaking: first, the study of the *nature and extent* of individual differences in psychological processes; and second, the discovery of the *interrelationships* of mental processes within the individual so as to arrive at a classification of traits and determine which are the more basic functions. Stern's text (1900) outlined a threefold problem: (1) What is the nature and extent of differences in the psychological life of individuals and groups? (2) What factors determine or affect these differences? and (3) How are the differences manifested? To what extent can we use handwriting, facial conformation, and other signs to help us analyze them?

These goals have remained primary from their day to ours, but a number of special emphases have become prominent in different periods. The first of these was the search for group tests which was given great impetus during World War I. Individual intelligence tests are obviously impractical when large numbers of people are to be classified. It seemed that it should be quite feasible to use some of the same types of material that had proved so useful in individual testing but to put them together in a form in which the answers to the questions would be short and definite enough to be accurately scored. This was successfully accomplished at the time of World War I. Five psychologists, under the direction of Robert M. Yerkes, undertook to see if they could produce something that would work in the army situation. Otis put at their disposal several types of test upon which he had been working. The results of their efforts were Army Alpha, a verbal test, and Army Beta, a non-verbal test, both of which could be given to large groups and scored by clerical workers with no psychological training. Since the mental-age concept was of little value in classifying *adult* soldiers, new ways of scoring had to be worked out, based on group norms. The fact that the research workers were provided by the army draft with a large and fairly representative sample of the American population on which to base their derived scores facilitated the solution of the problem. Work on the development of various types of derived scores based on norms for different populations has continued up to the present. A great number of group tests of intelligence have been constructed since 1918 to meet the almost unlimited demand in schools, from kindergarten to college and graduate school.

The second line of research had as its aim the development of *non-verbal* tests of intelligence. For many purposes, tests of either the Binet type or the ordinary group type were found to be useless. If the individual to be tested is deaf, he cannot, of course, hear the questions in an individual test. If he is illiterate, he cannot answer questions requiring that he read and write. If he is deficient in his knowledge of the language of the country in which he lives, he cannot be expected to distinguish himself on a vocabulary test. Furthermore, many psychologists felt that tests depending on some school knowledge were inherently not valid as measures of basic native mental capacity. Psychologists who devoted their efforts to this problem have brought forth a wide variety of performance and non-verbal tests, including form boards, puzzles, mazes, block-design problems, and many others. There are both individual and group tests of this sort, and they form an important set of tools for the applied psychologist. It has become increasingly evident as time has passed that such tests do not measure exactly the same mental capacity as the verbal tests do, but once this fact is understood their usefulness is in no way diminished. If they are worth less to us than we expected as *substitutes* for the typical verbal intelligence test, they are worth more as *supplements*. With an increasing amount of statistical knowledge and clinical experience, we have become clearer as to what traits various types of tests measure and what situations call for these traits.

Thus a third direction that research has taken is a turning away from the search for *universal* intelligence tests suitable for all human beings under all circumstances. Test-makers have found that it is impractical if not impossible to develop tests which will be equally valid for preschool children, college students, and illiterate adults. Separate tests are needed. It has also become increasingly apparent that intelligence itself has many aspects. Much of the work of recent years has been concerned with identifying these aspects and developing separate tests for characteristics such as spatial judgment, numerical ability, and verbal ability. The relationship between these separate *factors*, as they are called, and general intellectual ability is still a very live issue. It will be discussed in some detail in Part II of this book.

A fourth and related direction of research has been toward the development of tests of specific talents and vocational aptitudes. A great deal of work has been done on the problems related to mechanical, clerical, and musical aptitudes, somewhat less on those related to talent in the field of art and to the capacity for understanding social situations and handling people. Most of this work has had a strong practical orientation. Its aim has been the production of tools that would be really useful in selection, placement, and individual guidance. These findings will also be discussed in Part II.

The fifth line of research has been toward the measurement, or at least the rather precise evaluation, of the *non-intellectual* traits of the individual, such as interests, adjustment patterns, and personality traits. Strong has devoted half a lifetime to research on vocational interests. A long procession of adjustment inventories stretches from about 1918 down to the present time, although it must be admitted that no single distinguished individual appears in it. In the 1930's an entirely new approach to the problems involved in personality measurement made its appearance, the so-called projective technique, in which the subject by interpreting some material such as an ink blot or an ambiguous picture furnishes an indication of his basic attitudes, drives, and problems. These methods are further removed than the others from the quantitative techniques we have been discussing, but any survey of research on individual differences cannot ignore them entirely. In order to delimit the field with which this book is concerned, we shall not try to cover the vast literature on these clinical techniques except for studies in which some clear-cut *quantitative* method of evaluating the responses of subjects has been worked out. To be familiar with studies where results are reported as verbal descriptions rather than numerical scores is indispensable to our grasp of individual differences in the broad sense. The clinical psychologist, the teacher, and the social worker need such familiarity. But the task before us here is the synthesis of *research* findings, and the quantitative methods have proved more serviceable for testing hypotheses, exploring relationships, and drawing conclusions.

Still a sixth research emphasis had begun to take definite shape by the late 1940's. It was the use of objective laboratory methods to investigate differences in personality and temperament. This was not really an innovation. Hartshorne and May (1928), many German psychologists throughout the 1920's and 1930's, and scattered research workers in Britain and America had all seen the advantages in analyzing personality differences by means of accurately measurable perceptual or motor responses rather than by means of self-report techniques like the personality inventories. By 1950, however, several large-scale research programs were oriented in this direction, and some challenging new ideas had been launched on the mainstream of our thinking about personality. One of the main contributions this work has made consists of some new *variables* to work with, characteristics that cut across the traditional line between ability and motivation, mind and emotions. This has opened up new horizons. When we know more about such characteristics as "field dependence" and "intolerance of ambiguity," it may be possible to organize all of our thinking about individual differences in some now unforeseen way.

In attacking all these types of problem, both old and new, there has been increasing emphasis, especially in the period since World War II, on large-scale, coördinated research programs rather than isolated studies. Results are now coming in from longitudinal studies that have been in progress a long time—Terman's work with gifted children, for example, and the California Guidance Study. Other programs consist of groups of related experiments organized around an important theoretical issue or practical need. The work of Eysenck and his associates at the Institute of Psychiatry in London and the work of the Committee on Human Development in Chicago are examples.

What this trend toward large research programs means is that we now have far more dependable evidence to use in answering the basic questions of differential psychology than we have ever had before. In many instances we need no longer piece together scraps of information obtained from a host of small and inadequate studies but can make a thorough examination of a reasonable amount of sound evidence. This makes it less possible than it once was to argue for a favorite theory and support one's position by dismissing the evidence against it. A whole body of data obtained by a reputable research institute cannot be ignored or ruled out as can a single questionable study based on a non-representative sample. Arguments about the ill effects of acceleration on bright children, for example, are obsolete since Terman and Oden's careful analysis of the problem became available (see Chapter 15). Arguments that heredity has nothing to do with psychological differences lose much of their weight when confronted with Kallman's impressive accumulation of facts and figures (see Chapter 18). The details about these and other issues will be discussed in later sections of this book. Many psychologists would certainly insist that none of these complex problems is *settled* as yet. The only point here, one that perhaps is not sufficiently appreciated by workers in these vineyards, is that the raw material out of which conclusions and generalizations are now being produced is vastly superior to the best we had twenty years ago.

Perhaps because of this, the present period is marked by a number of rapprochements or syntheses by means of which conclusions once thought to be squarely in opposition to one another have been reconciled. For example, the question about whether or not the IQ is constant has been rephrased. The California studies have shown that IQ's do change, but in orderly ways that can to a considerable extent be predicted if we have the necessary information about the age of each child when tested, the educational level of his family, and the period of time intervening between examinations. Hereditarians and environmentalists no longer divide themselves into two hostile camps. Increasing knowledge about what is inherited, how learning processes change various mental characteristics, and what kinds of environmental situations have favorable influences on mental growth has changed the whole pattern of the controversy.

The participation of laboratory workers in research on individual differences in personality, discussed as the sixth trend above, may mark an even more significant rapprochement. For many years, experimental psychologists constituted one distinct group, mental testers another. Experimental workers were familiar with complicated types of apparatus, controlled as many variables as possible, and thought in terms of stimulus and response, independent and dependent variables. Mental measurement specialists used tests consisting of questions or simple tasks, worked in natural settings rather than laboratories, and developed statistical procedures based on correlation rather than dependency analysis. Most of these distinctions have become blurred in the years since World War II. One of the best examples of this synthesis is the work of Witkin and his associates to be reported in some detail in Chapter 9. They have used both tests and apparatus, both correlational methods for clarifying the meaning of consistent individual traits, and analysis of variance methods for clarifying the effects of variations in stimulating conditions on the responses.

With all this emphasis on progress we must recognize that the science of human differences is still very young. The most interesting questions are still unanswered, perhaps even unasked. Meanwhile, human life goes on. Somehow, we must all adjust ourselves to those around us in some fashion and plan as intelligently as possible for ourselves and for each other. It is well that in doing this we use the best information that we have. The more complicated our world becomes, the more essential it is that we avoid any attempt to found human institutions on ideas about human nature that we know to be false. To proceed on the basis of tested evidence when such evidence can be obtained, to suspend judgment in cases where no conclusion is warranted, to formulate tentative courses of action in areas where doubt exists—these are the skills needed by the social scientist and applied psychologist. It is to be hoped that the study of what now is known about individual and group differences will contribute to the development of such skills.

CHAPTER 2

General Principles

VARIABILITY AMONG INDIVIDUALS—A UNIVERSAL PHENOMENON

WHEN THE dog-lover begins to hold forth on the unusual intelligence shown by his favorite animal, his friends are likely to listen to him with good-humored tolerance. But the farmer who insists that his cows differ widely in temperament and the laboratory experimenter who insists that his guinea pigs show marked individual characteristics will probably be met with extreme skepticism. The bulk of the research evidence, however, is on their side. More and more experimental reports in animal psychology note the fact that one animal of any given species is not like another. Even the one-celled animals show differences analogous in some ways to the ones that interest us in higher forms of life. There is evidence, for instance, that protozoa show changes in behavior with continued experience in a situation, a form of learning which seems to be an elementary sort of conditioned response. Razran (1933) reports that whereas the average protozoon takes 138.5 trials to "learn" this, the range from fastest to slowest is from 79 to 284 trials. Some experiments by French (1940), using paramecia as subjects, supply evidence on two other traits or characteristics. One is the tendency to form groups. By an ingenious method, French separated the "groupers" from the "free swimmers," kept them separate and in clear water for a half hour, and then put them back into separate food solutions to see if the grouping tendency persisted. It did, to a striking extent. Similar experiments were run to see whether tendencies to enter or not to enter solutions in which a small amount of some foreign chemical had been placed would persist. Again, differences turned out to be fairly large in some of the experiments and statistically significant in all. If it is shown that even the one-celled animals differ in what might almost be called a rudimentary sort of personality trait, how futile it would be to try to make all human beings alike!

Animal psychologists, using rats as subjects, have for some time been calling attention to individual differences in maze-running ability and in certain temperamental traits such as wildness (C. S. Hall, 1951). Geier, Levin, and Tolman (1941) have carried out an elaborate study in which they have identified four different traits upon which their rat subjects differ from one another, two of them "intellectual" traits and two "emotional" or "motivational" traits.

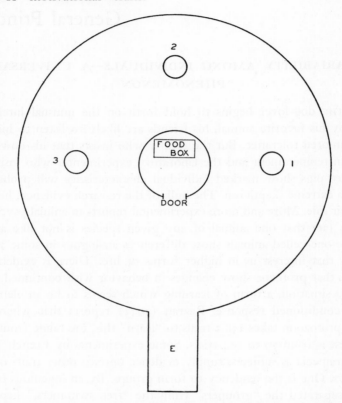

FIGURE 1. Design of problem box used in Fjeld experiment (Fjeld, 1934).

When monkeys are used as subjects, even more marked individual variability shows up. A typical study is that by Fjeld (1934) designed to measure for each animal the complexity of the problem he is able to solve. Figure 1 shows the sort of performance required.

To get the food box open, each animal was required to depress one or more of the plates in the floor. In Problem 1, the easiest problem, all he had to do was to depress Plate 1 and the door would open. In Problem 2, he must depress Plates 1 and 2 in turn, then the door opened; in Problem 3, Plates 1, 2, and 3. Problem 4 required him to depress 1, 2, and 3, reverse his direction, and step on 2 again. Problem 7 meant Plates 1, 2, 3, 2, 1, 2, 3. Out of a group of fifteen rhesus monkeys who served as subjects through the whole experiment, one was unable to learn more than 2 problems, whereas one learned 22. The rest varied all the way from 3 to 13. A similar study by Koch (1935) on Cebus monkeys gave similar results with somewhat less variability in performance from animal to animal.

Examples based on many other types of performance in many other species might be given, but enough have probably been cited to convince the student of human psychology that variation in mental characteristics is far from being an exclusively human phenomenon. Such studies are important for us in that they suggest that differences are universal and usually ineradicable. If this is the case we must learn to understand them, accept them, and use them in the building of our common society.

HUMAN CHARACTERISTICS IN WHICH DIFFERENCES HAVE BEEN MEASURED

Many types of measurement have been made on human beings. First, it is obvious to all of us that human individuals are not the same in size and shape. We have learned to expect and to make at least some provision for this kind of variation, though the army still sometimes has trouble fitting out the new recruit whose shoes are size 13, and women find that both the 32's and the 46's are sometimes hard to obtain at dress shops. Much first-rate work has been done in the field of anthropometric measurements. Not only gross height and weight, but the exact sizes of most of the individual parts of the body have been measured. Second, measurements have been made of the physiological processes, or the way various organ systems of the body function. Basal metabolism, the amount of calcium, sugar, acid, and hemoglobin in the blood, respiratory rate, pulse rate, and concentrations of acid and of urea in the urine are physiological characteristics in which individuals have been found to show definite, measurable differences. Third, accurate measurements have been made of motor capacities including such things as reaction time, speed of tapping, steadiness, and swiftness of blow. Fourth, much work on the measurement of sensory and perceptual differences has come from psychological laboratories. We know that individuals vary as to the keenness of their vision, hearing, and sense of smell. Some are much better than others at analyzing and remembering complex patterns of lines, colors, or sounds. Fifth, differences in intelligence and in the narrower processes of which it seems to be composed—memory, judgment, problem-solving, and the like—have been demonstrated in hundreds of studies at all age levels. Sixth, there are differences in achievement and knowledge among individuals who have had equal amounts of schooling. Seventh, special aptitudes and talents have proved to be measurable, at least in part. Eighth, interests and attitudes, beliefs and opinions, have been studied by quantitative methods which show how wide is the individual variation in these traits. And finally, considerable progress has been made in developing tests for the more subtle and elusive aspects of personality, and scores on such tests again point to significant differences between individuals.

We have done enough work now to feel confident that most if not all important human characteristics will eventually be amenable to quantitative evaluation if we can show enough ingenuity in the way we approach the problems. We have come to realize also that whatever we measure, there are always high-ranking and low-ranking individuals and others at all the in-between levels. The research on human beings corroborates the conclusions from animal studies—individual differences in measurable characteristics constitute a universal phenomenon.

TABLE I.

Frequency Distribution of Lung Capacity
(White soldiers 66.5 to 67.5 inches in height)
(Gould's data as reported by Wechsler, 1952, p. 28)

CUBIC INCHES	NUMBER OF MEN
Below 96	19
96-115	52
116-135	81
136-155	136
156-175	271
176-195	319
196-215	330
216-235	160
236-255	85
256-275	22
Above 275	16
	N = 1,491

THE NATURE OF DISTRIBUTIONS

As measurements of various human characteristics became available, it was necessary to work out methods of handling the data so as to bring order into them, make it possible to study them systematically, and provide for comparisons between the individual and the norms for his group. The first step in this procedure is to arrange the measurements or scores in an orderly table called a *frequency distribution*. The method is simply to tally all scores falling within each specified range of score points. The result is exemplified in Table 1.

It is easier to comprehend the significance of such arrays of figures if they are then portrayed in graphic form. Figure 2 shows how this distribution looks when graphed.

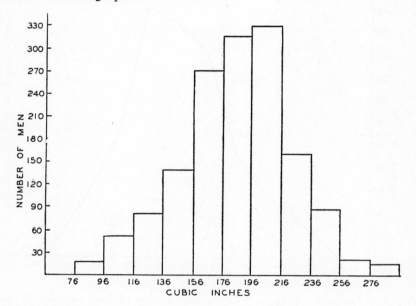

FIGURE 2. Histogram showing frequency distribution of lung capacity in 1,491 white soldiers (Wechsler, 1952).

A graphic presentation of the sort shown in Figure 2 is called a *histogram* and is the most common, most generally satisfactory way of graphing a frequency distribution. Measurements are always indicated as *distances* along the horizontal base line. Any convenient scale that will include the full range of obtained measures may be used. For these data, each unit of base-line distance represents an interval of 20 cubic inches of lung capacity. Bars are then erected showing how many individuals in the group obtain scores falling within that interval, and the scale along the side indicates how many *individuals* are represented by each bar. In this figure, each unit of height stands for 30 cases.

An alternative form of graphic presentation is the *frequency polygon.* Figure 3 is an example of such a figure drawn from the same data and to the same scale as the histogram in Figure 2. The only difference is that instead of bars a *point* is placed above the middle of each interval at a distance from the base line which represents the number of individuals whose measurements fall within the interval. Then these points are connected. Both these types of graph are used a great deal in presenting results obtained in differential psychology.

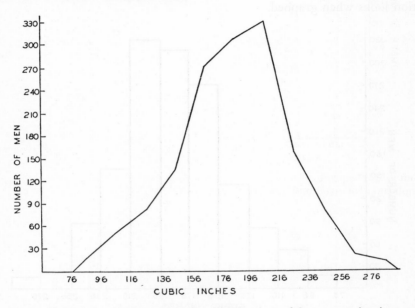

FIGURE 3. Frequency polygon showing distribution of lung capacity in 1,491 white soldiers (Wechsler, 1952).

A person who has never seen any sort of pictured distribution before, if asked to describe the shape of Figure 2, could not help noticing the short bars at the ends and the long bars at the middle. He would probably comment also on the fact that the height of the bars shows a gradual increase up to the middle and from there on a gradual decrease, giving a step-like effect similar to an old-fashioned stile over a fence. This shape has been found to characterize a great many distributions of human traits, when measurements are made on a large and unselected group of people. Figures 4, 5, and 6 are examples.

All of these distributions show the same general shape, high in the middle, gradually tapering off toward both ends. Figure 4 represents a simple

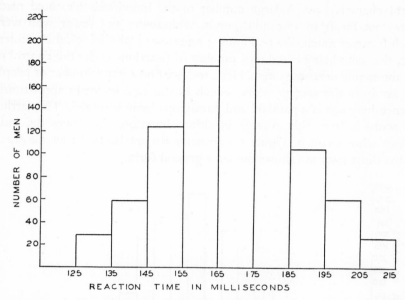

FIGURE 4. Frequency distribution showing reaction time to sound of 1,000 male applicants for machinist jobs in Paris (Fessard, in Woodworth, 1938, p. 336).

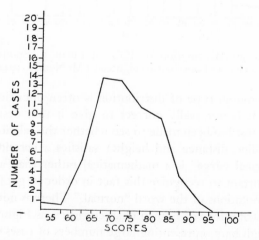

FIGURE 5. Frequency distribution of scores for autonomic balance. Each score is a weighted sum of five separate measurements of autonomic functioning (Wenger, 1941).

motor characteristic. A large number of the individuals measured made scores not far from 170 milliseconds, with fewer and fewer who were much faster or much slower. Figure 5 represents a physiological characteristic, the score being based on a number of functions under the control of the autonomic nervous system. Here, too, we find a large number of people not far from the average score, which in this case indicates approximate balance between sympathetic and parasympathetic activities. The farther the score is from this average in either direction, the fewer the individuals who obtain it. Figure 6 represents the intellectual trait measured by the Binet tests and shows the same general form.

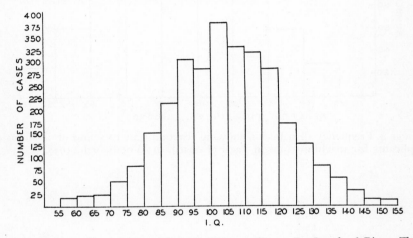

FIGURE 6. Frequency distribution of IQ's on Form L. Stanford-Binet Test, ages two and one-half to eighteen (McNemar, 1942).

This most common type of distribution is often uncritically called the *normal curve*. It is not really correct to give it that designation unless a mathematical test has been made to see whether the relationship between *x* and *y* (base-line distance and height) satisfies a certain mathematical equation. "Normal curve" is a mathematical rather than a psychological term. It is important to recognize this fact in order to get away from unwarranted connotations of the word "normal." There is nothing abnormal about other distributions of human characteristics, as Figure 7 shows.

When the high bars representing large numbers of cases are found considerably to the right or left of the middle, the distribution is said to be *skewed*. There are mathematical methods for determining the degree of skewness, but it can often be seen instantly when one looks at graphed data. Figure 7 is a distribution in which skewness is very apparent.

However, many biological, anatomical, and psychological measurements do seem to conform fairly closely to the mathematical normal distribution. That is because this is the form of curve that is obtained for repeated determinations of any event that is due to what the mathematicians call pure chance. Chance, in this sense, does not mean something outside the natural order in which cause and effect principles operate, but simply a phe-

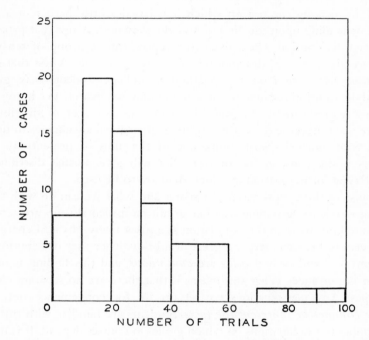

FIGURE 7. Frequency distribution showing individual differences in the ease with which conditioned eyelid responses are formed (Campbell and Hilgard, 1936).

nomenon with multiple causes so complex that they have never been isolated. Thus when one tosses ten coins at a time again and again, there is a very complicated interplay of forces which produce at each throw heads for some, tails for others. The most *probable* result in this situation is a combination of five heads and five tails. If the coins are tossed a thousand times, the distribution representing the frequency with which each number of heads, from zero to ten, is obtained, will closely approximate the normal curve. Measurements of physical and mental traits are also determined by a large number of independent factors, at present unanalyzable.

The effect is likely to be that when large numbers of subjects are measured, we tend to get the normal or chance distribution.

Because non-normal distributions are fairly common, sweeping generalizations which were the rule in earlier stages of research on human differences have had to be abandoned or revised. This is especially true with regard to *mental* characteristics that must be evaluated by means of tests. It is quite possible to change a skewed distribution into a normal one simply by making the test on which it is based a little harder or a little easier, depending upon the direction of the skewness. A test that produces a skewed distribution when given to a representative group of ten-year-olds may give a normal distribution for twelve-year-olds. A test that gives a skewed distribution on a population of college students may give a normal distribution for new recruits at an induction center. We know now that test scores can be manipulated to give us any sort of distribution that we want. Because there are definite mathematical advantages to be obtained from normal distributions, one of the aims of present-day test-builders is the construction of tests that will *give* normal distributions for the types of population in which they are to be used.

Because of these facts about test scores and what we can do with them, it is impossible to determine whether or not most mental traits are actually distributed normally in the population as a great many physical characteristics seem to be. But there is a great deal of evidence that distributions of both physical and mental traits are *continuous*, and this finding is of the highest importance. What this means is that there are no separate classes, no types. Any classifications we set up are for convenience only and *do not completely represent the facts*. Students are familiar with this idea as it applies to examinations on which grades in courses depend. It is necessary that a class be divided into A, B, C, D, and F groups at the end of a course, but there is always some unfortunate B man who is almost as high as the lowest person in the A group, and some fortunate soul who just barely obtains a D rather than an F. As far as we can see now, the same holds true in all classifications. We cannot say that one person has musical talent and another none, that one person is selfish and another unselfish, one introverted and another extroverted. There is probably no human characteristic that we do not *all* possess, to some degree. When sensitive measuring devices are developed to assess any trait, we find that the scores show a range from very little to very much of the trait in question, with no breaks in the distribution anywhere. We need to give some thought to this concept of continuous distribution because it involves a change in some of our most deeply ingrained habits of thinking about human beings. We have inherited a great number of classification systems which, from child-hood on, we apply almost unconsciously. It is perhaps the major contribu-tion that differential psychology has made so far to have demonstrated that all such systems, whether they divide people into the wicked and the righteous, the stupid and the intelligent, the beautiful and the ugly, or the neat and the slovenly, must necessarily falsify the facts. One of our major tasks is to learn to *think* in terms of continuous distribution, rather than classifications.

To describe the distributions which measurements of individual differ-ences have given us, it has been necessary to develop various statistical techniques. Some of them are extremely complicated and strike terror into the heart of the student encountering them with his first casual glance.

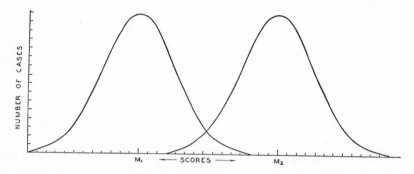

FIGURE 8. Two normal distributions which differ in central tendency.

The basic logic on which they rest, however, is relatively simple, once the concept of distributions has been assimilated. A little study of Figures 8, 9, and 10 will show what kind of statistical indices we *need* for describing the distributions.

It is evident that there are two ways in which two distributions, both of which appear to be "normal," may differ from each other. In Figure 8, the first distribution lies considerably to the left of the second distribution. Since distances from left to right along the base line represent scores or measurements, this shows that the *average* for Distribution 1 is consider-ably lower than the average for Distribution 2. It is this characteristic of each whole group of measurements for which the statistician uses some measure of *central tendency*. Figure 9 brings out the fact that even when two distributions have exactly the same central tendency, they may differ very markedly from each other in the degree to which they cluster around this average value. To describe this characteristic, the statistician has developed measures of *variability*. As Figure 10 indicates, it is quite possible for two distributions to differ from each other in *both* central tendency and variability. In this graph, Distribution 1 has a lower average, but is considerably more variable than Distribution 2.

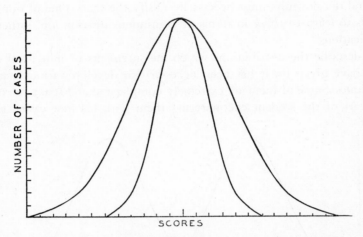

FIGURE 9. Two normal distributions which differ in variability.

The idea underlying the measures of central tendency is familiar to most persons, and, thus, easy to grasp. We learn in grade school to compute the *average* score for a group of individuals. The newspapers and popular magazines tell us of average incomes, average shoe sizes, average tempera-

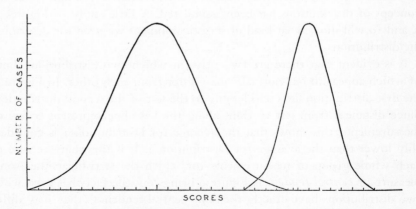

FIGURE 10. Two normal distributions which differ in both central tendency and variability.

tures. The scale in every ten-cent store carries a table of average weights for men and women of different heights. Thus, the student learns without difficulty, when studying distributions like those pictured in Figures 4 to 6, to look for the score represented along the base line which is at the *middle* of the distribution. It also seems natural for him to evaluate sets of figures that have not been graphed in terms of an *average* of some sort. We are always interested in average incomes, average scores, average temperatures.

The idea of looking for some indicator of the *variability* of the group we are studying is far less familiar. Yet it is of fundamental importance to anyone who wishes to understand human differences. It is obvious that two groups that differ greatly in this characteristic will need to be dealt with in different ways. If the range of IQ's of children in one fifth grade is from 50 to 150 and the range in another fifth grade from 90 to 110, the teachers will need to handle their classes differently even if the average IQ in both rooms is exactly 100. It is also true, though less obvious, that we need to know the variability of a group before we can adequately interpret any individual score. A student who gets a score of 81 on a course examination knows very little about where he stands if he is told only that the class average is 70. His next question is likely to refer to "how the scores run." He realizes that if they range from 20 to 140, his 81, though above average, will probably classify him in the C category. If they range from 50 to 90 he has hopes of getting a B. If 81 is the highest score in the class, he will naturally expect to get an A. We need for every distribution some index of its variability or spread, both in order to describe what the group is like and to evaluate the performance of any individual within the group. When this need was realized and a satisfactory way of expressing variability worked out, it became possible to rest a large and complex structure of statistical reasoning on this base.

There have been a number of ways of describing in a single summary figure the variability characteristic of a group of measurements, but one method has taken precedence over all the others for most purposes—the computation of the *variance*, or its square root, the *standard deviation*. Details of the computational procedures may be found in any elementary text on statistics. Briefly described, they involve obtaining the arithmetic mean (what we usually call simply the average score) for the group, subtracting it from each of the scores made by individuals, to get the deviations from the mean, squaring these deviations, and taking the average of the squared deviations. This gives us the *variance*, a figure that is used a great deal in testing statistical hypotheses with regard to data, as we shall see in later chapters. By taking the square root of the variance we obtain the *standard deviation*. This is a figure which for a normal distribution bears a certain fixed relationship to the whole group of scores, and thus is an invaluable tool to be used in the tasks outlined in the preceding paragraph—describing the group and evaluating individuals within the group.

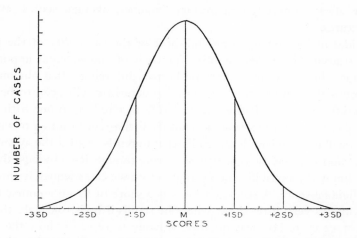

FIGURE 11. The significance of the mean and standard deviation in a normal distribution.

Figure 11 shows what these fixed relationships in a normal distribution are. In working with real data the horizontal base line always shows the range of scores in the group and the point marked M represents the score that turns out to be the mean or average. If in any normal distribution we measure off along this base line starting from M the distance corresponding to the standard deviation we have computed, we reach the positions shown by the points labeled +1SD and −1SD. If we examine the curve above the line between these points, and the area between the curve and the base line, which represents the number of persons getting scores within this range, we can see that approximately the middle two-thirds of the group fall into these two middle sections. If we continue the process of measuring off distances corresponding to the standard deviations along the base line and then examining the area under the curve that corresponds to the distance measured from the mean in both directions, we can see that approximately 95 per cent of the area is above the range between −2SD and +2SD, and the whole distribution is included between −3SD and +3SD. These relationships between area under the curve and distances from the mean along the *x*-axis have been worked out mathematically with great accuracy. While few obtained distributions of scores correspond precisely to normal curve specifications, the fit is often close enough so that the approximate areas we have been using become very convenient anchoring points for our thinking about a distribution.

An example or two will show how this works. If it is the general characteristics of the group rather than of any individual in it that interest us, we can get much of what we wish to know from the mean and standard deviation alone. In the example of the two different fifth grades given above, to state that 5A has a mean of 100 and a standard deviation of 17, whereas 5B has a mean of 100 and a standard deviation of 4, tells a teacher much about what to expect from the classes. In 5A, about two-thirds of the students will have IQ's between 83 and 117; about 95 per cent of them will have IQ's between 66 and 134; and the total range will probably be included between 49 and 151. In 5B, about two-thirds of the students will have IQ's between 96 and 104; about 95 per cent will have IQ's between 92 and 108; and the whole range will fall between 88 and 112. If there are in each case a few exceptions arising from the circumstances that the distribution is not exactly normal, they will probably not be striking enough to upset the general conclusions.

If we are interested in evaluating an individual's performance, knowing the mean and standard deviation of the group to which he belongs enables us to do this. In the example given above of the student whose score on a course test was 81, he needs only to know the mean and standard deviation of the group to enable him to judge how successful he has been. If the mean is 70 and the standard deviation 12 he knows that the point representing his score falls almost at the +1SD mark shown in Figure 11. He sees himself as above average but not strikingly so. About 83 per cent of the group probably have scored lower than he has, but some 17 per cent have scored higher.

Another way of explaining the usefulness of the mean and standard deviation as indices of central tendency and variability is to say that if we work with normal distributions, these two numbers alone give us about all the information there is in the whole set of scores. We do not need either a frequency distribution like Table 1 or a graph like Figure 2. The mathematicians did the work for us once and for all when they analyzed the relationships embodied in the basic normal curve equation. It is the task of the student of individual differences to become so familiar with this way of thinking about distributions of measurements that when he reads a mean and standard deviation in a published report of some new research he can make the correct inferences about the distribution from which these figures came.

In doing research work with a new test or a new group, however, it is always advisable to arrange the scores in a frequency distribution and it is often helpful to draw a histogram or frequency polygon. We must always remember that the relationships we have been considering hold only in *normal* distributions. Often an inspection of the graph of some new data suggests the possibility of a considerable departure from the normal form, and the frequency distribution permits us to test statistically, by methods we need not go into here, whether this departure is marked enough to invalidate the customary sorts of conclusions about the group and about individuals in it. This is common practice when a test is to be standardized for wide use, and norm tables based on the standard deviation of the standardization group are to be issued.

Let us summarize the basic facts that need always to be kept in mind about the nature of distributions. First, all distributions of measurable traits appear to be continuous. There is usually a gradation from very low to very high with the bulk of the cases falling somewhere in between. Second, many such distributions take a form which can be described fairly accurately by the mathematical normal curve equation. Such distributions are symmetrical and bell-shaped, with the largest numbers of cases falling at and near the middle and a decreasing number toward both extremes. Distributions of test scores which are skewed (non-symmetrical) or depart from the normal form in various other ways can often be made to approximate normal form more closely by changing the difficulty of some of the test items or using the test with a different group. It is an advantage in manipulating and interpreting test scores to have a normal distribution. Third, in describing a group or evaluating an individual's performance, it is necessary to consider both central tendency and variability. In normal distributions the mean and standard deviation are commonly used for this purpose. There is a fixed relationship connecting distances from the mean along the horizontal axis with areas under the curve. This enables us to draw conclusions relating the level of a score to the number of individuals in the group who scored above or below it.

THE MEANING OF MEASUREMENT

Up to this point we have been using the term "measurement" as though the same principles applied regardless of the sort of units to which the numbers refer. If we look back at Figures 2 through 7, we get some idea

of the variety of scales that have been used for measuring human characteristics—cubic inches in Figure 2, milliseconds in Figure 4, IQ's in Figure
6, number of trials in Figure 7. The unexplained word "scores" in Figure 5
does not tell us anything about the measuring units involved. Is it really
legitimate to present all these arrays of figures in the same way, and
apply the same mathematical procedures in all cases?

There has been a great deal of discussion of this issue among mathematicians and statisticians. To be sure, most of it has not troubled the
practical mental testers, since they were unaware that it was going on.
At first, a good deal of the comment resulted in condemning all conclusions resting on the mathematical analysis of "scores" not based on actual
physical units. In this narrow sense, "measurement" requires the comparison of the magnitude to be evaluated with some standard unit. Length
is measured by applying a ruler or yardstick to an object. Weight is measured by counting the number of standard objects it takes to balance the
object being weighed. The volume of any container is ascertained by
emptying into it the contents of smaller containers of known volume. For
magnitudes measured in this way, the numerical scale on which they are
represented starts from a true zero and proceeds by equal intervals. The
difference between ten pounds and twelve pounds means exactly the same
thing as the difference between 110 and 112. A twenty-pound object is
exactly four times as heavy as a five-pound object. We can add, subtract,
multiply, or divide such scores, and interpret the answers we get without
any ambiguity. Such figures indeed do not lie.

Measurements of height, lung capacity, and reaction time can obviously
be treated in the same manner, since they are expressed in definite physical
units. But how about variables such as IQ and autonomic balance? There
is obviously no kind of measuring stick or standard container by means
of which they have been defined. Zero on such a scale does not mean
none of the trait in question. Even the theoretical concept of a human
individual with *zero* intelligence or *no* parasympathetic response to stimulation is difficult to formulate. It can be seen that there is a real possibility
that if we treat these numbers as we do the others, the figures may "lie,"
and totally erroneous conclusions be drawn.

The more recent thinking about the meaning of mental "measurements"
has led to a broadening of our concept of what the general term means,
a differentiation of different *types* of numerical scale, and a clearer understanding of the kinds of mathematical treatment appropriate for each type
(Stevens, 1951). In this broad, inclusive sense, any kind of assignment of
numbers to objects or phenomena can be called measurement. Four levels

can be distinguished. At the bottom, the roughest variety or *nominal* scale comes into existence when objects are simply identified or classified by number. The numbers assigned to football players or to screws in different bins in a hardware store are of this type. Even with such crude categorizations research is possible, but most of our common mathematical procedures do not apply to them. The second level or *ordinal* scale comes into existence when the numbers assigned to individuals reflect a ranking that has been made with regard to some characteristic. A teacher may be asked to take handwriting specimens from 30 children and arrange them in order for general quality. If we then assign number 1 to the poorest, 2 to the next better, and continue numbering on to 30 for the highest, we shall have an ordinal scale. There are some methods of treatment appropriate for such scales which cannot be used at all with nominal scales. The third level or *interval* scale is one for which the numbers represent fixed distances along some known continuum or dimension, but for which any one number does not stand for a definite distance from zero. The Fahrenheit and Centigrade temperature scales are the best-known examples. The number of degrees in each case corresponds to the height of a column of mercury or some other substance, but when the thermometer reads zero it does not mean that there is no warmth at all in the surrounding atmosphere. Zero is an arbitrary figure and differs in its meaning according to whether a Fahrenheit or a Centigrade thermometer is used. When raters are instructed to evaluate individuals in such a way that the differences between ratings will be equal at all parts of the scale, we can think of their ratings as constituting an interval scale. The fourth level or *ratio* scale is one that has equal intervals throughout and a fixed zero point.

Although some psychological characteristics have been measured in physical units and can thus be treated as ratio scales, the majority of our mental measurements must be considered merely interval scales, if indeed they meet the requirements for even that level. Thus the distinction between mathematical treatments that can legitimately be used for interval and ratio scales becomes extremely important. First of all, because the zero point for the interval scale is arbitrary rather than fixed and meaningful as it is for the ratio scale, the absolute level of the numbers is meaningless. Twenty degrees on one thermometer can represent a higher temperature than thirty on another if the first happens to be Centigrade, the second Fahrenheit. With interval scales we do not have a built-in reference point to which all numbers are automatically calibrated. To make up for this lack we arbitrarily specify some reference point which enables us to interpret the rest of the numbers. For the Centigrade thermometer, zero represents the freezing point of water. In a distribution of test scores, we do not try to specify what zero represents, but we find what the *mean* is and measure our other distances from that. Secondly, with an interval scale, expressing one number as a fraction of another is meaningless and misleading. Since a zero score on a reading test does not mean zero reading ability and scores are not measured from this reference point, it is not legitimate to conclude that Tom, who scores 100, is twice as good a reader as Jim, who scores 50. If Sue scores 75, we can say she is 25 points higher than Jim and 25 points lower than Tom, but we cannot make a ratio or fraction and say that she is 1½ times as high as the one or ⅔ as high as the other.

As long as we keep it in mind, the rule that we must not divide one score by another when we are working with an interval scale does not constitute a serious limitation on our work. Most of the standard statistical procedures—the computation of means, standard deviations, and correlation coefficients, the analysis of variance, and the testing of hypotheses—can be carried on with an interval scale as well as with a ratio scale. There is a real question as to whether the differences between scores have an equal meaning at all parts of the scale for many of our test distributions, and thus there is a real doubt as to whether they qualify even as interval scales. However, the practical way of deciding such doubtful matters is to check whether the judgments about people we make when we treat scores as though the intervals were equal turn out to be sound. In general, they have done so, and we have continued to use means, standard deviations, and other interval-scale statistics on mental-test distributions.

We are realizing more and more, however, that we need not give up research activity in fields where even interval scores are impossible to achieve. If we can find *any* basis for assigning numbers to objects or to the responses people make, some kinds of research become possible. Rough, approximate correlations and judgments as to whether persons in different categories differ significantly are often first steps in the exploration of new areas where measurements of a high order cannot be obtained.

One of the things we need to understand as we think about individual differences is that though the terms "measurement" and "testing" are often used interchangeably in psychology, their boundaries do not exactly coincide. Measurement has been important in experimental psychology as well as in mental testing. Particularly in the area called *psychophysics* important principles and techniques have been worked out. *Psychophysics* can be approximately defined as the measurement of psychological magnitudes by physical means. Its fundamental task has been the measurement of *thresholds* or *limens*. The *absolute threshold* is the lowest level of stimulation to which a person is sensitive. The *differential threshold* or just noticeable difference is the smallest amount of *change* in the stimulating situation that will lead to a change in a person's perception of it. Individual differences in these sensory thresholds have been noted from the beginning. In many cases investigators have not been particularly interested in this aspect of their data, and in many cases they were working with too few subjects to draw any clear conclusions about it. But it is quite possible to use the procedures of psychophysics primarily for the purpose of investigating individual differences, as Pickford (1951) has done in the case of color vision.

Two circumstances have led to increasing attention to the individual differences reported in psychophysical experiments. One is the necessity, as in many specialized military training programs, of selecting persons who are exceptionally sensitive to certain kinds of stimulation. This has led to the standardization of various psychophysical procedures as tests that could be used to identify such persons. (This of course is not a new idea. The Seashore Measures of Musical Talent, first issued in 1919, were developed in just this way.) The other source of current interest is a possibility that some of these simple sensory thresholds may be related to important personality variables. Eysenck (1952), for example, has shown that measurements of dark vision are among the most sensitive indicators of the general "neuroticism" characteristic which he has been investigating.

Out of work in psychophysics have come procedures for quantifying *judgments* of all sorts, whether or not any physical magnitudes correspond to them. This line of development has brought methods for scaling products like picture postcards or handwriting samples, and measurements of a bewildering variety of attitudes toward particular nationalities, institutions, issues, or problems. Measurements based on such scales are also woven into the fabric of what we know about human differences.

The most general term that can be used for all the measurements with which one is working is *variable*. As the name suggests, this means simply a quantity whose magnitude varies. It may mean physical measurements, differential threshold determinations, test scores, or personality ratings. The variation we investigate may be from person to person or from day to day. Any ordered set of numbers constitutes a *variable*.

Although psychologists deal with all sorts of variables in their work, it is true that mental tests are of special importance. It is essential that anyone who is to read understandingly the results of the research on intelligence and personality have a clear concept of what a test is. It has often been defined as a *sample* of some type of human behavior that we wish to investigate. Thus if we wish to know how intelligently we can expect a person to act in life situations, we present under standard conditions some problems that call for an intelligent response and observe how he handles them. If we wish to know how rapid and well coördinated his hand movements will be on a job requiring such skill, we use as a test a standardized sample of the kinds of task he will be required to do. If we wish to know how well he reads, we try him out on a sample of reading material. For personality evaluation, we cannot actually sample his relationships to others and his behavior in crisis situations, but we can ask him questions as to what he customarily does, thus obtaining a report on a representative sample of his personal habits and attitudes.

The most important characteristic of a test defined in this way has always been considered to be its *validity*. To what exent does it actually measure what it purports to measure? In other words, what is the evidence that this test behavior actually constitutes an adequate sample of the behavior we are attempting to evaluate?

As mental testing has reached out in many new directions, it has become apparent that both this concept of what a test is and the concept of validity that goes with it are somewhat too narrow. Goodenough (1949), reviving an idea put forward years ago by Boring, has proposed that we supplement this notion of a test as a *sample* of some sort of behavior with another equally productive one—that a test may be regarded as a *sign* of some characteristic which we can proceed to investigate. There are many types of test whose usefulness has been demonstrated again and again, which fit better into this framework. As we have indicated above, one must stretch the sample concept to make it cover personality inventories. It seems to make better sense to consider that the answers a subject chooses on one of these inventories can be considered *clues* to some personality characteristics. Whether he really acts or feels as he says he does becomes immaterial. Our task in validating the test is to find out what sort of behavior these verbal responses are related to. It has been found time and time again that paper-and-pencil tests predict success in complex mechanical tasks as well as the so-called work-sample tests do. The test score constitutes a sign pointing to the kind of criterion performance to be expected of a person, but can hardly be considered a sample of it. With the increasing use of factor analysis to sort out the basic variables in batteries of many diverse tests, we are developing more and more tests which do not seem to constitute samples of any one type of observable behavior. But, taken singly or in combination, they do point to some aspects of characteristics that are important in life situations. Most of the projective tests similarly fit better into a "sign" than into a "sample" framework.

Along with this shift in our thinking about the meaning of a "test" have come new ideas about the old problem of validity. If we frankly say that until we have done a good deal of research with a new test we do not know what it measures, the important question becomes "What is this a test of?" rather than "Does it test what it purports to?" Even with tests like those of intelligence, where the originators thought they knew at the beginning what universe they were sampling, the experience of many test users over a long period of years has gradually modified and sharpened our understanding of what the scores tell us about individuals. (See Chapter 4.) With something like the "field-dependence" trait that Witkin and his associates ran into unexpectedly when they were looking for factors affecting perception of the vertical (see Chapter 9), the question of the validity of the rod-and-frame test, for example, was meaningless until a considerable body of research had been focused on the definition of the trait underlying the scores.

The monograph on test standards issued by the American Psychological Association in 1954 reflects this more complex and subtle thinking about validity problems. The authors distinguish between four kinds of validity evidence: (1) *content* validity, based on the demonstration that the test items constitute an adequate sample of the body of knowledge or kind of skill the test is set up to measure; (2) *concurrent* validity, based on evidence that the scores individuals make on the test correlate with other measurements about which more is known; (3) *predictive* validity, based on evidence that criterion scores or differentiations in some concrete field of endeavor or area of actual life experience can be forecast with better than chance accuracy by means of the test; and (4) *construct* validity, based on an analysis of the relationship of the characteristic measured to some hypothetical construct growing out of a whole body of research.

In studying individual differences we must be concerned with all sorts of measurements—nominal, ordinal, interval, and ratio scales, the measurement of thresholds and the quantification of judgments that psychophysical experiments produce, and mental tests of all varieties, whether conceived as samples or as signs. We must always try, however, to take into consideration what is known about the measuring instruments and the theories of measurement on which they are based, if we are to avoid the pitfalls of the past and build soundly toward the theoretical structure of the future.

THE DIRECTIONS RESEARCH TAKES

The first step in any research undertaking is to identify some trait that can be measured and show that individual differences do exist with regard to it. Sometimes, as in the case of intelligence, the trait is one that has become apparent to everyone from observation of children or adults in life situations. The task then is to construct some measuring instruments that will enable us to score subjects on sample situations. Sometimes a hypothesis with regard to a trait that ought to be measurable arises out of clinical work with individuals, as in the case of "rigidity" which a number of workers have been attempting to pin down. Sometimes the conclusion that a measurable trait exists comes about by pure accident when marked individual differences show up among subjects who had been expected to give uniform results in an experiment.

There are hundreds of traits with regard to which measurable individual differences have been shown. There is little we can do with such information, however, until more has been accomplished than simply to report that variability exists. Our concern in this book will be with traits for which research has been carried through one or more further stages, so that we actually know something about the trait that has been identified. A complete catalog of all the characteristics upon which human subjects differ, with references to the tests or experiments upon which the list is based, would be a valuable reference for research workers, but it would be of little value to students trying to organize their knowledge, or to teachers, social workers, and clinicians trying to apply their ideas to real situations. The facts and principles that have been most useful have been based on research that did more than to present a distribution, or a mean and standard deviation for a group.

At the very least, the investigator can be expected to get some evidence with regard to the *reliability* of the measurements he has made. A fact often lost sight of in our enthusiasm for a new testing technique is that a normal distribution for a group of scores will be obtained even if the results are due to pure chance. It is likely that if we gave only answer sheets for one of our intelligence tests to 1,000 subjects and asked them to select a response for each item without ever seeing the questions, the distribution of obtained scores would approximate the normal form although scores would undoubtedly be lower than they are when the test is given in the customary way. To some extent all test scores and measurements are determined by just such chance factors as are involved here.

We must always ascertain what part such chance determiners play. To do so, it has been customary to compute some kind of *self*-correlation. Either the test is repeated and the first set of scores compared with the second, or scores on one half—say the odd-numbered items, for example—compared with scores on the other half. In the extreme case cited above where responses on the answer sheet represent nothing but pure guesses, there is no reason to suppose that there would be any relationship between two sets of test scores obtained in any of these ways. If, at the other extreme, there is a high relationship, a marked tendency for individuals to come out with similar rankings on the two halves or the two administrations, we have evidence that a real source of differences between subjects is being measured.

As with the validity concept discussed above, the reasoning about reliability has become more complex and penetrating as the years have passed. It is realized now that coefficients obtained by different methods have somewhat different meanings. Cronbach (1949a) clarified the whole matter considerably by proposing that we distinguish between coefficients of *stability* (based on test-retest comparisons) and coefficients of *equivalence* (based on comparisons between different parts or different forms of a test).

In the special field of mental testing the blanket term "reliability" still seems to have some utility. In thinking about individual differences more broadly, however, it is more profitable for us to think in general terms of *sources of variability*. What we call *chance* is one such source and leads to low reliability coefficients. *Change* over a period of time is another, with or without special training during the interval between measurements. Methods are now at our disposal for getting clear-cut answers to questions about the sources of variability. They have great practical significance. If, for example, as has been shown with regard to some physiological characteristics, the differences between successive measurements of the same person are as great as those between simultaneous measurements of different persons, we can conclude that such measurements are of no value to us as indices of permanent personality traits, although as indices of current health or mood at specified times they may be quite useful. Or, to take another example, if the average differences between men with three days of training on a new job and men with one day of training are larger than the difference between the highest and the lowest man as measured on either occasion, the astute personnel manager will not be interested in a selection program for that particular job. Here obviously work methods which anyone can acquire are the principal source of variation. The first main kind of research that can be done, then, is to explore various *sources of variability* for any measured trait.

Another main type of research in individual differences has been the exploration of *relationships* among various measured characteristics. Two large subclassifications can be distinguished here. The investigator can relate the scores or measurements in which he is interested to other scores or measurements and search for meaningful hypotheses as to what the basic variables underlying all of them are. Or he can make use of a clear-cut *criterion* that he knows to be important in some area of applied psychology and ascertain how successfully his scores will predict it. The distinction here is not an absolute one. In the first type of study, *all* the traits considered enter into the procedure on an equal footing. Whatever we find out will apply to all of them. In the second type, the criterion is set apart from the others because we know it matters in real life, and our new variable, the "unknown," is interpreted in terms of its relationship to this "known." But there are many in-between stages, research designs that attempt to extract some meaning both from the relationships between "unknowns" and from the way in which each of them predicts a "known." We shall consider many studies of this general type in later chapters. But we can say almost categorically that individual differences in a single trait are of interest to us only when we can show how they relate to differences in some other trait, be it test, criterion rating, physical measurement, or developmental level.

A third important direction research has taken is the identification of *group differences* with regard to measured traits. Comparisons of distributions of scores made by males and females, Negroes and whites, "upper" and "lower" classes, psychotics and normals, "gifted" and "average" children, make up an important body of knowledge about human characteristics. Here again there is more than one way of using such comparisons. They may serve to define the trait to be measured, as in Strong's work where the scoring key for "Physician" interests is made up of only those items on which doctors differ in their responses from men-in-general. They may help to validate a test, as, for example, when evidence that a group of mechanics scores much higher than average men on a new test is used to support the author's contention that it is indeed a test of mechanical ability. More often, however, these group comparisons have been used to tell us something about the characteristics of the people in the groups rather than about the tests. There are some special hazards in such inferences which we shall discuss in greater detail later. We need to have some fairly adequate information about *either* the group *or* the test in order to draw useful conclusions of any sort. If we are not at all sure what a test is measuring and we have no way of knowing beforehand just how the groups to be compared differ, we are likely to be as much at sea when we finish a study as we were when we started. A good deal of the early work in the sex- and race-differences areas is subject to this cricitism.

A fourth type of research has been the developmental study. From the beginning of the work on intelligence measurement, the question of the *growth* of mental ability in children has been a focus of attention. At first, psychologists working on this problem tested groups of children of different ages and constructed growth curves by connecting the points that represented the averages. As time passed, more and more of them began to carry out *longitudinal* studies instead, testing the same individuals at different stages in their progress from infancy to maturity. This has turned out to be a much sounder procedure and has directed our attention to individual differences in the growth curves themselves. Investigations of age changes in adults were started somewhat later than the developmental studies of children, but they have taken on increasing importance as time has passed. At first they too employed cross-sectional methods, testing various age groups simultaneously. But in the early 1950's reports began to come in of longitudinal studies of adults, and the results they reported were as striking as those from the research on children had been. There has come to be general agreement among psychologists that studies of development should be of the longitudinal variety. Obviously this is a type of work that cannot be done on as small a budget as some of the other kinds.

Finally, a fifth and very important type of research that has been carried out with measured differences is the investigation of their *causes*. It is evident that this topic has something in common with the one we discussed first, that of identifying *sources* of variability. The difference is partly one of depth and partly one of time relationships. In identifying sources of variability, we are thinking about these particular *scores* we have obtained. To what extent are they accounted for by chance? What difference do the directions and other aspects of the testing conditions make in them? Is there a practice effect from trial to trial? In seeking causes, we think about the *traits* the test is measuring rather than about the scores themselves. Why do these children differ so widely in intelligence? Can we attribute the fact to differences in hereditary endowments, in general home conditions, in early childhood experiences, in opportunity for schooling, or in attitudes toward intellectual achievement? In a study of causation, a period of time, often a considerable period, must intervene between the measurements of causes and effects.

THE EXTENT OF HUMAN VARIABILITY

There is one group of questions that are in a different category from all these others we have discussed. How large are human differences, in general, in comparison with the magnitudes we have found ways to measure in the external world? Is there a difference in variability from one *trait* to another? Do men differ more with regard to intelligence, for example, than they do in stature or pulse rate? Such questions are connected with broad philosophical issues, and the answers one gives to them may be related to his religious, social, and political convictions. Many psychologists doubt, however, whether there is any way to attack them by research methods.

The one person who has made a serious attempt to do so is Wechsler. In his book *The Range of Human Capacities* (1952), he collected all the distributions he could find of various kinds of measurable characteristics. As an index of variability he used what he called the *range ratio*. Since he was only interested in the variability to be found in the healthy, non-pathological segment of the human race, he left out of his computations the highest and the lowest thousandth of each distribution. This would remove, for example, the measurements of dwarfs and giants, circus fat men and living skeletons, but would leave the great mass of people whose height and weight fall within the normal range. For each of these slightly curtailed distributions, he divided its highest by its lowest figure to obtain his range ratio.

Wechsler is impressed with the fact that differences between human beings, expressed this way, are relatively small. When we think of the enormous difference in size between the smallest and the largest living creatures, to say nothing of the objects in the inorganic world, the range ratio of 1.27:1 for human stature seems quite insignificant. When we think of the immense superiority of human intelligence over that of any of the lower animals, the ratio of 2.30:1 for mental age appears trifling. His conclusion is that the very large differences we find in income and social prestige certainly do not follow from natural differences, but are man-made exaggerations of those differences. Persons who prefer an equalitarian philosophy can take considerable comfort in these findings.

The most serious difficulty we encounter, however, when we attempt to draw any such general conclusion about human psychological differences, is that there is a whole class of measurements that we are compelled to leave out. It is only the ratio-scale distributions like those shown in Figures 3 and 4 that are susceptible to the kind of treatment Wechsler gives them. There is no question about the fact that 200 cubic inches of lung capacity is twice as much as 100 cubic inches. The person whose reaction time is 200 seconds is just twice as slow as the person who reacts in 100 seconds. As long as our scores are expressed in inches or seconds or pounds, we are on safe ground when we make such statements. Interval-scale distributions like those shown in Figures 5 and 6 cannot be handled in this way. The individual with an IQ of 140 is not twice as bright as the one with an IQ of 70. Each IQ point represents no definite unit to which a division on some measuring rod corresponds. We do not know what zero intelligence is. Any ratio we could set up between high and low performances would be misleading.

Certain questions in the field of differential psychology are thus unanswerable at present and perhaps forever. Questions involving comparisons of variability in different traits are of this nature, if the traits have to be measured by mental tests. Do people differ *more* in intelligence than they do in sheer memory, for instance? Do adults differ more than children? Is artistic talent or emotional stability or integrity of character a more variable trait than intelligence? The fact that IQ's run from zero to 200 and art-judgment scores from 50 to 125 means nothing at all, so far as these problems are concerned. Neither the IQ nor the art score represents an exact amount of anything. Zero does not mean that the individual has absolutely none of the ability involved. Five IQ points are not the equivalent of five points of difference in art score. Wechsler realizes this limitation and leaves out the complex characteristics that cannot be measured in physical units except for Binet mental age, Otis IQ, and a hard-learning test, all of which are subject to the criticism of not being measurements to which a ratio may be applied. But it is just these complex characteristics that are of most importance in human life.

Another objection that has been made to Wechsler's conclusions is that even when measurements can be made in physical units such as inches or seconds, the *psychological* units to which these correspond may be quite different in their magnitude and their significance. A runner whose speed on the hundred-yard-dash is 15 seconds at the beginning of the practice season can cut this down by one second with relative ease. But when he has reached the point where he is doing it in 10 seconds, a difference of one second represents a tremendous improvement—a step so great, in fact, that nobody has ever taken it. In factory production the fastest worker in a department may work at only twice the speed of the slowest, but the advantage this gives him in income and the standard of living that goes with it makes it appear that the ratio in psychological units would be considerably larger than 2:1. Because we cannot measure these psychological units in such a way as to make range ratios possible does not mean that we should ignore them.

The thing that we *can* do with psychological measurements of many kinds is to make distributions in the way that has been explained, express each individual's score in terms that will show where he belongs in the group, and accumulate information as to the practical significance in human affairs of derived scores of various levels of magnitude. This is a far more fruitful procedure than the attempt to describe in any absolute terms the variability of the human race.

If we cannot state how many times as bright as the village idiot Einstein is, we can say with some assurance what kind of contribution to human progress each is likely to make. If we cannot say that the aviation cadet with a score of 9 on the qualifying examination is nine times as talented as the man with a score of 1, our statistical data allow us to state with some assurance that he has *sixteen* times as good a chance to get through his elementary training. If we cannot say that the student with a college aptitude score of 120 is four times as bright as her classmate with a score of 30, we do know that the one is almost certain to pass, the other almost certain to fail in college competition. It may not be philosophically satisfying to leave the situation in these terms, but it answers our practical needs fairly well.

SUMMARY

Variability from individual to individual seems to be a universal phenomenon. As far down in the scale of life as it has been possible to go, individual organisms differ in the extent to which they show certain rudimentary psychological traits. One-celled animals differ in the readiness with which they modify their behavior with experience, and consistent individual tendencies toward such behavior as swimming in groups or tolerating chemicals in the water have been noted. Individual rats differ from one another in both learning ability and temperamental traits. Monkeys differ markedly in the complexity of problems they are able to solve.

In human subjects measurable differences have been shown to exist in physical size and shape, physiological functions, motor capacities, sensory and perceptual sensitivity, intelligence, achievement and knowledge, interests, attitudes, and personality traits.

When a set of measurements of any of these characteristics has been obtained, the first thing that is done is to arrange them in order of magnitude in a frequency distribution which can be presented graphically as a histogram or a frequency polygon. All measurable traits we have investigated give us continuous distributions, with no breaks between groups. The majority of the distributions show some resemblance to the mathematical normal curve, and it is usually possible to transform the data in some way for those that do not, so that normal curve statistics may be used. The two summary figures usually computed in analyzing a distribution are the mean and standard deviation, which constitute measures of central tendency and variability.

The types of measurement that have been used in differential psychology range all the way from nominal scales, which are nothing more than numbers used as labels for categories of objects or people, to ratio scales, which have true zero points and equal units. Because most mental-test scoring systems fall in the intermediate measurement categories, ordinal or interval scales, certain limitations must be kept in mind with regard to the mathematical treatments that are meaningful in such cases. "Measurement" is a broader term than "test" in psychology and takes in psychophysical work and the scaling of judgments and attitudes. Tests can be viewed in some cases as samples of the type of behavior we wish to investigate, in other cases as signs pointing to the characteristic we wish to assess. Somewhat different formulations of the meaning of the concept of validity and somewhat different sorts of research grow out of the two ideas.

The types of research study that have given us what we know about individual differences include the identification of measurable traits, the exploration of sources of variability in the measurements, the clarification of the relationships of each trait to other characteristics including life-situation criteria, the identification of group differences, inquiry into developmental trends, and studies of causation.

An ambitious attempt to assess the total amount of human variability and show how it varies from trait to trait has been made by Wechsler, using range ratios, or the ratio of the next-to-the-highest to the next-to-the-lowest individual scores in a thousand randomly selected cases. His conclusion is that variability in human capacities covers a relatively narrow range. The criticisms that the ratio method cannot be used on mental-test scores, and that for psychological traits measured in physical units the psychological units may not correspond to the physical ones, throw some doubt on the conclusion. At any rate, the more important task for differential psychologists is to gather information about what measured differences mean in life situations. Thus we can avoid arguments over questions that are at present unanswerable and discover the facts that are really significant in human affairs.

CHAPTER 3

Wresting Meaning From Measurements

SAMPLING—THE PROBLEM OF REPRESENTATIVENESS

In attempting to gather evidence on the kinds of research questions that have been outlined in the previous chapter, many problems have arisen, and we have gradually worked out acceptable ways of solving them. Perhaps the most fundamental of these is the problem of *sampling*. It is essential that the consumer as well as the producer of research data understand just what this problem is.

It is obvious when anyone begins to consider the matter that the pronouncements of psychologists about such things as, for example, the differences between males and females in dominance, the intelligence level of ten-year-old children, or the vocational interests of engineers are not based on a thorough study of all the individuals in the class they are describing. No-one has ever given any test to all the 75 million males and 75 million females even in this country alone, to say nothing of the rest of the world. No-one has tested all the ten-year-old children or all the engineers. What assurance have we that the sample that has been tested is typical of all the rest?

If no attention is paid to this at all, subtle kinds of bias are introduced into the conclusions we draw, and this bias may vary from one study to another. Persons who are working with children aged six through fourteen often obtain a fairly adequate sample of the population by accident, since our compulsory school laws insure that practically all the children within the age range will be in school. While no single grade school would be completely typical of all schools in the community, the state, or the nation, a combination of several of them in different geographical locations can often be used for research purposes. But with older or with younger populations, the problem of obtaining an adequate sample is far more difficult. Even at the high-school level, many students have left school to go to work. Unless we seek them out and test them along with the rest, our generalizations about adolescent characteristics will be in error to an unknown extent. Particular care must be taken not to generalize to the rest of the population from studies of college subjects, since college students are a selected group, both brighter and wealthier than the average. There is no one organization to which one can turn for representative samples of the adult population. Neither the luncheon club nor the labor union is typical of the whole world of adult men. We cannot find all the kinds of women we should like to study in a Ladies' Aid Group, a PTA meeting, or a Business and Professional Women's Club. A group of Negroes in a little southern town where policies of repression and discrimination have been applied for generations is not typical of the whole Negro race. But neither is a group of Negro children brought up under highly favorable educational conditions by parents who through unusual ability and determination were able to lift themselves far above the general level. If a graduate student sends out questionnaires to 1,000 people and 532 of them are returned, nobody knows just what kind of sample those 532 constitute. There is obviously some psychological difference between persons who coöperated and persons who did not. One important question that a student must learn to ask is, "On what sort of sample of the population are these reported results based?"

Technical means are now available for solving the sampling problem in a completely satisfactory manner. The mathematical concept to which all our statistical reasoning is related is the *random* sample. If we could take the names of all persons living in the United States, write them on little round discs so that they could be thoroughly mixed up, place them in an enormous hat, and then, blindfolded, draw out one name after another, we could secure a random sample of the U. S. population. Needless to say, such a procedure is impractical. Fortunately, we are not often attempting to draw conclusions for the whole U. S. population, so that it is not really necessary either. But it constitutes a sort of mathematical ideal which other sampling methods approximate as nearly as they can. The essential feature of random sampling is that one individual in the population from which a sample is drawn has exactly the same chance of being drawn as another.

It is in the field of public-opinion research that the greatest effort has been made to develop practical ways for obtaining samples that represent the population adequately. Most of us are aware that, in spite of some embarrassing exceptions, in general these polls give much more accurate results than they used to in years gone by. The most satisfactory sampling method they have found, and the closest to straight random sampling, is the *area* sample. As a basis or choosing a few persons among many, each part of the country is divided and subdivided until the pointer falls on a certain address in a certain block on a certain street. The interviewer goes to this place and asks his questions about soap or politics of the person who answers his knock. A reasonable substitute, much easier to work out, is the *representative* sample. One first studies the census reports which show the proportions of different income groups, different age groups, males and females, farm dwellers and city dwellers, Republicans and Democrats, Easterners, Westerners, and Southerners, in the population. Then he selects the right number of individuals in each category and thus puts together a group which, in the aggregate, will have exactly the same proportions of all these characteristics as the whole population does. In this way a few thousand will accurately represent a hundred million.

In studies using mental tests and other kinds of measurements that require a considerable amount of time from each subject, it has not usually been possible to be as careful and thorough about the sampling as the public-opinion pollsters are. Each study in the field of individual differences constitutes a unique challenge to work out some original way of making the sample to be studied as representative as possible. For questionnaire research, follow-up letters after the first appeal is made can often serve to increase the response very markedly. Toops (1926) in a classical study of this sort found that six follow-up letters, each using a different kind of appeal, brought 100 per cent replies in a study where response to the original questionnaire was only 52.7 per cent. Psychologists in Scotland in 1935 and again in 1947 gave individual intelligence tests to a completely representative sample of one age group by testing every child who had been born on February 1, May 1, August 1, and November 1, of a certain year (Scottish Council for Research in Education, 1939, 1949). Jones and Conrad (1933) gave free movies in order to draw in practically the whole population of the New England villages in which they were working. They then made home visits to obtain data from the individuals whose scores were still missing, thus including in their final sample about 90 per cent of total population of the place within the age range that interested them. Enough ingenious approaches to the sampling problem are now on record to serve as suggestions and sources of ideas to researchers launching out into new and unknown waters.

If we were to pay attention to *only* studies that have been based on adequate representative samples, a book on differential psychology would be a very thin volume. Fortunately, if we have enough different research reports to draw on, we can make use of much information that has come from frankly non-representative samples. By considering the results from several such biased groups simultaneously we can often come up with a reasonable conclusion that accounts for them all. If, for example, a certain kind of sex difference shows up in separate studies of ten-year-old children in one locality, college men and women in another, and husbands and wives at a PTA meeting in still a different spot, we are led to the conclusion that, at least in our culture, this *is* a sex difference not peculiar to the kind of group we happened to test. Or, if correlations of about the same magnitude between motor skill and intelligence are reported by all investigators whose subjects are mentally deficient children but not by those whose subjects are of better than average intelligence, this combination of facts makes possible a meaningful conclusion.

Furthermore, even findings about limited groups may have a great deal of practical usefulness. If there are important differences between high-school boys and high-school girls, that fact will have implications for education, whether or not the differences would be found in males and females generally. What we find out about the relationships between separate abilities in feeble-minded children can be useful in testing them, educating them, and placing them in employment whether or not we can expect to find such relationships in other groups. We must not generalize beyond our results. On the other hand, we must make use of everything we have. Some knowledge is better than no knowledge at all, and a conclusion with the weight of probability on its side is much better than complete ignorance.

What can be said with certainty about this problem of representative sampling is that it must *always* be kept in mind. The person doing research needs to concentrate on obtaining as satisfactory a sample as possible, considering the practical limits within which he operates. The person reading, evaluating, and applying research conclusions must take into consideration the information he has about the group or groups upon which results were obtained.

SAMPLING—THE MEANING OF STATISTICAL SIGNIFICANCE

There is another problem that arises from the fact that we do our research on samples, not on whole populations. Even in the ideal situation where two samples have been selected in a perfectly random manner from the same population, they do not give us precisely the same quantitative results. Suppose we have carried out the procedure described on page 47 and placed the names of all the residents of the United States in a hat.

Suppose too that we write each person's age after his name. Then we attempt to get a figure for the average age of the U. S. population by drawing a sample of 100 names and computing a mean. Because we do not quite trust our first result, we throw the name discs back in, shuffle them again, draw out another sample of 100 and compute another mean. Would the verdict as to the average age of the population be the same in the two cases? Common sense, as well as repeated experience with situations of this type, tells us that we would not get *precisely* the same answer. One old man of a hundred and two might show up in the second sample whereas nobody over eighty-five happened to be drawn in the first. The first sample might have happened to include twice as many babies under a year old as did the second. If we repeated the procedure time after time, the average of the *averages* would eventually give us a very accurate indication of what the population mean is, but any one sample would not.

This sort of difference between successive samples from the same population is what statisticians mean by *chance error* in any statistic. It would be more accurate perhaps to call it the error of sampling. It must always be taken into consideration when any sort of statistic is being computed. If, in the example of the previous paragraph, we happen to be interested in the variability of the population instead of its central tendency, we must remember that the standard deviations we compute from numbers that we draw will vary somewhat from sample to sample. If we are trying to find out the relationship between age and intelligence and we have an IQ as well as an age figure on each of the discs we draw for our sample, we can compute some index of correlation from the paired numbers, but we must remember that the correlation coefficient we compute from the next sample will not be exactly the same.

Unless we constantly remind ourselves of its existence, we are all too likely to forget about this chance sampling error when we are comparing two groups which we expect to differ, or correlating two sets of scores which we expect to be related to one another. Much confusion can arise from this source when we try to piece together the results that different investigators have obtained. One doctor tries out the effect of a new drug for treating the common cold. Fifty-five per cent of his 40 treated patients as compared with 45 per cent of the 40 untreated recover in three days' time. He announces triumphantly that his treatment is a success. But the next month another doctor, reporting the same kind of study, says that 48 per cent of his treated patients as compared with 52 per cent of the untreated recovered in three days' time. The results seem to conflict. What they actually mean, however, is that all these percentages—55, 45, 52, 48—

are within the range of proportions we might expect to get if we took samples of 40 cold sufferers at a time regardless of treatment and put down how many of them recovered in three days.

Or to take another example—one worker gives an intelligence test to both boys or girls in a certain kindergarten. Since the boys come out with an average IQ of 102, whereas the girls average only 99, he reports that boys at this age are brighter than girls. Another worker who tests the children in another kindergarten obtains average IQ's of 103 for girls and 101 for boys, and decides that it is girls who have the advantage at the preschool level. The issue seems to be deadlocked. Whom are we to believe? The most likely answer is that all four of these IQ averages are within the range of means we could expect to get if we tested successive samples drawn from a population of average children paying no attention to which sex they happened to be. No importance can thus be attached to either of the comparisons of boys with girls.

The term the statistician uses for the idea that a result is outside the range of those which sampling fluctuation alone is likely to produce is *statistically significant*. It is the most pervasive, universal concept in all of differential psychology, and is fundamental to quantitative research in a wide range of fields from agriculture to sociology. The problem for the statistician has arisen from the fact that in practical research undertakings we do not draw many samples so that we can observe the variation among them directly. A research worker is lucky if he can get *one* satisfactory representative sample of the kind of population he wishes to find out about. Thus the mathematical statisticians have expended a great deal of effort on the task of developing methods by which we can *estimate* from the information we have at our disposal about one sample, the amount of variation there would be in other samples from the same population.

Along with the conclusion that the results he is reporting are *statistically significant*, which means that he has reason to believe that they do not arise from chance errors of sampling, a research worker usually states a probability figure. He says that the difference or the correlation reported is significant at the 5 per cent level ($P = .05$) or at the 1 per cent level ($P = .01$) or even perhaps at the .1 per cent level ($P = .001$). Even after encountering them hundreds of times in textbooks and journal articles, students are often far from clear as to exactly what these probability values mean. The statement, $P = .05$, applied to a difference between two means, indicates that if one drew paired samples at random, less than five times out of a hundred would he get as much difference as these averages show. Thus if the researcher concludes that the groups he is comparing *differ* with regard to the trait measured, he has a 5 per cent probability of being wrong about his conclusion, a 95 per cent probability of being right. If his computations permit him to state $P = .01$, he can be still more certain that the groups actually differ. In this case his conclusion has a 1 per cent probability of being wrong, a 99 per cent probability of being right.

Quite often an inequality sign rather than an equal sign is used with the $P =$ value to express this idea. $P < .01$ means that the probability is less than one hundredth. $P < .05$ means that the probability is greater than five hundredths. A statement that $.05 > P > .01$ means that there would be more than one but less than 5 chance occurrences in 100 of the event the experimenter is trying to interpret.

Still another way of expressing the same idea is to say that a difference or a correlation coefficient is significant at the 5 per cent level of confidence. The percentage here refers to the probability of getting the result the author has obtained purely by chance.

The reasoning as it is applied to correlation coefficients is exactly the same. To say that a correlation coefficient is statistically significant shows that one has reason to believe that a figure of this magnitude would not have been obtained had one drawn paired numbers at random from a well-shuffled pool of numbers. But it is a *probability* judgment, not a yes-or-no, black-or-white decision. To attach to a correlation coefficient the appendage $P = .05$ means that had 100 random samples been drawn, only 5 of them would have given us a coefficient this high. Thus in concluding that the two traits to which the coefficient refers really are related, one has a 5 per cent chance of being wrong, a 95 per cent chance of being right.

If a person is to achieve a clear understanding of what the results that have been reported in differential psychology mean and to show good judgment in applying them, he needs to understand precisely what the concept of statistical significance means in order to be aware of what it does *not* mean. Around this point much confusion centers, probably because the word "significant" as we use it in our common speech carries a rich freight of connotations. It is a symbol of value as well as fact. What we do when we place the word "statistically" in front of it is to strip it of all this cargo it is carrying. The statement that a result is statistically significant means *nothing but* the fact that it is not accounted for by sampling fluctuations. The idea embodied in the research may be unimportant, the conclusion may have no practical application whatever, and the author may be a complete bore. It takes far more than statistically significant results to constitute a brilliant contribution to knowledge. But no amount of brilliance in planning a study and interpreting its findings can *make up* for the failure to check on statistical significance first. Unless one does this he runs the risk of expending all his brilliance in efforts to make sense of differences or relationships that do not exist.

METHODS OF ATTACK ON PROBLEMS OF RELATIONSHIP

The most important category of problems in the psychology of individual differences has been the investigation of relationships between measured traits. As was explained in the previous chapter, we can make little or no use of information showing that subjects differ with regard to any one characteristic until we have some other facts to put with it. Because this problem of trying to relate one kind of measured difference to another loomed large in the thinking of early workers such as Galton and Pearson, the correlation method was one of the first to be developed and widely used.

Like so many other things in psychology, the judgment as to whether or not two traits are related turns out not to be a yes-or-no matter. For example, if all students with high IQ's did well in school, all students with average IQ's made average grades, and all students with low IQ's did poorly, there would be no need to apply correlation procedures here. We could simply say that IQ and school success are related to one another, or that IQ predicts school success. But that, of course, is not the way things are. Not all of the high-scoring students do well. Some few even appear on the failure list. Among the average-IQ group are some with outstanding school records and some who rank far below most of their classmates. What we see when we examine IQ's and report cards for any group is evidence for a *tendency* toward a relationship without perfect correspondence.

The correlation coefficient, often represented by the symbol r, constitutes an efficient, economical way of describing such relationships. It is a number that looks like a decimal. Its sign can be either plus or minus, and its magnitude ranges between zero and 1.00.

The *sign* tells us whether the direction of the relationship is positive or negative. Most frequently this sign is plus and thus indicates that there is a tendency for high scores on one trait to be accompanied by high scores on the other, average scores on one to occur with average scores on the other, and low scores on one to occur with low scores on the other.

Sometimes, however, it is minus, and means that there is a tendency for high scores on one of the variables to occur with low scores on the other, and vice versa. In Table 2 one of the correlations is positive but those in which reaction time is one of the variables are negative. It is easy to see why this should be true. Reaction time is the only one of these three measures that indicates a good score by a *low* number. The smaller the subject's score, measured in hundredths or thousandths of a second, the faster he is. For the two other tests, scores run in the opposite direction. The higher the number of blocks placed in boxes, or cards sorted into piles, the better the person is performing.

TABLE 2.

Typical Correlations Between Block Packing,
Card Sorting, and Reaction Time

	BLOCK PACKING	CARD SORTING	REACTION TIME
Block Packing		.28	—.25
Card Sorting	.28		—.21
Reaction Time	—.25	—.21	

The numerical *size* of the coefficient tells us how *close* the relationship is between the two traits measured. If r is not much larger than zero, there is very little correlation between the two traits. If it approaches either 1.00 or —1.00, there is a high degree of relationship, and one of the traits of the pair can be used as an indicator or a predictor of the other. Most of the relationships we investigate in psychology give us correlation coefficients intermediate between these two extremes. The correlation between intelligence-test scores and school grades, for instance, usually turns out to be about .50. This means that it is more likely than not that a person will do about as well in his school work as he does on the test, but that there are numerous minor exceptions and a few major exceptions to the general trend. If we use the test score to predict the school record, we can expect to be somewhere nearly right in most cases but definitely wrong in a few.

One word of caution is in order here. Although a correlation coefficient looks like a decimal, it is not really a decimal fraction of anything and *must not* be interpreted as a percentage. A correlation of .50 does *not* mean that half the subjects get the same score in the two traits or that the figures in any way represent *half* of a perfect correlation. A correlation of .60

does not indicate three times as much relationship as one of .20. If we wish to evaluate how much two kinds of trait depend upon the same factors, the *square* of *r* rather than *r* itself is the index we use. Evaluated this way, a correlation of .60 indicates that common factors are responsible for 36 per cent of the variation among subjects in both traits. It is in fact *nine* times as large as the correlation of .20 which accounts for only 4 per cent of the variation. An *r* of .20 is of very little value to anybody in making decisions about individuals or groups. An *r* of .60 has considerable practical value.

The statistical significance of a correlation coefficient depends upon two factors: (1) the absolute size of the *r* (it makes no difference whether it is positive or negative) and (2) the number of cases on which it is based. Any small *r* (.00 to .20, for instance) is likely not to be significant unless it is based on a very *large* number of cases. Any correlation based on a small sample of people (say 25 cases or less) is likely not to be significant unless *r* itself turns out to be very large. A psychologist who knows the simple formulas needed to make such a significance test can easily determine whether any reported *r* is outside the probable range of coefficients one could get by random pairings of numbers. The consumer of correlational results should learn to look for the essential "P = .05" or "P = .01," especially when either the *r* or the N on which it is based is small.

There is another way of demonstrating that two characteristics are related at a given level of statistical significance without working out a correlation coefficient. It can be done by the use of the *chi square* (χ^2) method. This is a statistical technique that has many uses. What it tests is whether an obtained *distribution* differs significantly from some theoretical or expected distribution. It is particularly useful in problems involving the relationship of two traits that are difficult or impossible to quantify with any precision, where perhaps only a nominal scale is possible. Take, for example, Table 3, which comes from a study in which Munroe was trying to find out whether evaluations of emotional disturbance based on the Rorschach test were related to emotional disturbance as it showed up in the college situation.

All Munroe did was to *count the frequency* of students appearing in the different combination categories—good adjustment on the Rorschach along with good adjustment in college, good adjustment on the Rorschach along with frequent difficulties in college, and so forth. By setting up on the basis of the proportions in each class for one of the characteristics the distribution we would expect in the other if they were not related, we can always obtain an "expected" distribution against which the "obtained" distribution can be evaluated. If the discrepancies are large, we have reason to believe that the hypothesis of "no relationship" does not hold, and thus that the two traits *do* tend to go together. Probability reasoning comes in here again. Chi square tables which show the probability of getting figures of various magnitudes for different numbers of cells or categories make the task easy. The P-value reported with a chi square figure is the important item to examine when reading a research report of this kind. If P = .01, it means here that one would get this particular distribution for two *unrelated* variables only one time in a hundred. Therefore they must *not* be *unrelated* or independent of one another, but related.

TABLE 3.

Rorschach Adjustment Ratings and Adjustment in College

(Munroe, 1945, p. 40)

CRITERION	ADJUSTMENT RATING FROM RORSCHACH				
	A ADEQUATELY ADJUSTED	B SLIGHT PROBLEM	C MODERATE PROBLEM	D SEVERE PROBLEM	TOTAL
Seen by psychiatrist	5	6	8	24	43
Much faculty consultation	4	19	29	37	89
Committee rating "p" (problem)	3	1	8	5	17
Adequately adjusted	65	82	39	13	199
Total	77	108	84	79	348

$\chi^2 = 108.21$
C = .49
P = .001

Such a method does not of course tell us anything about how close the relationship is. It is possible, however, to obtain a derived measure called the contingency coefficient, or C. This looks like an *r*, and means somewhat the same thing as far as size is concerned. That is, a C of .50 would show a moderate degree of relationship, a C of .18 a very low relationship. It is not, however, a very good approximation of *r*. Its upper limit is somewhat short of 1.00, depending on how many classes or categories were used in computing the chi square on which it is based. It is useful only for making rough judgments and cannot be substituted for a correlation coefficient in any kind of precise computational work.

Much could be said about special correlation methods that have been developed for special types of data. It is enough here to mention that they are available and that practically any conceivable research problem in which the basic question is whether or not two characteristics are related is now soluble.

Many correlation studies are undertaken primarily for purposes of *prediction* rather than simply to show that two variables are related. The office manager wants not just a correlation coefficient but some information as to how much the use of this test will improve his selection ratios. The parole officer is interested in the extent to which personality evaluations can tell him which prisoners are likely to repeat their offenses. A set of techniques related to the correlational procedures has been devised for this special purpose. The general name applied to these predictive methods is *regression*.

In order to calculate regression coefficients, one variable, the thing being predicted, is designated the *dependent* variable. The other, from which one is predicting, is called the *independent* variable. There may be several independent variables all linked to one dependent variable. Thus one can set up a procedure for predicting report card marks from a combination of IQ, teacher's ratings, and socio-economic level. The report card marks are the dependent variables here (since they are assumed to *depend* upon the other characteristics) and the IQ's, ratings, and socio-economic indices are the independent variables.

SOURCES OF CORRELATION: FACTOR-ANALYSIS METHODS

While thousands of correlation coefficients have been published by psychologists who seemed to have had no curiosity about what they meant, there have been some workers from the very beginning who saw this as an engrossing question. Even before Binet published his first intelligence scale, the ancestor of so many others, Spearman was trying to account for the fact that the correlations between different varieties of mental ability tests always turn out to be positive. From 1904 on down to the present, the amount of attention devoted to *factor analysis*, as the mathematical analysis of correlations is called, has constantly increased.

The kind of reasoning on which the factor-analysis methods are based is an indirect or roundabout process. It is more like what an astronomer does as he tries to give an account of conditions on a distant planet, or what a geologist does when he tries to describe what the earth was like a million years ago, than it is like the customary activity of the laboratory scientist. It is largely this indirectness or deviousness in the original reasoning that confuses the beginning student. The necessity for it arises from the fact that the process we are interested in cannot be observed directly. The mental tester can no more see the abilities he is tapping than the geologist can look in on the events of a million years ago. Both must somehow contrive to make inferences from the data they have and to check the correctness of these inferences without ever seeing their basic variables at all.

What a scientist does when confronted with a problem like this is to construct a *model* (though not necessarily a concrete physical one) the workings of which would serve to account for the facts he is trying to explain. If the model really accounts for everything, it becomes an accepted explanation. If there are certain facts it cannot account for, eventually someone devises a better model which takes precedence over the old one.

In factor analysis, the easiest way to understand how this model-building works is to follow the reasoning Spearman did at the beginning. The facts he had to work with were that all cognitive tests correlate positively, and that some of these correlations are much higher than others. He said to himself: "Suppose that what we have in human nature is just *one* kind of cognitive ability. Call it 'g' for *general* ability. Some persons are more liberally endowed with this ability than others. Furthermore, some kinds of tests draw on it much more heavily than others. If this were true, what kinds of correlations would we get?"

Suppose we have five tests, A, B, C, D, and E. Suppose that their "g" loadings are .9, .8, .7, .6, and .5. If the correlations between them are the product of their loadings in this factor they have in common, they would look like this:

	"g" (.9) TEST A	(.8) TEST B	(.7) TEST C	(.6) TEST D	(.5) TEST E
"g"					
(.9) A......	.81	.72	.63	.54	.45
(.8) B......	.72	.64	.56	.48	.40
(.7) C......	.63	.56	.49	.42	.35
(.6) D......	.54	.48	.42	.36	.30
(.5) E......	.45	.40	.35	.30	.25

The characteristic that became the basis for the whole Spearman system of factor analysis is apparent when one looks at this model table. It is what he called "hierarchical order." All the correlations decrease regularly from top to bottom and from left to right. Furthermore all the columns are proportional. That is, $\dfrac{.81}{.72} = \dfrac{.72}{.64} = \dfrac{.63}{.56}$, etc.

Spearman then could reason with some cogency: If we take a table of intercorrelations derived from actual test scores and arrange them in order from high *r*'s to low ones and then find that the columns in *this table* are proportional to one another, we shall be able to conclude that the "g" model *fits*—that correlations between tests can in fact be accounted for by a single "g" factor which is represented in the different mental performances to different degrees. And we can work backward from the correlations to obtain the "g" loadings for these tests.

Such reasoning can never show us with certainty that "g" *is* what produced the correlations, any more than the geologist can say definitely what happened to the dinosaurs. Some other model, for all we know, might account for the observed facts equally well. But a theory that gives us even a *possible* explanation for hundreds of disconnected facts constitutes a powerful tool in our thinking and a great stimulus for further research.

At the present time, fifty years after Spearman first presented this idea, we have evidence that this simplest of models is not adequate to explain all the facts. We have found it necessary to shift to a *multiple-factor* model which shows how the correlations could be produced if there were in each person a set of more or less independent abilities. In any individual some of these are better developed than others. In any test, some are required to a much greater extent than others, and tests can be constructed in such a way as to draw on a single ability almost entirely.

The principal area of controversy in factor analysis now centers around whether models that account for the correlations on the basis of *only* these separate independent factors are superior to those that postulate *both* "g" and factors of more limited scope. Even these two types of model are being brought closer together than they once were by new methodological developments.

We shall not try to explain here the elaborate computational procedures that are required for a modern factor analysis. It is enough that the reader, the consumer of factor-analytic research, be familiar with the end results that he is likely to encounter, so that he will know what to make of a table of factor loadings and how to avoid pitfalls that arise in their interpretation.

Table 4 is an example of the sort of final results a factor analysis gives us. It shows the *loading* each factor has in each test. (The concept of *loading* is a sort of metaphor. Each test is thought of as a vehicle carrying a certain amount of one or more of the abilities. Another way of explaining it is that the loading of a certain factor in a certain test shows us the extent to which this factor determines the scores individuals make on the test.) The mathematical work that produces these loadings does not tell us *what* the factors are. The names that get attached to them are based on a careful scrutiny of the pattern of loadings the table (or "matrix," in technical factor-analytic language) shows. Let us see how this works by examining Table 4.

TABLE 4.

Rotated Factor Matrix Based on Centroid Analysis of 21 Tests

(Thurstone and Thurstone, 1941, p. 91)

	I (P)	II (N)	III (W)	IV (V)	V (S)	VI (M	VII (R)	RESID- UALS
1. Identical Numbers ..	.42	.40	.05	−.02	−.07	−.06	−.06	.08
2. Faces	.45	.17	−.06	.04	.20	.05	.02	−.12
3. Mirror Reading	.36	.09	.19	−.02	.05	−.01	.09	.12
4. First Names	−.02	.09	0.2	.00	−.05	.53	.10	.02
5. Figure Recognition..	.20	−.10	.02	−.02	.10	.31	.07	−.17
6. Word-Number	.02	.13	−.03	.00	.01	.58	−.04	.04
7. Sentences	.00	.01	−.03	.66	−.08	−.05	.13	.07
8. Vocabulary	−.01	.02	.05	.66	−.04	.02	.02	.05
9. Completion	−.01	.00	−.01	.67	.15	.00	−.01	−.11
10. First Letters	.12	−.03	.63	.03	−.02	.00	−.00	−.08
11. Four-Letter Words ..	−.02	−.05	.61	−.01	.08	−.01	.04	−.05
12. Suffixes	.04	.03	.45	.18	−.03	.03	−.08	.10
13. Flags	−.04	.05	.03	−.01	.68	.00	.01	−.07
14. Figures	.02	−.06	.01	−.02	.76	−.02	−.02	.07
15. Cards	.07	−.03	−.03	.03	.72	.02	−.03	.13
16. Addition	.01	.64	−.02	.01	.05	.01	−.02	−.03
17. Multiplication	.01	.67	.01	−.03	−.05	.02	.02	.01
18. Three-Higher	−.05	.38	−.01	.06	.20	−.05	.16	−.12
19. Letter Series	−.03	.03	.03	.02	.00	.02	.53	.02
20. Pedigrees	.02	−.05	−.03	.22	−.03	.05	.44	−.02
21. Letter Grouping	.06	.06	.13	−.04	.01	−.06	.42	.06

In the first place, since these loadings are on the correlation scale running from .00 to 1.00, and since they too are subject to sampling errors, it is customary to pay no attention to those which are near zero. The identification of the factor rests primarily on loadings of .30 or higher. When we look at Column I, where the loadings for the first factor are found, we find loadings above .30 for only three tests—Identical Numbers, Faces, and Mirror Reading. What is it that these three tests have in common? Thurstone decided that perceptual speed was the one ability they all required, so he called this factor P. Next we examine the loadings for Factor II. The tests on which they occur are Identical Numbers, Addition, Multiplication, and Three-Higher. Even without looking at the test papers themselves, the nature of this factor seems obvious. Thurstone called it N, because working with numbers is what these four tests require. We shall have more to say about the "primary mental abilities" represented in this table in a later chapter.

The reader who has never studied the mathematical theory and the compuţional procedures of factor analysis must necessarily take the loadings he is given in a table like this one without questioning their numerical accuracy. He has a perfect right, however, to make up his own mind as to what they show about the abilities or personality characteristics being investigated. The description and naming of the factors is a matter of psychological judgment, not mathematical skill. Instead of simply reading through the names that a factor analyst has given his factors, it is always a good plan to examine the factor loadings for oneself. There is often room for a considerable difference of opinion as to just what it is that several tests have in common. Sometimes these differences can stimulate important new research activity.

Even if one does not know anything about the mathematical procedures by means of which the "factor matrix" comes into existence, there are certain limitations and defects in it of which he should be aware. It is not as precise and rigid as many non-mathematical readers believe it to be. At several stages in the complicated sequence of steps that must be taken, estimates or informed guesses are required. Mathematically, the *loadings* constitute distances measured along geometrical reference axes, and there is often room for some disagreement among skilled workers as to just where these reference axes should be placed with respect to the points that represent the tests. The encouraging thing is that in spite of the uncertainties that are an ineradicable part of the factor-analytic methods, a great deal of agreement has been achieved. Another equally skillful person working independently from Thurstone's data would probably not produce *precisely* the same set of factor loadings that we find in Table 4. But the loadings would be similar enough so that they would warrant exactly the same *conclusions* about the factor composition of the tests. It is these conclusions that we are working for. There is nothing sacrosanct about the exact loadings themselves. Let us then think of factor analysis as an *aid* to psychological judgment, a methodological tool designed to help us construct a useful body of theory about how traits determine test scores and the other measurements of individuals.

METHODS OF INVESTIGATING GROUP DIFFERENCES

On first glance, the setting up of a study to show whether two groups in the population differ with regard to some psychological trait looks easy. This is probably one of the reasons why we have had so many of such studies comparing the intelligence, for example, of boys and girls, whites and Negroes, or farm- and city-dwellers. Actually such studies involve a number of problems and difficulties. One must plan what he does carefully if he expects to be able to draw clear-cut conclusions from his results.

The first of these complexities has to do with the task of getting representative samples, a problem that has been discussed in an earlier section. When two or more groups are chosen on the basis of convenience, it can often happen that each of them is *un*representative of the population from which it comes in a different way. Measured differences between them, in such cases, may do nothing more than to reflect these combined biases. Suppose, for example, we wish to try out a new algebra test. A college freshman mathematics class is an easy place to get subjects. When we average the scores we find to our amazement that the average for the girls in this class is ten points higher than that for the boys. How shall we account for this result in view of the almost universal finding that the sex difference in mathematics favors males? First of all, we should realize as was mentioned before, neither college boys nor college girls are really representative of the population in general. Furthermore, in a freshman mathematics class, the two sex groups may well select themselves on an entirely different basis. The girls here may be the high-school students who did unusually well in this subject and decided to take more of it in spite of the fact that their sorority sisters frown on it. The boys may be those who avoided mathematics in high school because they had less than the average amount of interest and ability in it and are only subjecting themselves to it now because they have been told they must have it as a prerequisite for later courses in other areas. The special selective factors are such as to wipe out the customary sex difference and produce a difference in the opposite direction. The important point is that it shows us nothing about differences between males and females *as a whole*. If we expected to draw any such conclusions, we have wasted our time in working with this particular group.

There is much discussion of such selective factors in the literature of differential psychology. As psychologists have become more aware of them they have made determined efforts to minimize them. Where it is impossible to avoid them because of practical difficulties in getting good representative samples, we can often resist being led astray by them if we try out hypotheses about group differences in various diverse settings. As has been stated earlier, when several studies have been reported, often a reasonable conclusion can be drawn even if all of them are biased one way or another. It helps with such interpretation if the research worker reports what kinds of biases he thinks his sample may represent.

Another problem in group comparisons is that of making sure the tests or measurements to be used are suitable for the purpose. Intelligence tests have often been criticized in this connection. They were developed expressly for the purpose of comparing each person with the others in the group to which he belongs. An eight-year-old can be compared with other eight-year-olds because we can make the assumption that all these children have had an approximately equal opportunity to develop the mental skills the test requires. All have been to school for at least two years. All have seen books, heard radios, gone to movies. When we shift over to a comparison of the averages of different groups of children, there is a basis for considerable doubt as to what the differences mean. We cannot immediately conclude that one group is brighter than the other. The difference may represent some discrepancy in the opportunity that has been given to develop these mental qualities. The complexity of the problem is increased by the fact that the different varieties of intelligence test—even the different types of question within the same test—do not correlate perfectly with one another, so that some may be affected in one way, others in another, by whatever influences differentiate the groups we are comparing.

This basic doubt as to what group differences in intelligence test scores and similar "measurements" mean has led some psychologists, sociologists, and anthropologists to the conclusion that we would be better off to give up completely any attempt to use such tests for group comparisons. However, the fact that we already have the results of hundreds of such studies "in the record," so to speak, and that they are constantly being cited by writers and speakers bent on proving a point, suggests that it might be wiser to analyze what they do show than to try to suppress them. There are by now so many studies comparing boys with girls, Negroes with whites, and high-status groups with low-status groups, that it is possible to draw much sounder conclusions from the sum of them than could have been drawn from any one alone. Instead of phrasing the question, "Do these groups really differ from one another in intelligence and other mental traits?" we can ask simply, "What do the well-documented differences between groups on mental tests mean?" Then we can proceed to put together all the pieces of evidence that may enable us to answer it.

When two groups at a time are to be compared, the soundest way to decide whether the difference between them is statistically significant is called the *t*-test. (In the older literature and in some of the current work, one is more likely to encounter what is called the "critical ratio" which serves the same purpose.) The reader can understand what the comparison has shown, even if he knows nothing about how these statistics are computed, if he looks for the probability value, P = .01, P = .05, or perhaps P < .01 (P *is less than* .01) and remembers that it stands for the proportion of the time one would get differences of the magnitude shown in the study if he were simply drawing samples of this size at random from a box full of numbers that covered the range these scores do.

The more general statistical method of which the *t*-test is just a special case is called *analysis of variance*. By using it we can compare three or more groups simultaneously and decide whether the differences among them are greater than chance sampling fluctuations would lead us to expect. In such studies where several groups rather than just two are used, the verdict about statistical significance is usually stated as an "F-test." This too is always accompanied by a P-value which is to be interpreted in the same way as the others we have discussed.

The analysis of variance often serves as an alternative to the correlation coefficient or chi square in demonstrating that two variables are related to each other. Suppose, for example, we have three groups of subjects which we designate simply as old, middle-aged, and young, and give to all of them a test of the ability to memorize new materials. By computing the appropriate variances we can arrive at an F-ratio that tells us what the probability is that these groups are *not* really different in memorizing ability. If this probability of "no difference" is low, meaning that the probability of a real difference is high, we can conclude that the ability to memorize is significantly related to age. A glance at the means will tell us which direction the relationship takes. In this case it would almost certainly be negative, since the old memorize less well than the young. This method does not tell us how close the relationship is, but if our question is simply, "Are the two characteristics related?" it often works as well as the correlation method does.

PROBLEMS INVOLVING CAUSATION

Neither the correlation methods nor the group-difference methods tell us anything about the causes of the differences between individuals. Experience has shown that we must be constantly on guard against jumping to conclusions about causation from such evidence. Take, for example, the low positive correlation which has consistently shown up between socio-economic level and IQ. This may mean, as some have contended, that the more favorable environments produce more intelligent individuals, that is, that the socio-economic condition is the cause, the IQ the effect. But it may just as easily mean that more intelligent individuals are more successful in the competion for this world's goods, that is, that IQ is the cause and socio-economic status the effect. Causal factors may be working in both directions, that is, the IQ may to some extent determine the economic level, which in turn may influence the IQ. Still another possibility is that some third variable such as education is actually the causal factor and that the apparent relationship between IQ and socio-economic level arises from the fact that they are both related to this "something else." The point is that there is no way we can extract from the correlation coefficient itself the information as to which of these hypotheses is correct.

Many psychologists realize this ambiguity in the causal interpretation of correlations, but fail to recognize similar pitfalls when group difference results, such as those coming from analysis of variance studies, are examined. Suppose it is found, for example, that children known to have been weaned early are significantly more unstable emotionally than those known to have had a longer nursing period. Does this prove that early weaning produces or causes neurotic tendencies? Not necessarily. It is quite possible that both the early weaning and the emotional difficulties in the children are caused by neurotic tendencies in the mothers, leading them to reject unconsciously the responsibilities of motherhood. The children may have inherited such neurotic tendencies, or they may have reacted to many other evidences of them besides the early weaning. Again the point is that such a study as this simply cannot tell us what the causal relationships are.

Problems of causation are especially complex and intricate, as many philosophers have pointed out. In one sense, everything in the universe is the cause of each event which occurs. In another sense, nothing can be known with certainty to be the *cause* of what happens since all that we can ever observe is some invariable *sequence* of the type: Event A is followed by Event B. Observation never shows the link between them. What we have are correlations, coming to us without any guarantee that the relationships they show will always be maintained. For practical purposes, however, we can and certainly do isolate factors which appear to exercise a determining influence on succeeding events. We mix certain chemicals and an explosion takes place. We predict when an eclipse will occur. We change our tariff laws, and certain economic consequences appear. We deny our child the evidences of our affection which are rightly due him, and he becomes refractory. We administer the proper treatment, and the sick man recovers.

It is the *time* factor characterizing these situations that makes it possible for us to refer to one as the cause of the other. Whether we say that the child's crying is the cause or the effect of the spanking that he gets depends on which comes first. It is this time factor that we must get into our experiments in differential psychology if we are to explore causes. The independent variables must be introduced prior to the time we measure the dependent variable. The experimental method requires that we: (1) measure, (2) introduce the new factor or factors, and (3) measure again. If we wish to know, for example, whether vitamin-B deficiency has an unfavorable affect upon school achievement, the thing to do is to test a representative group of children, put them on a diet deficient in vitamin B, and test again at the end of the experimental period. We might, of course, proceed in the opposite way by testing a group of children known to be deficient in vitamin B, putting them on a diet rich in this substance, and then testing them again. R. F. Harrell (1943, 1947) has in fact carried out an excellent study on this problem using an adaptation of this plan.

In order to make such studies in time at all conclusive, however, some supplementary steps must be taken. In the example given above, how do we know that improved scores on the second test are not simply practice effects? How do we know that they do not reflect some of the innumerable other influences to which children are exposed at home, in school, on the playground, or at the movies? How can we be sure that it is the nutritional factor rather than some of these others which has brought about the change?

The customary way of handling this difficulty is to use a *control* group. Subjects in this group are selected in exactly the same way as those who are to take part in the experiment. In some research designs, a control subject is *paired* with each experimental subject in respect to age, race, sex, IQ, and other characteristics that might influence results. Only the experimental subjects are exposed to the influence being investigated. The question at the end of the experiment is then, "Do the experimental subjects differ from the controls?" In Harrell's vitamin study, only half the orphanage children who were subjects were given the supplementary rations. All were tested before and after the experimental period. Since they had all been exposed to the same general environmental influences during that time, the difference between the treated and the untreated groups could be definitely tied in with the vitamin supplementation. (It was of course necessary to demonstrate that the difference between groups was statistically significant.)

The use of a control group in an experiment is a universally recognized essential of scientific procedure. Our problems in psychology have centered around the difficulty of making experimental and control groups truly comparable. To pair subjects is one method, but it is hard when we are investigating a new kind of trait to be sure that we have paired them for everything that may be related to it. Investigations of the effects of counseling, for example, have run into the difficulty that if a control group is set up by matching a non-counseled student with each student who voluntarily seeks a counselor's aid, the two individuals in each pair will not be alike in the characteristic most crucial for counseling success, namely, motivation for change or improvement. If persons in any experimental group think that they are being given special help or attention, increased motivation may lead to more improvement in performance than individuals in the control group show, no matter how carefully they have been equated in the first place.

There is no single best method to overcome these control-group difficulties. Whenever it is practically feasible, *randomization* in the choice of individuals for the experimental and control groups should be carried out. That is, names or numbers of all persons available for the experiment should be placed in one pool and assigned to the separate groups by tossing a coin or using a table of random numbers. Whenever it is possible, both experimental and control groups should be given some treatment that *appears* to be the same, so that no subject knows whether or not he is being exposed to the special experimental influence. In the Harrell vitamin study, for example, each child received a capsule each day. Not even the personnel of the orphanage knew which capsules contained the extra nourishment. It is always important when tests are to be given and scored that the examiners be kept in ignorance of which subjects are in the experimental and which in the control groups. Hard as they may try to be objective, examiners and raters tend to slant their judgments slightly in the direction of what they hope the experiment will show.

With the rise of analysis of variance methods which permit comparisons between more than two groups at a time, problems very difficult to attack by the old methods have been brought under experimental scrutiny. There are numerous problems in psychology for which it appears to be impossible to isolate the effects of one variable alone, controlling everything else. It is in just such instances that complex experimental designs based on analysis of variance are most helpful. (To maximize the student's confusion, such research plans in which the effects of several independent variables on a dependent variable are examined simultaneously are called *factorial* designs, though they have absolutely nothing to do with the *factor*-analysis methods for analyzing correlations. They grow out of quite different statistical soil. In spite of the similarity in the labels, it is necessary that one keep them separate in his thinking.)

Besides making possible research on problems where causal factors cannot be unraveled and examined one by one, the experimental designs based on analysis of variance have another advantage. By setting a study up in this way, the investigator obtains considerably more information for the same expenditure of time, money, and effort. It would be quite possible, for example, to plan a vitamin experiment in which one used the same group of subjects to test out the effects of as many as six or eight different kinds of treatment. Such a study would be planned so that a few subjects would get vitamin A alone, a few B, a few C, a few D, and so on through the vitamin alphabet. Some would get a combination of A and B, some A and C, some B and D, and so on through all possible combinations. At the end, the total amount of variation in test gains would be broken down into the parts associated with the different kinds of treatment, and the statistical significance of each treatment determined. Instead of answering one question, the experiment would have been made to answer several. If it should happen that vitamin B supplementation improves mental functioning only when accompanied by increases in vitamin C intake, this research plan would enable us to find this out, whereas simple comparisons of experimental and control groups might never have brought it to light. These combination effects are what is meant by the term *interaction* among variables.

Unfortunately for the statistically unsophisticated, research in psychology has progressed to the point where some familiarity with these less well-known ways of setting up experiments is needed by anyone who expects to read the psychological journals intelligently. Again, however, the distinction that has been made before between producers and consumers of research evidence can be maintained. All the consumer is absolutely required to know is the meaning of a P-value. In any study using analysis of variance, no matter how complicated, the question of whether any one factor has produced a statistically significant difference is finally expressed as an F-ratio with a P-value attached to it. A reader who thoroughly understands what this means in general can usually grasp the essential findings of a research report without too much difficulty.

SUMMARY

In carrying out research on individual differences, the investigator tries to secure as representative a sample as possible of the population in which he is interested. Statistically, a random sample is the ideal, but because of practical difficulties in achieving this, various methods have been devised for selecting individuals in such a way that the proportions of the sample falling into various subgroups—age, income, sex, and so forth—will be the same as they are for the total population. In interpreting the results of studies that have been made, selective factors in the samples studied must always be taken into consideration.

Any statistical-significance test is designed to evaluate the probability that the results which have been obtained in a research study could have arisen from chance sampling fluctuations alone. The smaller the probability value reported for any statistical result, the less likely it is that errors of sampling are responsible for the results obtained. What we are really trying to prove all the time is that our results are *not insignificant*.

The standard method of finding out whether two variables are related to one another is to compute a correlation coefficient. It is a number which may be either positive or negative and ranges in magnitude from zero to 1.00. A negative r means that above-average values in one variable tend to go with below-average variables in the other. A positive r means that persons in the group tend to get similar scores in both variables. The more r differs from zero, the closer is the relationship between the two traits under consideration, and the fewer will be the individuals with combinations of scores which differ markedly from the prevailing trend. In investigating relationships between variables that lend themselves to some kind of categorization but not to actual measurement or scoring, Chi square may be used to test the significance of the relationship, and a contingency coefficient derived from it will give a rough idea of its magnitude.

The factor-analysis methods have been developed for the purpose of making inferences about basic variables underlying the relationship between measured variables. By scrutinizing a table of factor loadings for a set of tests one can set up useful hypotheses with regard to the abilities or attitudes the tests require.

In setting up studies to find out whether groups differ from one another, the investigator needs to take particular care that the two samples to be compared really represent comparable populations and that the tests he uses are really applicable to problems of this sort. The reader must be on guard against both these sources of error in evaluating what he reads. The best significance test for differences between two groups is t; the best for three or more groups is F. A *low* value for P shows that the results are statistically significant.

Problems of what causes groups to differ or traits to correlate demand special care in planning and in evaluation. Time relationships are important. Control groups must be used whose members are not subjected to the experimental influence. By using factorial designs and analysis of variance, the effects of several kinds of experimental influence, singly and in combination, can be assessed in a single experiment.

PART TWO

Varieties of
Individual Differences

CHAPTER 4

Individual Differences in Intelligence

As HAS BEEN explained in the introductory chapter, the development of the whole field of individual differences has been bound up with intelligence testing. There were, it is true, some attempts to study variability in simple perceptual and motor characteristics just before the end of the last century. They had only a limited influence on the development of this field, however, as they seemed at the time to have few theoretical or practical applications. It was after Binet demonstrated that a human trait of major importance could be assessed in a quantitative way and that such assessments could actually make possible more valid judgments about individual children that active research on human differences really began. When in 1917 military psychologists showed that similar methods could help in the classification of adults as well as children, the stage was set for rapid development.

At the same time that this development has been bringing us to the place where we are now interested in the measurement of many human qualities besides general intelligence, it has also been supplying a constantly increasing amount of information about this trait itself. Question after question has arisen as work progressed and has become a focal point for controversy, a stimulus for research. Growing out of all the impassioned arguments, the painstaking calculations, and the concerted efforts to put good tests on the market, there has come a sizable body of knowledge about the meaning of intelligence, as we are measuring it. Teachers, personnel workers, counselors, and clinicians need to be familiar with these facts and principles. They have become part of the "basic science" underlying the human relations professions.

THE MEANING OF THE TERM "INTELLIGENCE"

Psychologists did not manufacture the concept of intelligence. Philosophers have pondered over it, teachers have evaluated it in their pupils, and the man on the street has assumed without question that he knows what it is. Dictionary definitions center around understanding or reasoning, taking effective action in new situations, and acquiring and utilizing appropriate information. People who use the word "intelligence" in casual conversation may mean any or all of these things.

Psychologists too have disagreed as to just what are the essential factors of behavior we label "intelligent." Some have emphasized adaptibility to new circumstances, some abstractness and complexity, some facility in the use of symbols. To some, intelligence has seemed to represent one central unitary trait, to others the sum or average of a great many separate and diverse mental abilities.

The thing that has saved psychology from bogging down in a mire of semantic confusion is the predominantly practical orientation of mental testers. Binet thought deeply and wrote wisely about the meaning of intelligence, but the tests that he developed justified themselves not so much by this "thinking about thinking" as by the success with which they identified mentally deficient children in schools. From his time on to the present, test development has been geared to practical problems. Illogical as it may seem, psychologists have found that it is not necessary to define intelligence in order to measure it. Experience in two world wars and many research undertakings has shown that men with quite different theories about the nature of intellectual activity can work together amicably on test-construction projects. Their aim has been to produce tools that people can use to make with more precision the judgment about individual mental capacities that they are already making on some basis.

Out of this procedure and in accordance with a point of view that became very popular in science during the 1930's came the so-called "operational" definition of intelligence—"intelligence is what these tests measure" (Boring, 1923). Logically there are some difficulties with this approach. An intelligence test, if we consider its construction as well as its administration, is hard to describe in terms of a clearly definable set of operations, and no two tests involve exactly the same ones. The thinking that psychologists have done along these lines, however, has been of considerable value. It has clarified the distinction between *intelligence*, the broad and somewhat ambiguous term of common speech, and "intelligence," the narrower, more limited trait with which our tests are concerned. Although a psychometrist thoroughly familiar with tests such as the Binet and the Wechsler may not be able to give a simple definition of the trait measured, he does have a fairly clear conception of what it does and does not include. In practical situations the increasing clarity and precision with which we can describe "what our tests test" constitutes real progress.

We have pinned down what we mean by test intelligence in two ways. One is by the study of the questions and tasks in the tests themselves and the relationships between them, an *internal* type of analysis. The other is by a study of the correlations of test scores with various criteria *external* to the tests themselves, such as grades in school or success ratings of Army officers. At first glance it would appear that the internal type of analysis would be easier to make than the external, as its raw materials become available as soon as the test has been given. As a matter of fact it is the external type, the correlation with criteria, that is simpler and has furnished useful data earlier in the history of intelligence testing. It is only recently that statistical techniques that are really adequate for analyzing internal relationships have been developed.

It is, of course, easy enough to examine the questions and tasks that have proved themselves most satisfactory for intelligence testing from Binet's time down to the present. In verbal tests, subjects have been asked to define words or recognize their meanings, work simple arithmetic problems, complete analogies, analyze similarities and differences, recognize absurdities, follow directions, and answer common-sense questions. Performance tests have been made up of form boards, picture puzzles, pictures to be described, pictures to be completed or arranged in order, mazes, and drawing assignments. Some have been given with time limits, some without. But when we try to identify something that all these tasks have in common, logic and intuition fail us. Do they really all require the same intellectual trait, or are many different capacities involved? Can a person be good at one of these things but poor at the others? If so, what does an "intelligence" rating mean so far as he is concerned? Answers to such questions were not obtainable from direct observations of test materials until factor-analytic methods were brought to bear on them. This research will be summarized later in the chapter. We shall turn first to work which has delineated the relationship of "intelligence" to non-test variables.

THE RELATIONSHIP OF "INTELLIGENCE" TO AGE

One obvious fact that gave psychologists a means of attacking the intelligence-testing problem is that children become brighter as they grow older. With the best teaching in the world the average five-year-old will not master counterpoint nor the average ten-year-old symbolic logic. What Binet and his successors have tried to work out is a pool of items, questions and tasks that sample mental abilities typical of the various age levels. The diversity of types of items noted in the previous section arose from the consistent application of this most basic criterion. *Any* task of an intellectual nature that can be evaluated and scored has been considered a suitable item for intelligence testing if it can be shown that older children are significantly better at it than younger children. Intelligence as measured in children is first and foremost a matter of developmental level.

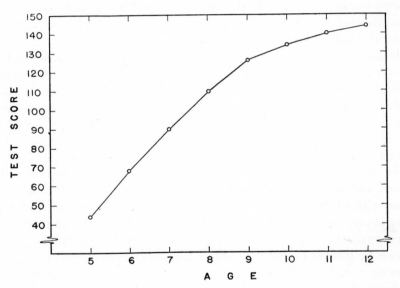

FIGURE 12. Graph showing average scores of successive age groups on Otis Quick-Scoring Test, Alpha, 1939.

Thus if we plot total score on any such group of items against chronological age for a representative group of children, we obtain a rising curve often referred to as a mental-growth curve. For example, the Otis Quick-Scoring Mental Ability Test for children in the primary grades gives us the curve shown in Figure 12. We can see at a glance that older children get higher scores than younger ones. The exact nature of the relationship between age and intellectual capacity cannot, however, be evaluated from such a diagram. The trouble is that we have no information as to the meaning of the units in which the test scores are plotted. Is each question the equivalent of every other question? Does the difference between scores of 50 and 60 have the same meaning as the difference between 90 and 100? We do not know. Thus the shape the curve should take is not determined.

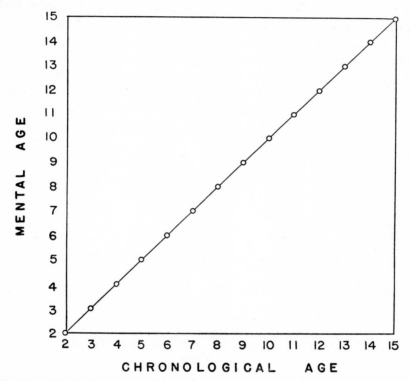

FIGURE 13. Graph showing average mental age for each chronological-age group on any mental-age scale.

If we use the mental-age scores usually obtained from Binet-type individual tests as our units, we still are in no better position to describe the course of mental growth in children. For a test standardized in this way, the average achievement of a representative group of children at a given age becomes the standard. Thus for each change in chronological age, the standardized test results show us exactly the same amount of change in mental age, as long as we are considering group averages rather than individual scores. For this reason, the "curve" of mental growth appears always to be a straight line like that shown in Figure 13, up to the age at which intellectual maturity is reached. It still does not tell us anything about what the real course of mental development is like.

During an earlier period of mental testing a number of psychologists were interested in finding some statistical technique that would get around these difficulties and enable them to plot a curve that would really picture the course of mental development in children. It is quite obvious that this should not be a straight line indicating the *same* amount of change each year from early childhood to maturity. Any observation of the way children change as they grow older shows that a year makes more difference in the younger ones than in the older ones. The difference between the problems and tasks that can be mastered by average five-year-olds and by average six-year-olds, for example, appears to be far greater than the difference between the abilities of thirteen-year-olds and fourteen-year-olds.

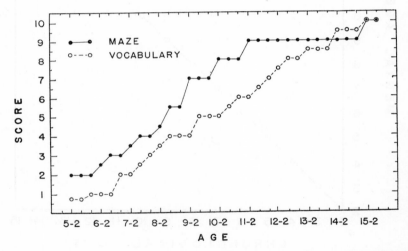

FIGURE 14. Age trends on two subtests of the Wechsler Intelligence Scale for Children (Wechsler, 1950a).

Several mathematical procedures for what is called "absolute scaling" of intelligence tests have been worked out. (An absolute scale is one that starts from zero and proceeds by equal steps to its highest value.) It is not necessary that we go into detail about these scaling procedures and the mental-development curves they generate. It has become apparent as time has passed that this whole search for a universal mental-growth curve was an unprofitable undertaking. Various assumptions had to be made as a basis for the mathematical treatments that were given the scores, and these are now seen to be untenable, or at least unprovable.

Several lines of research have led to the conviction now generally held that mental-growth curves are of doubtful validity. One has to do with differences in the patterns of the curves obtained using different varieties of test item. Figure 14 illustrates this point. The curve for the maze test rises rapidly and reaches a plateau at about eleven. The curve for vocabulary rises evenly and slowly. At one stage in the history of mental testing, research workers believed that these differences in rate of improvement on different kinds of task were not too important, since each specific task was thought to be only an indicator of the general and innate quality we call intelligence. The factor-analytic studies we will turn to later have shown that the relationships between kinds of test material are much more complex than this, so that we can not consider them interchangeable indicators of one general ability. Thus we are not justified in piecing together a single over-all growth curve from these specific curves of different shapes. It seems now that if there are such things as general laws of mental development that can be expressed as mathematical functions of age, they are more likely to be separate equations for separate processes than a single equation for the process as a whole.

A second reason for abandoning the search for a universal mental-growth curve is tied up with our increasing awareness of the interaction between native capacities and environmental influences. If we think of a general mental-growth curve as a way of portraying the natural development of pure native capacity, we know now that it cannot be achieved even as an abstraction. At every stage, development itself depends upon the opportunities for learning available at that stage. Later development is always an outgrowth of what the *interaction* of original capacity and learned changes have made of the person up to that time. This becomes especially clear when we consider a specific question that has stimulated much discussion and controversy among "growth-curve" thinkers: "At what age is the development of intelligence completed?" Early test-makers, basing their judgments on their standardization data, chose sixteen as the point where increases with age ceased. Many users of the tests became convinced that fourteen was nearer to the true figure. As more different special groups were compared, it became clear that intelligence-test scores increased with age beyond fourteen *if schooling continued* but remained constant or declined slightly in groups no longer in school. R. L. Thorndike (1948b), for example, showed that average scores for 1,000 students increased consistently year by year up to the age of twenty-one and one-half. P. E. Vernon (1951) reported an analysis of scores made by recruits of different ages in the British armed services. Decline in average score set in earlier for those in non-intellectual jobs than for those in intellectual jobs. The effect of this longer period of mental growth in persons remaining at school is clearly demonstrated in a study by Lorge (1945). He went back to the records of 131 boys who as eighth-graders in 1921-22 had been given a number of psychological tests. Twenty years later he gave them the Otis intelligence test. For subjects whose initial intelligence level was the same, the later score varied according to the amount of schooling. Those who had gone to college averaged considerably higher than those who had dropped out during the high-school years. The numbers in most of the subgroups are small, and no significance tests are given, but the trend is unmistakable. Husen (1951) shows that the same sort of relationship holds in Sweden. Such findings make it appear unlikely that we shall ever be able to give a single answer to the question, "At what age does mental growth cease?" We shall always have to say, "That depends."

Another source of dissatisfaction with generalized growth curves has been the constantly accumulating evidence that growth is an *individual* matter and that curves based on group averages tend to mask more than they reveal. One of the special questions about which controversy and research have centered is, "How constant is the IQ?" It is only recently that carefully analyzed results from several child development centers have begun to show us the directions in which answers to this question lie.

Practically speaking, there are a number of reasons why a child's obtained IQ may vary considerably from year to year, even if his intellectual status has not changed. One is the fact already mentioned that different tests do not draw on exactly the same kinds of ability. Even when the same measuring instrument, such as the Stanford-Binet, is used on different occasions, the items on which his score depends may not tap exactly the same aspects of intelligence. Non-verbal tests have a greater influence on scores at the lower age levels; educational deficiencies become more of a handicap at the upper age levels. Another problem in evaluating IQ constancy is that *variability* differs for different tests, or even for the same test at different age levels. This can be true even when the test has been standardized so as to give an *average* IQ of 100 at every age. An example will perhaps make this effect clear. If a six-year-old takes a test for which the standard deviation is 10 IQ points in the standardization group, and three years later takes another test for which the standard deviation is 16 IQ points, an IQ of 148 on the second test is actually the equivalent of an IQ of 130 on the first. On both occasions the child has scored three standard deviations above the mean, at or near the top of a normal distribution. What looks at first like a considerable improvement in IQ is only a statistical artifact. There has been no real change at all in intellectual status relative to his age group.

Once they understand these two sources of error in evaluating IQ change, teachers and clinical workers can avoid them. Errors arising out of differences in what is being measured by various tests can occur at all brightness levels. The errors arising from differences in variability for different tests or age levels are more marked the farther the individual is in either direction from the average. Very bright children and very dull ones thus may *appear* to change more than average children do.

After we have allowed for these sources of error, however, we find that there is apparently some real fluctuation in intelligence from age to age. Some children become brighter as they grow older, some become less bright in comparison with their age-mates, and some move up and down on the intelligence scale in an apparently random manner. Changes that frequently occur do not by any means cover the whole IQ range. The probability that a six-year-old moron will develop into a gifted sixteen-year-old with an IQ in the upper register is negligible, but there is a real possibility that a boy who in the first grade appears to be only slightly above the average of his classmates will be leading his class when he reaches high school.

The principal source of our knowledge about these IQ changes is a study that has been going on at the University of California for a long period of time. Forty children, representative of the Berkeley population (considerably above the national average in mental ability, however) have been followed through from birth to the age of eighteen, with tests at frequent intervals. Reports by Bayley (1949) and by Honzik, Macfarlane, and Allen (1948) throw considerable light on the problem of IQ constancy. The findings can be summarized under a few principal headings. Most of them have been corroborated by results from other less extended investigations.

In the first place, infant tests, those given during the first year or year and a half of life, are useless for predicting later intellectual status. It is a curious fact that the correlations of first-year tests with later intelligence measures, though very close to zero, tend to be *negative* rather than positive. The persons destined to reach the highest ultimate level average slightly lower in scores reflecting rate of early development than do those who will be of lesser stature. The correlation is so slight, however, that it is not worth speculating about. The important point is that indices of the rapidity of infant development give us no clues at all from which we can predict later IQ. (This generalization does not hold for extremely feeble-minded children or those with gross organic defects. An idiot who makes no progress at all during the first few months of life may be recognized as abnormal long before he reaches the age when valid predictive tests can be given.)

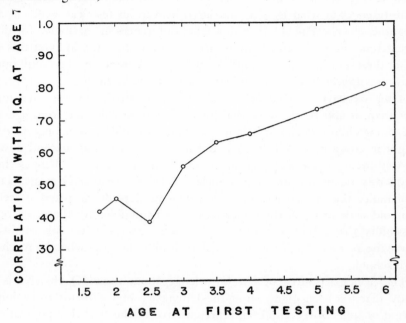

FIGURE 15. Correlations of preschool tests given at different ages with Stanford-Binet intelligence-test scores at age seven (Honzik, 1938).

The second general finding is that the degree of relationship between intelligence tests given at different age levels depends upon both the age at first testing and the length of the time interval between tests. Figure 15 illustrates the way in which correlation with a later test rises as both these factors are changed. A test given at two has very little predictive value. One given at four has considerably more. If later test scores are related to those obtained at the age of six or older, correlations of .7 or .8 are the rule. Six, the customary age for entering school, seems to represent a sort of turning point. From this age on there is enough IQ constancy to give intelligence tests definite predictive value, at least over limited periods of time. Husen (1953) reports test-retest correlations of .7 or higher for a number of Scandinavian groups.

The third important finding, much more evident in the later California studies than in those reported earlier, is that even a dependable correlation of .8 leaves room for marked fluctuations in individual cases. Honzik, Macfarlane, and Allen (1948) show that it is *possible* for a change of as much as 50 IQ points to occur during the school years. Changes of 30 or more points are noted in 9 per cent of the cases, changes as great as 15 points in 58 per cent of the cases. Only 15 per cent of the California group show *less* than 10 points of IQ change. While a change of 15 or 20 IQ points is not great enough to lift a person from the "normal" to the "very superior" category or to drop him from "normal" to "moron," it is enough to make an appreciable difference in the valuation of his potentialities that teachers and others are likely to make. Some of these reported IQ shifts are explained by differences in the variability of the IQ distribution at different age levels. The Stanford-Binet test (Form L) has a standard deviation of 12.5 points at age six and of 20.0 points at age twelve, according to Terman and Merrill's standardization data (1937). But even when all IQ's are transformed into standard scores to rule out this source of variation, much of the fluctuation from age to age still remains.

The California investigators have made a special effort to identify influences in individual lives that might help to account for IQ changes. Case studies of children with unusually regular or unusually irregular growth trends do show that there is a tendency for irregularity to go with life histories characterized by unusual variations in disturbing and stabilizing factors. The connection is far from clear, however. Some persons with disturbing experiences show very stable mental growth trends. The most clear-cut relationship that is evident so far is that between a child's final level of mental development and the educational level of his family. The child from a well-educated family is more likely to increase than to decrease in IQ as time passes. The correlations between parents' and children's intellectual status become higher as children get older (Bayley, 1954). Such findings fit in with those already cited, the Lorge study (1945), for example, which show that test scores are related to educational influences. Their meaning will be discussed in more detail in the next section.

The California studies have shown that it is unsound practice to use a single IQ obtained during the childhood years as an index of a person's permanent intellectual capacity. The conclusion is reinforced by the results of a similar study in Colorado reported by Hilden (1949). In this investigation 30 children, like the Berkeley group above average in mental ability, were tested annually from early childhood to maturity.

Variations from test to test were comparable to those reported in the other study, ranging in individual cases from 7 to 46 IQ points. The author shows that a practice effect does not account for the increases. He also cites evidence for the conclusion that a person's final IQ can be predicted more accurately from the *highest* IQ obtained before the age of twelve than from the *average* of all the scores up to that age. This will be a useful bit of practical knowledge for teachers and clinicians if other studies support it.

In spite of the qualifications brought to our attention by the longitudinal studies, a mental-test score is as good an indicator as it ever was of the level a child *has reached* in his intellectual development. As such it is an enormously useful tool. Perhaps the cautions recently expressed with regard to the IQ will lead us back toward a greater emphasis on the *mental age,* or some statistical equivalent, as a way of emphasizing present status rather than permanent endowment. Those responsible for the guidance of children need to realize that a single intelligence test can never be used as a basis for a definite judgment about what a child will be able to do several years hence. Each new decision, at successive stages of development, calls for a recheck. Although extreme changes occur only very rarely, changes from "average" to "superior" and vice versa are relatively frequent. We must remember, however, that we do not know how to *produce* such changes in an individual, and that the older he is the less likely it is that a marked shift will occur. To seize on the evidence accumulated in mental-growth studies as proof that anyone can be a genius if he wants to (or if his parents want him to) is fully as unwarranted as to cling to the belief that a person's intelligence is fixed for all time by the age of six. The fact that the IQ is not completely constant does not render it completely meaningless.

Besides their implications for practical judgments that must be made in the schoolroom and in the clinic, these facts we have been discussing are important in planning and interpreting other research. Whenever the effects of some special influence are to be determined—vitamins, teaching methods, foster homes, or play therapy, for example—it must always be remembered that many children show marked increases in IQ without any identifiable special treatment at all. Therefore the study must be designed to show that in the experimental group either the average shift in an upward direction is greater or a larger number of individuals show upward shifts, than in a comparison group not exposed to the influence being investigated. Too often a few extreme cases showing a striking amount of change are cited as evidence for the effectiveness of a certain method of treatment. Taken by themselves they prove nothing, since we know that such extreme cases occasionally occur regardless of circumstances.

Logically a complete discussion of the relationship of intelligence measurements to age requires a consideration of early and later maturity as well as childhood. When large groups of adults first became available for testing at the time of World War I psychologists were struck with the fact that the curve of mental development form the early twenties on appeared to be a *falling* one. The older the group was the lower its average turned out to be, and this decrement with advancing years became more and more noticeable throughout middle and old age. As psychological work with adults continued, however, the true relationships were seen to be more complex. The pattern or organization of abilities shifts with the years, and some kinds of capacity show much greater age differences than others. As results of longitudinal studies on the same individuals at different ages became available, the meaning of the group differences previously found became still more doubtful. Able subjects tested on different occasions did not show the decline during their forties that the group difference studies had led us to expect (see Chapter 12). Since all these findings can be brought together more clearly after we have taken up the subject of the patterning of mental abilities, the detailed facts about age trends in adults will be presented in a later chapter rather than here.

THE RELATIONSHIP OF "INTELLIGENCE" TO SCHOOL SUCCESS

From the beginning, intelligence measurement has been more or less closely tied in with school situations. The judgments teachers naturally make about the relative brightness of individual pupils has constituted a readily available criterion by means of which test items could be evaluated. If the teachers' judgments were accurate and infallible, we should of course need no tests for children. But if, on the other hand, our tests showed no relationship to these judgments, we should certainly question their validity. What we would expect to find, and what we get when we try it out, is a moderately high but far from perfect correlation between teachers' judgments and test scores.

One thing that the research with tests has shown is that the variation in intellectual level in any one age or grade group is much greater than the average teacher assumes it to be (Cook, 1947). In a typical schoolroom where no grouping on the basis of ability has occurred, the range of mental ages is five years at the primary level, six years at the intermediate level, and eight or more years at the secondary level. When we put test scores into mental age terms we find that the dullest child in a sixth-grade class may be functioning at the level of an average nine-year-old, the brightest at the level of the average fifteen-year-old. School assignments requiring that a child understand abstract terms or reason about complex processes are easy enough for those near the top of this group, but for those at the bottom they may be completely meaningless.

The *correlation* between measures of general intelligence and grades given for school achievement, though it is only moderately high, is remarkably consistent over the whole range of school situations. Either individual or group tests chosen so as to be suitable for the age group where they are used regularly correlate from .4 to .6 with school marks. Various qualifications can be appended to this statement. Tests calling for verbal reasoning tend to give higher correlations than those of the performance type. Predictions of grades over long periods of time are not nearly so accurate as predictions over short periods. Some school subjects are more closely related to measured intelligence than others are. But even when we consider these complications and the variation they produce in the size of the reported correlations from study to study, the general consistency of the correlations from first grade through graduate school constitutes impressive evidence that our tests are revealing some general intellectual factor upon which success in school depends.

Correlations of this magnitude are of considerable value in making predictions that will help students chart their courses. Examination of Figure 16 shows us that while we cannot hope to predict very accurately just what grade-point average any individual student will make, we can determine the range within which his grades are likely to fall and thus answer various specific questions that may arise. It is plain, for example, that the majority of students with stanine ratings of 1, 2, or 3 do not achieve the grade-point average of 2.00 or higher that the university requires. The great majority of students with stanine ratings of 8 and 9, on the other hand, show averages above 2.5 and thus probably qualify for special honors programs. About persons in the middle ranges with stanines of 4, 5, and 6, less definite statements can be made. It appears that they are much more likely than not to achieve the 2.00 minimum, but a fair proportion of them attain honors levels, and a few fail completely. One of the things that keeps correlations between intelligence and scholarship from being any higher than they are is that failure can occur at all levels of brightness. Figure 16, for example, shows that one of the students with a stanine of 9 makes a GPA of less than 1.00, and GPA's at or near zero go with stanines ranging all the way from 2 to 7. Some reasons for this state of affairs are obvious. Success in school calls for effort and participation in the work of the class, and bright students as well as dull ones can be lacking in these essentials.

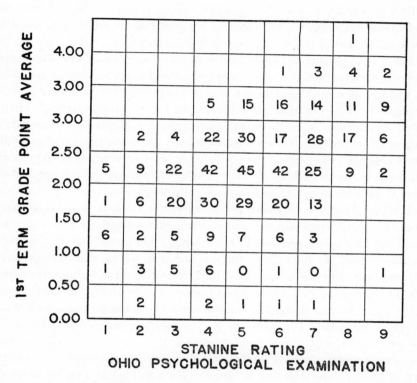

FIGURE 16. Scatter diagram showing relationship of scholastic aptitude test scores to college success for 589 University of Oregon freshmen. ($r = .43$).

When instead of grades based on teachers' judgments, scores on tests of school achievement are correlated with intelligence-test scores, somewhat higher coefficients are usually obtained. Correlations reported between group tests (more dependent on reading skill than individual tests) and standardized measures of school achievement often run as high as .8. This fairly close relationship between intelligence, especially as evaluated by means of group tests, and school-achievement tests has at times led psychologists to conclude that intelligence tests were nothing *but* tests of schooling. It should always be remembered, however, that within any group made up of individuals who have had *equal* educational opportunities, whether it be a group of first-graders or a group of graduate students, there are marked *individual* differences in both variables—measured achievement and tested intelligence. Equal education does not tend to eradicate these differences. Thus the test score would seem to reflect something more basic than the influence of schooling. There are individual differences in the capacity for profiting by education, and it is these differences that intelligence-test scores reflect.

Long-term predictions from intelligence-test scores also lend some support to the conclusion that the tests measure basic educational aptitude. A number of studies have shown that if school laws are such as to permit students to drop out after their fourteenth or even their sixteenth birthdays, intelligence tests given in grade school will predict with a fair degree of success how far up the educational ladder different students will go. Those who drop out at the ninth-grade level average lower than those who reach the twelfth grade. Those who attend college average higher than those who stop with high-school graduation.

It is useful for anyone who must interpret test scores to know something about the intellectual requirements of the higher educational levels. Studies by Embree (1948) and by Wrenn (1949) indicated that the average Stanford-Binet IQ for college entrants was 118, for bachelor's degree recipients 123, and for advanced degree recipients 126. Persons receiving Ph. D.'s averaged 141. These and all other studies of this problem, however, stress the fact that there is much variation in the groups which these averages represent. The *range* of IQ's for degree recipients in Embree's sample was from 95 to 180. In a supplementary study he showed that colleges vary widely in their intelligence requirements. In some, the average IQ of the students is as low as 100, in others as high as 133. In Wrenn's study, 10 per cent of those ultimately receiving Ph. D.'s scored below the average of entering freshmen at the colleges they attended. Thus the interpretations we make must always be in terms of probabilities. It is *unlikely* that a boy with an IQ below 100 will be able to graduate from college. It is *improbable* that a person with an IQ below 125 will succeed at a first-rate graduate school. In making such judgments we must always keep in mind also the qualifications already discussed with regard to IQ constancy over long periods of time.

Intelligence tests show consistent, dependable relationships to occupational level as well as to educational level. We are accustomed to ranking jobs on a prestige scale with the professions at the top and unskilled labor at the bottom. This ranking is not identical with what it would be for income or for social utility, but it is made by various groups of people quite consistently (Deeg and Paterson, 1947). Ball (1938) in 1937 determined the rating on one of these standardized occupational level scales for each of 219 men who had taken a group test of intelligence as children in 1918 or in 1923. For the 1923 group, the younger ones at the time of the follow-up, the correlation between test scores and occupational level rating turned out to be .57. For the older 1917 group, it was .71. This would suggest that there is some tendency for individuals to gravitate toward an occupational level in keeping with their measured intelligence.

Results of the tests given to large numbers of men in the Armed Forces during both world wars point in the same direction (see Chapter 13). The professions, probably because they require long periods of advanced education, rank highest in test scores. Business and white-collar occupations rank next highest, then skilled labor, then semi-skilled labor, and finally unskilled labor at the bottom. Needless to say, here too there is a great deal of variability within groups. Some of the unskilled laborers score as high as any of the professional men.

These relationships with educational level and with the aspects of occupational placement that depend upon schooling are the clearest evidence we have as to what intelligence tests are measuring. But they in turn require clarifications before we can glibly characterize the tests as measures of learning ability. What is it *about* learning that depends upon intelligence? Do the bright learn more *rapidly* than the dull, do they keep on learning *longer*, or do they learn *different things?* These are urgent questions when we wish to use tests for such purposes as the selection of workers. For a job requiring a preliminary training period, is it advisable to choose applicants with the highest score? Just what does "learning ability," often used as a synonym or euphemism for intelligence, mean?

Fortunately there has been enough research centered around these issues so that we can differentiate between what intelligence tests do show and what they do not. In the first place, if what we mean by learning ability is the *rapidity* with which a person improves with practice on any motor or intellectual skill, then we can say quite definitely that intelligence tests do *not* measure it. The most complete evidence on the point comes from a series of studies by Woodrow (1938, 1939, 1940) in which a group of students were given a number of practice periods on a variety of different tasks. Before and after this series of practice trials they took intelligence and special aptitude tests. The analysis of the correlations showed that there was no one general learning ability accounting for improvement on all the tasks. Some subjects made faster progress on one, some on another. Thus there was no basis for an identification of intelligence with general learning ability. Furthermore there was no significant relationship between any of the scores representing *gain* with practice and intelligence. In a later study, Woodrow (1946) analyzed correlations between IQ and gains from year to year in the scores obtained by school children on standardized achievement tests. In general, these results also showed almost no relationships between gain and intelligence, although the period from fourth to fifth grade did produce a few significant correlations. Another study done by Simrall (1947) shows that even when the types of material the subjects work with in practice periods are highly similar to the types of material in the intelligence test, gains during practice are still not significantly related to test scores. Such findings fit in with our common observation that average and dull students often progress as rapidly as bright students in football, automobile driving, accordion-playing, or using an adding machine.

How then do the consistent and fairly high correlations between intelligence test scores and measures of school achievement come about? Tilton (1949) has called our attention to another factor that must be considered when we speak of "learning ability." School success involves not just increasing skill in the performance of simple tasks but continuous progress from the simple to the more complex. In arithmetic, for example, we are not content to have children practice, year after year, the simple addition of two-place numbers. If we were, we should probably find that the dull child showed as much improvement as his brilliant classmate. But what we do in our schools is to lead students on from addition to subtraction, multiplication, division, fractions, decimals, and square root. The more rapidly a child's mental capacity is *growing* the better he is able to keep up with the constantly increasing complexity of what is to be learned. The child with an IQ of 80 is handicapped all through school not because he is slow or inept at learning things which are within the capacity of all the children of his age level, but because he is never *ready* to grasp new and more complex ideas at the time when they are ordinarily presented to children of his age. Tilton's study (1949) shows that one obtains substantial correlations between intelligence and gains in school achievement if this difficulty factor is allowed to operate. He obtained a correlation of .49 between intelligence rating and gains on a history test by omitting from the test all the easier items, those answered correctly by 45 per cent or more of the group at the beginning. It seems then that if a test is designed so that a person must learn the more difficult things in order to improve his score on it, the advantage goes to persons with higher IQ's.

The fact that gains from fourth to fifth grade were correlated with IQ in the Woodrow study (1946) cited above becomes intelligible from this viewpoint. The achievement test was one designed for the fourth grade and up. Thus it was undoubtedly more difficult for the fourth-graders than for any of the other grade groups. At the level where it was difficult, correlations between intelligence and gains appeared. Another study by Tilton (1953) shows that at the fourth- and fifth-grade level gains in all the school subjects are positively correlated.

We see then that the euphemism "slow *learner*" is not really an accurate characterization of the dull child. "Slow *developer*" would be closer to the true state of affairs during the elementary-school period. If he seems to have taken two years to master what his brighter classmates mastered in one, this is not because he learned more slowly but because it took him longer to reach the level of mental development at which these things could be learned at all. This change in interpretation fits in with the fact, quite familiar to teachers, that at the high-school and college ages which correspond to the leveling-off period in mental growth no amount of time spent by the dull on the same materials which the bright grasp with ease seems to produce mastery of them. There probably is a fair proportion of the adult population who are incapable of understanding integral calculus, Platonism, or international finance. One hesitates to be overly dogmatic about such a negative conclusion, however, since a change in the way problems and materials are formulated, organized, and presented sometimes reduces the level of complexity enough to bring them within the range of much more limited minds. To develop ways of doing this is a constant challenge to educators, in and out of schools.

Around the kinds of relationships we have been considering can be grouped a large number of miscellaneous studies reporting correlations between adult scores on intelligence tests and a variety of criteria. Tests correlate with occupational level, but not with degrees of success within an occupation. (See Wells, Williams, and Fowler, 1938.) In the military selection and training programs, tests correlate with grades given by instructors, which probably depend somewhat upon grasp of abstract concepts, but not with more "practical" criteria. (See Jenkins, 1946.) That this is not simply a matter of "book learning" is suggested by H. A. Smith (1949) who found that intelligence was correlated with gains on a standardized biology test in both an experimental group taught by the use of films and a control group taught in the customary way. In school or out, intelligence tests show us not how quickly individuals will "catch on" or how much they will improve their performance of some task they are

clearly capable of doing, but whether or not they will be able to advance
to the more complex, intricate, and difficult types of lesson or job.

It follows from this conclusion that we should never underemphasize
the learning ability of persons at the low end of the IQ scale. Some of
the research that has been done with the feeble-minded will be discussed
in a later chapter, but it is well to remind ourselves at this point that such
people can learn things within their range of mental ability as rapidly as
anyone else.

THE RELATIONSHIP OF TESTS TO EACH OTHER

Studies of mental growth and of the relationship of test scores to school
success have taught us much about the meaning of individual differences
in measured intelligence. The other principal pillar upon which our understanding of intelligence rests consists of research on the relationships
between various intelligence tests. The idea that each person is endowed
with a fixed quantity of mental ability, and that it will show up however
we choose to measure it, has faded with the years. Mental organization
has turned out to be vastly more complex than the early mental testers
suspected that it was. Several kinds of evidence force us to recognize that
intelligence is neither a single unitary quality nor a simple summation of
separate, unrelated traits. Let us examine this evidence.

The first type of results which bear on the problem consists of correlations which have been obtained when both verbal and performance tests
of intelligence have been given to the same subjects. If the individuals in
the group are all of approximately the same age so that large differences
based on maturity level alone are ruled out, the correlations between the
two varieties of test seldom run higher than .5 or .6. Gaw's (1925) study
on children of about thirteen found correlations of .41 for boys and .49
for girls between Binet IQ and scores on fourteen unselected performance
tests. Verbal and performance halves of the Wechsler-Bellevue test correlate .67 with each other when used with representative groups of adult
subjects comprising the whole intelligence range (Wechsler, 1950 b).
For the Wechsler Intelligence Scale for Children, the reported correlations
between verbal and performance sections are .60 at age seven and one-half,
.68 at age ten and one-half, and .56 at age thirteen and one-half.

In general we can say that the correlations between verbal and performance tests are of about the same magnitude as the correlations between
verbal tests and school marks. (Performance tests characteristically show
a somewhat lower correlation with measures of school success than verbal

tests do.) In interpreting both correlations we recognize that only a part of what is being measured is a common trait represented by the scores we have correlated. Verbal intelligence is not identical with performance intelligence. Neither is identical with brightness in school. There is a common core of something underlying all of them, but it is only a *core*. Each has with it a considerable amount of substance peculiar to itself.

Another signpost pointing to the conclusion that intelligence is not a unitary trait is the finding that some types of test which are highly correlated with one another during childhood differ greatly in the extent to which they are affected by advancing age or illness. For example, vocabulary is an excellent indicator of *general* intelligence in children, as it correlates highly with most other types of intellectual activity. If a single test must be given to a child in order to ascertain the mental level at which he is functioning, a vocabulary test is more satisfactory than any other. But in adults past middle age and patients suffering from brain injury and schizophrenia, vocabulary is not closely related to various other assessments of intellectual level (Wechsler, 1950 b). Performance tests show more impairment of mental functioning in such cases than do verbal tests; memory tests show more than information tests; analogies items show more than comprehension items. There are many more such differences. In order for them to occur there must be some degree of independence in the functions measured. If intelligence were a single unitary quality it would decline as a whole.

Another striking demonstration that intelligence is not a unitary quality is the occurrence from time to time of the so-called *idiots savants*, feeble-minded persons with one highly-developed talent of some sort. Cases on record include instances of mechanical aptitude, musical talent, proficiency in arithmetic, phenomenal memory, and marked skill in drawing or painting. Of recent years, since tests have been available, it has been possible to make thorough studies of such persons so that actual documentation rather than just hearsay evidence testifies to the enormous discrepancy between general level of ability and skill along some special line. Scheerer, Rothmann, and Goldstein (1945) have reported on one of these children whom they studied intensively between 1937 and 1943.

In 1937 an eleven-year-old boy, L., was presented by his mother to the writers for neuropsychiatric and psychological consultation. The complaints about L. summed up to this: he could never follow the regular school curriculum like a normal child, or learn by instruction. His general information was alarmingly substandard; he had made progress in only a few school subjects, and even in these, his achievements were very limited.

His motivational and behavior peculiarities had been an early concern of his parents. He had never shown interest in his social surroundings or in normal childhood activities. On the other hand he had always excelled in certain performances.

The first impression on meeting L. is that of an erratic and hyperkinetic child, driven by an urge to keep in constant motion. He seems also to be governed by an ever recurring impulse to move all four fingers of each hand rapidly in a definite beat, rubbing them against the thumbs (in a snapping-like motion without the snaps). Alternating with extreme inattentiveness, self-preoccupation and restlessness he displays a friendly poise and stereotyped politeness, as when responding to or addressing people. Most of the time L. appears motorically or otherwise self-absorbed and socially aloof. However, he shows one unique interest in his human surroundings—an amazing phenomenon exhibited in the first minutes of the examination. Spontaneously the boy asks each of us, "When is your birthday?" Given the date, he answers in a fraction of a minute, "Dr. G.'s birthday was on Saturday last year and Dr. S.'s birthday was on Wednesday." A glance at the calendar proves him correct. We call others to the scene, and with amazing swiftness, L. gives correctly the day of the week of every person's birthday. Moreover, he can tell at once exactly which day of the week a person's birthday was last year or 5 years ago, and on what day it will fall in 1945, etc. More closely examined, L. proves capable of telling the day of the week for any given date between about 1880 and 1950. Conversely, he can also give the date for any given week-day in any year of that period, e.g. the date of the first Saturday in May 1950, or of the last Monday in January 1934, etc. As much as we could determine he makes no mistakes in his calendar answers. Though L. unquestionably takes delight in the recognition of his feat, he never seems aware of its extraordinary character in the same sense as a normal person (e.g., the reader of this, if he could master such a task). On the other hand, it is known that, since his 7th year, he had developed a persistent interest in the birthdays of everyone he meets. For some time he has been surprising people he met only once by volunteering their birthdays "on sight." This, of course, happened to the writers on many occasions. In conjunction with this specific memory he almost inevitably will know the day and date of his first visit to a place and usually the names and birthdays of all the people he met there. He never fails to look for the date when he sees a newspaper, which otherwise does not interest him in the least.

The authors go on to describe other aspects of L.'s peculiar talents; his impressive skill in remembering and manipulating numbers without any general superiority in arithmetic, his excellent spelling ability, but lack of knowledge of or interest in the meaning of the words, his interest in opera and ability to play by ear coupled with a complete inability to profit from musical instruction. His IQ on the Binet test was 50.

As has been explained in the previous chapter, our understanding of what the complex inter-relationships among tests mean has been greatly facilitated by a statistical technique called factor analysis. It enables us to deal with large numbers of correlation coefficients at the same time and to erect mathematically a structure that serves to account for the varying sizes of these coefficients in terms of hypothetical factors or abilities which different tests require to different extents. In the case of a simple problem, it is easy to see without using any mathematical procedures the kind of reasoning that is involved. For example, one correlation coefficient between an arithmetical reasoning test and a reading test does not tell us much about the ability the tests measure. This correlation could reflect general intelligence or simply reading skill, since problems must be read to be solved. But let us add to the initial battery of two tests two others—an intelligence test that requires no reading and an arithmetic test that requires no reasoning but only simple manipulation of numbers. Then let us study all the correlations between the four tests and we may be able to decide between the different possible hypotheses. If they all show correlations of about the same magnitude, some general ability will need to be postulated. If the correlations between intelligence, arithmetical reasoning, and reading are all much higher than those between simple arithmetic and the other tests, it will look as though the manipulation of numbers constitutes a separate ability.

The necessity for mathematical factor-analytic methods in the carrying out of this type of thinking about abilities arises because a relatively small number of tests produces a large number of correlations and they cannot all be kept in mind at once. We can manage well enough with four tests and the six correlations we obtain from them, but for twenty tests we have 190 correlations and for fifty tests 1,225 correlations. Factor analysis does part of the work for us and simplifies the material before we attempt to interpret it.

If we remember always that factor analysis is only an extension of the method we find it quite natural to use when we wish to make an inference about mental traits on the basis of correlation coefficients, we may find the whole process less strange and difficult. We will also be reminded of the limitations of the method. As has been explained previously, it does not give us unequivocal mathematical statements of what the basic abilities are. It simply rearranges the information contained in the correlation coefficients. The psychologist doing the study must still name or identify the factors—name them in such a way that they fit the pattern obtained from the correlations. There is nothing mathematical at all about this naming process. And there is nothing *unique* about the mathematical solution. Another sort of rearrangement might fit the data just as well. Thus the factor analyst can only say, "This is *one* combination of traits which would serve to account for the relationships we have found between these tests." Another research worker may propose another set of traits based on equally sound mathematical and psychological reasoning, which will account for the relationships equally well. The choice between them must be made on the grounds of simplicity, usefulness, and congruence with the whole body of psychological knowledge. This is why there are so many arguments among factor analysts and why there is as yet no completely satisfactory account of the way mental abilities are organized.

In spite of these limitations of the method, however, factor analysts approaching the problem of mental organization from very different directions have found themselves meeting on common ground. By now the differences in interpretation are much less striking than the similarities. The most basic of the differences still not completely resolved has to do with types of solution of the factor problem preferred by American and British psychologists, respectively.

The British workers were the ones who initiated this line of research. Since the early years of the century Spearman, and later his students and colleagues, have been working on various aspects of a theory centered around the idea that mental tests all measure to some extent one basic intellectual ability. In *The Abilities of Man* (1927), Spearman summarized a vast amount of significant research. He showed that the inter-correlation for many test batteries containing a wide variety of materials and types of items *could* be accounted for in terms of the one characteristic he called "g." To him it seemed to represent the total *mental energy* available to an individual, while the "s" or specific factors in different tests stood for the engines through which this energy was applied. The data showed that "g" is most efficiently measured by questions and items we should ordinarily label "reasoning" tests, where the individual is asked to discover the relationship between two things or to identify something from its relationship to something else. For this kind of thinking Spearman coined the term *noegenesis*.

However, Spearman himself, and others using the methods he developed, encountered some test batteries in which not all of the correlation between certain tests could be adequately accounted for in terms of "g" alone. This seemed to occur in studies where several tests of somewhat similar content were included in the battery to be factor-analyzed. If there were, for example, two tests of vocabulary, or two tests of the form board type, the correlations between the two members of each pair were higher than their "g" loadings indicated that they should be. Out of this discrepancy grew the idea of "group" factors representing abilities less broad than "g" but broader than "s." Thus has developed the *hierarchical* theory of mental organization.

The clearest statement of this rather complex theory as to what intelligence consists of can be found in *The Structure of Mental Abilities* by P. E. Vernon (1950). What the theory means is illustrated in Vernon's diagram as reproduced in Figure 17. We can apply this kind of theory

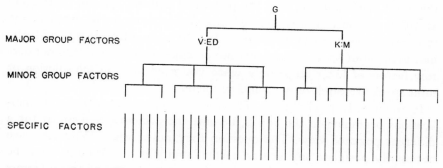

FIGURE 17. Diagram illustrating the hierarchical theory of mental organization (Vernon, 1950, p. 22).

both to tests and to persons being tested. If it is tests we are classifying in accordance with the system represented in Figure 17, we would evaluate them first with regard to their "g" loadings. (The factor loadings, derived from the correlations, answer the question, "How necessary is the ability under consideration for success with this test?") After this we can sort them out into two principal categories according to whether they require in addition to "g" the verbal-educational abilities important in all kinds of school work (v:ed) or the practical knack of understanding concrete things important in various mechanical jobs (k:m). We may if we wish make a still finer classification of tests by further subdividing the group that falls into each of the two main categories. Within the "v:ed" group, separate verbal and numerical abilities can be distinguished and tests of course differ in the extent to which they draw upon them. Within the "k:m" group, spatial and mechanical abilities can be separated.

It is doubtful, however, how useful these finer differentiations of ability are. Vernon presents statistical evidence that in the school, military, or industrial situations where applied psychologists work, the relevant criteria can be predicted fairly well by using only the "g," "v:ed," and "k:m" ratings. The other narrower group factors contribute so little to the total variance in test and criterion scores that they can safely be ignored. Specific factors, including such things as temperamental and character traits, background and experience, as well as specific talents and aptitudes, are of more importance in job situations than are the abilities at the minor group-factor level in Figure 17. Moursy (1952) has presented evidence for the suitability of the hierarchical scheme in accounting for correlations among twenty tests for a group of ten- and eleven-year-olds.

The point of view of the British factor analysts can be summed up in this way: try always to keep the pattern of abilities you are postulating as *simple* as you can. Measure "g" first and account for as much of the test variance as you can in terms of "g" alone. Supplement this with the measurement of broad educational and practical abilities. Separate out narrow factors of lesser scope only when you need them in the solution of some special research or personnel problem.

In America L. L. and T. G. Thurstone, in an important series of publications beginning in the 1930's, became the principal spokesmen for a different point of view. The question they raised was, "Why must we necessarily postulate any *general* mental ability at all? Would it not be possible to account for correlations between tests in terms of group factors alone, factors which inevitably overlap to some extent?" To put this idea into common-sense terms, we can easily conceive of five numerical tests that correlate with one another simply because they all require an ability to manipulate figures, not because of "g." But one of them may also correlate with a reading test because it requires that the problems to be worked must be read. Another may correlate with a test calling for the sorting of geometrical figures into categories because in both cases rapid perception of details is involved. Such tie-ups make it possible for all the correlations to be positive even if there is no one ability common to all tests. L. L. Thurstone worked out the mathematical techniques for what he called multiple factor analysis. By these methods it is possible to find a *set* of separate factors that account for the correlations in a battery of tests. (Remember that no mathematical system can guarantee that this is the *only* way the correlations can be explained. Solutions are not *unique*.) The multiple factor methods have been so successful that they have constituted the basis for the vast majority of American factor-analytical work done since they were formulated.

In his first large-scale study L. L. Thurstone (1938) assembled a battery of fifty-six psychological tests including as wide a variety as possible. Some had to do with seeing relationships between geometrical figures in space. Some were concerned with mechanical relationships such as are found in arrangements of gears and pulleys. Some required computation, some reasoning from syllogisms. The subjects were 240 volunteer college students. Nine "primary abilities" were identified from the tables of factor loadings. Later 1,154 eighth-grade children were given a similar battery of tests in a research undertaking designed to find out whether the same "primary abilities" would turn up in a group that was younger and less highly selected. Seven of them did (Thurstone and Thurstone, 1941). Still later evidence was presented (T. G. Thurstone, 1941) for the differentiation of six of the same factors in kindergarten children.

The primary mental abilities appearing in both college and eighth-grade studies were as follows:

S (space). Visualization of geometrical figures in different positions in space.
P (perceptual speed). Quick noting of details. (The interpretation of the loadings of different tests in this factor is somewhat less certain than for S.)
N (number). Quickness in making arithmetical computations of all sorts.
V (verbal meanings). Grasp of ideas and meanings of words.
W (word fluency). Speed in manipulating single and isolated words.
M (rote memory). Facility in memorizing words, numbers, letters, and other materials.
I (induction). Ability to extract a rule common to the materials of a problem or test.

Many other investigators have confirmed Thurstones' findings for factors V, N, S, and M. The distinction between the two verbal factors V and W was an unanticipated finding, and the meaning of W is still not completely clear. British psychologists have for a long time been interpreting a similar fluency factor they encountered in their studies as a temperamental rather than an intellectual characteristic (Eysenck, 1952). For both the perception and the reasoning factors, correlations were low enough in these original studies to suggest the existence of several rather than single factors. Goodman (1943a, 1943b) noted, for example, that the average correlation of the various perceptual tests in the Primary Mental Abilities battery he was using with a group of engineering freshman was only .36.

One of the lines of development most prominent during and since World War II has been the breaking down of Thurstone's "primary" abilities into others more homogeneous and narrower in their scope. If we analyze a battery of tests all of which have something to do with a single one of the primary abilities, we find that this ability splits up into others still more "primary." Thus Carroll (1941) identified nine verbal abilities in place of the two Thurstone had reported. L. L. Thurstone

(1944a) found ten perceptual factors, eight of them represented in enough tests so that they could be identified with special aspects of perception such as "speed and strength of closure" or "susceptibility to illusions." (These will be discussed in some detail in Chapter 9.) Guilford (1947) has summarized some of the outcomes of research done for the Army Air Force. There is evidence for the existence of at least twenty-seven identifiable factors. Several are spatial in nature, three represent different aspects of reasoning, and four have to do with memory. There is fairly clear evidence (Michael, 1954) that two separate abilities, space and visualization, are involved in what Thurstone originally labeled S. The work of Guilford et al (1954), of Corter (1952), and of Adkins and Lyerly (1952) has resulted in the recognition of several varieties of reasoning ability. A monograph by French (1951) lists and describes fifty-nine factors which have been reported in the literature.

Studies planned for special purposes are pointing to new varieties of ability as well as to subdivisions of those originally labeled "primary." Guilford and his associates, analyzing the abilities of high-level personnel, have reported a number of these. "Creativity" factors, for example, were isolated when tests were included that could be scored according to the uncommonness or the cleverness of the responses (Guilford, 1950).

Along with the fragmentation of the set of primary mental abilities first reported and the addition of new ones to the list has come an increasing realization that all these abilities are not really *independent*. If subjects in a study are scored on the factors themselves, these scores correlate positively with one another. This state of affairs leads to a factor analysis of *factors* and the identification of what are usually called *second-order* factors. When this fact first came to their attention psychologists on both sides of the Atlantic, including Thurstone (1944b), were quick to point out that we had here a basis for "rapprochement" between British and American viewpoints. A second-order general factor might well be the "g" on which Spearman had been insisting. The fact that Spearman's methods made it rise to the top first and Thurstone's picked it up in the bottom last would be more or less immaterial if its *existence* had been demonstrated both ways. Subsequent work has complicated this problem by producing evidence for not just one but *several* second-order factors showing up in intelligence-test materials. In this connection Rimoldi's (1948, 1951) analysis of scores made on a large number of tests by a group of Argentine school children aged eleven to fourteen, is pertinent. Three second-order general factors were indicated. The first of them seemed to be much like Spearman's "g" in that it showed up most strongly in tests requiring "noegenesis." The nature of the other two second-order factors was less clear.

For the practical worker attempting to apply the results of research to the problems he faces in school or industry, the importance of these second-order factors is that they extend and support the idea that has been prominent since the early days of applied psychology—that abilities are positively correlated and that there is such a thing as general *level* of intellectual competence upon which special talents and skills are superimposed. A person high in one kind of intellectual performance is quite likely to be average or above in others.

It was thought for a time that the generality or specificity of mental abilities was primarily a function of age, but later evidence has made this hypothesis untenable. McNemar (1942) demonstrated that a large general factor underlay the various problems and materials in the 1937 Stanford-Binet test for children, but L. V. Jones (1949) showed that the correlations could be accounted for just as well in terms of several primary abilities. (They were probably both right. An analysis in terms of second-order factors would probably have given evidence for a general factor as well as for the separate ones.) The Thurstones (1941) stated that factors were more highly correlated with one another in the eighth grade than in the college group. Garrett (1938, 1946), reanalyzing two previous studies, found higher correlations between factors for younger than for older children. Studies by Garrett, Bryan, and Perl (1935) and by Asch (1936) seemed to support this conclusion. However, more recent work by Curtis (1949), by Chen and Chow (1948), and by Doppelt (1950) indicates that age is not the variable that determines how important the general factor is. The Curtis study points to something else instead. Here a representative group of nine-year-old boys and a similar group of twelve-year-old boys were given ten tests designed to measure N, S, and V as well as "g," in two different *difficulty* levels. Holzinger's factor-analysis method which takes out a "g" factor before analyzing group factors made it possible to compare "g" loadings directly in the two age groups and at the two difficulty levels. The age groups did not differ with regard to the "g" component in their scores, but the difficulty levels did. The easy form produced a larger general factor than the difficult form did.

This difference in the difficulty of tests used in different age groups, something that was not controlled in the earlier studies, probably accounts for some of the difference in the generality or specificity of traits which was at first thought to arise from age differences. Another possible variation is *selection* in the groups tested. The fact that college populations are much more highly selected on an intellectual basis than grade-school or high-school groups are would tend to produce lower correlations between different intellectual abilities and thus suggest less generality. This conclusion fits in with facts summarized by Anastasi (1948) showing that in the Army group of young adults, similar in age but not in selection to Thurstone's college population, substantial correlations between traits were the rule rather than the exception.

The more glowing accounts of the clarification and efficiency that factor analysis was destined to bring to work in educational psychology and vocational guidance have been toned down as research progressed. For one thing, there is the question of how permanent or how changeable ability patterns are. At an intermediate age level in children (12-15), Swineford (1949) obtained test-retest correlations of from .3 to .8 for factor scores on the same tests given in sixth and in ninth grade. This indicates some consistency over the period, but hardly enough so that we could predict the pattern of an individual's development with enough accuracy to be helpful. At an earlier age level, L. E. Tyler (1953) found that fourth-grade primary mental abilities scores could be predicted as accurately from the total scores the children had obtained three years earlier as from the separate factor scores. It was general mental level that was most constant over this three-year interval. Patterns of high and low scores did not retain their shape. We need more information about the constancy of mental ability patterns at later ages.

Another finding making for caution in the use of primary mental abilities scores in guidance is that these scores often do not seem to correlate with the kinds of school criteria we might expect them to predict. Shaw (1949), for example, using as his subjects 591 high-school students, shows that it is only V (verbal) of the Primary Mental Abilities battery that shows consistently high correlations with school grades in most courses. There are in addition some moderately high correlations with R (reasoning) and a few that are significant with N (number). The other special scores do not correlate with grades in any course. It is to be noted that even the coefficients that show a significant relationship are not always in the subject areas where we would expect them. "N," for example, correlates to the extent of .43 with writing correctness, .19 with science, and .32 with quantitative thinking. We must not jump to conclusions about what an individual is best at from his factor scores.

What is needed most is more research relating factors to various criteria. Eysenck (1952) has worked out a method for doing this. Since most of his work has been on attitude and personality variables rather than intelligence, it will be discussed in a later chapter. Michael (1949) has reported an important study of Army Air Force tests given to two groups of fliers, 815 West Point Cadets, and 356 Negro cadets of much lower socio-economic background. He included the pass-fail criterion among the variables to be factor-analyzed. By doing this he was able to discover that even though most of the factors were the same for the two groups, their relationship to flying success was quite different. For the West Point group, success was most closely connected with pilot interest, spatial ability, and psychomotor coordination. For the Negro group it was connected with kinesthesis, perceptual speed, and spatial ability. It is apparent that only one of the three factors most closely related to the criterion is common to the two groups. Thus it appears that even if we knew what factors predicted what for a certain kind of people, we still could not be sure that the relationship would hold for another kind.

At this point perhaps we can pull together what all these studies representing both the British and the American viewpoints have taught us about the nature of what we loosely call intelligence. The type of theory fitting all the facts best is a hierarchical system similar to the one Vernon proposes. Intelligence is *both* one thing and many things. When we attempt to measure its general component we always leave some portion of the intellectual performance of our subjects unaccounted for. When we attempt to measure narrower abilities separately—verbal, spatial, perceptual—we always find that something they have in common makes scores on the separate traits correlate positively with one another. To describe an individual's mentality accurately we need to specify both *level* and *pattern*.

Authorities do not agree completely on the reasons for this hierarchical structure. P. E. Vernon (1950) attributes the partial breakdown of general intelligence into more specialized things to the influence of education. Because verbal and numerical abstract materials constitute most of the school curriculum, the specialized cluster of mental traits he calls "v:ed" develops. Children who take well to school work become high in the cluster as a whole; those who are less influenced by school rank lower. (The standard individual and group intelligence tests which have been used most in this country measure a mixture of "g" and "v:ed" and thus correlate well with school criteria, as the previous section has shown.)

Burt (1949) explains the hierarchy of abilities in a somewhat different way. To him the place of any kind of ability in the hierarchy depends upon its simplicity or complexity. Simple sensory processes, at one extreme, are almost completely specific. (An individual with unusually keen vision shows no tendency to excel in hearing, tasting, or smelling.) Work of persons like tea-tasters, for example, reminds us that there are highly specialized sensitivities and skills bearing little if any relationship to one another. Perceptual and motor processes produce factors of a little broader scope, such as perceptual speed and steadiness. The comprehension of relationships or "noegenesis," the process represented by "g," is at the other extreme from the sensory processes with regard to complexity, and it is a unitary trait that can be measured as a whole in each individual. Such a view does fit in well with what we have found to be true in life situations. If we wish to select workers for some highly specialized assembly-line task, we find it necessary to measure specific dexterity at certain kinds of arm and hand movements. If we wish to select college students who will do superior work in any field, a general intelligence test will serve about as well as a specialized test in one field alone. The study made by Moursy (1952) also supports this view of the meaning of the hierarchy.

One aspect of this hierarchical theory of intelligence has a bearing on a variety of problems in differential psychology—race differences, social class differences, and intelligence trends from generation to generation, for example. Much work that was done *before* we developed this theory now needs to be rethought in terms of it. As we have seen, it appears that there is a general intellectual ability in which individuals differ, but it also appears that we are never able to measure it in its pure state by means of any single test. As we encounter "g" in the individual, it is always combined with some of the "primary" and "specific" abilities, abilities which seem to be based in part on schooling and incidental learning. This fact makes group differences on test scores (or IQ's based on them) difficult to interpret. Is it "g" in which the groups differ or is it one of these other things? We shall consider the detailed evidence on this point in later chapters. Here we simply point out the existence of the problem.

Where group-difference studies have a bearing on the nature-nurture problem, it is especially important that we consider carefully what our results really show. P. E. Vernon (1951) speaks for a considerable number of psychologists when he advocates that we stop trying to use intelligence tests for research in eugenics. The fact that "g" is inextricably bound up with other factors makes comparisons of scores for families of different sizes or children from different regions ambiguous. He has concluded that we cannot hope to use our present tests to tell us whether one *group* is more intelligent than another. R. B. Cattell (1944) represents another point of view. He has attempted to develop a culture-free intelligence test which by being equally fair to all groups tested will control the "non-g" factors. His way of doing this has been to construct the test out of perceptual materials unfamiliar to all subjects. The available evidence on this test is still insufficient to permit us to be sure that it is in fact equally fair to all groups regardless of cultural background. It seems possible that dealing with perceptual materials of the paper-and-pencil variety requires a response set more easily developed in some cultures than in others. Some consideration of this problem will be included in the chapter on race differences.

SOME OTHER ANALYSES OF INTELLIGENCE

The research we have been considering constitutes what might be called the main stream of work on the intelligence problem. There have been, however, other currents of thought which might conceivably take us in a somewhat different direction as time passes.

Hofstaetter (1954) reports a factor analysis of a novel sort, since the correlations on which it is based are those between scores on the same test at different times rather than the customary correlations between different tests at the same time. The original matrix consisted of the figures obtained from the California developmental study reported in Bayley (1949). The results give rather clear-cut evidence for three factors characterizing different *periods*. Number one, with heavy loadings on tests given during infancy, he called sensori-motor alertness. Number two, with its heavy loadings on tests given in the preschool years, he called persistence or rigidity. Number three, with heavy loadings on tests given during the school years, might be called "g." Thus it would seem that the trait measured by "intelligence" tests may gradually shift over from one sort of thing in very young children to a quite different sort of thing in school-age boys and girls.

Other workers have concerned themselves directly with biological or physiological aspects of mental capacity. It is a puzzling fact about tests of the types we have been talking about heretofore, the descendents of Binet's first scale, that most of them do not indicate in any consistent way the effects of even quite extensive damage to the brain. Since there is general agreement that the brain is the organ upon which intelligent behavior depends, this fact has led some physiologists and psychologists to doubt their adequacy as intelligence measures. A number of investigators have applied themselves directly to the problem of what the effects of brain damage on mental characteristics are.

The most influential of these has been K. Goldstein. In a monograph by Goldstein and Scheerer (1941) the important distinction between *abstract* and *concrete* behavior is elaborated. This is a difference that shows up in its most marked form on sorting tests or other tests of concept formation. The person who is high in abstract ability is able to think of individual things in categories and is able to shift easily from one system of classification to another. Given a miscellaneous collection of little toy objects to sort, for example, he can place all the cars in one box, all the pieces of furniture in another, all the animals in a third. If asked to sort them in some other way, he may decide to place all wooden objects in one pile and all metal ones in another, or he may classify them on the basis of size, color, or some other attribute. In contrast to this, the person who is limited to a highly concrete kind of mental activity may be almost helpless with such a task. He may be able to place together the things which he has used at one time, such as a knife and fork or a pencil and paper, or he may be able to put two red objects side by side if their color is almost identical. But he cannot think in categories. The fact that such conceptual thinking does differentiate between unimpaired and brain-damaged persons gives it a sort of *biological* validity. It raises the question, "Could this process of abstraction *be* intelligence?" If we assumed that it is we could develop tests that would measure it more accurately and directly than our present standard tests do. The composite of subtests of which they are now composed includes many items that call for abstraction but many others that do not.

Halstead (1947, 1951) has also been working with brain-injured subjects. His findings have led him to contrast "biological" with "psychometric" intelligence (the ability measured by our standard tests). He has made factor analyses of the correlations between some specifically devised tests in both normal and brain-injured groups. There is evidence for four factors, the first resembling Goldstein and Scheerer's abstract ability:

A. The *ability to categorize* and form concepts of wide generality on some rational basis.
B. *Cerebral power.* This shows up especially in flicker-fusion tests where persons high in the factor can distinguish between a steady and an unsteady light at much higher rates of alternation than can those in whom the ability is low.
C. *Direction or modality.* This has to do with the avenue or special talent through which intelligence is manifested.
D. *Memory* or organized experience of the individual.

Using such a system of thinking about intelligence results in a different kind of description of an individual from the one we would formulate using such factors as Thurstone's. We would have to include an evaluation (a) of his abstract or conceptual ability, (b) of the power he can bring to bear on a problem, (c) of the directions in which his intellect has been developed, and (d) of the reservoirs of knowledge he possesses.

These factors have something in common with those which a Swiss psychologist Meili (1946) (reported in Myers, 1947) has obtained, using well-educated adults and school children as his subjects. The factors he obtained from the correlations are not to be thought of as special abilities but rather as separate *aspects* of intelligence. They can all be expected to appear in every intellectual performance, but their relative importance varies from one situation to another and from one person to another. The factors are:

1. *Plasticity*—the ability to break up a structure and organize it in a different way.
2. *Complexity*—the ability to grasp complex structures clearly and precisely.
3. *Fluency*—the ability to pass rapidly from one idea to another.
4. *Globalization*—the ability to bring separate ideas into a single whole.

In a later paper, Meili (1949) argues against the naming of factors obtained from factor analysis on the basis of the apparent composition of the tests in which they appear. He holds that an analysis of the type of mental process involved is a sounder basis for identification.

It may well be that Goldstein's abstract ability, Halstead's Factor A, and Meili's Factor 4 are all expressions of the same basic process. The other factors Halstead and Meili have presented do not match up quite so well. All of them, however, may represent significant aspects of intelligence as yet inadequately understood, aspects that it would be worth while to explore with many kinds of subjects, children and adults, educated and uneducated, normal and abnormal.

Still another approach to the problem of what intelligence means is found in the work of Piaget (1947). Instead of constructing tests to measure a trait that is assumed to be qualitatively the same from one age to the next, Piaget made careful observations of the kind of adaptive behavior infants and young children spontaneously engage in. He has distinguished several stages in the growth of intelligence, each built on the preceding one but showing new features. The basic processes which he calls *assimilation*, the incorporation of new experience into existing "schemas" or patterns, and *accommodation*, the modification of existing schemas in response to the impact of the environment, are present from the beginning. At the earliest stage, however, when the baby turns his head toward the nipple, thus demonstrating the existence of a simple schema, Piaget would not call the mental process intelligence. It is only when the child achieves the power of detaching himself from the pattern and thinking about it from different points of view that genuine intelligence can be said to be operating. So far, Piaget's emphasis has been principally on the uniform stages in development rather than on individual differences. If one wanted to concentrate on the differences in rate of growth, however, or the age at which each successive stage is achieved, there is no reason why a new type of mental-age scale could not be constructed in accordance with the theory. Piaget (1947, p. 153) mentions one study carried out along these lines.

SUMMARY

The fact that intelligence tests were developed to meet practical needs rather than to solve theoretical problems has meant that from Binet's time down to the present their primary value has been in practical situations. We still have difficulty in formulating a precise definition of the intelligence our tests measure, but with the accumulation of data of different sorts resulting from the widespread use of these instruments we are now able to say with some precision what they do and do not show. We know that for a child a test indicates how far along he is in the mental *development* that goes with growth toward maturity. We know that tests predict with a fair degree of accuracy how successfully individuals, children or adults, will be able to grasp the complex and difficult ideas that are presented in school. With regard to the controversies that have shaken the world of mental testing, we now have facts that compel us to take a middle position. The IQ is neither completely constant nor entirely unpredictable from one age level to another. Intelligence is neither pure "g" nor a simple combination of independent traits. With such information to guide us we can make sound judgments about individuals in school, office, or factory and can develop special tests for special purposes.

There are some promising leads for future research along theoretical lines in the theories of Goldstein, Halstead, Meili, and Piaget. It may be that further progress in understanding what intelligence means will come not so much from manipulation of scores obtained from the standard tests we are now using as from careful analyses of qualitative differences in the way in which mental work is done.

CHAPTER 5

Individual Differences in School Achievement

It has been in our schools more than in any other one place that individual differences have come to our attention. There they raise many questions and create many problems. They complicate the teacher's task and call for skills that go far beyond the making of assignments and grading of papers. They make it possible for newspaper reporters to come up with "shocking" exposures of ignorance in some students who have spent many years in our public schools. They create difficulties for curriculum planners, forcing them to recognize that however sound are the objectives for any one age or grade level, some pupils will achieve them and others will not. Perhaps their greatest importance comes from the fact that as each person during his own schooldays comes up against the realities of individual differences, he develops feelings of pride or inferiority, anxiety or defensiveness, which he will carry the rest of his life.

THE EXTENT OF THE DIFFERENCES

Teachers and students alike have always been aware that differences existed, but it is only since the development of standardized achievement tests that we have realized how great they are. These achievement tests constitute a development and refinement of the traditional examinations on school subject matter. For research purposes they have a number of advantages. Their content is based upon a wide sampling of material that a number of well-qualified teachers agree should be a part of the course in question rather than upon any one person's judgment. Their form is objective and definite so that the student understands the questions and the scorer can mark the answers right or wrong without ambiguity. Their norms are as representative as possible of all students of the age or grade level for which the test is intended.

One of the commonest ways of stating this normative information is for the publishers to give the score on the test that corresponds to the *average* score for each grade. Then each individual's score can be interpreted in terms of the grade placement to which it corresponds. If William makes an arithmetic score of 6-3 in this notation, it means that he knows as much about this subject as the average child who has finished three months in the sixth grade.

Such grade-norm scores make us aware of the tremendous differences between children in any one grade or class. Hildreth (1950) has summarized some of these results. In one group of seven-year-olds scores ranged from the first- to the sixth-grade level. For a group of ten-year-olds the range was from the first- to the ninth-grade level. In one study using age norms rather than grade norms the range of educational ages in a group of children all of whom had spent three and a half years in school was from six to fifteen. In other words, the lowest in the group knew no more than the average child just beginning school, whereas the highest was already at the level of high-school students.

TABLE 5.

Selected Percentile Norms for Metropolitan Achievement Test in English Usage, Grade 8

(Hildreth, Bixler, *et al.*, 1948)

PERCENTILE	SCORE	GRADE EQUIVALENT
98	258	Above 11
90	244	11.4
75	233	9.6
50	222	8.2
25	209	6.9
10	197	5.9
2	179	4.8

Tables 5, 6, and 7 give some figures taken from the norm tables furnished with two tests in common use, the Metropolitan Achievement Tests and the Iowa Every-Pupil Battery. Both tests have been standardized on several thousand children fairly typical of the school population. In addition to the sort of information cited in the previous paragraph about the extremes of school accomplishment in any one grade, these tables show how wide the "middle half" is, the group between the 25th and the 75th percentiles which we would probably consider average for each grade.

Table 5 shows that for English achievement at the eighth-grade level the distance from the 25th to the 75th percentile represents almost a three-year range. Table 6 shows that for reading comprehension this middle-half distance is one and one-half years for the third-graders, two and

TABLE 6.

Selected Percentile Norms for Iowa Every-Pupil Test of Silent Reading Comprehension

(Spitzer *et al.*, 1947)

3RD GRADE		5TH GRADE	
PERCENTILE	GRADE EQUIVALENT	PERCENTILE	GRADE EQUIVALENT
99	8-2	99	9-8
90	6-0	90	8-4
75	4-9	75	7-2
50	3-9	50	5-9
25	3-3	25	4-8
10	2-6	10	4-0
1	1-9	1	2-9

TABLE 7.

Selected Percentile Norms for Iowa Every-Pupil Test of Arithmetic

(Spitzer *et al.*, 1947)

5TH GRADE		9TH GRADE	
PERCENTILE	GRADE EQUIVALENT	PERCENTILE	GRADE EQUIVALENT
99	7-2	99	11-6
90	6-5	90	11-0
74	6-2	74	10-6
50	5-9	50	9-9
25	5-3	25	8-4
10	4-9	10	7-5
1	4-2	1	6-5

one-half for the fifth-graders. In general, the higher up the educational ladder we go the greater this spread becomes, at least until we reach the level at which compulsory school laws no longer apply and selection cuts off the bottom portion of the distribution. This increase at the higher levels is shown in Table 7 for arithmetic. The middle-half range is about a year for fifth-graders, over two years for ninth-graders. Similarly, the distance from 10th to 90th percentiles is less than two years for fifth-graders but more than three and one-half years for ninth-graders.

Figure 18 represents some similar results at the college freshman level. Even though some unofficial selection has occurred so that those who are lowest in the verbal skills have probably not applied for admission to college, there is still a vast difference in the facility with written language that different students bring to their college tasks. We can appreciate just

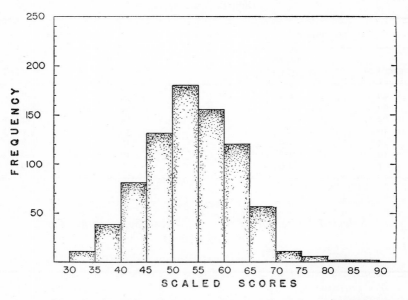

FIGURE 18. Distribution of scores on Coöperative English Test (Effectiveness of Expression) for 795 University of Oregon entering freshmen.

what this means in practical terms when we realize that a scaled score of 50 represents the performance of the average high-school graduate who has had an average amount of training in the subject and that the standard deviation of this scaled score distribution for average high-school students is set at 10. Thus a score of 34, which would be found in the lowest interval shown on Figure 18, is almost two standard deviations below the mean and corresponds to the average for the seventh grade, according to the norms furnished by Coöperative Test Service. On the other hand a scaled score of 80, near the top of the Oregon freshman distribution, is three standard deviations above the mean and corresponds to a percentile rank of 97 on the norms for college *graduates*.

These have been samples of the sort of variability in school accomplishment that is the *rule*, not the exception, in schools where the problem has been investigated. By far the most exhaustive and thorough of such investigations was a study carried on in Pennsylvania colleges and high schools from 1928 to 1932 and reported in detail in the monograph by Learned and Wood (1938). The purpose of the whole undertaking was to evaluate the educational system of the state in terms of what students who came through it actually knew. Examinations were carefully designed with questions organized under broad headings representative of the objectives of general education in any school—such headings as "Tools of Scientific Investigation," "Ancient Cultures," and "Contemporary Western Civilization." The tests were highly reliable and gave high enough correlations with college grades so that it was clear that they were measuring what teachers think students should know. In 1928 they were administered to college seniors throughout the state. In 1930 they were given to college sophomores. In 1932 they were readministered to the same subjects, now seniors in college, so that gains could be studied. In 1933 and 1934 a large number of high-school seniors took some of the tests. Figure 19 summarizes some of the findings on the examinations taken by all three groups—high-school seniors, college sophomores, and college seniors. This part of the total examination was called a "general culture" test and included questions on fine arts, history and social studies, world literature, and natural science.

This graph shows two things very plainly. First, there is a wide spread of scores within each of these groups of students who had spent the same amount of time in school. Second, there is a large amount of overlapping *between* groups. One person among the high-school seniors succeeded in answering only 25 questions out of the more than 1,200 he was asked. In contrast, another twelfth-grader answered more than 600 of them correctly. In the sophomore group the range is from 25 to 755 points, in the senior group from 45 to 805. It is perhaps a little unfair to judge variability from the exceptional cases at the extremes of the distributions, but even if we look at the middle half of each, the spread within each group is still considerably greater than the average differences between them. There *is* an average difference, obviously. In general we can say that the median for each of the higher groups falls at about the 75th percentile of the group below it. But this means that roughly a quarter of the lower group of students is made up of persons who already know more than the average person with two years more of schooling. As many as 10 per cent of the high-school seniors are always above the college senior average.

Learned and Wood analyzed the variability in a number of ways. There were large differences between colleges and between majors within the same college. In general, engineering students averaged highest, candi-

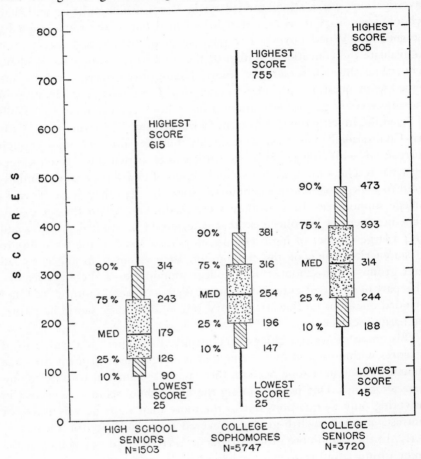

FIGURE 19. Distribution of scores on a General Culture Test for Pennsylvania students in three groups—high-school seniors, college sophomores, and college seniors (Learned and Wood, 1938, p. 18).

dates for Bachelor of Arts and Bachelor of Science degrees in liberal arts colleges only slightly lower, and business and education students considerably lower. Non-degree students in teachers' colleges stood at the bottom of the list with an average score *below* the average for high-school seniors. These findings were not uniform for all colleges within each classification, however. Engineering schools and liberal arts colleges differed considerably from one another. In one liberal arts college, 85 per cent of the sophomores were above the statewide mean for college seniors; in another, 75 per cent of the sophomores were below the statewide sophomore average. The inescapable conclusion is that there is no one standard of achievement that is "normal" for a certain educational level. Grading systems and course standards which assume that there is are founded on an illusion.

TABLE 8.

Differences in Major Groups on the SSCQT Test
(based on more than 74,000 cases)

(ETS Developments, 1953)

MAJOR	PER CENT PASSING	
	1951	1952
General Arts	48	49
Humanities	52	54
Social Sciences	57	55
Education	27	30
Business and Commerce	42	35
Physical Science and Mathematics	64	69
Engineering	68	68
Biological Sciences	59	62
Agriculture	37	44
All Fields	53	54

The testing program which was conducted in colleges throughout the country during 1951 and 1952 using the Selective Service College Qualification Test corroborates these findings about differences in colleges and in major groups almost perfectly. Since the SSCQT is an intelligence test rather than an achievement test, this parallel suggests that it is student ability rather than teaching efficiency in which the groups and institutions differ. Table 8 shows the percentage of students in different subject-matter areas who met the standard set for "passing" the test, a standard which for freshmen was the equivalent of a score one standard deviation above the mean for the general population. It is clear that science students are high, education students low. In a summary by Chauncey (1952) the extent of the variation from college to college is made clear. In some colleges as few as 35 per cent of the students taking the test received a passing grade; in others the per cent passing was as high as 98. Thus the students in the lower half of their classes in some institutions, so far as grades are concerned, are actually more capable than the students in the upper half of their classes in other institutions.

To return to some of the other results of the Learned and Wood study: it was clear that within any one school or class, the youngest students averaged highest, the oldest lowest. (Selection and promotion policies of the 1920's have something to do with this, since it was customary for brighter students to progress faster and reach any given level at an earlier age than duller students did. Under a policy that discourages the "skipping" of grades the same results might not hold.) The authors of the monograph illustrate their point about the lack of relationship between the time spent in school and the amount of knowledge gained by analyzing what the composition of a college graduating class would have been if individuals had been awarded diplomas on the basis of tested knowledge rather than hours and credits. Assuming that the top fifth of the student body was ready for graduation, Learned and Wood showed that this group would have consisted of 28 per cent of the senior class, 21 per cent of the juniors, 19 per cent of the sophomores, and 15 per cent of the freshmen. The mean age of this group would have been 20.6, nearly two years lower than that of the seniors. In place of the 3½ per cent who graduated before they were twenty-one under the traditional system, 52 per cent of the group graduated on the basis of knowledge would have been below this age.

Having the college seniors retake the examination they had taken as sophomores made it possible for the investigators to examine *gains* as well as ultimate attainments. Great variability showed up here also. Some individuals gained more than others; some colleges increased their average score more than did others; some subject-matter areas showed more increase than others. However, correlations between scores obtained on the two occasions were consistently high. Although there were some shifts in the positions of individual students in the distributions, they were not large or numerous. For the total score on the test, the correlation over the two-year period was .90. The lowest correlation was .70 (fine arts), the highest .92 (grammar and vocabulary). There is an overwhelming probability that a student who is superior as a sophomore will still be superior as a senior.

SOURCES OF THE VARIATION IN SCHOOL ACHIEVEMENT

Why do some students have at their command so much more knowledge than others at the end of any specified length of time in school? The question has been behind thousands of research studies and has stimulated endless discussion among educators. In spite of all these efforts, we can still give only a partial answer. The best predictions we can make of an individual's probable achievement are of limited accuracy. We have accounted for only about half the variance; the other half still eludes us. The importance of knowing even as much as we do know about the factors and influences affecting school success must not, however, be minimized in a society like ours that places a great deal of emphasis on education.

In the first place, there is abundant evidence for a consistent dependable relationship between school achievement and *intelligence*. In the previous chapter we have cited this relationship as evidence for the validity of the intelligence tests. It must be admitted that there is some circularity in the reasoning if we now use the same figures to prove that school success depends upon intelligence. This criticism of the whole mental-testing movement was once more cogent than it now is. As we have shown, our understanding of what intelligence tests are measuring no longer rests exclusively on the correlations with school criteria. Other lines of research —growth studies, factor analyses, and observations of abnormal groups— have helped to determine our present views. We know too from school prediction studies that intelligence tests do not tell the whole story. Intelligence is related to academic achievement but not synonymous with it.

Correlations vary somewhat from study to study but the bulk of them range between .30 and .80. The median would be about .5. This is not pure random variation. High correlations are typically obtained under some circumstances, low ones under others. There is, first of all, the purely statistical factor of *selection* in the group for which predictions are made. If the variability of the distribution has been curtailed through the elimination of low-scoring individuals, high-scoring individuals, or both, all correlations will run *lower* than they otherwise would. If this were the only factor affecting them, we would expect intelligence-achievement correlations to be lower for high-school than for grade-school groups, and lower for college than for high-school groups. They would naturally be lower also in colleges practicing rigorous selection than in those admitting all applicants. While there is a tendency for this differentiation to characterize reported correlations, it is not as marked as it might have been had not more highly discriminating tests been developed for the more highly selected groups. We do not use the Stanford-Binet or the Army General Classification Test for predicting college scholarship. Instead we develop difficult intelligence tests specifically for this purpose, tests which make as many accurate discriminations within the selected group as the easier ones did within wide-range groups. In evaluating reports of relationships between intelligence and scholastic achievement, the suitability of the tests used to the intellectual level and range of the groups tested must always be taken into consideration.

Another general finding is that intelligence tests are more highly correlated with scores on achievement *tests* than they are with grades given by teachers. We can summarize in a rough way the trends shown in many studies by stating that correlations with grades are usually below .5, those with achievement-test scores above .5. Is this because teachers are not very good judges of school accomplishment and tend to award marks too much on the basis of coöperativeness, agreeableness, and effort, or is it because intelligence measures are not independent enough of learned information and thus have a good deal of common content with achievement tests? Both reasons probably operate. Teachers do judge pupils partly on the basis of characteristics other than mastery of subject matter. Many authorities hold that it is right that they should. On the other hand, scores on verbal intelligence tests are based to some extent on schooling. It is a well-known fact that performance tests give consistently lower correlations with school criteria than verbal tests do.

It is interesting to note, however, that achievement tests based on quite different philosophies with regard to the aims and methods of education correlate about equally well with verbal intelligence. Beginning about 1930 there was a protest among educational psychologists against the current methods for the selection of content used in school examinations, both standardized and informal. This led to important changes in some achievement tests put on the market for wide distribution and use. Instead of being made up of items on disconnected facts, the questions centered around knowledge more closely related to the basic objectives of education, things like the understanding of concepts and the application of principles to new situations. R. W. Tyler (1936) reported that the correlations between scores obtained on these tests and on those of the traditional type were not high (.31 to .58). T. R. McConnell (1940), however, obtained much higher coefficients, averaging .87, between information and application sections of examinations in the same subject-matter areas. Probably no general statement can be made as to how closely related the two types of test are. It would all depend upon methods of teaching and on specific characteristics of the tests. But it seems clear that both types of test do correlate about equally well with intelligence measures. Lorge (1949) summarizes the evidence from several studies on this problem.

Although type of test is not a factor producing differences in correlations with intelligence, subject-matter *area* is. Such correlations tend to be highest for reading and English, somewhat lower for science and the social studies, lower still for mathematics, especially geometry, and negligible for music and the arts. Table 9 from the Learned and Wood study (1938) shows these trends for high-school groups in one large city.

TABLE 9.

Correlations of Achievement Test Scores in Various Subjects with Scores in the Otis Intelligence Test

(Learned and Wood, 1938, p. 143)

SUBJECT	r
English	.74
Algebra	.68
General Science	.64
Civics	.62
Biology	.52
American History	.50
Physics	.48
French	.46
Plane Geometry	.43
European History	.42
Ancient History	.42
Trigonometry	.34
Chemistry	.33
Latin	.30
German	.28

One further factor upon which the magnitude of the correlation between intelligence and school achievement seems to depend is the length of the time interval between the two measures. As one might expect, short-range predictions from intelligence-test scores are more efficient than long-range ones. Bailey (1949) reports correlations of from .53 to .80 for random samples of lower-grade students when intelligence and achievement tests were given during the same school year. The figures were lower (.47 and .67) when first-grade intelligence tests were correlated with fourth-grade achievement. (Correlations of the different group tests used with the Binet would suggest that the test giving the .67 coefficient was a better measure of intelligence than the one giving the .47.) This is still a substantial relationship over the three-year period. Travers (1949), summarizing predictions made over still longer intervals, reports correlations of from .21 to .58 between intelligence as measured in the lower schools and *college* scholarship. The .21 is based on the longest time interval, that from first grade to college. Plainly it would be an unsound procedure for lower-grade teachers to make definite predictions about the aptitude of individual children for advanced education.

Along with the interest American psychologists have shown in breaking down general intelligence into a number of more limited mental abilities have come parallel attempts to predict success in *specific* school subjects on the basis of special abilities. Two types of research can be distinguished here. In one type, an achievement test in one academic field is used as the basis for prediction in the same field—mathematics tests to predict subsequent mathematics grades, social science tests to predict social science grades, or foreign language tests to predict foreign language grades. In the other type, scores on "primary" mental abilities identified through factor analysis are used to predict grades in subject-matter areas one might logically expect to be related to them—V to predict English grades, S to predict geometry grades, N to predict arithmetic grades, for example. So far the first type of research has been the more successful.

Tests of the first variety, the so-called "prognostic" tests of achievement in various subject-matter areas, do seem to produce somewhat higher correlations with grades than intelligence tests do, especially at the college level. They are not, however, outstandingly high, seldom running above .7. (See Travers, 1949, p. 162.) The Iowa tests (Lindquist, 1948) and the battery developed at Yale (Crawford and Burnham, 1946) are particularly useful. There are many college personnel problems in connection with which the increase in predictive accuracy from the .5 which is about the maximum for intelligence tests to the .7 obtainable from these batteries has real practical value. One study reported by Olander, Van Wagenen, and Bishop (1949) shows that prognostic tests for arithmetic can be developed even at the first-grade level. These tests correlated to the extent of about .5 with arithmetic achievement three years later. It is doubtful, however, whether this represents a significantly better prediction than could have been made by means of an intelligence test alone. In any case, there seems to have been little interest in predicting success of specific kinds in school children.

Specialized prognostic achievement batteries are time-consuming and expensive. Many educators have hoped that as the tests based on factor analysis came into common use they would accomplish the same purpose more efficiently and economically. It seemed reasonable to expect that some kinds of school work would be related most closely to verbal ability, others to memory, and others to facility with numbers. As has been explained in the previous chapter, these hopes have not been supported by the correlational findings. Most of the work has been done with the Thurstone

Primary Mental Abilities battery at the college level, but what evidence there is from high-school studies corroborates the conclusion. Verbal and Reasoning factors are the only ones giving consistently significant correlations with scholastic achievement, and they correlate about equally well with everything.

Even the separation of scholastic aptitude tests into separately scored verbal and quantitative sections, as in the American Council on Education and Graduate Record examinations, for example, has been of doubtful value. Correlations vary considerably from place to place and from class to class, so that it is difficult to summarize trends. It seems to be true that L (linguistic) scores give higher correlations than do Q (quantitative) scores with grades in English and in all subjects that depend on reading. It is not true, however, that Q scores give consistently higher correlations than L scores do with mathematics and science grades. Sometimes the correlations of such grades with L and Q are about equal, as in Super's study (1940), sometimes L is a more satisfactory predictor, and in general the total score gives better predictions than does either of the subscores alone (D. M. Barrett, 1952).

One set of tests, designed especially as tools to be used in educational guidance, represents a compromise between the specialized achievement tests and the factor-analysis batteries. It is the Differential Aptitude Test developed by the Psychological Corporation (Bennett, Seashore, and Wesman, 1947). It includes not only tests for primary mental abilities such as verbal reasoning or space relations, but also aptitude tests like mechanical reasoning that make no pretense of being factorially "pure," and tests like language usage that are clearly based on material covered in the school curriculum. Doppelt and Wesman (1952) have summarized evidence from two predictive studies that shows there is a clear tendency toward specialized prediction in the expected directions. Numerical ability as measured here correlates with success in areas where quantitative thinking is required; space relations and mechanical reasoning correlate with science grades. Again, however, there are some of the same confusions and inconsistencies that have shown up with the other tests. Verbal reasoning tends to give the highest correlations with everything. It often predicts success in mathematics as well as the numerical test does. Conversely, this number factor seems to correlate with English almost as highly as with mathematics. Validity studies with the Differential Aptitude Test battery are continually in progress, and new generalizations may emerge as they are completed. Meanwhile the best rule to follow as one tries to make judgments about individuals in school is to be extremely cautious about predictions based on specialized tests that *appear* to involve the same mental abilities as the criterion predicted.

On this rather confused and uncertain issue, the extent to which special mental abilities determine success in specialized kinds of intellectual activity, British psychologists have taken a different position from Americans. The way they view the problem is in keeping with their general preference for keeping the theoretical structure they are postulating as simple as possible. P. E. Vernon (1950) has given the most complete statement. The evidence he summarizes indicates that a considerable part of the differences between individuals in school achievement can be accounted for in terms of differences in "g." Another part of the variation arises from differences in the "v:ed" factor, which could be characterized as aptitude in "book learning," and which can be measured by tests of vocabulary, arithmetic, spelling, or general information. There is also a third, *non*-intellectual factor which he labels X, a complex of personality traits, interests, and background characteristics. Except in groups so selected or specialized that they are high in all three of these main factors determining school achievement, Vernon feels that it is hardly worth while to look for special aptitudes which may have something to do with scholarship in one area alone. Their effects are so small in comparison with the main factors that measuring them can add very little to the accuracy of our judgments. Attempts to identify separate rote memory and reasoning abilities in school tasks or to differentiate various reading skills from one another have not produced convincing evidence that these traits can be broken down into independent abilities. The idea of basing our judgments of students on the best evaluations we can get of "g," "v:ed," and the X-factor is appealing in its simplicity, and it is in accord with the correlational data obtained so far.

Whether or not we adopt Vernon's system, the necessity for evaluating X, the motivational factor, is always with us. Several converging lines of evidence point to its importance. For one thing, the trend in dozens of reports on predicting college grades is for the highest correlations to be those with some measure of previous school achievement. In Garrett's summary (1949) of a large number of such studies, the median correlation with scholastic aptitude test scores was .47, and the median correlation with high-school grades .56. A weighted combination of the two has turned out to be a consistently better predictor of college grades than either taken separately. Evidently something in addition to scholastic aptitude is represented in the grades students make. Coöperativeness, agreeableness, persistence, and willingness to work could all be involved.

Another set of facts pointing in the same direction is the almost universal tendency for girls to get better school marks than boys. No higher in measured intelligence, girls do seem to average somewhat higher than boys in these non-intellectual traits making for success in school.

SCHOOL ACHIEVEMENT AND MEASURED MOTIVATIONAL CHARACTERISTICS

When personality inventories first became available, educators hoped by the use of these tools to do a better job of predicting and thus improving school achievement of individuals. It seemed reasonable to anticipate that students with stable, well-adjusted personalities would be better able to make use of their abilities than would students with personality disturbances. These hopes have been dampened if not extinguished by reports of near-zero correlation between scholarship and every conceivable variety of adjustment inventory at all educational levels (Donahue *et al.*, 1949, pp. 171-172). The only relationship that appears with any consistency at all throughout these studies is a small positive correlation between introversion and grades. Introversion scores on personality inventories usually show *negative* correlations with adjustment scores. Thus if items representing the two kinds of trait are included in the same test, as they often are, the tendency for introversion and scholarship to be *positively* related may counteract any slight tendency there may be for general adjustment and scholarship to be *negatively* related. The only conclusion that is at all important for practical purposes is that any degree of adjustment or maladjustment, as measured in personality inventories, may occur with any degree of success or lack of success in school work.

Interest inventories have produced results somewhat more impressive than have adjustment inventories, but reported correlations are still too low to be of much practical consequence. A few such correlations have turned out to be as high as .4 or .5 (Super, 1949, Chs. 17 and 18), but the great majority are in the .30's or lower. It is interesting to note that the highest relationships reported for both the Kuder and the Strong tests are in science fields. This suggests the possibility that interest has more effect upon achievement in some areas than in others. Some workers have been of the opinion that correlational procedures are not the most suitable means for exploring whatever relationship there is between interests and achievement. Interests could be very important in determining whether a person chooses a course of study and persists in it, and still have little to do with the grades obtained in the course. A certain ambiguity with regard to the meaning of scores obtained on either the Strong or the Kuder blanks also complicates the problem of interpreting correlations obtained with them. Neither of these instruments measures the *intensity* of the person's interest in a kind of activity and this may be the very factor upon which school achievement depends.

After projective tests came into common use for the evaluation of personality characteristics numerous attempts were made to relate their findings to school achievement. One of the most successful of these was the study reported by Munroe (1945). Using a check list to register the number of indicators of maladjustment each Rorschach record showed she obtained a correlation of .49 between adjustment scores and college grades. Since the adjustment scores were correlated to only a negligible extent with intelligence-test scores, they enabled the advisers responsible for helping individual students to make a considerably better judgment about each person's prospects for college success than could have been made from the ability test alone. Cronbach (1950) in another college did not get a correlation of this magnitude between Rorschach adjustment levels and grades. In this instance adding Rorschach scores to intelligence scores raised the over-all correlation from .45 to only .49. Such an increase in predictive power is not enough to justify the use of the personality test. Why these two studies using similar methods should differ in their results is still an unanswered question, one that calls our attention to the complexity of this field of research and the necessity for caution in generalizing from one group of students to another. Colleges differ in their educational goals and in the bases upon which grades are given. Students are selected differently in different places and have different attitudes toward their school tasks. All these things are likely to affect the correlation between grades and personality factors to a greater extent than the correlation between grades and intelligence.

Instead of trying to apply personality tests that have been worked out with other purposes in mind, some investigators have developed special inventories of motivational characteristics involved in school success or special scoring keys for the Rorschach or MMPI. This can be done by the use of item-analysis methods. The standard procedure is to identify by some means a group of *over*-achievers, students who make better academic records than their intelligence test scores would have predicted for them, and a group of *under*-achievers, those whose record is poorer than the prediction. The responses of the individuals in the two groups to each item of a biographical questionnaire, personality inventory, projective protocol, or interest blank can then be tabulated. Items on which the difference between the two groups is large enough to be statistically significant can then be combined into a scholarship prediction inventory.

An essential feature of this type of research is the procedure called *cross-validation*. We cannot prove that a test constructed in this way is really a valid instrument unless we try it out on a new group of students whose responses were not used in the development of the special scoring key. The reason for this is that the groups initially selected may differ from one another in a variety of *chance* ways as well as in the fact that one group is made up of better students than the other. Therefore *some* of the items we select will reflect these chance differences rather than the trait we are attempting to measure. But because they *are* chance differences they will not characterize new groups composed of different individuals. Thus, the correlation we obtain between test scores and scholarship in a new group shows us the extent to which we have identified *real* differences between good and poor students in general rather than chance differences between the persons who served as subjects in the initial try-out of the test.

On the whole research workers who have used these methods and constructed what we might call "tailor-made" personality tests for predicting scholarship have been more successful than those who have worked with scores on "ready-made" tests. In several such studies the Minnesota Multiphasic Personality Inventory has been used as a pool from which to select items (Altus, 1948; Owens and Johnson, 1949; Gough, 1949a). These studies demonstrate that it is quite possible to select a group of items that will correlate to a moderate extent with scholarship (about .4) and to a negligible extent with scholastic aptitude, *in the group whose responses were used for the tabulation*. These keys have not usually stood up well, however, under cross-validation. In new groups the correlation with grades has decreased and the correlation with intelligence increased enough so that there is little to be gained by the use of the new measure. Such modest gains may be worth the effort in some situations, it is true, and some studies have been more successful than others in achieving them. Gough's Ac (achievement) scale on the MMPI correlated .25 with grades and only -.02 with intelligence in a high-school group different from the one on which it was derived. Because of the low correlation between the two, the multiple correlation with grades was .68 as compared with the .62 between grades and intelligence test scores alone. One interesting point brought out in Gough's series of studies is the difference between high-school, college, and graduate-school groups. It takes different sets of items to achieve maximum prediction of scholarship at these three levels.

Selecting items from an item pool made up especially for the purpose has on the whole resulted in more efficient scholarship prediction inventories than have been obtained through the use of items from a standard instrument designed for other purposes, such as the MMPI. Borow (1945) worked out a set of items giving a correlation of .30 with college grades in a cross-validation sample. Gough (1953) located a set of sixty-four items that correlated more than .5 with scholarship. While these scores are also related to some extent to IQ (about .3) they add enough new information about students so that prediction of grades is significantly improved by their use. Even more striking success with the identification of motivational factors related to grades obtained in college has been reported by Holtzman and Brown (1953). Their inventory correlated .57 with scholarship in a group of men and .56 in a group of women. Using it along with scores on the ACE test produced multiple r's of .63 for women and .73 for men in the cross-validation sample.

What can be said about the traits represented by the combinations of items that have been sorted out by contrasting good students with poor ones? Gough thinks that the following characteristics are primarily involved:

1. Optimistic self-confidence, self-control, capacity for sustained and diligent application.
2. Acceptance of conventions, rejection of the frivolous and diversionary; orderliness, planfulness, and basic seriousness of purpose.
3. Personal efficiency, vitality, and integration.
4. Acceptance of others, denial of ill-will and animosity, absence of interpersonal friction, emphasis on equanimity and rationality.
5. Sense of academic effectiveness, good study habits, sense of accomplishment. At the college level self-sufficiency and independent judgment play a larger role than they do at the high school level.

This composite description is quite similar to qualitative descriptions teachers give of their good students. Thus the item-analysis studies corroborate our convictions that these qualities of character and personality are important, but so far they tell us nothing about the source of such qualities or methods of developing them. If we wish simply to predict who will succeed, it is useful to have this information. If we wish to change conditions and methods in ways that will improve scholarship, we need to know more.

Some workers, such as R. C. Myers (1952), have tried to find items of biographical information that would account for the motives related to scholarship. Results have not been impressive. Others, like Neidt and

Merrill (1951), have tried to measure attitude toward education. They obtained a correlation of .36 between favorable attitudes and scholarship, suggesting that the relationship is in the expected direction but is not high. The most promising leads have come from the studies of social-status differences. Havighurst and Taba (1949) present detailed evidence for a tie-up between social status, reputation ratings, and school achievement. Lower-class children fall below those from the middle and upper classes in ratings given them for character traits and in scholarship. The relationship of these things to social class seems not to be a straight-line one. It is the middle-class children who show the highest motivation and the most anxiety about school achievement.

The nature of the motivational differences has been made a little clearer by Hieronymus (1951). He developed three separate measurements, socio-economic *status*, socio-economic *expectation*, and attitude toward *education*, to use with IQ in the prediction of scores on the Iowa Tests of Educational Development. The subjects were about 600 ninth-graders. The achievement tests, which showed a close relationship to intelligence (r's of .80 for the boys, .78 for the girls), were related to a statistically significant extent to both socio-economic status and socio-economic expectation. The r's for status were .26 for boys, .35 for girls. Those with expectation were .42 for boys, .29 for girls. Attitudes toward education were related more closely to socio-economic expectation than they were to achievement. In other words, *upward mobility* in the social-class hierarchy makes for favorable attitudes toward school and for better grades. The special attitude scales devised by Hieronymus would probably not add much to the prediction of achievement-test scores from intelligence, but they point toward motives that operate in children's school work. The author was not so much interested in predicting achievement as he was in finding out what determines these socio-economic expectations.

Many counselors have been interested especially in the under-achievers, students who over a long period of time obtain marginal or failing school grades in spite of outstanding mental ability. B. A. Kirk (1952) has suggested that such a pattern of behavior is an expression of hostility, and Kimball (1952) has obtained some evidence that this motive operates in such cases. He asked 17 extreme under-achievers along with 100 other boys from a private school to fill out a sentence completion test especially prepared to elicit motives affecting school achievement. (In a projective test of this kind the subject finishes a sentence such as "My father is _____" with the first idea that comes to him.) The boys whose school work fell far below their abilities differed significantly from the others in the evidence they gave of a negative relationship to their fathers and of guilt and anxiety over aggression.

In other individual cases, motives and good work habits growing out of family expectations sometimes compensate for what looks like clearly inadequate ability. Dearborn (1949) describes one such case in detail.

To emphasize the fact that the problems of the counselor or guidance officer are never quite solved by any of the above considerations, and perhaps fortunately so, if he is to maintain an inquiring and open mind, I present the following puzzler:

In this case the socio-economic, cultural, and occupational background, the personality, character, and industry of the student were all "tops," but the scholastic rating (amply tested) was around an IQ of 98 and the scholastic achievement was of a corresponding order. When one of the most esteemed and experienced headmasters of one of the best preparatory schools of this country advised the boy's parents that the boy, who was then seventeen and according to the classification in his school a year from college, was not "college material," the parents were extremely disappointed and sought the advice of the Harvard Psycho-Educational Clinic. The father was a leading practitioner of medicine and had for years hoped that in due course his son would take over his practice. The boy, not only as a dutiful son, but also of his own free will and desire, was of the same intention. After conferring with the boy and his parents and confirming the above statements, I, as Director of the Clinic, advised that, if he had the grit, and really wanted to become a physician, was not too exacting in his choice of a college, and had the patience to stick with the job, his and his parents' ambitions could be accomplished. After another year at school, his record was not good enough to enter college on certificate and admission by college board examinations seemed out of the question. At this time the headmaster did me the honor of paying a visit to say that I was making a mistake in encouraging the boy to go on to college and professional school...., that a boy of his sterling character and integrity, set up in business or in farming in a small community, would come to be one of the leading citizens and towers of strength in the affairs of his community and withal a happier man than he would be if he should persist in his efforts to follow in his father's footsteps. Who can say?

By registering for extension and night courses in an urban university he finally gained admission to regular standing, but after a couple of years he gave up the effort and took a blind alley job in a department store. Pretty well discouraged and near to a nervous breakdown, he found or was helped to a job as athletic coach in a small preparatory school. Here in association with instructors who were college graduates, he was encouraged to make another try and four years ago this June, after ten years of effort, was graduated from a leading college of medicine.

Then, after two years in the service, he took up the practice of medicine in his father's office, where he is associated with a younger brother—a more recent graduate in medicine. This June he is to be married, and will, we shall assume, live happily ever afterwards.

In this instance, the student's socio-economic, cultural, and occupational background was a relatively more important factor than the more usually primary criteria—scholastic aptitude, rank in school, scholastic achievement, and headmaster's recommendation. (Dearborn, 1949, pp. 195-196.)

Almost every experienced counselor would be able to cite such cases. It is their existence that keeps our correlations from being any higher than they are. When counselors try to evaluate motivation, however, and make clinical predictions based on these evaluations, Sarbin's study (1943) shows that their predictions are no more accurate than those a clerical worker could make, grinding out grade-point averages by means of a regression equation based simply on entrance-test scores and high-school scholarship. We are in the position where we can say with great certainty that motivational factors are important determiners of achievement, but we cannot explain just what they are or how they will operate in an individual case.

THE RELATIONSHIP BETWEEN SCHOOL ACHIEVEMENT AND SUCCESS IN LATER LIFE

The exhortations of teachers and assembly speakers emphasizing the value of a good school record in the world outside the schoolroom rest on all too little dependable evidence, as the more cynical of the student listeners intuitively seem to know. A summary of most of the information that is available on the subject has been made by Trout (1949).

The most thoroughgoing studies have been made on groups of college graduates. Here there does seem to be a fairly high relationship between academic achievement and later success, particularly at the upper intelligence levels. Of the men qualifying for Who's Who, more than three-quarters are college graduates and more than one-quarter hold doctor's degrees. When follow-up studies are made of college graduating classes, the persons rated most successful turn out to be predominantly honor students. Phi Beta Kappa members are more successful than the general run of college students when success is evaluated either by achievement of Who's Who status or by salary. Such studies do not of course separate intelligence from grade-getting. It is quite possible that the success of honor students is a reflection primarily of their high ability and has little to do with what they learned in college or with non-intellectual qualities contributing to their high scholarship. There is one piece of follow-up research, however, that permits us to differentiate the effects of school achievement from those of intelligence alone. It is the analysis of the later careers of gifted children, by Terman and Oden (1948), which will be reported in some detail in a later chapter. This study does point out the fact that even among persons of outstanding intellectual ability there are wide variations in life success, and that some of the sources of the variations are identifiable in the school record. But the recent findings of Jepsen (1951) with regard to male graduates of Fresno State College should make us cautious about drawing general conclusions, since no relationship was found in this case between income and grades, for the whole group or within the separate professions.

Data on secondary-school graduates, scarce as they are, do not lend much support to the generalization that good students live successful lives, except for the fact that good students more often go to college and thus place themselves in line for advantageous positions. Several studies suggest that it is the leaders in extracurricular activities rather than the scholars who get along best (Trout, 1949). Thorndike's eight-year follow-up of more than 2,000 children tested in the eighth grade indicated that school achievement correlated very little with any of the criteria except success in clerical work, and even these correlations were relatively low (E. L. Thorndike *et al.*, 1934). We still know far too little about what happens to school drop-outs and failures and almost nothing about how the school record is related to non-financial criteria such as social adjustment, satisfaction in one's work, and contribution to community life.

SUMMARY

At all school levels enormous differences exist with regard to what individual students know. At ten, some fifth-graders have learned more than the average high-school students know at sixteen. In a typical group of high-school students, some will be reading and writing at a fourth-grade level while others will know more than the average college sophomore. Changes in educational procedures or in methods of testing and grading have not eradicated such differences. Intelligence, particularly its verbal aspects, seems to account for the largest single portion of this variability, somewhere from 20 to 50 per cent, depending upon methods of selection in the group. What the other 50 to 80 per cent of the variability in students means is far from clear. To a slight extent it reflects differences in specialized mental abilities, verbal, numerical, spatial, and so forth, but they seem to be important mainly in groups already selected on the basis of general intelligence. To a larger extent it is related to motivational differences, but so far ways of identifying just what they are or of evaluating them accurately in individual cases have eluded us.

It appears that for college students, already selected to a considerable extent on the basis of intellectual ability, a good academic record gives a favorable prognosis for success in later life. For persons closer to the average in intelligence who do not go to college, there is little evidence that high grades predict future success, but data are too inadequate for any general conclusion.

CHAPTER 6

Individual Differences in
Vocational Aptitudes

THE PRACTICAL DEMANDS

"I'D LIKE to take one of those aptitude tests." Again and again this request confronts the psychologist. Sometimes the person who makes it is a young veteran just out of the service and at a loss as to how to reëstablish himself in civilian life. Sometimes it is a woman of forty forced suddenly, through a death or divorce, to find some way to earn her living outside her home. Often it is a high-school boy conscious of the many possibilities lying before him but needing help in choosing between them. Through newspaper and magazine stories, through lectures or conversation, people have heard that it is possible for tests to reveal the pattern of a person's talents and weaknesses—that it is no longer necessary for square pegs to pass their lives in futile struggles to fit themselves into round holes. How much can we do for such individuals?

In other settings, managers of stores, offices, and manufacturing plants are seeking tests that will indicate which applicants are most likely to do well on various jobs. Mr. Henry must hire a new general office clerk. All of the five girls he has interviewed are attractive high-school graduates with some commercial training. Is there any way of determining which of them will be quickest and most accurate in her tasks of filing correspondence and sorting incoming mail, or which will be most dependable and industrious? The Blair Insurance Company is putting into operation a new plan for training representatives and inducting them into their duties, but since this is going to cost them $1,000 or more for each man they take on they wish to be as certain as possible that those they select will make good insurance men in the end. In hundreds of such situations, vocational aptitude tests are in great demand.

When we come to apply the knowledge we now have of tests we can see that there is an important difference between the selection situations where we are picking out the best person for a job, and the counseling situations where we are picking out the best job for a person. Many tests which can be used successfully in selection are just not good enough for counseling. The difference lies in the amount of concern one must feel about errors in judgment. In many selection situations such errors are not too important. Let us say, for example, that of the office clerks Mr. Henry hires in the course of a year 75 per cent are successful without the use of any tests at all. A testing program that can increase his percentage of good choices to 85 per cent will save the company money and make for better attitudes among the workers. He need not worry too much about the 15 per cent who still do not make good or about the equally large number that his tests have rejected, some of whom might actually have been more satisfactory than the girls he chose. But in a counselor's office where Lloyd Everett is trying to decide whether to major in journalism or engineering, much is at stake for him personally. If an engineering aptitude test misclassifies 25 per cent of the students who take it, Lloyd must know this fact and take it into consideration when he makes his decision. The fact that the test is "right" 75 per cent of the time leaves him still doubtful as to whether he is one of the majority for whom it predicts correctly the later course of events or one of the minority for whom it does not. It is because *all* existing aptitude tests make these errors in prediction that reputable psychologists in vocational counseling positions refuse to let final decisions as to what individuals should do with their lives rest on tests alone. Since the limitations vary from test to test, the task of drawing valid conclusions from a combination of several of them presents complex problems.

Besides this distinction between kinds of situations in which tests are used there is another complication which needs to be clarified. It was easy to assume in the days when special tests for various aptitudes were first being developed that the individual differences which they revealed were fixed ineradicable characteristics based perhaps on differences in neural structure. But at the same time other psychologists were finding out more and more about learning and the *changes* that take place in human beings over long and short periods of time. Thus in regard to vocational aptitudes as with intelligence there has been a tendency for both research workers and technicians to separate into two camps—those who assume that abilities are relatively unchangeable and who emphasize the importance of *selection*, and those who assume that anybody can learn anything he wants to and who emphasize the importance of *training*.

The truth lies somewhere in between, and is considerably more complicated than either of these extreme views. Success with some jobs and some educational programs is more dependent upon having a certain pattern of abilities to start with than is success in other areas. Age makes a difference; so does motivation. There are certain general principles that are becoming apparent, but they are not as simple as many consumers of tests think they are.

ESSENTIAL CHARACTERISTICS OF APTITUDE TESTS

The most important of the characteristics a useful aptitude test must have is *predictive validity*. This means that in developing the test it is imperative that the author obtain some evidence with regard to the relationship between scores and later success in real-life situations. It is only on the basis of such evidence that we are justified in making predictions about an individual from his score. To get such evidence the test-maker will first look for some *criterion* of success in a certain type of work or schooling. For one occupation it may be the amount of insurance sold over a three-month period; for another it may be the rating a foreman makes of the quality of each man's work. Whatever the criterion is that he selects, he then correlates test scores with criterion scores for a trial group of subjects and thus obtains what is called a *validity coefficient*. This is simply a special variety of correlation coefficient, a number somewhere in the range between zero and 1.00 which shows how closely test performance and criterion performance are related. (See Chapter 2 for fuller discussion of validity concepts.)

How valid are the vocational tests in common use? Ghiselli and Brown (Ghiselli, 1949; Ghiselli and Brown, 1951; Brown and Ghiselli, 1952) have searched the literature since 1919, when work on such tests was just beginning, for evidence on the question. The median validity coefficient for the tests giving the best predictions of *training* criteria in various occupations is .42. The mean validity coefficients when some aspect of performance on the job is used as a criterion cover a wide range from near zero to about .8. The authors call attention to a fact that has been too often unrealized or ignored by applied psychologists. Tests that predict training success best are not necessarily the ones that furnish the best indication of job performance. In many instances a different set of special abilities is involved in learning a job from the set that is required in carrying it out. Thus in using aptitude tests we must always analyze first what we wish to find out. For types of human activity for which training programs are long and expensive—physician or airplane pilot, for example—ability to learn the skills may be the essential characteristic we wish to get information about. But for many kinds of industrial or clerical jobs for which training programs are relatively short, it is the level of performance on the job itself which counts most.

Another validity problem which deserves more attention than it has so far received centers around the prediction of *long-range* success. For most occupations we do not know whether the workers who do well during the first few months are the persons most likely to stay with the work and advance in it. Worbois (1951) compared 1948 and 1929 ratings of 75 electric-power station operators. The two sets of criterion ratings with a 19-year interval between them correlated only .33. However, the test battery that had been used in the 1929 selection study still seemed to have an appreciable validity for predicting the 1948 criterion. Strong's long-range validity studies of the Vocational Interest Blank will be discussed in a later chapter.

The counselor or personnel worker who tries to give his clients or employer sound information on the basis of vocational tests must also keep in mind the limitations of prediction based on correlations of only moderate size. In evaluating persons who have very low scores we can be fairly certain that they lack some quality necessary to successful performance. In evaluating those who have very high scores we can be fairly certain that they have what it takes, although no one can guarantee that they will use what they have. But for a large group of persons scoring in the middle ranges it is difficult to predict with any certainty whether their criterion performance will be above or below the requirements that have been set.

Another characteristic of vocational tests, as of other varieties, is *reliability*. This is often confused with validity, but actually has quite a different meaning. It refers to the accuracy or precision with which the test measures whatever characteristic it does measure, or its freedom from chance errors of various sorts. It too is usually expressed in terms of a correlation coefficient, but this is always some variety of self-correlation—one form of the test versus another, one administration versus another, or one part versus another. Reliability coefficients average much higher than validity coefficients, many of them being above .90. If the test we are using has a high reliability we can be quite sure that the person's score gives us a true indication of his approximate rank in the group with which he is being compared. If the test has only a moderate reliability—say .6 or .7—we do not have this assurance and it is risky to try to make very sharp distinctions between subjects whose scores are close together in the distribution. The man who scores twelfth from the top in a group of 100 may actually have more of the ability being measured than the man who ranks seventh. In a test of questionable reliability, chance determiners of the scores that subjects make—such things as lucky or unlucky guesses, temporary physical or emotional states, and confusion over instructions, for example—can thus make it difficult to judge how high each person really is with regard to the ability the test is designed to measure. (For more complete discussion of reliability, see Chapter 2.)

Psychologists using tests must form habits of selecting those that are as reliable as possible and of taking this factor into consideration in connection with all judgments they make of individuals. The most common source of confusion and error with regard to reliability, however, is the failure to distinguish it from validity. We are so accustomed to thinking of "reliable" as synonymous with "dependable" or "good" that we tend to extend the reliability concept far beyond its technical meaning where tests are concerned. Reliability is not nearly so important as validity in testing practice. The most reliable test in the world does us very little good in evaluating a person if we have no idea *what* it is measuring. We can allow for inaccuracies in our judgments of people, but there is no way to allow for ignorance.

In addition to furnishing evidence that enables us to assess the validity and reliability, a test-maker should also furnish *norms*. These give us a picture of the range of scores actually obtained in a group representative of the kind of persons who will be taking the test. By using norm tables we can evaluate individual scores, compare scores made by different persons on the same test, and compare scores made on different tests by the same person.

The device most commonly used for accomplishing these purposes is the percentile rank. Percentile norms of some sort are furnished with most standardized tests. In constructing such tables, test-makers work out a frequency distribution showing how many of the subjects in the standardization group have scores *lower than* each separate score. If, out of a group of 100 tool-maker apprentices, 45 have scores below 39 on a test of mechanical aptitude, then 45 is entered in the percentile column of the norm table opposite raw score 39. When the test is used, a man who makes a raw score of 39 will be assigned a percentile rank of 45 on tool-maker apprentice norms. If, out of a group of 1,265 entering college freshmen, 1,047 make scores below 90 on a scholastic aptitude test, then

90 in the norm tables will appear opposite the percentile rank of 83 (1,047 ÷ 1,265). Tables 10 and 11 are examples of norm tables furnished by the publishers of the Minnesota Clerical Test.

TABLE 10.

Percentile Norms for Minnesota Clerical Test
—General Employed Population

(Andrew and Paterson, 1946)

| CENTILES | WOMEN | | MEN | |
	TEST 1 NUMBERS	TEST 2 NAMES	TEST 1 NUMBERS	TEST 2 NAMES
100	200	196	179	198
90	157	159	121	122
80	140	143	108	107
70	126	131	97	96
60	117	120	90	86
50	109	111	83	78
40	103	102	75	69
30	97	93	67	60
20	87	80	57	48
10	77	65	45	34
1	33	2	7	0

TABLE 11.

Percentile Norms for Minnesota Clerical Test
—Employed Clerical Workers Only

(Andrew and Paterson, 1946)

| CENTILES | WOMEN | | MEN | |
	TEST 1 NUMBERS	TEST 2 NAMES	TEST 1 NUMBERS	TEST 2 NAMES
100	200	200	198	196
90	178	187	176	166
80	166	178	162	154
70	158	173	151	143
60	151	161	141	134
50	144	152	135	126
40	137	145	129	119
30	129	136	121	112
20	119	125	114	105
10	106	111	104	97
1	65	63	68	62

It can readily be seen that there is nothing fixed or absolute about the percentile rank corresponding to any given score. It depends entirely on the group with which one is being compared. If we refer a raw score of 100 on the name-checking test to Table 10 and Table 11 we find that for women in the general population it would mean a percentile of 37. For men in the general population, the same score would give a percentile of 74. For women clerical workers, the percentile would be only about 8. People who use percentiles should form the habit of noting always the group on which they are based. Unless one knows that, the figures mean nothing.

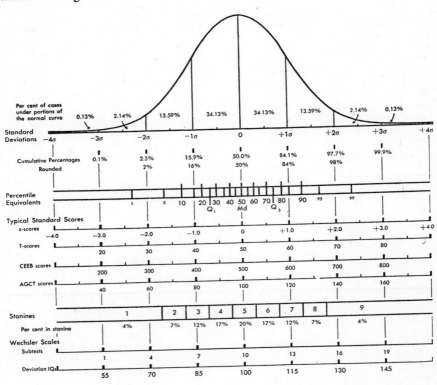

FIGURE 20. Relationships between various types of derived scores
(H. G. Seashore, 1955).

Another type of equivalent score very often used in norm tables is the *standard score* based on the mean and standard deviation of the group with which an individual is to be compared. As has been noted in Chapter 2, in a normal distribution the standard deviation can be used as a unit for measuring how far from the average an individual score is. Figure 20 shows the essential relationships.

When we learn that an individual's place in the distribution is one standard deviation above the mean, we get a fairly clear picture of how high he is. Similarly, if we know that one person is 2.4 standard deviations below the mean and that another is .8 standard deviations above, we can mentally assign them their places by visualizing the distribution. Many test-makers are now furnishing with their tests norm tables which systematize the information contained in the mean and standard deviation units. If the mean of a test given to a standardization group turns out to be 80 points and the standard deviation 20 points, then a raw score of 80 in the norm table would appear opposite a standard score of 0 (no distance at all from the mean). A raw score of 82 would appear opposite a standard score of 0.1, a raw score of 84 opposite a standard score of 0.2, a raw score of 100 opposite a standard score of 1.0. In the reverse direction from the mean, a raw score of 78 would correspond to a standard score of —0.1, a raw score of 74 to —0.3, and a raw score of 50 to —1.5. It is customary to get rid of decimal points in such systems of derived scores simply by *multiplying* all standard scores by some number. Usually this is 10, but any other figure can be used if we wish. The army psychologists, for instance, used 20 in developing norms for the General Classification Test. To get rid of minus signs in the norms it is customary to add some number to all of them. Most often this has been 50, but 100 has been quite frequently used. The relationship between scores, or their usefulness in showing us where in a distribution any individual belongs, is not affected by the multiplication or the addition, so long as all the standard scores are treated in the same way. Table 12 is an example of standard score norms.

The system in which all basic standard scores have been multiplied by 10 and added (algebraically) to 50, shown in Table 12, has become very common. Such scores are variously known as T-scores, derived scores, scaled scores, and so, on. Referred to such a system, a derived score of 70 indicates that an individual is two standard deviations above the mean. A score of 35 means that he is one and one-half standard deviation units *below* the average.

Another variety of standard scores that has been increasingly used since the Air Force psychologists devised it is called the *stanine* (*stan*dard *nine*-division scale). According to this system, the half standard deviation unit in the middle of the distribution is assigned the middle rating of 5.

TABLE 12.

*Standard Score Norms on the USAFI Test
of Educational Development I*

RAW SCORES		STANDARD SCORES
95	....	75
94	....	74
93	....	72
92	....	71
91	....	69
90	....	68
89	....	67
88	....	66
87	....	65
86	....	64
85	....	63
84	....	62
82-83	....	61
81	....	60
80	....	59
79	....	58
78	....	57
77	....	56
75-76	....	55
74	....	54
73	....	53
71-72	....	52
69-70	....	51
67-68	....	50
65-66	....	49
63-64	....	48
61-62	....	47
59-60	....	46
58	....	45
56-57	....	44
55	....	43
54	....	42
52-53	....	41
50-51	....	40
49	....	39
48	....	38
46-47	....	37
45	....	36
44	....	35
43	....	34
42	....	33

Half standard deviation units are marked off in both directions from this. Figure 20 shows these relationships.

In a normal distribution there is a constant relationship between percentile scores and standard scores of all varieties. A person who understands this can transform scores from one to the other frame of reference at will. Percentile scores are based on *areas* under the curve; standard scores are based on *distances* along the horizontal axis. Figure 20 shows the percentile equivalents of standard scores.

The error one must be especially careful not to make is to confuse derived or T-scores for which the mean has been set at 50 with percentiles for which the mean is also 50. Both low and high scores have quite different meanings on the two scales. A T-score of 70, since it is two standard deviations above the mean, is actually very high, and corresponds to a percentile of 98.

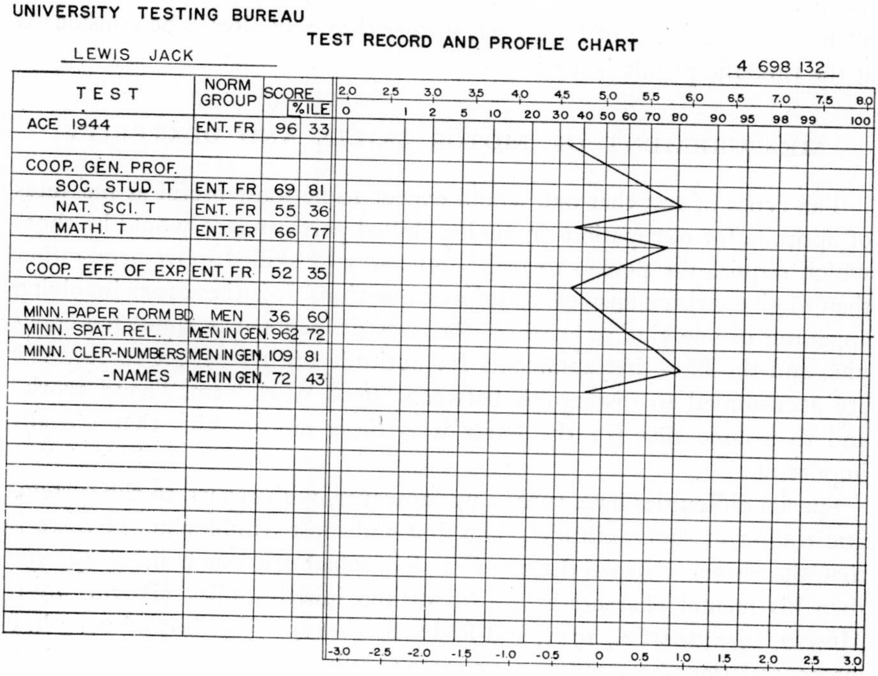
UNIVERSITY TESTING BUREAU
TEST RECORD AND PROFILE CHART
LEWIS JACK
4 698 132
TEST
NORM GROUP
SCORE
%ILE
2.0 2.5 3.0 3.5 4.0 4.5 5.0 5.5 6.0 6.5 7.0 7.5 8.0
0 1 2 5 10 20 30 40 50 60 70 80 90 95 98 99 100
ACE 1944 ENT. FR 96 33
COOP. GEN. PROF.
SOC. STUD. T ENT. FR 69 81
NAT. SCI. T ENT. FR 55 36
MATH. T ENT. FR 66 77
COOP. EFF. OF EXP. ENT. FR 52 35
MINN. PAPER FORM BD. MEN 36 60
MINN. SPAT. REL. MEN IN GEN. 962 72
MINN. CLER-NUMBERS MEN IN GEN. 109 81
-NAMES MEN IN GEN. 72 43
-3.0 -2.5 -2.0 -1.5 -1.0 -0.5 0 0.5 1.0 1.5 2.0 2.5 3.0

FIGURE 21. A vertical profile showing both standard scores and percentiles.

After the raw scores on a number of tests that have been given to the same person have been expressed as either percentiles or standard scores, the most common method of bringing them all together for quick inspection is the profile or psychograph. There are many varieties of these. An example is shown in Figure 21.

A counselor making use of the profile shown in Figure 21 would note at a glance that Jack Lewis, although he is below average in scholastic aptitude in general, is fairly high in social studies and mathematics and in the numbers section of the Minnesota Clerical.

The principal caution one needs to observe in profile interpretation is to avoid making too much of small differences, particularly when they are near the middle of the percentile scale. There may be very little difference between percentiles as far apart as 35 and 65 when the inaccuracy in the scores which we have discussed under *reliability* has been taken into consideration. It is important also that the percentiles or standard scores defining the profile be based either on the same norm group or on groups that are similar in their characteristics. If this is not possible, one should at least specify the norm groups, as has been done in the second column of Figure 21, so that they will always be considered at the time the profile is used.

MEASUREMENT OF MOTOR SKILLS AND DEXTERITY

The types of test that one would expect to be most useful as measures of aptitude for occupations involving skilled performance would be those which require the person to make some sort of skilled movement rather than to give written answers to printed questions. It is these tests involving apparatus of one kind or another—formboards, pegboards, simulated cockpits, and the like—that applicants for aptitude testing expect to see. We are accustomed to distinguish between "head work" and "hand work" and to assume that for the latter it is these motor skills that are all-important.

Special difficulties have turned up, however, with regard to the systematic testing of such aptitudes. The first and most troublesome of these is that the motor characteristics of an individual are much more *specific* than his mental characteristics. All of the initial studies (Perrin, 1921; Muscio, 1922; Garfiel, 1923; and R. H. Seashore, 1930) showed very low intercorrelations between various motor ability tests. Table 13 is typical.

There are a few fairly high correlations such as that of .63 between the motor rhythm and the speed-rotor tests and the one of .56 between the pursuit-rotor and the pursuit-pendulum. On the whole, however, we would have to conclude that excellence in one of these performances furnishes no basis for a prediction as to how well an individual would be likely to do in another. Psychologists interpreting these findings to personnel workers have emphasized that for selection and guidance purposes, it is necessary to develop tests for *specific* types of motor coördination involved in specific jobs. Just any dexterity test will not show whether an individual is likely to make good in repetitive factory work. He may be good at skilled movements involving the use of his fingers, but poor at work with small tools. He may be quick at movements of hand and wrist, but slow in his finger movements. It is interesting to note, also, that practice on motor skills does not tend to make them any less specific. Buxton and Humphreys (1935) practiced a group of subjects on tapping tests and eye-hand coördination tests until they reached a level of skill at which they were no longer showing any improvement from day to day. At the beginning of the practice trials, the correlation between scores for the two types of test was .25. At the end of the practice trials it was .16, showing that there was still only a very slight tendency for scores on the two performances to correspond.

TABLE 13.
Intercorrelations of Eight Motor Skill Tests
(Seashore, 1930)

TEST	ATAX	P.M.	K.P.R.	S.D.	M.R.S.	P.P.	S.R.	B.S.P.
Ataxiameter	..	.19	.12	−.15	.03	.16	.12	.15
Pursuitmeter	.19	..	.29	.18	.17	.14	.09	.26
Koerth Pursuit Rotor	.12	.29	..	.25	.40	.56	.33	.26
Serial Discrimeter	−.15	.18	.25	..	.29	.33	.08	.32
Motor Rhythm Synchrometer	.03	.17	.40	.29	..	.36	.63	.43
Pursuit Pendulum	.16	.14	.56	.33	.36	..	.23	.44
Speed Rotor	.12	.09	.33	.08	.63	.23	..	.38
Spool Packer	.15	.26	.26	.32	.43	.44	.38	..

Both Seashore and Adams (1933), however, and Humphreys, Buxton, and Taylor (1936), showed that there was a more general factor which seemed to determine scores on steadiness tests. All the correlations which they reported between different steadiness tests were in the neighborhood of .50. Humphreys, Buxton, and Taylor also showed that this factor was closely related to success in rifle marksmanship. Not only did the test scores differentiate clearly between members of the rifle team and ordinary students, but the correlation between test scores and coaches' ratings was .77. Thus it appeared that there might be motor aptitudes that would show up as group factors if motor-skills tests were subjected to factor analysis.

Several investigators became interested in this problem and reported their findings in the years just before World War II. R. H. Seashore (1940) brought together the results of a number of such studies, including his own. He showed that the correlations between tests of reaction time, serial discriminative action, speed of tapping, pursuit coördinations, motor rhythm, and gross muscular coördination, and the factor loadings based on these correlations, cannot be explained in terms of either the specific musculatures or the specific sense fields involved. He suggested instead that the group factors indicate *patterns of movement*, regardless of the particular musculature used in each performance.

During World War II, complex motor-skills tests were developed in connection with the Air Force selection program where they made a substantial contribution to the validity of the test battery as a whole. Fleishman (1953) has summarized what factor analyses of these tests indicated. He lists seven factors which were found quite consistently:

A. Reaction time. (Speed of making a predetermined response to a presented stimulus.)
B. Tapping. (Speed of oscillation of arm or fingers.)
C. Manual dexterity. (Arm-hand coördination and speed.)
D. Finger dexterity. (Rapid manipulation of objects with fingers.)
E. Steadiness. (Accuracy of making arm-hand positioning movements which minimize strength and speed.)
F. Aiming. (Ability to carry out quickly and precisely a series of movements involving eye-hand coördination.)
G. Motor kinesthesis. (Ability to make precise postural or body adjustments to kinesthetic cues.)

Besides these there were three others for which corroborative evidence from different studies were less clear: Psychomotor coördination, Ambidexterity, Psychomotor precision.

There are still some uncertainties in this area which stand in the way of the application of factor-analytic results to personnel situations. The tests that contributed most to the prediction of Air Force criteria were not simple measures of separate factors but complex apparatus tests designed especially for the one purpose for which they were used. There is no evidence that the sum of any set of separate factor measurements, weighted or unweighted, would give as good results. Furthermore, psychologists have not yet been able to decide with any certainty whether psychomotor skills constitute primarily an *aptitude* problem or a *training* problem. Much of the research in this field, especially of recent years, has been concerned with factors governing improvement during training rather than with individual differences.

Besides the experimental and the personnel psychologists, two other groups have done some research on psychomotor skills. Research workers in physical education have made factor analyses. Ordinarily they include in their initial matrices correlations based on a wider range of measurements than psychologists use—such things as size, weight, strength, and large-muscle coördination. Larson (1941) reports factors typical of those which have been found by various workers using this type of data: Speed, Large-Muscle Coördination, Strength ("dynamic" differentiated from "static" strength), Sensori-motor Coördination, and Motor Educability.

A study reported by Hempel and Fleishman (1955) was the first to incorporate large-muscle and small-muscle tests in the same battery. The subjects who took the forty-six tests (twenty-three of the manipulative variety, twenty-three of the physical proficiency type), were 400 Air Force trainees. The factor analysis produced fifteen factors, but none of them overlapped the two areas. Factors representing correlations between different manipulative tests were similar to the ones Fleishman had previously reported. Those on which the physical proficiency tests showed high loadings were similar to those which physical educators had previously reported. The finding that gross and fine types of motor skill are independent of one another constitutes a useful addition to our knowledge in this area.

The other group of workers that may eventually contribute more than it has so far to our understanding of psychomotor abilities consists of developmental psychologists who are taking an increasing interest in this problem because of its importance in the child's total adjustment. The *Oseretsky Tests of Motor Development*, published in Russian in 1923, were translated and made available for general use in the United States in 1946. These tests, six at each age level, were designed to give measures of "motor age" analogous to the Binet measurement of mental age. Holbrook (1953) used five of the six types of test in this battery, and worked out a new standardization for American children between the ages of four and twelve. There are tests of speed, general static coördination, simultaneous movement, general dynamic coördination, and dynamic manual coördination. Oseretsky's tests for "synkinesia" (associated involuntary movements) were omitted. Both Holbrook and Degardin (1949), who studied 150 Belgian children, found that the separate tests at each age level showed rather low correlations with one another. This is what we would expect from the work on motor abilities of adults. Both Degardin and Holbrook also found that there was a fair degree of individual consistency from year to year. Holbrook found that scores on these tests were not related to sex, IQ, or socio-economic level, but that a well-adjusted group of children was superior to a poorly-adjusted group.

In summarizing the research on psychomotor abilities, it can be said that while no general factor of motor aptitude analogous to "g" exists, the separate abilities are not as narrow and specific as the early investigators thought. A number of group factors, such as steadiness and manual dexterity, have been discovered through factor analysis. Psychologists attempting to measure aptitudes must always remember, however, that the fact that a test is named *Manual Dexterity* constitutes no guarantee that it actually measures the manual dexterity *factor*, and the fact that a job seems to require manual dexterity gives no assurance that this test will predict success in it. The measurement of motor skills for selection and guidance purposes is still fraught with difficulties.

FACTOR ANALYSIS AND APTITUDE TESTING

One of the important developments during the 1940's and 1950's has been the application of factor-analytic methods to problems of vocational testing. Some of the impetus for this movement came from military psychologists during World War II who realized that factor analysis could be used along with the customary methods of test validation to furnish continuous information with regard to the abilities underlying the correlations between tests and criteria (Guilford, 1948). Thus hypotheses as to what should be added to existing test batteries in order to improve the selection of special kinds of workers could rest on something besides unanalyzed "hunches." Some of the demand has come from guidance workers who see that with a short battery of non-overlapping tests standardized on the same group it ought to be possible to give an individual as much information about his own strengths and weaknesses as he now gets from a much larger number of tests assembled in hit-or-miss fashion.

The United States Employment Service took the lead in developing such a test battery. For years they have been standardizing short tests which can be used in various combinations to assess aptitude for a wide variety of specific occupations from File Clerk to Zig Zag Machine Operator (Stead, 1942). It was a natural step to make a factor analysis of the intercorrelations between these tests to ascertain how many separate abilities were involved and what they seemed to be (Occ. Anal. Div., 1945). So that the factors would not represent relationships peculiar to any one geographical area, nine separate analyses were made in widely separated parts of the country. A total of fifty-nine tests and 2,156 subjects were represented. Most of the same factors appeared repeatedly in different analyses. These were as follows:

O—General intelligence
V—Verbal ability
N—Numerical ability
S—Spatial ability
P—Perceptual ability as applied to geometrical figures or material requiring
  no formal educational background
Q—Perceptual ability as applied to words or numbers
A—Aiming ability. Accuracy or precision of movement
T—Time or speed
F—Finger dexterity
M—Manual dexterity
L—Logic or reasoning

These have been assembled into a two-and-one-half-hour counseling battery which is being widely used in employment offices throughout the country to identify the group or family of occupations for which an inexperienced worker shows the most aptitude.

A number of other counseling batteries based directly or indirectly on factor analysis have been put on the market. In many ways they are superior to the separate aptitude tests which have for so long been the stock-in-trade of school guidance workers and vocational counselors. There is one defect, however, that until it is corrected outweighs all these advantages. The evidence for their *validity* in predicting behavior in life situations outside the testing room is all too often lacking. It must of course be collected by the same laborious methods that were used with aptitude tests of the old-fashioned variety. Before we can conclude that a boy who is high in S and P should enter an apprenticeship for a mechanical trade—or before we can allow *him* to draw such a conclusion from the tests alone—we must know that S and P scores derived from this particular battery are correlated with mechanical success. Criticisms of test batteries for inadequate validity data must always be made as of a definite time. Important information may be reported the day after the criticism goes to press. The point is simply that applied psychologists who contemplate the use of these tests in their own activities should be sure to scrutinize carefully the evidence that has been presented as to what criteria the scores are known to predict.

RESEARCH ON OCCUPATIONAL DIFFERENCES

The basic question that needed to be answered before individual differences in special abilities could be utilized intelligently in the world of work was the question as to whether different occupations really required different patterns of ability. Some extensive evidence on this problem was accumulated by Dvorak (1935) working with the Minnesota Employment Stabilization Research Institute. This was an agency set up in 1931 to study economic and psychological aspects of unemployment. One of its undertakings was to test large numbers of employed and unemployed workers in various occupations. For each test standard-score norm tables were constructed based on a group of subjects chosen in such a way as to be representative of the whole urban employed population of Minnesota. In studying the pattern of scores for any individual or occupational group, standard scores based on these norms were used.

The tests sampled educational ability (usually called general intelligence), clerical ability, mechanical ability, and dexterity. The first comparison of profiles was between men office clerks and garage mechanics. Figure 22 portrays graphically the average-score profiles for the two groups.

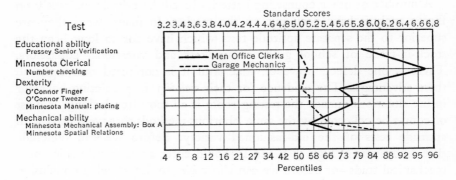

FIGURE 22. Occupational ability patterns of men office clerks and garage mechanics. (Reprinted by permission of the University Press, University of Minnesota, from Dvorak, *Differential occupational ability patterns*, 1935.)

Various statistical tests back up the impression one gets from looking at these profiles that there is a significant difference in the pattern of abilities. The clerical workers are considerably higher on the educational and clerical tests, somewhat higher on all the dexterity tests, but lower on the mechanical tests. Measures of overlapping indicate that only 3.7 per cent of the mechanics exceed the median score of the clerks on the number-checking test, but 71.4 per cent of them exceed the clerks' median on the spatial relations test. A supplementary analysis of groups of garage mechanics working in different places (Figure 23) shows that there is little or no difference in these patterns of abilities.

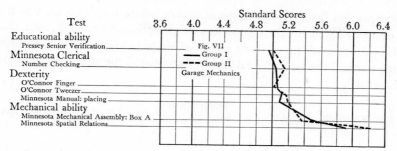

FIGURE 23. Occupational ability patterns of men garage mechanics employed in two different places. (Reprinted by permission of the University Press, University of Minnesota, from Dvorak, *Differential occupational ability patterns*, 1935.)

Another comparison was made between women office clerks and retail saleswomen (Figure 24). Again a marked difference is apparent. Not only do office workers tend to be higher in everything, but they are highest on the very test in which the saleswomen are lowest, so that the profiles have an entirely different shape.

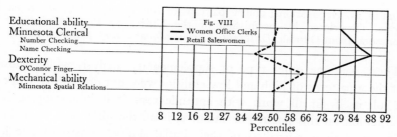

FIGURE 24. Occupational ability patterns of women office clerks and retail saleswomen. (Reprinted by permission of the University Press, University of Minnesota, from Dvorak, *Differential occupational ability patterns*, 1935.)

Dvorak also attempted to find out whether profiles of individual workers were sufficiently similar to the average profile for their occupation so that they could be classified by a person who knew nothing about the individuals except their test scores. Profiles of 90 employed women office clerks and 68 employed retail saleswomen were chosen at random from the research files and given to a vocational psychologist to sort into the two groups. His judgment turned out to be correct in 92.4 per cent of the cases.

Degree of success in the occupation seemed to be related to how *high* some or all of the scores were, rather than to their pattern. Figure 25 shows profiles for various groups of nurses where the A group was made up of those rated by their superiors as exceptionally capable, and the D and E groups made up of those rated definitely below average. The intelligence test and the two clerical tests differentiated the success groups most satisfactorily.

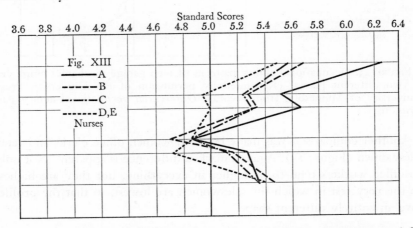

FIGURE 25. Occupational ability patterns of four groups of nurses rated for success. (Reprinted by permission of the University Press, University of Minnesota, from Dvorak, *Differential occupational ability patterns*, 1935.)

There was one other type of supplementary analysis which showed that these patterns of high and low abilities were not created by work on the job itself. In all work with aptitude tests it is important to have information on this point. For instance, if all the girls who work in an office for a time, regardless of their initial ability, come to make high scores on tests like the Pressey Senior Verification and the Minnesota Clerical, then we would hardly be justified in using these tests to evaluate *aptitude* in girls who have not yet had this office experience. Dvorak assembled the evidence on this question for the specific tests used in this study and showed that training and experience in kinds of work related to each test had a negligible effect on the score.

Following this exceptionally thorough study, a similar investigation was made by Dodge (1935) in New York. The subjects were unemployed men and women who came to the Adjustment Service for guidance. Differences were in the same direction as in the Minnesota study, but they were less clear cut, and there was so much variation from individual to individual within each group that profiles would have been of very little use for vocational guidance purposes. It is probable that the particular tests used in this research were not very well chosen to bring out distinctive occupational characteristics. The omission of mechanical aptitude tests and the inclusion of the Bernreuter Personality Inventory might have served to blur any distinctions that did exist. Dodge did, however, make one useful suggestion—namely, that *minimum* profiles would be of more value for guidance than *average* profiles. This idea is supported by Dvorak's finding that it was the general level of scores on differentiating tests that distinguished between successful and unsuccessful workers. The Employment Service psychologists have applied this idea in the procedure they have set up for the use of the General Aptitude Test Battery mentioned in the previous section. In evaluating a candidate's fitness for a certain type of work, the counselor checks his test profile to see whether his scores on the tests which count for that occupation are above the minimum.

This question as to which is more important, the pattern of abilities or their general level, is still a live one. Its relationship to the controversy over the nature of intelligence which we have discussed in Chapter 4 is apparent. Here as on the intelligence issue, the British psychologists have stressed the importance of all-round level of ability. In vocational as in academic situations they tend to think in terms of "g." Vernon (1950) has presented the clearest statement of this point of view. In referring to observations made in military personnel programs, he says, "The layman's notion that there exists a niche or special type of work ideally suited to the specialized aptitudes of each individual appeared to be much less true than the view that all types of work and all employees fall along a single high-grade to low-grade continuum." (Vernon, p. 122)

He cites several types of evidence for this conclusion. One is just this general experience with military selection problems. The fact that people from all walks of life learned highly specialized military duties as successfully as they did seems to him to be significant. Just what sort of occupation they had previously been following, unless it happened to coincide exactly with what they were assigned to do in the Services, mattered very little. Retail tradesmen learned to be engine-room mechanics as easily as civilian machinists did. No type of mechanical experience seemed to assist radio or electrical mechanics to learn their jobs. Women with very non-mechanical backgrounds succeeded at skilled engineering jobs. The military psychologists came to place a great deal more emphasis on school and work records showing stability and educational "drive" than on evidence of specific aptitudes. A more systematic type of evidence which Vernon presents comes from factor analyses of job elements as assessed by occupational experts, training marks in Service schools, and objective measures of workshop ability. Each of these analyses showed a large general factor accounting for from 30 to 40 per cent of the variance in individual performance. It must be remembered, however, that the factor-analysis methods used were such as to maximize general factor loadings. Rotation might have produced an alternative interpretation, as in the case of intelligence measures.

However, it has become increasingly clear that in much of the American work carried through from the special-aptitude point of view there is also considerable support for the conclusion that general level of ability is important in occupational situations. When correlations between the different mechanical aptitude tests and the different parts of the Army General Classification Test were worked out for 5,000 men representative of the entire army population in age and educational attainments, the coefficients obtained were all high. Reading and vocabulary correlated with arithmetic to the extent of .81. Mechanical information correlated .77 with total score on the AGCT (Anastasi, 1948). We have noted in discussing the Minnesota studies that general level of scores was the factor that was related to degrees of success within an occupation. The work of Ghiselli and Brown (1951) has shown that there is much more generality than specificity in what occupational tests predict. Spatial relations tests tend to correlate almost as highly with clerical as with mechanical criteria, for example.

Thus as in the case of the controversy over intelligence, the progress of knowledge has shown that the truth lies somewhere between the two extreme positions. For the psychologists using tests as tools, particularly the vocational counselor, this state of affairs serves to complicate his task. It makes it impossible for him to give many of his clients the kind of service which they expect from testing. There are many persons whose general level of ability classifies them with unskilled or semi-skilled workmen, persons who have no one special aptitude that stands out above the rest. There are others whose general level is so high that they are almost certain of success in any professional training they decide to enter. Both groups are likely to be disappointed with the contribution aptitude testing makes to their vocational decisions. There are, however, many more people at intermediate levels of general ability for whom it may make considerable difference whether they capitalize on their strongest or their weakest special aptitudes. Furthermore vocational planning can never be based on abilities alone. Interests, past experience, and present circumstances must all be considered.

USE OF VOCATIONAL TESTS IN SELECTION

As has been explained earlier, the use of tests for selection of workers is a simpler and more satisfactory business than the use of tests in vocational counseling. The question, "Which person can I recommend for this job?" can be answered more straightforwardly than the question, "Which job can I recommend for this person?"

There are a number of reasons for the difference. One of them has already been discussed. It does not matter much to the employment psychologist whether his judgment is wrong in the case of an individual worker if his total percentage of satisfactory placements is high. It does not matter particularly to him whether the validity coefficient of any particular test is high, if he can show that it adds *something* to the accuracy with which success on the job can be predicted. He can use as indications of aptitude general intelligence measures, personality evaluations, and items of biographical information, as well as specifically vocational tests. Although it may be of some value to him to know what kind of mental process a test requires, he can proceed without such knowledge on a purely empirical basis.

The one technical problem that has stood out in connection with this task has been the *weighting* of scores which are to be used in combination to predict a criterion. The most satisfactory method developed for this task is called *multiple regression*. The term "regression" is roughly synonymous with "prediction," and "multiple regression" refers to prediction of criterion scores from multiple measurements. As would be expected, the weights to be given the various test scores and other items of information depend upon the correlation of these scores with criterion scores. But the process is not quite so simple as it would be if we could assign a weight of 2 to a test with a validity coefficient of .60 and a weight of 1 to a test with a validity coefficient of .30. The predictive value of correlation coefficients is not directly proportional to their size. Furthermore, correlations *between* the tests have to be taken into consideration if the scores are to be properly weighted. A test correlating .30 with the criterion may add little or nothing to the prediction if it measures only abilities that are adequately sampled by other tests in the battery.

It is not necessary here to explain the mathematical techniques that are used to determine from the correlation coefficients what weight should be given the score on each test. The regression equation that results from such procedures is of this type:

$$Y = 1.56 + 1.49\, x_1 + .06\, x_2 + 3.94\, x_3$$

Where Y stands for a person's predicted criterion score:

x_1 stands for his score on the first test.
x_2 stands for his score on the second test.
x_3 stands for his score on the third test.

If an individual applicant's scores are as follows: first test, 25; second test, 42; third test, 7; his predicted criterion score, the best forecast we can obtain of his probable success on the job, would be 1.56 + 1.49 (25) + .06 (42) + 3.94 (7). In this case Y turns out to be equal to 68.91. If the criterion figure represents the number of seams completed per hour on a certain type of garment, and if anything over 50 is considered satisfactory, this applicant with a predicted criterion score of almost 69 looks like a good prospect.

Since available tests never sample all the factors involved in job success, such regression equations will never give us absolutely accurate predictions of criterion scores. If the tests are well chosen, however, we can expect a majority of the individuals in a group to show levels of achievement fairly close to the predictions for them, and we have methods for estimating in advance the amount of error to expect.

In evaluating a selection program the vocational psychologist usually computes a *multiple correlation* coefficient showing how close the relationship is between the criterion scores actually obtained on the job by subjects in this trial group and the scores that would have been predicted for them from their test performances. The symbol for this is R, and it can be interpreted in the same manner as an ordinary product-moment correlation. Values range from .00 to 1.00, and an R of .50 or higher is considered fairly satisfactory. A more meaningful way of showing how close the relationship is between predicted criterion scores and scores actually obtained is to arrange them in a table like Tables 14 and 15 or a graph like Figure 26. Table 14 shows that if an employment interviewer directs into the job of cardpunch operator only those persons who are in the highest third of the applicants according to test scores, 52 per cent of them will be in the highest third in the occupation, 29 per cent will be in the middle third, and 19 per cent will be in the lowest third. Of those who make the test scores in the *lowest* third, 57 per cent fall in the lowest third on the job, 26 per cent in the middle third, and 17 per cent

TABLE 14.

Per Cent of 234 Operators of Card-Punch Machines in Each
Errorless Production Criterion Score Group
According to Battery Score Groups

(Stead, Shartle, Otis, *et al.* 1940)

	PER CENT OF CARD-PUNCH-MACHINE OPERATORS IN CRITERION SCORE GROUP		
BATTERY SCORE GROUP	LOWEST THIRD	MIDDLE THIRD	HIGHEST THIRD
Highest Third	19%	29%	52%
Middle Third	23	45	32
Lowest Third	57	26	17

in the highest third. Generally speaking, of those who score high on the test, more than four-fifths can be expected to be at least average workers on the job. Of those who score low on the test, less than half can be expected to be average or above on the job. Thus, while use of such a test battery will not completely eliminate unsatisfactory workers and in many cases predictions made about individuals turn out to be wrong, it does make possible a large number of correct judgments.

TABLE 15.

Per Cent of Subjects in Each Sales Criterion Score Group According
to Battery Score Groups for Three Samples
of Department Store Salespersons

(Stead, Shartle, Otis, *et al.* 1940)

	PER CENT OF SUBJECTS IN CRITERION SCORE GROUP		
BATTERY SCORE GROUP	LOWEST THIRD	MIDDLE THIRD	HIGHEST THIRD
Highest Third	14%	36%	50%
Middle Third	32	30	38
Lowest Third	53	36	11

Figure 26 illustrates an even more successful test-development project, the Air Force selection research during World War II. The diagram makes clear that only 5 per cent of the group making the highest stanine score was eliminated from training as compared with 80 per cent of the group in the lowest test category.

The multiple regression method of using some kinds of measurements to predict some kind of success has been used in hundreds, perhaps thousands, of individual studies. It makes possible the utilization of many kinds of tests that are of no value when used alone. All measurable human characteristics become grist for the regression mill—size and strength, knowledge of arithmetic, finger dexterity, non-verbal intelligence, number of children, information about government, attitude toward nursing.

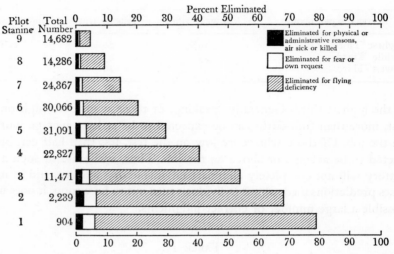

FIGURE 26. Percentage of candidates eliminated from primary pilot training classified according to stanine scores on selection battery. (Reproduced from "Psychological activities in the training command, Army Air Forces" by the Staff, Psychological Section, Fort Worth, Texas, in *Psychological Bulletin*, Washington, D.C., American Psychological Association, Inc., 1945.)

Thus in many vocational areas where it has not proved feasible to single out any one aptitude and measure it, it is known that a number of measurable traits in combination do show a moderate correlation with success. This has been standard practice, for example in developing selection programs for professional schools. There is no one "legal aptitude" or "scientific aptitude," but test *batteries* can be developed which are of real help in selecting students who will succeed in training.

There is one essential feature of the regression method which rules it out in many testing situations. The tests to be tried out and weighted must be administered to a fairly large group of subjects in order to give us the data on which a regression equation can be based. For these particular subjects the test results serve no practical purpose. By the time we know what weights should be given their test scores, the criterion itself is available and constitutes a much more adequate basis for judging them than the tests do. It is subsequent groups of *similar* subjects for whom predictions can be made at the time tests are taken. A counselor in his office interviewing clients singly cannot *derive* regression equations, though he may apply them if they are available from previous research. A personnel psychologist working for a small company that employs no more than twenty persons at any one type of work cannot derive regression equations. Correlations based on such small numbers are too inaccurate to be trusted as the basis for weights. The regression method is a two-step procedure. The weights to be attached to various kinds of measurements cannot be used in the group from which they are derived. It lends itself better to large-scale than to small-scale operations.

One development that has taken on considerable importance from the time of World War II onward has been the combination of factor analysis with multiple regression procedures (Guilford, 1948). If at each stage of the research in test development the inter-relationships between different kinds of tests can be scrutinized for evidence as to what qualities they have in common at the same time that their relationships to work criteria are being examined, it is possible to make increasingly good guesses about what to *add* to a test battery to improve its correlation with the criterion.

Another important modification of regression methods has been the use of *discriminant functions*. In such equations weights are assigned to tests in terms of two or more criteria at once, so that the number which one comes out with for a person indicates which of these types of activity he is *better* fitted for. Such methods would seem to have considerable value both in counseling and in personnel situations where all man power must be utilized in one way or another—in other words, where there are no *rejectees*.

One final comment can be made about regression methods. Most people, psychologists and personnel workers as well as students, tend to think of regression equations as rather rigid, inflexible ways of forecasting what their clients are likely to achieve. They point to multiple correlations of .50 to .60 as evidence that such predictions are far from adequate. What they often fail to realize is that *clinical* predictions made subjectively by skilled experts who try to take everything into consideration tend to be not more but *less* accurate than these statistical predictions. The best review of all available evidence on this point, along with a penetrating discussion of its implications, is available in a book by Meehl (1954). The limit to the predictive accuracy we have so far been able to achieve for any criterion is in general represented by an R of about .6. Adding more subtle, less easily quantifiable variables appears to reduce the accuracy of predictions rather than to increase it

WHAT WE KNOW ABOUT VOCATIONAL APTITUDES: AN EVALUATION

How much have we achieved in our attempt to develop methods by means of which individual differences in people can be matched up with individual differences in jobs? It is clear from the discussion above as well as from general observation that there are still a great many square pegs in round holes, in spite of the efforts we have made. How can we account for these inadequacies?

In the first place, work based on the theory that there were separate broad aptitudes for separate broad fields of work was unable to progress beyond a certain point. There does seem to be a definite kind of ability we can call mechanical aptitude. It involves primarily the knack of seeing how parts fit together in a complex pattern. L. L. Thurstone (1951a) describes it as "ability to visualize a flexible configuration." A large-scale, carefully planned research project at the University of Minnesota (Paterson et al., 1930) resulted in a group of tests that could be used to measure this aptitude: the Minnesota Paper Form Board, the Minnesota Spatial Relations, and the Minnesota Mechanical Assembly. They have been in constant use ever since that time, and a number of other tests of the same type have been devised. The ones that define the "k:m" factor the British psychologists talk about are very similar. Clerical aptitude, which seems to involve primarily the quick and accurate perception of details, also lent itself to simple measurement. The Minnesota Clerical Test (Andrew and Paterson, 1946) is the most widely used instrument.

But when we turn from the mechanical and clerical fields to other areas, not only are the tests less satisfactory, but the classification of abilities based on occupational differences does not seem to fit. Most skilled and semi-skilled occupations, for example, require dexterity in the use of hands or fingers, but there seems to be no *one* ability we can label "dexterity" that is common to them all. What we have instead are a great many specific finger and hand skills, to varying degrees improvable through practice and training. Similarly in music, the attempt to get some one general measure of musical aptitude has failed. The Seashore Measures of Musical Talent, even if given under conditions that will get rid of troublesome sources of unreliability, get at specific sensitivities such as pitch, rhythm, and timbre, but leave out some of the most important qualities a good musician must possess. Art tests are even less adequate. Most of them measure only taste or judgment, not creative ability, and the evidence for the relationship of their scores to success in artistic pursuits is not impressive.

Faced with these facts, we have gradually been changing not so much our testing practice as our theoretical approach. Instead of accepting a ready-made classification of what is to be measured, based on what appear to laymen to be distinctive characteristics of various kinds of work, psychologists are now in a position to develop their own classification. Factor analysis has been a powerful tool in this undertaking. Instead of a set of distinctive vocational aptitudes, we can proceed on the assumption that the primary variables we have discovered in our investigations of intelligence, achievement, perceptual and motor abilities, interests, and personality traits are the basic traits to be measured. We are coming to see that it is the level and the combination of these basic qualities that distinguish each occupational field or individual occupation, rather than any single "aptitude."

In the multiple regression methods we have the means by which these different kinds of information about individuals can be brought into optimum relationship with criteria of success in various occupations. In the discriminant function methods we have the means of evaluating which of several possible placements constitutes the best "fit" for a person. For rougher evaluations, there are methods involving critical scores on tests by means of which a deficiency that might be serious in connection with some occupational plan can be identified.

It is in this direction that the "growing tip" of research in vocational psychology is advancing. But for persons whose work requires them to apply psychological techniques rather than to develop them, the older formulations centered around concepts of mechanical aptitude, clerical aptitude, finger dexterity, and so forth may still be more useful than the newer ideas. The counselor in a small high school or the employment interviewer in a small office cannot carry out research studies to determine what combination of measured abilities best answers the questions he faces in the clients he interviews. For such workers *validity* is the crucial concept. A test of clerical aptitude that has been shown to correlate respectably with a wide variety of clerical criteria is more useful than precise measurements of P, S, V, and so forth that have never been tried out in employment situations. For the time being, a pragmatic attitude which enables one to utilize any means that are available for meeting practical needs must be encouraged.

We have learned, however, as work has progressed, not to expect too much of any variety of aptitude test. There seems little likelihood that the correlations between tests and criteria can ever be increased enough so that we can be *certain* whether a given individual will be able to succeed in a given field of work. Negative judgments are perhaps a little sounder than positive. Tests will often tell us if a person is seriously deficient in some trait known to be necessary in some occupation. But for persons who have more than the minimum of each of the abilities essential for a type of work, success depends on so many things, including subtle kinds of motivation and chance features of the particular work situation, that we cannot expect to predict it with great accuracy. The vocational psychologist sees his job in limited but realistic terms as one of reducing the number of misplacements and helping individuals to make wise decisions about their occupational futures. It is perhaps time that we discarded completely the analogy of pegs and holes of any shape. People are far more complex than this, and the job a psychologist does must necessarily involve far more than the simple matching of men with jobs.

SUMMARY

So-called "aptitude" tests are in great demand for guidance and selection purposes. In order to be interpretable, a test must have been used for a long enough period of time so that clear evidence is available as to the kind of criteria it predicts. Validity coefficients for the aptitude tests in common use are only moderately high, so that a psychologist must expect a certain number of wrong judgments about individuals who have been tested. High reliability and adequate norms are also important in tests upon which vocational decisions are to rest. Percentiles and various kinds of standard scores are used in norm tables.

Work on motor skills has suggested that such aptitudes are highly specific. As correlations between tests were factor-analyzed, factors like reaction time and manual dexterity have emerged, but the background of knowledge that is necessary if we are to apply measurements of psychomotor factors to vocational guidance problems has not yet accumulated. A number of general counseling batteries based on factor analysis have been published and promise to be of considerable value when evidence with regard to their predictive validity has been obtained.

Work on occupational ability patterns has established the fact that workers in different kinds of jobs do differ significantly in their tested abilities, so that guidance or selection on the basis of test scores is a feasible undertaking. In counseling situations, the most useful way of combining scores from several tests is the profile or psychograph. In selection situations, multiple regression methods are applicable.

The concept of "aptitude" as a basic psychological variable is being replaced by classifications of basic abilities coming from factor analysis. In many practical situations, however, aptitude is still a useful concept, and aptitude tests are among the most useful tools psychologists have at their disposal.

CHAPTER 7

Individual Differences in Personality

As THE scientific study of human individuality has progressed, it has become increasingly apparent that differences in personality are fully as important as the differences in mental abilities which the first tests were designed to measure. Anyone who is responsible for hiring or supervising workers soon realizes that he must make his judgments partly on the basis of their personal characteristics. Success often depends upon how high a man's morale is, how consistently he can drive himself to work, and how well he gets along with his colleagues, as much as it depends upon his aptitude and skill. Teachers have never lost sight of the importance of motivation in the schoolroom. They know that laziness or rebelliousness can play havoc with a child's school record regardless of his IQ level. From military classification to marriage counseling, in all types of situations which require that people work together, personality must constantly be evaluated.

DIFFICULTIES AND COMPLICATIONS

The quantitative study of personality has presented what seemed at times to be insuperable difficulties. To begin with, the word "personality" has a variety of meanings and is interpreted in different ways under different circumstances. The words "character" and "temperament" are sometimes used as synonyms for "personality," but usually they carry a somewhat narrower connotation. "Character" is most commonly applied to the *volitional* qualities of the individual, "temperament" to his *emotional* qualities, whereas "personality" can be stretched to cover all of these and his abilities and appearance as well. If the person planning research on personality defines the concept too broadly he finds it impossible to develop any sort of classification system around which experiments can be centered. If he defines it too narrowly he may leave out what some other workers consider essential aspects of it, and thus obtain results that cannot be integrated with those of previous investigations. As in the case of intelligence, however, continued work has cleared away some of the confusion, and psychologists have been able to reach some agreement on what they are *measuring* even though they cannot say with assurance *what* personality essentially *is*.

Psychology inherited from its pre-scientific ancestors some useful ways of looking at individual personalities. One of these approaches is through the classification of people as *types*. As early as the fifth century B.C., Hippocrates gave us a two-fold system based on body build, the *habitus apoplecticus* and *habitus phthisicus*. The later famous Greek physician, Galen, proposed a four-fold classification based on the predominance of different "humors" or biochemical fluids in the body. His four main types were the sanguine, the choleric, the phlegmatic, and the melancholic. Variations of these classifications have appeared under many names right down to our own century, and have been supplemented by typologies based on other aspects of observable personality. Spranger, basing his analysis on literature, analyzed the basic *values* men seem to live by, and elaborated six fundamental types: the theoretical, economic, aesthetic, social, political, and religious. Jaensch, basing his system on observations of eidetic imagery, described what he called a T-type, or integrated person, as opposed to a B-type or disintegrated person. Kretschmer attempted to relate a physical typology not too different from the early one of Hippocrates to a classification of temperaments, and tied the system in with the two major varieties of psychosis, schizophrenia and the manic-depressive states. William James sorted people out into the tough-minded and the tender-minded. But more popular than any of these systems has been the Jung classification into extraverted and introverted types. The fact that such typologies have appeared to many thinkers in many centuries to be a way of bringing some order into the complex realm of personality differences has kept us from dismissing them too lightly. The fact that they are so various and so confusing has led us to look beyond the verbal formulations for evidence that can enable us to sift out the convincing from the merely plausible and to locate the unities underlying the diversity.

Another approach to personality study carried over from pre-scientific days is the concept of *traits*. In our common everyday living, the natural way to describe a person is to mention his outstanding traits or qualities. We say, for instance, that John is thoroughly honest, somewhat shy, or very kind and considerate. More than typologies, this approach has lent itself to at least a rough kind of quantitative scaling. Thus a teacher, without making any sort of measurement at all, is able to say with considerable certainty that Ed is more sociable than Hugh, who in turn is more sociable than Roger. It seemed natural then for psychologists to start with single traits in their efforts to measure whatever in personality is measurable.

The trouble with traits as the basic variables of personality study is that they are in some ways too narrow and in others too broad. So many separate characteristics have been described in this way that the task of working out measurements for all of them assumes formidable proportions. Allport and Odbert (1936) have shown that there are from 3,000 to 5,000 words used in the languages of civilized people to describe personal qualities. It is obviously going to be impossible to measure personality in any complete way if in order to do so we must measure even 3,000 different characteristics. The proliferation of personality "tests" that have been put on the market is an outgrowth of this state of affairs. Hundreds of tests have been devised for traits that seemed important to one psychologist or another. Leafing through a reference volume such as the Mental Measurements Yearbook (Buros, 1953) gives one some idea of their variety. There are tests for common-sense traits like self-reliance, friendliness, and stability. There are other tests for psychiatric-sounding traits like hypochondria and schizothymia. Some test-makers prefer a two-ended type of statement such as nervous-composed, ascendance-submission, or "Bohemian unconcernedness vs. conventional practicality." The reader of either the Allport and Odbert list or the Mental Measurements Yearbook finds himself thinking, "But surely there aren't as many separate personality traits as all this. Surely there must be some simpler way of describing personality differences in people."

Yet in another sense, these traits personality testers have been trying to measure are too broad rather than too narrow. They imply a consistency in an individual from time to time and from situation to situation which observation of ourselves and others shows us does not exist. Hartshorne and May (1928) brought this fact to our attention years ago in interpreting the results they had obtained in attempting to measure such qualities as honesty, generosity, and self-control in children. A person who gets an average score for generosity may be generous to his playmates but not to his brother and sister, and he will probably be much more willing to give away some sorts of toys than others. What then does the score on generosity mean? The fundamental psychological facts are the ways he acts and feels in these real situations. His "generosity" score actually covers up these basic facts and thus may be more misleading than helpful when we are trying to understand the boy. Because of this difficulty in the use of trait concepts, some psychologists have been inclined to abandon them and to try instead to develop ways of measuring each person's unique way of organizing his own experience. For many practical purposes, however, trait evaluations with all their ambiguities are more useful than more penetrating analyses of individual idiosyncracies. Trait concepts do make possible the comparison of one person with another.

Fortunately, as in the case of intelligence measurements, correlational techniques and the factor-analysis methods based on them have shown us how to bring some semblance of order into this confused realm. Traits are not completely separate and independent of one another, and some are much more fundamental than others in the structure of a personality. At their narrowest they merge into the myriad little characteristics of specific acts and experiences; at their broadest they become indistinguishable from what theorists of all the centuries have described as basic types. Thinking in terms of this hierarchy of personality traits has led to some very productive research. We will be discussing it in more detail later.

There is another kind of difficulty that has stood in the way of the exploration of personality differences. Tests for any kind of psychological characteristic have to be *validated* before we can be at all sure what they are measuring. As long as we are dealing with an ability of any kind, it is not too difficult to find some life situation in which different degrees of success seem to depend at least to some extent upon the postulated ability. Any correspondence between the degree of success shown by our subjects in the test and in the life situation constitutes evidence as to what our test is measuring. It is always difficult and often impossible to apply the same methods to personality measurements. What shall we use, for example, as a criterion for "optimism" or "determination"? There seem to be no life situations where success depends on the possession of either of these qualities to the extent that school success depends upon intelligence. If we rely upon the correspondence between test scores and ratings made by persons who know our subjects, we are emphasizing outer appearances rather than inner realities. What we need for validation purposes are situations that will show what a person *is* rather than how he *appears*.

The one ready-made situation that test-makers have had at their disposal is the psychiatric hospital and clinic. Psychotic and neurotic syndromes develop in some individuals, not in others. If we can think of these syndromes as the extremes of personality tendencies found to a lesser degree in many if not all normal people, we have a way of validating tests of some traits by ascertaining whether or not psychiatric patients obtain extreme scores on them. To a visitor from some other planet where psychologists have not been active it might seem a curious fact that we have so many more tests for maladjustment than for adjustment. We can measure neurotic tendencies much more successfully than leadership, delinquent tendencies much more successfully than altruism. The main reason for this state of affairs is that we have a means of validating the measurements in negative directions, an asset that we do not have for the positive traits. Furthermore, the practical demands for tests have come primarily from the agencies dealing with personalities that have proved to be in some way inadequate, and thus research has tended to center around their problems.

METHODS OF MEASUREMENT

Quantitative research on individual differences in personality has made use of four principal methods. The first of these is *ratings*. If one is accustomed to describing individuals in terms of traits such as sociability or dependability, it is an easy step to the assigning of numbers from 1 to 5 or from 1 to 7 to represent the strength of the given trait in a person. For practical purposes these ratings have never been superseded by more elaborate methods. When the manager is trying to decide whether to employ Mr. Barnes in his store, he is most interested in the kind of impression the man has made upon his previous employers. This is the sort of thing that ratings will tell him. They will not tell him much about the basic characteristics of Mr. Barnes—what his deepest desires and his system of values are like—but his employer does not *need* to know these things.

For the psychologist interested in personality theory, however, such knowledge is not only relevant but absolutely essential. When he studies ratings of observed traits, he finds that such data have a number of serious defects. For one thing, they are made by outsiders and thus represent the mask or the face a person shows to the world rather than the self behind the face. There is of course some relationship between these inner and outer selves—in many cases they appear to be much alike—but the relationship is complex and may differ from one person to another.

Thus Mrs. Halliday keeps her windows shining clean and her furniture free from dust because she loves her husband and gets a deep satisfaction out of her role as homemaker. Mrs. Berwick produces the same results because of an obsessive irrational fear of dust and disorder. Ratings of the two for cleanliness would be similar, but there is a world of difference in the personalities to which the ratings apply.

Furthermore, ratings inevitably have in them something of the personality of the rater as well as the person rated. Consequently, two sets of ratings of the same group of subjects often do not agree very well. Because of the shape life has imposed upon his perceptual apparatus, one rater sees some things in those he observes where another sees different things. No matter how hard we try to be objective, our own personalities affect the judgments we make of the personalities of others. When it is necessary to use ratings in a research study this defect can be corrected to some extent by using several judges and assuming that their idiosyncrasies will cancel out in the general average. This procedure works more successfully for some traits than for others, and there are correlational techniques for testing its adequacy.

The apparent unreliability of ratings may arise from confusion about personality theory rather than from defects in the rating method itself. A clear theoretical orientation shows one what to rate. It seems quite apparent in the example given above that "cleanliness" is not really a personality trait, but a symptom of something else. It is because judges of personality start with different theories and interpret surface traits or habits in different ways that they come out with ratings that do not agree. In research settings where psychologists are proceeding according to clearly defined theoretical formulations, there is little difficulty in obtaining a satisfactory degree of agreement in ratings.

There is almost no limit to the kinds of traits that have been rated in studies of personality. Psychiatric ratings of patients have been used as basic data for correlational studies of syndromes or symptom-complexes, and as criteria for the validation of tests. Observers have been asked to rate the behavior of subjects in standard situations, their expressive movements, or their projective test protocols. Individuals in groups have been asked to rate one another, and ingenious ways of obtaining these judgments, the sociometric and "Guess Who" procedures, have been worked out. Statistical methods for handling all sorts of special rating problems have been developed. With all their defects, ratings have contributed much to our knowledge of personality.

The second type of personality "measurement" that has been widely used is the questionnaire or self-report inventory. This requires that the subject answer questions about himself—what he does, what he likes, how he feels. This method also has its defects, some obvious, some not so immediately apparent. The one usually noticed first is that the score depends to a large extent on the subject's honesty. There is no reason why he cannot say "yes" to the questions having to do with good traits and "no" to those having to do with undesirable traits if he wishes to. This particular defect is more serious in practical situations where personality is being evaluated than it is in personality research. The applicant for admission to a professional school, for example, has a powerful motive *not* to be honest about his less admirable qualities, since he believes that his whole future depends upon his being allowed to obtain the professional training. The same person in a psychological laboratory may make a very satisfactory subject, particularly if conditions are set up to insure complete anonymity of results. In still another situation, one in which he is seeking psychotherapy, he may have a tendency to choose the *unfavorable* answers in order to prove that he does indeed need help. Such effects of the subject's interpretation of the test situation cannot all be classified as deliberate dishonesty. To a large extent they may be quite unconscious, a natural and unavoidable part of the total complex of motives that are operating. Some technical improvements in the construction of tests of the questionnaire type have obviated these difficulties to some extent. The widely used Minnesota Multiphasic Personality Inventory, for example, has special keys designed to indicate whether the person taking it was trying to show himself in a good or a bad light, and to correct the score for such tendencies. "Malingering" keys on various tests were developed during World War II. By paying some attention to the way a person is *likely* to interpret a specific testing situation, a psychologist can avoid using inventories for purposes that are inappropriate. However, even when such precautions have been taken, there is still some residual doubt about the meaning of the answers to the questions. Even the score of a completely honest subject is somewhat ambiguous. Much of motivation is not accessible to conscious awareness. The answers we give to questions about ourselves doubtless have some relationship to unconscious motives, but they do not reveal such basic factors directly.

Whether or not answers can be taken at face value would not matter if we were in a position to validate personality tests against good outside criteria of the traits to be measured. We can if we like consider each "yes" or "no" answer (or each black mark on an IBM sheet) as a bit of behavior in response to a verbal stimulus. If it can be shown to be related to other kinds of behavior, it is useful for personality evaluation. Thus if "I dislike black cats" is always answered "yes" by housewives and "no" by career women it becomes an index to whatever the personality trait is that determines this choice of life pattern. This completely empirical approach has determined the choice of items in the Strong Vocational Interest Blank (to be discussed in more detail in the next chapter) and the Minnesota Multiphasic Personality Inventory. The reason it has not been used more often is that clear-cut criteria for sorting human beings into categories are scarce. Men and women, people in different occupational groups, and psychiatric patients with different diagnoses have so far furnished the more clear-cut groupings making possible the empirical selection of valid personality items. Whenever a research worker can identify a new kind of natural grouping, it then becomes possible to identify personality tendencies that go with it.

Another approach to the validation problem that has become increasingly popular is to correlate responses to test questions with *one another* rather than with outside criteria. By this means clusters of items can be found which hang together and thus seem to have some common root in personality. The term *factorial validity* is applied to traits discovered in this way, traits which do appear to have some consistency, generality, and stability. What must always be remembered, when we use tests that have been developed in this manner, is that there is no real evidence as to what the traits are or how they will show themselves in life situations. Perhaps they should always be called simply A, B, and C, or X-1, Y-2, and Z-3, rather than "dominance" or "introversion." Until some evidence of predictive validity is available for these tests, they cannot help with practical judgments that must be made of students, patients, or applicants for jobs. It is clear that a high score on a group of items all *appearing* to measure dominance may reflect any one of a number of things—an unwillingness to admit shyness, a stereotype characteristic of a certain socio-economic subculture, or the effect of a certain kind of schooling. If we use such scores to select salesmen or discussion leaders, we may choose the very persons who are likely to be least successful at such tasks. Factorial validation cannot be a substitute for tryout in life situations.

One further difficulty, less often discussed than the previous ones, characterizes personality measurement by questionnaire. In using as a score the number of items answered in a certain way, we make the assumption that more separate manifestations of a given trait mean a greater intensity or a larger amount of it. But is this necessarily true? Is a patient who has a variety of obsessive-compulsive symptoms really worse off than the one whose only abnormality is an overwhelming urge to set things on fire? Admittedly this is an extreme example. Probably in most cases a larger number of symptoms does indicate a greater degree of maladjustment. It would seem, however, that this limitation restricts the degree of validity that can be obtained for personality inventories even if all other validation problems can be solved.

During the 1940's and 1950's projective or expressive methods of personality evaluation became enormously popular among psychologists. The basic idea underlying them is simple: Since personality can be thought of as the consistent manner in which a man interprets and organizes his experience, the way to measure it is to present him with ambiguous non-structured or partially-structured materials and note what he does with them. Literally hundreds of possible methods for doing this have been tried, and hardly a month passes that someone does not propose a new system. The leader of the procession, however, has been the Rorschach test with its ten inkblots for subjects to interpret.

The advantages of the projective methods are their flexibility and freedom, and the opportunity they afford for observing the person as a whole rather than trying to reconstruct him from separate trait scores obtained on separate tests. His intelligence and his emotions, his memories and his hopes, all coalesce in one of these protocols. Clinical experience has left little doubt that a sensitive, experienced interpreter can gain a large measure of intuitive understanding of an individual from his responses to projective tests. They have become indispensable in clinical work.

There are difficulties, however, when we try to use them as research instruments to help us understand the nature and organization of individual differences in personality. For one thing, quantification is a problem. To use results in regression equations or factor analyses we must have *scores* rather than qualitative descriptions. If we simply add answers of a given kind, as is often done in the case of Rorschach W, M, or FC responses, we are discarding the most distinctive and valuable contribution a projective technique has to offer, the opportunity for evaluation of each aspect of a record against the background of everything else in it. But if, on the other hand, we use this clinical approach and ask the interpreter to *rate* the subject for introversion, ego strength, and anxiety, we have reverted to the very *trait* approach to personality that we hoped to avoid by using projective methods.

A more important source of ambiguity in research based on projective tests, as well as in their application in practical situations, is the problem of validity. No less than in work with inventories it is essential that some evidence be forthcoming of a demonstrated relationship between test performances and behavior in real life situations. Because a test like the Rorschach purports to cover such a broad range of personality qualities the question of its validity becomes very complex. It is not enough to show that skilled judges can match case histories and Rorschach records as a whole. We need to know something about the validity of each of the separate kinds of judgments. Do large numbers of movement responses show creative talent of some sort? If not, what do they show? Are all varieties of color response related to the same aspects of personality? Does a "small detail" score of 20 out of 100 total responses mean the same as a score of two out of ten? Such are the questions that Rorschach validation research must take under consideration, and the other projective methods face similar problems.

There is a fourth main type of personality evaluation which in spite of its long history has not come into general use. It is usually called the *objective* method because it involves the measurement of something the subject *does* in a situation rather than what he *says*. Measures of *behavior* and measures of *physiological changes* like blood pressure and respiration rate can be classified under this heading. The most ingenious collection of behavioral tests to be used in large-scale research was that assembled during the 1920's for the Character Education Inquiry which was reported in the three much-quoted volumes by Hartshorne *et al.* (1928, 1929, 1930). The tests for honesty, for example, included one in which children were placed in a situation where they would have an opportunity to copy answers from an examination key and one in which coins were left in boxes with the puzzles they were working. "Service" tests included opportunities to decide whether a score should count for oneself or for the group and whether prized articles should be given away to less fortunate children. One of the inhibition tests required a subject to refrain from touching some interesting small object until his task was done.

Recently two of the leading research workers in the field of personality have revived the interest in objective personality tests and have developed some new techniques. R. B. Cattell (1948a) has attempted to get at such things as perseveration, fluency, speed of judgment, fluctuation of attitudes, and suggestibility. Eysenck (1947) has measured motor control, level of aspiration, persistence, and personal tempo. Both of these investigators have included in their test batteries physiological measurements such as dark adaptation and the psychogalvanic response. Their results and conclusions will be discussed a little later.

The reasons why these methods have been used less widely than ratings, questionnaires, or projective techniques are not hard to find. For one thing, in educational, industrial, and clinical settings, data like these cannot be obtained without great difficulty. Much of the testing must be done individually, complicated apparatus is often required, and hours of each subject's time may be needed. Furthermore, situations like many of those from which Hartshorne and May obtained their scores only occur in the presence of an individual's own social group. One test that attempted to assess personality traits objectively in a practical way by means of handwriting, the Downey "will-temperament" test (Downey, 1923), became enormously popular after it was first published but fell into disrepute when validity studies failed to support the author's statements as to what was being measured. There is at present no convenient way for a clinical worker or personnel man to evaluate personality through behavior. Even for research programs, tests of this type have certain disadvantages. Scores tend to be unreliable since they are easily influenced by various chance determiners. Different tests which should logically be expected to measure the same trait show only low correlations with one another. The average intercorrelation for Hartshorne and May's nine tests of "deceitful behavior," for example, was only .227; for tests of "service," it was .201. Such findings led to doubt as to whether one could get at broad personality traits in this way—whether, in fact there were any such things as broad personality traits.

It was the development of the new and more powerful factor-analytic methods which focus on the *pattern* of the intercorrelations rather than their size that has lead us to take another look at the objective test methods. They do have the great advantage over all the others, that a subject's scores are unbiased. Neither his own need to make a good impression nor the reputation he holds with others can influence them to any great extent. Traits identified by carrying out factor analyses of such scores may thus be more stable and less ambiguous than those identified by means of the other kinds of measurements.

The thing about personality measurement that has been most encouraging during the 1940's and the 1950's is that investigators using different methods have come out with similar results. Some traits familiar to psychologists who have been working with ratings and personality inventories appear with greater clarity in the interpretations of projective protocols. Characteristics similar to those differentiating between neurotic and normal soldiers have been identified in school children. As statistical techniques for handling complex combinations of scores have been improved, it has become increasingly possible to analyze these resemblances. There is still much confusion, but some order is beginning to appear.

BASIC PERSONALITY VARIABLES: NEUROTICISM

The first and broadest of the personality variables which has been measured in many ways is general *neuroticism* or emotional instability. Much of the work of Eysenck reported in the three books *Dimensions of Personality* (1947), *The Scientific Study of Personality* (1952), and *The Structure of Human Personality* (1953b), has been directed to the definition and description of this trait by factor-analytic methods. The fact that it is defined in negative terms, as "neuroticism" rather than as some superior quality, is a natural result of the sociological fact mentioned above—that persons who get into difficulties requiring psychiatric help constitute a group it is convenient to use in validating personality tests. Eysenck has taken full advantage of this opportunity for validation. He has developed a procedure called *criterion analysis* to supplement the factor analysis of correlations between personality test scores and obtain evidence as to what the factors represent. After showing that the tests which come out with the highest loadings on the first, most general factor based on individual differences in normal non-psychiatric subjects are the same tests that most clearly differentiate neurotic patients from people in general, he concludes that this particular set of tests measures a continuous variable which can reasonably be called "neuroticism" even in normal people. They differ from the patients not in any absolute, qualitative way, but simply by having less of the trait the tests measure. Some of them, of course, have more than others.

Eysenck and his associates have carried on detailed research of various kinds with regard to this basic trait. They prefer to use objective tests to measure it—such things as motor dexterity, dark vision, and body sway. The largest groups of subjects have been normal and neurotic soldiers, but differences on the neuroticism factor have also shown up in school children, mental defectives, students, and unskilled factory workers (Eysenck, 1952). Eysenck has assembled considerable evidence that ratings, personality inventories, and the Rorschach test all measure this same trait along with whatever else they are measuring.

Such an interpretation makes good sense to clinical workers as well as experimentalists. Those who are familiar with the kinds of profiles of scores obtained from the Minnesota Multiphasic Personality Inventory, for example, know that the easiest thing to observe about an individual record is its general elevation. Factor-analytic studies have corroborated these impressions that separate symptoms of maladjustment tend to correlate, thus giving the impression that some individuals are "worse off" in all ways than are others. The first judgment a skilled interpreter is likely to make of a Rorschach record has to do with the *degree* of personality difficulty it indicates. It has proved feasible to develop check lists of Rorschach characteristics in order to get a quantitative measure of neurotic tendency for use in diagnosis or research. Both the Munroe inspection method (Munroe, 1945) and the Bühler basic score (Bühler *et al.*, 1949) are grounded in this kind of reasoning. Factor analysis of Rorschach scores has pointed to a factor that can reasonably be called neuroticism (Eysenck, 1952).

One of the most valuable contributions made by Eysenck's work of delimiting and defining this variable has been the clear separation of neuroticism from tendencies in the direction of psychosis or complete mental breakdown. Confusion over this issue has for years handicapped both the personality theorists and the applied psychologists who attempted to develop usable personality tests. The question essentially is, "Is a neurotic condition or syndrome a less severe manifestation of the same personality traits that lead to psychosis, or are two separate traits or dimensions involved?" The criterion-analysis procedure outlined above has made it possible for the first time to answer the question unambiguously. The figures show (1952, Ch. 6) that neurotic and psychotic tendencies are two completely different dimensions of personality though both are continuous with traits existing in normal people. The nature of the proof involved in this rather complicated kind of statistical analysis is that the tests which define the neuroticism factor in normal individuals differentiate clearly between diagnosed neurotics and normals, but they do not differentiate at all between diagnosed psychotics and normals. Another quite different family of tests must be used to differentiate psychotics from normals.

The nature of the evidence that these two personality variables are independent of one another can be seen in Figure 27. It represents the average scores for the three groups on two tests. With regard to the Word Connection List, neurotics differ markedly from normals while psychotics make practically normal scores. But with regard to the test of Length Estimation, psychotics differ markedly from normals, whereas neurotics score at the normal level. This difference in the pattern of scores obtained from the two abnormal groups was apparent in most test combinations and showed up very clearly in the factor analyses based on the correlations. Because "neuroticism" and "psychoticism" are continuous variables, rather than all-or-none characteristics, a perfectly sane individual well within the normal range may show some behavior suggesting that of psychotic patients and some like that characteristic of neurotics. All of us probably have a certain amount of both traits as part of our basic human nature. Because the two tendencies are independent, we must not use the one as an indicator of the other. The anxious, nervous man, or the girl who is subject to hysterical fainting spells is no more likely to be hospitalized for schizophrenia or manic-depressive psychosis than is the person without such neurotic symptoms.

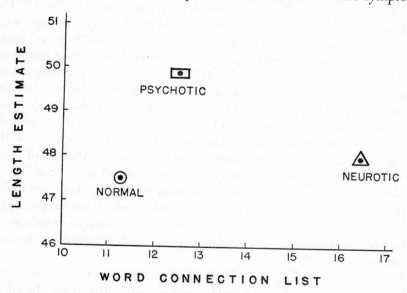

FIGURE 27. Differences in average scores made by neurotic, psychotic, and normal subjects. (Reprinted by permission of the Macmillan Company from Eysenck, *The scientific study of personality*, 1952, p. 224.)

There is one question growing out of the work on the neuroticism factor that has not been so satisfactorily answered. It is, "What is the obverse or opposite end of this continuum?" "What is the meaning of unusual *freedom* from tendencies leading to a psychiatric diagnosis in one of the neurotic categories?" It is the concept or interpretation that gives us trouble rather than the test results themselves. On Eysenck's battery of objective tests there are some subjects in the normal group who are unusually good at the tests of dexterity, persistence, and motor control, unusually free from worries, annoyances, and suggestibility. Who are these people, and how can we expect them to behave in real-life situations? What can we call "neuroticism" at the opposite or "good" end of its distribution? This is of course the same problem that was discussed earlier in regard to personality measurement in general. We lack for subjects at the high end of the scale the kind of criterion information that psychiatric study gives us for persons at the low end.

There are, however, some suggestive results. A number of investigators, working entirely with normal subjects, and applying factor-analytic methods to carefully obtained ratings of personal characteristics, have reported a factor the negative extreme of which is usually called "e" for "emotionality" and the positive extreme "w" for "will." The earliest of these studies was reported by Webb (1915). Ratings were made of two groups of students and four groups of children on thirty-nine traits grouped under headings of "Emotions," "Self-qualities," "Sociability," "Activity," and "Intellect." Correlations were analyzed by Spearman's method, which as explained in a previous chapter identifies the most general factor first and then extracts factors of lesser scope from the residual correlations. As might be expected, the "g" factor, representing general intellectual ability, was the first thing to appear. It is the second factor, relatively independent of intelligence, that is of most interest to us here. Webb called it "w" and defined it as "consistency of action resulting from deliberate volition or will." Traits producing high "w" ratings are: tendency not to abandon tasks from mere changeability; tendency not to abandon tasks in face of obstacles; kindness on principle; trustworthiness; conscientiousness; and perseverance in face of obstacles.

Since 1915, something resembling this "w" factor has shown up again and again in quantitative personality studies, particularly those based on ratings. Burt (1939), who has made several such studies on children, has been most explicit about the meaning of the factor, which he calls "general emotionality." At one extreme it represents neurotic instability, at the other dependability and persistence. P. E. Vernon (1953) would prefer to call the trait "dependability-undependability."

It would be easy to identify "w" with another trait arising from a quite different type of research, the Hartshorne and May character study described above (1928, 1929, 1930). They worked out for each child a variability score based on the standard deviation of his twenty-one scores on separate tests. These standard deviations can reasonably be considered measures of consistency or integration. Correlations between integration scores and various separate traits resemble those obtained by Eysenck and others for freedom from neuroticism (1953b, pp. 136-139). Maller (1934) who carried out a factor analysis of tests for honesty, coöperation, inhibition, and persistence, found that one general factor accounted for the correlations. It appeared to be the same as this "w" or integration factor. He describes it as a "readiness to forego an immediate gain for the sake of a remote but greater gain."

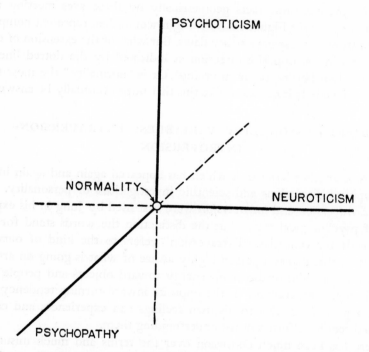

FIGURE 28. Hypothetical relationship of three personality dimensions.

It is impossible to be certain that a factor coming out of one study is identical with a factor coming out of another in which both subjects and tests are different. What is needed is some coördinated research in which various methods that have shown promise can be applied to the same groups. If it turns out, for example, that the *same children* get high scores on ratings defining Webb's "w" and tests defining Hartshorne and May's "integration," and low scores on tests defining Eysenck's "neuroticism," the nature of the underlying personality variable will be much clearer than it now is and we can proceed to find out what its sources are, how it affects behavior, and how amenable to change it is. We are a long way as yet from such certainty, and some pieces do not quite fit into the picture. The set of qualities we have been labeling "w" could as easily be seen as the obverse of psychotic as of neurotic trends, and the kind of person we label "psychopathic personality" would appear to be especially low in these character qualities. Yet Eysenck has shown that "psychoticism" is a separate trait from "neuroticism" and that the psychopaths too are different from neurotics (1952, p. 151). It would be possible to represent these facts geometrically by three axes meeting at a common origin as in Figure 28. The origin would then represent complete *freedom* from all these personality flaws. But what of the extension of each of the axes in the opposite direction as indicated by the dotted lines in the figure. Do they represent anything? Or is "normality" the most than can be achieved? It is questions like this that must eventually be answered.

BASIC PERSONALITY VARIABLES: EXTRAVERSION-INTROVERSION

There is another basic trait which has appeared again and again in the philosophical discussions and scientific investigations of personality. The terms *extraversion* and *introversion* were first used by Jung in his exposition of psychological types, but the distinction the words stand for had been made for centuries. "Extraversion" refers to the kind of outward orientation that makes a person highly aware of what is going on around him and causes him to direct his energy toward objects and people outside himself. "Introversion" is the opposite inward-turning tendency that makes a person sensitive to his own feelings and experiences and causes him to direct his efforts toward understanding them.

There has been much confusion over the terms and much misunderstanding. According to Jung's reasoning, they are not mutually exclusive categories. Both trends are a part of everyone's psychological make-up, and if one of them is not in evidence in one's behavior he looks for signs of its unconscious operation. Furthermore, Jung did not equate extraversion with sociability as many psychologists have done. For Jung the introvert was not necessarily shy, seclusive, or socially maladjusted. When social behavior is used as the touchstone, introversion becomes confused with the neuroticism we have been describing. The lack of agreement between different theorists and different research workers as to the exact meaning of the terms makes for a situation in which psychologists use them with more hesitation than does the man in the street.

Work with personality questionnaires has made us very much aware of this fact that introversion-extraversion mean different things to different people. During the 1920's several different inventories were published by Laird, Heidbreder, Marston, Conklin, and others (see Symonds, 1931, pp. 195-205). There was little evidence for the validity of any of these blanks, largely because of the difficulty of obtaining a usable criterion for the trait. Furthermore it became increasingly apparent that the different tests did not correlate very well with one another. It was quite possible for a person to come out as an introvert on one test, an extravert on another. P. E. Vernon (1938) found in summarizing correlations reported for various kinds of personality inventories that the average correlation between different tests of introversion was only .36 and that this figure was practically identical with that obtained when introversion tests were correlated with those which were supposedly measuring neurotic tendency. Such findings caused questionnaire assessments of introversion-extraversion to fall into disrepute. In fact, they caused a large number of psychologists to take a dim view of the whole concept.

Eysenck (1947), using objective personality tests and factor-analysis methods, has come out with much more solid evidence that introversion-extraversion is a meaningful basic dimension of personality. He found first that the psychiatric diagnoses of neurotic patients were of two main types which he called *dysthymia* and *hysteria*. "Dysthymia" covers those conditions where the main feature is anxiety and depression, and seems to characterize introverted personalities. "Hysteria" covers the condition marked chiefly by physical conversion symptoms and by inability to work or to take responsibility, and is a disorder to which extraverts are subject. Patients in the two groups are clearly differentiated by many of their test performances. On "level of aspiration" tests, for example, subjects in the introverted group show large discrepancies between the goals they set for themselves and their accomplishments, whereas the extraverts set their sights much lower and do not underestimate their past performance so much. On tests given to airplane pilots where precise organization of motor responses were required, the dysthymics (introverts) showed overactivity and restlessness, whereas the hysterics (extraverts) showed boredom and failure to concentrate on the task. In still a different sort of experiment, it was shown that extraverted patients were much more amused by cartoons than the introverted were, the greatest differences showing up on those with sexual themes. The fact that these same sorts of objective tests show similar differences between persons who are within the normal range leads Eysenck to think of introversion-extraversion as another personality continuum along which individuals, normal or neurotic, can be ranked. However, most of the studies he reports in which such tests were used in connection with practical problems—employability of the feeble-minded, work adjustment of unskilled laborers, selection of students and of nurses—do not give much evidence for its utility (see 1952, Ch. 7). One especially interesting finding was that severe neurotics after the brain operation called leucotomy showed significant changes in the direction of extraversion. Since this is just what had been predicted about the effect of the operation, it constitutes some evidence for the theoretical structure on the basis of which the prediction was made. We can sum up by saying that the research work of Eysenck and his associates has furnished strong support for the idea of an introvert-extravert dimension *in neurotics*, but that the significance of the trait in normals is still somewhat uncertain. It may be that other criteria are needed to demonstrate its influence. Salesmen, for example, might constitute better subjects than do unskilled laborers for such a study. It may be that differences in extraversion do not correlate with degrees of success on any job, but that they make for differences in the way the job is done. There is interesting research to be done on such questions.

In the everyday work that clinical psychologists do, it has been the Rorschach test which has been most used to evaluate this dimension of personality. One of the standard combinations of scores used as a basis for personality interpretations is the ratio of the "movement" total to a weighted sum of the color responses. Predominance of movement has been though to indicate introversive trends, predominance of color what Rorschach called "extratensive" trends. The difference between this form-ulation and that based on Eysenck's test results is that introversion and extraversion are thought of as two separate traits rather than the extremes of a single one. Not only is it possible for a person to fit in somewhere between the two extremes but he may be outstandingly high in both. Un-fortunately for our attempts to tie together the results of many kinds of personality studies, careful research has thrown considerable doubt on the validity of this particular line of interpretation of Rorschach records. (See Hertz, 1952, for summary.) The meaning of both movement or color scores seems to be less obvious and more complex than was at first supposed.

There is one idea with regard to the introversion-extraversion con-tinuum that has had wide currency and been discussed in hundreds of papers. It is the hypothesis that the contrasting psychiatric diagnoses of schizophrenia and manic-depressive psychosis represent the extremes of in-troversion-extraversion. According to this theory, the schizophrenics are exaggerated introverts, manic-depressive patients exaggerated extraverts. Often the idea has been tied in with the theories about the relationship between physique and temperament (Kretschmer, 1925) which we will take up in more detail in a later chapter. The best evidence on this question comes from Eysenck's study (1952, Ch. 6) of what he calls the psychotic dimension. The subjects were 100 normal people and 100 psychotics, of whom 50 were manic-depressive and 50 schizophrenic. On the basis of the tests that he used he was able to obtain no evidence at all for the idea that the two psychotic states represent opposite ends of a single continuum. "Psychoticism" seemed to be a trait totally different from "neuroticism," but schizophrenics as a group differed from manic-depressives simply in being somewhat less "psychotic." One study, however well designed, does not settle an issue of this magnitude. There is a real possibility that this particular battery of tests did not include the kinds of performance or situation that would allow differences between types of psychotics to show up. But negative findings like these should at least make us cautious about conclusions that introversion and schizophrenia are different degrees of the same thing.

In summing up what we know about introversion and extraversion we can say that while there is some experimental evidence for the existence of such a basic personality variable, we are as yet in no position to apply our knowledge of it in day-to-day judgments of people. Apparently the only tests that measure it satisfactorily are physiological and behavior measures such as Eysenck has utilized. Because they require considerable apparatus and skills that clinical psychologists and personnel workers are not likely to have developed, they have not been considered to be suitable for use in most practical situations. The types of test that are commonly used there, inventories and projective methods, do not measure the trait in a clear manner. (Some of Eysenck's tests could certainly be adapted for clinical use if psychologists were to become more familiar with them.) Furthermore, we do not yet know enough about the relationship of introversion-extraversion to outside criteria to make much use of a score for the trait even if we did have it. We might be able to judge the type of neurotic symptom to which a person is susceptible, but we could not say anything about psychotic tendencies. Although it is commonly assumed that extraverts make good salesmen, and introverts predominate among artists and musicians, we really have no evidence on which to base such opinions. Perhaps eventually introversion-extraversion will turn out to be one of the most important categories in personality study. As yet we must suspend judgment.

MORE COMPLEX FACTOR-ANALYTIC RESEARCH

British and American psychologists have differed in their approach to personality measurement just as they have in their work on intelligence. The factor-analytic methods used in Britain encourage interpretation in terms of a few broad characteristics such as neuroticism and introversion. The methods preferred in the United States lead to interpretations in terms of a much larger number of basic traits.

One main line of research here has been the analysis of correlations between item responses on personality questionnaires. The aim is to locate clusters of responses which can then be examined in an attempt to determine what tendencies they represent. Guilford and Guilford (1936, 1939 a and b) and Martin (1945) have made a number of such factor analyses of inter-item correlations and have come out with thirteen differentiable traits. They have named and described them as follows:

S—Social Introversion-Extraversion (sociability as against shyness).

T—Thinking Introversion-Extraversion (introspective as opposed to objective orientation of the thinking process).

D—Depression (cheerful optimistic disposition as opposed to chronic depressed mood).

C—Cycloid disposition (stability of mood as opposed to marked fluctuations).

A—Rhathymia (happy-go-lucky or care-free disposition as opposed to inhibition or over-control).

G—General Activity (tendency to engage in overt activity as opposed to inertness).

R—Ascendance-Submission (social leadership vs. social passivity).

M—Masculinity-Femininity (resemblance to characteristic masculine vs. characteristic feminine responses).

I—Inferiority Feelings (confidence vs. lack of confidence in oneself).

N—Nervousness (calmness vs. jumpiness, irritability).

O—Objectivity (tendency to view oneself and surroundings objectively vs. tendency to take things personally).

Co—Coöperativeness (willingness to accept things and people as they are vs. over-criticism and intolerance).

Ag—Agreeableness (lack of quarrelsomeness as opposed to belligerent, domineering attitude).

Lovell (1945) factor-analyzed the correlations between total scores on these thirteen personality variables looking for a smaller number of traits of broader scope which could be used in place of the thirteen to describe a personality. Four of these so-called "superfactors" seemed to account for most of the relationships. She called them:

I. Drive-Restraint (high loadings on general drive, carefreeness, sociability, and social ascendance).

II. Realism (high loadings on objectivity, masculinity, freedom from nervousness, and freedom from inferiority feelings).

III. Emotionality (high loadings on stability of emotional reactions, freedom from depression, and extravertive orientation of the thinking process).

IV. Social Adaptability (high loadings on lack of quarrelsomeness and tolerance).

Another analysis of the Guilford data by L. L. Thurstone (1951b) produced seven major factors in place of the original thirteen, described by the adjectives:

1. Active.
2. Vigorous.
3. Impulsive.
4. Dominant.
5. Stable.
6. Sociable.
7. Reflective.

The trouble with work of this kind is that the answers which subjects give to the questions in a personality inventory must necessarily be doubtful indicators of what their real personality traits are. There is a possibility that the Guilford and Lovell factors represent different kinds of *test-taking attitude* rather than basic categories in experience or behavior. It is something to have shown that the things subjects are willing to say about themselves fall into these patterns. Corroboration is needed from other kinds of research before we can be sure that these are the basic dimensions of personality.

The work of R. B. Cattell, as reported in numerous journal articles and several books (1946-1950), is the most ambitious attempt anyone has made to combine factor analyses of ratings, questionnaires, and objective tests into an organized whole and to integrate the results with non-mathematical classifications of personality. The plan of the over-all research program was to identify basic factors from separate studies based on ratings, questionnaires, and objective tests, and then to apply all three methods to a single group in order to determine whether the same factors would show up for all three.

He started with ratings. The problem of *what to rate*, one of the continuing difficulties in personality study, was solved in an ingenious manner. His basic assumption is that language development over a period of many centuries has by now given us *words* for all the personality traits that are discernible in human beings. Thus if we include all the traits for which there are *names* we will have a list defining what Cattell calls the "total personality sphere." After identifying clusters of traits on this sphere, factor analysis should give us clues as to the source traits from which these clusters grow. Cattell took his basic list of trait names from the dictionary prepared by Allport and Odbert (1936), and supplemented it with names from psychiatric and psychological literature. In order to reduce the number to workable size, a psychologist and a student of literature went over the list carefully, grouping all synonyms together. Ratings were then obtained on 100 adults for each of these 171 characteristics. After this enormous number of ratings had been intercorrelated, traits were grouped into *clusters* by putting together all those which correlated more than .45 with each other. By making some minor omissions it was possible to reduce the number of clusters to thirty-five. Then 208 male adults, representing quite a wide range of the population, were rated on each of the thirty-five variables. Correlations between these ratings constituted the raw material for the factor analysis. The resulting basic factors were described as follows:

A. Cyclothymia vs. schizothymia.
B. Intelligence vs. mental defect.
C. Emotionally mature, stable character vs. demoralized general emotionality.
D. Hypersensitive infantile emotionality vs. phlegmatic frustration tolerance.
E. Dominance vs. submissiveness.
F. Surgency (optimistic enthusiasm) vs. melancholy shy desurgency.
G. Positive character integration vs. immature, dependent character.
H. Charitable, adventurous rhathymia (happy-go-lucky attitude) vs. obstructive, withdrawn schizophrenia.
I. Sensitive, imaginative, anxious emotionality vs. rigid, tough poise.
J. Neurasthenia vs. vigorous, obsessional, determined character.
K. Trained, socialized, cultured mind vs. boorishness.
L. Surgent cyclothymia vs. paranoid schizophrenia.

Subsequent analyses of personality ratings have in general confirmed the interpretations from the first one. In another group of 133 men, college students this time in place of the more diversified sample originally used, a factor analysis of ratings, completely independent of the first one, turned up ten of the same twelve factors along with one new one (R. B. Cattell, 1947). A similar rating study of 240 college girls (R. B. Cattell, 1948) produced nine factors which it seemed possible to equate with those obtained from men's groups, although the reader of the report is left in some doubt as to just how well all the names fit. (The naming of traits from factor loadings is the most subjective and questionable part of the work.) **Fiske** (1949) showed that when psychology graduate students were rated three ways on twenty-two of the Cattell variables—by classmates, by staff members, and by self—and separate factor analyses carried out, there was considerable resemblance between factor loadings obtained from the three kinds of evaluation. Fiske called his five principal factors: (1) Emotional control, (2) Social adaptability, (3) Conformity, (4) Inquiring intellect, and (5) Confident self-expression. Whether these can be exactly identified with any of the Cattell traits listed above is not certain. There is some similarity.

The most crucial phase of the Cattell research program has been the analysis of scores obtained from questionnaires and from objective tests to see whether they could be matched up with the rating factors (R. B. Cattell, 1948, 1950). The plan was to use the same 370 students as subjects in all the studies so that it would be apparent whether or not the same individuals stood high in a trait when it was measured in different ways. The fact that many of these subjects fell by the wayside before the project ended makes the final results somewhat ambiguous. On some of the objective tests the number is as low as 77, and only 35 finished all the special physiological measures. As the results stand, the factors from the three media do not really match up very well. Only three factors seem to be the same for all three kinds of measurements, and because of the small N's involved in some correlations these are not too certain (Cattell and Saunders, 1950). In a more recent study Cattell and Gruen (1953, 1954) have used similar methods to identify personality factors in eleven-year-old children.

Still another question in which Cattell has been interested is whether other varieties of *correlations*, when factor-analyzed, will identify the same or similar basic traits. Two studies (A. K. S. Cattell, R. B. Cattell and Rhymer, 1947; R. B. Cattell and Luborsky, 1950) have explored possibilities of P technique, in which a battery of tests and ratings is given to one person on a large number of occasions rather than to a number of people on one occasion. It appears that the factors representing day-to-day fluctuations are similar to those representing differences between individuals, but as in the other studies considerable subjectivity is involved in the matching of factors.

In evaluating the contributions made to our knowledge of personality by these complicated and time-consuming factor-analytic investigations, we can say that while they have not as yet accomplished as much as they set out to do they have been of considerable value. They have not given us an unambiguous picture of personality structure in terms of which we can describe the chief ways in which one person differs from another. But they have given us new tools and new ideas with which to work. Inventory-type tests representing the Guilford variables (Guilford and Zimmerman, 1949; Thurstone, 1950) and the Cattell variables (R. B. Cattell, Saunders, and Stice, 1950) have been published. They promise to be useful in many kinds of research. The other kinds of measurement Cattell has used, such as ratings, objective tests, and physiological indices, are clearly described in his publications. Thus they too are available for further investigation. More important than these tools, however, may be the formulations that have arisen from this completely empirical attempt to find out what kinds of personality traits tend to go together. They constitute a stimulating source of new *hypotheses* about personality. These can be tested in diverse ways. At present these personality variables have little if any practical significance to applied psychologists, but they may eventually lead to the development of techniques that will have such practical value.

OTHER WORK ON BASIC TRAITS

There are some theoretical formulations with regard to basic dimensions of personality that are not readily fitted into the frameworks discussed so far. The most influential of these is the psychoanalytic theory of character types based on different stages of psycho-sexual development. The term *oral character* describes an habitual mode of adjustment which resembles that of very young children at the stage when love is still equated with food. Such persons are passive, dependent, receptive, and given to all sorts of oral gratifications such as eating, drinking, and smoking. The *anal character* constitutes a fixation on some of the traits arising from conflicts with the parents over toilet training. Such persons are frugal, obstinate, and orderly. Some writers describe also a *urethral character*, in which ambition and competitiveness are salient traits, and a *phallic character* which is aggressive and provocative.

The ideal or norm, in this system of description, is called the *genital character*. It represents the person who has achieved genuine maturity, and thus is free to love, to give, and to achieve. He is not troubled by incompatible attitudes of love and hatred toward the same persons, and his feelings toward the world are optimistic and confident.

Without necessarily accepting the Freudian theory as to the origin of these types in psychosexual development, it is possible to examine them and try to determine whether they represent consistent personality tendencies in individuals. There have been a few studies showing that the kinds of behavior involved in each trait do tend to cluster. R. R. Sears (1943), for example, found that the "anal" traits of stinginess, obstinacy, and orderliness were correlated significantly in the ratings fraternity boys gave one another; and Goldman-Eisler (1951), Blum (1949), and Blum and Miller (1952) obtained correlations in the expected direction between various traits thought to be a part of "orality." Eysenck (1953b, p. 126) has reminded us that the demonstration that a trait like "orality" exists does not tell us anything about its origin. But it may give us useful research leads.

Another idea growing out of psychoanalytic thinking which has been very fruitful in its applications is that of the "authoritarian" personality (Adorno et al., 1950). During the course of their work on Anti-Semitism and other varieties of prejudice it became apparent to the investigators that all of these prejudiced attitudes grew out of a common matrix which could be thought of as a personality type. A scale called the F-scale (prefascism) was devised to measure the personality variable directly. A high scorer on this scale is characterized by: (1) repression rather than awareness of his own unacceptable motives; (2) externalization or projection which leads him to suspect and blame others and to avoid introspection; (3) conventionalism or conformity; (4) an orientation toward others in terms of power rather than love; (5) rigidity rather than flexibility. "Authoritarianism" seems to be independent of "neuroticism" and "psychoticism" since both low and high scores on the F-scale can be found among neurotics undergoing treatment and among hospitalized patients. Vigorous research programs in many places are investigating the relationship of the trait to other aspects of personality and behavior.

A trait related to another part of psychoanalytic theory is often used descriptively by clinical workers in their diagnoses of cases. It is usually called "ego-strength." The idea is somewhat related to a matter discussed earlier in the chapter, the need for concepts to represent positive aspects of the personality. The ego, as analysts see it, is the part of the person that copes with reality. Some individuals seem to have more of this coping ability than others do, so that they can endure large amounts of psychological stress. Barron (1953) selected the sixty-nine items from the Minnesota Multiphasic Personality Inventory that were related to success in psychotherapy and decided after inspection of the differentiating items that the scale was measuring ego-strength. If his findings are corroborated by further work, an important new variable will have been added to the list.

Pascal (1951) and Sipprelle (1954) have identified a characteristic they call *psychophylaxis*, meaning resistance to psychological stress, which seems to be important in the make-up of research scientists they have been studying. This trait would seem to have something in common with Barron's ego strength. The search for these *positive* personality variables is one of the most promising current activities, but so far it is too early to evaluate the results.

PERSONALITY ORGANIZATION—THE COMPOSITE PICTURE

The work that has been discussed constitutes only a fraction of the attempts that have been made to measure individual differences in personality. French (1953) lists no less than forty-nine factors, each of which has been reported in two or more factor-analytic investigations. A number of investigators have been interested in expressive movements and the qualities that can be assessed from voice or handwriting (P. E. Vernon, 1953, Ch. 4). Some have approached the problem from the standpoint of the arts and tried to judge personality from drawings or from choices of art objects. Rosenzweig (1945) has attempted to measure characteristic types of response to frustrating situations. The measurement of different varieties of interest and attitude is such a well-developed field in itself that we are giving it a separate chapter. Browsing through the psychological journals for any month suggests several new proposals for evaluating personality.

For the person who is primarily interested in the practical applications of all this work several conclusions can be drawn. In the first place, it is quite feasible to assess, by any one of a number of available methods, how stable or sound an individual's general adjustment is. The quality Eysenck calls "neuroticism" and Vernon "undependability" is the most obvious thing that shows up in ratings, questionnaires, or objective tests. In the second place, clinical workers familiar with the peculiarities and limitations of the available methods of assessment can get a considerable amount of information as to the *direction* of the maladjustment that a subject shows. Is he headed toward neurotic handicap or psychotic breakdown? Is he a person who *suffers* mentally and physically from anxiety or is his anxiety repressed and disguised? What are his characteristic ways of relating himself to other people? These latter evaluations are not *measurements* of personality but somewhat intuitive descriptive judgments based on things the subject says and does in test situations. In the third place, methods for the evaluation of positive personality qualities that make for outstanding success in life situations are as yet not very satisfactory. Probably the old-fashioned kinds of evidence, such as ratings and letters of recommendation, are still more useful than anything the psychological laboratories have turned up. (What interest tests have to contribute will be discussed in the next chapter.)

Although these practical values from research on the measurement of individual differences in personality are as yet somewhat limited, the theoretical picture has become much clearer than it was a decade ago. It appears now that it may eventually be possible to describe personality characteristics in terms of a hierarchy similar to that postulated for abilities. Figure 29, taken from Eysenck (1947), illustrates this. It is based on the correlations that have been obtained for all sorts of personality measure-

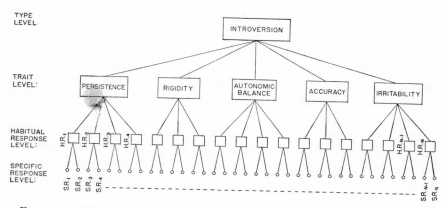

FIGURE 29. Diagrammatic representation of hierarchical organization of personality. (Reprinted by permission of The Macmillan Company from Eysenck, *Dimensions of personality*, 1947, p. 29.)

ments. Specific bits of behavior show some consistency with one another, thus defining what Eysenck calls the *habitual response* level. These habitual responses, in turn, are to some extent correlated, thus defining what we call *traits*. The traits too tend to group themselves into clusters which constitute *types*. Much of the confusion and many of the conflicting results coming from various quantitative studies disappear when we think in terms of such an organization. Factor-analytic methods like those used by most American investigators identify *traits* first but obtain *types* as second-order factors when trait measurements are correlated with one another. British factor-analytic methods locate *types* first, *traits* afterward. Ratings based on observed behavior usually stand for personal qualities at the habitual response level; questionnaire scores are more likely to be concerned with the trait level.

If the system represented by Figure 29 can be supported by the research needed to develop workable methods of assessment at all levels, we shall be able to analyze personality in the following way:

Henry M. is a man with an average amount of general stability or freedom from abnormal trends (type level). He tends to be introverted rather than extraverted (type level). Of the *traits* related to this type, however, he shows only shyness and subjectivity to a noticeable degree. In rigidity and irritability he is about average (trait level). Shyness is most marked in social groups involving both sexes and in meeting strangers. In classroom and business situations and on the speaker's platform he expresses himself without hesitation (habitual response level).

Eventually we may be able to evaluate any personality in this orderly way, proceeding from top to bottom of the hierarchy. But there are many gaps to be filled in before this will be possible, and there are perhaps definite limits to the progress that can be made in this direction. For a person is not only a combination of traits but a *process* in time. What he is becoming, the direction he is going, is inherent always in what he is at any one period. This is especially apparent in the case of a child, but the constant movement in time characterizes adults as well. Because of this fact many serious students of personality have little interest in research on quantifiable traits and their relationship to one another such as we have been discussing in this chapter. At present these processes of change seem not to be quantifiable.

Another limitation on the usefulness of any type of personality measurement is the well-known fact that the *situation* in which a person finds himself has a considerable influence on his behavior. Thus a full knowledge of a man's personality characteristics will never enable us to predict very accurately what he will do in situations different from those in which we have observed him. The most crucial feature of the framework within which traits operate is made up of relationships to other people. These too in their diversity and individuality have so far resisted quantification. We cannot get into a regression equation a man's lurking suspicion of one companion, his unconscious effort to impress another. This too has made some thinkers doubtful of the value of personality measurement.

Still another question that has not been answered to everyone's satisfaction has to do with the possibility of *unique* traits. All the work we have discussed so far presupposes continuous trait distributions by means of which we can measure a person by comparing him with others. Some personality theorists have stubbornly insisted that to describe personality in this way is to lose the very essence of it. Stephenson (1953) has produced an eloquent statement of this point of view and elaborated a method for carrying on scientific research even with a single case.

It is an advantage to recognize that there are other ways of approaching the study of personality and that there are limits to the accuracy with which we can understand or predict by means of tests, at least those available to us now. Such knowledge makes it possible for us to use tests intelligently for purposes for which they are appropriate but to supplement them with non-quantitative methods whenever it is necessary. There are many situations in which we do not need to know exactly what a man will do about the specific incidents of which his job consists, but simply how stable or dependable he is. But if we must trust him with a delicate and important task of negotiation we must know more about him. It may be unnecessary at the beginning to know just how a patient will react to the personnel and activities of a hospital if we can establish beyond the shadow of a doubt that he is in fact schizophrenic. But in order to plan his treatment intelligently we need more information. The understanding of the complexities of personality is an involved, intricate, eternally fascinating undertaking. In carrying it out we need all the help that novelists and dramatists can give us, as well as the insights of psychotherapists and personality theorists. But it is not too much to hope that personality measurements may do an important part of the work for us. They can constitute a valuable check on hypothesis and speculation. They can suggest new and perhaps more fruitful hypotheses. They can lead to ways of organizing information otherwise too complex to be grasped. Like all quantitative methods they are *tools* which we must use as intelligently and skillfully as we can.

SUMMARY

The study of individual differences in personality has been beset with difficulties, many of which have been only partially overcome. It has been difficult to define exactly what it is we wish to measure. The validation of tests has been hampered by the dearth of real-life criteria of the traits with which they deal. Much more work has been done on deficiencies than on personality strengths.

The principal methods of measurement have been ratings, questionnaires, projective techniques, and objective tests such as actual behavior in a standardized situation. Factor analysis has been used with all these types of measure to explore relationships and reduce the number of separate traits.

Eysenck has produced evidence for three broad variables: neuroticism, psychoticism, and extraversion-introversion. Guilford and Cattell have used factor-analytic methods to identify a much larger number of more narrowly defined traits. Other trait formulations growing out of psycho-analytic theory have been supported by at least a small amount of quantitative evidence.

It seems now that some sort of hierarchical arrangement with broad general characteristics at the top and specific responses at the bottom will be needed to organize what we know about measurable personality differences.

CHAPTER 8

Individual Differences in
Interests and Attitudes

WHILE A large part of their attention has been devoted to the measurement of mental abilities and of personality traits making for maladjustment, psychologists have always realized that other aspects of individuality are in some ways more obvious and important than these. As we think of our friends and associates or listen to the conversation of new acquaintances, what we are most likely to notice are their characteristic interests and attitudes. We may not be able to judge how bright a high-school student is, but we can be sure as to how he feels about English literature and photography. We cannot usually tell how neurotic or introverted our next-door neighbor is, but a few moments of back-fence conversation will suffice to classify him as a rock-ribbed Republican with strong religious and patriotic sentiments.

As long as the science of individual differences was conceived as a division of human knowledge that was to include only hereditary characteristics, interests and attitudes did not seem to fall within its boundaries. Nobody seriously considers the possibility of genes for scientific interests or socialism. To many observers, an individual's assortment of interests and attitudes seems to represent a hodgepodge of miscellanea assembled from here and there, a collection that can perhaps be described but hardly ordered in any systematic fashion. It is often assumed that such traits are shallow and superficial in comparison with the kinds of traits that we have discussed in previous chapters, and that they are too changeable to permit any assessment.

Applied psychologists, however, both in occupational counseling and in social psychology, found these aspects of personality so vital for their work that they proceeded to develop ways of evaluating them. As research data accumulated, it became increasingly apparent that interests and attitudes are *not* superficial and that they are less changeable than many "deeper" psychological traits. Furthermore, regularities about the way they are organized consistently show up. These lead to interesting theoretical generalizations. What started as purely practical research can now play an important part in the building of personality theory.

HOW INTERESTS ARE MEASURED

Much of what we know about occupational interests rests on work that has been done with the Strong Vocational Interest Blank. First published in 1927, this test has been given to thousands of persons in both counseling and research situations. A large bibliography has accumulated.

The system of scoring used for the Strong, novel at the time the blank was first brought out, has become one of the most useful methods in personality measurement. What Strong did was to collect several hundred items of many kinds [1]—occupations, school subjects, recreational activities, self-ratings—and to ask the respondent to mark each one indicating whether he liked it or not. Figure 30 illustrates what the respondent's task is like. Each scoring key was constructed by tabulating the responses of a group of successful men in some one profession or occupation and comparing the percentage of this group endorsing each response with the percentage characteristic of men in general. Any response for which the difference in percentage was statistically significant became a part of the scoring key for this particular occupation. Weights were attached to items according to the size of the difference. In developing the "Engineer" key, for example, Strong found that 47 per cent of men in general as compared with 60 per cent of his engineers marked the first item of the blank, "Actor," D for Dislike. This led to the inclusion of the D response on "Actor" as part of the Engineer scoring key, with one point of credit. A little farther down the list, on the item "Author of technical book," 59 per cent of the engineers said L (Like) whereas

---

[1] The adequacy of the original item pool is a matter of some importance in cases like this where such a large structure of research rests on a single foundation. It is very difficult to evaluate this. Fryer (1931) gives the clearest account of what happened during the early 1920's when work on interest inventories was getting started. About 1,000 items were collected in Yoakum's seminar at Carnegie Institute of Technology. Various people made up inventories for special purposes during the next few years. Items from the original pool were used, discarded, or replaced by new ones according to whether or not they seemed to be making any sort of occupational differentiation. There is no way now of determining what "universe" Strong's items represent. This does not matter so far as the practical uses of the blank are concerned, but it makes for ambiguity in our attempts to fit the results into any theoretical structure.

VOCATIONAL INTEREST BLANK FOR MEN (Revised)

By EDWARD K. STRONG, JR.

Professor of Psychology, Stanford University

Published by STANFORD UNIVERSITY PRESS, Stanford University, California

It is possible with a fair degree of accuracy to determine by this test whether one would like certain occupations or not. The test is not one of intelligence or school work. It measures the extent to which one's interests agree or disagree with those of successful men in a given occupation.

Your responses will, of course, be held strictly confidential.

GENERAL DIRECTIONS

In order that your test may be scored accurately, it is important for you to follow the directions carefully:

1. Use only the special pencil for the test.
2. Do not write on the test booklet. All responses must be made on the answer sheet.
3. Fill in the blanks at the side of the answer sheet.
4. Answer spaces, made by dotted lines on the answer sheet, are numbered to correspond to the numbering of the items in the test. You are to decide how you wish to mark the question, then blacken with your pencil the Answer Space that corresponds to this answer.

Example: Do you *like*, or are *indifferent* to, or *dislike* children? The answer sheet is as follows:

L   I   D   where **L** means *like*
                          I means *indifferent*
                          D means *dislike*

If you like children, you should black in the space below **L,** like this:

L   I   D

Do not encircle or make check marks.

Go over the pencil mark two or three times with firm pressure. Make a solid black mark. If you make a mistake, erase the black mark completely; do not merely cross it out. Be very careful to touch your pencil on the sheet only when blacking in between the dotted lines, otherwise electrical contact may be made by the scoring machine, thus causing wrong answers.

Please do not mark on this test booklet at all. The arrangement of questions in columns of 25 each corresponds with the same arrangement on the answer sheet.

FIGURE 30. Strong Vocational Interest Blank, first page. (Reprinted from *Vocational interest blank for men—form M* [revised] by Edward K. Strong, Jr. with the permission of the author and of the publishers, Stanford University Press. Copyright 1938 by the Board of Trustees of Leland Stanford Junior University.)

only 31 per cent of the men in general gave this response. This greater difference meant than an L response to "Author of technical book" received three points of credit on the "Engineer" key (Strong, 1943, p. 75). The advantage of this variety of scoring key is that it has a certain amount and kind of validity built into it. We may not be able to describe in psychological terms what it is that distinguishes engineers from other men, but we know that there is *something*. In practical counseling situations, such empirical validity in a measuring instrument is a very valuable characteristic. By 1954, Strong had developed keys for forty-five different occupations. A women's blank with keys for twenty-five occupations has also been made available.

Scores based on item analysis have certain peculiarities that need always to be kept in mind. While there is some doubt as to what kind of a scale the scores on a test of ability or achievement constitute (see Chapter 3), there is a double dose of doubt with regard to scores like these. On the Engineer scale, for example, the norms show that the average score for engineers is 112. If Harry Higgins comes out with a score of 200, what does that indicate about him? He seems to be much more like engineers than the average successful engineer is. This is a confusing, rather meaningless statement. What we must not conclude is that he has more interest *in* engineering than the average engineer, or that he is likely to be more *successful* than the average. There is no evidence at all that within any one occupational group, degrees of success are correlated with magnitude of Strong score. Some of the ambiguous results that have been correlated with other types of ability and personality measurements may arise from this basic ambiguity with regard to what sort of scale the measurements constitute.[2]

Strong himself has centered most of his research around broad categories set up in such a way as to represent the degree of certainty we can feel that an individual really belongs to an occupational group. Strong's A rating includes scores ranging all the way from a half standard deviation below the mean to the top of the distribution, thus covering the range over which it seems reasonable to say, "This individual unquestionably fits into this occupational group." "B+," "B," and "B−" stand for ranges of scores below the average for an occupational group, thus representing increasing amounts of doubt as to whether an individual belongs in it. What a "B" score means is that a person has *some* attitudes in common with men in the occupation, but other attitudes that are different. A "C" score indicates that he shows little or no resemblance to persons in this particular occupa-

[2] Strong's most recent work, a long-term follow-up of men first tested in college, indicates that the size of the score is related to *remaining* in the occupation represented by the key in question. Men with scores well above the average for a norm group are considerably more likely to be found in an occupation corresponding to it twenty years later than are men who made just average scores on the scale. (Personal communication)

Machine-scoring

KUDER PREFERENCE RECORD
VOCATIONAL
FORM CM
Prepared by G. Frederic Kuder, Editor, *Educational and Psychological Measurement*
Professor of Psychology, Duke University

This blank is used for obtaining a record of your preferences. It is not a test. There are no right or wrong answers. An answer is right if it is true of you.

A number of activities are listed in groups of three. Read over the three activities in each group. Decide which of the three activities you like most. You have been given a separate answer sheet; each column on the answer sheet corresponds to a page in the booklet. When the answer sheet is correctly lined up with the booklet, there are two spaces for marking answers on the same line as each activity. Make a heavy, black mark with the special pencil in the left-hand space following the activity you like **most**. Then decide which activity you like **least**, and make a heavy, black mark in the right-hand space following this activity. Be sure that the letter by the space you mark is the same as the letter in front of the activity in the booklet.

In the examples below, the person answering has indicated for the first group of three activities, that he would usually like to **visit a museum most**, and **browse in a library least**. In the second group of three activities he has indicated he would ordinarily like to **collect autographs most** and **collect butterflies least**.

EXAMPLES

Put your answers to these questions in column O.

P.	Visit an art gallery	
Q.	Browse in a library	←LEAST
R.	Visit a museum	MOST→
S.	Collect autographs	MOST→
T.	Collect coins	
U.	Collect butterflies	←LEAST

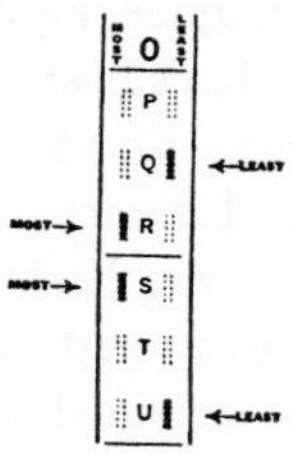

O
P
Q
R
S
T
U

Some of the activities involve preparation and training. In such cases, please suppose that you could first have the necessary training. Do not choose an activity merely because it is new or unusual. Choose what you would like to do if you were equally familiar with all of the activities.

In some cases you may like all three activities in a group. In other cases you may find all three activities unpleasant. Please show what your first and last choices would be, however, if you *had* to choose.

Some activities may seem trivial or foolish. Please indicate your choices, anyway, for all of the groups. Otherwise we cannot give you a complete report. Your answers will be kept strictly confidential.

Please do not spend a lot of time on one group. Put down your first reaction and go on. Do not discuss the activities with anyone. An answer is worthless unless it is your own judgment.

If you want to change an answer, erase your first answer completely; then mark the new answer in the usual way. Be sure that you mark all your answers with the special pencil.

Now go ahead with the activities on the next page.

Published by SCIENCE RESEARCH ASSOCIATES, 57 West Grand Avenue, Chicago 10, Illinois

FIGURE 31. Kuder Preference Record, first page.

tion. Research based on such letter grades, though it lacks the apparent precision of work with exact numerical scores, seems to rest on a sounder logical foundation.

The other widely-used method for measuring interests is the Kuder Preference Record. It was developed in a different manner from the Strong. Kuder assembled a set of items representing diverse kinds of activity—such as "visit an art gallery" or "collect autographs,"—and gave it to about 500 college students. He examined their responses to see if he could find a group of items that seemed to cluster together. The first such group was the "Literary" scale. Using this as a starting point, he continued to use correlational methods of item analysis searching for another cluster of closely related items that would have little or no correlation with the first one. Having developed a second scale by this means, he repeated the procedure, seeking still another set of items that would correlate highly with one another but negligibly with *both* of the first scales. Since 1934 when the work on the Kuder blank began, scale after scale has been added in this manner. Figure 31 shows what the test is like. Since 1948, ten scoring keys have been available for the *Kuder Preference Record—Vocational*. They are: Outdoor, Mechanical, Computational, Scientific, Persuasive, Artistic, Literary, Musical, Social Service, and Clerical. In 1953, Kuder published the *Preference Record—Personal*. It is built in the same manner as the vocational blank, but the scales represent preferences for different kinds of personal or social activity, described as follows:

A. Preference for being active in groups
B. Preference for familiar and stable situations
C. Preference for working with ideas
D. Preference for avoiding conflict
E. Preference for directing others.

When one carries on research with the Kuder tests or evaluates research that others have done, it is important that he keep in mind the distinctive characteristics of these scores. For one thing, the validity of the test as a measure of characteristics actually involved in any occupation is not guaranteed. The fact that a set of items hangs together and that all these items appear to have something to do with mechanical types of activity tells us nothing about men in mechanical occupations. The process of validating a test like this is a long and difficult task. With the passage of time, more and more of the essential information is being accumulated. Each successive Kuder Manual has summarized it and users of the blank need to be familiar with it. Another point that must be kept in mind is that a person's score represents what he says when he is required to *make a choice* of the best- and least-liked activity in a group of three. Thus each of a person's scores is dependent upon all the others. It is the combination or profile that is meaningful rather than any one score taken singly. Embedded in a different set of choices, an individual's score on the Clerical scale, for example, might be considerably higher or considerably lower than it turns out to be in this particular context. The fact that scores obtained from the Strong and the Kuder blanks represent different systems of measurement and that neither is a straightforward interval or ratio scale complicates research undertakings, whether we wish to relate either test to criteria of success or to determine the amount of agreement between them. The soundest procedure is probably to use the *judgment* made on the basis of the test as the experimental variable rather than to use test scores directly. Strong's letter grades and Kuder's reports of differential profiles for occupations are ways of accomplishing this purpose.

Another test devised to disclose the pattern of a person's motivation is the Allport-Vernon *Study of Values*. (The most recent revision is the Allport-Vernon-Lindzey Study of Values, 1951.) This, like the Kuder, requires the subject to make choices between alternatives, but the traits which the items represent were settled in advance instead of being identified from empirical research. The idea as to what the six basic interests are came from Spranger's book, *Types of Men* (1928). They are as follows:

Theoretical—interest in the pursuit of truth by intellectual means.
Economic—interest in useful, practical things.
Aesthetic—interest in beauty and artistic qualities.
Social—interest in helping people.
Political—interest in power or influence over people.
Religious—interest in mystical experience.

Because of the lack of external validation, the *Study of Values* has been little used in the practical business of counseling, but many research studies in which it has figured have suggested that it does reveal some basic attitudes. The scores here, of course, have the same limitations as the Kuder scores, since they are based on choices, so that each response depends on the subject's attitude to more than one thing.

Down through the years since the 1920's, when psychologists first started thinking seriously about measuring interests, there have been various attempts to evaluate them by so-called "objective" rather than "subjective" means. To do this requires that we set up some situation in which we can get an interest score from what a person *does* rather than from what he *says* about himself. The great advantage such objective tests would have is that scores on them could not be "faked." Some ingenious techniques have been proposed, but so far all of them have shown limitations which prevented them from coming into common use. Information tests centering around processes and terms in different occupations or areas of knowledge certainly reflect interests, but they also measure general intelligence. It is difficult to separate one from the other. Tests of how much a person remembers from different passages he has been allowed to read once tell us something about his interests, but reading ability and general habits of concentration also help to determine such scores. Another method which has been tried is to show movies of work in progress in different occupational settings and then to gauge an individual's interest in such work by the amount he can recall when the show is over (Super and Roper, 1941). Here too, other psychological characteristics besides interest probably figure, and the method has the further disadvantage that the large number of separate occupations we have in our society would make it impractical to show even short films of any considerable number of them. The Army Air Force psychologists during World War II did a considerable amount of research on objective interest measures (Super, 1949, pp. 477-480). Validity coefficients reported for these blanks were promising but not really satisfactoy (about .3).

Thus, the majority of research workers and counselors have continued to use tests of the inventory type, the Strong, Kuder, Allport-Vernon, and a number of others that are similar. We turn now to a summary of what we know about individual differences in interests on the basis of their experience with these inventories.

WHAT DO INTEREST INVENTORIES MEASURE?

One of the most striking things that extensive research has shown is that the patterns of likes and dislikes which identify a person as a member of a certain occupational group are very stable aspects of his personality. Strong (1951b) has accumulated follow-up data on a number of groups first tested during their college years and then retested many years later. The intervals are of different lengths for different occupational groups, the longest twenty-two years. Table 16 summarizes these results. When the set of scores originally making up a person's interest profile is correlated with the set of scores obtained after a long time interval, the individual correlations range from .67 to .88. For the 228 persons in the group with the twenty-two-year interval, the median r was .75. How close the relationship is seems to depend about equally on the length of the interval and the age of the subject at the time he first took the test. The

TABLE 16.

Permanence of Interest Scores

(Strong, 1951 b)

NO. OF SUBJECTS	EDUCATIONAL LEVEL	DATES TESTED	AGE AT TIME OF TEST	INTERVAL IN YEARS BETWEEN TEST AND RETEST	MEDIAN CORRELATION
33	11th Grade	——	17	.06	.86
148	11th Grade	——	17	1.25	.83
57	11th Grade	——	17	2.33	.81
50	College freshmen	1930-31	19	1	.88
50	College freshmen	1930-39	19	9	.67
50	College freshmen	1930-49	19	19	.72
50	College freshmen	1931-39	20	8	.72
50	College freshmen	1931-49	20	18	.72
50	College seniors	1927-32	22	5	.84
50	College seniors	1927-37	22	10	.82
228	College seniors	1927-49	22	22	.75
50	College seniors	1932-37	27	5	.86
50	College seniors	1932-49	27	17	.84
50	College freshmen	1939-49	28	10	.87
50	College seniors	1937-49	32	12	.88

TABLE 17.

Change in Letter Grade Scores on the Vocational Interest Blank for
181 Boys Tested as High-School Seniors and
Retested Two Years Later as
College Students

(Stordahl, 1954)

TEST		RETEST							
LETTER GRADE	N	% C	% C+	% B—	% B	% B+	% A	TOTAL	
A	804	2	3	6	10	19	60	100	
B+	761	4	6	13	21	26	30	100	
B	1,106	8	12	20	23	20	17	100	
B—	1,394	19	16	24	20	12	9	100	
C+	1,300	31	23	22	15	6	3	100	
C	2,599	68	15	9	5	2	1	100	

high level of the correlations generally would suggest, however, that permanence in vocational interest pattern is the rule, not the exception.

Trinkaus (1954) has reported results from a follow-up study of 308 Yale alumni about fifteen years after they first took the Strong test as college freshmen. Stordahl (1954) studied University of Minnesota students who had taken the Strong test two years before as high-school seniors. In both these studies, Strong's findings with regard to the stability of interest patterns was verified. Table 17 shows what Stordahl found with regard to letter grades. It can be seen that 60 per cent of the A's remain A after two years; 79 per cent of them are A or B+. The C's are even more stable, with 68 per cent remaining C and 83 per cent C or C+.

It is apparent from all these studies of interest stability, however, that there are *individual* differences with regard to it. Most persons change very little, but some few change a great deal. This fact shows up most clearly in studies of high-school students. Finch (1935), Taylor (1942), Carter (1940), and Taylor and Carter (1942) have shown that stability of interest pattern is the *rule* even for subjects as young as sixteen. But always in a few cases, the correlations between sets of scores obtained on two occasions turn out to be *negative;* in other cases they are so low that attempts to predict the later from the earlier interests would have been seriously in error.

Work on the Kuder has been less extensive, but here too there is some evidence that a fair amount of stability in obtained pattern is the rule rather than the exception. Reid (1951), testing college subjects, found a median correlation of .77 for sets of scores separated by a fifteen-month interval. Rosenberg (1953), with high-school subjects tested in the ninth grade and again in the twelfth, obtained correlations ranging from .47 to .75. Herzberg and Bouton (1954) have reported similar correlations for intervals up to four years. In all these studies, as in the Strong studies, there are marked changes in some individuals (Mallinson and Crumrine, 1952).

This question of why a minority of students change their scores over a period of time during which the majority have shown almost no change is of considerale interest to counselors. One of the most obvious possible reasons is a fact which must always be taken into consideration when interest tests are used. Like most personality inventories, these tests are easily faked (Longstaff, 1948). If a student has any reason to suppose that some types of response are more acceptable than others, the likes and dislikes he encircles on the Strong or the choices he makes on the Kuder will reflect this attitude. In such a case one would not expect him to get the same scores when retested under other conditions. It seems reasonable to suppose that when group testing is carried on in the schoolroom, some subjects may see the situation differently from others. To what extent such changes in sets or attitudes may account for the apparent changes in interest pattern has not as yet been investigated. In many counseling situations, and in all selection situations, the user of interest tests must be aware of the possibility that a score has been faked.

Another obvious possible reason for interest change is occupational experience. This one has been investigated and seems *not* to be important. Strong has shown (1943, Ch. 15) that a person's interest pattern develops prior to the selection of an occupation, and is not much affected by subsequent work experience. There is evidence in a study by Bordin and Wilson (1953), however, that curricular shifts in college freshmen are related in a rather complex way to interest changes on the Kuder test. The authors interpret this to mean that when reality factors force a change in an individual's self-percept, his measured interests change with it. In summary we can say that measured interests tend to have considerable stability, but that the meaning of interest changes in some individuals is still not understood, and that the problem deserves more attention than it has as yet received.

The second thing that Strong's extensive research permits us to say with considerable certainty is that measured occupational interests are tied in with the choice of a suitable occupation and the tendency to continue in it. Strong has centered his follow-up work around the validation of four propositions (Strong, 1943, p. 388).

1. Men continuing in occupation A obtain a higher interest score in A than in any other occupation.
2. Men continuing in occupation A obtain a higher interest score in it than do other men entering other occupations.
3. Men continuing in occupation A obtain higher scores in A than do men who change from A to another occupation.
4. Men changing from occupation A to occupation B score higher in B prior to the change than in any other occupation, including A.

On the whole it can be said that all the follow-up studies support these propositions. The most extensive evidence has been obtained for physicians (Strong, 1952b) and engineers (Strong, 1952a), but the figures for the group in general appear to follow the same pattern (Strong, 1951a). The men who stay with a profession over a twenty-year period are found to have had higher interest scores for that profession when they were undergraduates than the men who shift away from the occupation at some time during the twenty years. It is to be remembered that the scores were obtained prior to their entry into the profession, so that we cannot say that they are based on experience with the work itself. There is a possibility that the occupational choices and shifts that the subjects made were influenced by their knowledge of their interest test scores, since they seem to have been given the results in return for their coöperation in filling out the blank (Strong, 1943, p. 389). It seems unlikely, however, that this knowledge could account for the correspondences between scores and ultimate occupational placement, since students do not ordinarily make their decisions on the basis of one set of test scores. Aside from this one point of doubt, the evidence for the validity of the Strong blank as a measure of some kind of motivation that enters into occupational adjustment is impressive.

Further evidence of this sort comes from the Terman and Oden (1947) follow-up study of gifted children, to be discussed in greater detail in a later chapter. Almost twenty years after the subjects had first been studied as children, the 20 per cent of them who had turned out to be most successful were compared with the 20 per cent who had achieved the least. (These were all subjects who had possessed IQ's of 140 or higher in childhood, so that the general intelligence necessary for success was known to be present in all cases.) One of the most striking differences that was found between the two groups was with regard to vocational interests. A significantly larger proportion of the successful were engaged in occupations for which the Strong blank gave them an A rating. Furthermore, there were a larger number in the unsuccessful group who failed to show any clear pattern of interests on the Strong and whose occupational record showed many shifts from one thing to another (Terman and Oden, 1947, pp. 324-326).

Work with the Strong blank has thus suggested that occupational interests are related to stability and satisfaction in one's life work. There is little direct evidence on this point using other interest tests. Kuder has accumulated data from groups of persons in many different occupations (see Manual). In general his findings would fit in with the more extensive data from the Strong studies. Persons in a given occupation show the kind of profiles one would expect from them. Accountants are highest on Computational and Clerical interests; laboratory technicians show a peak on Scientific, salesmen on Persuasive interests. With this test as with the Strong, there are a few studies, cited by Kuder in the Manual, pointing to differences between satisfied and dissatisfied workers. Satisfied workers are more likely to have the pattern of interests one would expect to go with their jobs.

One study (Levine and Wallen, 1954) followed up 124 students who had taken the Kuder test in high school after intervals of from seven to nine years and classified the occupations in which they were working according to Kuder's categories. The authors then compared the interest scores on each scale for the group of subjects who were in the occupation corresponding to it and the group of subjects who were not. In almost all the comparisons there was a significant difference in the expected direction. Men who were now found in mechanical occupations, for example, had averaged 81.6 on the mechanical key at the time of the original Kuder test, as compared with 69.5 for non-mechanical workers. This difference is significant at the 5 per cent level. Others reach the 1 per cent level. This corroboration of Strong's findings would seem to indicate that interests are related to occupational placement regardless of the specific way they are measured.

Along with research on specific occupational groups, there has been a constant effort to systematize the knowledge about interests as it was obtained. An important question has been, "What are the principal *dimensions* of vocational interests?" If vocational counselors had to think in terms of a specific interest pattern for each of the more than 30,000 separate jobs that have been identified and described, their task of helping an individual find a suitable occupation would be impossibly difficult. Thinking in terms of families of occupations, each characterized by a common interest pattern, seems to be necessary.

For a test constructed in the manner of the Kuder, the titles of the scales themselves constitute such principal dimensions. The items included in any one scale are there because they correlate with one another and do not correlate with scores on the other scales. The table of intercorrelations in the Kuder manual shows that on the whole these separate scores have turned out to be quite independent of one another. There are a few moderately high correlations ($-.519$ between Persuasive and Outdoor, for example, and .544 between Clerical and Computational), but the great majority of them are near zero. The method by which this test was constructed does not guarantee that we have all the principal dimensions of interests represented in it, but it does organize the specific choices we do have in this way.

Work done with the Strong and similar inventories of likes and dislikes did not furnish any such ready-made system for classifying the kinds of interests we measure. Here the procedure has been to correlate the scores obtained by some representative group of people on all the various occupational scales and to examine these correlations for evidence of similarity between occupational scales. It is possible then to apply factor-analysis methods if we wish to do so. Strong has preferred to base his classification on the correlations themselves rather than on the factors derived from them. By including in each group the scales that correlate more than .60

with one another, he arrived at the following arrangement of men's occupations:

Group I: Artist, Psychologist, Architect, Physician, Osteopath, Dentist, Veterinarian
Group II: Physicist, Chemist, Mathematician, Engineer
Group III: Production Manager
Group IV: Farmer, Carpenter, Printer, Mathematics-Science Teacher, Policeman, Forest Service, Army Officer, Aviator
Group V: Y.M.C.A. Physical Director, Personnel Manager, Public Administrator, Vocational Counselor, Y.M.C.A. Secretary, Social Science Teacher, City School Superintendent, Minister
Group VI: Musician
Group VII: C.P.A. Partner
Group VIII: Senior C.P.A., Junior Accountant, Office Worker, Purchasing Agent, Banker, Mortician, Pharmacist
Group IX: Sales Manager, Real Estate Salesman, Life Insurance Salesman
Group X: Advertising Man, Lawyer, Author-Journalist
Group XI: President, Manufacturing Concern

The word "Group" is hardly applicable to III, VI, VII, and XI, since each is made up of only one occupation. Whether there is actually something unique about these types of work, or whether it just happens that as yet no keys have been constructed for occupations similar to them, cannot be determined. In using the Strong blank in counseling, emphasis falls on Group I, which can be called a "Human Science" type of interests; Group II, Physical Science; Group IV, Technical and Non-professional; Group V, Social Welfare; Group VIII, Business Detail; Group IX, Business Contact; and Group X, Verbal. Scales for measuring the interests of the group as a whole have been worked out in I, II, V, VIII, IX, and X.

Strong made a similar analysis of correlations for the women's blank. The fact that there are fewer separate occupational scales than for the men's blank makes the classification based upon correlations between them more uncertain. It is as follows:

Group I: Physician
Group II: Dentist
Group III: Mathematics-Science Teacher
Group IV: Nurse
Group V: Housewife, Office Worker, Stenographer
Group VI: Life Insurance Saleswoman
Group VII: Social Science Teacher, Y.W.C.A. Secretary
Group VIII: Social Worker, Lawyer
Group IX: English Teacher
Group X: Librarian, Artist, Author

The thing which has always characterized the results obtained in counseling situations where the women's blank is used is that what appears above as Group V is by far the most common variety of interest in girls. Factor-analysis results classify "Nurse" with this group also. It has been variously named "Non-professional interests," "Interest in working for the convenience of others," and "Interest in male association." Perhaps it might best be called "Typical Feminine Interests." The presence of this common core of similar likes and dislikes in the great majority of women and girls seems to constitute a factor differentiating feminine from masculine interests. No such standard set of attitudes has appeared in males. This sex difference may be one of degree, however, since there is a strong tendency for most high school boys to score high on the Group IV scales, which we might call "Typical Masculine Interests."

When working with the Strong test or others for which scoring keys have been constructed in the same manner, we must always remember that the method itself maximizes *differences* between various groups and does not really give them a chance to show how much they are *alike*. When we include a Dislike response to the item "Auctioneer" in the key for engineering interest because it is chosen by 83 per cent of the engineers as compared with 65 per cent of the non-engineers, the use of the scoring key does not tell us how unpopular this occupation is with everybody, a fact which is readily apparent when we look at the percentages themselves. Strong's cautions about this (Strong, 1943, Ch. 6) have not had the attention they deserve. When we correlate the percentages themselves for any two different groups—figures like the 65 and 83 given above—we find that there is considerable agreement among groups in the rankings they give the various activities. Some things are popular with all, others unpopular. The correlation between percentages for twenty-five and fifty-five-year old men, for example, is .88. For college men versus college women it is .74. For Engineers versus Life Insurance Men it is .68.

Another interesting finding with the Strong inventory is what has been called the "point of reference" phenomenon. If we compare physicians, lawyers, or ministers with men chosen as a representative sample of the great mass of American workers, we find that the scales developed in this way correlate very highly with one another. However, if we compare physicians, lawyers, or ministers with a group made up of men in the other *professions*, the scales we obtain are much more specific and do not correlate with one another to any great extent. Why is this? It seems to mean simply that professional men as a whole differ more from lower-level workers than physicians differ from lawyers. It is only when we leave out the lower-level men from our comparison group that the differences between specific professions get a chance to show up. This is where the "point of reference" concept comes in. From the standpoint of the unskilled worker, all professional men look alike. From a point closer to their own position, differences between them can be observed. Since Strong's work has been concerned almost entirely with groups of men in high-level occupations, we know little about whether this same tendency operates also in the reverse direction. Are railroad section men and janitors, for example, as distinguishable as physicians and lawyers? Work on such problems has been delayed because there is no practical demand for it. These jobs are not usually chosen deliberately, and thus they are not discussed in vocational counseling situations. It would be useful to know more than we now do about the interests of men in the occupations that include the bulk of the working population. Research which has been going on in the armed services may eventually throw some light on this problem.

An outgrowth of the realization that other factors besides the specific occupational group to which a person belongs help to determine the pattern of likes and dislikes he shows has led to the development of several non-occupational scales for the Strong blank. Most closely related to the foregoing discussion of the point of reference is the "Occupational Level" scale which was constructed by comparing item-response percentages for a group of unskilled men with those for a group of successful business and professional men. Another is the "Interest Maturity" scale made up of items which differentiated older and younger men. Another is the M-F scale made up of items on which men and women differ significantly. The most recent of these non-occupational scoring keys is the "Specialization Level" scale which differentiates between the interests of specialists and general practitioners in the field of medicine, and which probably indicates for other professions as well the extent to which an individual would find satisfaction in advanced study leading to specialized work in a narrow area.

As with all tests that come to be widely used in practice and research, evidence keeps accumulating about the nature of the trait that interest blanks are measuring. The thing we know with most certainty is that it is a motivational characteristic having to do with the choice of a certain type of occupation and the tendency to continue in it. It would seem, however, that such motivational characteristics are almost completely independent of the *abilities* that make for different degrees of success within an occupation. Correlations between numerical interest scores and occupational and educational criterion measurements generally turn out low, although there are a few reports which suggest that inclusion of interest tests in a predictive battery may add something to the accuracy of the prediction. (See Super, 1949, Chs. 17 and 18.) In only one occupation, Life Insurance Selling, has it been clearly demonstrated that men with "A" Strong scores on the key for the occupation make higher incomes than those with the lower letter grades (Strong, 1943, Ch. 19). The bulk of the evidence should make us very cautious about predicting *success* in a course or an occupation from interest scores.

In a more general sense, it is true, the Terman and Oden study of men and women who once were gifted children would point to some sort of relationship between interests and success. Persons who have interest scores very different from those characteristic of people in the occupations they enter, or persons who have no well-developed pattern of interests at all, are less likely to achieve all-round success than are the others for whom the correspondence between test results and life plans is closer. The question interest tests answer is, "Does this man have the outlook characteristic of men who have succeeded with this occupation?", rather than, "*How much* of the trait necessary for success does he possess?"

One study of the relationship of interest scores to scholarship was based on a more complex hypothesis. Fredericsen and Melville (1954) separated a group of engineering students into "compulsive" and "noncompulsive" subgroups. The hypothesis was that in the case of compulsive (thorough, perfectionistic) persons, one would not expect much correlation between interests and grades, since they would be likely to work hard at everything. In noncompulsive persons, however, one would expect a correlation between interests and grades to appear. Some might object to the means by which these investigators made the compulsive-noncompulsive judgment (by the use of the Strong Accountant scale and by a combination of vocabulary and reading speed scores). But the interesting result is that the predicted difference in correlations did occur. The coefficients were about zero for the compulsive, whereas a number of them were .3 or higher for the noncompulsives.

The attempt to fit interest measurement into general personality theory seems important to many psychologists who have done research with interest tests. There has been a considerable amount of research designed to explore the relationships between occupational interest scores and the *scores* on other types of personality test. Since interest, in the broad sense, is a matter of motivation, it might be expected that interesting correlations with other measures of motivation would be found. What we find when we examine research of this sort, however, is a whole succession of near-zero correlations between interest tests and the personality inventories which have grown out of psychiatric thinking. No one kind of interest appears to be consistently related to *maladjustment* in any of its common forms. In the most extensive study of this sort, Cottle (1950) administered the Strong, the Kuder, the MMPI, and the Bell Adjustment Inventory to 400 male veterans and then made a factor analysis of the correlations between subscores. Of the seven factors that could be identified, none was common to both personality and interest tests.

Such a result is not completely convincing because of statistical artifacts. We have already mentioned the ambiguity with regard to the nature of the measurement system represented by scores on the Strong scales. Since each of the tests Cottle used differed in the way the scoring keys were derived, it is perhaps natural that the subscores of any one of them would correlate with one another more highly than they correlated with scores on another test. Furthermore, the fact that different scores obtained from any one blank are based on responses to some of the same items makes for some extra correlation between them.

It seems unlikely, however, that such statistical complications completely explain the failure to obtain factors common to interest and adjustment inventories, since sizable correlations have been obtained when personality tests of a non-psychiatric variety are used. Some of the Strong and Kuder scales for measuring the same sorts of interest, for example, correlate to the extent of about .60 (Triggs, 1944a and b), different as they are in derivation and form. Subscores on the Strong also correlate with similar-appearing subscores on the Allport-Vernon Study of Values (Sarbin and Berdie, 1940), and factors obtained from such correlations show loadings based on both tests (Ferguson, Humphreys, and Strong, 1941). The bulk of the evidence would suggest that occupational interests and types of maladjustment are relatively independent of one another. There may be a few exceptions to this generalization. Steinberg (1952), for example, found that a group of neurotic veterans were lower than average on the Kuder Mechanical scale, higher than average on the Musical and Literary scales, suggesting their neuroticism may be related to preferences for imaginative rather than realistic activities. While the differences between groups on these three scales were statistically significant, two of them at the 1 per cent level, they were not large. They would not warrant a judgment that an individual with literary interests is maladjusted.

It is perhaps impossible completely to settle the question of the place of interests in the total personality by means of tests like the Strong and Kuder which were developed for specialized uses in vocational psychology.

There is no reason to suppose that such tests cover *all* the areas of human interests. There has been one factor-analytic study in which the variables correlated were based on an unusually broad survey of types of human motivation (Guilford *et al.*, 1954). Variables like *Aggression* and *Altruism* were thrown into the initial correlation matrix along with *Business* and *Mechanical* interests. A liking for humor and a need for affection were included along with preferences for outdoor activity or social science subject matter. For each motivational variable, the score was based on ten items to which the subject was asked to respond. Two huge correlation matrices, 95 x 95, resulted from the administration of these tests to 600 airmen and 720 officer candidates. The size of the groups makes for dependability of the factor loadings. There turned out to be twenty-four factors for the airmen, twenty-three for the officers. Seventeen of them were common to the two analyses. They were named as follows:

A. Mechanical Interest
B. Scientific Interest
C. Adventure vs. Security
D. Social Welfare
E. Aesthetic Appreciation
F. Cultural Conformity
G. Self-reliance vs. Dependence
H. Aesthetic Expression
I. Clerical Interest
J. Need for Diversion
K. Artistic Thinking
L. Need for Attention
M. Resistance to Restriction
N. Business Interest
O. Outdoor-Work Interest
P. Physical Drive
Q. Aggression

It is interesting to note that the specifically vocational clusters of interests still separate themselves out, even where all the scores are statistically comparable and each item is included in only one original test. Factors A, B, D, I, and N are similar to Strong's groups and to Kuder's scales. For some factors the correspondence with previous interpretations of basic interests is not so close. Instead of getting separate factors for musical, artistic, and literary types of interest, for example, the two basic aesthetic factors show up as Aesthetic Appreciation and Aesthetic Expression.

It is possible that a broader and thus more satisfactory interest inventory than any presently available can be constructed on the basis of factor analysis. The only one so far to be developed in this way is that of Guilford, Schneidman, and Zimmerman (1948), and this does not correspond in all particulars to what was discovered in the later and bigger factor analysis. For practical purposes, however, we must remember that it will take years to accumulate for such a test the body of validity information that makes the Strong blank so meaningful.

Why should clusters of likes, dislikes, and preferences centering around kinds of *occupations* show up as basic stable dimensions of personality? It seems obvious that one could not possibly be born with the interests of an engineer or a social worker, and that something about an individual's environment must shape his motivation into such patterns. Bordin (1943) has suggested that they represent the way in which the person sees himself expressed in terms of occupational stereotypes. This interpretation fits in with results Tyler (1955) has obtained from investigations of interest differences in young children. The earliest type of differentiation to show up is that between males and females. Even at the first-grade level clear sex differences are apparent. Among nine- or ten-year-olds, factors seem to represent more finely differentiated perceptions of the sort of person one ought or ought not to be. In boys, for example, the rejection of "sissy" behavior of all sorts seems to be one such factor around which interests are organized, and the rejection of "work" behavior seems to be another. In girls, the rejection of aggressive, violent kinds of activity acts as such an interest organizer.

It seems possible also that a person's *dislikes* are of more crucial importance than the *likes* in defining the pattern of his interests. When one examines the items that enter into the various scoring keys for the Strong blank, he finds that, in general, more *dislike* responses than *likes* are scored. An unpublished study of my own based on the Strong scores of 50 college boys indicated that scores based on *dislike* responses alone correlated more highly with full score than did scores based on *like* responses alone for all the group scales and for occupational level. The analysis of responses made by children to the items on the interest blank used in the study cited above (Tyler, 1955) pointed even more clearly to the importance of *dislike* responses in defining individual patterns of motivation. Nine- and ten-year-old children mark the "L" response for the great majority of the items on an inventory of activities appropriate to their age level. In order to distinguish between persons we have to direct our attention to the minority of these items upon which a fair number of *dislike* responses appear. The older and the brighter children tend to mark more dislikes than the younger and the duller. It seems that the individual differences in interests which the Strong reveals to us may develop through a process of gradual *ruling out* of whole sets of activities that are seen to be inappropriate. Very young children are enthusiastic about almost any new toy, game, or activity. Adults do not even consider for themselves a large proportion of the activities available to them.

The whole process of the development and meaning of differential patterns of likes and dislikes is complicated, however, and as yet very inadequately understood. There is some evidence that *too* restricted a range of interests is indicative of neuroticism or maladjustment (Berdie, 1945). Strong (1943, p. 339) cites a study by Jacobsen showing that for students of superior intelligence, the high-scholarship group gave like responses to far more items than did the low-scholarship group. J. E. Anderson (1952) has reported results for 3,200 children who were asked to respond to a list of chores and tasks. The better-adjusted children showed larger L:D ratios than the less well-adjusted. Another fact familiar to Strong users must also be fitted in here. As men pass from adolescence to adulthood their scores on Group V, social service occupations, tends to increase. Group V is the scale most dependent upon *like* responses.

There are not enough data to warrant any final conclusion as to the meaning of *like* and *dislike* responses, and some of the information we have seems to be contradictory. It would seem possible that the two types of response are not, as we have been assuming, opposite ends of the same continuum. A person's positive interests and enthusiasms may represent one process in personality development, his dislikes quite a different one. The latter, the process by which a person establishes the limits within which he, as an individual, will be content to function, has scarcely been studied at all. It may be that realistic limits, represented by a moderate number of clear *dislike* responses on an interest inventory, are conducive to the constructive sort of motivation upon which success depends, whereas a general negative or fearful attitude, which might be represented by a large number of *dislike* responses, goes with maladjustment.

One type of research finding that may be in some way related to the foregoing problem is the evidence for the high stability of C scores on the Strong test. The follow-up studies show quite consistently that C's and A's are less subject to change than the intermediate ratings are, but that C's are even more stable than A's. It is thus possible to name with more certainty the occupational groups to which a person does *not* belong than the ones to which he does belong. This is not identical with the problems of the significance of *like* and *dislike* responses, since both negative and positive answers contribute to both A and C scores. It should, however, remind us that we should look at both sides of the picture whenever interests are in question. Darley and Hagenah, in their forthcoming book on the clinical use of the Strong test, place considerable emphasis on *reject* patterns, which they define as groups of related scales on which all of an individual's scores are *below* the chance level.

We see then that interest measurement, which began with the practical task of constructing useful counseling tools, has reached the place where it is confronted with complex theoretical problems. The traits that interest tests are measuring must now be given a place in our thinking about personality. As yet there is no general agreement on what that place is. Strong, who undoubtedly has earned the right to first consideration, thinks of interests as simple qualities of pleasantness and unpleasantness which a person finds in his activities. Interests are discovered rather than learned. According to this point of view, they are part of what is "given" in human nature. It is no more necessary to explain them in terms of anything outside themselves than it is to explain why men find the odor of a rose pleasant, of garbage unpleasant. Darley holds that interests are expressions of basic personality *needs*, for security, for achievement and recognition, for prestige or power.[3] Bordin (1943) does not attempt to explain what interests themselves are, but tries rather to explain why an individual *says* what he does about himself when confronted by an interest blank. "In answering a vocational interest inventory an individual is expressing his acceptance of a particular view or concept of himself in terms of occupational stereotypes." (1943, p. 53) "Stereotype" needs to be defined broadly in this connection to include the salient characteristics of any socially defined group of people. The opinions a person has about sex differences, age differences, and social classes play a part in his responses. He is *locating* himself in this complex social structure as he sees it.

There is room for much interesting research here. As time passes and the results of old and new studies are pieced together, we shall be able to see which of these theories of interests or what combination of them best fits all the facts.

[3] The statement of the Strong and Darley views is based on a discussion of the theoretical basis of interests at a conference on *The Counseling Use of the Strong Blank* held at the University of Minnesota, Feb. 7-9, 1955. Proceedings are to be published by the University of Minnesota Press.

BASIC PATTERNS OF SOCIAL, ECONOMIC, AND POLITICAL ATTITUDES

The development of scales for measuring attitudes grew out of research that social psychologists wished to do on social problems. They were interested in finding out such things as whether groups with different economic backgrounds take different positions on political issues, or whether some experimental influence—a speech, for example, or a movie—changes the attitudes of subjects exposed to it. Although such group differences on specific issues have been reported since the early 1930's, individual attitude differences as an aspect of personality, and the nature of the basic attitude dimensions, have only recently come into prominence as research problems.

There have been two standard methods for the construction of attitude-measuring devices. Whichever procedure is to be followed later, the first step is to write a large number of simple statements representing all shades of opinion on the issue in question. In the Thurstone method of attitude-scale construction, judges then sort these statements into categories corresponding to discriminable differences in the attitude to be scaled. In building a scale to measure attitudes toward war, for example, a statement like "War is always wrong under all circumstances" would be placed in the extreme category at one end; a statement like "A country should declare war whenever its basic interests are threatened" would go into a category somewhere near the other end. Most statements would be classified in intermediate categories. Scale values are assigned to statements on the basis of the sortings the judges make. Once these values have been fixed, a respondent can be given an attitude score by simply averaging the numbers for the statements he endorses.

The second of the two most common methods of scale construction, originated by Likert, requires that the basic data be obtained from respondents rather than from judges. Items on both sides of an issue are presented to a large group of subjects similar to those whose attitudes are to be eventually measured. They are asked to indicate for each item their feeling about it, marking "Strongly Agree," "Agree," "Undecided," "Disagree," or "Strongly Disagree." By giving each of these responses a numerical weight, a total score for each respondent on the attitude can be obtained. Irrelevant and non-discriminating items are then pruned off by customary item-analysis methods, and the revised scale standardized for use in new groups. There are a number of other techniques for the construction of attitude scales, and various combinations of methods have been tried, but most of what we know about the relationship of attitudes to personality is based on work with Thurstone and Likert-type scales.

As with other types of measurement, factor analysis has been the favorite method used in the attempt to bring some order into a complex mass of data. A good summary of all this work is to be found in Eysenck (1953b). The problem for the factor analysts turned out to be somewhat different from the ones they had encountered in their work with ability measurements. No clear-cut simple structure emerged from the factor loadings. In other words, there seemed to be few if any specific attitudes that could be described in terms of one attitude dimension alone. More than one basic attitude seemed to be involved in the responses a subject made to any statement, whether it was about war, birth control, or communism. The most reasonable solution obtained by the typical American factor methods with rotation to something approaching simple structure was Ferguson's (1944). He named the three factors he had found "religionism," "humanitarianism," and "nationalism."

Eysenck (1953b, Ch. 7), using the typical English factor methods and utilizing a very careful selection of attitude items and respondents, came out with two main factors which he labeled R (radicalism vs. conservatism) and T (tough-mindedness vs. tender-mindedness). Figure 32 shows how specific attitudes are related to these principal dimensions. Pacifists, for example, are high in both radicalism and tender-mindedness. Those who endorse "My country, right or wrong," on the other hand, are both conservative and tough-minded. The strongest argument for the use of this structure to describe basic attitudes comes from a comparison of some well-defined political groups in England. The same items that defined the R factor were the ones that differentiated most clearly between Conservative and Labor party members. Working-class subjects were higher on the T factor than middle-class subjects, whatever their party affiliation, and both communists and fascists were higher on this T factor than were members of the three democratic parties.

Eysenck's results are not so different from Ferguson's as one might think if he examined simply the names of the factors. The relationships between attitudes are similar, but Ferguson's proposed factor axes would be at about a forty-five degree angle from Eysenck's. His "religionism" is defined by items in the conservative-tender-minded quadrant, his "humanitarianism" by items in the radical-tender-minded quadrant. Which of these systems one prefers to follow makes little difference. Eysenck prefers his primarily because it corresponds better to the distinctions

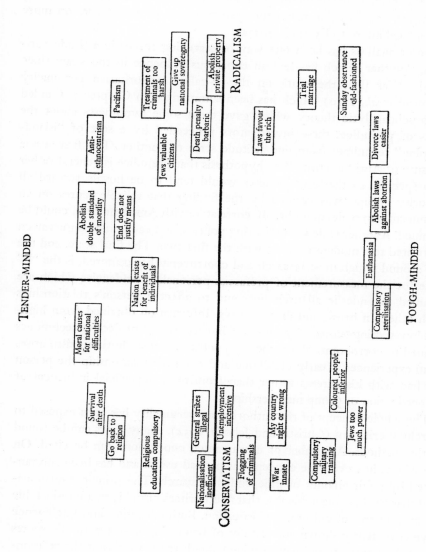

FIGURE 32. The two primary social attitudes (Eysenck, 1951).

society now makes. It is more natural to classify people as radicals and conservatives than as religionists and humanitarians. His demonstration that the pattern of relationships among attitudes is similar in England, Germany, and Sweden makes the system he has proposed take on more than a local interest (Eysenck, 1953a).

Factor analysis has been one way of searching for basic attitude variables. Another which has had an enormous influence in the years since World War II is the work on the so-called authoritarian personality (Adorno et al., 1950) which has been summarized in Chapter 7. Guided by psychoanalytic theory which gave them some hypotheses about the roots of prejudice, these investigators proceeded by a sort of "island-hopping" technique from one attitude scale to another. The first was a measure of Anti-Semitism. The hypothesis that prejudice is general rather than specific, so that Anti-Semites would tend to be hostile toward all minority groups, was verified by the finding that reliable scores on an Ethnocentrism scale, quite highly correlated with Anti-Semitism, could be obtained. Another scale for measuring political and economic conservatism correlated to a moderate extent with the first two. The final scale, and the one around which most research and controversy has centered, is the "F" scale for the measurement of prefascist personality tendencies which are assumed to underlie all prejudices and to affect a person's relationships with others in broad and diverse ways. Information obtained from high- and low-scoring subjects by means of interviews and projective techniques seemed to corroborate the authors' hypothesis that authoritarianism arises from experiences in early childhood and from the relationship the person has had with his parents rather than from more superficial influences of indoctrination or group membership.

The whole concept of the authoritarian personality has been exposed to searching criticism (Christie and Jahoda, 1954). Many flaws can be found in the methods. A number of unwarranted conclusions can be cited. On the whole, however, the concept has proved useful and has been substantiated by a fair amount of independent research. The principal qualification that has become evident is that "authoritarianism" is to a considerable extent a matter of cultural sophistication. Both education and intelligence have consistently shown correlations of from $-.4$ to $-.5$ with "F" scores when the groups tested have a wide enough range to permit the relationship to show up. It is still a possibility that childhood training is really the significant variable, since families at different social levels have different practices. But we cannot assume that the relationships between all the kinds of attitude items that make up the "E" and "F" scales will remain the same when we move from one cultural group to another. There is in this volume of critical studies some clear evidence that such relationships do change. (See, for example, pp. 135-136 and pp. 174-175.)

Eysenck (1953b, p. 239) shows that the syndrome of authoritarian attitudes can be understood as the opposite end of Ferguson's humanitarianism, or as a cluster falling in the quadrant defined by high scores on both conservatism and tough-mindedness in the Eysenck scheme (see Figure 32). Although he thus sees in this body of research nothing that contradicts the findings of the factor analysts, he holds that the isolation of dimensions ought to precede rather than to follow the accumulation of personality data.

Whichever of these systems of basic variables we choose to work with, we can recognize that it has been a genuine achievement to have laid bare enough of the basic structure of primary attitudes so that the systems can be made congruent with one another. These variables, whatever we decide to call them, may turn out to be among the most important traits we have succeeded in measuring. Their relationships to interests and to many other personality variables have yet to be explored.

SUMMARY

Interests were investigated first by applied psychologists who needed to take them into consideration in vocational guidance. The Strong and the Kuder blanks, developed in different ways, have come into general use. A large amount of work with the Strong blank over a long period of time has demonstrated that the characteristics it measures are remarkably stable and that they reflect aspects of motivation that are important in a person's adjustment to his work. Results with the Kuder over a shorter period point to the same conclusions.

Correlational analyses have shown that there is a limited number of broad types of occupational interest rather than a large number of specific interest patterns. These would seem to be based on self-concepts or roles the person sees himself as playing rather than on experiences with work itself, since they appear before he enters any occupation. Interest scores of any type have not usually correlated to a significant extent with neuroticism or maladjustment, but they are related to other kinds of personality variables such as values.

The basic dimensions of social attitudes, as measured by specific attitude scales, have been labeled "radicalism vs. conservatism" and "tough-mindedness vs. tender-mindedness" by Eysenck, who has carried out extensive factor analyses. This system of classification is compatible with most of the other factor-analytic evidence as well as with the "authoritarian" syndrome which has been investigated by a combination of clinical and statistical methods.

The sources of these stable interest and attitude patterns in individual personalities are still not well understood. It is thought that they grow out of childhood experience, but much research must be done before it is clear how this occurs. The effort to incorporate this material in personality theories has only recently been made.

CHAPTER 9

Individual Differences in Perception

DEVELOPMENT OF INTEREST IN THE TOPIC

IT WAS NOT until 1953 that *Psychological Abstracts* found it necessary to include in their index the heading "Individual Differences in Perception." Research in the field of perception has been going on unceasingly since the days when the early psychological laboratories were founded. The measurement of individual differences in intelligence, special abilities, and personality traits has almost as long a history. But until about 1950 very little had been done to connect the two. The possibility that the world might actually look and sound and feel differently to different persons, and that the same pattern of stimulation might carry different immediate meanings for different observers was not usually taken into account.

It is true that the early workers in the field of mental measurement did stress differences in sensory and perceptual characteristics. Galton (1883) devised tests of weight discrimination and sensitivity to high tones, and tried to find out what forms the imagery of different subjects took. J. McK. Cattell and Farrand (1896) published the results from a group of 100 college students on a battery of tests that included a considerable number measuring perceptual differences—keenness of eyesight and hearing, color vision, perception of pitch and of weights, sensitivity to pain, and time perception. Jastrow (see Peterson, 1925) displayed a collection of psychological apparatus and tests at the Columbian Exposition in Chicago in 1893, and invited interested persons to take them. They included tests of cutaneous and kinesthetic sensibility, such as estimation of the distance of an unseen movement of one's finger and the estimation of a surface by touch, as well as the common measures of visual acuity, color vision, and speed and accuracy of movement. At about the same time, J. A. Gilbert (1897) gave similar perceptual and motor tests to several hundred children and compared them with measures of physical growth. Thus even before 1900 it had been demonstrated that accurate measurement of differences in many perceptual characteristics was possible. Why then did half a century elapse before work of this sort again became a major research interest?

The reason seems to be that research in individual differences has a practical orientation and is continued only when some possibility for application presents itself. Especially at the time when differential psychology was just getting started, differences in measured traits needed to be correlated with criterion measurements of some sort before anyone took much interest in them. The aim of the early mental testers was to measure intelligence. When the evidence began to come in (Sharp, 1898-99; Wissler, 1901) that tests of this sort showed very little relationship to school success, the enthusiasm of psychologists for the whole mental-test movement was considerably dampened. Since tests of the kind that Binet and Henri (1896) had been recommending, tapping complex intellectual characteristics rather than perceptual sensitivities, stood up better under this kind of evaluation, they set the pattern for the later work, and the attempt to measure perceptual differences was largely abandoned.

The rise of Gestalt psychology and its signal successes in clarifying the nature of perceptual processes probably served also to play down the importance of individual differences. Gestalt workers focused their attention on phenomena for which striking similarities between subjects are the rule —apparent movement, figure and ground, tendencies toward closure and "pragnanz," the constancy effects. Since the aim of much of this research was to enable them to make inferences about the nature of the brain as an electro-physical system, individual differences were not explored. The phenomena can be demonstrated in every person who carefully examines his own experience, and it is not necessary to use large groups of subjects in order to demonstrate their existence. Thus many crucial studies were done with small numbers and without benefit of the types of statistical treatment that would show us how much individual variation from the reported mean performances actually occurs.

There was one of the perceptual characteristics the Gestalt psychologists had stressed that lent itself to quantitative treatment much earlier than the rest—the constancy phenomenon. Thouless (1951) has summarized some of his own work on the constancy phenomena, for which he coined the new term *phenomenal regression*, work going back as far as 1932. It is to be remembered that "constancy" refers to the tendency we all show to react to objects in space in terms of their *known* size, shape, and color rather than in terms of the image that is actually being projected onto the retina. As material for differential psychology, this family of experiments has the advantage of permitting very accurate measurement. Just how much size constancy a subject is experiencing can be determined by having him match a far object to a near one. The size of both objects and the distances to them can be measured as accurately as we like. Thouless showed that there were sizable, consistent differences in the matches made by different persons. Differences were significant at the .001 level. When the same group of twenty subjects was tested on two different occasions, the correlation between their scores was .876. In another study he showed that the correlation between size and shape constancy measurements for 53 subjects was .65, whereas the correlation between the means of the size and shape measures and color constancy determinations for forty-five subjects was .58. All of these correlations are significant at the .001 level. There can be no doubt that some persons have the constancy experience to a greater degree than do others.

Other studies of the constancy phenomena have confirmed Thouless in his conclusion that there are sizable individual differences, but have left some doubt as to how consistent they are from one type of experimental situation to another. Lichte (1952) gives data for 50 students on shape constancy, measurements which show a considerable range. The correlation of .88 and higher for sets of measurements on the same subjects taken a week apart shows that the differences are stable and accurately measurable as long as we confine ourselves to this one type of task. But Sheehan (1938) who made three kinds of constancy measurements—brightness, shape, and size—on her 25 student subjects found only low correlations between the separate varieties, suggesting that the same people are not necessarily object-oriented or stimulus-oriented in different situations. The question of how general these sets are is still an open one.

It was in connection with their investigations of the effects of attitudes, set, attention, or motivation upon perception that laboratory psychologists were most likely to find it necessary to take individual differences into consideration. In the earlier studies, such factors were usually thought of as something superimposed upon the standard experience of perception rather than as an inextricable part of it. Experiments were set up in such a way as to show that different verbal instructions can change the report subjects give of ambiguous figures, that indistinguishable pictures will more often be seen as food when subjects are hungry, or that experimentally induced frustration tends to disrupt the perceptual process. But it became increasingly clear that some set or attitude in the observer is *always* involved in a perception whether or not the experimenter takes any cognizance of it. As early as 1930, O. O. Anderson (1930) demonstrated the importance of these attitudes and the impossibility of establishing complete experimental control over them. He found that his subjects, three graduate students trained in introspective techniques, were at different times using any one of six attitudes in their perceptual response to visual and auditory stimuli: (1) casual survey of stimulus objects, (2) inquiring survey, (3) critical survey by the observer of himself observing, (4) critical particularizing survey of objects for accurate description, (5) personal valuation, in terms of pleasantness and unpleasantness, and (6) impersonal valuation of objects in terms of some conventional standard. The ease with which any particular set could be adopted differed from one stimulus object to another and from person to person. The attitude adopted in each case seemed to be an aspect of the perceptual experience itself rather than an extra ingredient contributed by the experimenter's instructions.

Gibson (1941) summarized a large number of experiments on "set" including those having a bearing on perception. The gradual extension of the meaning being given to the term "set" becomes very apparent in this series of experiments. At first it was considered a temporary condition created in a subject by the experimenter's instructions. It was soon realized that what was perceived was dependent also on habits developed by past experience and on general expectations arising from the pattern of the total situation. The concept of "set" was extended to include all of these conditions in the perceiver. For the purposes of this discussion it matters little whether "set" is the most appropriate term. The recognition that there are these personal determiners of perceptual experience has opened the way to the investigation of individual differences with regard to them.

In particular it has been the resurgence of interest in the relationship of *motivational* factors to perception, the "new look" in perceptual research, that has led to the active contemporary work on individual differences which we shall consider later in the chapter. It has coincided with a general shift of emphasis in differential psychology from the measurement of cognitive or intellectual traits to the measurement of temperamental or motivational traits. It is perhaps true that the early mental testers abandoned too soon their search for relationships between perceptual differences and significant aspects of intellectual functioning. Some research of the 1950's suggest that there may be more rich ore in this vein than the first prospectors concluded that there was (Krech and Calvin, 1953). But the relationship between perceptual tendencies and personality characteristics seems to be even more striking. Enough significant findings have already appeared to warrant a thorough exploration of this terrain.

THEORIES OF PERCEPTUAL TYPES

Although objective measurement of perceptual-personality relationships is a fairly recent thing, theories about such relationships have a much longer history. A great many typologies have been constructed contrasting persons whose typical ways of experiencing the world differ in one way or another. They are too numerous for detailed consideration, but they do serve as sources of hypotheses and as materials that can be used to corroborate the evidence we get from objective studies. A good summary is available in M. D. Vernon (1952, pp. 247-256).

One of the most frequently recurring of these typologies contrasts the *analyzers* with the *synthesizers*. The analytic observer concentrates on details and tends to see separate parts. The synthetic observer sees the field as an integrated whole but may miss some of its details completely. Various workers cited by Vernon make mention of the fact that subjects spontaneously adopt one or the other attitude in experiments on psychophysical relationships, illusions, or comparisons of complex geometrical forms. Subjects seem to be most successful at a perceptual task when they adopt the attitude that is natural for them.

Another somewhat similar typology contrasts *objective* with *subjective* perceivers. The distinction here is between rigid, narrow consistency in the approach to a perceptual task—such as reading a few letters at a time but getting them all right—and fluctuating, broad inspection with considerable subjective interpretation of what is seen. There is some support for the idea that this may be related to other personality characteristics in the finding by Angyal (1948) that obsessional individuals showed the objective pattern to tachistoscopic materials whereas persons suffering from anxiety or hysteria were more likely to make use of the subjective procedure.

Among children, *active* and *passive* perceivers have been differentiated. Whether this is really a distinction based on fundamental temperamental differences seems doubtful, however, in view of the fact that several investigators have shown the age of the subjects to be an important consideration. Children become more active as well as more accurate in their perceptions as they get older. Hanfmann (1941), however, has noted that intelligent adult subjects approach the task of sorting the Vigotsky blocks into categories in different ways to which the *active* and *passive* labels might well be applied. (*Conceptual* and *perceptual* are the terms Hanfmann uses.) Some of the subjects work rationally, attempting to formulate hypotheses as to what the correct solution might be. Others proceed by trial-and-error, guided by their immediate impressions of the stimuli.

Still another differentiation of basic perceptual attitudes has been called *confidence* and *caution* by Bartlett (1932). The confident observer reports all he sees of a complex presentation in a single glance, often reporting details not actually present. The cautious observer gives a careful, hesitating report, including less detail than was actually present. Bartlett also differentiated between *evaluative* and *non-evaluative* attitudes.

One of the most inclusive of all the proposed typologies based on perception was that of Jaensch (1938). (See Frenkel-Brunswik, 1954.) He contrasts the "disintegrated" S-type, whose perceptions are unstable, irregular, and not firmly tied to reality, with the "integrated" J-type, whose perceptions are systematic, logical, and realistic.

Another perceptual typology that has appealed to a large number of European psychologists contrasts *color reactors* with *form reactors*. (See Eysenck, 1947, p. 220.) A great many ingenious experiments have been devised using stimulus materials that will trigger one response if the subject is most sensitive to color, a different response if he notices the shape first. The theory has been that schizoid types of personality are form-conscious, whereas cycloid (manic-depressive) types are color-conscious. The evidence presented so far, however, does not establish the conclusion. We shall have more to say about this later.

Still another possible distinction is the one that has been made by Lowenfeld (1945) between *visual* and *haptic* types. The visually-minded person experiences the world primarily through his eyes. The haptically-minded person experiences the world primarily through touch and kinesthesis. In each case a person translates the experience that comes to him into the medium that suits him best. The haptic painter, for example, shows forms and textures in such a way that they can be sensed as if one were feeling them. The visual individual constructs in visual images some representation of what he encounters in the dark. Lowenfeld has devised some ingenious tests that can be used to determine how strong each of the tendencies is in a person and has shown that there is a high degree of consistency in the verdict the different tests give on an individual.

The reader who is familiar with the use of the Rorschach test for personality diagnosis will have noticed the similarity between a number of these typologies and the characteristics that are evaluated from a Rorschach protocol. The distinction between analyzers and synthesizers is obviously related to the interpretations of Whole, Large Detail, and Small Detail totals. The color-form typologies show some kinship with the procedures for scoring Rorschach determinants. The Lowenfeld visual-haptic classification suggests the weighing of the color total against the movement total, a basic Rorschach procedure. We can say without much hesitation that the Rorschach method grew out of the same psychological soil that produced these various typologies. The whole involved procedure of scoring and interpretation is a living monument to the conviction of many psychologists that personality can be understood through perception.

It is a sad fact, however, that in spite of hundreds of studies using the Rorschach method, the evidence for the validity of these separate perceptual variables is still as tenuous as the evidence for the other perceptual typologies. What evidence there is for the validity of the Rorschach consists largely of demonstrations that skilled interpreters, using *all* the responses a subject has given, can make sound inferences about him. The extent to which a W (whole) total or an M: C (movement vs. color sum) comparison actually enters into one of these judgments is hard to single out from the total complex in which it is embedded. The special research studies that have been made of separate Rorschach scores and their relationship to personality have been inconclusive and conflicting.

However, although at present Rorschach results cannot be used to support theories as to perceptual typologies, there is a good prospect that research on perceptual-personality relationships in general may eventually enable us to use such tests as the Rorschach far more skillfully than we now do. From this point of view it would seem that the detailed investigation of some basic perceptual variables is likely to be of more long-range value than the same amount of effort directed into attempts to validate existing tests. It is this hope which motivates much present-day research on individual differences in perception.

The various perceptual typologies have been presented in some detail in spite of the fact that good quantitative evidence for their meaningfulness does not exist. They can still be considered sources of hypotheses, starting points for research. It is apparent that there is a considerable amount of overlapping in the different systems. It would be interesting and not too difficult to find out, for example, whether, if a large number of the proposed tests were to be given to the same group of subjects, the same persons would turn out to be high in the *synthetic, subjective, active,* and *confident* variables. To bring some order and meaning into this proliferation of personality typologies is a research task for the future. We turn now to some of the more limited efforts of the recent past.

FACTOR-ANALYTIC STUDIES

The first large-scale quantitative investigation of individual differences in perceptual characteristics was published by L. L. Thurstone in 1944. The monograph is interesting in the first place simply as a source of information as to how much individual variation occurs in the kinds of perceptual processes that have been so exhaustively studied by laboratory psychologists. As has been said, their own publications usually do not give us this information. Table 18, for example, gives the frequency distribution for the Gottschaldt Test, Form B, which turned out to be in several ways the most interesting test in the battery. It requires the subject to locate in a complex configuration a simple figure that he has been shown. A part of a later revision of the test itself is shown in Figure 33.

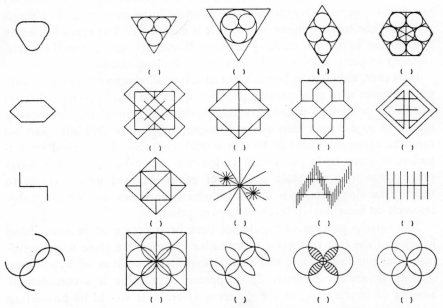

FIGURE 33. Four items from the Concealed Figures Test (Thurstone, 1951b).

The study was designed to use the factor-analytic method as a way of exploring the perceptual domain. Thurstone hoped to find out how many different perceptual variables it would be necessary to postulate in order to account for the perceptual processes and to get some idea of the nature of the basic differences between individuals. He felt strongly that it would be far more economical of time and effort to build our subsequent research with regard to perception-personality relationships around variables identified in this way than to center it around the typologies of the philosophical theorists or the intuitive categories of the practicing clinicians.

TABLE 18.
Scores of 186 Students on Gottschaldt Test B
(*Score represents the number of designs marked divided by the number of minutes required.*)

(Thurstone, 1944a)

SCORES	FREQUENCY
.4- .7	5
.8-1.1	6
1.2-1.5	14
1.6-1.9	24
2.0-2.3	33
2.4-2.7	28
2.8-3.1	16
3.2-3.5	21
3.6-3.9	14
4.0-4.3	5
4.4-4.7	7
4.8-5.1	7
5.2-5.5	2
5.6-5.9	1
Over 6.0	3

Forty tests were chosen to represent a wide variety of perceptual phenomena. Some were alternation tests, like the Necker Cube which flops back and forth as one watches it. Some were tests of closure, in which the subject's task is to see a clear simple figure under various distracting conditions. A number of well-known optical illusions were included. Response time and reaction time were assessed in several tests. Several of them involved conflicts between color and form. Size constancy, shape constancy, and brightness constancy tests similar to those Thouless had used were included. The Rorschach test was also given, but only two scores, R, the total number of responses, and W, the number of organized wholes, were used in the analysis.

The subjects were 194 volunteers, mostly University of Chicago students. The customary procedures of intercorrelating all variables, extracting centroid factors, and then rotating these factors to simple structure, were employed. Because this was a pioneer study, and there was little previous information that could be used as a guide in the interpretation of the factors, Thurstone preferred to try to describe each in general terms rather than to pin it down by a specific name.

Eleven factors were identified mathematically, but only seven of them could be given the detailed examination from which some conclusions about the nature of the perceptual processes could be drawn. Of the eleven, one was a residual, apparently due to chance errors in the original correlation coefficients. One was what factor analysts call a doublet, carrying high loadings in only the two Rorschach scores. Another one was also a doublet linking two scores that were both derived from the same test, although logically they seemed to represent different things. One factor showed up in only the tests of the intelligence or cognitive type which had been carried over into this study from the previous work on primary mental abilities.

Of the seven that had some significance for perception, three seemed to represent different kinds of speed—the familiar *reaction time*, speed of *perception* (where stimuli were easily recognizable), and speed of *judgment* (where some decision had to be made about what had been clearly perceived). The finding of three separate speed factors rather than one was one of the interesting results of the study.

Two factors seemed to represent specific kinds of experimental material—in one case illusions, in the other stimuli where alternations or reversals occur. There is evidence here that some persons are more subject to illusions than others are, and that the rate at which any of the alternating figures tends to reverse itself is a characteristic differentiating between individuals.

The most interesting of the factors from this analysis, and the ones that have stimulated most of the later research, were those concerned with *closure*. The Gottschaldt Test (called Concealed Figures in later studies, see Figure 33) had fairly high loadings on both of these closure factors, but the tests that clustered with it showed a somewhat different pattern of loadings in the two factor columns. After discussing various possibilities as to what aspects of perceptual closure the two factors might represent, Thurstone tentatively described the first as *speed and strength of closure* and the second as *flexibility in the manipulation of several configurations*. (Closure refers to the act of grasping and retaining a clear, coherent pattern in the stimulus materials.) In a later discussion of these closure factors, after more work that was planned especially to throw light on their essential nature, Thurstone (1949) described them thus: "The first closure factor C_1 (speed of closure) seems to facilitate the making of a closure in an unorganized field, the second closure factor C_2 (flexibility of closure) seems to facilitate the retention of a figure in a distracting field."

Yela (1949) after re-analyzing some mental test data that had been presented by Alexander in 1935, identified the factor Alexander had called Z and had not been able to define very successfully as the now familiar *speed of closure* factor. His description of it is one of the clearest statements of what it involves: "The subject will excel in this task if he can hold the given structure as a group of elements organized into a pattern and at the same time reproduce it quickly. . . . or is able to perceive the figure that completes the unfinished configuration. At the beginning of the task the elements integrate themselves into changing configurations that interfere with the completion of the final pattern. In all cases the final structure is arrived at by quickly rejecting the patterns that do not lead to the correct configuration and by the ability to synthesize the units given into a meaningful whole."

There have been a number of studies from the Chicago laboratory attempting to find out what other psychological traits are related to these perceptual factors. From the first study on, there is consistent evidence in the way the factor loadings are patterned that the flexibility of closure factor is related to reasoning ability (Botzum, 1951; Pemberton, 1952a). Hypotheses that one closure factor is linked with induction, the other with deduction, or that one represents "analytical," the other "synthetic" processes, are less well supported by the data. Pemberton (1952b) has also shown that persons who are high on the first perceptual factor differ *temperamentally* from those who are high on the second. She used a number of inventories and self-ratings of interests and emotional characteristics. These were all brought together into ratings of eleven broad traits, such as "socially outgoing," "systematic," and "energetic and impulsive." Among this group of 154 subjects, mostly graduate students, those receiving high *speed of closure* scores tended to have high self-ratings on the traits "sociable," "quick in reactions," "artistic," "self-confident," "systematic," "neat and precise," and "dislike logical and theoretical problems." Those with high scores for *flexibility of closure*, on the other hand, tended to rate themselves "socially retiring," "independent of the good opinions of others," "analytical," "interested in theoretical and scientific problems," and "dislike rigid systematization and routine." This looks like another sort of typology and suggests in its general outlines the extrovert-introvert classification that has been used in so many ways by so many people. It must be remembered, however, that the perceptual scores that define the traits Pemberton has studied are *not* at opposite poles of one continuum, but are actually *positively* correlated. While the correlation is not high, it is still true that an individual with an outstanding score on *speed of closure* is less likely to be low on *flexibility of closure* than he is to be high. Thus, in the lives of actual people, we should expect many of the temperamental traits from apparently opposite clusters to occur together.

One of the specific questions that Thurstone had in mind was the meaning of the difference between persons who respond primarily to form and those who respond primarily to color. In the 1944 study no factor of this sort showed up when the correlations between color-form tests were analyzed. In a later research project, however (Thurstone, 1953), evidence of a very interesting kind has been appearing. The test for color or form dominance consists of a film to be projected on a screen in such a way that the subject sees spots, apparently moving from one number to another across a clock face. The direction of the movement that the subject reports indicates to the experimenter whether he is reacting to the color or to the form of the spots. Thurstone reports that *form dominance* is a consistent, reliably measured trait that is related to a number of self-ratings on a temperament scale. The persons who are form dominant tend to be emotionally stable, socially dominant, and outgoing. *Color dominance*, however, does not show this clear-cut relationship to a group of temperamental traits and has not as yet been interpreted. A new finding from this study is that some subjects react consistently in terms of *direction* of movement rather than in terms of either form or color. Both the *up dominant* and the *down dominant* show distinguishing patterns of self-rated temperamental traits. The meaning of form and color dominance thus seems to be more complex than the typologists who have discussed it assumed that it was.

The direction Thurstone's research has taken of recent years has led him to incorporate individual differences in perception into a broader study aimed at the development of objective measures of temperament. (Objective measures can be defined here as they were in Chapter 7, as measurements based on what the subject *does* in some standardized situation rather than on what he says about himself.) A considerable number of ingenious tests have been assembled, including projective methods, verbal association tests, and psychophysical discriminations. The relationship of all these measures to temperamental qualities is being explored in systematic fashion (Thurstone, 1951, 1953).

Some factor analysts have been interested in individual differences on perceptual tests primarily as ability rather than temperamental indicators.

Perceptual speed (P) was one of the original primary mental abilities. Subsequent work showed it to be a composite of factors rather than a single one. Bechtoldt (1947) reported four perceptual speed factors we have already discussed. Three of them were interpreted as: (1) Choice-discrimination speed, (2) Facility in dealing with predetermined symbols, and (3) Facility in associational recognition. His subjects were University of Chicago students. Roff (1952), who based his factor analysis on seventy tests which had been given to large numbers of pre-aviation cadets (average sample size 480), came out with eight perceptual factors. One of them, Perceptual speed, showed a fairly high correlation with all the others. He called them: (1) Plotting, (2) Directional thinking, (3) Length perception, (4) Perceptual closure, (5) Sequential perception, (6) Complex reaction time, and (7) Perception through camouflage. There was one more factor, Movement detection, which was not correlated with perceptual speed and has not been reported in previous studies. For all these perceptual factors we need information about the predictive validity of such measurements. What kinds of workers, for example, need to score high on *Sequential Perception* tests?

Factor-analytic studies have given us clues as to what some basic individual differences in perception are. Preliminary reports indicate that these variables are related to both ability and temperament. Research on them thus occupies a strategic position in psychology.

FIELD-DEPENDENCE AND ITS PERSONALITY CORRELATES

Our current interest in individual differences in perception, as well as our knowledge about them, has been tremendously increased during the years since World War II as a result of a large-scale research program initiated at Brooklyn College by Asch and Witkin (1948) and reported in some detail in *Personality Through Perception* (Witkin *et al.*, 1954). The investigation began when they discovered that there were large and consistent individual differences in the ability of college subjects to bring themselves to a vertical position when placed in a situation where visual cues were misleading.

There were three separate kinds of test situation. In the Rod-and-Frame Test, the subject sat in a darkened room where all he could see was a luminous frame that surrounded a movable luminous rod. The frame could be tilted at any angle by the experimenter. The subject's task was to report on the position of the rod as it was moved a little at a time and to tell when it appeared vertical, disregarding the frame if he could. The angle between the setting of the rod he accepted and the true vertical constituted his score. In the Tilting-Room-Tilting-Chair Test, the subject sat in a small room in a special movable chair. The room could be tilted into any position and the chair could be tilted in either the same or in an opposite direction. Each trial started with different degrees of tilt. In some trials subjects were asked to manipulate the controls in such a way as to straighten the room. In other trials they were asked to straighten the chair. The angle made by one's adjustment with the true vertical again constituted his score. In the Rotating-Room Test the subject sat in a chair within a little room that was made to rotate around a circular track. Both chair and room could be tilted various amounts, and the subject was required in some trials to straighten the room, in others to straighten his chair.

The perceptual trait that these research workers succeeded in defining clearly and measuring accurately by these methods was "the ability to keep an object isolated from compelling background forces." Subsequent work centered around a number of questions. How consistent are individuals from one sort of task to another with regard to this trait? How stable are their scores over a period of time? Can the same characteristic be measured by other methods—perceptual tests that do not involve bodily orientation as a basic variable, or personality evaluations of the kinds clinicians have been using? Can group differences be identified—between the sexes, between children of different ages, between hospital patients and normals? The method they followed was first to set up some hypotheses as to the correlations one would expect to get between this variable and some other—for example, Rorschach records or interview protocols—and then to see whether the obtained correlations supported the initial hypothesis.

Only the results that seem most important for the general understanding of the meaning of individual differences in perception can be summarized here. First of all, this perceptual trait is clearly a stable, consistent characteristic, and shows itself in a variety of ways. Odd-even reliability coefficients on the various tests ranged from .69 to .91. Test-retest coefficients were of about the same magnitude even when there was a one-year interval. A group of 32 men retested after three years obtained scores on the Rod-and-Frame Test that correlated .84 with their original records and scores on the Tilting-Room-Tilting-Chair Test that correlated .89 with the first ones. For a group of 30 women the three-year correlations were .66 and .89. Correlations between the *different* orientation tests were on the whole lower, but most of them were significant at the one per cent level. Table 19 shows these figures. Furthermore, the trait is not specific to

TABLE 19.

Intercorrelations Between Orientation-Test Index Scores
(Number of cases: men = 46; women = 45)

(Witkin *et al.*, 1954, p. 66)

TEST	TILTING-ROOM-TILTING-CHAIR		ROTATING ROOM	
	MEN	WOMEN	MEN	WOMEN
Rod and frame	.64[a]	.52[a]	.25	.18
Tilting-room-tilting-chair			.51[a]	.62[a]

[a] Significant at less than 1 per cent level.

bodily orientation situations. The Embedded Figures Test, a variation of the Gottschaldt Test discussed in reporting on Thurstone's work (see Figure 33), correlated as highly with these scores as they correlate with one another. (See Table 20.) The kinds of measurements with which these scores did *not* correlate significantly turned out to be as helpful as the significant correlations in defining what the trait essentially is. It is only

TABLE 20.

Correlations Between Orientation and Embedded-Figures-Test Scores
(Number of cases: men = 46; women = 45)

(Witkin *et al.*, 1954, p. 85)

	MEN	WOMEN
Rod-and-frame		
Index score	.64[a]	.21
Tilting-room-tilting-chair		
Index score	.60[a]	.51[a]
Rotating-room		
Index score	.36[b]	.39[a]
Orientation index	.66[a]	.46[a]
(all three tests)		

[a] Significant at or below 1 per cent level.
[b] Significant at or below 5 per cent level.

in tests that require sujects to keep one aspect of a complex perceptual situation isolated from its background that this particular trait shows up. The scores correlate significantly with success on a Two-Hand-Coördination Test, for example, but not with measurements of body steadiness. The failure to get significant correlations with a test involving conflict between auditory and visual cues as to the location of a sound in space shows that something other than a simple preference for judgments based on visual impressions must be involved.

In a number of separate studies, ratings of the field-dependence trait were made using data obtained by means of other well-known methods of studying personality—interview, Rorschach, Figure-Drawing, and Minia-ture-Toy Play Situation. These were correlated with orientation scores. As a whole, the results supported the hypotheses the authors had formulated with regard to the nature of the basic personality variable, although there is some possibility that knowledge of subjects' orientation scores might have biased the judgments made in interview and test situations. Each also *added* something to the total picture of "field-dependence" and the way it operates in a personality. The final description of the trait making for success in the orientation tests included three aspects: (1) *activity* in deal-ing with one's environment as opposed to passive acceptance; (2) *aware-ness* of one's inner life along with good control over impulses; and (3) *self-esteem* and self-acceptance.

Studies of children of various ages showed that the trait is related, but not in a clear-cut linear fashion, to maturity. Thirteen-year-olds did better than eight- or ten-year-olds on all the tests, but the seventeen- and eighteen-year-olds on some tests made more errors than the thirteen-year-olds.

One of the most striking findings of all was that there were marked sex differences in all the kinds of samples tested—college students, children, hospital patients. Females seem to be markedly more field-dependent than males and thus less successful in these orientation tasks. These differences will be discussed in more detail in a later chapter when we are considering sex differences of all kinds.

GENERAL PERCEPTUAL ATTITUDES OR "ANSCHAUUNGEN"

What is in many ways the broadest and most comprehensive attack on the problem of individual differences in perception has been made by G. S. Klein and his students and associates at the Menninger Foundation. The theoretical framework for a whole series of experiments was clearly explained in a symposium paper by Klein and Schlesinger (1949) and a chapter by Klein a little later (1951). Looking at personality from a func-tionalist point of view, one can see that an individual's perceptions have *adaptive* properties. "They are the means we have for fending off, choos-ing, and admitting stimulation from the outside world which, with free entrance, would traumatize and overwhelm us." In psychoanalytic terms, it is the *ego* that we study when we analyze a person's characteristic ways of perceiving, and broad perceptual attitudes can thus serve as clues to the whole *ego-control system*.

It is because the word "attitude" has come to be used in the narrower sense of opinions about political or economic issues that Klein and his fellow-workers prefer the lesser-known German word *anschauung* as a label for this concept of a personal outlook on the world, an individual way of coming to terms with reality. They hope that by identifying the important varieties of *anschauungen* with regard to which individual differences can be measured they will make possible a fresh attack on the most challenging theoretical problems in the psychology of personality.

So far they have studied three sets of *anschauungen*: (*a*) leveling and sharpening; (*b*) attitudes of resistance to or acceptance of instability; and (*c*) physiognomic and literal attitudes (Klein, 1951). They have shown considerable ingenuity in sorting out separate variables and combining them in ways that permit them to use highly sensitive analysis of variance procedures. By this means they can show unambiguously whether their hypotheses are borne out by the data. Since the work on the "leveling-sharpening" dimension has been reported more completely than the rest, we shall take that up in some detail.

The first step was to use what had previously been observed as a basis for the setting-up of hypotheses. The theoretical distinction between levelers and sharpeners is an interesting one. Levelers tend to make a stimulus simpler and less differentiated if they can, either by reducing figure-ground distinctions or by assimilating new stimuli to a dominating organization. Sharpeners try to heighten figure-ground distinctions and exploit differentiation. One would then expect that persons in whom the leveling tendency is strongly developed would have great difficulty in extricating embedded figures from their backgrounds and in detecting gradual changes in a pattern of stimulation.

In setting up an experiment to prove that "leveling-sharpening" is a broad general tendency not specific to any one task, Holzman and Klein (1954) selected subjects who made extreme scores on a test involving "gradual change" and then tried them out on a test involving "assimilation of figure to ground." The test used in selection of subjects was carried out by presenting squares one at a time in random order in sets of five different sizes and asking the person to judge the size of each. After he had had three trials on each square from the smallest set, the very smallest of the squares was removed and the next size larger introduced without the subject's knowledge. After three trials with each of these (in random order) the smallest square was again taken out and the next larger one substituted. This process of gradual shift was continued until a set made up of the five largest squares had been presented. For example, the first series of judgments might be made on squares of 2-inch, 3-inch, 4-inch, 5-inch, and 6-inch sides. The second set would consist of squares of 3-inch,

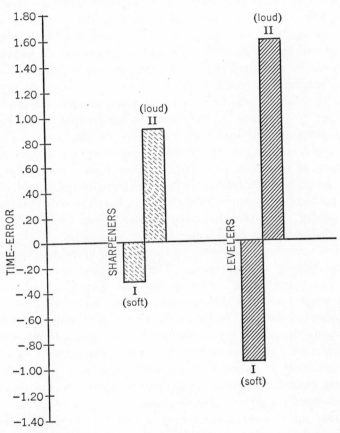

FIGURE 34. Differences in the performance of "levelers" and "sharpeners" on a test of auditory time error under two conditions of interpolated field (Holzman, 1954).

4-inch, 5-inch, 6-inch, and 7-inch sides. The final set would consist of 10-, 11-, 12-, 13-, and 14-inch squares. There were great differences in the accuracy with which subjects were able to *change* their size judgments as the general level of squares being presented changed. In the experiment reported by Holzman and Klein (1954), nine extreme "levelers," subjects whose judgments were very inaccurate under these conditions, were contrasted with nine extreme "sharpeners" on a test of visual time error. This test required that the subject compare the brightness levels of stimulus lights with the brightness of a standard light which he had first been shown. Between the standard and the variable light stimuli, dark, dim, or bright interpolated lights were used on different trials. The hypothesis was that

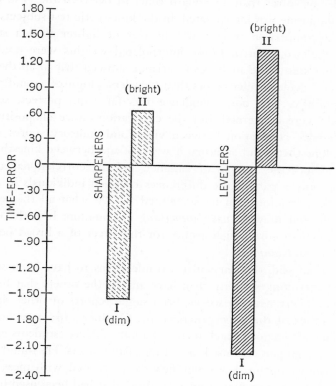

FIGURE 35. Differences in the performance of "levelers" and "sharpeners" on a test of visual time error under two conditions of interpolated field (Holzman, 1954).

the "levelers" would be more confused by this interpolated stimulation, less able to keep the different stimuli separate, and thus would show greater "time errors." The results of the analysis of variance bore out this hypothesis and showed that differences were statistically significant even with this small number of cases. There were, however, large individual differences *within* each group. "Levelers" are not all equally good at the assigned tasks; neither are "sharpeners."

Holzman (1954) extended the study to three different sense modalities. Selecting 21 levelers and 22 sharpeners in the same way, by their success in judging the size of squares presented in sets that were gradually shifting in size, he tried them out on the same sort of visual test that had been used before, and also on auditory and kinesthetic tests of similar type. In the auditory test subjects were asked to judge whether a comparison tone was louder or softer than a standard tone. In between the two, either a soft or a loud tone was interpolated. In the kinesthetic test subjects judged whether a comparison weight was heavier or lighter than a standard. Between the two, light or heavy interpolated weights were used. As in the previous study, the analysis of variance showed that in all these tasks "sharpeners" made smaller errors than "levelers." Figures 34 and 35 show this graphically. The correspondence was far from perfect, so far as individuals were concerned, but the correlations were all positive. The rank-difference correlation between visual and auditory scores was .25. Between kinesthetic and auditory it was .66, and between kinesthetic and visual .50. Both the analysis of variance and the correlational approach show that only a part of the differences between individuals in any one of these test situations can be accounted for by what all the tests have in common, but they do have *something* in common. It is the evidence for this common core which argues for the effect of a broad perceptual attitude or *anschauung*.

As has been said, this particular attitude seems to have been subjected to more penetrating scrutiny than have any of the others that have been postulated. There have, however, been single reports of other significant differentiations of the same general type. Gardner (1953) recorded first the number of categories each of his 50 adult subjects (students and Menninger Clinic employees) used in sorting small objects. He found that this score so simply obtained was significantly correlated with measurements of size and shape constancy, similar to those that had been used by Thouless (1932), and with the accuracy of judgments as to the brightness of lights. Observations of the way subjects went to work indicated that the subjects who sort into many categories appear to be more careful and intent, more sensitive to subtle differences. Is the attitude shown on this sorting test the same as the "leveling vs. sharpening" dimension? We do not know, as the same subjects were not tested under both sets of circumstances, but it appears that it may be.

Schlesinger (1954) hypothesized that the intrusion of personal values into perceptual tasks, a phenomenon around which much discussion has centered, might be more closely related to individual differences in the way persons are organized to cope with interference than to the strength of their personal needs. He set out to show that people do differ in the extent to which they stress "focusing" in their perceptions. The experimental task with which his 29 subjects were confronted was that of judging the size of discs that differed from one another in various irrelevant ways as well as in size—in such characteristics, for example, as color, weight, and texture. A personality inventory was then made up of items that appeared to have some bearing on "affective freedom." The correlations between size-judgment error scores and inventory scores was positive though rather low. It and the other types of analysis he carried out offer some support for his hypothesis but leave the nature of the "focusing" attitude somewhat unclear.

One other perceptual attitude upon which some experimental work has been done is that of "tolerance for instability." Klein and Schlesinger (1951) selected on the basis of Rorschach records ten subjects who could clearly be classified as "form-bound" and ten who could be classified as "form-labile." They then compared these groups on the scores they made for "range of apparent movement." When pictures are presented in succession at the right speed, subjects tend to see a single moving figure. If the interval between presentation is too long, however, one sees the two stationary figures in succession. If the interval is too short, one sees a single stationary figure. Klein and Schlesinger hypothesized that the less formbound subjects would show a *wider* range of time intervals at which successsive stimuli would be perceived as moving, since they would be less tied to the known objective properties of these stimuli. Here again the results of the experiment bore out the hypothesis.

A thing that lends interest to this particular study is that it connects up with another line of research on "intolerance of ambiguity" as an emotional and personality variable (Frenkel-Brunswik, 1954). In Frenkel Brunswik's work, children who had been chosen on the basis of high or low scores for ethnocentrism or prejudice were compared on various perceptual tests. The prejudiced subjects were slower to recognize a new picture in a series where one gradually changed over into another. (An initial picture of a cat, for example, would have one feature after another altered in successive presentations until it had become a clear picture of a dog.) Block and Block (1951) also showed that ethnocentrism scores in male college students were significantly related to intolerance for ambiguity as measured by a procedure involving the autokinetic effect (apparent movement of a stationary light in a dark room).

There have been various reports of individual differences in other perceptual characteristics such as after-image (Young, 1948) and flicker fusion frequency (Simonson and Brozek, 1952), but so far they have not been incorporated in any intelligible theoretical framework. There have also been a number of other methods proposed for getting at personality variables that appear to be similar to those hypothesized in the Menninger Clinic studies. The studies of esthetic choices by Barron and Welsh (1952) and Barron (1952) as well as the work of Smith and Klein (1953) on serial behavior patterns and Fisher (1951) on memory changes would seem to be of this nature. The theory of basic perceptual attitudes is far from being a finished structure, but even now it constitutes a framework around which such a structure may eventually arise.

IMPORTANCE OF THIS RESEARCH

We have discussed these perceptual experiments in considerable detail partly because the tests and the characteristics they are measuring are still unfamiliar to most readers. It is harder to see how a score is obtained on a tilting-room-tilting-chair test or a test requiring size judgments of squares in gradually shifting sets than it is to understand how an intelligence test is scored, simply because we have been exposed to intelligence tests again and again from our early youth on up. Furthermore, we are used to thinking of individuals in terms of IQ, reading age, or even cycloid-schizoid temperament, whereas to evaluate them for speed of closure, field-dependence, or tolerance for ambiguity seems as yet an unnatural procedure. The experiments reported in this chapter lead us in a different direction from earlier work in individual differences.

They are worth considering carefully because of the relationships that have already been demonstrated between the perceptual variables and a number of traits that have always been of the greatest interest to differential psychologists. On the cognitive side there is at least a slight possibility that experiments like these may help us out of some of the impasses we have run into in intelligence measurement. Perceptual scores seem to be related to scores on our standard intelligence tests (Witkin *et al.*, p. 477-478). There is evidence for a relationship between these variables and those Goldstein and Scheerer have been classifying as abstract and concrete attitudes. The work of Piaget showing how intelligence develops out of early perceptual "schemata" fits well into this framework.

On the other hand, these perceptual variables are clearly related to the traits we have been classifying as *non-cognitive*, the motivational or personality traits. It is especially interesting that various approaches to personality theory can be reconciled by means of the concepts that have been developing. As noted above, Klein finds it quite possible to think about *anschauungen* psychoanalytically as *ego* characteristics. They fit equally well into Adlerian "life-style" or Rogerian "self-concept" thinking. They even enable us to utilize the insights of typological theorists who have been beyond the pale for emancipated scientific psychologists who insist on quantitative rigor in their work. Both Klein and Schlesinger (1949) and Frenkel-Brunswik (1954) have been struck by the fact that the dimensions of personality they were revealing correspond rather strikingly to the Jaensch integrate-disintegrate classification. The principal difference is that we have attached an opposite value judgment to the quality. Jaensch's integrated type, the simple man of action who scorns complexities and does not even see fine distinctions, appears here as the rigid authoritarian whom we think of as a real problem to democracy.

This points to one other interesting relationship. These traits are important in social psychology as well as in branches of psychology concerned primarily with analysis of the individual. Enough work has been done by Frenkel-Brunswik and her associates to show that perceptual characteristics are a part of the complex syndrome that has been labeled the authoritarian personality. Thus the study of them may have something to contribute to our understanding of such problems as prejudice and totalitarianism.

Work on perceptual differences seems to occupy a strategic position in differential psychology. Not only does it tie together work being done in widely separated areas—intelligence measurement, clinical study of individual personalities, and research on basic social attitudes—but it suggests the possibility of measuring variables in which all of these psychologists are interested far more accurately than they can be measured by the techniques that have previously been used. The scores on these perceptual tests are *ratio* measurements, not the ordinal or interval scales we have had to content ourselves with in the other fields. The size of an angle, as in the Witkin experiments, or the error in size judgments, in those of Klein and Holzman, can be measured to any degree of accuracy we desire. The fact that the scale has a true zero point and equal intervals permits us to use any mathematical treatment we find that we need. The success with which the experiments of the Menninger group have wrested unambiguous conclusions from small numbers of cases has already been noted.

Dana (1954) has called attention to the importance of the concept of *personality orientation* as an organizational focus for research on personality. He definies it as *the relative resistance of the individual to the en-*

vironmental situation, and shows how many of the experimental findings and theoretical concepts we have been discussing can be incorporated under this one heading. What he seems to envisage is a new sort of "g" factor in personality study.

Whether a single broad concept is really adequate to cover these various dimensions upon which psychologists have been working cannot be decided on the basis of present evidence. We have, however, several clearly formulated, accurately measurable variables to work with: constancy, speed of closure, flexibility of closure, field-dependence, leveling-sharpening, and intolerance for ambiguity. It should be possible to find out how they are related to one another. And it may be that in this direction lies the personality theory of the future.

SUMMARY

Psychologists were measuring individual differences in perceptual characteristics before the beginning of the twentieth century, but lost interest in the problem when simple perceptual measurements proved not to be indicators of general intelligence. Both armchair theorists and experimental workers proposed various typologies, however, with regard to perception—analyzers versus synthesizers, color-reactors versus form-reactors, and the like.

A series of factor-analytic studies during the 1940's delineated a number of factors centering around perceptual speed which seem to be related to mental ability or aptitude of some sort. They also pointed with increasing clarity to two *closure* factors, speed of closure and flexibility of closure, which seem to be related primarily to temperament.

A series of studies centering around individual differences in the perception of the vertical under confusing conditions have isolated a perceptual trait called field-dependence and shown it to be related to personality characteristics that have been evaluated by clinical techniques.

Still another series of experiments on general perceptual attitudes or *anschauungen* has shown that subjects consistently manifest tendencies such as "leveling" and "sharpening" when tested in different types of laboratory situation.

The perceptual variables on which research has been done are of interest to psychologists who study abilities, personality, or social attitudes. They constitute a promising new approach to complex problems.

PART THREE

Varieties of Group Differences

CHAPTER 10

Sex Differences

HISTORY OF THE PROBLEM

No TOPIC in psychology is of more perennial interest than sex differences. Study after study, book after book, testify to the fact that research workers, writers, and readers consider the subject to be of paramount importance. Partly this interest comes from the need men and women feel to understand one another. Many social problems having to do with marriage and divorce, education, and working conditions depend upon such knowledge for their successful solution. Partly the multiplicity of studies is perhaps just a matter of convenience. Any psychologist who is trying out a new laboratory procedure or standardizing a new test can easily compare the performance of males and females, since his subjects, however chosen, divide themselves into these two categories.

Although there had been many books presenting theoretical discussions or general impressions even before 1900, quantitative research began at about the turn of the century and expanded very rapidly. The 25 references, only 10 of them directly psychological, that Dr. Woolley found to summarize in 1910 grew to the 327 that C. C. Miles covered in 1935. Much of the work done during this period was motivated by the desire to demonstrate that females are not inherently inferior to males. Over many centuries, in our culture and perhaps in most others, this had been the prevailing view. The fact that women were physically weaker than men had seemed to suggest an all-around weakness, including mental traits. The primitive idea that in reproduction the male was the active, form-giving agent whereas the female furnished only soil and nourishment continued to affect attitudes long after research on the mechanics of heredity discredited it completely as an explanation of the facts. But from 1900 on, the findings of the psychologists gave strong support to the arguments of the feminists. The *smallness* of the differences between the sexes in mental abilities and the possibility of accounting for such differences as there are on a sociological rather than a biological basis were the two conclusions that stood out. Differences between the sexes were minimized and overlapping of the two groups was stressed. Along with this emphasis on equality, however, a large amount of material showing differences in *patterns* of ability gradually accumulated.

Since about 1935 the emphasis has changed. Differences have again been stressed, but not for the purpose of demonstrating any general superiority or inferiority. Research has rather been directed to the more subtle qualitative differences in attitudes and emotional needs. Many of the studies have been related directly or indirectly to psychoanalytic theories which postulate basic emotional differences arising from biological rather than sociological sources. Many of them have been more closely tied in with research on culture and personality and are concerned with what the sex roles are in our present society and what they should be. We shall try to sift out from the vast mass of facts and figures now available the data that have contributed most to all these main currents of thinking.

SEX DIFFERENCES IN ACHIEVEMENT

Everyone who wishes to discuss the abilities of the two sexes must attempt an explanation of one unquestionable fact. It is this: history has recorded the names and achievements of a large number of men but of only a very small number of women. Ellis (1904) in his study of British genius found only 55 women in his total group of 1,030 persons. J. McK. Cattell's (1903) list of the 1,000 most eminent persons in the world lists only 32 women, and some of these were distinguished by circumstances such as royal birth rather than by intellectual achievements of their own. Castle (1913) collected a list of 868 famous women down through the ages. The highest degre of eminence, as indicated by amount of space in biographical directories, characterized women whom circumstances had made prominent—sovereigns, political leaders, mothers, wives, or mistresses of great men. More women attained eminence in writing than in any other profession. In the 1927 edition of *American Men of Science*, only 725 women were listed out of 9,785 entries, and out of the 250 names starred because of special eminence, only 3 were women. If it is an indisputable fact that society produces, now and then, a Marie Curie, it is just as true that it does not repeat the performance at all frequently.

Even in fields traditionally assigned to women, the most eminently successful persons are likely to be men. Interest in the arts is for us a feminine trait, yet there are very few women who have distinguished themselves as creative artists. Even in dress-designing and interior decorating, the leaders in the field are men. Most of the world's cooking may be done by women, but the great chefs of all time have been men. Acting is a field that has been open to women for a long time, but the great playwrights and producers are men. Wherever we look we find this same preponderance of male leadership and high achievement. For the differential psychologist, this is a fact to be explained and a spur to the research that may eventually supply the explanation.

In contrast to this situation with regard to *adult* achievement, all studies of *school* achievement agree that girls consistently make better school records than boys. Differences of this sort have been reported from a wide variety of investigations, using various criteria of school success. It is recognized that girls are less frequently retarded and more frequently accelerated than boys. More of them receive high marks and fewer of them receive unsatisfactory marks. When batteries of achievement tests rather than school ratings are used to evaluate school performance, the differences are less marked but are still, on the whole, in favor of girls. Interesting differences in the various sections of these tests show up in such studies (Terman and Tyler, 1954). Girls excel in English, spelling, writing, and art. Boys usually do better in arithmetic, especially arithmetical reasoning, history, geography, and science. Even in these subjects, however, girls often get better marks than boys when marks are based on teachers' judgments rather than tests. All the sex differences in school achievement in the various subject-matter fields are very small as compared with the total range of achievement in the school population. They would furnish no justification for setting up different schools or using different educational methods for boys and girls.

Several main lines of explanation have been offered for these differences in achievement, both those in school and those in the world outside. They will be simply mentioned at this point and discussed in more detail as the other data on sex differences are analyzed. It is evident, to begin with, that it would be difficult to account for both kinds of achievement differences by any hypothesis of general intellectual inferiority or superiority. If women are, on the average, less intelligent than men, why do they consistently do better at school? If, on the other hand, they are brighter than men, why do they not continue to demonstrate the fact after school days are over? Cultural and social factors are often proposed in explanation of the difference in the number of great men and of great women. For only a very small fraction of recorded history have women been given anything like an equal opportunity to achieve, and the dice are still loaded against them to some extent. Differences in special aptitudes constitute a possible explanation of the disparity in school achievement. The fact that girls consistently do better in verbal tasks would make for feminine superiority on all sorts of school work involving reading, writing, or reciting. Differences in rate of maturing are also sometimes used to explain the differences in school performances. Girls reach puberty, on the average, about two years earlier than boys. During the period preceding this change, they are taller, heavier, and more mature in their interests. However, this explanation of differences in intellectual achievement is less convincing than it once was, since a great deal of evidence has been accumulating that physical and mental characteristics are related only very slightly if at all. Differences in attitudes and personality traits may also be called in to account for the facts. Docility and submissiveness, usually considered feminine traits, enable girls to make a better impression on teachers than boys do. This inevitably shows up on report cards in other places besides the deportment column. These same traits would, to some extent, *prevent* their possessors from assuming positions of leadership in the world of affairs.

SEX DIFFERENCES IN TESTED ABILITIES

As long as psychologists considered that the intelligence tests they had devised were direct indicators of native intellectual abilities, they took some interest in comparing the IQ's obtained by girls and boys. All these early studies disclosed a consistent tendency for girls to get slightly higher IQ's than boys up to the age of fourteen. The differences were small, seldom more than four IQ points, but always in the same direction. Among high-school students, the opposite of this situation was found. Boys were consistently higher, and their superiority increased from the first to the last year of high school.

Development of sampling procedures has led to a perfectly clear-cut and obvious explanation of the superiority of high-school boys. Because of the fact that the males are the bread-winners in our society, they are likely to leave school earlier to go to work than girls do. The individuals most likely to leave are those for whom the school situation is least satisfying. In general, they are the ones who make lower than average scores on intelligence tests. To remove them from the group is automatically to raise the boys' average. Girls, on the other hand, are a little more likely to stay in school even if their intellectual gifts are limited, both because economic pressure upon them is less great and because, as has been noted in the previous section, they get along better in school than boys do. The result is that the scores are more typical of the unselected population average for high-school girls than for boys.

Analysis of results obtained with different types of problem and material has led to an explanation of the superiority of girls under fourteen on the basis of their slight advantage in everything having to do with verbal expression. If tests having a large verbal content are used in school surveys, girls come out ahead. On composite tests using a wide *variety* of content, there is usually no difference. Perhaps the best study that was ever made from the standpoint of adequate sampling of the population was done in Scotland (Scottish Council for Research in Education, 1939). All children in the whole country who were born on February 1, May 1, August 1, and November 1 in 1926 were singled out in whatever grade school they were attending and given Stanford-Binet tests. The average IQ's were 100.51 for the boys and 99.7 for the girls. The difference is not significant, and is about as small as one ever obtains between any two samples of any population.

A later Scottish study (Scottish Council for Research in Education, 1949) based on an equally good sampling, this time of children born in 1936, shows boys about 4 points higher on the individual test (Terman-Merrill, Form L) and girls about 2 points higher on the group test. Both differences are statistically significant because of the large number of cases involved, but the fact that they are small and in opposite directions lends no support to a conclusion that either sex is superior.

Since the good present-day intelligence tests are designed to be administered to both boys and girls in coeducational schools, test-makers deliberately try to exclude materials that would lead to consistently higher scores for either sex. What differences there are are balanced against each other so that neither group has an over-all advantage. The best analysis of the way this has been done in the most widely-used revision of the Binet test has been made by McNemar (1942). Test items showing large sex differences were excluded entirely from the final scale. In those which remain, items that give the advantage to girls are those involving esthetic responses, language, hand skills such as buttoning and tying knots, and social items such as guessing ages and distinguishing between types of appearance. Those in which boys excel are the mechanical and mathematical items and the picture absurdities which involve detecting what is foolish about a picture. A test like the Stanford-Binet includes about as many of one of these classes of items as of the other. Hence, total score averages do not differ. In summary, it can be said that since no way of measuring intelligence aside from the presentation of definite questions and tasks has been devised, there is no way of stating which sex is intellectually superior in any absolute sense. We can only say that males are superior in some respects, females in others.

The exploration of these special abilities has proven a far more rewarding task than the search for absolute differences. The first of these, touched upon in the previous discussion of intelligence tests, is the consistent difference in verbal ability. From infancy to adulthood, females express themselves in words more readily and skillfully than males. Throughout the grades and high school, they obtain higher scores on verbal sections of intelligence tests and do better work in English courses. It is to be remembered in this connection also that among the women who have been distinguished for great achievements, a large proportion have been *writers* (Castle, 1913).

Most of the available evidence seems to indicate, however, that it is in verbal *fluency* (what Thurstone has called W), rather than in the grasp of verbal meanings (V) that females are superior. Hobson (1947) and Havighurst and Breese (1947) both found that girls of junior-high age were significantly higher on W but not on V of the Primary Mental Abilities battery. In the Hobson study boys actually averaged higher on V; in the other there was no difference. Herzberg and Lepkin (1954) found senior high school girls to be significantly higher than boys on W for all three ages they were considering: sixteen, seventeen, and eighteen. In this case the seventeen-year-old girls were also higher on V. A large number of reading surveys show that girls of all ages tend to get better scores on speed, but not on vocabulary or comprehension (Terman and Tyler, 1954). When we consider also the evidence that girls learn to talk a little earlier (Goodenough, 1927), are somewhat superior during the preschool years in articulation, intelligibility, and correctness of speech sounds (Wellman *et al.*, 1931), and are less likely to be stutterers, it all fits in with the generalization that girls are more fluent, almost from infancy on.

With regard to mathematical ability, male superiority is the rule. It shows up more plainly on tests that require mathematical reasoning than on those that require simple computations. A number of studies of school achievement (Terman and Tyler, 1954) report significant differences in favor of boys in arithmetic tests requiring reasoning—what students call "story problems." At the lower age levels, kindergarten and below, where number tests involve simple counting or identification, and on tests for all age levels where only "mechanical" arithmetic is involved, differences do not appear. It is interesting to note that in the two factor analyses of junior high school children (Hobson, 1947; Havighurst and Breese, 1947) males did not excel on N, the ability having to do with manipulation of numbers. It is *solving problems* with numbers that boys manage more successfully than girls.

In judgment and manipulation of spatial relationships, a consistent male superiority has been demonstrated. Tests of the form board type, requiring that pieces be fitted together quickly and accurately, have been widely used as performance tests of intelligence and as indicators of mechanical aptitude. From preschool levels to adult, males are in general more successful than females with this sort of task. They excel, also, in various related mechanical-aptitude measures, such as mazes (Porteus, 1918), puzzle boxes, and tests calling for the assembly of small objects. One of the tests in this field is the Mechanical Comprehension Test by Bennett, calling for the observation of pictures in order to answer questions about mechanical relationships involved. He reports a large and highly significant sex difference (Bennett and Cruikshank, 1942). There is not a single one of the sixty items for which women average higher scores than men. Among high-school students, only one girl in twenty exceeds the boys' average. Most of the studies using factor analysis have reported that males score significantly higher on the Space factor or factors which seem to represent the most essential part of mechanical aptitude (Terman and Tyler, 1954).

Sweeney (1953) has reported a series of experiments on a kind of sex difference that may be related to the differences we have been considering in both the mathematical and mechanical areas. He was interested in problem solving in general, and used a variety of problems in his various experiments. The subjects in this research were college students. Males were significantly superior on all problems requiring what he called *restructuring*, situations in which the person must discard his first system of organizing the facts he has been given and try out new approaches. This difference between the sexes persisted even in groups that had been equated for general intelligence, verbal ability, mathematical ability, relevant knowledge, and various background factors. Taylor [1] has presented some evidence that the difference is primarily a matter of *attitude* toward problems and is susceptible to training.

A study by G. M. Gilbert (1942) suggests that differential training may account for the sex difference that is customarily found for musical talent tests. Among the groups of men and women students in twelve Eastern colleges who had been given the Kwalwasser-Dykema music tests,

[1] D. W. Taylor. Paper presented at the symposium on sex differences held at the meeting of the A.A.A.S. in Berkeley, Calif., December 27, 1954.

subgroups based on the amount of training in music were formed. Women were superior to men in the total indifferentiated group, but in the *untrained* there was no significant difference. Girls seem to be somewhat superior also on art ability, as it is commonly measured in the classroom (H. O. Barrett, 1950). To what extent this difference reflects differential training is not known.

In tasks involving dexterity or light, deft, swift movements of the hands the advantage is again with girls and women. It is difficult to make any absolute generalization with regard to this sort of ability since the dexterities have been found to be highly specific, and a person who is skillful at one type of movement may be below average in another. But on several of the tests commonly used to predict success in various occupations requiring dexterity, the O'Connor Finger Dexterity Test, the O'Connor Tweezer Dexterity Test, and the Purdue Pegboard, the averages for women are consistently better than those for men. (See test manuals.) It seems safe to conclude that in any industrial situation requiring dexterity and speed rather than strength, women workers, on the whole, can be expected to do at least as well as men, and in some performances they may do better. In sensory characteristics, such as hearing, eyesight, taste, and smell, sex differences are negligible, except for the fact that eye defects are less common in females than in males.

Most studies agree that females excel in memory. Memory tests in general use call for the exact repetition of a group of digits or words immediately after presentation, for the reproduction of geometrical figures that have been studied for a short time, or for the recitation of a story or paragraph that has been read aloud. In all these types of test, female superiority is the general rule. The situation is reversed occasionally where the material to be remembered is more familiar or interesting to males. In amount and range of general information, however, men and boys are superior to girls and women.

In the quick perception of details which constitutes the basic aptitude for clerical work of all sorts, women are definitely superior to men. Differences are large and unquestionably significant. Only 21 per cent of employed men clerical workers reach or exceed the median for women clerical workers on the widely-used Minnesota Clerical Test (see manual). Schneidler and Paterson (1942) have summarized data from several sources showing that at all age and grade levels, only about 20 per cent of the males exceed the median for females. This consistent sex difference is of considerable importance in vocational psychology.

One other type of sex difference which shows up with great clarity at the higher age and educational levels has to do with achievement in science. Some of the best evidence comes from reports on the Science Talent Search (Edgerton and Britt, 1944, 1947). Participation in this program is voluntary. Since each year two or three times as many boys as girls apply, one would expect the girls to be far more highly selected. In spite of this fact, highly significant differences in favor of boys have been obtained each year. These subjects are high-school boys and girls. At the grade-school levels, differences on achievement tests favor boys, but are less marked (Heilman, 1933). Primary and preschool studies shown no sex differences in abilities that might seem to underlie science achievement, abilities like comprehending causal relationships (McAndrew, 1943). Increasing male superiority in science is something that develops as a part of the educational process. One might speculate that it is a matter of the same difference in attitude that shows up in the Stanford problem-solving experiments discussed above.

To summarize, males are clearly superior on tests of mathematical reasoning, spatial relationships, and science. Females are superior in verbal fluency, most types of memory, perceptual speed, and dexterity. Some of these differences develop earlier and appear to be more fundamental than others.

In any discussion of *average* differences such as those that have been outlined, reference should again be made to the importance of noting *variability* as well as averages. In most of the abilities we have considered, differences between the *sexes* are so small, and differences between *individuals* of the same sex are so large that a given *individual* can be found who, regardless of sex, may show any degree of these special abilities. A distinction needs to be made between types of situation in which we may want to apply knowledge of human differences. If a *group* must be dealt with, as a whole, then average differences, even though small, may be highly important. For instance, if, because a nation is engaged in a war, one of its industrial plants finds it necessary to replace men with women workers throughout a whole department, and the personnel system and labor market conditions do not permit testing and selection, the difference between the two sexes *as a whole* on the type of task involved is decidedly worth knowing. If, however, the problem is to select *one* first-rate mechanical draftsman, then the sex of the applicants should not be the decisive factor. Although males usually excel in work of the sort, it is quite possible that one or more of the women among the applicants may be superior to any of the men. Group averages will not tell you what you want to know about individuals. The great Dr. Samuel Johnson was once asked, "Which has the most brains, man or woman?" His reply was, "Which man; which woman?" We cannot do better than to reëmphasize his remark.

One of the most plausible theories to explain the difference in achievement between the two sexes makes use of the concept of variability. For a time, it enjoyed wide popularity and was often referred to as one of the basic truths about sex differences. According to this theory, the principal way in which males and females differ has nothing to do with *averages*, but is a matter of range. Females are said to be clustered more compactly around the middle of the distribution with far fewer extreme deviates than males. Figure 36 shows graphically the way this theory would describe the difference in intelligence between the two sexes.

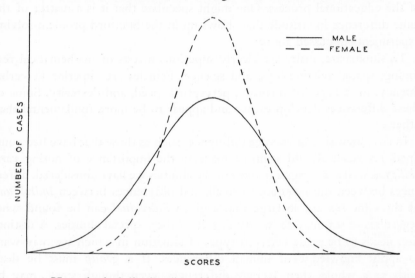

FIGURE 36. Hypothetical distribution of intelligence for the two sexes according to the theory of greater male variability.

Such a difference in the two distributions would explain very satisfactorily two indisputable facts. The first is the preponderance of males among eminent persons. The second is the surplus of males in institutions for the feeble-minded. Essentially, it means that males are more likely to run to extremes; females tend toward mediocrity.

In 1922, L. S. Hollingworth published the first careful analysis of sex differences in numbers of feeble-minded in institutions, based on 1000 hospital cases. The evidence pointed strongly to the conclusion that sampling factors, rather than any genuine sex difference, were at work.

In the first place, the women, on the average, were older at the time they were institutionalized. This seems to mean that because of the less responsible and independent position they occupy in American life and perhaps because of their greater docility and submissiveness, feeble-minded girls are better able to make some sort of place for themselves in their own homes and communities for a longer period of years, than are feeble-minded boys. This explanation is strengthened by Hollingworth's further finding that the women in the institutions had lower IQ's than the men, on the average. In other words, a girl has to be *more deficient* than a boy does in order to be recognized as feeble-minded and sent to an institution. These and other data in this study indicate that percentages of institutional inmates are figures of questionable value as a basis for conclusions about the whole population. About 1914, there was a considerable increase in the percentage of girls in institutions, largely because a contemporary emphasis on eugenic factors (in this case restriction of parenthood) made it seem more important that they be segregated. In summary, the argument for greater male variability based on findings at the *low* end of the intelligence distribution breaks down.

The most extensive information about the *high* end of the distribution comes from Terman's famous study of gifted children (Terman *et al.*, 1925). A school population of 168,000 in grades three to eight which was sifted for children with IQ's of 140 or higher yielded 352 boys and 291 girls, a ratio of about 6 to 5. Witty (1930), on the other hand, found no difference in the proportions of boys and girls in his high-IQ group, and Lewis (1945), who selected the top 10 per cent from a population of 45,000 grade-school children in several hundred widely separated schools reported a sex ratio of 146 girls to 100 boys. The fact that he used a test the verbal content of which tends to favor girls and selected a larger proportion of the total group than Terman did may account for the discrepancy. But it illustrates the difficulty we encounter in trying to evaluate this theory of greater male variability.

The student might think at first glance that this is a clear-cut statistical problem with an obvious statistical answer. But the many studies reporting the amount of variability for comparable male and female groups supply conflicting and inconclusive results. The main reason for this has been that until recently research workers could not agree as to whether they should use *absolute* or *relative* variability in a problem of this kind. Absolute variability is usually stated as a standard deviation (see Chapter 2) and registers simply how much spread there is in the actual distribution of obtained scores. But the fact that in many kinds of measurement (height, for instance, or mechanical ability) women's averages are considerably lower than men's automatically cuts down the possible range of scores for them. Therefore, many research workers have held that if we want to consider variability alone, apart from averages, we must correct for this discrepancy by dividing each standard deviation by the *mean* or average of the group to which it applies. This gives us what is called CV, or Coefficient of Variability. Thus, for height, a standard deviation of 13 inches for a group in which the mean was 65 inches would be equivalent to a standard deviation of 14 inches for a group whose mean was 70 inches. Both would have the same CV. Fortunately for the progress of mental measurement, this is one controversy over method that has been quite conclusively settled. Although the CV has some merit for measurements like height that come in equal units starting from zero, it is never mathematically permissible to form a ratio by dividing figures that are *not* in these definite units. An IQ of 100 does not represent 100 units of anything, and a zero IQ does not mean zero intelligence. We have no real idea of what zero intelligence would be. Certainly a score of 56 on a test of mechanical aptitude does not represent 56 steps beyond just no mechanical aptitude at all. Consequently, for mental measurements, the use of relative variability is *never* justified, and we can rule out at one stroke all the conclusions based on it. (See Chapter 3.)

The McNemar-Terman summary (1936) is the best compilation of significant results that bear on this problem. They find that for anthropometric measurements of all sorts, results vary from age to age, with adult men somewhat more variable than adult women. In educational achievement and in measurements of special aptitudes of all sorts, differences are very small and there is no consistent trend. On verbal intelligence tests, there is a consistent trend toward greater male variability. In twenty-nine out of the thirty-three comparisons they cite, the difference in standard deviations is larger than would be at all likely to occur in comparing different samples of the same sex. This trend is to some extent, however, dependent upon the type of test used, and some tests do not show it. The best evidence again comes from the Scotch study already cited where sampling factors were absolutely controlled. The standard deviation for the boys was 15.88, for the girls 15.26. While the figure is higher for the boys, the difference is small. On the whole, the hypothesis of greater male variability has not stood the test of research, and we must look elsewhere for our explanation of differences in accomplishment.

SEX DIFFERENCES IN PERSONALITY AND MOTIVATION

Interests

It is when we move into the area of non-intellectual traits that we begin to find large psychological differences between males and females of all ages. First of all, their *interests* differ markedly. The most comprehensive research is that carried on by Strong (1943). The method by which occupational scoring keys for the Strong blanks were obtained has been explained in a previous chapter. Sex differences were explored in a similar fashion. He tabulated item responses made by representative samples of men and women and attached scoring weights to those that showed large differences, thus obtaining an M-F (masculinity-femininity) key. In explaining this, Strong makes a point that should always be remembered when considering results of studies in which this and similarly derived scoring keys are used. The procedure tends to *exaggerate* differences between groups, by scoring only the items on which differences occur. Actually there are many more ways in which men and women resemble one another in their interests than ways in which they differ. However, certain kinds of item repeatedly show large sex differences. The distinctly masculine interests show up on items having to do with: (1) mechanical and scientific activities, (2) physically strenuous, adventuresome activities, (3) legal, political, and army occupations, (4) selling activities, (5) certain forms of entertainment such as smokers, rough-house initiations, and chess, (6) certain miscellaneous preferences, e.g., for outside work over inside, for working for oneself, etc.

The distinctly feminine interests are indicated on items having to do with: (1) musical, artistic activities, (2) literary activities, (3) certain kinds of people, especially the unfortunate and disagreeable, (4) certain forms of entertainment, e.g., fortune-tellers, full-dress affairs, and social-problem movies, (5) clerical work, (6) teaching, (7) social work, (8) merchandise, that is, looking at shop windows, displaying merchandise, etc., (9) certain school subjects, (10) miscellaneous characteristics. A more detailed description of the items thus classified can be found in Strong's book (1943).

When M-F scores based on these discriminating items alone are obtained for representative male and female groups, large and highly significant differences are found in all comparisons from adolescence to middle age. There is some overlapping between distributions, but very little. Only 3 per cent of adult men, for example, are more feminine in their scores than the average woman. No adult women are above the median for men, and only 1 per cent are above the 25th percentile.

It is to be expected, since this is the case, that men and women will also differ considerably in the scores they obtain on the occupational scales of the Strong test. This is found to be true. Women average considerably higher than men on the scales for occupations involving art, social service, and writing. Men score higher on the scales for science and business. Seder (1940) found, however, that if instead of comparing sample groups representing *all* men and women you choose groups of men and women in the same profession, the interests of the two sexes are practically indistinguishable. Men and women physicians, for instance, share the same likes and dislikes. Men and women life insurance agents, likewise, are very similar. The interests of women doctors are probably more like those of men doctors than they are like those of housewives.

Strong has developed a special interest blank for women before Seder's results suggested that if one wishes only to get at interests characteristic of an *occupational* group, a special test may not be necessary. Work with the women's blank, however, has pointed to another very interesting fact. As has been explained in Chapter 8, analysis of the correlations between scores has shown six main types of interests for men, along with some others of narrower scope. For women, similar correlational studies show that *one* type of interest pattern predominates so strongly over the others that very often it is the only thing that shows up. Crissy and Daniel (1939) who made one of the factor analyses that clarified this point called this interest factor, which appears to characterize as many as 90 per cent of graduating senior girls in high school, "Interest in Male Association." The name was chosen to represent what housewives, office workers, stenographers, and nurses have in common. It would be simpler and probably more correct to call the factor "Typical Feminine Interests," since it includes elementary teachers as well as housewives and office workers. It doubtless represents the general attitude and outlook of the woman who does not want a career for its own sake, but who is satisfied to pursue any pleasant congenial activity that offers itself until marriage, and perhaps afterward. One can get a fairly good idea of what it is by examining the content of one of the standard women's magazines—home, personal attractiveness, amusements, direct relationships with people. The comparative rarity of specialization of interests in women might well be one of the reasons for the dearth of high-level professional achievement which has been mentioned earlier.

Less extensive work with other interest tests has shown sex differences similar to those Strong has reported. On the Kuder Preference Record, boys average higher in the mechanical, scientific, computational, and persuasive areas, and girls average higher in the musical, artistic, literary, social service, and clerical areas (Traxler and McCall, 1941). On the Allport-Vernon Study of Values, men obtain higher average scores for theoretical, economic, and political values, indicating more interest in abstract ideas, more emphasis on practical success, and more desire for influence and power over others as goals for living. Women obtain higher average scores for aesthetic, social, and religious values, indicating more interest in art, more emphasis on religion, and more concern for the welfare of others as goals for living. Figure 37 shows these differences graphically.

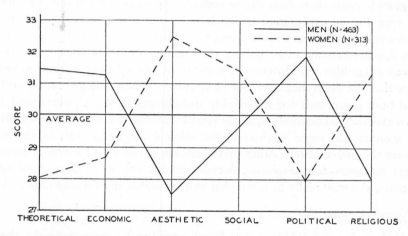

FIGURE 37. Composite psychographs of adult men and women on the Allport-Vernon Study of Values (Allport and Vernon, 1931).

A large number of studies of children's interests by many methods have indicated that boys and girls show marked differences no matter how young they are. As early as the kindergarten years boys engage in more active games calling for vigorous physical activity, whereas girls are more likely to enjoy dolls, paper activities, and games calling for skillful movements. In reading, movies, and radio girls show more interest in sentimental and domestic stories, whereas boys prefer adventure and violent action. When allowed to choose play materials, boys select building material and vehicles, whereas girls prefer articles of furniture and painting and modeling materials. (For a fuller discussion see Terman and Tyler, 1954.) There is no doubt about the fact that marked sex differences in interests develop very early.

Adjustment

When we turn from interests to evaluations of emotionality or "neuroticism" by means of pencil-and-paper questionnaires, we find that there is a consistent tendency for women's averages to be closer to the maladjusted end of the scale than men's are. On the Bernreuter Personality Inventory, for example, the norms show that women are more neurotic, less self-sufficient, more introverted, less dominant, less self-confident, and more socially dependent than men (Bernreuter, 1933). Sex differences of this sort, in contrast with the interest differences, do not appear in groups younger than the high-school age (Terman and Tyler, 1954). Does this mean that females become more neurotic or males less so as they grow up? This may be true, but an explanation which is at least as plausible as this is that as males and females learn more about the places in life they are expected to fill, females become more willing than males to confess what their emotional difficulties are. However, one study by Darley (1937) seems to indicate that the difference may not be spurious. When college students who had been given tests for identifying maladjustment were interviewed by two experienced counselors, it was found that the excess of neurotic trends in women was more marked in the clinical diagnoses than in the test scores themselves. Some other investigations of children by non-questionnaire methods—fear responses, nervous habits, and so forth—suggest also that females may really be somewhat more unstable emotionally than males.

Aggressiveness

If there is some evidence that females tend to be more neurotic, there is no doubt whatever that males tend to be more aggressive. This is one of the sex differences most universally found and shows up as clearly in pre-school children as in adults. It is apparent in teachers' reports of misbehavior in the classroom (H. D. Williams, 1933), and in statistics on delinquency and crime (Scheinfeld, 1943). Scheinfeld cites figures showing that in one fiscal year, 1939-40, for example, the total number of persons committed to federal and state prisons and reformatories was 62,692. Of this number, 60,083 were males and only 2,609 were females. Although the sex ratios are different for different offenses, and change somewhat with changes in social and economic conditions, there is no offense for which the number of females even approaches the number of males.

Although the "ascendance" or "dominance" evaluated by personality inventories is not the same thing as aggressiveness, it probably bears some relationship to it. Here too, males characteristically score significantly higher. On the Bernreuter dominance scale, high-school and college subjects, as well as older adults, show marked sex differences (Bernreuter, 1933). Similar differences show up for social aggressiveness on the Bell Adjustment Inventory (Bell, 1939).

Studies of young children by a variety of methods agree that quarrelsome behavior occurs more often in boys than in girls. The most interesting work on this question has been reported by P. S. Sears and associates (1951). The method that has been used in this series of studies is to bring children, three-, four-, or five-year-olds, individually into a room where they are allowed to do anything they like with dolls representing members of a family in a setting like a typical home. This constitutes a projective situation for children. They act out what they feel. In such a setting boys show significantly more aggression than girls. They are less likely to use the dolls in the customary stereotyped way, acting out common home situations, and more likely to engage in violent maneuvers such as stuffing the baby doll's head into the toilet bowl.

General Masculinity-Femininity

By far the most comprehensive study of all the personality traits in which sex differences occur is the one made by Terman and Miles (1936). The investigation had its origin years before in their discovery, while collecting information about gifted children, that the boys and girls in the experimental group differed markedly from each other in certain ways. Using these items as leads, they tried out a large number of questions on male and female groups of various ages, selecting for their final assortment those which gave statistically significant differences between group responses. The result is the test that they call the Attitude-Interest Analysis Blank, a non-descriptive title chosen so as not to give the individual taking it any clue as to its purpose. There are seven types of item included: Word Association, Inkblot Association, Information, Emotional and Ethical Response, Interests, Opinions, and Introversive Response. The authors give abundant evidence that scores on this test produce large and statistically significant differences between men and women of all ages, occupational levels, and degrees of education. There is very little overlapping of male and female distributions. Terman and Miles remind us that the method they used tends to exaggerate sex difference since the large number of associations, interests, and opinions on which men and women do *not* differ were discarded in constructing the scale. However, the fact that such a set of items can be selected indicates that there are genuine differences between the sexes in our culture.

The nature of these differences is summarized by Terman and Miles as follows: [2]

From whatever angle we have examined them the males included in the standardization groups evinced a distinctive interest in exploit and adventure, in outdoor and physically strenuous occupations, in machinery and tools, in science, physical phenomena, and inventions; and, from rather occasional evidence, in business and commerce. On the other hand, the females of our groups evinced a distinctive interest in domestic affairs and in aesthetic objects and occupations; they have distinctively preferred more sedentary and indoor occupations, and occupations more directly ministrative, particularly to the young, the helpless, the distressed. Supporting and supplementing these are the more subjective differences—those in emotional disposition and direction. The males directly or indirectly manifest the greater self-assertion and aggressiveness; they express more hardihood and fearlessness, and more roughness of manners, language, and sentiments. The females express themselves as more compassionate and sympathetic, more timid, more fastidious and aesthetically sensitive, more emotional in general (or at least more expressive of the four emotions considered), severer moralists, yet admit in themselves more weaknesses in emotional control and (less noticeably) in physique.

But we must define some of our terms more precisely, for instance, aggressiveness" and "self-assertion." The evidence is for initiative, enterprise, vigorous activity, outdoor adventure; "aggressiveness" need not imply selfishness or tyranny or unfair attack. The compassion and sympathy of the female, again, appears from the evidence personal rather than abstract, less a principled humanitarianism than an active sympathy for palpable misfortune or distress. In disgust, in aesthetic judgment, and in moral censure, the evidence is rather for the influence of fashion and of feeling than of principle or reason. Our evidence need not imply the possession of a "truer" taste or a more discerning conscience. (Terman and Miles, 1936, pp. 447-448)

It is plain from the data furnished by Terman and Miles that masculinity-femininity, as measured by their M-F scale, is no all-or-none trait. The various occupational groups differ, for instance. Among men, athletes and engineers have the most "masculine" averages; journalists, artists, and clergymen, the least "masculine." Among women, domestic employees are the most "feminine"; athletes and doctors, the least "feminine." Age groups differ also. Eighth-grade girls are more "feminine," eleventh-grade boys more "masculine" than any other age groups. Figure 38 shows some of these differences graphically.

Individuals within any one of the occupational or age groups differ among themselves. What we have is a continuous distribution rather than an exact classification.

[2] Reprinted by permission from *Sex and Personality: Studies in Masculinity and Femininity* by L. M. Terman and C. C. Miles, Copyrighted, 1936, by the McGraw-Hill Book Co., Inc.

Terman and Miles report in some detail on a supplementary study in which they investigated the attitudes of male homosexuals, as shown by the M-F scale. They found a marked difference between the 71 classified as *passive* (those who customarily played female roles in homosexual relationships) and the 46 classified as *active* (those who customarily played male roles). The PMH group (passive male homosexuals) obtained sig-

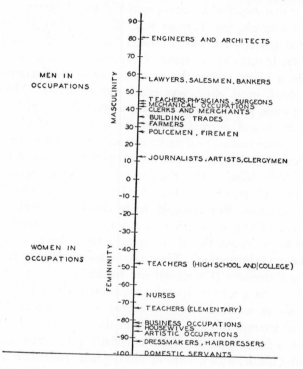

FIGURE 38. Mean M-F scores of various occupational groups (Terman and Miles, 1936).

nificantly more feminine scores than the average, the AMH group (active male homosexuals) slightly more masculine. All of the subtests with the exception of Exercise 4 (Emotional and Ethical Response) showed this characteristic femininity in the PMH group. It was most pronounced on Exercise 5 (Interests). The authors hasten to remind the reader that not all men who receive low M-F scores are inverts. They carried on some exploratory work with a special I (inversion) scale in which the weight attached to each item was based on the extent to which it differentiated between the PMH group and an average group of high-school boys. This item analysis showed, in general, that in the invert group, interests, attitudes, thought trends, and occupational preferences were characteristically feminine. Interest in art, music, and religion was common. Aggressiveness of all kinds was repudiated. Introvertive and psychoneurotic tendencies and excessive sex consciousness characterized the invert group to a greater than average degree. Case studies of eighteen of the individuals, together with the fact that *physical* measurements did *not* differentiate the homosexuals from normals, led Terman and Miles to place the emphasis on environmental rather than constitutional factors in the development of homosexuality. It was characteristic of a number of these subjects to have grown up in a home where the mother was over-affectionate and the father was dead, or if alive, was cruel and autocratic. Many of them reported the same pattern of having been treated as a girl. An overemphasis on neatness and niceness of behavior and a lack of vigilance against seduction by older homosexual males also seemed to be involved.

One source of confusion in the interpretation of scores made on the Terman and Miles blank is that the parts show little correlation with one another, so that it is possible for the same score to represent quite different patterns of responses. For example, high-school boys and engineers are both very masculine groups, with an average standard score of .75. The high-school boys obtain this score largely from Exercise 5 (Interests) and Exercise 3 (Information). They are below average in masculinity as measured by Exercise 4 (Emotional and Ethical Response). But it is precisely this Exercise 4 which gives the engineers their high score. The two groups are not as much alike as the averages of their total scores would suggest. In an attempt to clear up some of this confusion, Ford and Tyler (1952) made a factor analysis of the correlations between subtests on the Terman-Miles blank, with groups of ninth-grade students as subjects. For the boys, two factors were clearly shown, one an emotional characteristic that could be labeled "Toughness" or perhaps "Insensitivity," the other an interest factor like that that we have described in connection with the Strong test. For the girls the first factor seemed to be "Sensitivity," the second an interest factor. The analysis for the girls also gave some evidence for a third factor which seemed to have to do with the acceptance of a feminine social role.

Since Terman and Miles did their work, a number of M-F scoring keys for various other tests have been constructed. In interpreting results obtained with these, the relative independence of emotional characteristics and interests should always be kept in mind, since the scales are usually composites of the two types of item. Particularly we must be wary of making judgments of sexual abnormality from such scales. A man can have a large number of interests that are feminine in our culture without being homosexual.

Achievement Motivation

It has been apparent for a long time to vocational counselors dealing with young people that girls do not put as much emphasis on professional or occupational success as do boys. Left to their own devices, a large proportion of boys are likely to make vocational choices in the professional areas, whether or not their level of intelligence and academic success warrants such a choice. With girls the problem for the counselors is often of an opposite nature; many of them do not aspire to the positions their abilities would make possible. One of the techniques for measuring achievement motivation that has come into common use for personality investigations is the "Level of Aspiration" experiment. The subject is given a trial at some task, then asked what score he will try for on the next attempt. It is interesting to note that results using this method have substantiated what had been observed about sex differences in occupational ambitions. Walter and Marzolf (1951) tested ten boys and ten girls at each of four grade levels, fourth, sixth, eighth, and twelfth, with the Rotter "aspiration board." Girls of all grade levels showed significantly lower "goal discrepancy" scores—that is, they set their sights lower. Differences in aspiration level were not related to grade level or to achievement on subject-matter tests. The lesser degree of ambition, if one can call it that, was equally characteristic of younger and older girls and of good and poor students.

In the most original and thorough study of achievement motivation done so far, that reported by McClelland et al. (1953), striking sex differences again appeared. The method used in all these experiments was to score for achievement motivation stories written in response to pictures, both before and after subjects had been exposed to a sort of intelligence test presented in such a way as to stimulate achievement needs. Although statistically significant *changes* in responses to the pictures showed up in males under such circumstances, they were not apparent in females. An ingenious group of supplementary experiments served to show, however, that what the results indicated was not a lower general need for achievement in women, but rather that the needs they had were aroused in a different way. When *social* rather than *intellectual* acceptability was called in question by the situation set up between TAT test periods, achievement scores changed significantly in females but not in males. The authors think that this difference may be related to the greater importance of dependence on others for women and independence of others for men. It also has obvious bearing on sex differences in professional achievement.

Perceptual Characteristics

Striking sex differences in another sort of "dependence" have come out of the series of studies by Witkin *et al.* (1954) which have been reported in some detail in Chapter 9. Table 21 shows some of these differences on specific tests. What they add up to is that women are less able

TABLE 21.

Sex Differences on Perceptual Tests

(Selected from Table 8.1, Witkin *et al.*, 1954, pp. 156-157)

TEST SITUATION	NATURE OF SCORE	MEN		WOMEN		P
		N	SCORE	N	SCORE	
Rod-and-frame (Series 1, body tilted)	Degrees deviation of rod from upright per trial	136	12.4	258	16.9	.01
Tilting-room-tilting-chair (Series 1a, room adjustment)	Degrees deviation of room from upright per trial	136	11.5	258	17.7	.01
Rotating-room (Series 1, room adjustment)	Degrees deviation of room from upright per trial	45	17.5	50	13.0	.05
Embedded figures	Mean time in seconds to locate simple figure in complex	51	39.8	51	58.2	.01

to disregard the visual field in which the perceptual pattern they are trying to grasp is embedded. They cannot disregard the context of a perception and concentrate on it alone. Supplementary experiments with tests which did not show sex differences served further to clarify the nature of the trait involved. It is not that females are less able than males to use stimuli coming from their own bodies. In the tilting or rotating room tests carried on *with eyes closed*, women did as well as men. The difference lay rather in their tendency to utilize a procedure the authors call "passive-acceptance"—to assume at the beginning that the room was upright even when it was tilted as much as 56° rather than to utilize all kinds of perceptual clues by means of which they could have *analyzed* the true situation. Developmental studies showed differences of the same sort even at the eight-year level, but they did not become marked enough to be consistently significant statistically until the adult years.

One other type of sex difference which is perhaps related to the Witkin findings has been studied by Sandström (1953). He discovered the curious fact that if a subject in a completely darkened room is asked to point to a luminous spot of light, he finds it impossible to do this with any accuracy. The errors made by women are significantly greater than those made by men, and women are much more likely to show disoriented behavior. If Witkin's work indicates that females are more dependent on the surrounding field than males, Sandström's might be interpreted as evidence that they perform less well when no visual field is available and react in a more disturbed fashion to its absence.

BIOLOGICAL AND SOCIAL ORIGINS OF SEX DIFFERENCES

As in the other areas of differential psychology, there has been much discussion and controversy on the question of the extent to which sex differences arise from basic biological factors. This problem is set apart from the rest of the heredity-environment issue by the fact that in this case we know that the two groups do differ through hereditary causes in many ways—anatomical structure, hormonal composition, and so forth. The question is, "Do these anatomical and physiological differences we know to exist make certain kinds of psychological differences inevitable?"

It should be recognized, however, that physical masculinity or femininity is not so clearly an all-or-none quality as many people believe it to be. Embryologically the sex organs are practically indistinguishable for the first two months and have corresponding structures even when completely developed (Kinsey et al., 1953, p. 572). Both main types of sex hormones, the androgens and the estrogens, are produced in both males and females. It is in the balance or relative proportions of these different chemicals that the sexes differ. But this also varies considerably from individual to individual within the same sex. Masculinity-femininity, physically or psychologically defined, must be regarded as a continuum—or perhaps a number of continua—rather than as a fixed entity.

The psychoanalytic writers have been the principal defenders of the notion that differences in physiology and reproductive functions create different emotional needs in males and females, which are reflected in personality differences and should be taken into consideration in the planning of a good society. Most of their writing has been based on clinical study of patients rather than on the kind of quantitative research with which this book is concerned. There have, however, been a few quantitative studies supporting the psychoanalytic conclusions. Blum (1949) devised a new sort of projective test specifically for the purpose of measuring the kinds of psychosexual variables that the analysts have discussed—oral and anal tendencies, castration anxiety, and the like. Having gone through standard psychoanalytic textbooks for theoretical ideas, he made specific predictions as to the direction of sex differences that would appear in the various scores on the test. The most conclusive finding for our purposes was that for nine areas where it was possible to make such definite predictions, eight of the differences obtained from the responses of male and female college students were statistically significant in the predicted direction.

Another study utilizing a quite different approach also gives evidence for the kind of sex differences analytic theory postulates. Franck and Rosen (1949) asked their subjects, again college students, to make drawings from very simple stimuli, such as pairs of parallel vertical lines. They found that they could develop a scoring system for these drawings which differentiated between the sexes at a high level of significance. For instance, females tend to close in their drawings at the ends, males to leave them open. Females draw static objects, males moving things. Females draw flowers, rooms, and household furnishings, males vehicles and projectiles. It was such differentiations that formed the basis of the scoring system. The authors argued that most of the kinds of differences it reflected could not be explained on the basis of familiarity or environmental influence. Pokers as well as pans are household objects, but boys draw the former, girls the latter. Franck and Rosen considered the explanation to be rather that girls and boys differ in "body image," which, as they use the term, covers both structure and function. They explained how this general "body image" could constitute a set which could determine how an individual would deal with all sorts of ambiguous materials. Shepler (1951) has since shown that there is no relationship between masculinity-femininity assessed in this way and the trait measured by such tests as the Terman-Miles blank.

The fact that both the Blum and the Franck and Rosen studies used college subjects throws some doubt on the generality of the results. It is true, of course, that Terman and Miles, Strong, and others have shown that college men and women differ somewhat less from one another than do unselected groups, and thus one might reason that the obtained differences would have been even larger had the samples been more representative. Fortunately there is another study in which the subjects were eleven-, twelve-, and thirteen-year-old children, about 150 at each age, that furnishes corroborating evidence. Erikson (1951) asked these children in the California Guidance Study to "construct an exciting movie scene" from building materials and objects supplied to them. Honzik (1951) analyzed the productions in terms of content, and found the sort of sex differences to which we have already referred—the preference of boys for blocks, vehicles, and people in uniform, the preference of girls for furniture and people in ordinary dress. But Erikson showed that the differences go beyond these content preferences which might be purely a matter of cultural influence. When he analyzed the way in which the same materials were used, he found that boys tended to produce high structures, ruins, and scenes suggesting sudden arrest of motion, whereas girls set up static, open enclosures such as rooms. Again, as in the Franck and Rosen study, there was internal evidence that this was not just a matter of familiarity, and some sort of "body image" theory fits in well with what was found.

The second of Kinsey's research volumes (1953) calls into question many of the psychoanalytic generalizations but presents evidence for some kind of a basic biological difference in male and female sexuality. He stresses the fact that there is little if any difference in the anatomical or physiological bases of sex behavior in men and women. While the structures and specific sex hormones differ, the sensitive areas are the same or closely similar, and orgasm and the processes leading to it occur in the same manner. It is the *psychological* aspects of the sex response that show the clearest sex differences. Males have sex responses associated with a much wider variety of stimuli and situations than females do, so that they can be aroused in many more ways—by fantasies, by erotic pictures, by seeing male or female genitalia. Why this difference should exist is not clear to Kinsey, but it seems to arise from something deeper than differential cultural conditioning, since the same phenomenon can be observed in non-human mammals. He concludes after examining all the evidence with regard to neural and hormonal factors that there must be some sex difference in the cerebral cortex. This explanation seems hardly adequate, however, to explain the tremendous variability he reports with regard to female sexuality. A sizable proportion of women do seem to respond as strongly as men do to fantasy, sexual pictures, and so forth. It is interesting that in their range of sex behavior and attitudes, females seem to be *less* uniform than males. The theory of greater male variability does not apply here.

A somewhat different sort of biological explanation of sex differences has been proposed by Johnson and Terman (1940). They discuss in some detail the physiological characteristics that are ordinarily included under the term *homeostasis*. They show that in the maintenance of constant body temperature, the acid-base relationship in the blood, constant blood sugar level, and gonadal activity, males are somewhat more stable than females. They propose the hypothesis that there is a difference in "mental homeostasis" that accounts for many of the psychological sex differences. Women tend to be more sensitive to external influences, more easily thrown off balance by them. It is interesting to note that this explanation, proposed so long before, fits in with some of the differences in sexuality that Kinsey outlines and with the differences in perception found by Witkin and his associates.

As evidence that sex differences are not entirely cultural, Johnson and Terman cite four facts. First, differences have been found in very young children. Second, neurotic tendencies in women have shown no relative decrease as women have been allowed more freedom. Third, institutional groups such as orphanage children whose environments have been closely similar over long periods of time show the same sort of differences as groups in the general population. Fourth, a growing body of research on animals shows plainly that sex hormones can influence behavior.

The fact that biological explanations of the origin of sex differences have become more convincing as the years have passed does not mean that cultural influences are being ignored. On the contrary, the progress of research has made it possible for us to see more clearly the ways in which the two can interact. It seems now that it is possible for any degree of "masculinity" or "femininity" to occur in an individual of either sex, but that a girl growing up does find certain attitudes, interests, and personality traits more congenial than others and tends to acquire them, whereas a boy is likely to acquire another set. This slanting, this difference in tendency to acquire differential characteristics, is the factor that may have a biological basis.

There is little doubt that just what is acquired in the way of abilities, interests, and attitudes depends to a considerable extent on the culture in which a person grows up. Often cited in this connection is Margaret Mead's study of three primitive tribes (1935). Among the Arapesh, both sexes display what we would consider feminine characteristics. Among the Mundugumor, both sexes display what we would consider masculine characteristics. They are violent, aggressive, and competitive, lovers of action and fighting. Among the Tchambuli, the traits as we find them in our society appear to be reversed. It is the women who have the positions of power and take the responsibility for earning the living of the family, while the men engage in artistic and non-essential activities. Consequently, the women are impersonal, practical, and efficient, whereas the men are artistic, timid, sensitive, and dependent. (We have probably all seen families in our society where this is true.)

Although such extreme differences between societies are possible, there are many more groups that have been studied where the sex roles are somewhat like those we find in our own culture. Mead in her later book on the subject (1949) reëvaluates all this material.

It is the concept of *sex roles* that has helped to organize our thinking about the effects of culture. It seems now that it is the roles children learn to play that determine a great many of their attitudes and habits. It is not necessary that a little boy be trained specifically to like guns, practice football, and take responsibility. If he can grasp all at once what it means to be a man, he has a mental set which will operate in many diverse situations. There have been a number of studies designed to show what these roles are in our culture and how they affect development. Sherriffs and Jarrett (1953) and Fernberger (1948) have shown that college students have definite, consistent beliefs about the ways in which men and women differ. Tuddenham (1951, 1952), using a reputation test in which the names of individuals in a child's own school room or play group are matched up with various traits, such as "Good at Games," "Show-off," or "Friendly," showed clearly that even among children in the early elementary grades there are consistent differences in the type of trait correlated with popularity. In boys' groups, such traits as "Real Boy," "Leader," "Good at Games," and "Takes Chances" make for popularity. Among girls, traits like "Quiet," "Not a Show-off," "Not Quarrelsome," "Doesn't Fight," are related more closely to popularity ratings.

There is some evidence in a study reported by S. Smith (1939) that a general notion of male superiority develops in both boys and girls as they grow up. Girls and boys in each age group from eight to fifteen were asked to vote as to whether boys or girls possess to a greater degree each of nineteen desirable and fourteen undesirable traits. The striking fact was that the older the groups were the more favorable all the ratings made by *both* sexes were to boys. This is the more remarkable when we remember that during these school years the girls are consistently behaving better, having less trouble, and getting better marks than the boys.

Studies by Milner (1949) and by Rabban (1950) have been concerned with the interaction of sex and social status in role formation. There is evidence from both these studies that it is the personalities of the parents and the nature of the children's relationship to them that affect the learning of these sex roles. The Rabban study also shows that concepts of sex roles develop in very young children, although there is some difference between the sexes and the social classes with regard to this. By the four- to five-year level, working-class boys show an awareness of sex roles. Middle-class boys develop it about a year later. Middle-class girls are the slowest to develop a clear-cut sex role concept.

Even clearer evidence about the way in which sex-role concepts develop is furnished by a study reported by Sears, Pintler, and Sears (1946). In a standardized doll-play situation, three-, four-, and five-year-old children were scored for aggression. As in previous studies, there was a marked sex difference in the total amount of aggression shown. The next step was to compare the scores for children whose fathers were at home and children whose fathers were away in the Armed Services. The girls showed no difference in aggression whether they were from father-present or father-absent homes. But the boys from father-present homes were significantly more aggressive than the others. Differences were most pronounced in the three-year-olds. It would seem that by the age of three, boys whose fathers are at home develop a concept of masculinity permitting a considerable amount of aggression. Boys whose fathers are away develop the same concept, but more slowly. It is evident in their behavior by five but not by three.

The extent to which the marked differences in achievement we have noted at the beginning of this chapter grow out of differing concepts of sex roles is hard to estimate. In the long run, it would seem to be desirable that we formulate these roles in such a way that they are in harmony with biological facts, but permit and encourage both male and female participation in all the varied activities which go into the making of our society. Art, business, education, and science are enriched by the distinctive contributions men and women can make (Mead, 1949). In the short run, however, individuals who fail to come to terms with the prevailing opinions may be less happy than the ones who go along with such opinions even when they are wrong. Seward (1945) asked college girls to fill out an attitude scale on sex roles in postwar society. She then compared on a number of psychological tests the fifteen who were the most liberal in their views with the fifteen who were most conservative. There was some evidence that the conservatives were somewhat happier and better adjusted than the liberals. Whether this was the cause or the effect of the sex role differences would be hard to determine, but it illustrates the difficulties one encounters in thinking about changing such basic attitudes. As many writers on the subject have pointed out, the progress of science and the removal from the home of many kinds of work that were once done there makes the restriction of women's activities to home and family increasingly inappropriate. The wide range of abilities in both sexes makes it appear that sex typing of occupations is not appropriate either. But the *attitudes* that both men and women have grown up with fit these practices better than they do the actual economic and psychological facts, and too great a deviation from the accepted attitude makes for maladjustment. There lies our problem.

SUMMARY

Interest in psychological research on the topic of sex differences has grown by leaps and bounds since 1900. Tabulation of statistical information about eminent individuals has brought into sharp relief the fact that high achievement is very rare among women. In school achievement, however, girls usually excel boys. So far as tested abilities are concerned, there are some sex differences in the averages, but the distributions show a great deal of overlapping. Males tend to be higher in mathematical reasoning, spatial judgment, and science. Females average higher in verbal fluency, rote memorizing of most materials, perceptual speed, and dexterity. Careful analysis of what the distributions show has cast considerable doubt on the concept of greater male variability.

In interests, attitudes, and personality characteristics, much larger differences have been shown to exist, although even here there is considerable overlapping between distributions for the two sexes. Males show greater aggressiveness, females more symptoms of neuroticism and instability. Sex differences in likes and dislikes, in emotional and ethical attitudes, in the kind of success that is desired, in perceptual habits, and in sexual responsiveness to psychological stimulation have been shown.

There is evidence that the emotional differences are more closely tied in with fundamental biological differences than the ability differences are. In all these areas, however, concepts as to what the sex roles are seem to be of considerable importance.

CHAPTER 11

Race and Nationality Differences

PROBLEMS AND DIFFICULTIES

As HAS BEEN pointed out, the research worker in human differences does not start his work in a vacuum. His task is often not simply to make a beginning in a field where nothing is known, but to check up on convictions that are held with dogmatic certainty. Nowhere is this situation more evident than in the field of race differences. Up to the beginning of this century, there was scarcely a dissenting voice in the general consensus that definite mental differences in the various races paralleled their obvious physical differences, and that the white race was unquestionably superior to the others. G. O. Ferguson, in his monograph (1916), cites many such opinions. The eminent British scientist and pioneer in the field of differential psychology, Sir Francis Galton, held that if one postulated sixteen grades of mental ability between Aristotle and the lowest idiot the average Negro would be about two grades or one-eighth the total distance below the average white. Another common view, expressed by Tylor (1881), Odum (1910), G. Stanley Hall (1905) and others, was that adult Negroes were inferior to adult whites because their mental development stopped earlier. Whereas white children continued their mental growth throughout adolescence, Negro children had theirs cut short at about the age of twelve. Most writers on the subject agreed that it was in the so-called higher mental processes—such as reasoning, attention, foresight, and judgment—that these differences were most marked. Many were even willing to concede that in sensory and motor characteristics, keenness of the senses, quickness of response, and perception of slight details, some of the more primitive races excelled our own. Portrayal of the Indian scout in fiction embodies this opinion.

In general, the total effect of research done so far on the race-difference problem has been a tremendous *decrease* in the degree of certainty with which it is possible to hold such a view. Besides the problems inherent in any research on psychological differences between human groups, such problems as those of finding adequate tests or measuring instruments, securing representative samples of the population, and checking both the statistical and the practical significance of the differences between averages, there are some other special difficulties encountered in research on race. Because of the extreme urgency of race problems in modern society, it is particularly important that students of the social sciences be familiar with what these difficulties are. On the one hand, we must refrain from drawing unwarranted conclusions from data with certain inevitable limitations. On the other hand, we need to make full use of the facts that we have discovered, in situations where they are applicable.

The first of these special problems is that almost never are we able to carry out our psychological studies on *pure* races. Race is essentially a biological concept. The fact that a group of persons now living had in the remote past a common ancestry means that they have a number of physical characteristics in common, characteristics that set them off from groups of other remote ancestry in the same way that dachshunds are distinguished from cocker spaniels. The number of places where one may encounter pure races of human beings, in this sense, is extremely limited, and as transportation and communication facilities grow and expand into remote regions of the world, there will be even fewer of them. To add to the difficulty, in the places where we find groups of people who seem to belong to a single racial group, such as the True Negroes of western Africa, our common varieties of psychological test are not applicable. We cannot ask these individuals the questions in the Binet Scale and expect meaningful answers. Even if we should translate the questions into their language, so many of them refer to objects and experiences that are totally unfamiliar to Africans that the responses would still be of no use to us. Performance tests of intelligence are less obviously dependent on a certain standard background of experience and information, but we do not escape from the question of the effect on their scores of subtler factors like motivation, attitude, and experience with toys and pictures.

When we compare racial groups living in the same country and speaking the same language, such as Negroes and whites in the United States, the difficulty of classification becomes an important consideration. Wherever races have lived in close proximity for a number of years, considerable race mixture has occurred. This means that we will have within any so-called racial group individuals showing all different degrees of the physical characteristics that once differentiated this race from others. It may prove difficult or impossible, in such a case, to assign an individual *scientifically* to one race or the other. Anthropologists have given considerable attention to identifying the physical characteristics on the basis of which useful classifications of races can be made. The traditional criterion has been skin color, and the most widely used classification of human beings into the white, black, and yellow races, with red and brown races as possibly separate from these, is based on it. Other physical characteristics, however, are more reliable indicators of racial origin than is color. The pigmentation of the eyes and the color and texture of the hair show race differences. Measurements can be made of the shape of the cross-section of a hair which will show whether it approximates the round shape characteristic of straight-haired races or the flat shape that makes it kinky or woolly. Gross bodily dimensions such as stature and breadth of shoulders show significant differences from race to race. Cranial and facial measurements are also useful differentiating data. Genetically, all these racial traits seem to be determined by genes that vary *independently*, so that almost any combination of physical traits may occur in an individual whose ancestry includes persons of more than one race. As long as a racial group remains isolated, the traits will all seem to go together inevitably because the mother and father who endow their child with a set of genes for the typical skin color of his race will also pass on to him the genes for the other typical physical characteristics. They have no other kind to give him. When there has been an admixture of genes from another race, however, this will not be true. Negroes, for instance, as a whole, are relatively dark-skinned, long-limbed, and woolly-haired; but we have all seen so-called Negroes in this country who have light skins but woolly hair, dark skins but Caucasian features, dark skins and long limbs but straight hair, and so on. It is difficult in many cases to decide whether a person is or is not a Negro.

A caution with regard to racial classification systems based on anatomical measurements has arisen from the findings of Boas (1911), Hirsch (1927), and Spier (1929) that such characteristics once thought to be entirely determined by heredity, are subject to environmental influence. Children born in the United States are significantly different in these measurements from children of the same race and nationality born elsewhere, perhaps because of differences in nutrition and type of infant care. Thus we must recognize that our racial classifications are not clear-cut exact representations of facts about human groups, but only rough approximations to some biological differentiation assumed to have a genetic origin in the far-distant past and not yet entirely wiped out by migration and intermarriage.

Many biologists and anthropologists hold today that the most satisfactory means of differentiating between races is to compare the *distributions* for representative samples of the groups in question with regard to traits known to have a genetic basis (W. C. Boyd, 1950). Blood types have been the factors most commonly used in this way. If we look at the figures for three varieties of Americans, for example, we find that they distribute themselves as follows:

U. S. Whites	45 % O	41 % A	10 % B	4 % AB
U. S. Negroes	44.2% O	30.3% A	21.8% B	3.7% AB
North American Indians (Sioux)	91 % O	7 % A	2 % B	0 % AB

(Taken from UNESCO, *What Is Race?*, 1952)

If we use this method as a basis of classification we do not get clear-cut divisions. Chinese and Negroes differ less from white Americans than Poles differ from Frenchmen. Furthermore, it is obviously impossible to classify an *individual* by such methods. For any given person with a moderately dark skin and B-type blood, for example, how are we to know whether he belongs to the 22 per cent of the Negro race or to the 10 per cent of the white race whose blood is of this variety? Nevertheless, for analyzing the relationships between populations and tracing the migrations of the past, this study of distributions has been most helpful. The general concept it represents is an important basis for all our thinking about race. There is no absolute difference. The characteristics human beings show are the same. It is only the proportions that differ biologically.

There is still another vexing question related to the interpretation of research findings on race differences in a country like the United States. Historical and economic factors have produced a social structure in which persons of different races are exposed to quite different environmental influences throughout their lives. If anatomical proportions are not entirely determined by heredity, most psychologists agree that mental abilities and personality traits are even less so. Consequently, before we can answer the question as to whether there are fundamental *biologically-determined* mental differences between races, we must either make the proper allowance for the effects of unequal education and socio-economic status, or we must find groups of subjects of the races being compared who have not been exposed to these inequalities but who still are representative of their respective populations. In order to do the first of these things, we need to know a great deal more than we do now about the specific effects of all sorts of environmental influences on mental development, the subtle factors such as the emotional responsiveness and the goals and values of the family, as well as the obvious factors such as material standard of living and amount and quality of education. To do the second is practically impossible. We do not find, in this country, sizable groups of whites and Negroes for whom environmental influences have been equal.

Attempts to break this impasse will be discussed in the following sections. They are, so far and perhaps always, only attempts; and we must agree with those who hold that no biologically-determined mental differences between races have been *proved* to exist. What we must remember is that when we fail to prove groups *unequal*, we do not thereby prove them *equal*. We simply leave the question undecided. We find, however, when we analyze carefully what we need to know in order to make valid decisions about individuals and the social order, that the facts with which the research studies have supplied us can be of considerable practical value. It is from this viewpoint that the data discussed in this chapter are to be approached. Let us admit at the outset that we have no justification in the research evidence for the kinds of dogmatic convictions about the relative mental abilities of races that were once all too common and that are still current in much popular thinking. We do have, however, data that can enable us to avoid *wrong* conclusions and can help with both our day-to-day problems of classifying and educating people and our long-range problems of improving human society.

Most of the work on psychological race differences that will be taken up in this chapter has to do with the Caucasian, Negroid, and Mongolian races and the Nordic, Alpine, and Mediterranean subraces. There is also some research on American Indians, and on Malaysians in Hawaii. Just where these groups are to be classified is still somewhat a matter of controversy. Psychologists have usually compared the data they get using these groups as subjects with data on whites and let it go at that. Needless to say, in any of these studies the elaborate measurements of a variety of characteristics that would be necessary really to determine the race of any given subject (assuming this is possible in principle) have seldom been made. If a child lives in a Negro district of a city and is considered a Negro by his classmates, the research worker includes him in his Negro group. Because it is our custom to excommunicate persons of mixed blood from the white race, an undetermined number of the subjects listed as Negroes in the studies to be reported are partly white. This is also true of yellow-white comparisons, but to a lesser degree, since there has been less race mixture here. For practical purposes, this does not matter. What we want to study are the differences between the groups as society is now determining them.

EARLY RESEARCH ON SENSORY AND MOTOR DIFFERENCES

Some of the earliest work in race differences was designed to discover whether there were differences in vision, hearing, smell, reaction-time, and motor control between the primitive races and our own. In the early 1900's, reports were published of an anthropological expedition to the Torres Straits, giving the results of psychological tests of sensory and motor abilities of the natives (*Reports*, 1901-1903). In 1904, Woodworth (1910) tested 300 persons representing many primitive races at the St. Louis World's Fair. American Indians, Negritos from the Philippines, Malayan Filipinos, Ainus from Japan, Africans, Eskimos, Patagonians, and Cocopa Indians all were included in his group of subjects. There turned out to be very little difference between the sensory and motor abilities of any of these people and those of average white subjects. Indians and Filipinos were somewhat above the white norms for vision, but in hearing the averages of all the primitive groups fell somewhat below the white average. Circumstances might well account for these differences. The greater use of the eyes for comparatively unnatural types of activity on the part of white men might be expected to impair their vision to some extent. The greater emphasis on cleanliness and hygiene and the freedom from some forms of injury incurred under primitive conditions should give the white man a better-functioning ear. Woodworth noted also that stimuli such as watch ticks and clicks would be less familiar to the primitive subjects. In keenness of smell, all groups were very much alike. The one most important sensory difference Woodworth noticed was in regard to the sense of pain. Greater pressure on the skin was required to produce a report of pain in the primitive than in white subjects. This may, however, represent a difference in what subjects understand "pain" to mean. In tests of color matching, tapping, illusions, and handedness, no differences were apparent.

The only test similar to our present intelligence tests that Woodworth had at his disposal in those early years of the twentieth century was the Seguin Form Board test, in which a set of blocks of various shapes were to be fitted as quickly as possible into the holes where they belonged. Such tests are still widely used as non-verbal indicators of somewhat complex mental processes, though it is no longer held that they measure exactly the same abilities as tests based on language. On these tests, most of Wood-worth's subjects did about equally well and made scores about equal to those of white subjects. A few groups, however, the Igorot and Negrito from the Philippines, and the Pygmies from the Congo, were very much lower than the average. About this finding, Woodworth comments:

If the results could be taken at their face value, they would indicate differ-ences of intelligence between races, giving such groups as the Pygmy and Negrito a low station as compared with most of mankind. The fairness of the test is not, however, beyond question; it may have been of a more unfamiliar sort to these wild hunting folk than to more settled groups. (Woodworth, 1910, p. 181)

The investigation of sensori-motor differences is no longer considered an important research problem. Goodenough (1936), reanalyzing the Torres Straits and St. Louis Exposition data, has brought out the fact that psychologists may have abandoned this line of investigation too soon. Differences in visual, auditory, and cutaneous sensitivity, as reported in these early studies, may have some significance even though they are small. Since such traits can be measured directly and not by inference, as intelli-gence must be, there is merit in her suggestion that investigation of them be continued. However, there is increasing evidence from other research fields that it is not the efficiency of the sense organs themselves so much as it is the *use* people have learned to make of them that varies from group to group. The blind, for instance, do not have a more delicate touch sense than do their seeing neighbors, but their *learning* of a certain kind is more advanced. They have learned to make *discriminations* that are much finer than ordinary persons customarily need. The feats of Commando troops during World War II are as spectacular as anything Cooper's Uncas could boast, showing that white men can learn the Indians' keenness and control if their lives depend upon it and if they have the right learning situation.

Very little has been done so far to determine whether there are racial differences on the more complex kinds of perceptual traits we have dis-cussed in Chapter 9. There is one study by Thouless (1933) in which 20 Indian students were compared with 49 British students in what he calls "phenomenal regression," but which is ordinarily called perceptual con-stancy—the tendency to perceive an object in terms of its known physical size and shape rather than its actual projection on the retina. There was a difference between the English and the Indians, significant at the .001 level. The Indians saw things more as the retinal image would be, the English more as the object itself was known to be. Thouless mentions that this difference might account for the lack of perspective in Oriental art.

That perceptual differences can be cultural in origin is suggested by Thompson's (1951) report that children from three different Indian tribes differ in their characteristic responses to Rorschach blots. The Papago tend to see vague wholes, the Navajo obvious detail, and the Hopi differentiated, organized wholes.

The investigation of perceptual differences between races and cultures may again become an important line of research. So far, however, the large majority of studies have been concerned with differences in the complex mental abilities tapped by intelligence tests.

RESEARCH ON THE AMERICAN NEGRO

It was natural that comparisons of Negro and white intelligence should constitute a primary research problem in America. For one thing, subjects were easily available. For another, the race problem was and still is one of the most acute social problems in the United States. There was and still is urgent need for as much information as possible.

The earliest comparisons of white and Negro children were made on the basis of school surveys to identify backward children. It was found quite generally that there were more retarded Negroes than whites, that is, children who were over-age for their grade (B. A. Phillips, 1912). In spite of this frequent advantage in age, they consistently were getting poorer marks in school subject matter. Mayo (1913) reported the median mark of 150 white high-school pupils in New York as 66, whereas the median for the colored pupils was 62. Only 29 per cent of the colored pupils reached or surpassed the median white mark. Later studies, after achievement tests in the various subjects had been developed, disclosed similar facts (Bousfield, 1932; Busby, 1932; Cavins, 1928; Sackett, 1932). Whatever these facts may mean, there is practical unanimity among investigators about the facts themselves. Negroes do *not* get along so well in school as do white children in the same communities.

After Binet tests of intelligence became available, a number of studies were made comparing average IQ's for supposedly comparable groups of Negroes and whites. It is unnecessary to cite many of them since they show remarkable unanimity of findings. Average IQ's for Negro children practically always fell at least 9 or 10 points below those of white comparison groups. Pintner (1931) gave a good summary of these results up to about 1930. Many of these early studies paid no attention to the problem of checking the significance of reported differences. On the basis of what is known statistically about the Binet test ordinarily used in these investigations, it is possible to make a rough estimate as to the magnitude of the difference and the number of cases necessary to insure statistical significance. The smallest difference Pintner cited, from Strachan's report, was 9 IQ points. This would be statistically significant at the 1 per cent level if more than about 30 cases had been included in each of the comparison groups. Since Strachan had something over 14,000 whites and 6,000 Negroes, there is no doubt that the difference stands. Inspection of the other comparisons reported by various investigators corroborates the judgment of significance and warrants two definite summary statements:

1. Negro children averaged lower than white children on Binet tests.
2. Not more than 25 per cent of the Negro children scored above the median of the white distribution.

There have also been a large number of comparisons of Negro with white school children made in various parts of the country, using *group* tests of intelligence. Since good summaries of the results of the early studies are available in Pintner (1931) and Garth (1925), they will not be repeated here. It is difficult to evaluate this material in a quantitative way, since different group tests were used by different investigators and thus the IQ's are not comparable from study to study. It is impossible also to make any exact test of the statistical significance of the reported differences in studies where the author has not done this himself, but the magnitude of the differences and the large numbers of cases used in most investigations makes it seem impossible that the results can be explained by sampling fluctuations alone. It would appear from all this work that Negroes were even more handicapped on group tests of intelligence than they were on individual tests. The average Negro IQ for the studies that Pintner reported was 76, although because of the different tests used in different studies, this is a figure of limited meaning. The percentage of overlapping of the two distributions is a clearer indication of the way the groups compare. If the two groups were equal, this would be 50 per cent, since exactly half of one group would be above the average of the other. For the Negro-white comparisons that Pintner cited, this percentage varied from 1 to 33 and in no case reached 50. The consistency of the results from study to study was impressive.

Results based on the testing of school children were, however, not quite unanimous. Since it is often the case that exceptions to the general trend furnish starting points for the most significant new research, they are always to be noted especially. W. W. Clark (1923) tested 510 Negro and 4,326 white children in the city of Los Angeles. They were all pupils in grades three to eight whom he judged to be fairly representative of the school population. The median IQ of the Negroes was 104.9 and that of the whites 106.0. This difference is *not* significant. IQ's of both groups were slightly above average. Either a superior selection of Negro families migrating to Los Angeles or much more favorable environmental influences would have to be assumed in order to account for this non-typical result. A letter from Clark cited by Peterson and Lanier (1929) says, "These Negroes were the children of a high selection of parentage who had traveled extensively."

It may also be a fact of some importance that a more recent survey in Tennessee reported by Chapanis and Williams (1945) shows less difference between the Negro and white means than did the early ones. On the Kuhlmann-Anderson group test which was given to a large and apparently quite representative group of children between the ages of six and fifteen, there was about a 10-point IQ difference for all age levels.

TABLE 22.

Percentage of White and Negro Men Making Different Letter Grades on the Combined Scale for Intelligence in World War I

(Yerkes, 1921)

	WHITE MEN	NEGRO MEN	WHITE OFFICERS	NEGRO OFFICERS
NUMBER	93,973	18,891	1,385	95
A	4.1	0.1	49.2	14.7
B	8.0	0.6	31.2	24.2
C+	15.0	2.0	12.3	21.0
C	25.0	5.7	6.2	22.1
C−	23.8	12.9	0.7	5.3
D	17.1	29.7	0.3	10.0
D−	7.0	49.0	0.1	3.3

By far the most extensive program of adult testing by means of which whites and Negroes could be compared was the work of the Army psychologists in World War I (Yerkes, 1921). Results here seemed to confirm everything that other investigators had been finding with children as subjects. In every comparison where the scores for a group of Negroes and an equivalent group of whites were placed side by side, there was a significant difference in favor of the whites.

All in all, psychologists agreed fairly well up to about 1930 on the meaning of the figures that had been obtained. Negroes as a whole were definitely inferior to whites as a whole in intelligence tests. In discussing the subject, qualifications were usually added to head off unwarranted conclusions. Northern Negroes averaged considerably higher than Southern Negroes. *Variability*, as well as average figures, was an important consideration, and *individual Negroes* differed as widely in IQ as individual whites. But the idea of white race superiority seemingly stood firm.

The entering wedge for the widespread questioning of these conclusions which has characterized more recent writing on the subject was the problem of North-South differences. If instead of arranging the Army results in the way in which we have them above we make another sort of comparison, their apparent meaning is changed.

TABLE 23.

Average Scores on Army Alpha for Negro Soldiers from Three Northern States and White Soldiers from Three Southern States

(Benedict and Weltfish, 1943; N's added by Garrett, 1945a)

STATE	WHITES		STATE	NEGROES	
	N	MEDIAN ALPHA SCORE		N	MEDIAN ALPHA SCORE
Arkansas	618	41.0	New York	850	44.5
Kentucky	832	41.0	Ohio	152	48.8
Mississippi	665	40.8	Illinois	578	46.9

It is clear that several groups of Northern Negroes made higher averages on the Army test than several groups of Southern whites. The meaning of these comparisons between Northern Negroes and Southern whites was again widely discussed after the publication of the pamphlet, *Races of Mankind*, by Benedict and Weltfish (1943). Montagu (1945), Garrett (1945a, b, c, and d), and Alper and Boring (1944) have reanalyzed the data from different viewpoints. The results of their efforts can be summed up in two generalizations: (1) Northerners consistently scored considerably higher than Southerners of the same race; and (2) whites consistently scored considerably higher than Negroes of the same region. Whether the comparisons are made on the basis of Alpha scores alone (verbal test), or the combined scale, these generalizations as to what the *facts* are hold true. How they should be *interpreted* is another matter upon which there is as yet no universal agreement.

The characteristic differences in the intelligence-test scores of Northern and Southern Negroes was apparent in studies of children as well as of army recruits. One of the most extensive investigations of this factor was the one undertaken by Peterson and Lanier (1929), in which twelve-year-old children in Nashville, Chicago, and New York were given seven different tests, three of which were called ingenuity tests. One was called a "rational learning" test and required that the subject discover and remember the digits that stood for certain letters. Another was called a "mental maze" because it required that the subject learn and remember numbers representing alternate paths at choice points. The third was a disc-transfer test in which five discs of different diameters had to be transferred from one circle to another according to certain specified rules. Unfortunately, there is considerable question as to how representative some of the groups of subjects were of their respective races. The Chicago data are especially vulnerable to criticism, since the subjects were children connected with summer-playground activities, and we have no way of knowing what selective factors operate to bring some children to playgrounds and keep others away. In Nashville and New York, all children of the desired age level were tested in selected elementary schools. Since the New York white group was drawn almost entirely from a single school where over half the children were of a single nationality (Jewish), it is probably not representative of white children in general. However, the comparison between Nashville Negroes and New York Negroes seems to be valid from a sampling standpoint, and it is this which interests us most. On both the Myers Mental Measure, a group verbal intelligence test, and the Rational Learning Test there were highly significant North-South differences. Less than once in a million times would such differences occur from sampling causes alone. There is no doubt at all as to the superiority of the Northern Negro children on tests requiring the solution of novel problems as well as on the more traditional types of test material.

Two sorts of explanation were at first formulated to explain North-South differences, the *selective migration* hypothesis and the *educational opportunity* hypothesis. According to those who have stressed the first of these hypotheses, it is reasonable to suppose that there has been a continual draining off of the most alert, capable, and ambitious of the Negroes from the South into Northern cities where their opportunities are greater and their handicaps less marked. Consequently on any test of intelligence they can be expected to make higher scores than Negroes who have remained in the South. The chief weakness of this hypothesis is that it fails to explain why the scores of *whites* in Mississippi, Kentucky, Arkansas, Georgia, and the other Southern states are so low in comparison with the national averages. There has, of course, been some white migration out of these states also, but it is not clear that there has been any more of it than there has been from New England or the Midwest. The second hypothesis, held by those who explained these results in terms of educational and cultural influences, emphasizes the fact that ranks of the states for scores on Army Alpha correspond rather closely to their ranks for economic level and educational efficiency as judged by such indices as the percentage of daily school attendance, percentage of children attending high school, and the average per capita expenditure for education (H. B. Alexander, 1922). Since research on the construction and evaluation of intelligence tests has indicated that such tests are not infallible indicators of pure native ability and that educational experiences have some effect on scores, we can no longer ignore educational differences between groups being compared.

TABLE 24.

Results of Studies by Klineberg and Associates Comparing Groups of Negroes in New York with Different Lengths of Residence National Intelligence Test

(Klineberg, 1935)

INVESTIGATOR		LENGTH OF RESIDENCE					
		1-2	3-4	5-6	7-8	9 OVER	NORTHERN BORN
Lapidus	N ...	56	35	41	33	44	308
(boys)	Av. ..	64.21	66.86	72.32	83.58	84.64	86.93
	S.D...	29.5	29.5	33.2	29.1	30.4	28.9
Yates	N ...	58	50	57	45	50	359
(girls)	Av. ..	70.8	80.7	94.8	97.55	100	97.86
	S.D...	33.2	23	26.7	22.1	27.5	29.7
Marks	N ...	36	40	38	34	63	350
(boys)	Av. ..	87.53	78.7	81.18	85.82	96.19	90.78
	S.D...	29.9	37.5	28.4	31.5	32.3	35.1

The first thoroughgoing investigation set up specifically to test the selective-migration hypothesis was the one undertaken by Klineberg (1935). It consisted of a number of related studies on various phases of the problem. In one of them, school marks (expressed in percentile ranks) for children who moved away from three Southern cities were compared with the marks of those who stayed. Results were inconsistent and showed no general trend. Thus the average percentile rank for Birmingham migrants was about 45, whereas the Nashville average was 54. This obviously does not look like selective migration, although advocates of this interpretation counter with the objection that school marks are known to be highly unreliable indices of mental ability, and differences would have to be very marked to show up at all in this type of comparison.

TABLE 25.

Results of Studies by Klineberg and Associates Comparing Groups of Negroes in New York with Different Lengths of Residence Stanford-Binet

(Klineberg, 1935)

INVESTIGATOR		LENGTH OF RESIDENCE					
		LESS THAN 1 YEAR	1-2	2-3	3-4	MORE THAN 4 YEARS	NORTHERN BORN
Skladman ..	N ...	20	20		19	20	28
	IQ ..	81.8	85.8		90.3	94.1	98.5
	S.D...	9.14	7.91		8.42	12.6	9.47
Wallach ...	N ...	24	23	21	24	26	49
	IQ ..	80.5	84.0	85.9	85.1	87.1	85.2
Rogosin ...	N ...	18	17	19	22	21	50
	IQ ..	82.6	84.5	83.0	85.9	87.7	89.3

TABLE 26.

Results of Testing Different Groups of Ten-Year-Old Negro Boys with Pintner-Paterson Performance Tests

(Klineberg, 1935)

RESIDENCE	N	AV. MA	S.D.
Less than 2 years	20	7.25	3.03
2-5 years	20	7.65	1.85
More than five years	20	7.50	2.29
Total Southern-born	60	7.47	2.44
Northern-born	50	8.65	2.17

Klineberg also obtained data on groups of New York twelve-year-old Negro children who had lived in the city varying lengths of time. Out of the large amount of material he has included in his report, the results based on the National Intelligence Test (group), the Stanford-Binet (individual), and the Pintner-Paterson (individual performance) tests are shown in Tables 24, 25, and 26.

The first group of results reported in Table 24 shows a clear trend. On this linguistic group test of intelligence, in two out of three studies, length of residence in New York appears to be related to average scores. Why, in the Marks study, the one-to-two-year group should be so high is not apparent. Although differences between adjacent groups are not statistically significant, the larger differences shown in the table, those between groups with long and with short periods of residence in the city, are clearly significant. The results using the Binet tests, reported in Table 25, show that in one of the separate studies there was a very striking tendency for length of residence to be related to IQ. In this, the Skladman study, the average IQ for New York-born Negro children was 98.5, almost at the white norm. In the other two, however, differences between groups are very small, and the highest IQ reached by any Negro group is 89.3, which is still considerably below white averages. Unfortunately, Klineberg gives no standard deviation figures for the Wallach and Rogosin studies, so that it is impossible to estimate the probability that these differences are statistically significant. On the Pintner-Paterson Test, Table 26 shows that results are inconsistent and show no meaningful trend. The highest average score was obtained by the Northern-born group, the next highest by the group with two to five years of residence. These are probably sampling fluctuations. Here, too, the highest mental age reported, 8.6, is still considerably below white norms, since the subjects were ten years old. Klineberg also reports data indicating that residence in a Southern city has the same effect on National Intelligence Test scores as has New York residence, in spite of well-known deficiencies in educational and economic opportunities for Negroes in the South.

The Klineberg studies furnished some definite evidence as to the effect of improved environment in raising the average test score of a group. The ambiguity that remained arose from the fact that we did not know whether any one of the schools in which the investigators worked, or all of them taken together, were representative of the total Negro population of New York. As the figures stood there was as much fluctuation from school to school as from North to South. The New York-born children, for instance, in the Wallach study had an average IQ of 85.2, whereas the children with less than a year's residence in the Rogosin study, averaged 82.6, only 2.6 points less. What did these large differences between Negro *schools* in the North mean?

The picture has become clearer as a result of a more recent study carried on in Philadelphia by Lee (1951). He has obtained convincing evidence of the relationship between IQ and periods of time spent in Northern schools. The number of cases in each group was considerably larger than in the Klineberg study, ranging from 100 to 400. The same children were tested repeatedly after increasing periods of residence. Thus the effects of extraneous sampling fluctuations were ruled out. Still another feature of the study that turned out to be of special interest was the breakdown of the Northern-born group into those who had and had not attended kindergarten. Table 27 gives the results obtained with the Philadelphia Tests of Mental and Verbal Ability.

TABLE 27.
Mean IQ's on Philadelphia Tests of Mental and Verbal Ability

(Lee, 1951)

		GRADE IN WHICH TEST WAS TAKEN				
GROUP	N	1A	2B	4B	6B	9A
Philadelphia-born who attended kindergarten	212					
Mean		96.7	95.9	97.2	97.5	96.6
SD		14.3	14.8	15.0	13.9	14.2
Philadelphia-born who did not attend kindergarten	424					
Mean		92.1	93.4	94.7	94.0	93.7
SD		13.8	14.4	14.6	14.1	15.1
Southern-born entering Philadelphia school system in grades:						
1A	182					
Mean		86.5	89.3	91.8	93.3	92.8
SD		13.2	13.3	14.1	14.5	13.6
1B-2B	109					
Mean			86.7	88.6	90.9	90.5
SD			15.2	13.6	14.4	16.1
3A-4B	199					
Mean				86.3	87.2	89.4
SD				15.3	14.8	13.7
5A-6B	221					
Mean					88.2	90.2
SD					15.1	14.7
7A-9A	219					
Mean						87.4
SD						14.3

The lower part of the table shows a fairly consistent increase in scores whether it is read from left to right or from bottom to top. Southern-born children averaged about 87 when they entered the first grade and about 93 when retested in the sixth grade and in the ninth grade. Southern-born children who entered Philadelphia schools at the junior-high level (bottom right corner) tested at about 87, whereas those who had had some Philadelphia schooling averaged about 90, and those who had had all their schooling there averaged about 93. This cannot be explained on the basis of simply increasing familiarity with the test, since neither group of Phila-delphia-born Negro children shows the increase. Lee carried out the neces-sary statistical tests to prove that these trends are clearly significant at the one per cent level.

One of the most interesting comparisons shown in Lee's tables is that between kindergartners and non-kindergartners. At each testing period, those who had attended kindergarten averaged higher than those who had not. The difference was only about 3 IQ points (96.6 versus 93.7 at the time of the last test) but was significant and always in the same direction. Lee made no attempt to explain it. It could arise from either selective factors in kindergarten enrollment or a genuine effect of kindergarten training on intellectual functioning. We shall consider later some other re-search findings that may be related to it.

One other aspect of the Lee research is also worth noting especially. A number of the subjects took the Chicago Tests of Primary Mental Abilities and the Minnesota Paper Form Board as well as the general intel-ligence test. With the single exception of the Memory factor (M), on which the various subgroups did not differ, all of these special kinds of ability measurement showed exactly the same trends as did the general test—increasing scores with increasing length of residence, and higher scores for those who had attended kindergarten than for those who had not.

The Klineberg and the Lee research findings have shown quite con-clusively that more adequate educational opportunities serve to raise the average of Negro subjects on intelligence tests. The explanation of *North-South* differences on the basis of educational influences rather than selec-tive migration has become a matter of general agreement. The fact that the more recent studies report higher averages for Southern Negro children than the early studies fits in with this explanation, since education has improved over the years in many parts of the South. The question that re-mains is whether all the *Negro-White* differences can be explained on the basis of discrepancies in educational opportunity. Two studies leave us in some doubt about this. The first of these was done by Tanser (1939) in Kent County, Ontario. The ancestors of the present Negro population there moved to the region before the Civil War, in the days of the underground railroad. We have here an unusually favorable situation for research, since socio-economic status has been more nearly comparable for Negro and white groups there than it is anywhere in this country, and there has been at least a serious effort to secure complete *educational* equality since 1890. All Negro pupils, grades one to eight, in one urban and seven rural schools were tested. White pupils attending the same schools served as comparison groups. Results are shown in Table 28.

TABLE 28.

Negro-White Comparisons on Four Intelligence Tests

(Tanser, 1939)

TEST	N	WHITE IQ MEAN	WHITE IQ S.D.	N	NEGRO IQ MEAN	NEGRO IQ S.D.
National Intelligence Test	386	103.6	16.5	103	89.2	15.9
Pintner Non-Language Test	387	110.9	19.0	102	95.2	13.3
Pintner-Cunningham Primary Test	155	97.6*	....	54	82.8*	....
Pintner-Paterson Performance Tests	211	109.6	22.4	162	91.0	19.0

* These averages are medians rather than means, and no variability figures are given.

It is interesting to note that on *all* tests, language and non-language alike, there is a consistent difference of 15 to 19 IQ points between comparable white and Negro groups. Tanser does not state whether or not the differences are significant, but it is a simple matter to make appropriate statistical tests from the data he provides, and they leave no doubt about the matter. Whatever it is that is producing this differential, it is not chance.

There is some evidence in Tanser's report that even in an area like this where racial discrimination is at a minimum, one does not entirely avoid differences in socio-economic status, with their possible effects on intelligence measurements. Tanser states that in the *urban* schools where testing was done the average socio-economic level of the homes from which the white children came was considerably higher than that of the homes of colored children. In the rural groups, he thought that this difference did not exist. It is interesting to note that whereas significant differences in race averages are shown for both urban and rural schools, such differences are smaller for the rural groups. Urban white children score higher than do rural white children. For Negroes the reverse is true. Furthermore, school attendance figure show that all Negroes attended school a smaller percentage of the time than did the whites. For the total group of whites tested, school attendance averaged 93.38 per cent. For the total group of Negroes, it averaged 84.77 per cent.

It must always be remembered, on the other hand, that the difference in environmental advantages may be to some extent an effect rather than a cause of the differences in intelligence. The fact that in the urban communities of Ontario, the Negroes predominate in the unskilled jobs paying low wages might mean that in the course of the occupational sifting-out process that continually occurs many of them naturally have gravitated toward work of that level. We cannot easily disentangle cause from effect in complex social situations of this sort. Our only recourse is to be on guard against drawing too-easy conclusions.

The other study in which environmental factors have been more nearly equalized than is customary is the one by Bruce (1940). Her work was done in a locality in South Virginia where the economic level of both whites and Negroes was unusually *low*. It thus furnishes a valuable complement to Tanser's at the other end of the scale. The subjects given the group test of intelligence (Kuhlmann-Anderson) were 521 white and 432 Negro children from nine matched pairs of schools. Their ages ranged from 6.0 through 12.9. Out of this number, 86 whites and 72 Negroes were selected as a representative group to be given individual tests, the 1916 Stanford-Binet and the Arthur Performance Scale. The results are as follows:

	WHITE IQ	NEGRO IQ
Kuhlmann-Anderson	88	72
Stanford-Binet	90	76
Arthur	94	77

As would be expected in a backward region of this sort, all IQ's are considerably below average, but the Negroes are 14 to 17 IQ points lower than the whites. This, of course, might mean that the Negroes are even more retarded environmentally than are the whites—that the whites are poor, but the Negroes even poorer. To obtain further evidence as to whether this possibility might explain the results, Miss Bruce used the Sims Score Card, a method of evaluating economic level, to pick out a *paired group* of white and Negro children, presumably of equal economic status.

These comparisons also indicated a definite differential, not quite so large, but still significant.

	WHITE IQ	NEGRO IQ
Kuhlmann-Anderson	83	73
Stanford-Binet	86	77
Arthur	89	77

From 9 to 12 IQ points still separated Negro from white performance. Bruce reported one other significant finding. The difference between races was about equally marked for all kinds of material used in the tests. Negroes were no more handicapped on tests based on general information than those involving new situations. They were no more handicapped on speed tests than on power tests. The differences characterized all the types of task that we include in intelligence scales.

In view of what biologists and anthropologists have said about the nature of races, psychologists have become increasingly reluctant to interpret such Negro-white differences as evidence for any sort of inherent white superiority. To account for whatever difference is left over after educational influences have been equated, two main types of explanation have been invoked. Discussions of the problem do not always keep clear the distinction between them. The first of these possibilities is that tests designed for white subjects may not really measure Negro intelligence. The second is that some influence during development may actually be depressing the level of Negro intelligence.

Many have argued that our tests are not fair to Negroes, and thus may have no meaning when applied to them. Some have insisted that most tests are too *verbal* for people whose percentage of illiteracy is high. Others have questioned the emphasis on *speed* which they say fits poorly with Negro temperament. Still others have questioned whether the *motivation* of Negro and white groups is actually comparable, especially when tests are given by a white examiner. Evidence on all these points is scanty and somewhat hard to interpret because it comes from many different age groups and locations. We might ask ourselves first, is there any evidence that Negroes may achieve more than their test scores would lead one to predict? Here the report of Stalnaker (1948) on the Pepsi-Cola scholarship program has some bearing. In order to be sure that Southern Negro high-school students would have an opportunity to participate, the sponsors awarded scholarships to the highest-scoring Negro applicants in each state even if they ranked considerably below the level of the white students to whom awards were made. Stalnaker reported that 55 out of the 59 Negro students chosen in this way were succeeding under competitive conditions at first-rate colleges. In general, however, the bulk of the studies covering the whole intelligence range rather than just this upper segment indicate that Negroes show the same deficiencies in their school work that they do on the intelligence tests themselves.

On the question of the appropriateness of verbal tests, there is at least one study, reported by Anastasi and D'Angelo (1952), which shows that among five-year-old preschool children in a day-care center, the Negroes were slightly lower than the whites on measures of sentence length and structure but not on the Goodenough Draw-a-Man Test. The fact that the sex difference on the language ratings were in an opposite direction for the two racial groups (Negro boys higher than girls, white girls higher than boys) makes some sort of cultural explanation seem reasonable. Goodenough (1926), however, had encountered as much retardation on the Draw-a-Man Test as was being found on verbal tests. In general, Negro-white differences have shown up whatever special variety of test has been used. Coppinger and Ammons (1952) found that their Negro grade-school subjects averaged about two years below the white norms on the picture vocabulary test. Hammer (1954) found his Negro subjects to be somewhat higher on the language section than on the non-language section of the California Mental Maturity Scale. McGurk (1953), after having test questions sorted into "cultural" and "non-cultural" categories by 78 judges, found that there was more difference between groups of white and Negro high-school students who had been equated for age, school attendance, curriculum, and general socio-economic level on the "non-cultural" than on the "cultural" items.

Explanations of racial differences as nothing but differences in motivation have little evidence to support them. Motivation does not seem to make that much difference. Maller and Zubin (1932) and Benton (1936) did not get significant increases in group intelligence-test performance by introducing rivalry, or offering a prize. Klugman (1944), using the Stanford-Binet test and money incentives, also failed to produce a significant improvement. His subjects included both white and Negro children. G. F. Boyd (1952), who used a level-of-aspiration procedure with groups of white and Negro children in a Northern, non-segregated school, found that the Negroes showed significantly higher aspiration levels than the whites of the same intelligence level. Canady (1936) who investigated specifically the effects of "rapport," the relationship between a Negro subject and a white examiner (again in a Northern, non-segregated school, however), found that while there was a slight tendency for children to score higher when tested by an examiner of their own race, in general the pattern of gains and losses upon retest was comparable with what is usually obtained when a racial factor is not involved. The hypothesis of Hammer (1954) that Negro children are handicapped in intelligence tests by a severe degree of "neuroticism" is not convincing. His measure of "neuroticism" consisted of ratings of the drawings the children made of a house, a tree, and a person, and such drawings are themselves at least as closely related to intellectual as to motivational characteristics.

Although it has been often mentioned as a possible basis for differences in score, it seems very doubtful whether a general speed factor enters in. Rhodes (1937), Lambeth and Lanier (1933), and Moore (1941) all failed to get significant Negro-white differences in psychomotor speed when the task was a simple one, although Peterson, Lanier, and Walker (1925) and Klineberg (1928) had noted a certain indifference to speed in some Negro groups.

To summarize, there is little or no evidence that the first type of explanation in terms of factors peculiar to the *test situation* accounts for the Negro-white differences we have obtained. It is not always realized, that if we could prove to everyone's satisfaction that differences *were* purely a matter of test score and had nothing to do with functioning intelligence itself, it would take away some of the justification for our efforts to equalize opportunities for the less favored groups. As has been often said in earlier pages, we are not assuming any longer that our tests measure pure *native* intelligence, and thus we are not attaching any racial stigma when we say that the evidence points to a lower average level of intellectual functioning among Negroes than among whites in the American population. It may well have been produced by environmental inequalities, but it is real and it does have its effect upon relative achievements. Can we formulate any reasonable hypotheses about the way in which such a difference comes about?

It would seem that the time is ripe for a more penetrating analysis of *specific* intellectual differences and where they come from. Hebb (1949) presented a very fruitful new concept when he discussed the effects of early *perceptual* learning on intellectual development. Piaget (1947) has approached the problem from a somewhat similar point of view. Is there any evidence that Negro-white differences can be explained in terms of differences in what is *learned* at early stages of development? There is no research related specifically to this issue, but there are a number of extremely suggestive studies getting at it obliquely. First of all, there have

been several studies in which groups of institutionalized criminals or delin-
quents have been matched in different ways and compared. At first glance,
they might seem to be very unrepresentative subjects, but actually there
are advantages in using them rather than such groups as school children
or college students. We can be more certain that at least some of the
environmental and motivational factors that are hard to control are constant for white and Negro subjects. Machover (1943) compared a group
of 50 Southern Negroes who had migrated to New York after the age of
sixteen with a group of New York-born Negroes matched with them for
scores on the Comprehension and Similarities tests of the Wechsler-Bellevue scale (an individual intelligence test widely used for adults). The
Negroes from the South were most inferior to the New York Negroes
on the Digit Symbol, Block Design, and Picture Arrangement subtests.
The combination of these suggests some sort of *perceptual* defect. The cul-
turally restricted group seems not to get the meaning of the stimulus material as clearly somehow as the group with the better educational background. In this study where all groups were initially matched by Comprehension and Similarities scores, differences between Northern Negroes and
whites were small. It was the one type of difference between Southerners
and Northerners that stood out. Franklin (1945) and De Stephens (1953)
have given the Wechsler-Bellevue test to delinquent Negro boys and
have also reported special deficiencies on the Block Design and Digit
Symbol subtests. Both these studies agree that Negro subjects are deficient
also on the Arithmetic and the Picture Completion subtests. Picture Completion would fit in with the hypothesis of a perceptual defect. Clarke
(1941), who compared white and Negro delinquent boys on the Stanford-
Binet test, found that when the two groups were matched for over-all
IQ, the Negroes were superior to the whites on Dissected Sentences,
Memory for Sentences, and Vocabulary, but inferior to them on Arithmetical Reasoning, Repeating 5 Digits Reversed, and Picture Absurdities.
This agrees with the two previous studies in pointing to some special difficulty with numbers. The Picture Absurdities Test again involves perception of visual material.

A study by Davidson *et al.* (1950), whose subjects were white and
Negro psychoneurotics matched for age and intelligence level, shows a
similar pattern of differences on the Wechsler-Bellevue test, with Negroes
scoring lower on Arithmetic and on all the performance subtests. The
authors interpret this as a culturally-conditioned difference in psychomotor speed. In view of the fact that the largest single subtest difference is
on the Picture Completion Test, which is not ordinarily a speed test at all,

it would seem more reasonable to interpret these results also as differences in some kind of perceptual ability and in skill with numbers.

The well-documented fact in the Lee study cited above that Negro children who had been to *kindergarten* consistently scored higher than the others fits in with the idea that perceptual training makes a difference. Relevant too is a report by Tomlinson (1944) indicating that preschool Negro children score significantly higher on the Binet than their older siblings do, and one by F. Brown (1944) reporting Negro averages almost as high as white for Minneapolis kindergarten children.

Two studies show clearly that perceptual discrimination can be *trained* and that Negroes benefit particularly from such training. Eagleson (1937) trained his 50 white and 50 Negro subjects, all high-school students, to move a marker into a position that would bisect the length of a bar. After each trial the subject was told how much in error he was and in which direction. Whites were considerably superior in the first trial, but as the experiment progressed the difference constantly diminished. Eagleson concluded, "Since training has been found to decrease the average error, the difference between the two groups for the first setting may be interpreted to mean that the white group had had more experience in this kind of activity than the Negroes at the beginning of the study." One wonders if the same conclusion would not apply with equal cogency to the other perceptual differences we have been outlining.

Boger (1952) shows that perceptual training does influence scores on group intelligence tests. His subjects were Negro and white primary school children, about 50 of each, in small rural Virginia schools. Two group intelligence tests were given in January and again in May. In the intervening months, half of the children, both white and Negro, were given practice periods with problems involving visual perception, discrimination, and spatial relations. The materials included scrambled comic strips, hidden picture puzzles, designs to be copied, and the like, and gave practice in following directions, noting details, detecting likenesses and differences, and coördinating hand and eye movements. The results showed significant increases in most of the tests for the experimental but not for the control groups, and the Negroes gained more than the whites. While the white children who had had the experimental program still scored higher in May (average IQ 101 on the Language section and 106 on the Non-Language section of the California Test), the Negro averages had come up to 84 on the Language section and 98 on the Non-Language. Retests the next October showed that gains had been maintained.

One further line of evidence fits in with the hypothesis that the failure of Negro children to learn to make complex perceptual discriminations may serve to handicap them in developing the sort of intelligence called for both in tests and in school work. Newland and Lawrence (1953) reported scores made by Negro children from Nashville and its vicinity on the Chicago Non-Verbal Examination, which is another *picture* test of various kinds of mental ability. On this test too, Negroes scored from two to three years below the white norms. But it was apparent that the test was discriminating scarcely at all at the lower levels because of the piling up of zero and near-zero scores. Table 29 compares the Negro distribution

TABLE 29.

Distributions for Negro and White Six-Year-Olds on the Chicago Non-Verbal Examination

(Newland and Lawrence, 1953. Brown, 1940)

	NEGRO	WHITE
80-84		2
75-79		3
70-74	1	7
65-69		16
60-64	1	12
55-59		29
50-54	3	43
45-49	2	31
40-44	2	35
35-39	2	26
30-34	12	26
25-29	9	22
20-24	13	18
15-19	9	21
10-14	16	14
5- 9	32	6
0- 4	40	7
N	142	318
Mean	15.3	41.1
S. D.	14.1	17.6

for six-year-olds with that given by A. W. Brown (1940) in the original standardization data. The figures suggest that the majority of the Negro six-year-olds may not be getting anything at all out of the pictures on the test booklet. It may be more important to find out why than to compare their average score with that of the white group.

The hypothesis of a perceptual handicap originating in the meagerness of early childhood surroundings but perhaps remediable at later age levels if it can be identified is certainly not *established* from data available so far. The most that can be said for it is that it accounts for some research findings not easily explainable in other ways. The interest that has been generated in perceptual problems generally during recent years (see Chapter 9) may eventually produce conclusive evidence on this question along with others. It need not be pointed out that the practical implications are far-reaching. It might even be that kindergartens are of more crucial importance than colleges in the program of equalizing educational opportunities for students of different races and all cultural levels.

The special difficulty with arithmetic that has shown up in study after study should also be investigated. Is it related to the perceptual habits we have been discussing? Is it representative of the whole "v:ed" factor the English psychologists stress, the special ability involved in school success? (See Chapter 4.)

In making practical applications of research findings on race differences, we must always remember one all-important fact: A difference between *averages* tells us nothing about what to expect of any given *individual* in either group. IQ's of white children range all the way from a hypothetical zero to an occasional 200. The same can be said for Negro children. Jenkins (1948) has summarized studies of gifted Negro children. It is a significant fact that IQ's as high as 200 have been found among Negro children in the public schools. It is important for such individuals themselves and for society that their exceptional abilities be developed and used for the good of all. We must judge each person, white or Negro, on his own merits. A thorough understanding and acceptance of this principle would wipe out the most flagrant types of injustice and discrimination.

One of the minor problems taken up in many of the studies of race differences is the relationship between intelligence-test scores and amount of white blood. In most investigations, Negroid characteristics such as skin color, width of lips, or width of nostrils have been used as criteria of mixed ancestry. The Ferguson study already cited, using a subjective classification based largely on skin color, reported that the larger the proportion of white blood, the higher the score on the analogies and the completion tests. Peterson and Lanier obtained positive relationships between intelligence-test scores and lightness of skin in their Nashville group, but found no relationship between test scores and Negroid characteristics in their New York group. Klineberg found no relationship between skin color and other Negroid characteristics and either intelligence or length of residence in New York. Tanser, classifying his subjects on the basis of information supplied by Kent County residents, found that the mixed bloods did somewhat better on the National Intelligence Test than did the full bloods and that the larger the proportion of estimated white blood, the higher was the score. It is probably best, however, to draw no conclusion with regard to this problem. Just what mixture of genes has determined the racial characteristics of any present-day Negro, is, as we have said, an unanswerable question. Herskovits (1928) has shown that in selected groups of Howard University students whose ancestry is quite definitely known, the variability of any one of the racial traits commonly used as criteria is so great as to render it a very unreliable indicator of degree of mixture. He has also shown that within the Negro group, a process of *social* selection on the basis of skin color is going on. To the extent that groups of higher social level have greater educational and cultural advantages, some correlation between skin color and test score might occur entirely apart from racial factors. There is certainly no evidence for the opinion held by many people that hybrids are *less* able than persons of pure race. But there is also no clear conclusive evidence that mixed bloods are more intelligent than pure Negroes.

There has been little satisfactory evidence presented on the question of whether or not there are characteristic personality differences between Negroes and whites in our society. The few studies using questionnaires or projective methods have been based on samples that are probably not typical, and they have shown no clear trends. There may be some interesting questions on this area, but so far there is not much to be said about them.

RESEARCH ON THE AMERICAN INDIAN

A number of studies have reported the scores of Indian children on intelligence tests. Pintner (1931), summarizing available research up to about 1930, reports IQ's ranging from 69 to 97. Since these are based on different tests, the only general statement that is warranted is that Indians as a group average considerably lower than whites on standard intelligence tests. There is another significant fact, however, which comes out especially in the study by Jamieson and Sandiford (1928). Although their 717 Indian subjects could all speak English, and some of them came from homes where only English was spoken, they obtained very much better scores on non-verbal than on verbal tests of intelligence. Average IQ's on the two verbal tests used, the Pintner-Cunningham and the National Intelligence Test, were 78 and 80. On the Pintner-Paterson Performance Scale and the Pintner Non-Language Test the average IQ's were 92 and 97, differing very little from the 100 which is average for white children. Differences in cultural factors as well as language would seem to be reflected here.

Such an interpretation receives further support from the study by Dennis (1942) on Hopi children. The test he used was the Goodenough Draw-a-Man Test. For young children in our culture, scores on this test have a rather close relationship to scores on the standard Stanford-Binet intelligence tests. The score is based on the number of details the child gets into his drawing, such as fingers, eyes and ears, hair, and articles of clothing, and affords a fairly good indication of how complex and finely-differentiated his concepts are. Dennis's subjects, 152 Hopi children ranging in age from six to ten, obtained an average IQ of 108.3—several points *higher* than the white children's average. He attributes this superior showing to special practice, arising from the attention given the human figure in Hopi decorative arts. The fact that it was the boys, not the girls, whose scores were outstanding, fits in with this interpretation, since the boys are the ones who from early childhood are trained in the arts for which the tribe is famous. Havighurst, Gunther, and Pratt (1946) have also shown that several groups of Indian children average higher than whites on the drawing test, and that Indian boys tend to do better than Indian girls. It may be that this test is for such groups more of an *achievement* test, showing what has been *learned* about drawing the human figure, and less of an intelligence test than it is in our culture. Such findings as these should be examined further for their bearing on the problem of the relationship of perceptual learning to intelligence.

Studies of the Indian like those by Tanser and Bruce of the Negro, equating economic and educational advantages for the two races, have not been made. Therefore, it is impossible to make any definite statement as to the source of average differences. It can be said with considerable certainty that Indian averages are considerably below white averages on tests involving a high degree of abstraction and the understanding of verbal concepts. In tests involving reasoning *in terms of concrete materials* and manipulation of spatial relationships, there is some evidence that the two races do not differ. In making use of these findings, we should remember that it is the abstract, verbal test materials that afford us our best prediction of school success, so that we should expect Indians as a group to be less well adapted than whites to the kind of school work customary in our civilization. We should also keep in mind as always the variability of the two distributions, so that we do not lay too much stress on averages. Some individual Indians are far above the white averages on all sorts of intelligence tests; some individual whites have scores as low as those of the lowest Indians.

RESEARCH ON CHINESE AND JAPANESE

In contrast with the findings for Negroes and for Indians, investigations of Chinese and Japanese intelligence have shown them to be little below the white averages, in spite of language handicaps. Pintner (1931) in summing up available studies, shows IQ's on Binet tests running from 85 to 98, with all work on non-language tests showing the Orientals to be equal to or above the American norms. Since there is no study in which economic level, educational advantages, and selective factors have been controlled, these findings may indicate only that the culture from which Japanese and Chinese school children come is intellectually more closely related to our own than the Negro and Indian cultures are. The fact that Oriental children can be expected to do about as well as American children in school work is the principal practical conclusion which is justified. Again the factor of variability should be kept in mind. Chinese and Japanese individuals vary all the way from idiot to genius.

RESEARCH ON NATIONALITY DIFFERENCES

During the 1920's, after the Army test results had been published, there was a flurry of research on the comparative intellectual level of the various nationalities whose people had been immigrating to this country in large numbers. Army data, as analyzed by Brigham (1923), ranked the nationalities in order ranging from North Europeans who were highest to South Europeans at the bottom. The two groups at the top, English and Scottish, were nationalities for whom English is the native language. Various people have reported similar findings for children of foreign-born parents in American schools. A good summary of this work is found in Pintner (1931, pp. 459-462). In most of these investigations Jewish, English, and Scotch have ranked somewhat above American norms, Irish, Germans, and Scandinavians have been about average, and South Europeans and Mexicans have been below American norms. Goodenough (1926) published results for 2,457 public-school children who were given the drawing test described above. Since this test is completely non-verbal, the factor of whether or not English had been spoken in the child's home would not be expected to affect the scores, although, as the studies of Indians have subsequently shown, other environmental factors may. The general hierarchy was similar to that in the other studies—Jewish at the top, English and Scotch about average, Mexicans, Indians, and Negroes at the bottom.

The tendency of Jewish groups, from whatever European country they originated, to score at or above the American average has been apparent in all the studies of nationality differences. Since they would have the same language handicap as other groups growing up in foreign-speaking homes, this is a significant detail. Brill (1936), summarizing available studies up to 1936, criticizes them all on the basis that neither socio-economic level nor language handicap has been controlled. What evidence there is, however, seems to warrant the conclusions that Jewish children in Great Britain and the United States are at least equal to non-Jewish children of similar socio-economic status, and that they are superior to most other foreign-born groups.

An explanation of nationality differences which was rather widely quoted for a while and is still sometimes defended postulates intellectual differences between the subgroups of the white race in Europe: the Nordic, Alpine, and Mediterranean. Unfortunately for those who are attracted by the surface plausibility of this hypothesis, it has not stood up under critical investigation. Brigham, who in 1923 proposed this explanation, abandoned it completely in 1930. The grounds for repudiating the conclusions he had drawn from the army results were largely statistical. By that time, it was becoming apparent that the so-called combined scale the army psychologists had used was not a sound basis upon which to rest any comparisons, since the various subtests in the Army Alpha, Army Beta, and the Stanford-Binet did not give scores that were identical in psychological meaning. Since no one of these tests could be used with all groups of subjects, there was no way of making valid comparisons between them. Brigham's conclusion was that comparative studies of national and racial groups could not be made with existing tests.

Other criticisms of work on nationality differences have also been pointed out. There is of course the problem of language handicap. Even for children born in this country, the learning of another language before English or the acquisition of two languages at once would have its effect on intelligence-test scores and make it impossible to use these scores as indices of intellectual level. It is quite possible that European languages differ in this respect, and that some operate as more of a handicap to the rapid learning of English than do others. The summary of the available research by Arsenian (1945) indicates that any such handicap so far as test score is concerned does not represent a permanent intellectual handicap and that bilingual children grow up to be fully as bright as those acquiring only one language during childhood. The other important consideration in interpreting nationality comparisons is that we have no way of knowing how representative the immigrants are of the population of the country from which they come. If the North Europeans were in general drawn from a higher socio-economic level in their own country than were the South Europeans, that fact alone would serve to explain differences in test score without recourse to any supposed difference in the average intellectual levels of the respective countries. We have no satisfactory way of analyzing these selective factors. Consequently results of testing different nationalities *in this country* cannot be used as a basis for judgment of the nationalities in general. Obviously any derived explanation, such as the Nordic-Alpine-Mediterranean hierarchy, rests on even shakier ground since the exact racial mixture in each of the countries considered can only be vaguely surmised.

TABLE 30.

Comparison of National and Racial Groups on a Performance Scale

(Klineberg, 1931)

GROUP	PROVINCE	VILLAGES COVERED	PERFORMANCE AVERAGE	SCALE SCORES RANGE
1. German Nordic	Hanover	17	198.2	69-289
2. French Mediterranean	Eastern Pyrenees	12	197.4	71-271
3. German Alpine	Baden	10	193.6	80-211
4. Italian Alpine	Piedmont	10	188.8	69-306
5. French Alpine	Auvergne & Velay	19	180.2	72-296
6. French Nordic	Flanders	13	178.8	63-314
7. Italian Mediterranean	Sicily	9	173.0	69-308
8. All Nordics			188.5	63-314
9. All Alpines			187.5	69-306
10. All Mediterraneans ..			185.2	69-308

A few investigators have attempted to compare these nationalities or races in their own countries. The most satisfactory of these studies is the one by Klineberg (1931). He tested a large number of ten- to twelve-year-old schoolboys in rural sections of Germany, France, and Italy. He chose the subjects according to criteria that would give him supposedly unmixed samples of Nordic, Alpine, and Mediterranean races. The tests used were six of the short performance tests from the Pintner-Paterson scale, mostly of the form board or puzzle type. Results are shown in Table 30.

What these results show very definitely is that for this type of test the important differences are not *between races* but between different samples of the same race. Differences between races are negligible and do not even approach statistical significance. Differences between French and Italian Nordics or French and Italian Mediterraneans, for example, are fairly large and statistically significant. Klineberg attributes these differences to some sort of cultural factors. It would be interesting to know just what they are. It must be remembered that these were not verbal tests and for this reason are not directly comparable to tests upon which many of the differences between immigrant groups in this country have been based. Furthermore, the tests he used are not well adapted to subjects at the age level with which he was working. Had he used seven- and eight-year-old subjects for whom these tests are best suited, the results might have been different. (At older ages, performance tests such as simple form boards tend to be measures more of the *speed* with which the individuals can make the necessary hand movements than of the intellectual factors involved in solving spatial problems.)

Another attempt to test Europeans on their home ground was made by Franzblau (1935). The subjects were approximately 300 school girls in each of four groups, Danes in Denmark, Italians in Italy, Danish-Americans, and Italian-Americans. Socio-economic levels for the four groups were equated as well as possible. A non-language test was used, the International Intelligence Test. There was no statistical evidence that the Danes and the Italians in Europe differed at all, although the Danish-Americans received significantly higher scores than the Italian-Americans. This study would suggest strongly that differences between nationality groups in this country may result from selective factors rather than differences in the parent populations.

One other study bearing on both race and nationality differences is of considerable interest. S. Smith (1942) tested the public-school population of Honolulu with ages between ten and fifteen in 1924, and again in 1938. Three kinds of test were used: non-verbal, spoken English and printed English. The interesting fact is that differences between pairs of racial groups were highly significant both in 1924 and 1938 and that the rank order of the races was about the same on the two occasions. (For convenience, *race* is used in this report to include some groups better classified as nationalities.) High-scoring races both times were the Korean, Chinese, Japanese, and white. Low-scoring races were the Portuguese, Hawaiian, and Porto Rican. The effect of the educational system that had been in effect during the fourteen-year interval had been to raise the averages for *all* these groups but *not* to reduce the differences between them. In fact, groups scoring high in 1924 showed more improvement than did groups scoring low. This study tells us no more about the intelligence of the population in the countries from which these groups originally came than the others that have been cited, since selective factors are unknown and probably unknowable. But it does strongly suggest that, whatever their source, we cannot expect differences between groups in the population to be eradicated by education.

There has been, especially in the years since World War II, much interest in the problem of personality differences between national groups. Books have been written by anthropologists, psychiatrists, and social psychologists, as well as by foreign correspondents, in which "national character" in some particular country is described and accounted for. The fact that such generalizations have not been made or tested in quantitative form places them outside the scope of this book. Quantitative research that has been carried out on national products—jokes, plays, folktales —also falls more naturally into social psychology than into a discussion of individual differences.

The principal reason for the lack of quantitative data is of course the difficulty of devising measuring instruments. It is hard enough to develop a personality test that is valid for individuals with the same general cultural background. Problems multiply when we attempt to compare persons with different languages, different kinds of schooling, and different values. Most verbal questionnaires are ruled out because of doubts as to what the words mean when translated into another language. Projective methods such as the Rorschach will be of more value when we are sure just what they are measuring. Objective tests such as those which Eysenck has been using (see Chapter 7) are even more promising. So far, however, in this area there is nothing of importance to report.

SUMMARY

Research on psychological differences between races is extraordinarily difficult. Added to the problems of classifying individuals correctly are problems of selecting measuring instruments equally fair to all groups and allowing for the differences in environmental influence that race prejudice has created. Psychologists have in many cases short-circuited these problems simply by ignoring them. Consequently, what we often have are data on groups classified according to current social custom based on tests that may or may not be suitable.

Under these circumstances, average scores made by Negro groups on intelligence tests are consistently and significantly lower than those made by white groups in the same places. The fact that Northern Negroes score significantly higher than those in the South, and that averages increase with attendance at Northern schools, shows that deficiencies in education are involved, at least to some extent. The effect on mental development of restricted educational and cultural surroundings in early childhood has not yet been satisfactorily analyzed.

Indians also score considerably below the white norm in both verbal intelligence and school achievement tests. There is evidence, however, that some groups of them are about as high as whites on non-verbal tests, and may score even higher on types of performance in line with their special training and experience. Chinese and Japanese groups usually score near the white norms.

Among immigrants to this country and their children, mental testers in various places have found that a hierarchy exists, with Jews, Scandinavians, Germans, and English-speaking groups at the top, and South Europeans of all nationalities at the bottom. Two studies done in Europe have served to discredit the hypothesis that this constitutes a Nordic-Alpine-Mediterranean racial hierarchy and to explain the findings in terms of selective factors that brought persons from different strata of the European population to the United States.

Research on personality differences between races and between nationalities awaits the development of satisfactory measuring instruments.

CHAPTER 12

Class Differences

CLASS DIFFERENTIATION IN THE UNITED STATES

THE AVERAGE American is likely to respond with heated denial to any statement that he lives in a class society. True, he may have listened often to the complaints of his adolescent son and daughter that a certain ruling clique runs the high school. But he feels, as the son and daughter themselves do, that this one high school is probably exceptional and that either a transfer to another school or a well-planned reform movement would clear up the situation. He has probably read *Kitty Foyle* and *H. M. Pulham, Esq.* and *Alice Adams* and recognized some of their prototypes among people he knows. But the problems involved in marrying beneath one's class, he thinks, may be serious in Boston or Philadelphia, but not in his own more progressive city. After all, was not America founded and built up as the "land of opportunity" where one man is as good as another and where anyone who wishes to work and struggle can make himself a fortune or carve out a distinguished career in politics?

Of recent years, considerable evidence has been accumulating that American communities do show a definite class structure. The methods by which these facts have been obtained are much like those used by a social anthropologist in studying a primitive society. The research worker goes to live in the community. After making friends with as many people as possible so that they trust him and feel free to talk to him, he interviews a great many individuals of all ages and uses the information they give him as a basis for his analysis of social structure. Large-scale research of this sort has been carried on by Warner and Lunt in a New England community which they call Yankee City (1941); by Davis, Gardner, and Gardner in a southern community which they call Oldtown (1941); and by Warner, Havighurst, and Loeb, in a midwestern community which they call Midwest (1944). The Lynds' work on Middletown (1929, 1937) and West's *Plainville, U. S. A.* (1945) contribute information from other sections of the Midwest. The criteria that they use in determining what class an individual belongs to and what classes the community contains are those that show unequivocally which people are accustomed to associate freely with one another. The social clique is the basic unit. People are of the same class if they may normally (*a*) eat or drink together as a social ritual, (*b*) freely visit one another's families, (*c*) talk together intimately in a social clique, or (*d*) marry into each other's families. All these investigators are impressed with the high degree of agreement that all informants show as to just where any given individual belongs in the social hierarchy.

In Yankee City and Oldtown, six distinct classes could be differentiated on this basis. The following diagram shows what they are:

| Upper upper class |
| Lower upper class |
| Upper middle class |
| Lower middle class |
| Upper lower class |
| Lower lower class |

The upper classes, though making up a small fraction of the population numerically, are the families with the most influential positions, the largest incomes, and homes in the best part of town. The distinction between "upper-upper" and "lower-upper" in both the Eastern and Southern cities is based on family. A person qualifies for the highest class only if, in addition to having wealth and position, he also belongs to one of the old, established families with what Americans consider an aristocratic heritage. In the Midwest, this distinction is less important. The upper middle class is made up of business and professional men who are leading citizens in community activities but lack wealth and social prestige. The lower middle class persons are predominantly minor clerical or retail workers who live in smaller homes nearer the "wrong part of town." The distinction between "upper-lower" and "lower-lower" is based largely on moral considerations. "Upper-lowers" are poor but honest and ambitious. "Lower-lowers" are considered shiftless, dirty, and disorderly.

In the midwestern studies the class structure is somewhat different. Havighurst and Janke (1944) analyze it as follows for the community they studied:

Class A   Wealthy families (2 per cent of population)
Class B   Professional men, officials, and leading business men (6 per cent of population)
Class C   Small business men, lesser professional workers, some skilled workers, white-collar workers (37 per cent of population)
Class D   Semi-skilled workers and laborers, hard-working and respectable people (43 per cent of population)
Class E   Lowest occupational groups with poor reputation in the community (12 per cent of population)

These groups correspond fairly well to the five classes below the "upper-upper" in the Yankee City and Oldtown research. In Plainville, the distinction between the upper half and the lower half is more marked, based as it is on a geographical separation. The "better class" live on the prairies, the "lower class" back in the hills.

It is fortunate that we have these findings from several different parts of the country to compare, since differences as well as similarities in the class structure are apparent. The important conclusions for our purposes are twofold. First, wherever a thorough empirical study of the way in which people in a community regard each other has been made, it shows some sort of class differentiation. Second, economic factors of occupation and income seem to be involved in all of these distinctions, although other criteria, such as membership in clubs and organizations and religious affiliation, enter into them with different weights in different places.

The task of analyzing the class structure of any community has been facilitated through the publication by Warner, Meeker, and Eells (1949) of the monograph *Social Class in America*, which describes in detail two methods that can be used to make such an analysis. The first, which they call *Evaluated Participation*, requires that a number of persons in the community be interviewed. What these informants say about other individuals, the categories in which they place them, the designations they use for these categories (such as "upper crust" or "poor whites"), the nature of the institutions with which they are identified, and several other kinds of information are used. The second, much simpler method gives what they call an *Index of Status Characteristics*. It was found that an excellent prediction of the class positions of individuals in a group could be made by assessing four characteristics and giving them approximate weights. The four were: (1) Occupation, (2) Source of income (inherited wealth, salaries, welfare, etc.), (3) House type, and (4) Dwelling area. The correlation between the *Evaluated Participation* and the *Status Characteristics* indices was .97. Thus in many studies it is feasible to use the second, not requiring interview information for its computation, as a good substitute for the first.

An indirect gain growing out of this work is that it enables us to make better use of a body of research that has related psychological measurements (IQ, for example) to socio-economic indices, or to occupational level alone. Since differences in occupational level alone are so closely tied in with the complex differences in social status that influence a growing child in many ways, we are able to form plausible hypothesis about the meaning of a large number of correlations that were reported in the literature in the years prior to the research on social class.

DIFFERENCES BETWEEN CLASSES IN MENTAL ABILITY

A direct attack on the problem of whether there are differences between social classes in mental abilities has been made by Havighurst and Janke (1944) and Janke and Havighurst (1945). They selected batteries of tests to be given to all ten-year-olds and all sixteen-year-olds in the small city they call Midwest. The battery for ten-year-olds included the Stanford-Binet, the Cornell Coxe (a non-verbal test of intelligence), the Iowa Silent Reading, the Minnesota Paper Form Board (measuring judgment of spatial relationships), an adaptation of the Minnesota Mechanical Assembly Test for boys and a new mechanical assembly test of their own devising for girls, the Porteus Mazes, and the Goodenough Drawing Test. For sixteen-year-olds the battery included the Stanford-Binet, the performance tests from the Wechsler-Bellevue Scale, the Iowa Silent Reading, the Minnesota Paper Form Board, and the two assembly tests. Their aim was to include both verbal and non-verbal tests of intelligence along with tests of the more specialized reading and mechanical aptitudes. There were no children from either Class A or Class B in the ten-year-old group. For the sixteen-year olds, these two classes were combined to give nine cases altogether. One of the good features of the study is that practically the entire population of ten-year-olds was included, and evidence was given that the 29 sixteen-year-olds who had to be left out because of inaccessibility or failure to coöperate did not differ to any extent in IQ from the rest. Thus the effects of unknown selective factors are not distorting the results. Tables 31 and 32 show the means on the tests for the various social status groups.

TABLE 31.

Means of Social Status Groups on Psychological Tests— Ten-Year-Old Children

(Havighurst and Janke, 1944)

SOCIAL STATUS	N	STAN-FORD-BINET	CORNELL COXE	GOODE-NOUGH	IOWA SILENT READING	PAPER FORM BOARD	MECH. ASSEM.	MECH. ASSEM.	PORTEUS MAZE
							T-SCORE		
		IQ	IQ	IQ	SCORE	SCORE	BOYS	GIRLS	MENTAL AGE
C	26	114	116	107	99	22.5	52.5	56.0	12.7
D	68	110	110	102	99	21.3	49.2	49.5	12.8
E	16	91	96	91	88	15.7	46.9	41.3	10.4

TABLE 32.

Means of Social Status Groups on Psychological Tests— Sixteen-Year-Old Children

(Janke and Havighurst, 1945)

SOCIAL STATUS	N	STANFORD-BINET	WECHSLER BELLEVUE	IOWA SILENT READING	PAPER FORM BOARD	MECH. ASSEM.	MECH. ASSEM.
						BOYS	GIRLS
A B	9	128	118	58.0	44	46.8	62.1
C	44	112	109	51.0	40	51.6	52.0
D	49	104	102	48.9	31	48.8	48.5
E	13	98	103	45.6	31	53.0	45.9

The authors give also the standard deviation and total range of score for each group. Statistical tests show differences between the two lowest groups to be the most significant for the ten-year-olds. It is to be noted that these differences show up on *all* tests except the paper form board and the mechanical assembly test for boys. Among the sixteen-year-olds the differences between the A-B group and the others are the most significant. Again they show up consistently on *all* tests except the mechanical assembly for boys. Contrary to an opinion that has often been stated, the class differences are *not* more marked on verbal than on non-verbal tests. Since scores on the Minnesota Mechanical Assembly Test have been shown to depend partly on familiarity with the items, it seems likely that this factor explains why differences on it alone are not significant. Lower-status children may actually have a greater opportunity to try tasks of this kind.

Havighurst and Janke also analyzed differences between boys and girls, and between urban and rural children. The sex differences were very slight and not statistically significant. There was a consistent tendency for urban children to do better than rural on intelligence and reading tests, but most of the differences were not large enough to be clearly significant, with this number of cases. It is the class differences that emerge as the most clear-cut findings. Even here, not too much weight can be placed on one study, especially when the number of cases is small.

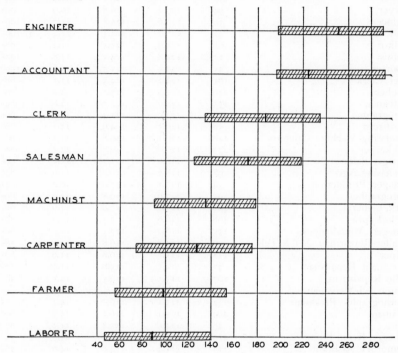

FIGURE 39. Scores on Army Alpha obtained by soldiers in World War I who reported various preservice occupations (Yerkes, 1921).

A later study in the same community by Schulman and Havighurst (1947) reported similar results for vocabulary. Using a test that enables one to estimate the total vocabulary of the person who takes it, they found that differences between Classes B, C, D, and E were again significant at the five per cent level. The average estimated vocabulary for Class B subjects was 45,600 words as against 28,800 for Class E subjects. Again the differences between boys and girls and between urban and rural subjects was not significant.

TABLE 33.

Mean GCT Standard Scores, Standard Deviations, and Range of Scores of 18,782 AAF White Enlisted Men by Civilian Occupation

(Harrell and Harrell, 1945)

OCCUPATION	N	M	MEDIAN	STANDARD DEVIATION	RANGE
Accountant	172	128.1	128.1	11.7	94-157
Lawyer	94	127.6	126.8	10.9	96-157
Engineer	39	126.6	125.8	11.7	100-151
Public-Relations Man	42	126.0	125.5	11.4	100-149
Auditor	62	125.9	125.5	11.2	98-151
Chemist	21	124.8	124.5	13.8	102-153
Reporter	45	124.5	125.7	11.7	100-157
Chief Clerk	165	124.2	124.5	11.7	88-153
Teacher	256	122.8	123.7	12.8	76-155
Draftsman	153	122.0	121.7	12.8	74-155
Stenographer	147	121.0	121.4	12.5	66-151
Pharmacist	58	120.5	124.0	15.2	76-149
Tabulating-Machine Operator	140	120.1	119.8	13.3	80-151
Bookkeeper	272	120.0	119.7	13.1	70-157
Manager Sales	42	119.0	120.7	11.5	90-137
Purchasing Agent	98	118.7	119.2	12.9	82-153
Manager, Production	34	118.1	117.0	16.0	82-153
Photographer	95	117.6	119.8	13.9	66-147
Clerk, General	496	117.5	117.9	13.0	68-155
Clerk-Typist	468	116.8	117.3	12.0	80-147
Manager, Miscellaneous	235	116.0	117.5	14.8	60-151
Installer-Repairman, Tel. & Tel.	96	115.8	116.8	13.1	76-149
Cashier	111	115.8	116.8	11.9	80-145
Instrument Repairman	47	115.5	115.8	11.9	82-141
Radio Repairman	267	115.3	116.5	14.5	56-151
Printer, Job Pressman, Lithographic Pressman	132	115.1	116.7	14.3	60-149
Salesman	494	115.1	116.2	15.7	60-153
Artist	48	114.9	115.4	11.2	82-139
Manager, Retail Store	420	114.0	116.2	15.7	52-151
Laboratory Assistant	128	113.4	114.0	14.6	76-147
Tool-Maker	60	112.5	111.6	12.5	76-143
Inspector	358	112.3	113.1	15.7	54-147
Stock Clerk	490	111.8	113.0	16.3	54-151
Receiving and Shipping Clerk	486	111.3	113.4	16.4	58-155
Musician	157	110.9	112.8	15.9	56-147
Machinist	456	110.1	110.8	16.1	38-153
Foreman	298	109.8	111.4	16.7	60-151
Watchmaker	56	109.8	113.0	14.7	68-147
Airplane Mechanic	235	109.3	110.5	14.9	66-147
Sales Clerk	492	109.2	110.4	16.3	42-149
Electrician	289	109.0	110.6	15.2	64-149
Lathe Operator	172	108.5	109.4	15.5	64-147
Receiving & Shipping Checker	281	107.6	108.9	15.8	52-151
Sheet Metal Worker	498	107.5	108.1	15.3	62-153
Lineman, Power and Tel. & Tel.	77	107.1	108.8	15.5	70-133

TABLE 33—(*Continued*).

OCCUPATION	N	M	MEDIAN	STANDARD DEVIATION	RANGE
Assembler	498	106.3	106.6	14.6	48-145
Mechanic	421	106.3	108.3	16.0	60-155
Machine-Operator	486	104.8	105.7	17.1	42-151
Auto Serviceman	539	104.2	105.9	16.7	30-141
Riveter	239	104.1	105.3	15.1	50-141
Cabinetmaker	48	103.5	104.7	15.9	66-127
Upholsterer	59	103.3	105.8	14.5	68-131
Butcher	259	102.9	104.8	17.1	42-147
Plumber	128	102.7	104.8	16.0	56-139
Bartender	98	102.2	105.0	16.6	56-137
Carpenter, Construction	451	102.1	104.1	19.5	42-147
Pipe-Fitter	72	101.9	105.2	18.0	56-139
Welder	493	101.8	103.7	16.1	48-147
Auto Mechanic	466	101.3	101.8	17.0	48-151
Molder	79	101.1	105.5	20.2	48-137
Chauffeur	194	100.8	103.0	18.4	46-143
Tractor Driver	354	99.5	101.6	19.1	42-147
Painter, General	440	98.3	100.1	18.7	38-147
Crane-Hoist Operator	99	97.9	99.1	16.6	58-147
Cook and Baker	436	97.2	99.5	20.8	20-147
Weaver	56	97.0	97.3	17.7	50-135
Truck Driver	817	96.2	97.8	19.7	16-149
Laborer	856	95.8	97.7	20.1	26-145
Barber	103	95.3	98.1	20.5	42-141
Lumberjack	59	94.7	96.5	19.8	46-137
Farmer	700	92.7	93.4	21.8	24-147
Farmhand	817	91.4	94.0	20.7	24-141
Miner	156	90.6	92.0	20.1	42-139
Teamster	77	87.7	89.0	19.6	46-145

Although this is the first time that the relationship of test scores to social status in a community has been specifically determined, the relationship of IQ to socio-economic level is one of the best documented facts in mental test history. From the time when Decroly and Degand (1910) first called attention to the fact that children in more favored economic groups made scores higher than Binet's norms, one investigator after another has called attention to the differentiation of test scores by occupation. When the army psychologists tested large groups of men in World War I, they were impressed with the hierarchy of average scores running from professional men at the top to day laborers at the bottom. Figure 39 shows the trend.

Similar findings for World War II, based on the scores of 18,782 white enlisted men of the Army Air Forces Air Service Command, were reported by Harrell and Harrell (1945). Table 33 shows these results. A more detailed analysis of the AGCT scores of over 80,000 white enlisted men in the Army, a representative sample made up of about 2 per cent of the total at the time, has been presented by Stewart (1947). The same hierarchy is shown.

The trends are obviously the same in the figures from both armies. The average score for men in the professions is at least one standard deviation unit above the mean. (In the AGCT test, the mean is 100 and the standard deviation 20.) Office workers and business men average from one-half to one standard deviation above the mean. People in the skilled trades show averages about at the mean. Semi-skilled workers are slightly below the mean, unskilled workers definitely below. In studying these figures, however, one must not forget the factor of individual differences within each group. The teamsters, the group with the lowest average in Table 33, have at least one man with a score of 145, far above the professional average. In general, the standard deviations show a greater variability in the groups at the *bottom* of the scale than those at the top. Educational requirements for professional and white-collar positions may account for this fact. It is not likely that a moron will ever be able to qualify as an engineer, lawyer, or accountant. However, it is quite possible for a brilliant man to be working as a truckdriver, lumberjack, or miner. The Stewart study brings out another fact which can be noted if we examine the scores representing the bottom of the range in the first column of Table 33. The variation in *low* scores for occupations is much greater than in average or high ones. This is true for occupations at the top of the hierarchy as well as those at the bottom. Table 33 shows, for example, that it is possible for a man to be a teacher, draftsman, or pharmacist even if his intelligence score is about one and one-half standard deviation units below the mean. (The low score for teachers was 76.) No engineer or chemist scored below 100. Evidently some jobs have a definite lower limit whereas others do not.

Simon and Levitt (1950) have given us figures showing the same sort of hierarchy for the Wechsler-Bellevue Test, although the fact that their 8,000 subjects were not selected to constitute a representative sample of the employed population would keep us from putting too much confidence in the occupational averages themselves. Foulds and Raven (1948a) have demonstrated the same differentiation between occupational levels in Scotland. Here the men were all employees of the same company, a plant manufacturing photographic equipment. The most important extra information we get from both these studies is that occupational differences in intellectual level are not confined to one sort of test material. They occur on both verbal and performance tests, both vocabulary and non-verbal reasoning.

TABLE 34.

Mean IQ's of Children According to Fathers' Occupations

(McNemar, 1942)

FATHERS' OCCUPATIONAL CLASSIFICATION	CHRONOLOGICAL AGES			
	2-5½	6-9	10-14	15-18
I Professional	114.8	114.9	117.5	116.4
II Semi-professional and Managerial	112.4	107.3	112.2	116.7
III Clerical, Skilled Trades, and Retail Business	108.0	104.9	107.4	109.6
IV Rural Owners	97.8	94.6	92.4	94.3
V Semi-skilled, Minor Clerical and Business	104.3	104.6	103.4	106.7
VI Slightly Skilled	97.2	100.0	100.6	96.2
VII Day Labor, Urban and Rural	93.8	96.0	97.2	97.6

When children are classified on the basis of their fathers' occupations, the same sort of differentiation is apparent. There have been dozens of reports emphasizing this finding, and their unanimity makes it necessary to point them out individually. The most dependable figures are those cited by McNemar (1942) from the data collected in the standardization of the Terman and Merrill revision of the Binet test. This sample is more representative of the total white population of the United States than any that had previously been obtained. Table 34 gives IQ's for children classified according to their fathers' occupations.

Children of professional men average highest, children of farmers and day laborers lowest, and the others somewhere in between. There is, of course, much overlapping between adjacent groups. However, the authors point out that only about 10 per cent of the day laborers' children exceed the mean for the professional men's children, and only about 10 per cent of the professional group fall below the general average. Stupid children can be and are born to parents of all levels, but they are much *less common* in those of higher economic status. Similarly, unskilled parents may have unusually bright children, but not many of them do. Terman and Merrill also bring out the fact that the difference is as marked for the youngest age group, those from two to five and a half, as it is for the oldest, fifteen to eighteen. This is important because for the younger ones the environmental differences have had a much shorter time to influence the scores.

Furthermore, a much larger proportion of the tests at the lower level are non-verbal. A thorough survey of a large number of studies, all showing this same trend, is available in Loevinger (1940).

TABLE 35.

Estimated Average IQ's for Different Occupational Levels

(Johnson, 1948)

	STUDY CLASS	CHILDREN			ADULTS	
		TERMAN-MERRILL	DUFF AND THOMPSON	ARMY ALPHA	CATTELL	AGCT
I	Professional	116	115	123	132	120
II	Semi-professional Managerial	112	113	119	117	113
III	Clerical, Skilled Trades, Retail	107	106	108	109	108
IV	Rural Owners, Farmers	95	97	97	—	94
V	Semi-skilled, Minor Clerical	105	102	101	105	104
VI	Slightly Skilled	98	97	98	—	96
VII	Day Laborers	96	95	96	—	95

D. M. Johnson (1948) has brought together the results of five large-scale studies on intelligence and occupational level. He made the figures for different tests comparable by using their means and standard deviations to put all the distributions onto the same scale as the Stanford-Binet. Treated in this manner, the averages from the different studies in this country and Great Britain show a remarkable amount of agreement. The largest discrepancies are at Level I. It might well be that Cattell's group was more highly selected than the American samples. It would be expected that the averages for the children of professional men would fall somewhat below the averages for the men themselves, because of regression toward the mean. Aside from these readily explained irregularities, the table gives a clear picture of the occupational hierarchy. We must remember, however, that these are *average* figures. The variability within each group cannot be ignored.

There is another whole body of research in which *scales* for measuring socio-economic status have been used instead of a classification of occupations. By this means, each individual can be given a quantitative score for status, and the scores can be *correlated* with other variables. Four principal types of scale have been devised. The first is simply a rating of occupational level alone. The Barr Scale and the Minnesota Scale for Occupational Classification are of this type. The second, represented by the Sims Score Card or the Chapin Living-Room Equipment Rating Scale, uses home characteristics, including furniture and equipment, as an index. The third, best exemplified by the Index of Status Characteristics we have discussed in a previous section, uses a composite of occupational level, source of income, and home type and location. The fourth, more recently developed by Gough (1948a and b, 1949b), is made up of personality items that have been found to correlate with status, such as literary-esthetic attitudes, social poise, and positive, dogmatic opinions. It has the advantage of being less easily "faked" than the others, since the subject does not know what it is measuring, and there is some preliminary evidence that discrepancies between scores on this and on status scales of the other types may measure tendencies toward social mobility.

In general, correlational studies using socio-economic indices of any of these types have corroborated those based on occupational differentiation. Adults and children from the more-privileged homes test higher than those from the less-privileged homes.

There is one group in the population for whom this generalization does not seem to hold, namely, *infants* under a year or a year and a half of age. Furfey (1928), for instance, found no tendency for babies from homes scoring low on the Chapman-Sims Scale for measuring socio-economic status to be inferior in mental development to those from more favorable environments. Bayley and Jones (1937) found that during the first eighteen months intelligence-test scores and ratings on the California Socio-Economic Index were not significantly related. More recently Irwin (1948) has shown that infants from professional and white-collar families differ significantly from those being reared in laboring-class homes in the number of different types of sound they use and the frequency with which they use them. But these speech or language differences are statistically significant only after the eighteen-month level, not before. This exception does not invalidate the general conclusion about the relationship of intelligence to occupational level, since it has been clearly shown that mental tests before eighteen months show little if any correlation with later mental-test scores either. But it is an interesting fact.

There are a number of studies that show us that the relationship between intelligence and status is not confined to any one country or to any one segment of the population. Several British reports have already been mentioned. Livesay (1944) has shown that in Hawaii the average intelligence-test scores of high-school seniors are related to the income level of their parents. Sirkin (1929) found the same sort of relationship in the Soviet Union between intelligence scores of elementary-school pupils and the occupational and educational level of their parents. In this country, Robinson and Meenes (1947) have shown that the relationship holds for Negroes as well as whites.

Besides showing that both men themselves and their children are differentiated according to occupational level, research has also shown specifically that intelligence-test scores made by children can be used to *predict* their later occupational level. Ball (1938) determined in 1937 the occupational rating on the Barr scale of 219 men who had been given the Pressey Mental Survey Test in 1918 or in 1923. For the 1923 group the correlation between test score and occupational level was .57; for the 1918 group it was .71. Both these figures show a substantial relationship, more pronounced where the interval has been longer.

There is some evidence that income, in itself, is not the deciding factor. The tables and graphs cited above tend to place professional occupations higher than the managerial occupations which on the whole pay higher salaries. A study by Wells, Williams, and Fowler (1938) in which the comparisons were between groups of men in the same business organization, with similar training and cultural opportunities, differing only in income, shows no difference between groups on ability tests. The hierarchy of occupations seems to be based more on the amount of training they involve and their prestige in the community than on what they pay. Warner *et al.* (1949) found that the *source* of the family income gave a better prediction of status than did the *amount*.

There is clear evidence that occupations do have different prestige values in our society and that these values have important effects on the occupational choices of individuals (Super, 1942). Deeg and Paterson (1947) in 1946 asked for rankings of twenty-five occupations from four groups of subjects: (1) college freshmen and sophomores; (2) college juniors, seniors, and graduate students in a vocational psychology class; (3) seniors in an academic high school. The occupations on the list had been used by Counts (1925) in 1925 for a similar study. Table 36 shows the prestige rankings given in the two studies which were separated by an interval of over twenty years.

It is interesting to note that in spite of a depression, a war in which unprecedented numbers of workers went into industry, and a flourishing vocational-guidance movement, the ranks on the two occasions are strikingly similar. The professional men still stand at the top. The unskilled and service occupations stand near the bottom. Welch (1949), using the same list of occupations, found that the ranking given them by 500 stu-

TABLE 36.

*Comparison of Social Status of Twenty-five Occupations
Obtained in 1925 and 1946 **

(Deeg and Paterson, 1947)

OCCUPATIONS	RANK ORDER BY COUNTS 1925	RANK ORDER BY DEEG AND PATERSON 1946
Banker	1	2.5
Physician	2	1
Lawyer	3	2.5
Supt. of Schools	4	4
Civil Engineer	5	5
Army Captain	6	6
Foreign Missionary	7	7
Elem. School Teacher	8	8
Farmer	9	12
Machinist	10	9
Traveling Salesman	11	16
Grocer	12	13
Electrician	13	11
Insurance Agent	14	10
Mail Carrier	15	14
Carpenter	16	15
Soldier	17	19
Plumber	18	17
Motorman	19	18
Barber	20	20
Truck Driver	21	21.5
Coal Miner	22	21.5
Janitor	23	23
Hod Carrier	24	24
Ditch Digger	25	25

* The ranks are based on the median rank assigned to each of the occupations by 450 persons in 1925 and by 475 persons in 1946. The occupations are listed according to the rankings obtained by Counts in 1925. The correlation (*rho*) between the two rankings is .97.

dents in an Indiana teachers' college was similar enough to give a correlation of .98 with the Deeg and Paterson ranking. Hall and Jones (1950)
obtained a very similar prestige ranking in England for 30 occupations
chosen to represent the entire range. Medical Officer, Company Director,
and Solicitor (lawyer) were ranked highest; Barman, Dock Laborer, and
Road Sweeper stood at the bottom. All groups agreed on this prestige
ranking—men and women, old and young, upper and lower classes. Himmelweit *et al.* (1952) showed that English adolescents agreed with the
adults on the ranking of eight occupations taken from the Hall and Jones
list.

Differences between occupations in average intelligence levels and in
prestige ranking have been established beyond the possibility of any argu-

ment. Controversy centers around what they *mean*. They are important to people in countries with democratic ideals because of their bearing on social mobility. The question is one of the extent to which these differences are standing in the way of the equality of opportunity we prize so highly.

Intelligence-test scores are related to school success, and the school is the principal channel through which mobility occurs. The traditional type of academic work is ill-suited to the needs of persons of below-average intelligence, yet it is only by means of the academic curricula that a person can attain one of the occupations carrying the high prestige values. Does this "load the dice" against a large fraction of our population, and promote a rigid class structure? The problem has many facets. We shall take up briefly only those aspects of it on which some clear evidence has been presented.

For one thing, intelligence differences do not constitute the *whole* problem. A number of studies show that it is not inadequate mental ability alone that forces lower-class children out of school. As indicated above, all levels of IQ occur in every social class, and because the great majority of our citizens fall into one of the lower classes, even a small *percentage* of high-scoring children at these levels adds up to a large total number. A considerable proportion of such bright lower-class children do not go to college. Many do not finish high school. Bingham (1946) summarized figures from testing done during World War II which showed that of the men classified Grade I on the AGCT (more than 1½ standard deviations above the mean) only about one-fourth were college graduates and 5,000 had not even finished grade school. Sibley (1942) analyzed 23,000 school records of Pennsylvania children who had been in the sixth grade in 1926 or 1928. Their subsequent school progress was related to *both* IQ and father's position. As far as college was concerned the most intelligent individuals had a 4 to 1 advantage over the least intelligent, but those from the highest occupational levels had a 10 to 1 advantage over those from the lowest. It was usually assumed, when such figures began to appear, that lack of money was the principal reason for school drop-outs among bright students. Although this is undoubtedly a factor, more recent scrutinies of what the class structure means to adolescents, Hollingshead's *Elmtown's Youth* (1949), for example, or Havighurst and Taba's *Adolescent Character and Personality* (1949), have indicated that it is partly a matter of emotional attitudes and motivation.

The problem still remains, however, as to what the differences in average intelligence levels for the different socio-economic classes mean. As with regard to so many other specific issues, argument on this one has tended to revolve around the general heredity-environment controversy. This has perhaps tended to obscure a question of more importance. It seems quite probable that there are some differences between classes based on differences in native ability. It would be difficult to account for the wide distribution of IQ's *within* a given class (or within a single family, for that matter) without postulating such differences. But admitting this still leaves us with the problem of whether *some* of the differences in class averages may be environmentally determined, and if they are, just what such differences mean.

As in the case of the Negro-white differences taken up in the previous chapter, two kinds of explanation, not always clearly distinguished from one another, have been proposed. They do, however, have quite different implications for education and for social planning in general. The first type of explanation holds that our present intelligence tests are not fair to lower-class children. The hypothesis is that they are actually as intelligent as the middle- and upper-class groups, but because the questions asked them do not give their ability a chance to show up they are consistently underestimated and discriminated against. The remedy would be to devise more adequate tests. The second type of explanation, fitting in with Hebb's and Piaget's emphasis on the importance of early learning in intellectual growth, holds that by the time they reach school age lower-class children have not, on the average, developed mentally to the level that more privileged groups have reached, and that the differences widen as years pass. The remedy would be to find out what kinds of early learning are indispensable to later intellectual development, and to plan for all children educational experiences that would promote it. What evidence do we have that would enable us to choose between these two types of environmental explanation?

The most thoroughgoing investigation of the first of them has been carried out under the auspices of the Committee on Human Development at the University of Chicago. Results have been published in a monograph by Eels *et al.* (1951). In this large-scale study, a number of standard intelligence tests were administered to all the nine- and ten-year-olds and all the thirteen- and fourteen-year-olds in a small Midwestern city, subjects whose social position had been identified by means of the Index of Status Characteristics. High-status groups were then compared with low-status groups, item by item, on all the tests. The main finding, the one which the author considers the principal support for his hypothesis of test unfairness, is that some items showed a much greater status difference than others did. Only 37 per cent of the items for the nine- and ten-year-old group, however, and 9 per cent of them for the thirteen- and fourteen-year group showed differences which were too small to be significant at the 5 per cent level. In general, verbal items seemed to show more status difference than did non-verbal items, but there were many exceptions.

Do these findings really indicate that the tests are unfair, or could they be interpreted equally well as evidence for status differences of a more fundamental kind? In the report on the many separate analyses made during the course of the research, there are some facts pointing toward the second alternative. For one thing, there are only 19 items out of 334 at the younger level and 3 out of 324 at the older level for which the difference between high- and low-status non-ethnic Americans does not favor the high group *to some degree.* Had the number of subjects been larger, all the other differences, though small, might also have been statistically significant. If the experience of the groups had been qualitatively different, one might have expected that some types of item would have favored the low-status children. Secondly, in a number of cases, a priori judgments about items on which status differences would have been expected because of differential familiarity with the content were not supported. Familiarity seemed not to be the most important determiner of success on test items. Thirdly, the factor that did seem to be important in producing large status differences on both right and wrong alternative answers was the quality of *abstractness* in the item itself. This we have discussed as an aspect of intelligence in Chapter 4. Low-status children have more trouble with similarities items, for example, and show more of a tendency to choose literal interpretations of proverbs. Out of the 25 items Eels chose for special consideration because of the large status differences they showed, 12 cannot be accounted for on the basis of *any* reasonable hypothesis as to how the environments of the two groups differ. Scrutiny of these items (Eels *et al.*, pp. 316-317) suggests, however, that they require either a complex classification or the following of complex directions. This sounds like "g." The progress of research using the Davis-Eels Test of General Problem-Solving Ability, which has been developed from items showing the least status difference, should tell us whether it is possible to divorce intelligence from social class and measure it independently. The crucial question with regard to such a test will be "What does it measure?" If it is not correlated with school achievement, what shall we use as a criterion of its validity?

On the second of the two types of explanation, that environmental factors can facilitate or hinder the development of effective intelligence itself, there is a considerable body of research which we shall present in Chapter 18. We still do not know, however, what it is that matters most about lower-class surroundings in the early years, nor the extent to which handicaps incurred during these years can be remedied at later stages. A more penetrating analysis of both the mental processes and the environmental influences will be necessary before we can say for certain what the intelligence differences between social classes mean. In the meantime, for practical purposes, it is important that we emphasize the variability within each social group and try to create conditions in which each *individual* will be able to achieve up to the limit of his potentialities.

URBAN-RURAL DIFFERENCES IN MENTAL ABILITY

A class distinction that cuts across the occupational hierarchy we have been considering in the previous section is urban-rural differentiation. The relationship of intelligence-test scores to this factor has been pointed out repeatedly by a wide variety of investigators in many different parts of this country and of Europe (Pintner, 1931, pp. 251-253). Figures cited by McNemar (1942) from the Terman and Merrill standardization data can be considered fairly typical of what is generally found. These are shown in Table 37.

TABLE 37.
IQ Data for Urban, Suburban, and Rural Children

(McNemar, 1942)

	(AGE—2-5½)			(AGE—6-14)			(AGE—15-18)		
	URBAN	SUBURBAN	RURAL	URBAN	SUBURBAN	RURAL	URBAN	SUBURBAN	RURAL
N..	354	158	144	864	537	422	204	112	103
M..	106.3	105.0	100.6	105.8	104.5	95.4	107.9	106.9	95.7
σ...	15.7	16.1	15.4	14.7	16.8	15.5	16.5	15.7	15.9

Suburban averages are almost identical with urban averages, as would be expected from the fact that the suburbs are populated almost exclusively by city people. The rural children average about 10 or 11 IQ points lower at all ages except the lowest, for which the difference is only about 5 points. Terman and Merrill's sampling of the rural population was less complete and representative than that of the urban population. They feel, however, that if it had been more satisfactory, differences would have been even more marked.

The school surveys referred to above indicate that rural children score lower than city children on tests in the various school subjects. There is little information as to how they compare on tests of special aptitudes. Shepard (1942) compared 104 children in two Kansas cities with an equal number of New York City children, using paired groups matched for occupational level of the parent, chronological age, sex, and place of birth (native or foreign). Besides the Otis test of intelligence, he included in his battery two tests calling for judgment of spatial relations, a mechanical assembly test, and a musical-aptitude test. Results showed New York children to be superior on the Otis test, and Kansas children to be superior on the spatial and mechanical tests. On the music test, the Kansas children were slightly higher, but the difference was not statistically significant. There is some doubt as to the weight that should be given this study as an indicator of typical urban-rural differences, since the Kansas group would be considered *rural* only by a New Yorker. In Kansas, a population of 12,000 constitutes a fair-sized city. It may be that regional rather than urban-rural differences are involved.

There is no argument among social scientists as to the *existence* of urban-rural differences in test scores; the controversy centers around what they mean. Again we encounter in discussions of this problem a hereditarian explanation and two types of environmental explanation not always clearly distinguished from one another. No one explanation will acount for all the research findings. From the hereditarian viewpoint, *selective migration* is the important factor in urban-rural differences. It is assumed that the most able individuals from farms and small towns are the ones most likely to move to the cities. Among those who prefer to stress environmental differences, some try to show that the intelligence tests we commonly use are not fair to country children and thus the results tell us nothing about actual intelligence. Others hold that there are real differences in intellectual ability, but that they arise from the educational handicaps under which rural children often grow up.

So far as selective migration is concerned, direct evidence for its occurrence is somewhat scarce, but there is some. The best study is by Gist and Clark (1938). High-school students in a number of rural communities in Kansas were given the Terman intelligence test in 1922-23. In 1935, information was obtained on 2,544 of these individuals to determine whether or not they had migrated. Over 70 per cent of them had left their home towns, 38 per cent having moved to urban communities. Table 38 shows how the moving is related to IQ. It should be read down the columns rather than across the rows.

TABLE 38.
IQ Distribution of Migrants and Non-Migrants
(Gist and Clark, 1938)

IQ	PER CENT OF GROUP MOVING TO CITIES	PER CENT OF GROUP REMAINING IN COUNTRY
105 and over	26.97	17.46
95–104	33.82	29.87
Under 95	39.21	52.66

Of the group that moved to the city, about 27 per cent had high IQ's, and about 39 per cent had low IQ's. Of the group that remained in the country the corresponding percentages were 17 and 53. For persons in the average group the difference was small. Statistical tests showed all these differences to be highly significant. The authors noted also a tendency for the migrants to large cities to be significantly superior to the migrants to small cities and for the non-farm rural residents to be superior to the farm group. Less extensive studies showing the same trend for several small towns in the South are on record (Mauldin, 1940; G. A. Sanford, 1940). On the other hand, Klineberg's extensive research (1938) tends to minimize its importance. He obtained intelligence- and achievement-test records for the children of migrants from rural regions in New Jersey. Scores were expressed in percentiles based on the total group taking the same test from the same teacher. The average percentile rank for the whole group of migrants was 47.5, which is just a little under the 50 which would be average for the whole population. In other words, these results show no tendency for the bright to leave and the dull to stay. Unfortunately there is a considerable amount of purely seasonal migration in this particular region in connection with the harvesting of crops, and it was not possible to distinguish the temporary from the permanent migrants. Klineberg feels, however, that the reasons for migration are very complex and differ from place to place. Consequently nothing can be said with any certainty about the relative intelligence of people who leave rural for urban areas. What we need are a number of studies in different parts of the country similar to that of Gist and Clark. It would then be possible to determine how widespread and universal selective migration is.

The best evidence for the hypothesis that rural children score lower because of environmental handicaps comes from a group of studies that have demonstrated an *increasing* deficit in rural children as they grow older. If we could depend upon the adequacy of Terman and Merrill's rural sample, we would have some evidence for this in Table 37. In the two-to-five-and-a-half-year group, the average IQ for farm children is almost 101. At the later ages it is more than 5 points lower. As has been said, McNemar feels that the rural sample is not complete enough to warrant any definite conclusion. However, there are a number of special investigations of children in isolated areas that show this same trend unmistakably. Among the best known are those of Gordon (1923), who tested canal-boat and gypsy children in England. While these are not rural samples of the population, the isolation and the lack of educational advantages are the same sort of handicap that farm children face. It was estimated that the school attendance of the canal-boat children was only 5 per cent, that of the gypsy children only 35 per cent, of the total school year. The average Binet IQ for the entire group of canal-boat children was 69.6. For the 82 gypsy children it was 74.5. There was a marked, consistent tendency for the older children to get the lower scores. The correlation between age and IQ was —.755 for the canal-boat children, —.430 for the gypsies. When different children from the same family were tested, the older one almost invariably obtained a lower IQ than the younger one did.

In this country, similar work has been done on children from southern mountain regions. Hirsch (1928) who examined 1,945 school children in various mountain regions in Kentucky using the Pintner-Cunningham and the Dearborn group tests of intelligence found the following average IQ's:

Age	5-6	7	8	9	10	11	12	13	14	15 and up
IQ	86.6	85	81.1	79.2	78.6	77.2	75.4	73.1	74.6	81.1

A general downward trend is apparent, the rise in the top category being attributable to the inclusion in the sample of a number of high-school students, who are a select group in communities like this. Sherman and Key (1932) gave a number of tests to children living in four remote hollows in the Blue Ridge Mountains and in one small village in this region. Again there was a consistent tendency for the older children to get lower scores. Asher (1935) tested mountain children in southeastern Kentucky. On the Myers Mental Measure, IQ's declined from 83.5 at age seven to 60.6 at age fifteen. Wheeler (1942) in 1940 gave the Dearborn Intelligence Test to over 3,000 children in East Tennessee, repeating a testing program which had been carried out in 1930. During the ten-year period there had been a great improvement in educational and cultural opportunities in this area.

The results showed that the average IQ for the region had increased about 10 points, from 82 to 92. There was, however, almost exactly the same tendency for IQ to decrease with age. In 1930 the decline had been from 95 at age six to 74 at age sixteen. In 1940 the decline was from 103 at age six to 80 at age sixteen.

These findings are usually interpreted as supporting the second of the environmental hypotheses outlined above, the hypothesis of educational handicap, but they may also point to the first. If the fact that tests are devised by professional persons using content appropriate to city children is responsible for the urban-rural differentiation, then we might expect that the factor should operate more strongly at the upper age levels where test scores are more dependent on vocabulary, general information, and skills acquired in school. It is impossible to decide between the two interpretations on the basis of the facts that have been presented. Shimberg (1929) worked specifically on the problem of whether the content of tests enters into rural-urban differences, using information tests of her own devising. Each test consisted of twenty-five items of general information chosen from a much larger number, and scaled or arranged in order of difficulty according to the percentage of children who could pass it in the group to which it was originally administered. For one test, a group of city children was used in this preliminary scaling; for the other, a group of country children. The two tests were then administered to large numbers of urban and rural children. The important finding was that farm children showed a consistent superiority over city children on Information Test B, the one scaled on rural subjects. Interestingly enough the superiority of city children on the urban scale was not so marked. The fact that this was purely an information test limits the conclusions that can be drawn from the study as to intelligence-test materials in general, though Shimberg makes the point that general information plays a part in many of the tasks set by most intelligence tests. Jones, Conrad, and Blanchard (1932) have also shown that the difficulty values of the items in the Stanford-Binet test, determined from the percentage of children passing each one, are different for rural subjects in New England than for the urban subjects on which the 1916 revision was standardized. The rural group was most inferior on three types of test items: (1) tests involving the use of paper and pencil; (2) tests involving experience with coins, street-cars, etc.; and (3) distinctly verbal tests.

There are a few research findings, however, that point in the reverse direction and prevent us from attributing all urban-rural intelligence-test differences to this familiarity factor alone. Klineberg (1931) in his European study cited in Chapter 11 found rural children consistently inferior to city children. The tests he was using were entirely non-verbal, and it is difficult to see how the content could have given the urban groups any great advantage. Since they are *timed* tests, a temperamental factor of speed of response might be involved, but there is little clear evidence for this. Another bit of conflicting evidence comes from the 1932 Scottish survey cited earlier. The striking fact (Scottish Council, 1939) is that there were *no* urban-rural differences. The figures are as follows:

	N	MEAN	SD
The Four Cities	319	100.86	15.29
The Industrial Belt	393	99.19	16.18
The Rural Areas	162	100.92	14.52
More Isolated Rural Areas	47	101.79	13.13

The one factor that would appear to be most important in explaining why a kind of difference found in the United States and various parts of Europe did not appear in Scotland is that educational opportunities there have been completely equalized. Schools in the country are said to be just as good as the city schools.

The matter is complicated still further by the fact that the later Scottish survey, in which all children born on six days in 1936 were given Binet tests eleven years later, does show city children slightly but significantly ahead of country children. The urban mean was about 105 as compared with a rural mean of about 101. (Scottish Council, 1949, p. 53.) It may be that conditions have changed. It is also possible that the 1937 Terman-Merrill Revision of the Binet test which was used in this study favors city children a little more than did the 1916 Stanford-Binet which was used in the previous one. At any rate, differences in Scotland are apparently much smaller than in many other places where such comparisons have been made.

In accounting for urban-rural differences, then, no one type of explanation will account for *all* the facts. It seems more reasonable to conclude that a combination of causes is producing the findings. Many tests are probably penalizing rural children to some extent. This would need to be analyzed for each individual test to determine how large a handicap it imposes. Simply to include rural children in the group on which the *norms* are based does not solve the problem, since it is the selection and scaling of the test *items* that are at fault. The Scottish study strongly suggests that one or both of the other two factors producing differences outweigh this one in importance. It may well be that the relative importance of selective migration and educational handicap varies in significance from place to place and from study to study. Some selective migration has been shown to occur. Marked educational deficiencies have been shown to characterize various rural regions, and their relationship to lowered test scores at the older ages has been well documented. We can sum up by stating that country children, almost everywhere they have been tested, obtain lower averages on intelligence tests than do city children. There seems to be no one simple explanation for this fact.

CLASS DIFFERENCES IN PERSONALITY TRAITS

General observation would suggest that there are wider differences between social classes on personality characteristics of various kinds than on measures of ability. What evidence do we have that this is true?

There is a considerable body of evidence for significant class differences in interests, attitudes, and values. Strong (1943) has found that one of the most clear-cut differentiations he was able to make was that between professional and laboring men. L. E. Tyler (1941) has shown that high-school girls taking a college preparatory course, who represent middle and upper social classes, differ in a number of respects from those in other high-school curricula. They are less hampered by traditional views as to "woman's place," more tolerant in their attitudes toward minor types of misconduct, less fearful. Mosier and Kuder (1949) have developed five preference scales having to do with personal characteristics rather than work activities, and have shown that they differentiate between men employed in different types of occupations. E. L. Phillips (1950) was able to develop three scales for the measurement of upper-, lower-, and middle-class attitudes by putting together items that differentiated significantly between junior high school pupils classified into the three groups. Gough's (1948a) status scale mentioned in a previous section was constructed in much the same way. His analysis of the types of items to which upper- and lower-status groups respond differently is particularly helpful in understanding the nature of the differences. He lists five categories of items on which class differences occur:

1. Literary-esthetic attitudes.
2. Social poise, security, self-confidence.
3. Denial of fears and anxieties.
4. "Broad-minded," "emancipated," and "frank" attitudes toward moral, religious, and sexual matters.
5. Positive, dogmatic, and self-righteous opinions.

Public opinion surveys on political and economic issues have shown significant differences between classes on many specific points. Many of them can be summed up by saying that people at the lower occupational levels are more concerned with *security*, people at the upper levels with *advancement*. J. W. McConnell (1942) found that wage-earner and white-collar workers in New Haven, Connecticut, differed in their attitudes about jobs, politics, family relationships, and education. The white-collar worker thinks of his job as a way of getting ahead and expects to move up into a better one; the wage-earner's chief concern is with safeguarding what he has. The white-collar worker wants a government that will be efficient but not curtail individual initiative; the wage-earner wants a government that will protect his economic security and raise his standard of living. Wage-earners characteristically marry earlier than white-collar workers and show less freedom in choosing mates from classes other than their own. White-collar workers are more likely than wage-earners to see education as a means of advancement. A. W. Jones (1941) showed that different groups in the population—business leaders, technicians, farmers, teachers, office workers, factory workers, and a number of others—showed highly significant differences in their attitude toward property rights. Business leaders averaged at almost the maximum score so far as respect for corporate property rights was concerned, whereas union members showed very little of this attitude. Kinsey *et al.* (1948) have shown that there are class differences among males but not among females in sex practices that are thought to be wrong.

The most comprehensive analysis of attitude differences on various matters has been presented by Centers (1949). He has shown that classes differ in their job satisfaction, in aspirations for their children, in opinions about the place of women in society (lower groups less liberal), and in the reasons they give as to why some persons succeed more than others. Centers (1950, 1951) has also been particularly interested in what interviewees say when asked to *identify* the class to which they belong. He has shown that though there is a clear-cut relationship between occupation and class identification, it constitutes by no means a perfect correlation. Most people whose jobs classify them in what we have been calling the lower classes say that they belong to the "working class," but some in each group answer "middle" and some "upper" to such a question. Both the overlapping between classes in the kinds of responses public opinion analysts get to all their questions and this evidence that people do not always identify their own class the way the analysts do serve to remind us that the lines we have been discussing throughout this chapter are not sharp ones.

With all these differences in interests and attitudes, the question still remains as to how much difference there is in more basic aspects of personality structure. There is a hypothesis which has grown out of the work of social anthropologists that differences in methods of child-rearing produce fundamental differences in personality. In this connection Davis (1943) has described what happens at various levels of Negro society, and many observers have thought that his generalizations apply equally well to white social-status levels. The chief difference he points out is that the lower-class child is not taught to inhibit his aggressive and sexual impulses, as is the middle-class child. He seeks immediate gratification rather than deferred satisfaction. There is as yet little quantitative evidence for these conclusions, although Milner's (1949) intensive analysis of 30 adolescents at the middle-status levels seems to point to some "group-typical" characteristics that fit in with the hypothesis that in the training of middle-class children, inhibition and conformity have perhaps been overly emphasized. Havighurst (1952), summarizing what has been reported about class differences in personality, concludes that there is too much difference *within* any class to make the hypothesis of a basic personality structure characteristic of each subculture tenable.

Results using personality questionnaires are ambiguous. Auld (1952) has summarized a large number of separate studies using a variety of so-called personality tests. In many cases, no difference between classes at all appears; in many others, it is small and not statistically significant. It is a fact worth noting, however, that in studies that have shown significant differences, the advantage lies with the upper-level groups. They turn out to be less neurotic, more dominant, more stable. The anxiety that the social anthropologists have stressed as an inevitable concomitant of the inhibition of impulses toward sex and aggression seems not to result in a greater frequency of neurotic attitudes.

Much clearer evidence that the general level of mental health is higher among the more privileged classes comes from two large-scale psychiatric surveys. R. E. Clark (1949) classified 12,168 male first-admissions to mental hospitals in the Chicago area into nineteen large occupational groups. Age-adjusted rates were calculated for each. What we might call "rate of breakdown" for each occupation was then correlated with some of the other figures characteristic of it. Highly significant correlations were obtained. Among white patients, for example, income-level correlates —.83

with "rate of breakdown," prestige level —.75. For Negroes the coefficients are somewhat lower but still strongly negative: —.53 for income, —.60 for prestige. The same kind of relationship holds when figures for the various diagnostic categories are analyzed separately, with the one exception of manic-depressive psychosis, which apparently occurs with about equal frequency at all occupational levels.

Many other specific questions are being put to the research data in a similar survey being conducted at New Haven, Connecticut. A preliminary report by Redlich *et al.* (1953) substantiates the Clark conclusion and presents some extra facts. In this investigation all patients receiving any sort of psychiatric treatment on Dec. 1, 1950 constitute the experimental group. It thus includes persons treated in physicians' offices as well as patients in public and private hospitals. A five-step classification of socio-economic level has been used. Results show in an unequivocal way that psychiatric difficulty is much more common the farther down the social scale we go. Furthermore, there are clear-cut class differences in both type of disorder and kind of treatment. At the two upper levels, about two-thirds of the patients are diagnosed as neurotic, about one-third as psychotic. At the lowest level, only 8 per cent are given the neurotic label, 92 per cent the psychotic label. Schizophrenia is nine times as prevalent at the lowest level as it is at the two upper ones. The majority of patients at the two upper levels receive psychotherapy, the majority at the lowest level no treatment at all except hospitalization, or organic therapy of some sort. These differences in diagnosis and treatment are not of course independent of one another, and may arise partly from the fact that neurotic states of mind are more likely to be recognized by upper-class individuals than by those in lower classes, who in any case could not afford psychotherapy. The one thing about which both these studies leave little doubt is that there is a highly significant *negative* relationship between social level and mental illness.

SUMMARY

Sociologists are devoting considerable attention to the analysis of the class structure of our contemporary American society. Studies in different parts of the United States have shown that five or six distinct levels can usually be differentiated. The upper classes are numerically small but command a considerable amount of prestige. Recent studies in a Midwestern community show that the social-status groups differ in average level of intelligence. This finding fits in with occupational intelligence differences which have been reported again and again since the test data for soldiers in World War I first became available. There is a definite relationship between average intelligence and average occupational level, although among individuals in any given occupation there is a wide intelligence range. Probably both innate intellectual differences and environmental handicaps are involved.

Another intelligence difference that has been consistently reported is the tendency of urban groups to score higher than rural groups. Of the types of explanation that have been proposed to account for this finding, the selective migration and the educational handicap theories seem most reasonable. It seems likely that both factors are affecting results and that their relative influence varies from one location to another. The fact that test questions and tasks are not equally fair to rural and urban children is another possible explanation, but the finding that in some places farm children score as high as city children would lead us to discount the importance of this factor as compared with the others.

There are probably significant class differences in personality traits as well as ability, but the problem has not been adequately explored. The most clear-cut differences found so far are in interests and attitudes and in rates of occurrence of mental illness. The advantage in all these comparisons rests with the middle-class and upper-class groups.

CHAPTER **13**

Age Differences

REASONS FOR CONSIDERATION OF AGE DIFFERENCES

THE TOPIC of differences between the generations is one of perennial interest in a world where people of all ages must somehow live and work together. High-school boys and girls take note of the ways their parents think and act and then draw their own conclusions. Middle-aged adults look at adolescents in puzzled wonder. Often they come out with sweeping and not complimentary generalizations about young people. Toward the aged most middle-aged persons show either protectiveness or impatience, and both of these attitudes imply a tacit assumption that old people are less able than they once were. If required to formulate his ideas as to how the generations differ, the man on the street would be likely to say something like this:

"Everybody knows that young people are quicker than older ones— faster in their movements, quicker to learn new things. They're a lot more adventurous too, always wanting to try something new to get a new thrill. They are likely to be more radical, more hot-headed, less steady, than older people are. Men in their forties are slower, though their judgment is better. You don't find so many radicals among them, and they are a lot more settled in their attitudes. Old people are a little feeble, of course, though some of them manage to keep on working. They can't learn anything new very well, and they are often kind of tiresome because they insist on telling the same stories over and over, living in the past."

This is more or less the prevailing attitude, as we find it in ourselves and our friends. Unlike various other cultures such as the Chinese, we have quite consistently emphasized youth as the golden age of life. Until recently America has been predominantly a nation of young men and women. The sort of achievement we have admired most in the pioneer,

the cowboy, or the self-made business man is the kind of thing that requires vigor, aggressiveness, and youthful energy. For many people, all
the years after the first twenty are a prolonged anticlimax.

One reason why it is important now that we become as well informed as
possible about what the differences between generations actually are is
that the age composition of our population is rapidly changing. Improved
medical techniques have saved for middle age and even destined for
senescence a great many individuals who would otherwise have died in
early youth. Emigration from Europe, which once brought in a steady

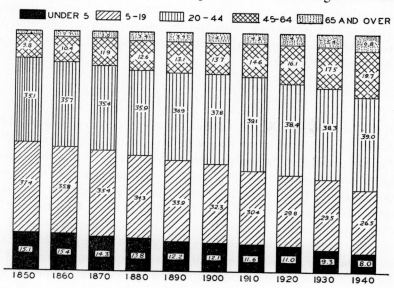

FIGURE 40. Percentage distribution of total population of the United States by
age, 1850 to 1940 (Dublin, 1942).

stream of young people, is down to a very small figure. The birth rate until
recently was declining. Figure 40, taken from a paper by Dublin (1942),
shows what these trends have been doing to our population. The increased birth rate since World War II can be expected to change these
proportions somewhat, but not drastically.

Many interesting comparisons can be made between figures for 1850
and figures for 1940. The proportion of infants and young children declined from 15.1 to 8.0. The proportion of children from five to nineteen
declined from 37.4 to 26.5. The other groups gained. The percentage of
young adults twenty to forty-four was only slightly higher in 1940 than
it was in 1850 but the group from forty-five to sixty-four was over twice

as large. There was a large relative increase in the group over sixty-five also, but they still comprised only a small fraction of the population. Whether we like the thought or not, we are rapidly becoming a middle-aged nation. Just what changes this will involve in our social and economic institutions remains to be seen. But in adjusting ourselves to such changes, it is imperative that we attempt to find out what psychological differences, if any, actually exist between people at the different age levels.

In this chapter we will not concern ourselves with the differences between children and adults. The fields of child and adolescent psychology have been intensively cultivated and have developed a body of literature too large to be covered in a course on human differences in general. We shall confine ourselves here to the differences among *adults* of various ages, the age trends after maturity.

PROBLEMS AND DIFFICULTIES

Of the problems discussed in Chapter 3, two have been special stumbling blocks in the path of research on age differences. The first of these is the problem of getting satisfactorily representative samples. Growth studies of children have demonstrated the value of longitudinal rather than cross-section methods. In a longitudinal study the *same individuals* who form the initial sample are measured again from time to time. Thus the research worker knows that the groups of people he is comparing differ in age alone. Any change noted must be a change that comes with age. In a cross-section study, the measuring of different age groups is carried out at the same time, which means, of course, that the persons comprising each sample are not the same ones. We can never be sure in this type of research whether the differences between the ten- and the fifteen-year-olds are actually changes that come with age or whether the samples differ also in some other respects. It has been impractical to carry on longitudinal studies of the whole life span of any sample of adults. If we had information about the characteristics of a fairly large group of adults tested at twenty, and again at forty and at sixty, it would be of tremendous value in answering our questions. Obtaining this information, however, constitutes a project of such magnitude that to carry it out was for a long time impossible. Since World War II some studies of this type have been set up, and first reports from them are now available.

In cross-section studies where groups of different ages are tested at the same time, the sampling difficulty is primary. Where are we to go to get a group of adults who will be as typical of the whole *adult* population as the sample of children we can find in almost any elementary school is of the total *child* population? All organized groups of adults are *selected* in some fashion and none represent men and women as a whole. Church groups, luncheon clubs, labor unions, women's clubs, and inmates of homes for the aged constitute selected samples. Huge draft armies, like those of World War I and World War II give us more nearly representative samples of male America than have been obtained in any other way. It is to be noted that the first important comparisons of different age groups were made in a study of the test scores of officers in World War I. Had someone been able to persuade applicants for ration books to stay and be tested, we might have been able to get as adequate a sample of women, though it is doubtful whether it would ever have been possible to get all members of a large group to coöperate in such a plan. Investigators have solved the sampling problem more or less satisfactorily in various ways. We shall note what their solutions were as we proceed, and it is well always to keep this difficulty in the back of one's mind in attempting to interpret the findings of research.

The other special difficulty is that of getting mental measurements equally fair to persons of all ages. A test is not a measuring rod but a standardized *situation* in which a sample of an individual's behavior may be taken. The psychological situation may not be the same for persons differing widely in age. To the child in school, any task is something to be completed as satisfactorily as possible. He has been subjected to a long training period in which he learns that the rewards come to him who does the assignments whether or not they look silly or pointless. The chances are that an adult long out of school will not react in this way. If the problem given him does not constitute a challenge, he sees no reason for struggling with it. If the questions are stated in childish terms or the materials give an impression of immaturity, the situation they represent for an adult is not the same as the situation they create for a child, and comparisons of scores do not really tell us what we want to know. Recognition of the fact that age differences vary with the type of material used has led to some of the most significant work done in this area. We should keep this fact in mind also as we scrutinize research findings.

AGE DIFFERENCES IN GENERAL INTELLIGENCE

Some of the first evidence on the question of age differences in intelligence came from an analysis of World War I army test data (Yerkes, 1921). Enlisted men were almost all relatively young, but the 15,385 officers whose scores formed the basis of this study were men of all ages from eighteen to sixty. Table 39 shows the results obtained.

TABLE 39.

Average Army Alpha Scores of 15,385 Officers in World War I

(Yerkes, 1921)

AGE	AVERAGE SCORE
Under 20	150
20-24	146
25-30	143
31-40	133
41-50	125
51-60	120

The steady decline from the youngest to the oldest age groups is the most striking finding. There was, of course, a great deal of overlapping, and the variability *within* any one age group was far higher than the differences between the groups. Many sixty-year-olds did better than the average man of twenty. Many twenty-year-olds were below the average man of sixty. But the general trend was clear-cut and consistent.

Jones and Conrad (1933) also used Army Alpha to test practically the entire population of nineteen New England villages. They were able to get an unusually good sample of the population of all ages by giving free movies to which everyone was invited, and requesting the audience to take the intelligence test as well as a short test on the movie they had just seen. They found much the same general age trends as had the army psychologists. Figure 41 shows what their findings were.

The highest scores were made by people between the ages of nineteen and twenty-one. With one exception each age group, from here on up, scored a little lower than the preceding one, so that the average for fifty-five-year-olds was the same as that for eleven-year-olds.

Jones and Conrad then made separate analyses of the scores on the eight subtests of Army Alpha. It was interesting to note that on Information and Vocabulary there was no decline until the age of sixty. The three subtests showing the *greatest* decline with age were Analogies, Common Sense, and Number Series. The one thing these three seem to have in common is the fact that they necessitate quick adaptation to *new* situations. This sort of differentiation in the age trends for different types of test item has been substantiated by all the later research.

One of the most elaborate of these studies planned especially to clarify the differential decline of abilities is that of Weisenburg, Roe, and McBride (1936). Their method of getting an adequate sample of the population of all ages is also particularly interesting. Their subjects were hospital patients in orthopedic and surgical wards. Persons in this situation have a great deal of time on their hands. If they are approached in such a way as to

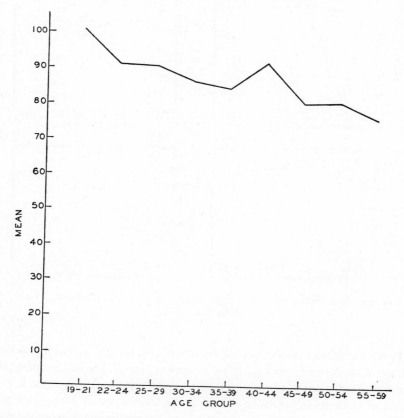

FIGURE 41. Age differences in scores on Army Alpha for total rural New England sample (Jones and Conrad, 1933).

win their coöperation and interest, they are available for a great many more tests than an investigator is usually able to give. Weisenburg, Roe, and McBride show evidence that their sample, though small, was quite representative of the population from which it was drawn. While they had only seventy patients, aged ten to fifty-nine, they gave each one a number of tests requiring ten to fifteen hours altogether. Some of their results are shown in Figure 42.

It is clear from their results that the verbal tests show only a slight decline with age. For the non-verbal tests, the decline is very marked and begins early. For verbal tests, the least decline is found for vocabulary and word knowledge, the most decline for analogies.

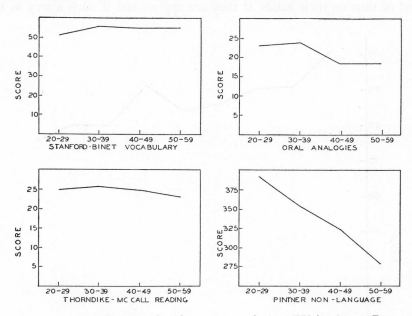

FIGURE 42. Age differences for four types of test (Weisenburg, Roe, and McBride, 1936).

Further evidence on the lack of decline in vocabulary and well-practiced mental skills comes from a study by Sorenson (1933). He had a sample that was admittedly not representative of the general population since it consisted of students in extension classes at the University of Minnesota, who were largely elementary and junior high school teachers. He arranged them in five-year groups from fifteen to sixty-five, equating schooling and occupational level. The scores showed that for these people who are constantly working with books, vocabulary actually increases with age. Reading scores show no age trend.

There have been several other studies on populations of varying educational background that corroborated Sorenson's findings with regard to vocabulary. Just how long the increase in vocabulary continues is not so clear as the fact that the increase occurs. Christian and Paterson (1936), for instance, showed that for their group of parents and relatives of college students, the sixty to sixty-nine year group was higher than any of the others. Heston and Cannell (1941) who tested a large number of rural men and women through the Farm Security Administration found a slight persistent rise through fifty-five, a slight drop after that. Shakow and Goldman (1938), who equated all their age groups so that each constituted a representative sample of the educational attainment that was standard for the time in which the subjects were growing up, found vocabulary level remained constant through the seventh decade and declined after that. Thorndike and Gallup (1944) gave a short vocabulary test to the same representative sample of the American voting population that is used in the Gallup polls. Vocabulary level remained practically constant from twenty through sixty, declining slightly after that.

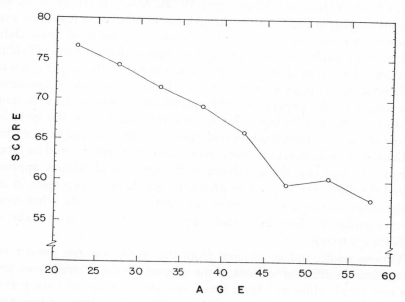

FIGURE 43. Relationship between general intelligence and age in adults (Vincent, 1952).

Studies in Great Britain have given similar evidence of a decline in general intelligence level with the years, along with the maintenance of vocabulary level. The most conclusive figures are those reported by Vincent (1952) who standardized a new verbal intelligence test on more than 7,000 civil service employees ranging in age from twenty-one to sixty. With the exception of one group, the forty-five to fifty-year olds, who scored unusually low, the other means show a straight linear relationship with age, as Figure 43 demonstrates. Summarizing the age trends in most of the large-scale studies where some sort of general intelligence test has been used, Vincent shows that they agree remarkably well. The mean annual decrement over this range from twenty to sixty is about .03 of a standard deviation, regardless of which test is used.

Foulds and Raven (1948b), using as subjects groups of adults employed in the same plant, show that the decline is apparent on the Progressive Matrices (a general intelligence test using geometric figures as material), but not on the Mill Hill Vocabulary Test. This is exactly what the American findings would have led one to expect.

The most ambitious investigation of many aspects of the problem of psychological differences between age groups was the Stanford Later Maturity Study (Miles and Miles, 1932; W. R. Miles, 1933). In 1930, 863 persons ranging in age from ten through eighty-nine were tested. In 1932 another 1,600 persons were added. Subjects were obtained from clubs, lodges, and church groups by paying the organization for each individual they sent. This method of selection is well adapted to secure persons with an interested, coöperative attitude, but could hardly provide a representative sample of the population. This qualification must be kept in mind as we interpret the findings. One noteworthy feature was the inclusion of 190 of the *same* individuals in both the 1930 and 1932 studies. For these individuals actual *changes* in score over a two-year period could be ascertained. The fact that this difference in the *same* people closely approximated the difference in separate groups of people two years apart in age is significant in that it enables us to put more faith in all the other cross-section studies we have been analyzing. It suggests that they really do indicate age trends.

Various results and conclusions from this major research project will be outlined in different sections of the chapter. So far as intelligence tests are concerned, Miles and Miles found averages that repeated the pattern by now familiar to us, as Figure 44 shows. There is evidence of increasing scores up to eighteen, a constant level maintained during the twenties, a slight decline in the thirties, more in the forties, and an increasing amount from there on. By the age of fifty, over one year of mental age has been lost; by the age of sixty almost two. The average mental age for eighty-five-year-olds is eleven years seven months. We must remember, of course, that this group of subjects is not a representative sample of the whole population. Figure 44 shows it to be a superior group intellectually, since the average IQ for the twenty-year-olds was considerably above the 100 that would be expected for people in general. The trends, however, are similar enough to those brought out in the analysis of the army data and in the Jones and Conrad study so that we can be sure they are not the result of selectivity alone. The most important *additional* fact that can be noted from Figure 44 is that the trend is similar for groups with different educational backgrounds, though the college-trained *individual* may be superior to the grade-school average even to an advanced age.

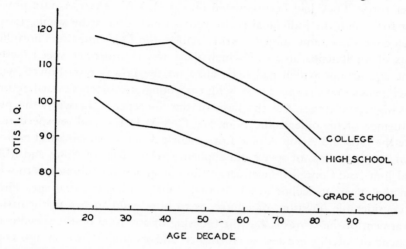

FIGURE 44. Age differences in intelligence test score for groups reporting different amounts of formal education (Miles and Miles, 1932).

Another study reported by Sward (1945) substantiates this finding. His subjects were all university professors. Forty-five men in the age range sixty to eighty were matched with men from the same departments in the age range twenty-five to thirty-five. The tests included many types of material often used in intelligence measurement—ingenuity, artificial language, synonyms and antonyms, symbol-digit, word meanings, number series, analogies, and arithmetic. On six of the eight tests there were significant differences in favor of the younger men. On only one, synonyms-antonyms, was there a significant difference favoring the older subjects. Again vocabulary shows up as the one kind of score not showing an age decrement.

The principal value of the Miles and Miles research is that it emphasized the differences in age trends from one type of test to another. For one thing, they showed that the decline is greater for speed tests than for power tests. (Speed tests are those in which the individual is scored on how much he can finish within a limited time. Power tests are those in which his score depends entirely on the difficulty of the tasks he can do when given all the time that he needs.) The evidence points to a decrement even in power tests, however, by fifty.

A study by Lorge (1936) focuses attention on this difference in age trends for speed and power tests. He used three age groups: twenty to twenty-five, twenty-seven and one-half to thirty-seven and one-half, and over forty. They had been equated on the C A V D test, a pure power test for which the individual is allowed as much time as he wants. Lorge then gave these same subjects Army Alpha, the Otis, and the Thorndike tests of intelligence, in all of which there is a considerable speed factor. The age groups which had been alike on the power test showed wide discrepancies on the speed tests, with the youngest subjects as usual getting the highest averages. On the basis of the discrepancy between the performance of his older subjects on the C A V D test and on speed tests like the Otis and Army Alpha, Lorge worked out a mathematical *correction* factor for loss of speed and applied it to the data of Miles and Miles and Jones and Conrad. The effect of this correction for slowness is to wipe out the apparent decline in intellectual ability with increasing age. There is considerable question, of course, as to how valid such a mathematical treatment of the scores is, but the focusing of attention on the speed component of intelligence-test performance and its importance in age comparisons has been a valuable contribution.

With the increasing use of the Wechsler-Bellevue Test for the measurement of adult intelligence, a considerable amount of material showing age trends in the different subtests has become available. So far as total scores are concerned, Wechsler's standardization data show the same trends as all the other studies (Wechsler, 1941). But there are consistent differences between types of test which are reported in study after study of older men and women. The Information test shows the least age decrement, the Digit Symbol test the most. Fox and Birren's (1950) fifty subjects in the sixty to sixty-nine year range, chosen so as to be fairly typical of the population at that age, scored highest in Information, Vocabulary, and Comprehension, lowest on Digit Symbol, Picture Arrangement, and Block Design. These results agree with those from previous studies. Whatever it is that the Digit Symbol test requires, it is the intellectual characteristic that falls off most strikingly with age.

The one factor-analysis study that has attempted to classify the abilities tapped by the Wechsler-Bellevue Test (Balinsky, 1941) has not left us very clear as to what the abilities are. Balinsky shows that there is more evidence for "g" at the older age levels than in young adults. The fifty to fifty-nine year olds are more like the nine-year-old children than like the intermediate groups, in that all the subtests show higher correlations with one another. But the group of tests that show the highest loadings in this general factor at the older age levels includes two that have been shown to decline markedly with age, namely Picture Arrangement and Block Design, and one that has been shown to decline little if at all, Information. Thus this factor analysis does not tell us anything about what the differential decline means. It is evidently not "g" as a whole that falls off.

One other report on the Wechsler-Bellevue Test should be considered, since it contains a finding somewhat at variance with previous studies. Corsini and Fassett (1953) tested 1,072 adults entering San Questin prison, and made an age classification in five-year steps from fifteen to seventy. Older groups made lower scores than the younger on most of the performance tests, as they usually do. But on most of the verbal tests, the older prisoners were not just equal but actually *higher* than the younger. Those in their fifties made higher scores than those in their teens on Information, Comprehension, Arithmetic, and Digit Span. They were approximately equal on Similarities. There may of course be selective factors at work. It would be gratifying to believe that a life of crime is attracting a less intelligent segment of our population now than it did in the days when the present middle-aged criminals were choosing their careers.

One study (Schaie *et al.*, 1953) tested 61 older men and women, aged fifty-three to seventy-eight, on the battery of Primary Mental Abilities Tests developed by Thurstone to measure what factor analyses had shown to be relatively independent components of intelligence. Older subjects were most handicapped on the Space and Reasoning tests, least handicapped on Number and Verbal Meanings. This is about what one would have predicted from studies based on other tests.

During the early 1950's first reports began to come in of some longitudinal studies of adults, reports that seemed to *contradict* the conclusions from all the previous cross-sectional studies. The most challenging of these is the one by Owens (1953). What he did was to arrange for the retesting in 1949-50 of 127 males who had taken Army Alpha thirty years before at the time they entered college. Instead of scoring lower on the second occasion than they had on the first, this group averaged significantly *higher*. This was true for a number of the separate subtests as well as for total score. There was no subtest on which scores had decreased significantly and only three out of the eight on which the change in an upward direction was slight. Bentz (1953) has reported some results over an eight-year interval that substantiate the Owens conclusions. His subjects were Sears Roebuck executives. Those who were thirty-five years or under at the time of the first administration of the American Council Psychological Examination showed significant *improvement* on retest. Bayley [1] has found that members of Terman's "gifted children" group who as adults took a high-level intelligence test twice, with about a ten-year interval between the two administrations, also showed a significant increase over the period.

The meaning of these results from longitudinal studies is still unclear. Why should they diverge so sharply from the findings obtained from cross-sectional studies? It is true that the subjects in all three of these studies are middle-aged rather than old, and there is still time for decline to occur. But the evidence for a straightforward linear relationship such as that shown in Figure 43 has been so consistent that we would have predicted that Owens' group after thirty years would have averaged almost a whole standard deviation below their original score ($30 \times .03$). In the other studies we would have expected a decline of one-fourth to one-third of a standard deviation. It is true that the subjects in these three studies were all well-educated individuals, but the Miles and Miles and the Sward results cited above seemed to indicate that similar trends characterize groups of all educational levels. Further reports based on longitudinal studies will be eagerly awaited.

In summarizing the large amount of work that has been done to compare the intelligence levels of adults in different age groups, there are three types of finding we must keep in mind. First, so far as total score is concerned on almost any kind of intelligence test, cross-sectional studies have shown a peak in the twenties, a gradual decline to about fifty, and a much steeper decline thereafter. Longitudinal studies have cast doubt on the inevitability of the decline from twenty to fifty, at least for educated people. Second, the trends are different for different kinds of material. Vocabulary, general information, and power tests in general show no decline up to fifty, and actually show an increase for some groups. From fifty on, a gradual falling off even in these abilities would seem to be the rule. Performance tests in general, and the Digit Symbol test in particular, show marked decreases at the older levels. Third, within every age group there is a wide range of scores. It is absolutely impossible to determine a person's intelligence from his age alone. Decisions that have to be made about hiring older workers in industry, letting eighteen-year-olds vote, lowering age requirements for public office, and drawing up pension and retirement

---

[1] Personal communication.

plans will be made more intelligently by persons who are thoroughly conversant with these facts.

AGE DIFFERENCES IN OTHER ABILITIES

In making decisions about the employment of older workers it is often important to know which special abilities decline with age. Miles and Miles, in the Stanford Later Maturity Study, made an admirably complete survey of many measurable traits. Tests of vision and visual perception, tests of dexterity and motor coördination of different parts of the body, a test of judgment, in which positions of objects were determined from scale size, tests of memory for new materials, and an ingenious test of imagination by means of kinephantoms or shadow pictures were included. Some of the results are shown in Table 40. The highest group averages for each set of scores is arbitrarily given a value of 100 and the others indicate percentages of this standard comparison figure.

TABLE 40.

Average Performance of Different Age Groups on Various Tests *

(Miles, 1933)

PERFORMANCE	B (10-17)	C (18-29)	D (30-49)	E (50-69)	F (70-89)
	%	%	%	%	%
Visual Perception	100	95	93	76	46
Motor Skills					
Rotary	90	100	97	89	72
Reach and Grasp	92	100	98	88	70
Finger Extension	87	100	98	99	71
Foot Reaction	85	100	96	94	71
Comparison and					
Judgment	72	100	100	87	69

* 100 indicates highest group average. Others are stated as percentages of this.

From this table it can be seen that motor skills, contrary to common opinion, are not the earliest to mature and the quickest to decline. In all motor abilities included in this study, the peak comes in the eighteen to twenty-nine year group rather than in the adolescent group, and the thirty to forty-nine year group averages almost as high. Even in the fifty to sixty-nine year group there has been only a negligible decline, although it is very noticeable in subjects beyond seventy. Judgment also, as measured in this study, holds up fairly well to the advanced ages. The earliest to mature and to begin its decline is visual perception.

There is interesting evidence from other studies that all the sense organs show considerable loss of efficiency with age. Deafness to high pitches is a common symptom of middle age (Webster *et al.*, 1950). The vibratory sensitivity of muscles and joints has been shown to decrease (Pearson, 1928). Taste, smell, and pain all show the same trend. There is an actual decrease in the number of taste buds in the tongue as an individual's life goes on.

The loss in the efficiency of perception is even greater, however, than the physiological changes in the sense organs themselves. One study by Price (1931) shows that even with properly-fitted glasses, older subjects are considerably inferior to younger ones. In this evaluation, various kinds of materials—letters, figures, colors, and groups of lines—were presented for a very short interval of time in a tachistoscope, a piece of apparatus designed especially for this sort of exposure. Average scores for the different age groups are shown in Table 41.

TABLE 41.

Average Visual Perception Scores for 684 Male and Female Subjects

(Price's results, from Miles, 1942)

N	AGE	MEAN SCORE	SD
24	16-17	115	17.9
18	18-19	111.7	16.0
41	20-24	109.9	14.3
39	25-29	111.2	19.3
45	30-34	102.8	16.7
43	35-39	106.6	18.7
45	40-44	105.0	17.7
44	45-49	103.4	19.8
60	50-54	99.5	21.9
53	55-59	88.6	21.5
52	60-64	90.2	19.8
52	65-69	82.5	20.8
39	70-74	75.0	20.5
23	75-79	68.0	22.9
10	80-84	52.0	16.8
2	85-89	55.0	10.0

There are some minor fluctuations, but the general trend is steadily downward. A rough check indicates that with means, standard deviations, and numbers of cases of the magnitude of these, a difference of ten points is about the amount necessary to be statistically significant. This would indicate that there is no *significant* decline before the fifties. After that it is more marked. Weston (1948) also furnishes evidence for a slowing up of visual perception, even within the age range of nineteen to forty-seven years. An interesting feature of this study is that subjects retested after a five-year interval showed the same decrement as did different groups five years apart in age, thus indicating that this represents a real decline and not some bias in the samples tested. Another finding with some practical implications was that increasing the illumination improved the performance of the older subjects more than the younger.

In studies of other aspects of visual perception, Chapanis (1950) and Boice, Tinker, and Paterson (1948) found that color vision does *not* show the characteristic decline with age, although there is some conflicting evidence on this point. (See Shock, 1952.) Dark adaptation (Birren, Bick, and Fox, 1948) declines significantly.

In sheer physical strength, there is a falling off with age, but it is perhaps not as great as it is commonly assumed to be. Fisher and Birren (1947) compare the age curves they obtained for 552 male industrial workers with those reported by previous workers. They all correspond fairly closely. The peak comes in the decade of the twenties. Decline is gradual during the next forty years, until by the age of sixty the average is about 16.5 per cent less than the average for the twenty-year-olds.

In comparing learning efficiency for subjects of different ages, the most widely quoted study is that of E. L. Thorndike and associates (1928). (It is to be remembered that learning ability is *not* synonymous with intelligence. Our intelligence tests measure learning ability for *only* complex, abstract sorts of material, and recent work indicates that they do not predict very well the *rate* at which even this type of material will be learned. See Chapter 4.) Thorndike used a great variety of tasks and materials. His verdict, which has been much publicized, is that adults twenty-five to forty-five learn at nearly the same rate and in nearly the same manner as they would have learned the same thing at fifteen to twenty. The small numbers in the various separate studies and the doubtful representativeness of the samples make it impossible for us to judge how much of a decrement there really was in the older groups.

A better-controlled study is that carried out by F. L. Ruch (1934) as a part of the Stanford Later Maturity Study. He was most interested in the differences between *types* of tasks in respect to the ease with which they could be learned by young, middle-aged, and old individuals. Results support Thorndike's findings that the older subjects learn a little less readily than the younger, and that the deficit increases with age. It is more marked in tasks involving interference with old habits than in tasks in which old habits can be used. It was easier, for instance, for the older subjects to learn to follow with a stylus a moving object seen directly than one seen in a mirror. It was easier for them to learn pairs of words that had a meaningful relationship to each other than to learn nonsense materials or false multiplications.

In a more recent study by Hanes (1953), the efficiency of what he called "perceptual learning" was investigated. Subjects were 180 prison inmates divided into three age groups: twenty to thirty-four, thirty-five to forty-nine, and fifty to seventy. Three kinds of material were presented in a tachistoscope: correct arithmetical statements (e.g., $6 \times 3 = 18$), incorrect statments (e.g., $20 \div 5 = 7$), and nonsense statements (e.g., $14:3 = 12$). Following Ruch's conclusions, his hypothesis was that the false materials would show the greatest difference between age groups, the true materials the least difference, and the nonsense materials an intermediate amount. These hypotheses were not confirmed by the results. There was a consistent decline with age for all three types of material, and the nonsense material seemed most difficult for the older groups. The author's report suggests, however, that this particular procedure may have tested sheer speed of perception rather than learning, and if so, this general decline in everything is just what previous studies would have led us to expect.

There has been a good deal of interest in the question of memory decrement among older people. A study by J. G. Gilbert (1941) is concerned with the decline in memory ability as applied to various sorts of tasks. She compared 174 subjects, aged sixty to sixty-nine, with an equal group aged twenty to twenty-nine who had been paired with them for vocabulary on the Stanford-Binet test. (Vocabulary is being used in much current work as an indication of the intellectual *level* the individual has attained, regardless of whether he functions efficiently at that level or not.) How the subjects were selected is not specified. As in previous studies, the average differences in all the memory tests were significantly in favor of the younger group, but there were marked variations in the extent of these differences. Older people were very nearly as good as younger on simple repetitions of digits forward or backward. They were considerably inferior on learning paired unrelated words or Turkish-English vocabulary. It is interesting to note also that the *brightest* sixty-year-olds showed less decline than the average.

Since 1946 there has been in progress at Cambridge University a research program which promises to tell us more than has any previous work about what happens to special abilities and skills with advancing age. Welford (1951) has described the program as a whole and given examples of the experiments and the results so far obtained. What these workers have been trying to do is to *analyze* complex skills into their component parts, and to determine not only how successful people in different age groups are with the tasks set for them, but just *how* they do them. Studies have been made of both "manipulatory" skills such as throwing at a target and "mental" skills like solving an electrical problem. The investigators time separately the different parts of the sequence of things that must be done, and study the separate time curves they obtain from persons of different ages. This project has shown rather conclusively that the *methods* by means of which older individuals accomplish a skilled act change even more than the scores for the whole performance do. The older individual distributes his time differently from the younger. In general, the results show that the time needed to grasp the meaning of the stimulus and decide what to do increases more than the time the movements themselves require. In a study by Szafran (1951), in which the subject was asked to point at the target whose position corresponded to that of a light presented to him in a stimulus panel, older men were slower to initiate movement, and kept the pointer on the bullseye longer. The time required for the actual movement of the pointer was the same in all age groups. Under another experimental condition in which red goggles made it impossible for a subject to *see* anything in the room except the filament of the stimulus light, it was the time spent in searching for the target that increased significantly in older subjects.

A similarly planned study of a serial learning performance by Kay (1951) shows that the difference between twenty-year-olds and thirty-year-olds is chiefly a matter of speed, and the difference between thirties and forties more a matter of accuracy. Groups older than fifty show marked decline in both. One particularly interesting outcome of this study, based on an analysis of errors, is the evidence that older groups show exaggerated tendencies toward the very types of mistake that are most troublesome for people in general. Thus they demonstrate in exaggerated form what this particular learning process involves. It is not that they cannot grasp the general pattern of the sequence of numbers or of positions they are supposed to learn. It is *modifying* a pattern that is not quite correct that they find most difficult. The same error is repeated again and again.

It is too early to summarize in any general terms what all of this coordinated research is teaching us about motor and mental skills at different ages. One idea—that by shifting to some different procedure it is possible to maintain a complex skill even when strength and speed of perception decline—is the most useful conclusion so far. It is likely that workers in many jobs have always done this quite unconsciously. This fact may help to account for the well-known findings with regard to automobile accidents (De Silva, 1938), that while younger drivers are unquestionably quicker and more competent at the separate skills required—steering, coordination, brake reaction, and the like—middle-aged drivers have far fewer accidents. In the process of compensating for loss of speed in some of these reactions, the older men and women may actually achieve a more efficient pattern of driving skills as a whole. Motivational factors may also enter into the accident-rate difference, of course.

In summary, the conclusions that can be drawn with regard to age differences in special abilities are:

1. A gradual decline in all types of measurable ability sets in after thirty but does not become marked until well after fifty.
2. Sensory and perceptual abilities decline most and earliest.
3. Motor abilities hold up well until late middle age, but there is a change in the methods by which tasks are done.
4. Decline in learning ability varies with the type of material to be learned.
5. There are wide individual differences, so that in any age group some persons are superior to the average for groups much younger.

AGE DIFFERENCES IN PERSONALITY

By far the most thorough investigation of all aspects of the interests of adults we owe to Strong (1943). Data which he has accumulated on men ranging in age from fifteen to fifty-nine have made possible a thorough analysis of changes in likes and dislikes over this age range. The main conclusion that can be drawn from Strong's tables is that interests change very little throughout the entire adult life span. There is a surprising stability in the pattern of likes and dislikes that the individual shows even during adolescence. What changes there are more likely to come between the ages of fifteen and twenty-five than from twenty-five to fifty-five. There are only a few types of items that show any consistent trend when the figures for twenty-five-year-olds are compared with those for fifty-five-year-olds. Liking for activities and occupations involving writing shows a slight decrease. Liking also decreases for items suggesting change or interference with established habits and customs. In this connection, however, it is interesting to note that fifteen-year-old boys also show less liking for change than do the twenty-five-year-old men, who seem to be the least conservative group. In the words of Strong's summing up:

The primary conclusion regarding interests of men between twenty-five and fifty-five years of age is that they change very little. When these slight differences over thirty years are contrasted with the differences to be found among occupational groups, or between men and women, or between unskilled and professional men, it must be realized that age and the experience that goes with age change an adult man's interests very little. At twenty-five years of age he is largely what he is going to be and even at twenty years of age he has acquired pretty much the interests he will have throughout life.

With regard to age trends in other personality traits, less can be said with certainty. In the Stanford Later Maturity Study there were very few significant differences between age groups in scores on the Bernreuter Personality Inventory. There was some tendency for dominance scores to be lower in older men, but there was a great deal of individual variability. Older people reported more handicaps and more feelings of inferiority. Psychiatrists have noted that older people show more feelings of anxiety and guilt, more intolerance and conservatism, and increasing tendencies toward regression, or the repetition of childish adjustment techniques. Since a psychiatrist's patients are by no means representative of the population as a whole, too much weight cannot be placed on this sort of evidence. It is true, however, that older persons are more likely than younger to have *need* for a psychiatrist's services. Statistics on rate of admission to mental hospitals for the different age groups in the population show a steady increase up to sixty-five, and a sharp rise from there on. Older people are evidently more susceptible to extreme maladjustments, but an analysis of the figures by types of mental disease indicates that it is the *organic* rather than the functional conditions which show the steady increase. Malzberg (1935) has brought together a considerable amount of statistical information showing age trends for the principal types of psychosis. Figure 45 shows which types predominate at different ages.

Among young persons, admissions to hospitals are mainly for the schizophrenic and manic-depressive psychoses. Among the middle-aged, alcoholism and paresis take their toll. For those beyond middle age, cerebral arteriosclerosis and the brain deterioration that produces senile psychosis are the primary causes of commitment. There seems to be no psychiatric evidence that the personalities of *healthy* older persons are less stable or less capable of making good adjustments than those of younger persons. As individuals age, however, they become more vulnerable to physical conditions of various sorts which bring mental deterioration along with them.

There have been a considerable number of studies using personality inventories with adults of different ages (Kuhlen, 1945), but there is very little consistency in what they report about age trends. Adjustment seems to be poorer in old age than it is in middle life, but there are large dif-

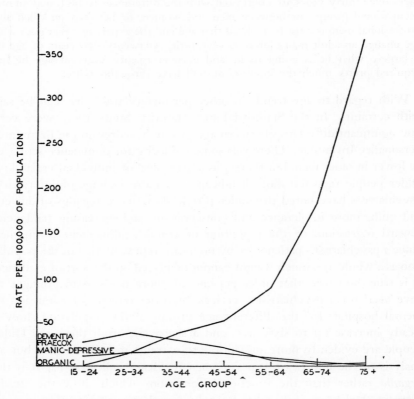

FIGURE 45. Age differences in first admissions for various psychoses (Malzberg, 1935).

ferences among individuals in this regard. One direction in which research is moving is the analysis of these adjustment differences to find out what they are related to (Cavan *et al.*, 1949). A few studies have supported the commonly accepted notion that conservatism increases with advancing years, but the research as a whole does not demonstrate this (Shock, 1952). The data on motivation and job satisfaction are too inadequate to warrant any conclusions. In general, age differences in personality as measured by questionnaires have turned out to be far less significant than sex or occupational differences seem to be.

There have been a few Rorschach studies of old people (Davidson and Kruglov, 1952; Chesrow, Wosika, and Reinitz, 1949; Prados and Fried, 1947; Klopfer, 1946). Considering the fact that none of the samples used in these studies was large or representative, the results agree remarkably well as to the kinds of responses older adults do and do not give. The most noticeable feature is what Rorschach workers call *constriction*, a dearth of all the types of answer that make a record rich and interesting. The total number of things seen in the blots is low. Both movement and color responses are scarce, and the variety of content is limited. When we try to interpret what these trends mean with regard to personality, however, we find ourselves blocked by our lack of knowledge as to the validity of separate Rorschach scoring variables. We cannot be at all certain that these findings mean low drive, narrowed interests, decreased emotional responsiveness, feelings of insecurity, rigidity, or low intelligence, as would be assumed if they were encountered in young adults or psychiatric patients.

There is incidental evidence for the insecurity and lack of confidence in oneself from qualitative observations reported by research workers investigating other things. Sward (1945) and Welford (1951), for example, mention the reluctance of older men to be tested. Davidson and Kruglov (1952) describe the self-deprecatory, cautious attitudes with which the subjects approached the Rorschach. It would seem that there is a considerable amount of insecurity in older people, but there is room for some difference of opinion as to what it means.

Most psychologists would probably say that personality and adjustment difficulties are not *inevitable* accompaniments of the biological process of aging. They are rather the product of the situations in which aging people find themselves, and their reactions to those situations. There is consequently a growing interest in old-age counseling. A pioneer in this endeavor was Dr. Lillian Martin who, upon retirement from Stanford University at the age of sixty-five, started a clinic for old people in San Francisco. In such centers, evidence has been accumulating that when adjustment has been disturbed by unfavorable circumstances, it is still possible to recreate constructive attitudes. You *can* teach an old dog new tricks.

AGE DIFFERENCES IN ACHIEVEMENT

There is another entirely different approach that has been made to the problem of age differences. It involves the analysis of biographical information showing the ages at which man's best work has been accomplished.

Lehman (1953) has been making a thorough survey of this problem in many areas of human achievement. His method is to take a standard reference book which selects the outstanding contributions in a field, then to list these works and if necessary have them rated for importance by

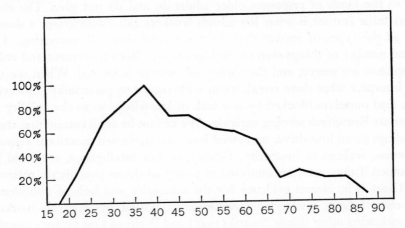

FIGURE 46. Ages at which great paintings were produced. The highest figure has been assigned a value of 100 per cent and the others rendered comparable (Lehman, 1942).

present-day authorities in the subject, and after that ascertain the age of the man who made each contribution. Results are reported in graphs like Figure 46 showing the relative numbers of great works contributed by men of each age range. (Figures are corrected to allow for the decreasing number of people still living in each successive age group.)

This type of presentation has the advantage of showing at a glance both the *peak* years, when the largest volume of work is done, and the *spread* or the range of ages at which eminent achievement has occurred. Figure 46 shows us, for instance, that relatively more masterpieces of painting are produced by men in their thirties than by any other age group. There is no age, however, from fifteen on, that has not produced some masterpieces. Most of the curves tend to resemble Figure 46 in shape, showing marked skewness. Thus the mean would not be a satisfactory indicator of central tendency.

For a great many other fields, Lehman's figures show similar age distributions. The peaks come during young adulthood. For several fields they are as follows:

Games and Sports (baseball players, pugilists, auto racers)......... 25-29
Science (chemistry, physics, inventions) 30-34

There is little difference from one period to another or from one country to another (Lehman, 1954).

A similar study by Adams (1945-46) seems at first glance to contradict Lehman's findings. Adams listed the date of the most important contribution made by each of more than 4,000 scientists born since 1600. By subtracting the date of the man's birth from the date at which his principal contribution was made, he obtained the age at which the work was done. The median of this age distribution turned out to be forty-three, about ten years higher than the peak for scientists reported by Lehman. The discrepancy is only apparent, however, and arises from the difference in the way these figures are handled. The skewness of the distributions both Lehman and Adams are working with makes for medians much higher than the peaks.

It is not clear what the full implications of these well-documented facts are to the student of differential psychology. We have a complex of psychological and sociological factors impossible to unravel at present. Do the trends represent a decline in mental ability making high achievement increasingly difficult after "life begins at forty"? Do they mean that there are important changes in motivation as life proceeds? Do they mean that our society is organized in such a way that the middle-aged individual is too much involved in various other duties to give his time and attention to creative work? Adams shows that different causes operate in different cases—prolonged ill health, administrative duties, change of occupation. It is important for us to remember that great work has been produced by persons of all ages. Goethe was over eighty when he wrote Faust, Part II. Adams quotes a sentence from a letter written by F. D. Drewitt years ago which sums up about all we know here:

Humans vary, as apples do, some ripen in July, others in October.

AGE DIFFERENCES: INTERPRETATIONS AND CONCLUSIONS

It was noted at the beginning of this chapter that certain special difficulties in carrying on research in age differences should put us on guard against too rigid an interpretation of the reported findings. Because of the limitations on methods of getting data, there are at least five possible explanations of the differences that have been found in cross-sectional studies: (1) the biological process of aging, carrying with it various effects on performance; (2) the deterioration of functions through disuse, making for poorer test performances on the part of persons who have not had recent practice in similar activities; (3) motivational differences between age groups; (4) sampling errors, since different people are tested at the different ages; and (5) social change, which means that the older subjects have had quite a different background of experience from those who are younger. Kuhlen (1940) has emphasized particulary the last of these factors. He shows in two tables age differences reported in various psychological studies and census data indicating social changes. Tables 42 and 43 show these figures.

TABLE 42.

Selected Data Indicating Differences Between Age Groups
(Kuhlen, 1940)

	AGE					
	20-29	30-39	40-49	50-59	60-69	70-79
Intelligence-Test Score	39	35	34	30	26	23
Report Liking for Bridge	63%	54	40	31	..	..
Report Never Attend Movies	18%	33	50	61	72	80
Height (employed men in centimeters)	171	169	168	167	166	..

It can readily be seen that there is at least a possibility that data in Table 43 explain trends shown in Table 42. Just as the same improvements in nutrition and public health that have increased the life expectancy from forty-eight to fifty-seven years might be expected also to increase the average size of the population, so the reduction in illiteracy and the increase in public education might be expected to raise somewhat the average tested verbal intelligence. In other words, it may be that the sixty-year-olds get the intelligence test score of 26 shown in Table 42, 13 points lower than the twenty-year-olds, not primarily because they have fallen off in intellectual ability, but because they were growing up in the 1880's when few people went beyond grade school, magazines and books were scarce, and the opportunities for intellectual growth were in general more limited than they are now. The fact that the same sorts of age-decline curves have been noted for groups who have had various amounts of formal education would indicate that this cannot be a complete explanation, but it

TABLE 43.

Selected Data Indicating Social Change

(Kuhlen, 1940)

	YEAR				
	1890	1900	1910	1920	1930
Per Cent in Secondary School	7	12	16	33	51
Illiteracy	13	11	8	6	4
Magazine Circulation (per 100 population)	..	9	20	21	27
Per Cent in Towns Over 8000 Population	29	33	39	44	49
Life Expectancy (males in years) ..	..	48	50	54	57

is a factor that we should not lose sight of. Similarly, the fact that older men and women are likely to have grown up in rural communities rather than cities would have something to do with their lack of interest in movies and bridge, and perhaps a number of other items on interest tests. The increasing use of longitudinal studies should clear up some of these ambiguities.

The importance of educational influences on trends with regard to mental abilities has been stressed by P. E. Vernon (1948). He analyzed the scores of naval recruits between the ages of fourteen and twenty, obviously below the age when biological deterioration of any sort sets in. Measures of "g" showed some increases from fourteen to seventeen, but the increase was more marked in students than in those who had left school for work. Men in lower-level occupations showed decreasing averages from seventeen to twenty, whereas the scores of men in more intellectual types of work increased. Achievement scores in such areas as spelling and arithmetic fell off rapidly in those who left school at fourteen, but mechanical and spatial scores showed an increase even in persons who did not get any technical education. Such findings should make us cautious about broad general statements with regard to age trends.

In applying the knowledge we have about age differences, we should never lose sight of the factor of *overlapping* from one age group to the next. Reaction time, for instance, is one function which declines with age, yet Miles showed that 25 per cent of the seventy-year-olds were as quick as the average for the whole group. If a job requires fast reaction time, many men of seventy can qualify for it more satisfactorily than many men of twenty. The curves that have been shown are *group* curves.

They show you nothing about any specific individual. The same principle that was emphasized for sex and race differences applies here also. Differences between the individuals in a group far outweigh the differences between *averages* of groups.

Statistics show that, for better or worse, the average age of our population is increasing. To clear the way for youth so that as much as possible can be accomplished during the years before forty, to establish social conditions that will keep mental vigor at its maximum throughout the life span and encourage continued achievement, to select persons for jobs on an individual rather than an age basis, to furnish clinical services that will maintain good adjustment in the middle-aged and old—these are some of the tasks which challenge us. More research is urgently needed. Meanwhile let us make good use of that which we have.

SUMMARY

Census data for the past century show increasing proportions of middle-aged and old people. The proportions of children and adolescents in the population have been steadily declining, although absolute numbers at this level have increased. The proportions of individuals twenty and older have been steadily increasing.

The use of intelligence tests with adult groups has shown that age brings a decline in the total score obtained on such tests, but that the magnitude of the decrement depends to a large extent on the type of task involved. Scores on vocabulary tests and tests involving elementary-school subject matter stay up throughout middle age. Scores on performance tests and tests requiring rapid adaptation to new situations decline markedly. Speed tests decline more than power tests. Longitudinal studies, however, have shown increases rather than decreases up to the forties.

In the field of special abilities and aptitudes, the greatest decline is for perceptual tasks of all kinds. Motor skills are maintained fairly well throughout middle age. Learning and memorizing are somewhat less efficient with advancing age, especially the learning of skills that involve the breaking of old habits. Personality differences between various age groups are slight, and the possibility of excellent adjustment for older persons has been demonstrated.

For most types of outstanding achievement, the peak years come before forty, although persons of all ages have produced masterpieces and important ideas.

There are several possible explanations of the differences that have been found between age groups. Just how much of each difference is to be attributed to the biological process of aging itself, and how much to other less inevitable factors is a task for future research to clarify.

CHAPTER 14

The Mentally Deficient

DEFINITIONS AND CLASSIFICATIONS

FOR MANY people, it is an encounter with a feeble-minded individual that first makes tangible and vivid the fact of intelligence differences. Down through the centuries, men have been puzzled about these human creatures who in some ways appeared so different from themselves, yet in other ways were so like them. Societies have been compelled to make some provision for them—in their institutions and in their philosophies. We can easily find, in attitudes of our own time, traces of the attitudes and theories that have prevailed in former times.

Through most of recorded time, some *supernatural view* of all mental abnormality has prevailed. Persons who were mentally ill were thought to be possessed by demons driving them from within. Idiots have in some places received special veneration as purehearted children of God, unsullied by the evil of the world. In other times and places they have been thought to be the victims of witchcraft.

Although it had been advocated as early as the fifth century B. C. by the Greek physician Hippocrates, the *medical view* of abnormality did not become common until the nineteenth century. Mental deficiency began to be considered as a disease, to be treated by physicians in the same spirit in which they would treat inadequate development of a leg or an arm or a lung. Much work on treatment was done in the early nineteenth century by Itard, in France. He was interested in determining how much could be done for the so-called wild boy of Aveyron. This child, discovered at the age of eleven or twelve in a French forest, had apparently grown up like an animal with no human influences. Itard spent five years attempting to train the boy in human ways of thinking and acting, giving up the task finally because there seemed to be no prospect of bringing him up to normal. The general conclusion has been that the "wild boy" was probably a feeble-minded child to begin with, and the comparative failure of these treatment methods served to make physicians less optimistic about *curing* mental deficiency.

But the method that Itard used, later developed and systematized by Seguin, who in 1837 founded the first school devoted primarily to the education of the feeble-minded, has constituted a major contribution to education. He called it the physiological method. It was aimed at the development of the mental faculties and functions directly rather than at the imparting of knowledge or information. Under this system each sense was trained separately. The pupil was taught to make finer and finer discriminations in vision, hearing, touch, and even taste and smell. He was given special training in movements and coördinated actions such as cutting, folding, and using tools. He was trained in attending, memorizing, and imagining. With advancing knowledge of the way the mind works, we no longer think of intelligence as a composite of faculties that can be separately trained. We know that it is not possible to make the feeble-minded individual normal by such methods as these. Nevertheless they are of great value in enabling an individual who is limited in the more complex intellectual abilities to make the best use of those assets that he has. Incidentally, the form board that Seguin devised for training his pupils to recognize and use geometrical shapes has become one of our standard performance tests of intelligence for the lower mental-age levels.

With the development of intelligence tests, what might be called a *psychometric* view of mental deficiency became common. It was apparent from the study of test-score distributions like those in Chapter 2 that while persons who had been classified as feeble-minded on other grounds almost invariably scored low, no definite and absolute dividing line could be set between the normal and the subnormal. To many psychologists the most reasonable procedure seemed to be to set some arbitrary boundaries which they would not adhere to too strictly in classifying individuals. Because it seemed to fit in best with observations of the adjustment that persons managed to make in society, an IQ of 70 was usually set as the bottom of the normal range. This standard was originally based on the 1916 Stanford-Binet test, but it seemed to work fairly well with the later individual tests of similar type. (Undoubtedly the figure has often been applied wrongly to IQ's derived from test distributions showing quite different standard deviations from the Binet.)

It has been customary to distinguish three *grades* or *levels* of mental deficiency, and these also have been recast in psychometric terms. Persons in the lowest group are called *idiots*. Even when their mental development is complete, they are never able to care for their personal needs, guard against common physical dangers, develop speech, or master simple occupational tasks. Persons in the next higher group are called *imbeciles*. They are capable of caring for their personal needs, guarding themselves from danger, and mastering simple routine tasks. They learn to speak but show a marked poverty of ideas, and seldom learn anything from the ordinary school curriculum or acquire any but the simplest occupational skills. People at the highest level among the mentally deficient are called *morons*. They are capable of supporting themselves, at least under favorable circumstances, though they often lack judgment about handling their finances and meeting their responsibilities. They learn to read and write, but the only meanings they can grasp are the more literal and concrete ones. Abstract concepts such as truth, integrity, or suspicion mean little or nothing to them.

In IQ terms, the classification that has been most commonly used is that which Terman set up in 1916:

Dullness, rarely classifiable as feeble-mindedness	80-90
Borderline deficiency, sometimes classifiable as dullness, often as feeble-mindedness	70-80
Moron	50-70
Imbecile	20-50
Idiot	Below 20

For several reasons no reputable psychologist holds that these figures should constitute the sole basis for decisions about an individual with regard to institutionalization, placement in a special class, or the like. The classification was based in the first place on an intelligence test that is no longer used, and we know that individual scores vary somewhat from one test to another. The unreliability inherent in mental measurement means that each IQ is to some extent inaccurate. The boy who scores at 49 might well have a "true" IQ of 51, which would place him in the moron rather than the imbecile category. But more important than these statistical reasons for refusing to base judgments on test results alone is the fact that feeble-mindedness is now considered to be as much a *sociological* as a psychological concept.

Most of the subsequent sociological definitions and classifications have grown out of the criterion of social adequacy set up in England in the Mental Deficiency Act of 1913 and its subsequent revisions. According to this view a person is feeble-minded if he lacks the mental ability to manage his own affairs with ordinary prudence. Doll (1946) has enlarged and refined this concept, defining the feeble-minded as those individuals "who are socially incompetent because of serious degrees of intellectual subnormality resulting from subnormal psychosomatic development." The concept involves four essential attributes: social incompetence, intellectual retardation, developmental arrest, and constitutional deficiency. If any one of these factors is missing, the condition is something other than feeble-mindedness. A satisfactory diagnosis must be based on a consideration of the individual's mental level, his developmental history, his social adjustment up to this time, his personal characteristics, his aptitudes and skills, and as much supplementary information as is available. Doll has emphasized the importance of this kind of thorough diagnosis in individual cases. The label "feeble-minded" should not be used unthinkingly.

To aid in measuring these social attainments with something like the precision with which the purely intellectual characteristics can be evaluated, Doll (1953a) has devised a type of scale similar to the Binet tests, but measuring *social* rather than mental age. The Vineland Social Maturity Scale is made up entirely of items having significance for adjustment in society. For example, at the III-IV year level, such things as "buttons coat or dress," "helps at little household tasks," and "washes hands unaided" are included. At the IX-X year level we find such things as "cares for self at table," "makes minor purchases," and "goes about home town freely." Although performances of this sort are correlated with intelligence as ordinarily measured, the relationship is far from perfect, and some children are further advanced in these social skills than they are in intellectual abilities of an abstract nature.

A variant of the sociological view of feeble-mindedness has been proposed by McCulloch (1947). It is one that has probably been tacitly accepted by many other workers in this area. McCulloch argues convincingly that mental deficiency is essentially an *administrative* concept related to our institutions more closely than to anything else. These special homes, schools, and colonies have been set up to take care of persons who show gross social incompetence with mental retardation. Individuals are committed to them for different reasons, and practice varies somewhat from time to time. McCulloch holds that our important task is to improve the kinds of treatment given in such institutions so as to enable them to increase the social competence of those they serve until it is above the tolerance level of the community. It is not so essential that we define precisely the sort of persons who are eligible for their services. In guiding his work by this concept, a doctor or social worker might judge a child mentally deficient simply because it appeared that a school for the mentally deficient in his community would be able to help him.

All of these viewpoints—the supernatural, the medical, the psychometric, the sociological, and the administrative—have some influence on our thinking and practice with regard to the mentally deficient. From the days of the demonological explanations there have survived to our own time some inarticulate fears and anxieties about the unknown—feelings that there is something mysterious or monstrous about such people. From the days of the predominantly medical explanations there have been carried over both uncomfortable feelings about psychological taints, and a body of knowledge about treatment for those conditions that do have definite physical causes. A mother asked a psychologist on one occasion if there was any danger involved in letting her little boy play with an imbecile child in the neighborhood. "Is there any chance," she asked, "that Joe might catch what Jerry has?" Obviously some misunderstanding of the medical concept was involved. The psychometric view has influenced the legislation that has authorized special institutions and educational programs in many states. Even where it is not the sole or principal basis for diagnosis, an intelligence test constitutes a valuable check on subjective judgments of a kind that are often very difficult to make. The sociological view is most influential at present, to judge by the writings and speeches of the leaders in this special field, but there is no clear consensus as to how the ideas are to be applied. Controversy often centers around the exact meaning of various terms that may be used synonymously, such as *feeble-minded*, *mentally defective*, *mentally deficient*, *intellectually retarded*.

Because of this plurality of approaches, research findings are more ambiguous than in many other areas where the groups to be compared are sharply defined. Much of the research has been done in institutions with subjects who are very diverse in all their characteristics except low intelligence. It would seem that there is even considerable diversity in intelligence itself, since individuals are often committed because of problem behavior of some sort and the mental defect may be only apparent. Tizard *et al.* (1950) found that more than half the cases in a group of high-grade institutionalized males with which they were working had IQ's above 70, regardless of which test they used. In this institution a considerable number of IQ's in the neighborhood of 100 were turned up. Thus a real question arises with regard to some of those persons now officially classified as feeble-minded. Is their intelligence level actually low? Other studies have been carried out in the community, usually as an outgrowth of special classes in the public schools. They have customarily used psychometric classifications primarily or exclusively as a basis for their choice of subjects. When such "low-IQ" individuals turn out to be much more satisfactory citizens than they were expected to be, a different question im-

mediately arises. Were they actually feeble-minded, in a social or behavioral sense?

Confronted with such ambiguities and differences in research approaches, the best we can do is to take up some of the specific questions
that have been asked, analyze the evidence that has been obtained, and
try to put together as much of it as seems to fit. Since community problems force us to take action with regard to the mentally deficient, it is
better that we base such action on some knowledge than on none at all.

WHAT HAPPENS TO MORONS?

From the practical standpoint, this is the most important of the research questions and fortunately it is the one to which evidence now
available permits us to give the most clear-cut answer. Of the different
subclasses of feeble-minded described in previous pages, morons constitute by far the greatest social problem because there are so many of them.
Even among persons who are institutionalized, the figures reported by
Whitney and Caron (1947) show that morons constitute something like
half of the total defective population. Since they are much less likely to be
institutionalized than are persons at the imbecile and idiot levels, they constitute a much larger fraction of the mentally deficient with whom schools
and community agencies deal. The fact that they usually do not differ in
appearance from persons whose intelligence is normal and that their deficiency is not accompanied by physical symptoms easily diagnosed by a
physician makes it harder for communities to give them the special help
or consideration they need. They must struggle to maintain themselves
in competition with others who have a considerable advantage over them
from the beginning.

Until fairly recently, most clinical psychologists and social workers
would have made rather pessimistic predictions for such individuals. The
account Wembridge (1931) gave, for instance, of the difficulties faced by
the inhabitants of Moronia is both amusing and eloquent, as the following
excerpts indicate:

It was my duty at one time to interview a young man, Flora's mental coun-
terpart, on trial for the murder of a policeman. The little fellow had been part
of a hold-up party, in which he was either the cat's paw for cleverer members
of the group, or had misunderstood directions, or was too drunk to know what
he was doing—or any one of several explanations, none of which could he
give himself. He was gentle and good-natured, simple and entirely vague as
to the whole affair, for which he was later electrocuted. Even the bailiff, in-

clined to be severe over the murder of an officer on duty, looked at the mild little murderer with some misgivings.

"It seems hard that policemen must be at the mercy of stupid little fellows like David, and hard that the first notice any one takes of David is to electrocute him," I remarked.

The bailiff peered at him in doubt. "Can I do anything for ya, Dave?" he inquired gently, but murmured in an aside, "He ain't got a chancet. He shot him all right and before witnesses, and that gets the chair."

Then he puffed away down the corridor shaking his head, while Dave smiled pleasantly and remarked, "I'm off the booze, all right. Excuse my necktie." The policeman's widow, and Dave's widow, the policeman's orphans and Dave's orphans, the arrest, the trial, the chair—all because Dave could not exercise the foresight and imagination which he did not possess, respect the law which he could not grasp, and think quickly in a new emergency when he could not think at all. His children will go through the same routine, and we all foresee it—all but Dave. He meditates upon his necktie, and then is seen no more.

Of course, the real victims of such tragedies are the children. Many are the remedies that have been suggested—none, perhaps, adequate. Certainly none has been adequately tried. Early discovery of morons is granted as desirable, but what then? Reduction of the number of their offspring is also regarded by most people as desirable. But by what means? Segregation? That means money from the taxpayers. Sterilization? That means fright, opposition, and general panic. No granting of marriage licenses? That means the elimination of something which the moron is only too ready to do without. Birth control? Illegal, or morons cannot understand it, or it is irreligious—or what you will. Education of the feeble-minded for unskilled labor? Does that solve the problem of the delinquent tendencies of children reared by a moron mother? And so it goes. In the mean time they multiply. Today they compose from five to ten per cent of the population of the United States—according to how dull they must be to be included.

As Flora, Lucille, and Chuck advance in age from twenty to forty, their escapades become less amusing, and even the most callous reporter does not consider them suitable for his pages. They are doing as well as they can, considering their training, their talents, their temptations, and the heavy burdens laid on their weak shoulders. But they and their pale babies are recognized as disasters. They are still subject to the same diseases and healed by the same means as we. Their children die from epidemics like flies, but they pass their germs on to our children before they go. Their children see ours in automobiles, and steal them from us. Our girls must dress in fashion, and so must theirs, even though our boys pay the bills. All of them flock gladly toward any frivolity or indecency which we commercialize. And ever the grim chorus chants monotonously in the background—"The villainy you teach us we will execute, and it shall go hard but we will better the instruction."

It is too dreadful and too stern a refrain for such frail little clowns as Chuck and Flora, and their children. And in the final tragedy, who are the villains and who the victims—They or We? (Wembridge, 1931, pp. 18-21)

But this sort of anecdotal material, interesting as it may be to read, does not answer the important questions. We need quantitative evidence as to the sort of adjustments such persons actually make.

The results of a number of follow-up studies now make it abundantly clear that in spite of the handicap of low intelligence, as measured by our customary tests, the great majority of morons who have been given special training in school make good after they get out. Results have been reported from several different areas and covering various periods of time as different from one another economically as were the depression, war, and postwar years. The study that has covered the longest period was one carried out in Nebraska. Baller (1936) in the first follow-up of "opportunity-room" students managed to locate 95 per cent of the group, all over twenty-one at the time of the study. He compared the figures for this "under-70" IQ group with those for a high-normal group, IQ 100 to 120. He found that only 7 per cent of these so-called feeble-minded had been placed in institutions. Educationally they had, of course, done far less well than the normal group, having completed an average of four to five grades as compared with the normals' twelve to thirteen. (Nevertheless it is interesting to note that *one* of the low-IQ girls did manage to get through high school at the age of twenty-two.) In marital status, the feeble-minded girls had the same score as the normal controls, 59 per cent married. For the boys there was a substantial difference, only 33 per cent of them having married as compared with 52 per cent of the normal group. The sub-normal were producing more children, a situation that could be attributed at least partially to the fact that the subnormal girls had married younger. Court records for the subnormal group were several times as frequent as for the normal (25 per cent versus 4 per cent in juvenile court, 18 per cent versus 6 per cent in police court) but the large majority had had no court record of any kind. The employment record of the sub-normals was not as satisfactory as that of the normals, but 83 per cent of them had been self-supporting at least part of the time. Whether or not individuals were making satisfactory adjustment seemed to depend upon factors other than IQ. For girls marriage was the differentiating factor, and personal appearance and domestic training were important insofar as they led to it.

This Nebraska research project takes on special interest because of a second follow-up reported by Charles (1953), made when the subjects had reached an average age of forty-two. Again the number located constituted a remarkably high proportion of the original group, over 73 per cent. Only nine individuals were in institutions, an even lower number than in 1935. The death rate had been somewhat high for this age group, 25 out of the 151 who could be traced having died, and deaths by violence or accident had been more common than in the population at large. A larger proportion of the group now had police records (60 per cent of the males), but the citations were largely for minor violations. Both the marriage rate, 80 per cent, and the average number of children, two, were now *lower* than the national average. As in 1935, 83 per cent were at least partially self-supporting, and their records showed that as the general economic situation had improved there had been decreasing need for relief. The jobs at which they were working covered a wide range of skill and salary levels. They were by no means all in the lower brackets. Their homes also varied quite widely. Detailed case studies showed a variety of kinds and degrees of adjustment. For the most part, their children were doing satisfactory work in school. The study confirmed the major conclusion of the first one—that special-class students on the whole become useful citizens.

Another large-scale study, results of which point in the same direction, is that of Kennedy (1948). This is a report of a survey carried out in 1944-47 on morons who had been identified in a census of defectives taken in 1937. The group of 256 morons was compared with a group of 129 non-morons which had been matched with them for characteristics other than intelligence—such as age, race, sex, nationality, and father's occupation. The average age of the subjects at the time of the follow-up was 24.5. There were some significant differences between the two groups with regard to work success, antisocial activity, and social participation and leisure interests. But there was a notable absence of significant differences in most respects. On marital adjustment and on economic indices such as income, staying on the same job, and agency relief, there was little or no difference. Seventy-five per cent of the morons were self-supporting, more than a fifth of them received top ratings by their employers, and about four-fifths of them had no court record.

Other studies of lesser scope corroborate the conclusions. Hegge (1944) found that during the war years of 1941-42, 88 per cent of the 211 parolees from Wayne County Training School were employed in fairly permanent jobs on which they made from $40 to $60 weekly. Muench (1944) located after an eighteen-year interval 18 individuals whom tests had rated mentally deficient in 1925. All of them were working, making from $38 to $55 per week, and showed no special problems. McIntosh (1949) discovered from a questionnaire sent to 1,000 graduates of a Canadian trade school for "non-academic" boys that almost 98 per cent were working, and that the wages they were making were comparable with those of industrial workers as a whole. Even those whose initial IQ's had been below 60 were self-supporting in 76 per cent of the cases. Mullen (1952) tells of a rather informal follow-up carried out by a committee of Chicago teachers of the handicapped indicating that not more than 15 per cent of the group is unemployed. He also cites reports from Detroit, Cleveland, and the U.S. Department of Labor which give similar figures for a number of other cities and various time periods. O'Connor (1953) reports similar findings in England. There is a remarkable uniformity in all these publications. Mentally deficient persons who have had the benefit of special class training make a good occupational and social adjustment, and the less intelligent within this limited range do as well as the more intelligent. It is characteristics other than IQ that distinguish between the successful and the unsuccessful. It should be noted that these are all follow-up studies of individuals in some sort of special class. They do not tell us anything about people who fail to receive such education. On the other hand, they do not, of course, prove that it is the training that produced the good results.

The most controversial of these reports was that of Schmidt (1946) who compared the subsequent development of 254 children trained in three experimental centers in Chicago with that of 322 trained in the ordinary rooms for the retarded. The mean initial age of the subjects was 12.5, and the average IQ's at the five centers ranged from 51 to 63. The progress of the groups was evaluated every eighteen months during the three-year period covered by the study, and a follow-up was made five years after it ended. The principal feature of the educational program at the experimental centers was its individualization. Each child was helped to improve his or her appearance, skills, and work and study habits, and was given guidance in locating work and making plans for the future. The report on the social and vocational adjustment of the group at the time of the follow-up is very favorable, as the reports we have considered from similar groups elsewhere have been. Eighty-five per cent of these children went on with some sort of voluntary education after the compulsory attendance at the special center was over; 92.5 per cent were employed full time for more than four out of five of the postschool years. The jobs they managed to hold covered a wide range of clerical, skilled, and semi-skilled occupations. There had been little need for assistance from social agencies.

It was not this part of the report around which the argument focused, however. The thing that psychologists found hard to believe was the assertion that the IQ's of the members of the experimental group had increased so markedly by the end of the time span covered in the study that most of them were intellectually within the normal range. During the three-year school period the mean Stanford-Binet IQ shifted from 52 to 72. By the end of the five-year follow-up the mean was 89, and about 86 per cent scored at the "dull" or "normal" rather than the "feeble-minded" level. Improvement of the same magnitude showed up on tests of school subject matter and on personality tests. The control group showed none of these desirable changes.

Questioning of Schmidt's conclusions has centered mainly around the accuracy of her figures. S. A. Kirk (1948) attempted a thorough critical evaluation of the report. His doubts as to its accuracy arose from two sources: (1) peculiarities in the report itself, such as failure to explain how persons who were reading at the first-grade level could have taken the Bernreuter Personality Inventory, and (2) discrepancies between Schmidt's initial IQ distribution and the figures obtained from Board of Education statistics and special-class records during the period of the study. Schmidt (1948) countered with the charge that Board of Education statistics in the city in question are known to be unreliable. She refused to make her original data available on the grounds that such an action would not be fair to subjects who have a right to assume that all the information regarding them is confidential.

There the matter rests so far as the Schmidt report itself is concerned. What other evidence do we have with regard to the important question it poses: "Can some sort of education help a moron to become normal?" Some of the most convincing data come from the Nebraska follow-up study by Charles (1953) which has been described above. Twenty-four of these subjects were given a Wechsler-Bellevue Test. The mean IQ's were: Verbal, 72; Performance, 88; Full, 81. Here also we have scores which fall in the dull-normal rather than the feeble-minded range. Charles concludes that the original scores were probably in error, but it would seem equally reasonable to assume that some genuine improvement had occurred, since the data on social adjustment in the community support such a view.

Kephart (1939) has also reported striking IQ changes following a special educational program. Sixteen boys, aged fifteen to eighteen, whose initial IQ's ranged from 48 to 80, were placed in an experimental group for a kind of training different from that which had been previously tried. They were given problems to work on and required to develop their own methods of solving them. After the training period, it was found that the average IQ on the Stanford-Binet test had risen from 66 to 76. All except one of the boys had gained. One factor here creates some doubt as to the meaning of the change. A part of the special training included the detection of absurdities and illogical parts in material presented to the subjects. Since a number of the Binet items are of this type, the increase might reflect merely an improvement in the quality of the answers to this one kind of question. In that case it might or might not indicate improvement in the ability to carry on reasoning of other sorts. An analysis of the data to show what items improved from one testing to the next would have been helpful.

Soon after the Schmidt study appeared, Hill (1948) reported his findings with regard to 107 special-class pupils in Des Moines who were retested after a time lapse of about three years and nine months. The educational program for such pupils is described as being quite similar to Schmidt's, but its effects on IQ here were negligible. There was practically no change at all in the mean, and downward shifts were as common as those in an upward direction.

There is one factor that may help to account for the conflict between these reports—the factor of age. The special classes reporting the largest IQ changes have been those set up for *adolescents,* and it is interesting to note that in the Hill report, all of the average changes for groups over ten years old at the time of the first testing *were* in a positive direction. It could be that in these children who develop slowly, *readiness* for academic training comes several years later than it does for the average child. If so, it would be advisable to postpone attempts to teach them to read, write, and figure until the preadolescent years. This is all very much in the realm of hypothesis rather than fact, however. There simply is not enough clear evidence to enable us to decide the matter.

One research program (Skeels and Dye, 1939; Skeels, 1942) would seem to point in just the opposite direction and emphasize very *early* environmental stimulation. These investigators placed thirteen young children ranging in age from seven to thirty months in a home for the feeble-minded. Initial IQ's ranged from 35 to 89 with a mean of 64.3. In the home, they were placed in the wards to be cared for by feeble-minded girls who lavished on them a great deal of attention. According to Skeels, this turned out to be an exceptionally stimulating psychological environment for the infants because they had an opportunity to handle many kinds of play materials and try out all sorts of activities. After a few months of this treatment (varying in length from individual to individual) all of the children showed IQ increases of from 7 to 58 points, with a mean increase of 27.5. The average IQ of the group after the "psychological prescription," as he calls it, was about 92. Eleven of the thirteen were then placed for adoption in fairly good homes. Two and a half years later, their average IQ was about 96, showing that gains had been maintained. The contrast group consisted of twelve children who were kept in an orphanage with no special treatment at all. Their average IQ went *down* from about 87 at the beginning to about 61 at the end of the experiment. The increase for the one group and the decrease for the other are both statistically significant. The one difficulty that stands in our way when we try to draw conclusions from the figures, however, is that all the children were so young at the time of the first test that it could not be considered a good predictor of later test results under normal circumstances (J. E. Anderson, 1940). Furthermore, there is the statistical phenomenon called *regression toward the mean*, which signifies in simple terms that in successive testings errors tend to correct themselves. There is some error in every test score. If it happens that a person scores lower than he should the first time through such chance factors, he is likely to score somewhat higher on the next occasion when chance factors are no longer working in his favor. Conversely, a score that is unduly high the first time is likely to be lower at the next testing. Since the contrast group averaged fairly high for orphanage children and the experimental group unusually low, they cannot be considered statistically comparable. Some increase in the low IQ's and decrease in the high ones can be accounted for on the basis of regression alone.

It seems unlikely, however, that by recourse to statistical artifacts one can explain away *all* of the improvement Skeels reports. Since this report came out, much has been said about the devastating effects of impersonal institutionalization upon children (Spitz, 1945-46) and the importance of "mothering" (Ribble, 1943). Although quantitative evidence on this question is scarce, it now seems a tenable hypothesis that more attention during the early years could make for somewhat more rapid intellectual development. Viewed in this manner there is no conflict between this hypothesis and the previous one. For children who mature slowly, whatever the reason, schooling may produce its best effects when they have reached the stage of complete readiness for it. A rich and stimulating environment in infancy may have some effect on the rate of development itself.

These are challenging ideas for all who are concerned about problems of the mentally handicapped. We need to know why some morons apparently become brighter while others remain dull. One study by Guertin (1950) may have some relevance. He picked out a group of 25 institutionalized patients who had shown marked IQ increases and a control group matched with it for age, sex, IQ on admission, and length of institutionalization. The research question was, "Is there any material in the case histories of these subjects who improve which differentiates them from those who do not improve?" Statistical tabulations showing the incidence of various favorable and unfavorable conditions in the case histories did not show any significant differences, but clinicians could *judge* the likelihood of IQ change from their reading of these case histories. Their judgments were correct in from two-thirds to three-fourths of the cases. It turned out that different judges were paying attention to different features of the individual's background and previous experience. The social worker who was emphasizing the adequacy of early family relationships made more "hits" than the psychologist who was looking for emotional handicaps and sensory disabilities.

These results are only suggestive. More research focused on the characteristics of individuals who do or do not gain under training programs would be of great value. The attempt by Kephart and Strauss (1940) to differentiate between endogenous and exogenous forms of mental disability is a program we shall consider in the next section. They have accumulated data showing that the *endogenous* cases, in whom no physical or neurological cause of the mental deficiency can be identified, show increases in IQ as a result of the training school program, whereas the *exogenous*, in whom there has been some sort of brain injury, show decreases. This kind of differentiation corresponds quite closely to the ideas of Doll (1953b), who has consistently maintained that there is a difference between the *true* feeble-minded in whom some actual neurological defect exists, and those who are simply intellectually retarded but not really feeble-minded. The real feeble-minded individual, according to this way of thinking, never becomes normal.

Whatever the facts may eventually turn out to be with regard to IQ changes, it is well to keep in mind for practical purposes that the optimism that has arisen in some quarters with regard to the curability of mental deficiency is not justified. In comparison with the whole range of IQ's in the population, the amount of upward shift in even the studies reporting the most striking results is only moderate. Retarded children may perhaps become less retarded; they do not become brilliant. Morons manage to support themselves in the community; they do not enter professional schools or become community leaders. Most parents of feeble-minded children must come to terms with the realization that there is nothing that can be done that will enable these boys and girls to catch up with normal children.

CHARACTERISTICS OF THE INSTITUTIONALIZED
FEEBLE-MINDED

Psychologists have done a considerable amount of research on patients in custodial institutions for the feeble-minded. Conditions under which they must work impose some limitations on such studies. Although the clinical types of idiot and imbecile that are readily identifiable by physical signs can usually be left out of the group on which the experiments are based, it is often not possible to differentiate between exogenous and endogenous cases. Thus many generalizations carry with them a certain amount of ambiguity. We do not know whether they apply to non-institutional as well as institutional cases, and it is possible that a single subgroup within the total group may be producing the trends the figures show. In spite of these limitations, some of the findings are real contributions to our knowledge about persons whose intelligence is limited.

The first of the generalizations often made is that the process of mental growth and decline in the feeble-minded follows a course somewhat different from that characteristic of normal subjects. The IQ ratings tend to *decrease* with age throughout the childhood and adolescent years instead of remaining approximately the same (Kuhlmann, 1921; Sloan and Harman, 1947). The lower the IQ, the *earlier* mental growth ceases. Kuhlman summarized these trends for 639 patients tested repeatedly over a period of ten years. The idiots showed no increase in mental age after fifteen. Imbeciles reached their ceiling at fifteen or sixteen, morons at seventeen, and borderline cases at eighteen. More recently, C. W. Thompson (1951) has furnished some figures that fill in the last part of the age curve. Her study of 137 subjects who originally had Binet IQ's of 50 to 69 when tested at sixteen or afterward showed a decline which set in considerably earlier than it does in normal subjects. Thompson used types of test material that have been most useful for showing differences between age groups in investigations like those reported in the preceding chapter. Morons in their thirties were significantly lower than morons in their twenties on all ten tests. On only four of them has any difference between normal twenty-year-olds and thirty-year-olds been reported. Curves for the moron leveled off after thirty in much the same way that curves for normal groups of adults have often been shown to level off after sixty. For these feeble-minded subjects, as for normals, there was no difference between successive age groups on the vocabulary test. Thompson ties in these findings with medical studies which indicate that the feeble-minded have a shorter life span and an accelerated aging process. The picture suggested is one of a weaker organism growing more slowly and not so long, and deteriorating more rapidly after the peak is reached. The qualifications mentioned at the beginning of this section apply here, however. Studies of non-institutionalized morons like that of Charles (1953) do not show this phenomenon of early peak and decline. Selective factors related to institutionalization rather than low intelligence by itself may be involved, or the institutional environment may have a depressing effect on intelligence.

Another research question leading to generalizations of considerable importance to practical workers has been, "How *general* is the handicap? Are the feeble-minded equally deficient in all directions?" A part of the answer to these questions is furnished by the well-documented stories of *idiots-savants*, persons who gave every indication of having some one talent developed to an extreme degree. The report of Scheerer *et al.* (1945) on L, the eleven-year-old boy with an IQ of 50, who was so phenomenally good at numbers, has been discussed in the chapter on intelligence. A number of equally striking examples of mechanical aptitude, musical or artistic talent, and ability to memorize have been described.

These are very exceptional cases, however. In general, persons whose IQ's are low tend to be below average on other test performances. Sloan (1951) compared 20 feeble-minded with 20 normal children on a test for six kinds of motor proficiency (ability to make skilled, coördinated movements). The feeble-minded were significantly inferior on all of them and showed the greatest handicap on the complex tests calling for the most integrative activity. At the adult level, Cantor and Stacey (1951) tested 175 mental defectives, IQ 42-82, with the Purdue Pegboard, and found that they averaged considerably below the norm for men in general. An IQ of 60 showed up here as a critical point in the distribution. Subjects lower than this were considerably inferior to those higher. In England, Tizard *et al.* (1950) gave some portions of the General Aptitude Test Battery to 104 males at the moron and borderline level. They scored below average on all four factors—spatial aptitude, form perception, dexterity, and motor speed. It is interesting to note that they were more deficient in motor speed than in anything else. Their mean was about two and a half standard deviation units below the reported norms for this, whereas for spatial aptitude it was only one standard deviation below. The fact that these three independent studies point up the motor deficiency of persons diagnosed as feeble-minded should be kept in mind, since it is not in line with what many people think. It is a common opinion that persons who cannot work with their heads will be good at working with their hands. Unfortunately this is not true.

A more hopeful aspect of these studies of special aptitudes in the feeble-minded is the *variability* of their distributions with regard to any of these measurements. The average may be low, but some individuals are very good. Cantor and Stacey show, for instance, that on the different subtests of the Purdue Pegboard, from 4 per cent to 28 per cent of the feeble-minded score above the general average. Tizard *et al.* found that a sizeable fraction of their group had high enough scores on one or more of the special tests so that they would have good prospects for employment. Perhaps we can paraphrase Orwell's "All animals are equal, but some are more equal than others," and say, "All special abilities tend to be low, but some are lower than others" in any individual feeble-minded person.

A type of study indirectly related to this work on special aptitudes has attempted to find out what *aspects* of intelligence are most and least deficient. The most thorough study here is the one by Magaret and Thompson (1950) who made an item analysis of the responses mental defectives succeeded and failed with in the Stanford-Binet test. They then compared these tabulations with those which had been obtained from average children and from superior children who were younger in years than the feeble-minded group, but had the same *mental* age. As had been suspected, the pattern of successes and failures was somewhat different for the low-ability group. They were better at some things, poorer at others. The items they did least well with, however, were those that McNemar (1942) had shown were the best measures of "g." In other words, the most serious deficiency of the mentally deficient individual is lack of general intelligence! On questions calling for more practical knowledge and less abstract reasoning, they did somewhat better.

Sloan and Raskin (1952) have reported an ingenious study which also shows that the answers adult mental defectives give to some kinds of questions show greater maturity, practicality, and realism than the answers of children of comparable mental ages. For example, the question, "If someone gave you an elephant, what would you do with it?" prompted a majority of the feeble-minded subjects to think of ways of getting rid of it, whereas the majority of normal children seemed not to realize the practical difficulties they would incur if they kept the animal. Pattern analyses using tests like the Wechsler-Bellevue have usually found that mentally deficient groups make a relatively better showing on the performance subtests than on the verbal subtests. All of these findings can be roughly summarized in the statement that the feeble-minded, though their over-all mental ages would classify them with children, may differ from children in having somewhat more ability to deal with practical situations and concrete materials than their mental age would lead us to expect.

Another way in which feeble-minded persons have been shown to differ from normal children of the same mental age is with regard to what Kounin (1943) has called *rigidity*. His ingenious experiments are based on Lewin's theory that an individual's personality becomes more definitely differentiated into separate "regions" as he gets older. The boundaries between these regions also become more rigid with age, so that it is more difficult for the older person to change his attitude at will. Because of his poor potentialities for development, the feeble-minded person never develops a very complex or highly differentiated mental structure. But rigidity increases with age as it does for the normal person, so that an increasingly stereotyped kind of behavior results. Thus a feeble-minded person is content to repeat a simple act over and over again, since he is not bothered by competing desires and tendencies. The concept of rigidity is still more than a little hazy. Different workers have been using the word with different meanings and tests designed to measure the trait often show little or no correlation with one another. But whether or not his theoretical explanation is correct, Kounin's results, as well as much general observation, seem to show that feeble-minded individuals often do seem to have a greater than average tolerance for monotonous, repetitive activity. Brand *et al.* (1953), using a different method of measuring rigidity, have obtained results similar to Kounin's showing an increase in rigidity with age. They think, however, that this may be a result of institutionalization rather than of age itself.

A third very important research question is, "How well do the feeble-minded *learn?*" This issue has been clouded by the common interpretation of measured intelligence as general learning ability. The assumption that learning ability is the characteristic that intelligence tests measure would naturally lead one to expect very little progress from low-scoring individuals. Actually, as we have shown in the chapter on intelligence, the two terms are far from synonymous, and most of the evidence shows IQ to be quite unrelated to the *rate* at which learning takes place and to the *amount* of material learned. Research investigation of learning in the feeble-minded has not had the attention its practical importance warrants. McPherson (1948) located eleven experimental studies, the earliest one reported in 1904. Taken all together, these studies show that although a *minimum* intellectual rating seems to be required for a given task in order that any learning at all may take place, above that minimum there is no consistent relationship between errors or rate of improvement and psychometric rating. (The two earliest studies are out of line with the rest on this point, but the rest of them agree well.) This lack of relationship is not affected by the number or length of the practice periods. It seems to characterize the whole learning process. Changes in motivation influence learning in the feeble-minded, as in normals, and the same sort of transfer from one performance to another occurs.

One of the most important effects of all the research on the mental characteristics of persons who have been classified "feeble-minded" has been to make us aware of the individual variation that exists within the group. This label "feeble-minded" is no more helpful than any other label if we wish to understand an individual. Chipman (1946) has called attention to the many kinds of individual differences there are within a homogeneous psychometric group, and has illustrated the point by diverse case studies of actual persons. This emphasis can give teachers and social workers a new slant on the work they are doing.

PERSONALITY DIFFERENCES IN THE FEEBLE-MINDED

The emphasis on viewing each mentally deficient person as an individual with his own unique combination of assets and liabilities rather than simply as a typical example of a diagnostic category has been accompanied by new interest in the personalities of low-ability people. It would be difficult to say which was cause and which effect, but the influence of the whole trend on our thinking is very apparent to anyone who examines the literature in the field since World War II.

Some of this emphasis seems to be related to the increasing use of projective tests, especially the Rorschach and the Thematic Apperception Test. The personality inventories that have played such an important role in investigations of normal, psychotic, and neurotic persons never figured very prominently in work with the feeble-minded, since low reading ability and a very limited stock of word meanings made it impossible for such persons to answer the questions on such blanks. Projective tests can of course be administered to low-ability subjects as easily as to those whose intelligence is normal. From the time of Rorschach's first publication to the present there have been a considerable number of reports on the feeble-minded. They have been well summarized by Sarason (1953).

One major aim, the primary one in Rorschach studies, has been to develop more adequate methods of *diagnosis*. Psychologists have long been dissatisfied with psychometric diagnosis based exclusively on the Binet and similar tests. They welcome the chance to utilize diagnostic signs from another quite different procedure in making difficult decisions as to whether a person is or is not feeble-minded. Certain characteristics of the Rorschach record do seem to be typical for low-ability subjects. Their total number of responses tends to be low. They give few finely-differentiated, well-organized whole responses. They are less accurate than average in their perception of the form of each blot and find it difficult to integrate form with color. Human-movement responses are scarce, and the range of content represented by their answers is narrow. It is thus possible to make a list of indicators of feeble-mindedness and use it in diagnostic work.

The problem that has arisen when this procedure has been followed is that a certain number of individuals who would clearly be considered feeble-minded on the basis of both intelligence tests and behavior do not show these Rorschach signs. There is considerable variability in the distributions for the feeble-minded, as there is for normals. What shall we conclude with regard to such a person whose Rorschach record gives no sign of mental abnormality? One answer, proposed by Jolles (1947), Sloan (1947), and others, is that what appears superficially to be feeble-mindedness may really be an emotional disturbance which prevents the individual from utilizing the ability he has. Such a condition is called *pseudo-feeble-mindedness*. According to this view, such persons should not be treated as genuinely deficient cases, but should be given some sort of psychotherapy in order to remove the handicaps to efficient functioning.

The weakness in this idea lies in the doubtful validity of Rorschach scores as personality measures. Because we are not sure just what kind of mental process the production of any given type of Rorschach response calls for, we are really in no position to judge what the occurrence or non-occurrence of any type means with regard to mental handicap. Evidence that feeble-minded persons with "normal" Rorschach records are any more normal in their behavior has so far not been presented. Until we have it, we must suspend judgment on the whole hypothesis. The line of work, however, has been valuable in that it has pointed out the possibility of pseudo-feeblemindedness and has developed interest in it as a field for research.

What the Rorschach studies do clearly show, and what is still more clearly indicated by work with the TAT and similar picture-story tests, is that there are large individual differences in personality within the feeble-minded group, and that problems and anxieties are common (Sarason, 1953). We are becoming increasingly aware that the indirect effects of a mental handicap and its accompanying circumstances may be as important as the deficit itself. There are especially likely to have been inadequate parent-child relationships in such cases. Anxiety, feelings of guilt and hostility toward others, discouragement, and depression are very likely to develop. It was a surprise to many psychologists to find in the mental defective evidence of a rich fantasy life and an internal struggle with many of the same problems that plague us all (Beier *et al.*, 1951).

O'Connor (1952) has shown that the same objective tests of neuroticism that have proved so useful in defining and measuring the trait in normals (Eysenck, 1952) can be utilized to measure instability in the feeble-minded, and that the employability of an individual is significantly related to the way he scores on this trait. This finding may well serve to explain some of the results of the follow-up studies considered in a preceding section. The persons of quite low intelligence who are unusually stable or non-neurotic are probably the ones most likely to make good on jobs in the community.

Both the possibility of pseudo-feeblemindedness and the realization that mentally defective persons have emotional problems have led in recent years to some emphasis on psychotherapy for persons in this group. Axline (1949) has reported that some retarded children gain as much as 20 IQ points as a result of play therapy. Other children do not show this increase in intelligence. Presumably the high gainers are pseudo-feebleminded rather than genuinely low. The case that Sarason (1953) makes for psychotherapy rests on the fact that it can help the person, whether or not the diagnosis of feeble-mindedness was correct in the first place, to overcome behavioral handicaps and change crippling emotional attitudes. Research which shows how much good such treatment does will be very valuable.

PROGRESS IN DIAGNOSIS

Another trend that down through the years has characterized research on the characteristics of the feeble-minded as a group has been an increasing *differentiation* of diagnostic categories. The first distinction that became apparent, although it was not generally made until the nineteenth century, was that between *subnormality* and *abnormality*. Even yet in the eyes of the common-sense observer there is little distinction between the person who has "lost his mind" and the person who has never had one. Professionally and scientifically, however, we now differentiate very sharply between psychotic conditions on the one hand and mental deficiency on the other. We realize that many psychotic patients are highly intelligent, even when their bizarre associations branch off in strange directions. The fact that a person can be *both* subnormal *and* maladjusted to the point of neurosis or psychosis, as discussed in the previous section, does not mean that the two conditions are the same.

The next kind of differentiation to become common separated various clinical types of feeble-mindedness. We shall not go into detail about them here, since their diagnosis and treatment is primarily a medical problem, though it does have its psychological aspects. The *Mongolians*, so-called because of slanting eyes giving them a superficial resemblance to the Mongolian race, the *intracranial birth lesion* cases, where motor symptoms such as paralyses, tremors, and incoördination accompany the mental deficiency, the *microcephalics* with their small heads of a characteristic "sugar-loaf" shape, the *hydrocephalics* whose heads are unusually large because of the pressure of cerebrospinal fluid within the brain, and the *cretins*, who represent extreme cases of thyroid deficiency, are the most common of these special varieties, but there are many other rarer conditions which are met in medical practice.

Whenever research is able to identify a specific cause for a specific type of feeble-mindedness, it opens up possibilities for treatment or prevention of that particular condition. The evidence presented by Yannet and Lieberman (1944) that incompatibility between mother and fetus with regard to the Rh factor in the blood may be the cause of mental defect in from 3 to 4 per cent of institutional cases is an example of work of this sort. Knowing what we now know about this hazard, it should be possible to prevent such cases of mental defect completely.

The great majority of persons now classified as feeble-minded, however, do not show any clear differentiating characteristics. They are what Sarason has called "garden-variety" mental defectives. If their families show a high incidence of deficiency they are usually classified as "familial." If there is no such family history they are simply labeled "undifferentiated." The diagnostic question of most urgency at present is whether this large group can be split up into subtypes which call for different kinds of treatment. One distinction several authorities think can be made differentiates between persons who simply represent the low end of the intelligence distribution and persons whose brains have been injured or damaged in some way, although the injury may not show itself in the motor symptoms that are easy to recognize. Considerable work has been done on this problem at Wayne County Training School by Strauss, Werner, and others. (See Sarason, 1953, Ch. 2, for a good summary.) Results of various tests suggest that *exogenous* (externally caused) cases of mental deficiency differ from *endogenous* (internally or naturally caused) cases in perception, thinking and behavior. The exogenous individual is likely to be more incoherent and confused when he tries to copy a geometrical pattern, less successful at sorting objects into categories, and more erratic and uninhibited in behavior than an endogenous defective of the same mental age. There is a good deal of overlapping in the distributions, however, and there are no dependable neurological signs that enable one to be certain that all cases showing exogenous types of behavior have actually incurred some injury to the nervous system. The idea is an interesting one and has served as a clear-cut hypothesis around which research could be organized.

Doll (1953b) has proposed a somewhat similar distinction. He would differentiate between the mentally *deficient*, who simply lack some of the potentiality for development that characterizes normal children, and the mentally *defective*, who have sustained some sort of injury to the central nervous system. If this injury is diffuse enough to produce disorders in multiple areas, but no striking symptoms in any one, he proposes that we call it *neurophrenia* and set up research procedures to find out more about it.

For practical purposes, in institutions and special classes, it is as yet impossible to make such distinctions. In this chapter we have used the terms *retarded, deficient, defective*, and *feeble-minded* interchangeably, and that is the way they have been used in most of the literature. The time may come when we no longer group together all cases that have in common only one characteristic, namely, what appears to be low intelligence. Perhaps with the development of differentiated diagnosis and individualized education we shall be able to dispense with the label "feeble-minded."

SUMMARY

Feeble-mindedness has been approached from supernatural, medical, psychological, sociological, and administrative points of view.

There is general agreement that diagnosis should rest primarily on a social criterion, the individual's capacity for handling his own affairs "with ordinary prudence." However, mental tests have proved to be very useful in contributing to the diagnosis. Three levels of deficiency are usually differentiated: the idiot, with IQ below 20; the imbecile, with IQ between 20 and 50; and the moron, with IQ between 50 and 70.

A number of follow-up studies have provided evidence that the majority of morons who are given special schooling make satisfactory adjustments in their communities, supporting themselves and keeping out of trouble.

There is some evidence that measured IQ for such persons increases over the years, but this conclusion is still doubtful because of inadequacies in the research designs.

In general, mentally deficient individuals are comparable in intellectual achievement to children of equal *mental* age. The two groups differ, however, in some respects, and both special abilities and personality characteristics may vary a great deal among persons of the same IQ level. It has been clearly demonstrated that the feeble-minded can learn, and the feasibility of psychotherapy for them has been suggested.

Attempts are being made to increase the precision with which diagnoses can be made. There is some evidence that natural dullness or lack of ability can be differentiated from defectiveness arising from injury to the central nervous system.

CHAPTER 15

The Unusually Gifted

THE PROBLEM OF GENIUS

CIVILIZATION RESTS on the shoulders of its great men. In every age there are a few individuals whose achievements are so exceptional that the ordinary common-sense principles we use in understanding human nature do not seem to apply to them. How shall we judge a Richard Wagner, for example? Does the fact that he produced music of unparalleled splendor excuse his irresponsibility, his conceit, his disloyalty to his friends? Is it necessary for the really great man to be ruthless in his demands on those around him and to snatch from his society what his insatiable spirit craves? How shall we know who the really great men of our own time are? Can we identify them in childhood, by outstanding achievements at an early age? How shall we stimulate their efforts? Is it better to make them happy and secure in the essentials of life, or will they under such conditions become smug and self-satisfied, and cease to achieve anything of importance? Will genius overcome all environmental handicaps, or do certain conditions stifle it completely? The whole field bristles with questions. Much has been written and said, and it will be the task of this chapter to sift out the dependable facts from the chaff of opinion and speculation.

The definition of genius is not easy. Probably it is made most satisfactorily on the basis of *eminence*. The person who far excels the average performance in some field is called a genius. The field, however, makes a difference too. We do not honor our athletes, our hairdressers, and our tightrope-walkers by this designation. It is the artists of all kinds, the scientists, and the statesmen that we include in our halls of fame. There is some justification for this distinction on the basis of *permanence* of the contribution an individual makes to our culture. The great book influences the thinking of millions of persons for centuries; the pattern a great statesman sets for the government of his country influences the course of history for many years. A good working definition would be, then, that the genius is the highly-gifted individual who produces contributions to civilization whose effects persist far beyond his own time. Lange-Eichbaum expresses the idea when he says that the genius is the bringer of values.

There is a widespread general opinion that there is something queer or abnormal about genius. Partly this belief grows out of the "sour-grapes" attitude so common among human beings, the satisfaction that comes from being able to say, "I know I'm not brilliant, but thank God, I'm normal!" But it has been noted also by writers as far back as Aristotle that men of genius often show pathological characteristics. The most influential exponent of this view has been the Italian criminologist, Lombroso (1896). In *The Man of Genius*, he gives example after example of famous men who showed various kinds of abnormality. Among more recent writers, both Lange-Eichbaum (1931) and Kretschmer (1931) have also emphasized the relationship of genius to psychopathology. Witty and Lehman (1929, 1930) have cited many additional examples which lend support to the theory. Among literary men they cite Poe, Byron, Dowson, Heine, Sappho, Shakespeare, and Oscar Wilde as great writers who were driven by inner frustrations and conflicts. Poe's own eloquent words which they quote constitute a clear statement of the belief in the essential instability of genius:

I am come of a race noted for vigor of fancy and ardor of passion. Men have called me mad; but the question is not yet settled, whether much that is glorious, whether all that is profound, does not spring from disease of thought, from moods of mind enacted at the expense of general intellect.

What are we to make of this sort of evidence? The safest procedure seems to be to apply the kinds of standards of judgment that we have discussed in previous chapters. Anecdotes and individual cases prove nothing except the almost unlimited variability of the human race. Of course there are insane men of genius, but is the proportion of abnormal individuals significantly higher than it is in the population as a whole? Of course even the sane men of genius behave strangely at times, but so do we all. Are the instances of queer behavior any more frequent among them than among ordinary people? Psychologists are inclined to challenge theories like those of Lombroso and Kretschmer, and find them valuable only as sources of specific hypotheses which can be subjected to statistical tests.

Another perennially interesting question has to do with the relative weights to be assigned to personal and social factors in high achievement. There are numerous instances of inventions propounded simultaneously by two or more people working independently when the time was ripe for their appearance. Thus we have a Bell-Magendie Law and a James-Lange theory of the emotions. Many sociologists have stressed the fact that social influences are at least as important as constitutional endowment in the production of high achievement. William James (1927), in an essay first published in 1880, took exception to the extreme sociological and geographical views that had been propounded by Herbert Spencer and Grant Allen. His thesis was that the function of society and the geographical environment is not the *production* of genius but its *selection*. By fostering and increasing the influence of certain types of man, and by destroying what is incompatible with itself, a given environment makes certain achievements possible, but it does not produce the men capable of making them. The logic of James' reasoning is still an impressive answer to those who would insist that "the age makes the man." The argument as to whether the age makes the man or the man makes the age is a part of the general controversy over heredity versus environment. In its extreme form it has largely died down. The question is now one of *relative* importance and *specific* environmental influences. Is it possible, for example, for a mediocre man to be catapulted to greatness if the pressure of unusual circumstances is strong enough? Are there "mute, inglorious Miltons" who find no outlet at all for abilities of a high order? What kinds of family and school situations discourage and thwart genius? In what surroundings does it thrive and flower? We shall examine what evidence there is on these points later in the chapter.

In studying the problems of genius there are basically two approaches. One is to select individuals who are unquestionably eminent and collect all the information possible about them. The other is to pick out children who show unusual promise, and follow their development. In carrying out the first of these plans one can do various things. He can collect statistical data showing both the biological and the sociological characteristics of the settings in which the unusual individuals appear. He can study biographies and attempt to analyze and classify the psychological characteristics of the individuals themselves. The most elaborate refinement of this biographical method is the method of historiometry used by Cox (1926) in her epoch-making study. She not only noted and tabulated but managed to *quantify* the evidences of high ability that were available in the biographies of great men, so that a numerical estimate of their childhood intelligence was possible. If one starts from the other direction and studies children who may some day become great, he may either make complete case studies of individuals in their early years to be kept on record for future reference, or he may carry on mental measurement of large groups of these promising children and analyze the group characteristics now and later.

There are difficulties which one encounters in doing either of these things. In choosing groups of eminent persons to be studied, some criterion is necessary. Unless this is satisfactory, and unless a fairly complete group of persons who satisfy it is obtained, the kind of sampling errors that have been criticized in Lombroso and in Kretschmer can easily be made. Individual cases whose lives support any kind of theory one wishes to devise may be found. The safest criterion is some objective indication of the amount of attention each person's achievements have commanded, such as the amount of space devoted to him in the standard biographical dictionaries. Another kind of criterion is based on ratings by experts in the field in which the individual's achievements have been made; and some investigators have had chemists rate chemists, musicians rate musicians, writers rate writers, and so on. It is of course true that this sort of selection gives us *eminence* rather than ability as such, but if we adopt the fairly objective definition of genius suggested at the beginning of this chapter, we are on safe ground. It may well be that some individuals who merit very few lines in a biographical dictionary have more exceptional qualities than the ones who rank high, but we must judge them as society does if we are to do this type of research.

In order to be sure what the judgment of society is, however, it is usually desirable to let some time elapse after the person's career is over. Many men who constitute important figures in their own day are completely forgotten twenty years afterward. This means that we have a sounder criterion of eminence if we study great men who have died than if we try to study so-called genius in its own day. Thus another difficulty arises, because the biographical data available on great men of the past are incomplete. Often just the information that would be most useful to the psychologist is missing from the record. Biographers are likely to stress the periods in a person's life when his most important work was going on. The psychologist is most interested in the circumstances and the motivation leading up to that work. Consequently the study of eminent persons as a research method is limited in its scope. Only certain types of information, and those not the most crucial, can be discovered this way.

The work with gifted children by-passes some of these difficulties. It does not leave to chance the recording of the essential information about childhood years. For each of the subjects of the study the psychologist can collect data about intelligence, special abilities, personality traits, and family circumstances. There is still, however, a sampling difficulty. *Which* children shall he include in the group whose careers are to be followed? Whatever the criterion is, it must be used consistently so that bias resulting from the investigator's opinions is ruled out. The criterion that has been most common has been intelligence-test scores supplemented by teachers' ratings. This assumes that there is a relationship between genius and intelligence. A study of this kind must amass data on a large number of subjects. We know that only a few of them will set the world on fire, but since we have no way of knowing now *which few*, we must include them all. Whether or not the research on gifted children will answer the important questions about the psychology of genius is still uncertain. It will be many years before the final judgments can be made. But the facts so far accumulated about the highly intelligent child and his development have considerable practical value in themselves whether or not they answer the more profound questions.

STATISTICAL STUDIES OF EMINENT INDIVIDUALS

There have been a number of statistical surveys of data on record about famous persons since Galton (1952) began this type of research in 1869. Some of them have been concerned with biological information which might be related to the Lombroso theory of degeneracy and pathology in men of genius. The results on the whole do not support any such conception. The average age of the fathers of American men of science, at the time of the subject's birth, according to J. McK. Cattell (1915, 1917a and b) was thirty-five. The parents thus tend to have been in the prime of life when the child was born. The great man is more likely to be the first-born than any other member of the family. He is most likely to come from a family in which there have been other eminent individuals. In Galton's study (1952) for instance, the 977 eminent men included had a total of 739 eminent relatives. Great men as a whole seem to be more vigorous than the average. C. C. Miles and Wolfe (1936) analyzed biographical data on fifty representative geniuses to get ratings of their mental and physical health during childhood. They show that the distribution of ratings is at least as favorable as that for children in general. Only 2 per cent show definitely frail health, only 8 per cent serious mental and emotional weakness. There is a difference between imaginative geniuses and men of action. Among the poets and artists there is a higher percentage of instability than among the statesmen and leaders. On the whole, however, no relationship between genius and mental pathology is demonstrated. Adams (1945-46) noted that the average life span for scientists born since 1600 was considerably longer than the typical life span for their period.

Galton and many later writers have interpreted the evidence as supporting a hereditary theory of genius. Into the first-rate families are born superior children from among whose number will come our first-rate men and women. Critics of this viewpoint have been quick to point out that in families like the Huxleys and the Adamses it is not just the germ plasm that is superior. A child in such a home receives physical care, mental stimulation, educational advantages, and motivation to high achievement far beyond the average. As has been said above, surveys of the biological facts about genius discredit the Lombroso theory of degeneracy and give evidence that the hereditary endowment of the great man is superior. They do not prove, however, that this good endowment is *all* that matters.

Out of the surveys of eminent men has come also considerable sociological information. Such persons are much more likely to come from the higher than from the lower occupational levels of the population, as Table 44 shows.

TABLE 44.

Occupational Distribution of Fathers of 282 Eminent Men and Women of all Countries

(Cox, 1926)

OCCUPATIONAL LEVEL	PERCENTAGE
Professional and nobility	52.5
Semi-professional, higher business and gentry	28.7
Skilled workmen and lower business	13.1
Semi-skilled	3.9
Unskilled	1.1
No record	0.7

Certain regions are much more likely than others to produce geniuses, as Table 45 shows; but with the passage of time, the relative proportions from different parts of the country change. This might be a result of either migration of first-rate families to the newer regions or the improvement of educational facilities in these areas.

More important than any of these miscellaneous facts about great men is the definite evidence that they were highly intelligent from childhood on. There are, of course, famous anecdotes. We read how the little Mozart began composing at five, played for the emperor at six, and wrote an opera

TABLE 45.

*Numbers of American Men of Science Born in Eastern
and Midwestern States, 1903 and 1932*

(Cattell, 1933)

PLACE OF BIRTH	NUMBER OF CASES (PER 1,000 ENTRIES)	
	DATA GATHERED IN 1903	DATA GATHERED IN 1932
Massachusetts	134	72
Connecticut	40	16
New York	183	128
Pennsylvania	66	48
Illinois	42	88
Minnesota	4	32
Missouri	14	40
Nebraska	2	20
Kansas	7	32

at eleven. Sir Francis Galton's letter to his sister, written the day before his fifth birthday, in which he catalogs his accomplishments, is well known:

My dear Adele:
　I am four years old and I can read any English book. I can say all the Latin substantives and adjectives and active verbs besides 52 lines of Latin poetry. I can cast up any sum in addition and can multiply by 2, 3, 4, 5, 6, 7, 8, 9, 10.
　I can also say the pence table. I read French a little and I know the clock.

Francis Galton
February 15, 1827

　But there are other cases of men like Edison who were reported by their teachers to be dull in school. Thus there was a great need for a systematic attempt to bring together information about the childhood mental characteristics of geniuses, the task which was accomplished by Cox (1926). The subjects were 301 persons objectively rated as outstandingly eminent. As much biographical information as possible was brought together for each of them, and three experienced psychologists estimated the person's IQ on the basis of the items that showed what he was able to do at specified ages. It is interesting to notice that the more information there was available about individuals, the higher the rated IQ's turned out to be. Superior mental ability, of the type we are identifying readily in children today by means of intelligence tests, characterized *all* of these eminent individuals without exception. No individual was rated below average on the basis of available childhood information. The average for every type of leader considered was above 140. For most of them it was 160 or above. These results enable us to place far more confidence in the research on gifted children than would otherwise be warranted, since they furnish strong support for the belief that the leaders of tomorrow are among the gifted children of today.

TABLE 46.

High Personality-Trait Ratings of One Hundred Geniuses in Childhood

(C. C. Miles, 1954)

(Ratings are averages of two raters on a seven-point scale, +3 to −3, when o is the assumed average of the general child population.)

Intellectual Traits:

Mental work devoted to routine studies	1.7
Independence of thought	1.8
Keenness of observation	1.9
Strength of memory	2.0
Quickness of apprehension	2.0
Originality, creativeness	2.1
Profoundness of apprehension	2.3
Mental work devoted to special pursuits	2.4

Social Traits:

Trustworthiness	1.7
Conscientiousness	1.7
Wideness of influence	1.7
Intensity of influence on intimates	2.0

Self-traits and Motivation:

Desire to be a leader, to impose his will	1.7
Correctness of his own self-appraisal	1.7
Correctness of self-appraised special talents	2.0
Belief in his own powers	2.0
Force of character as a whole	2.0
Devotion of effort toward distant goals	2.0
Strength of will in perseverance	2.3
Persistence in the face of obstacles	2.3
Steadfastness of effort	2.5
Desire to excel in efforts	2.6

Other characteristics as well as mental ability were rated for Cox's sample. The same background factors of high family occupational level noted by Galton and others were brought out by this study. Breadth, intensity, and kind of interests also distinguished these persons from other children. They were more likely to have demonstrated strong intellectual interests in childhood. In rated character and personality traits they were also above average, as Table 46 shows.

Such ratings can be criticized because of their subjective nature. Psychologists, it could be argued, knowing that the persons they were rating had been outstanding in achievement, might be prejudiced in their favor in evaluating all these traits. Biographers probably have recorded more of the eminent person's good than of his bad traits. However, this work at least suggests strongly that genius involves a complex of favorable personality characteristics as well as a high degree of ability.

STUDIES OF GIFTED CHILDREN

In 1922, Terman et al. (1925) embarked upon the most ambitious developmental study that had ever been attempted. Its object was a direct attack upon this problem of genius. The method was essentially very simple. Canvass a given region (in this case, the state of California) for all the children having abilities of a very high order. Collect information, as extensive as possible, about the abilities and personal traits of each person. Then make follow-up studies every few years to find out what they are accomplishing. There are two groups of questions that can be answered by this type of research. First, what, generally speaking, becomes of gifted children? How well do they maintain their early superiority? Second, *which individuals* from this selected group accomplish work of the quality that will rank them with the geniuses we have been considering? How do they differ from the others? Is there any way we could have identified them in childhood? Conversely, what do the failures among the group seem to lack? Is it characteristics of the individuals themselves or handicapping effects of bad environments that hold them back?

The initial investigation, reported in *Genetic Studies of Genius*, Vol. I, was based on 1,000 preschool and elementary-school children and 300 high-school pupils with IQ's of 140 or above. Teachers' judgments as well as IQ's were used in making the initial selection. The first important follow-up study, reported in *Genetic Studies of Genius*, Vol. III (Burks et al., 1930), was made seven years later. The next follow-up, reported in the *Thirty-ninth Yearbook* of the National Society for the Study of Education, was made in 1935-36. A summary of the whole project to date and a detailed report on the follow-up studies made in 1940 and in 1945 was published in *The Gifted Child Grows Up* (Terman and Oden, 1947). This was particularly important since it showed what has happened to the subjects after they have grown up, left school, and begun their careers. Later follow-up reports will be still more significant.

The first important result of this work was a usable body of knowledge with regard to gifted children as a group. Since this group included about nine-tenths of the highest IQ's in a population of 250,000 public-school children, its size and completeness makes the findings unusually dependable. In the first place, statistics about the *families* from which the children came showed striking similarities to those that had been accumulated about eminent men and women. There was the same preponderance of high occupational level, 31 per cent having fathers belonging to the professional class, 50 per cent to semi-professional and business occupations, 12 per cent to skilled labor, and 7 per cent to semi-skilled or unskilled occupations. (It is to be remembered in evaluating such figures that there are many *more* non-professional than professional men in the population. The fact that 31 per cent of these children came from professional homes is noteworthy because not more than 5 to 10 per cent of the working population is classified at this level. However, high IQ's do occur at all levels, as the 7 per cent whose fathers were laborers show.) The educational level of the fathers and mothers of the gifted children was considerably higher on the average than that of the general population. The frequency of insanity in their families was much below the population average. Parents tended to be above average in general health and in the prime of life at the time the children were born. The gifted child was more likely to be the first-born than to occupy any other position in the family.

In physical and developmental characteristics, the gifted group showed a consistent superiority. Their averages at each age exceeded the age norms for children as a whole in a wide variety of anthropometric measurements, including height, weight, general physical development, and muscular energy. The gifted children were superior to the average in the rate at which they had learned to walk and talk. Puberty was somewhat earlier than normal. General health, as determined from physicians' ratings, was better than average, and symptoms such as headaches, stuttering, and nervousness were relatively uncommon. Of course there were wide individual differences in all these things; but the old stereotyped picture of the child prodigy as a weak, sickly, frail little person with a vastly over-developed brain was demolished completely.

Educational accomplishments were particularly outstanding. About 85 per cent of the children had skipped one or more half-grades, and their teachers thought that some 80 per cent were entitled to still further promotion. Their school work was most superior in subjects like debating, history, composition, literature, grammar, general science, geography, civics, reading, and arithmetic—subjects that require verbal comprehension and abstract reasoning. They were least superior in subjects such as physical training, art, and shop work. (The gifted child is actually at a disadvantage in the ordinary schoolroom in these things, since the physical and muscular development on which complex coördinations depend is not correlated to any significant extent with mental development. Thus the fact that he is likely to be from six months to several years *younger* than the average child in the *grade* means that he may appear deficient in these skills, even when development is normal or above for his *age*.) The stated preferences of the gifted children for different kinds of school work showed the same trends as their accomplishments, though they were also inclined to give the same high preference ratings to games and sports as normal children do. Versatility rather than one-sidedness characterized these bright children. Achievement tests showed high scores in *all* subject-matter fields.

The gifted children showed a wide range of interests and an active play life. Their play interests were quite similar to those of average children, except that they tended to prefer games that are favorites of children somewhat older than they, as might be expected from their greater mental maturity. The greatest contrast between gifted and average children was with regard to reading and other distinctively intellectual interests. They had learned to read unusually early, often with little or no instruction. They read more than twice as many books as the average children of the same age, and included in their lists much more good literature, such as poetry and drama, science, history, biography, and travel. They made twice as many collections as average children, and these were more likely to be of scientific interest and value.

In many character and personality traits, the group was considerably superior to the average. Table 47 shows some of the comparisons between gifted and control children on various rated traits. It is apparent that it was in the *intellectual* traits and the motivation that lead to achievement that the greatest differences occurred. In most social traits the two groups did not differ. On tests of emotional adjustment there was a highly significant difference in favor of the gifted group. Though there are all sorts of individual patterns represented in the group, the general tendency is plainly for good personality development to accompany high intelligence.

Fortunately there have been enough other studies of gifted children by various persons in other parts of the country to make it plain that Terman's findings are not limited to a particular group of California individuals. In New York, in Chicago, in Kansas City—wherever the investigations have been made, the same general superiority of the children with high IQ's has been apparent.

TABLE 47.
*Teachers' Ratings of Gifted and Control Children
on Various Personality Traits* *

(C. C. Miles, 1954)

TRAITS IN WHICH GIFTED CHILDREN DIFFER LITTLE FROM CONTROL CHILDREN		GIFTED		CONTROL	
		BOYS	GIRLS	BOYS	GIRLS
Fondness for groups	M	6.2	5.6	6.1	5.9
	SD	2.1	2.2	2.1	2.0
Freedom from vanity	M	5.9	5.4	6.1	5.6
	SD	2.7	2.3	1.9	2.0
Sympathy	M	5.8	5.2	6.3	5.7
	SD	2.1	2.1	1.8	1.8
Popularity	M	6.4	5.7	6.5	6.2
	SD	2.0	2.0	1.8	1.9

TRAITS IN WHICH GIFTED CHILDREN DIFFER SIGNIFICANTLY FROM CONTROL CHILDREN		GIFTED		CONTROL	
		BOYS	GIRLS	BOYS	GIRLS
Leadership	M	6.3	5.8	7.2	7.0
	SD	1.9	2.0	2.1	2.2
Desire to excel	M	4.2	3.6	6.1	5.6
	SD	2.2	1.9	2.4	2.0
Conscientiousness	M	4.8	4.0	6.2	5.4
	SD	2.5	2.2	2.3	2.2
Common sense	M	4.2	4.1	6.2	5.9
	SD	1.9	1.9	1.8	1.8
Perseverance	M	4.4	4.1	6.4	6.1
	SD	2.1	1.9	2.2	2.0

TRAITS IN WHICH GIFTED CHILDREN DIFFER LARGELY AND SIGNIFICANTLY FROM CONTROL CHILDREN		GIFTED		CONTROL	
		BOYS	GIRLS	BOYS	GIRLS
Desire to know	M	3.5	3.9	6.3	6.2
	SD	1.9	2.1	2.0	2.1
Originality	M	4.4	4.5	6.8	6.9
	SD	2.1	2.1	1.9	1.9
General intelligence	M	3.1	3.1	6.4	6.2
	SD	1.6	1.8	1.9	1.8

* Smaller numbers indicate superior ratings.

The heart of this kind of research, however, is not in the initial survey, but in the follow-up studies. What becomes of children like this as they grow up and take their places in society? Terman's first follow-up was published in 1930 as Vol. III of *Genetic Studies of Genius* (Burks *et al.*, 1930). Since the subjects were about six years older than they had been at the time of the first testing, most of them had moved up to the next school level. Most of the children originally in elementary school were now in high school; most of those originally in high school were now in college. One fact stands out as of paramount importance from the data collected at this time: the educational superiority of the group was being maintained in the large majority of cases. There was a slight drop in both average IQ and average achievement quotient $\left(\dfrac{\text{Test Age}}{\text{Chronological Age}}\right)$, probably to be explained on the basis of the regression phenomenon discussed in the previous chapter. When one selects for initial study a group far above the general average, any part of the high scores that is the result of chance errors in an upward direction is likely to be corrected at the time of the next testing, thus producing a slight decrease in the average score. It may be significant, however, that the loss in IQ for the girls was 14 points as compared with a 3-point decrease for the boys. Changes in either developmental rate or intellectual motivation seem in the case of the girls to have supplemented those due to regression alone. But even in cases where a considerable decrease had occurred, the individuals were still well above average, and the Stanford-Binet IQ's averaged 143 for the boys and 135 for the girls. More students than before were now accelerated in school. School records showed consistent high achievement in all academic subjects. Character ratings and personality test scores were still high. With regard to this point also, the tendency for superiority to be maintained throughout the school years, data from other parts of the country support the Terman findings.

In the follow-up reports published by Terman and Oden (1940, 1947) we now have a wealth of information about the subjects up to the age of approximately forty. We can summarize much of it around a number of research questions to which the investigators turned their attention. First, has the superior intellectual status been maintained? Getting an answer to this question is not so simple as it might appear at first glance. The tests on the basis of which the IQ's of the subjects were determined in childhood have much too low a "ceiling" for superior adults. It was necessary for Terman and his associates to develop a new very difficult test they called the Concept Mastery Test, and then by giving this along with better-known tests to college students, to arrive at statistical estimates of the IQ's to which its scores correspond. The final conclusion was that there had been some slipping back toward the average intelligence level. Whereas the whole group had averaged 3.2 standard deviations above the general mean as children, they now average about 2.1 standard deviations above.

R. L. Thorndike (1948a) using a different type of "bridge" between the Concept Mastery scores and the norms for the general population, arrived at an even lower figure. He estimated that Terman's group now average about 1.7 standard deviations above the general population. Only about half the drop can be accounted for by the regression effect. The rest is not due to chance. When all this has been said, however, the important fact remains that the group as a whole is still very high. Translating the facts into percentile terms, Thorndike shows that half the group would still score above the 95th percentile and the other half would spread out between the 75th and 95th percentile points on a test designed for the common man. There would be no low or even average scores. The report of Bayley and Oden [1] that retests on the Concept Mastery Test after a ten-year interval showed an increase in score would seem to suggest that what drop there was in some subjects may have occurred during the school years rather than later.

A second question had to do with the physical and mental health of the group. Results of the later follow-up studies corroborate those of the earlier ones in showing predominantly good health and adjustment. While about 5 per cent were now rated seriously maladjusted, 80 per cent showed no emotional difficulties whatever. Comparison figures for people as a whole are not obtainable, but this incidence of difficulty appears to be low rather than high.

A third question might be, "Has the group as a whole been successful in life?" Here the answer is outstandingly positive. School success was as marked at the later as at the early stages. About 90 per cent of the group entered college, and more than two-thirds of them graduated. Graduate study leading to advanced degrees, outstanding scholastic records, and election to honorary societies was common. Participation in extracurricular activities and a considerable amount of self-support accompanied this academic success. The fact that there were some failures and many mediocre records, however, indicates that high intelligence does not guarantee such favorable outcomes.

The occupational status of these young adults was also very satisfactory, whether evaluated by general level attained or by income. The percentage of unemployment was far lower than the general population figure. Approximately 71 per cent of the gifted men were in professional or higher business fields as compared with less than 14 per cent of California males as a whole. There was a marked sex difference in this area, however. Occu-

---

[1] Personal communication.

pational level and income were both much lower for the women than for the men in the group.

A fourth set of questions centered around marriage and family life. The marriage rate was as high as it is for the population as a whole, and the evidence indicated that both marital happiness and sexual adjustment were slightly more satisfactory than they are in available comparison groups. The spouses were intelligent also, but did not score quite so high on the Concept Mastery Test as did the subjects themselves. The average IQ for children who had been born to them so far was 128.

Perhaps the most illuminating part of this study is a comparison of the 150 individuals rated most successful (Group A) with the 150 rated least successful (Group C). (The C individuals were not necessarily failures by general standards, but they had not lived up to the promise of their childhood years.) A number of significant differences showed up, although the two groups overlapped so much with regard to each characteristic that it would not have been possible to predict for any individual child whether or not he was to be successful. In Group C, the intellectual level had dropped since high-school days so that these subjects were at the time of the follow-up significantly lower than the others on the Concept Mastery Test. Ratings on desirable personality characteristics—self-confidence, perseverance, integration toward goals, absence of inferiority feelings, and even common sense—averaged lower for the C's, whether they were made by wives, parents, or by themselves. There were more cases among them where scores on the Strong Vocational Interest Test did not match career choices. Both slight and serious maladjustments were far more common among them. But it was the variables included under "Family Background" that showed the largest differences. Far more of the A's than of the C's came from homes of high occupational and educational status. There was a significantly larger proportion of broken homes among the C's, and the C subjects themselves had had twice as many divorces as the A's. This study furnishes striking evidence that background and motivational factors can help to determine how effectively high intelligence will be utilized.

A report that this is true even during the school years comes from Lewis (1941). This study also is part of a large research project in which the 10 per cent scoring highest on the Kuhlmann-Anderson intelligence test and the 10 per cent scoring lowest were singled out for special study. Since the total sample included almost 50,000 grade-school children from 310 communities in 36 states, the results have the statistical reliability that goes with large numbers. In this particular comparison, high-ability children whose scores on school achievement tests averaged at least a year lower than their mental ages were contrasted with those whose achievement was at least a year higher than their mental ages. The groups differed in much the same ways that Terman and Oden's A and C adult groups did. Ratings made by their teachers prior to any of the testing showed the over-achievers to be more dependable, original, and self-reliant. They reported more intellectual interests, such as reading, collecting, and music. A larger proportion of them came from the professional classes, and fewer of them from semi-skilled and unskilled occupational classes.

One side issue on which Terman and his co-workers attempted to get information was the question of whether acceleration in school is really as unsatisfactory a way of handling gifted children as many administrators and teachers believe it to be. The comparisons of those who had been accelerated from two to four years with the others indicated that there had been no unfavorable effects. All the indicators of social adjustment and mental health ranked accelerated individuals high. Pressey (1949) has made a number of related studies of the same problem and has come to the same conclusion. There are of course individual exceptions, but as a whole the under-age students are superior in both social adjustment and educational achievement.

The studies of Terman and the Stanford group have told us much about children who score high on intelligence tests. There is some question as to how much bearing they have upon the question that interested the earlier research workers most, the origin and meaning of genius. One would not, of course, expect anywhere near all of the high-scoring children to attain the distinction to which the term refers. In Galton's ingenious scale for evaluating eminence, even the lowest level of eminence—that represented by successful English judges and bishops—was defined as the point reached by only one in 4,000 of the general population. The rare, illustrious characters in history were placed above the point reached by only one in a million. Terman and Oden's group now includes the director of an atomic research laboratory, a professor in a medical school who has made over one-hundred research contributions, and four writers making from $40,000 to $50,000 yearly. We cannot say for certain that no Newtons or Shakespeares have shown up, because it often takes years before the greatness of a truly great man is recognized. The fact remains, however, that most of these subjects are successful but not outstandingly creative. It is perhaps unfortunate that the word "genius" was used as a label for high-IQ children when the Terman study began.

There are many present-day students of the problem who feel that the

140 IQ used in the early studies was too low to serve as a demarcation line for intellects of genius quality. Hollingworth (1942) was particularly interested in the very rare boys and girls with IQ's above 180. She assembled some fascinating case material on those she had an opportunity to study. In these extremely high individuals, creativity and originality are likely to be evident even in early childhood. The following excerpts from the report on Child D, whose IQ was 184, illustrates this kind of achievement: [2]

Imaginary land. From the age of about four years to about the age of seven, D was greatly interested in an imaginary land which he called Borningtown. He spent many hours peopling Borningtown, laying out roads, drawing maps of its terrain, composing and recording its language (Bornish), and writing its history and literature. He composed a lengthy dictionary—scores of pages—of the Bornish language. The origin of the words *Borningtown* and *Bornish* is not known. It seems possible that D's imaginary land may have arisen out of the mystery of being born.

Gift for music. D has had piano lessons for several years, and he has displayed remarkable ability to deal with the mathematical aspects of music. He composed music before he had any instruction in playing musical instruments. He read certain booklets which came with Ampico and decided to compose. He can compose music which he cannot himself play.

Gifts for form and color in drawing. D's talent for color, for drawing and design, has been marked from the time he could wield a pencil. His drawings, paintings, and designs would fill a book by themselves.

D loves color, and one of his favorite playthings has been a sample folder of silk buttonhole twists of three hundred shades. Between the ages of eight and nine years he would go over and over these, classifying the colors in various ways, scoring them for beauty, and naming them to satisfy his appreciation of them. Some of these names will give an idea of his appreciation:

spotted pale	spoiled pink
darkling green	soft light pink
shame blue	meadow beauty pink
dark darking green	cat black
regular green	royalest red
paper white	apron blue
alien white	beau yellow
feeling blue	visitor's green

One of his favorite games (aged eight to nine years) was to assign a numerical value to each of the 300 shades and then to list them for "highest honors." "Royalest red" nearly always won in these contests.

Originality of new concepts and new words. From earliest childhood D has felt a need for concepts and for words to express them that are not to be

[2] Quoted by special permission from *Children Above 180* by L. S. Hollingworth. Copyright 1942 by World Book Company.

found in dictionaries. His occupation in this field he calls "wordical work." Some examples are recorded by his mother in the following note dated December, 1916.

"Was having his dinner and being nearly finished said he didn't care to eat any more, as he had a pain in his actum pelopthis. He explained that his actum pelopthis, actum quotatus, serbalopsis, and boobalicta are parts of the body where you sometimes have queer feelings; they don't serve any purpose. He said he also had a place called the boobalunksis, or source of headaches; that the hair usually springs out from around the herkadone; that the perpalensis is the place where socks end, and the bogalegus is the place where legs and tummy come together. He also named one other part, the cobaliscus or smerbalooble, whose function is not explained. The definitions are exactly as he gave them in each instance."

Invention of games. D has invented many games. To illustrate this aspect of his mental capacity, there are his designs for three-handed and four-handed checkers. D held that these would be better games than two-handed checkers because they are more complicated. A description of the games invented by D, together with his mathematical calculations concerning the chances and probabilities in each, would fill many pages. (Hollingworth, 1942, pp. 123-127)

Hollingworth felt that activity of this sort bore much more resemblance to adult genius than the ordinary sort of school work does. So far, however, it has not been reported that any of her small group of eminent children has attained a high degree of adult eminence. (D, whose childhood achievements are catalogued above, died in 1938 at the age of twenty-eight.)

Terman and Oden (1947) also included a special chapter on a group of 47 men and 34 women singled out for special study because their childhood IQ's had been 170 or above. The best general summary of the findings is that this group differs in no essential way from the group as a whole. The percentage of successful achievement is a little higher both in school and in occupational life, but there is no sharp dividing line. These investigators feel that above 140 IQ it is not the intelligence level that determines the degree of creativity. There is no particular advantage in an IQ of 180.

Hollingworth (1940) has also pointed out that the tendency for good personality adjustment to accompany high intelligence is not as apparent for the extremely high as for the moderately high individuals. Probably the optimum IQ range for good adjustment is from 130 to 150. Above that level certain problems arise which Hollingworth classifies as follows: (1) problems of physique (being weaker and smaller than their classmates and thus susceptible to bullying); (2) problems of adjustment to occupation (preferring self-direction to direction by others); (3) problems involved in "suffering fools gladly" (difficulty in getting along with teachers and classmates who are inferior to them intellectually); and (4) problems created by isolation (the impossibility of finding friends with their own interests and goals). All of these problems are most acute when the child

FIGURE 47. Musical composition produced by Child D at age 8 years 7 months (Hollingworth, 1942, p. 124).

is of elementary-school age; after he gets into the secondary school and college, the intellectual level of those around him is more nearly equal to his own. Witty (1940) also has called attention to the fact that some gifted children who appear satisfactorily adjusted when first tested increasingly develop undesirable trends in the direction of either laziness or cynicism.

Terman and Oden's report does not show any clear tendency for the very high subjects to be less well-adjusted adults than the rest. It is interesting to note, however, that the 1928 ratings, made when the children were in their middle teens, did show a significant difference in this direction, a difference which was greater for the girls than for the boys. Even at the time of the 1940 rating, almost twice as many of the women in the high group as in the total group were seriously maladjusted. Although the number determining this percentage is small, there still seems to be a possibility that the girls with unusually high IQ's may have more adjustment difficulties than do the boys. The fact that differences appear most clearly in the 1928 follow-up rather than earlier or later would suggest that children of this sort tend to have some trouble during adolescence but usually manage to overcome it successfully.

Thus with the progress of research on the gifted child, more and more emphasis has been placed on proper handling and training. We cannot safely assume that because a child's intelligence is high, that he will sail through life more easily than his classmates. The average elementary-school curriculum suits him little better than it does the moron. If he is to develop to the limit of his potentialities—and society has a tremendous interest in seeing that he does—he should get enough special attention to enable him to make the most of his intellectual powers, develop habits of work and concentration, and maintain adequate contact with his fellow men. Just what changes in the regular school program this must involve is as yet an undecided issue. Programs of acceleration, segregation, and enrichment all have their enthusiastic supporters. Good results have been obtained under all of them. Perhaps the most important thing is to make sure that someone understands the child as an individual. Then whatever special treatment is available can be used to his best advantage.

STUDIES OF LIVING SCIENTISTS

Because of the importance of scientific work during World War II and in the postwar years, public attention has been focused on the need for scientists. Questions have been raised that are more practical and concrete than those that grew out of people's interest in the general problem of genius. What combination of abilities does it take to make an outstanding scientist? What motives and personality traits enter into his choice of career? Why are some men more productive than others?

The most important series of studies in this area has been carried out by Roe (1951a, 1951b, 1953). The subjects have been biologists, physicists, psychologists, and anthropologists, in each case men who are agreed to be among the most eminent, perhaps *the* most outstanding persons in their respective fields. Though the numbers are small (about 20 in each professional group) the methods of study have been very intensive and have focused on personality characteristics, family backgrounds, and motivation. Biographical material and information about attitudes were obtained from interviews. The Rorschach and the Thematic Apperception Tests were given and analyzed. A new high-level intelligence test made up of verbal, spatial, and mathematical sections was administered. Information from all these sources was brought together in a case study of each individual. It is these case studies themselves rather than any of the summary figures that are the most interesting part of the Roe monographs, since they show how diverse and individual these men are.

It is difficult to summarize data of this sort in any meaningful way. The subjects, biological, physical, and social scientists, most often came from professional and middle-class homes. In many cases some event occurred during childhood that led to a feeling of *apartness*—something like the death of one parent, a serious illness, or a physical handicap. There seemed to be no general pattern for the choice of a vocation. Some decided early, others much later. In some cases a teacher was very influential; in others childhood hobbies developed into adult work. The possibility of doing research was a decisive factor in many cases. The projective test protocols and the interview data would suggest that these are not particularly well-adjusted groups, in our ordinary sense of the term. There would appear to be a considerable amount of basic insecurity, with work itself serving as an adjustment technique in many cases. The social scientists differed somewhat from the physicists and biologists in that they were more concerned with human relations. They volunteered more biographical information and gave twice as many Rorschach responses. On the whole, however, individual differences far outweigh group differences.

As was expected, there were some group differences in the pattern of abilities shown on the V S M intelligence test (Verbal, Spatial, Mathematical). Interestingly enough, there was a considerable range of total scores on this test. This indicates that while these men all are high in general intellectual ability, some are much higher than others. Furthermore, the ones with the lower scores are just as successful as the higher ones. This corroborates Terman and Oden's conclusion that above a certain level differences in intelligence are not related to success.

Terman (1954) has examined the records of the California men to see what factors differentiate between those who have become scientists and the others. Out of about 500 items of information, including test scores, ratings, and biographical data, only 108 items differentiate at the 5 per cent level of significance. The majority of these items have something to do with *interests*. Scores on the Strong test show the clearest pattern, but interest in science as rated in childhood by parents, teachers, or the children themselves also shows up with high frequency on the records of those who later became scientists.

Much light may eventually be thrown on the problem of what makes a scientist by follow-up studies of the young people who are selected each year in the Science Talent Search. Edgerton *et al.* (1948) have already given us one such report, a three-year follow-up of the first year's winners. The important fact is that these boys who surmounted the very stiff hurdles set up for them, the Science Aptitude Test, the personal data and scholarship record, and the essay on "My Scientific Project," and who then were chosen as the most outstanding of the applicants who qualified, were all at the time of the follow-up making excellent records in science at the colleges where they had gone.

All these studies would seem to show that the one thing scientists have in common besides high intelligence is a compelling interest in their work. In other personality traits they are very different from one another. If we are to produce more scientists, the task of the educational system would seem to be to foster this interest and to encourage creative, independent work in students who are capable of doing it. But we know very little as yet about what produces such interests in the first place.

THE COMPLEXITY OF "GENIUS"

It is plain that psychology has not yet solved the problem of genius. The research on gifted children has been an important first step, but it will be years before the findings tell us the things we really need to know. The work thus far has, however, enabled us to discard the obviously untenable hypotheses and formulate sounder ones. It is these that can be subjected to further test, as time goes on.

In the first place, we are now in a position to say quite definitely that high intelligence, defined as the quality measured by tests like the Binet, is a *necessary but not a sufficient* characteristic of genius. In other words, all geniuses are highly intelligent, but not all highly intelligent individuals are geniuses. Unless a person has a high degree of the ability we call intelligence, the chances of his producing any work of immortal significance are negligible. But if he has this brilliant intellect, he still may fail to make a mark in the world. Why?

For one thing, there is a possibility that intelligence is not identical with creativity. All those who have worked with high-IQ children have been impressed with the fact that some are creative and original, whereas others are not. Since 1950 there has been some research especially designed to investigate creative thinking (Guilford, 1950; L. L. Thurstone, 1950a). Ingenious tests have been devised, tests requiring subjects to find new solutions rather than simply to give correct answers. Factor analysis of such tests (Guilford *et al.*, 1952) produces factors that call for names like *Ideational Fluency* and *Adaptive Flexibility*. Undoubtedly such abilities are correlated with intelligence as ordinarily measured, but intelligent persons do not all show them to the same extent. Genius then may be partly a matter of a *kind* of intelligence we have not yet succeeded in measuring very satisfactorily.

Besides this, we can fill in from our knowledge of case studies and biographies a catalogue of some other characteristics that appear to be involved in high achievement. One is certainly *special* ability of some kind. What little evidence there is indicates that gifted children are not much more likely than the average to be talented in art, music, or mechanics, though they often stand out in scientific and writing activities (Wilson, 1953). But unless they happen to have some outstanding talent or interest, some basis for specialization, they will fall short of the highest levels of achievement. Every college counselor is familiar with the case of the high-ability student who finds it extremely difficult, almost impossible, to choose a major. If he forces himself to choose on a purely arbitrary basis, such a person is likely to continue to try to cultivate the talents he has had to pass by. The line between the versatility which is an asset and the diffuseness of effort which is a liability is often a very fine one.

Some powerful motivation would also seem to be essential to those who would do great work. Here if anywhere the examples cited by Lombroso and Kretschmer of neurosis and other mental abnormalities are applicable. For some men, neurotic tensions act as a constant driving force. If they have the right combination of abilities, the neurosis can furnish the power to mobilize them. Such men are intensely unhappy most of their lives, but they turn out great work. An overpowering interest seems to serve the same motivational purpose in more fortunate individuals. The scientist is often a man of this sort. Some problem or complex of problems focuses his attention early in his career. From then on his life is a constant search for the solution. Some day perhaps we shall know more about why some men but not others are gripped in this way by dominant interests. Other motives such as ambition, love, or desire for revenge can probably serve to drive the engine of genius, if they are powerful enough. It is likely that most work is done under the impetus of a combination of motives. The unfortunate thing about exceptional motivation is that so far we have no idea how to *produce* it. If a highly-gifted individual lacks it, we must stand by and see his talents wasted. Prodding and urging are futile.

Other qualities are desirable supplements to these essentials. Galton emphasized physical stamina, and many others have called attention to the protracted difficult labor required for all tremendous achievement. Many eminent men have, however, been sickly and frail, so that health would not seem to be a primary characteristic. Good habits of *work* are an advantage also. Many a promising writer has fizzled out because he could not bring himself to write regularly; many a brilliant would-be scientist fails because he never can organize his time in a way that leaves him free to do the necessary experiments. But the fact remains that there are lazy, unsystematic people who turn out inspired creative work from time to time, so that good work habits also are a supplementary rather than an essential characteristic. One might go on adding to this list indefinitely traits that would be desirable for a genius to have and that selected individuals do show to a high degree.

If we cannot identify all the factors entering into the development of genius, we have unraveled some of them. On the basis of what we know we are even now in a position to single out the children from whom, under favorable circumstances, great achievements may be expected. It is to our advantage to create for them those favorable circumstances through the education we offer them. The more we find out about environmental factors and their effects, the more skillfully we shall be able to accomplish this purpose. The more we find out about the hereditary backgrounds from which they emerge, the more intelligently we can proceed to the adoption of social policies that will lead to the production of as many superior individuals as possible.

SUMMARY

In their work on the problem of genius, psychologists have attempted to avoid philosophical speculation and to concentrate on two kinds of research: (1) the analysis of the characteristics of individuals who have achieved eminence; and (2) follow-up studies of gifted children.

Statistical surveys of eminent individuals have shown that, contrary to much popular opinion, they are likely to be stronger and more vigorous than the average man. They come predominantly from the upper occupational classes and from regions where a high level of education prevails. Analysis of biographical information shows that they were highly intelligent from childhood on and that they were superior to the average in character and personality traits. Case studies of scientists show them to be very diverse in their personality traits.

Studies of gifted children have shown that they too are superior to the average in health and physical size and strength, that they come predominantly from the upper occupational levels, and that their play life and range of interests, their character and personality traits are superior to the average. Early academic superiority is maintained throughout the school years. The most recent follow-up of Terman's original group shows that the great majority of the gifted have been successful in their chosen occupations, though few if any have as yet achieved work of genius quality. Hazards in the way of the satisfactory adjustment of gifted children, particularly those with the extremely high IQ's, have been pointed out, and the schools are trying various methods for meeting the special problems of this group.

The body of research evidence which has accumulated would lead us to conclude that high intelligence, though essential to genius, is not synonymous with it. Special abilities, motivation, habits of work, and probably many other factors must all be combined in the production of outstanding achievement.

PART FOUR

Factors Producing Differences

CHAPTER 16

The Relationship of Mental
To Physical Characteristics

INTRODUCTION

PROBABLY no belief has been more tenaciously held among people of all times than the conviction that it is possible to judge an individual's mental characteristics by the way he is put together physically. Novelists describe the build, facial shape, coloring, and clothes of their characters in such a way as to accentuate the inner qualities which they assume are expressed by these things. Intelligent men and women who "pooh-pooh" the idea of fortune-telling in general still feel that "there may be something in this palmistry or phrenology." Books explaining personality in terms of the endocrine glands obtain wide and enthusiastic acceptance. Employment interviewers develop their own systems of judging prospective employees by appearance. Habits of thinking in such terms are ingrained in our language in such expression as "high-brow," "long-headed," or "thin-skinned."

The investigation of these relationships is an important scientific problem. It *is* desirable that we be able to make good sight judgments of people. Hundreds of life situations require us to make the attempt. But here, as in so many other areas covered by differential psychology, it is important to remember that a *wrong* judgment is worse than a suspended judgment or no judgment at all. The trouble with most of our rule-of-thumb methods is that they may lead us to make serious errors. It is the task of the psychologist to check up on what the popular beliefs are and then to discover what physical characteristics, if any, really *are* related to mental ability and personality.

There are special reasons why people's conclusions on this subject are likely to be faulty. The scientist along with the man on the street is susceptible to these errors and must constantly guard against them. First, human beings are very prone to base their beliefs on a few outstanding instances and to neglect the much more numerous examples that do not support them. It is this tendency that keeps superstitions alive and active. The untrained observer is likely to remember the one person he knows who broke a mirror just the night before his house burned down and to forget that mirror factories are constantly turning out replacements for other broken mirrors in houses still standing. Similarly, if a person has one intellectual friend with a high forehead or one timid associate with a receding chin, his opinions tend to be determined or confirmed by his contact with these cases.

Second, attitudes and prejudices with which people approach their personal relationships or their scientific research actually enter into their judgments of mental characteristics. Even if the man with the receding chin is possessed of more than the average force of character, he is likely to be adjudged a weakling until he proves himself otherwise. The slim, aristocratic-looking boy may get better marks in school for the same quality of work than his pudgy neighbor does. The sales manager who thinks size is related to aggressiveness may rate the tall salesmen on his staff higher than the short ones. In scientific research, wherever evaluation of personality is based on *ratings* by other people, we must watch out for this source of error. When tests are used, it is not important.

Third, any unusual physical characteristic may appear to carry personality characteristics along with it because of the way in which its possessor sees *himself*. These *indirect* effects of physical characteristics on personality can easily be confused with direct causal relationships. Careful study, however, will always show the difference, since in a group of people, examples will occur in which the same physical trait carries with it mental traits that are quite opposite. Take, for instance, the case of the weak, undersized child handicapped in infancy by a long illness. He may be shy, withdrawn, and retiring. On the other hand, he may try to compensate for his weakness by being noisy and troublesome in school and terrorizing younger children. These indirect effects of physical characteristics on personality are highly important, but there is nothing constant about them that we can use to help us make sight judgments of people. Only detailed study of an individual will show what his physical endowment means to *him* and how he is reacting to it.

Fourth, it must be remembered that relationships holding at the extremes of the distribution of human characteristics do not necessarily hold throughout the average range. There are numerous pathological conditions that produce abnormal personality characteristics, but unless conditions really *are* pathological, no abnormalities appear. Some idiots, we have noted in a previous chapter, have extremely small heads. This does *not*, however, warrant a conclusion that the smaller your head is, the nearer you are to idiot status. The cretin's feeble-mindedness, along with definite physical symptoms, arises from an extreme thyroid deficiency; but that fact tells us nothing about the relationship of thyroid functioning to intelligence within the normal range. Extreme cases of various kinds often do suggest hypotheses which we may check by research. In themselves they do not *prove* anything about people in general. With these cautions in mind, we can proceed to the discussion of what the research workers have found.

STRUCTURAL AND ANATOMICAL CHARACTERISTICS

Physical Size and Intelligence

There is a widespread popular belief that bright children are likely to be puny and underdeveloped physically, and that great thinkers are characterized by underdeveloped bodies as well as by overdeveloped brains. Scientists and writers, on the other hand, ever since Galton's epoch-making study of men of genius, have tended to support the view that all-round superiority goes with intelligence. What are the facts on the question?

Starting with Porter's investigation (1895) of 35,500 St. Louis school children, there have been a number of studies in which the *average* heights and weights for children of different degrees of intelligence have been compared. Early investigators were handicapped by the lack of any objective measure of intelligence. They had to rely on criteria like age-grade location and teachers' judgments. Most of them found that physical differences between mental ability groups were very slight. In Porter's work, for instance, the weight of nine-year-old boys still in Grade I (presumably the dullest group) averaged 55.87 lbs. For grade 2, the average was 57.64; for grade 3, 59.66; for grade 4, 61.75. The trend fits in with that we have already discussed in regard to gifted children. The bright children do average slightly heavier.

How *slight* this relationship is, however, became more apparent when intelligence tests replaced ratings, and the correlation method replaced simple comparisons of averages. It is the correlations that tell us what we really want to know, because they afford us an estimate of how strong the trend is in all individuals in the group. Table 48 summarizes what various investigators have found, using correlational methods. Studies using partial correlation techniques have been omitted, since as Paterson (1930) has shown, they are peculiarly susceptible to statistical sampling errors.

TABLE 48.

Correlations between Intelligence and Physical Size in Children

(Results summarized from Paterson, 1930)

INVESTIGATOR	PHYSICAL VARIABLE	N	CORRELATION
Murdock and Sullivan (1923) ..	weight	600	.16
	height	600	.14
Abernethy (1925)	weight	29 to 61 (different ages)	—.06 to .21
	height	29 to 62 (different ages)	.01 to .25
Gates (1924)	height	115	.06
	weight	115	.10

For studies like those of Abernethy where the number of subjects in each age group is relatively small, we would expect fluctuation in the r's from sample to sample, since there is about one chance in three of drawing a sample of 29 that will produce a correlation of .19 or higher from a population in which there is no correlation at all.[1] But in studies like Murdock and Sullivan's, the fact that there are 600 cases makes the sampling error very small. There would be almost no chance at all of obtaining an r greater than .12 if there were actually no correlation in the population. Thus we can be fairly certain that there is a slight tendency for brightness and physical size to go together, but the relationship is so low as to be of no practical importance in judging children. Any sort of combination of height and IQ can occur. The few studies in which adults have been used as subjects show similar results. If anything, correlations average even nearer the zero point.

Another whole family of research workers have felt that it was *shape* rather than absolute size that was correlated with intelligence. Various morphological indices based on the relationship of weight to height have been worked out. Usually they are expressed in such a way that persons whose height is greater in proportion to their weight get the higher scores. The work of Naccarati (1921) on this problem reported correlations running from .11 to .44 between morphological index and intelligence as meas-

[1] The standard deviation of the sampling distribution of r's from a population with zero correlation is:

$$\frac{1}{\sqrt{N-1}}$$

ured by various tests in various groups of students. The number in each group was too small to make any one of the coefficients very reliable. Later workers, attempting to check up on this hypothesis using more adequate samples, obtained less striking results. Heidbreder (1926) for instance, found that for 500 freshman men, the height-weight ratio correlated with scores on the college ability test to the extent of only .03. Sheldon (1927) found that the correlation between a psychological test and an index based on twelve physical measurements was only .14. Garrett and Kellogg (1928) found an r of .10 between height-weight ratio and psychological test score. It seems, then, that the relationship between body build and intelligence, if it exists at all, is too slight to be of any practical importance in judging people.

Head Measurements and Intelligence

Another considerable group of investigations is devoted to the question of the relationship of head measurements to intelligence. Ever since Gall formulated his system of phrenology at the beginning of the nineteenth century, popular interest in head size and shape as indicators of mental characteristics has been keen. Even though the psychological theories on which phrenology is based have been outmoded for generations, practicing phrenologists still do a good business. To organize research to check on their theories would be futile since we know already that the shape of the brain does not conform to the shape of the skull, and that separate faculties like memory, judgment, and generosity are not mediated by specific brain areas and could not possibly be lodged beneath the bumps that the phrenologists study.

The investigations that psychologists have planned and carried out have been designed to test two less fantastic hypotheses: (1) Is there a significant tendency for head size to be correlated with intelligence? and (2) Is the degree of "long-headedness" or "broad-headedness" correlated with intelligence? In connection with the first problem there are on record a number of studies reporting differences in *averages* between groups of differing mental ability. These figures, on the whole, support the hypothesis. Feeble-minded and dull persons have smaller heads than average. Eminent adults and gifted children have larger heads than average. Galton's classical study of Cambridge University students in 1888 showed that the honor men's head averaged slightly larger than those of men who just passed. As has been explained in connection with body size, however, these differences in *averages* really mean very little unless we know something about the distributions on which they are based. The later, more carefully planned studies used correlation methods. A number of these coefficients are summarized in Table 49.

TABLE 49.

Correlations between Head Size and Shape and Intelligence as Reported by Various Investigators

(Results summarized from Paterson, 1930)

INVESTIGATOR	MEASUREMENT	GROUP	N	CORRELATION
Pearson	Head length	Cambridge students	1,010	.11
	Head breadth	"	1,010	.10
	Cephalic index	"	1,010	—.06
	Head length	School boys age 12 yrs.	2,298	.14
	Head breadth	"	2,298	.11
	Cephalic index	"	2,298	—.04
	Head length	School girls age 12 yrs.	2,165	.08
	Head breadth	"	2,165	.11
	Cephalic index	"	2,165	.07
Pearl	Head circumference	Bavarian soldiers	935	.14
Murdock and Sullivan	Head diameter	Elemen. and high school students	596	.22
Sommerville	Head length	Male college students	100	.10
	Cephalic index	"	100	.01
Reid and Mulligan	Cranial capacity	Male medical students	449	.08
Sherman and Hull	Various measurements	Freshman engineering students	78	.23 to .34

The trend of these coefficients is clear. Even the highest one cited, .34, is only slightly above the chance level for this small number of cases. The fact that the large majority of them are *positive*, diverse as are the groups on which they are based, fits in with the trend brought out in the studies based on averages. They are, however, so small as to be of absolutely no practical value. The only important dissent from this conclusion has been registered by Porteus and Berry (1920). They found evidence in the measurements of 10,000 students in Australia that cranial capacity, when either unusually large or unusually small, tended to be associated with mental inferiority. Since no correlations were given, and the figures that would be required for an evaluation of the statistical significance of the reported trends were not included, it is impossible, as Paterson has shown (1930, pp. 102-112), to decide whether Porteus' evidence really does contradict the rest.

Research on facial characteristics, coloring, and so forth has been just as unrewarding. The most thorough studies on this problem were done under the direction of Hull (1928). Convexity of profile, blondeness, and a number of specific facial measurements gave correlations with scholarship and personality ratings that were all within the chance range. Regardless of what physiognomists, authors, or personnel men may say, there is nothing we can observe about the structural characteristics of a face that will tell us what we want to know about the person. Whether his expressions and movements, or the way he *uses* these strucures, can be revealing, as we all tend to believe, is a question that can only be answered by adequate research.

Hands

There have always been some reputable psychologists, along with a large number of charlatans, who have insisted that the shape and markings of a person's hands can tell us something about his mental abilities and personality. The most recent spokesman for this idea is Wolff (1947). She presents some detailed tables showing characteristics that were present in the hands of 115 high-grade mentally defective boys, and makes the statement that interpretations of personality made from information about the hands were correct in about 85 per cent of the cases. The rationale given to account for this relationship is that some hand characteristics reflect endocrine functioning at different growth periods and that the muscular development and the crease lines show what kind of habitual reactions have been built into the individual. As it stands the evidence is not very convincing, but the hypothesis might be considered as one worthy of further research.

Physical and Mental Growth

Another type of research has been concerned with the relationship of physical *growth* to mental development. Do a child's bones and brain develop at approximately the same rate, and if so, would it be fairer to use the so-called anatomical age or physiological age rather than the actual chronological age as a standard by means of which to determine mental retardation or acceleration? In a series of papers, Pryor (1905, 1906,

1908) and Rotch (1910) reported a new method for obtaining a quantitative index of skeletal development by analyzing X-ray photographs of the hand and wrist. Thirteen stages in the gradual transformation of cartilage into bone could be identified. Since that time, this method of measuring maturity of the body has been widely used. Other indices such as number of permanent teeth and age of pubescence have furnished supplementary information. Wherever any of these indices have been correlated with IQ, the resulting coefficients have turned out to be negligible. More of them are positive than negative, as with the other physical variables we have considered, but very few are higher than .20, and most of them fall definitely within the chance range. (See Paterson, 1930.) There seems to be little doubt that physical and mental development proceed at independent rates in the individual. We cannot use one to measure the other.

It has become more and more apparent, however, that the fact that correlations between physical and mental development are low and of little practical significance does *not* mean that physical characteristics are unimportant. The kind of indirect effect mentioned at the beginning of the chapter is something that must always be assessed if we wish to understand a person. Barker *et al.* (1953) have made the most comprehensive analysis of what they call the *somatopsychological* relation between physique and behavior. Because his size, shape, appearance, and strength help to determine the psychological situation in which a person finds himself, by setting limits to what he can do and by serving as stimuli to himself and others, they have far-reaching effects that do not show up in correlation coefficients since they differ from person to person. To understand them we must study the individual, not just his measurements and test scores. There is abundant evidence in the studies reported by Stolz and Stolz (1944), Levy (1929, 1932), Jacobson (1945), and M. C. Jones and Bayley (1950) that various aspects of physique constitute sources of dissatisfaction and anxiety about the self, and of favorable or unfavorable evaluations by others. Physical and mental characteristics are related to one another in unique ways in individual cases.

DISEASES AND PHYSICAL HANDICAPS

The general, common-sense opinion is that physical condition has a marked effect on intellectual functioning. Time after time students explain their inadequate performances on examinations in terms of the cold from which they are suffering or the sleep that they failed to get the night before. Teachers are taught to observe closely the physical defects shown by their pupils and to expect better school work, once these are corrected. How much truth is there behind these beliefs?

Physical Defects and Intelligence

A number of studies have used simple group comparisons, either classifying subjects according to physical conditions and comparing the IQ's of the groups, or classifying them according to IQ and comparing the groups for defects. It has been surprising to find that many kinds of defects show no relationship whatever to intelligence. A number of studies on malnutrition show groups of undernourished children to be fully as bright as those who are well-fed. Defective teeth are just as common among the normal as among the dull. Children with diseased tonsils do not differ intellectually from those with normal tonsils, as Figure 48 strikingly shows.

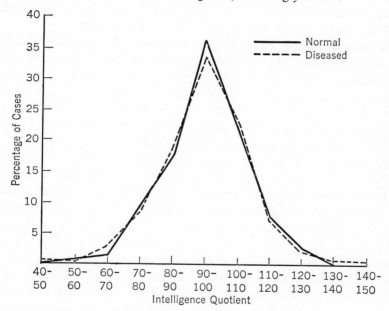

FIGURE 48. Frequency distributions for groups of children with normal and diseased tonsils (Rogers, 1922).

There is some evidence from the early study by Ayres (1909-10) and the surveys by Sandwick (1920) and by Kempf and Collins (1929) that dull, normal, and bright groups of children are differentiated by total number of defects of all sorts, although some other school surveys (Mallory, 1922; Stalnaker and Roller, 1927; Westenberger, 1927) have failed to substantiate these findings. Smillie and Spencer (1926) show that lowered intelligence tends to accompany hookworm infestations. The average IQ for the very heavily infested cases in a hookworm "area" was 76.3, whereas for the children free from the condition it was 90.2.

The studies in which correlations have been computed between the *extent* of the defects and intelligence are more meaningful than the group comparisons. With few exceptions, these all run very low. Condition of teeth, nutritional status, condition of cervical glands and tonsils and adenoids all give correlations of .15 or lower. (See Paterson, 1930, Ch. 6.) Since the data on which they are based have been obtained by many different investigators working in a wide variety of places in England and the United States, we are justified in concluding that the relationship in general is low and insignificant. The one defect for which the comparison of group averages showed most difference, hookworm, gives a correlation of .30[2] with intelligence. This is still too low to warrant the assertion that it is a major factor making for intellectual differences.

The most reasonable explanation of whatever slight relationships have been found between physical defects and intelligence is in terms of the class differences we have already discussed in some detail. The poorer socio-economic groups have a larger number of uncorrected defects; they also average somewhat lower in IQ. The important correlation is the one between socio-economic status and intelligence, and we have already seen how difficult this is to analyse into cause and effect.

One other type of study has been carried out in connection with some physical defects. "Before-and-after" studies, designed to show whether or not the correction of the defect increases the intellectual level, are particularly interesting. It is important that a control group be used in this type of research to make sure that whatever change is noted arises from the elimination of the defect and not from some other unanalyzed factor in the situation. This has been done for malnutrition, for dental caries, and for tonsils. In general, such studies have shown the effect of the treatment on the IQ to be negligible (Paterson, 1930). Feeding a child well and attending to his teeth and tonsils do *not* make him brighter, whatever enthusiastic champions of public health measures may say. The physical benefits must be valued on their own merits.

Illness and Intelligence

Even the common belief that temporary illness depresses examination scores seems to be unwarranted. The most convincing evidence on this point comes from a study made during World War I when it was neces-

[2] Computed by Paterson from Smillie and Spencer's data.

sary to test a group of men who had been recently inoculated for typhoid fever (Paterson, 1930, pp. 204-205). The average score for these 178 men was 67.7 as compared with an average of 67.1 for 7,167 men not recently inoculated. When the average score for those who reported that they were feeling the after-effects was compared with the average for those who were subjectively not affected, the figures turned out to be 67.4 and 67.9.

All the averages are so much alike that it must be concluded that in general, the illness had no effect on the performance. Paralleling these findings are the figures reported by A. J. Smith (1950) showing that there is no consistent relationship between the menstrual cycle and industrial efficiency in women workers. It is still possible that certain *individuals* are so upset by their physical ailments as not to be able to concentrate on the tasks assigned them, and the good psychometrician is always on the lookout for such cases in individual testing. But, on the whole, regardless of what people may think of their own test performances, they are not necessarily handicapped when they do not feel well. Whether they would be able to carry on serious mental work for long periods of time under those circumstances is, of course, another problem.

The question as to whether longer periods of illness might have a depressing effect has also been considered. In a careful comparison between 101 children who had had poliomyelitis a year before the study began and a control group, E. L. Phillips, Berman, and Hanson (1948) found that there had been a 1.5-point drop in IQ for the polio group as compared with a 2-point increase for the controls. While the difference is statistically significant (at the 2 per cent level), it is too small to be of any practical importance. Harris (1950), who obtained ratings of 58 of these same subjects two years after the illness on a variety of personality traits, found that they were indistinguishable from the controls.

Two Kinds of Handicap

There are two kinds of physical condition that do have definite effects on mental functioning. The first includes the illnesses affecting the central nervous system itself. Birth injuries and various abnormal brain conditions have already been mentioned in the chapter on feeble-mindedness. The relationship here is clear-cut. An injured or defective brain does not develop normal intelligence. Encephalitis lethargica is a disease that affects the central nervous system. There is evidence from several studies that the IQ may drop after this disease, and that the decrease is greater in younger than in older children. Dawson and Conn (1926) explain these results in terms of an arrest of mental development at the level the child has reached when the disease strikes. Various unfavorable personality changes also often follow encephalitis, the neurological basis of which is still not understood.

The second group of defects that impair mental development are those which constitute such an extreme sensory handicap that they cut down greatly the stimulation the individual gets from his environment. Blindness and deafness are the most common examples. Contrary to popular belief, deafness, when it is congenital and complete, constitutes more of an intellectual handicap than blindness. It is difficult to make exact comparisons between the IQ's of children with either of these handicaps and the norms based on children in general, since test materials and administration have to be modified. The average IQ of blind children has been estimated at about 90, and there is a greater-than-average proportion of feeble-minded among them. Minor visual defects do not constitute any handicap at all. Some studies even show that bright children have a larger proportion of such defects than dull ones do, perhaps because they read more. Pintner (1928) has shown that the average IQ's of totally-deaf children of different ages fall in the 80's even on his non-language test. Deaf children are still more retarded on educational tests in all subject-matter fields. Minor hearing losses may, in contrast to minor visual handicaps, be related to subnormal IQ's and unsatisfactory school work, according to Sterling and Bell (1930). Since the development of intelligence depends upon a constant interaction between the growing individual and his environment, and since at the higher levels, the amount of information he can embody in concepts determines the complexity of his intellectual achievements, it is natural that relationships of this nature should hold. The person who is completely deaf is most handicapped because of his failure to acquire language at the time most children are learning it. That there can be outstanding individual exceptions to these trends—Helen Keller, for example—goes without saying. Much of the work on the training of the handicapped is directed toward making achievement of this kind possible.

In summarizing all the work on the relationship of physical defects to intelligence, Paterson (1930) stresses the point that nature has thrown strong safeguards around the central nervous system, upon which intellectual functioning depends. Had it been possible for any minor illness or injury to disorganize the thinking processes, it is probable that the human race would not have lasted as long as it has. This viewpoint makes the research findings seem reasonable. The general conclusions are that no physical condition except one that acts on the central nervous system itself has a serious effect on intellectual efficiency, at least for limited periods of time, and that no developmental handicap except one that severely restricts the individual's contact with his environment and his mastery of language has a serious effect on his IQ. In a generation when so many children and adults throughout the world have been subjected to unprecedented physical deprivations and hardships, there is some small degree of comfort in these facts.

PHYSIOLOGICAL FACTORS

With the tremendous increases that recent years have brought in our knowledge of the endocrine glands, blood composition, electrical activity of the cortex, and other biochemical and biophysical processes, it is only natural that considerable research should have been done on the relationships between these factors and mental abilities or personality traits. As yet there is more confusion than order in the results that have been reported, but some general statements can be made.

Blood Composition

A number of studies have attempted to correlate various aspects of blood composition with mental characteristics, and a number of hypotheses have been proposed: (1) that alkalinity is correlated with excitability; (2) that proportions of creatinine, phosphorus, and cholesterol are correlated with specific personality traits such as good-nature and perseverance; (3) that *variability* of blood composition from day to day is related to emotional instability. For each of these ideas there is about as much evidence for as against. One investigator, using a small number of cases, finds a trend in one direction; another with a different small group finds an opposite trend. The study by H. Goldstein (1935) demonstrates one of the reasons for this inconsistency. His subjects were nineteen college men. Each of them was given blood tests twice a week for ten weeks, and was asked to fill out the Bernreuter Personality Inventory and the CAVD intelligence test. The most striking finding was the great variability in the same individual from time to time. In all except one of the variables tested (cholesterol), there was as much variation in the twenty measurements of the same individual as in one measurement for the nineteen individuals at any given time. For instance, the person whose blood was most alkaline one week might be average or even low in alkalinity the next week. The person who was very low in blood sugar on one trial might be fairly high the next time. What this means is that there is little prospect of getting significant correlations between blood concentrations taken at any single time and personality traits. There did seem to be a little evidence for the third hypothesis connecting blood variability with emotional instability, since individual variability from day to day was correlated to the extent of .41 with the neurotic-tendency score on the Bernreuter test. With only nineteen cases, however, it was impossible to be sure that this represented an actual relationship.

Allergies

Another line of research has attempted to relate various mental characteristics to allergies. Here also results are conflicting and inconclusive. A few studies seem to indicate that allergic children are brighter than the average (Balyeat, 1929), but others show no difference (Riess and De Cillis, 1940). Figures suggesting that allergic children are more ascendant, extroverted, and emotionally unstable than non-allergic children are similarly indecisive and contradicted by other figures (Chobat *et al.*, 1939; Riess and De Cillis, 1940; Rogerson, 1943). The best conclusion would seem to be that no one has yet *demonstrated* a relationship between allergies and mental traits. It may exist, however, and if so, it remains for further research to clarify what it is. The psychoanalysts who have been working in the field of psychosomatic medicine feel that they have strong clinical evidence that specific types of allergy develop in specific types of personality.

Hormones

With the growth of physiological knowledge about the endocrine glands and their functions, a lively search for mental correlates of glandular functions has been going on. The fact that suggests the possibility of such correlations is the finding that glandular disturbances are unusually frequent in behavior problem children. Lurie (1938), for instance, found in his analysis of 1,000 problem children that 20 per cent showed some glandular abnormality, and in 10 per cent this appeared to be a causative factor in the child's behavior. The thing that makes it difficult to attribute any specific personality trait to the functioning of a specific gland is that quite different patterns of behavior may arise from the same apparent cause. Inadequate thyroid functioning usually produces a condition of sluggishness, dullness, and lack of energy. But some children with this same physiological defect show instead motor restlessness, destructiveness, and speech disturbances. The most likely explanation is that the behavior disorders are a *reaction or adjustment* on the child's part to the way he feels and his recognition of the fact that he is different from his fellows. They are thus indirectly rather than directly connected with the glandular disturbances. Since these patterns of adjustment are highly individual matters depending upon everything else in the person's experience, we would not expect to find general correlations between physiological and personality variables.

The relationship of sex-hormone production to various aspects of masculinity and femininity has also been a research topic of some interest. In general, as Beach (1948) has pointed out, the higher a species is in the evolutionary scale the more its sex behavior is determined by social factors and learning rather than by hormonal influence directly. However, there have been a few studies that suggested that some correlation between endocrine and personality measurements persist in human subjects. Sollenberger (1940) reported some relationships between the urinary excretion of male sex hormone and the interests and attitudes of adolescent boys. Stone and Barker (1939) showed that premenarcheal and postmenarcheal girls differed significantly in their interests. In both these studies, since the subjects were adolescents, the interest differences might have occurred, of course, as a result of individuals' awareness of their own maturing, rather than as a direct consequence of the presence of sex hormones in the blood. It is impossible to separate the physiological from the *somatopsychological* effects. It seems less possible to account in this way, however, for the correlation of .58 that Levy (1953) obtained between maternal behavior and duration of menstrual flow for 72 women whom he interviewed. Just how much relationship there is between sex hormone concentration and personality is still an open question.

The one measurement of glandular functioning for which some definite relationship to mental ability is at least a possibility is basal metabolism. This is a measure of oxygen consumption in the body, which depends upon the functioning of the thyroid gland. When basal metabolism is low, it is standard medical practice to use thyroid medication. It has, of course, been known for a long time that an extreme degree of thyroid deficiency results in the type of feeble-mindedness called cretinism. The question is whether less extreme deficiency in persons falling within the average range carries some mental deficiency along with it. The strongest evidence for such a relationship comes from two studies by Hinton (1936, 1939). He obtained under very carefully controlled conditions the basal metabolic rates for 200 orphanage and private-school children in the Chicago area. He then gave each one a Binet test and an Arthur performance test to get both a verbal and a non-verbal index of intelligence. For the total group, aged six to fifteen, the correlations were as follows:

Binet IQ vs	BMR	.71
Arthur IQ vs	BMR	.74

Analysis of the figures by separate groups showed coefficients in the .70's for all groups from six through eleven. Above that age they were considerably smaller. Hinton interpreted this to mean that the relationship holds most strongly during the childhood years of growth and is upset by the metabolic changes associated with adolescence. Shock and Jones (1939), in their careful analysis of the measurements accumulated in the California adolescent study, did not find a significant relationship. None of the physiological variables they tested, basal metabolic rate, blood pressure, pulse rate, and vital capacity, were correlated significantly with mental ages on the Terman Group Test. These findings are not necessarily in conflict with Hinton's, since the ages of all the California subjects were within the adolescent range at which Hinton indicates that the relationship begins to break down. It would be very desirable to have supplementary research checking on the Hinton results with other subjects in other places since the point is an important one. In the desert of stunted vegetation that the low correlations between physical and mental traits suggest, these r's of .70 and above stand out like landmarks. Although a considerable period of time has passed since Hinton's study was reported, there seems to have been no repetition of the work which would support or refute the conclusions.

Nutrition

One of the most flourishing fields for research since World War II has been nutrition. The possibility of improving intelligence or personality by enriching the diet in one way or another is a very appealing one. The largest of the studies investigating the effects of dietary *deficiencies* was carried on during the war years by Keys *et al.*, and has been reported in detail in their book *The Biology of Human Starvation* (1950). The 36 young men who underwent a radical decrease in food intake over a period of six months were subjected to all sorts of tests and examinations. In general, the result seemed to substantiate those obtained previously in showing that mental *abilities* changed very little. Drive and motivation, however, were markedly decreased, and marked neurotic characteristics appeared both in the subjects' behavior and in their responses to the MMPI test (Schiele and Brozek, 1948). It is interesting to note that neurotic manifestations differed from person to person and that there were marked individual differences in the capacity to withstand this stress.

There is some possibility that in younger children dietary deficiencies may impair mental functioning as well as personality, and that proper treatment may improve it. Examined superficially, results with regard to the B-complex vitamins seem to be conflicting. Guetzkow and Brozek (1946) and O'Shea *et al.* (1942), present some evidence that deficiencies do not impair intelligence nor supplementation improve it. R. F. Harrell (1947), on the other hand, in an unusually well-controlled study of 60 paired groups of orphanage children, showed that adding extra thiamin to the diet produced significant changes in intelligence test scores and in performance on tests of learning and visual acuity. Bernhardt *et al.* (1948), applying similar treatment to eleven-year-old children in Toronto, where identical twins were used as experimental subjects and controls, did not find any significant differences that could be attributed to the thiamin. Contradictory as they seem, taken as a whole these results make sense. The absence of any effect in the first two studies is explainable on the grounds that they used *adult* subjects. As we have noted previously, mental ability, once fully matured, is quite resistant to change. The difference between the two studies on children can be understood if we assume that the diet of Harrell's orphanage group was somewhat deficient at the beginning, whereas the Toronto children, living in their own homes, were probably well-nourished enough so that the extra thiamin was neither needed nor utilized. Most of the studies of IQ change in children following upon any sort of environmental change indicate that it is easier to produce IQ increases by improving unsatisfactory surroundings than by making an already good situation even better. This point will be considered in more detail in the next chapter.

Perhaps the most controversial of the reasearch problems has been the attempt to improve the intelligence of feeble-minded children by giving large doses of glutamic acid. This is an amino acid which it was thought might be used by the brain in the synthesis of acetylcholine, a chemical that plays an important part in nerve action (Gadson, 1951). The earlier studies, especially those by Zimmerman *et al.* (1948, 1951), were so loosely designed that their results could not be said to prove anything. The two investigations that were well planned and included adequate control groups for comparison purposes report results that seem to be in flat contradiction. Ellson *et al.* (1950) concluded from their comparison of two matched groups of 30 feeble-minded subjects that there was no significant difference between those who received glutamic acid therapy and those who did not. Albert *et al.* (1951), who also treated low-IQ school children, alternating four-month glutamic acid periods with four-month periods in which a placebo was given so as to use the group as its own control, found differences in IQ increase significant at the .001 level between treatment and control periods. They account for the difference between their findings and those of Ellson *et al.* on the grounds that they used glutamic acid itself, whereas sodium glutamate was the medication used in the Ellson study. There may be some biochemical reason why the glutamic acid cannot be utilized when administered as a salt. In any case, changes reported by *all* investigators so far are small, less than 5 IQ points, on the average. There is no present prospect of making feeble-minded children normal by means of this treatment. Observations of the behavorial changes that accompany the IQ increases suggest that the effect may be emotional and motivational rather than intellectual. By making the child more alert and active, glutamic acid may enable him to make better use of the intelligence he has.

Electroencephalograms (EEG)

Another group of investigators has been attempting to establish a relationship between electroencephalograms or "brain waves" and mental traits. Work on the recording and analysis of the electrical potentials generated in the brain has proceeded at a rapid pace. Much of the analysis has used what is called "alpha activity" as a standard. Alpha waves are those with a frequency of about ten per second which seem to characterize normal children and adults in a relaxed waking state. It has been established by Travis and Gottlober (1936, 1937) that a person's brain waves do show individuality, can be identified with a high degree of agreement by different judges, and are consistent from day to day. Whether these individual differences in EEG are correlated with psychological traits of any sort, however, is less certain. Kreezer (1940) obtained correlations in the .30's between Alpha Index and mental age for Mongolian idiots whose mental ages ranged from 1.5 to 7.5 years. Since in these cases brain damage might produce both the abnormal EEG's and the feeble-mindedness, it is impossible to generalize from this special group to non-pathological cases. In a similar study in which the subjects were 46 familial mental defectives with no obvious physical pathology, Kreezer and Smith (1950) found that there was some correlation between Alpha Frequency and mental age, but it was too low for statistical significance. Knott, Friedman, and Bardsley (1942) report a correlation of .50 between Alpha Frequency and IQ for 48 eight-year-old children, a coefficient which is statistically above the chance level. For twelve-year-olds, however, the correlation was only .12. The decrease here might be due to adolescent changes which upset the relationship. Since this is the only evidence so far for a correlation between EEG and intelligence in normal children, we must suspend judgment on the point until more data are available. One study of adult aircrew candidates (Shagass, 1946) demonstrates fairly conclusively that Alpha Frequency is not correlated with intelligence in adults. In the area of personality characteristics, there are reports from various clinics and schools showing that a large proportion of behavior problem children have abnormal brain waves, many of them of an epileptiform nature. Attempts to correlate alpha activity with scores on personality inventories (Henry and Knott, 1941) have so far not met with success. Saul, Davis, and Davis (1949) have reported some very striking relationships between the EEG patterns of 136 adult patients and their predominant personality characteristics as they became apparent during psychoanalysis. (It is in line with all the evidence as to the persistence and distinctiveness of these EEG "brainprints" that they did not change during psychotherapy.) The very passive individuals had high Alpha Indices. Women with strong masculine trends or maternal drives had low Alpha Indices. Frustrated, demanding, hostile, aggressive women had mixed or irregular records. These findings are reported in a descriptive way that makes any check on the statistical significance of the relationships impossible, but this method of searching for personality characteristics that patients with a certain type of EEG have in common appears promising.

Great strides have been made in electroencephalographic work since World War II through the use of new methods of analyzing the record of electrical activity in the brain into its components (W. G. Walter, 1953). Much of this work has been designed to throw light on brain functioning in general, but some attention has also been paid to the relationship of individual patterns to personality. In addition to types based on the predominance of the three principal types of waves—alpha, delta, and theta—Walter and his co-workers have set up distinctions based on the way in which a person's EEG record *changes* with stimulation. It is a familiar fact that alpha activity which is elicited from electrodes at the back of the head when the eyes are closed usually disappears when the eyes are opened, or when the person is asked to make some mental effort. But some individuals, according to Walter, show no alpha rhythm at any time. These turn out to be persons who think by means of visual imagery. The opposite type, in which alpha rhythms persist even when the eyes are open, are those who tend toward auditory or kinesthetic rather than visual perceptions. Here again the detailed evidence is not presented, and much of the discussion is speculative, but the ideas are extremely interesting. Are we meeting Lowenfeld's *visual* and *haptic* types in a new setting? (See Chapter 9.)

Autonomic Balance

Another important line of research has been the attempt to measure the functioning of the autonomic nervous system as a whole rather than isolated physiological variables. Using indices that appeared promising from previous work, Wenger (1942) put together five measurements that would evaluate *autonomic balance*, or the extent to which sympathetic or parasympathetic reactions predominate in a person's makeup. He showed that such scores were stable from day to day and that they distributed themselves in something like a normal distribution. What evidence is there that they are related to psychological characteristics? In a study of 87 children, aged six to thirteen, Wenger (1947) picked out the ten with extreme sympathetic scores, and contrasted them with the ten obtaining the extreme parasympathetic scores. One would expect the S group to be more reactive, excitable, unstable, and inhibited, the P group calmer, better nourished, and more phlegmatic. Using a number of indices of personality characteristics—ratings, personality test scores of the parents, and the like—Wenger made specific predictions with regard to the differences between his two groups. The differences turned out to be in the predicted direction for most of them, but only a few were of clear statistical significance using these small numbers. Inspection of the distributions indicated that it was only at the extremes that personality differences could be anticipated. For the bulk of the subjects with scores near the middle of the sympathetic-parasympathetic distribution, no predictions could be made. In a later large-scale study of Army Air Force men, Wenger (1948) used a number of methods for assessing the meaning in personality terms of scores for autonomic balance. One comparison was made in order to check the hypothesis that men with scores toward the sympathetic pole would show a tendency to become anxious in stress situations. Groups of men who had been returned from duty suffering from either operational fatigue or outright neurosis were compared with preflight cadets. As the hypothesis would have led one to predict, these anxious airmen scored significantly higher in sympathetic activity. The fact that other returnees did not differ from the cadets seemed to indicate that it was not simply exposure to combat that produced the difference. Another type of what might be called validation, in which autonomic balance scores were correlated with scores on personality inventories, was less successful. Some of the correlations were statistically significant, but they were all low. This state of affairs might reflect the inadequacy of the personality tests rather than the inadequacy of the physiological measure, but the doubt remains. As things stand, the nature of the relationship between autonomic balance and temperament is still obscure.

Patterns of Physiological Response

More recently, it has begun to look as though the important differences may be related to *patterns* of response rather than responsiveness as a whole. Lacey (1950) and Lacey and Van Lehn (1952) have demonstrated that such individual patterns exist, and that they are consistent from one occasion to another. For example, when exposed to a mild stress, one person may show an increase in systolic but not in diastolic blood pressure. For another person, just the opposite may be true. Another individual may show no blood pressure changes at all but a marked increase in heart rate. Terry (1953) made a factor analysis of twenty-two autonomic measures obtained from 85 male college students under rest and under mild stress conditions. There seemed to be evidence for three separate autonomic factors: conductance, heart period, and blood pressure.

The investigation of *patterns* of physiological response that are consistent for the individual is one of the most promising current research undertakings. Outstanding work in this area is being done by R. J. Williams, a biochemist who has been making an eloquent case for simultaneous studies of the individual from all possible viewpoints. (*The Human Frontier*, 1946; *Free and Unequal*, 1953.) Research done by Williams and his colleagues has already shown that there are metabolic patterns that are distinctive for individuals. These are illustrated in Figure 49. Individual A is unusually sensitive to potassium chloride, and shows a predominantly alkaline urinary reaction. Individual B, on the other hand, is most sensitive to creatinine, and shows an acid urinary reaction. Some of the difference persists even when the subjects are placed on exactly the same diet.

Research such as Lacey's on autonomic patterns and Williams' on metabolic patterns may point the way to a new utilization of physiological measures for the understanding of psychological differences. They will require methods of statistical analysis different from those we have been accustomed to use. Simple correlation procedures are not applicable. Indeed there is a possibility that the generally low level of correlations that have been obtained in this area may reflect our failure to handle the data correctly rather than an absence of significant relationships. Much more

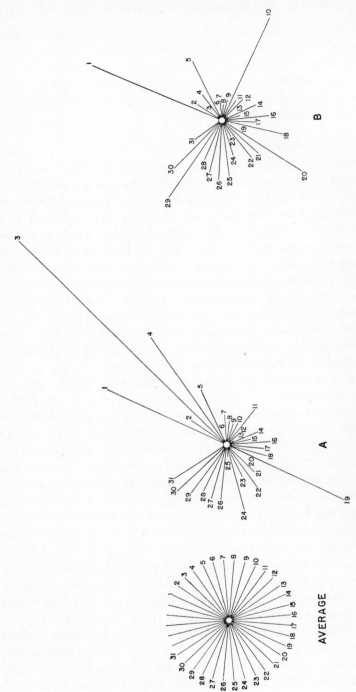

FIGURE 49. Physiological patterns of two different persons as compared with a hypothetical "average" person. Numbers 1-5 represent taste sensitivity to different substances. Numbers 6-16 represent salivary constituents. Numbers 18-31 represent urinary constituents (Williams, 1951).

work must be done, however, before we can be sure just how significant this work on physiological patterns of response is.

PHYSIQUE AND TEMPERAMENT

Related to the foregoing kinds of research but branching off in a somewhat different direction is the age-old question as to whether people with different types of physique have different types of constitution carrying along with them distinctly different temperaments. It is a very important question because of its relationship to many areas of social planning. If there are distinctly different temperaments, then, as Sheldon has so aptly pointed out, to house, clothe, feed, and educate them all the same way is sure to result in widespread maladjustment. Medical research has shown that there are important constitutional factors in susceptibility to various diseases. The long-thin types are more likely to get tuberculosis; the short-thick types develop high blood pressure and its attendant difficulties more easily. The question is, "Are there psychological differences of any kind which consistently accompany differences in physical type?"

The work of Kretschmer (1925) was very important in stimulating discussion and research on the problem. He was interested primarily in the predispositions to psychoses of different kinds. A large proportion of the patients we find in our mental hospitals are suffering from either manic-depressive psychosis, which is a cyclical condition characterized by extreme mood swings from excitement to depression, or schizophrenia, which is characterized by a withdrawal from reality, a cutting oneself off from the world outside. It is natural that a hypothesis should have developed that the manic-depressives are the extroverted, emotionally responsive people who have eventually let these emotions run away with them completely, whereas the schizophrenics are the introverted, seclusive, lonely individuals who finally decide to live completely within themselves. Any observer of actual patients in a clinic or hospital knows that the differentiation is far less clear-cut than this explanation implies, but it seems to be true in a general way, and it has formed the basis for much thinking about predisposing factors in psychotic breakdowns. Kretschmer's hypothesis was that the short-thick types of person whom he called *pyknics* are the ones with the extroverted personalities predisposing them to manic-depressive psychosis, whereas the long-thin types that he called *asthenic* or *leptosome* tend to be introverted and thus predisposed toward schizophrenia. He also postulated an *athletic* type with measurements intermediate between those of the pyknics and the leptosomes, and a *dysplastic* or mixed type in which the different parts of the body do not match. Kretschmer compiled data on over 4000 abnormal cases and found interesting differentiations as shown in the following comparisons:

BODY TYPE	SCHIZOPHRENIC	MANIC-DEPRESSIVE
Pyknic and mixed pyknic	12.8%	66.7%
Leptosome and athletic	66.0	23.6
Dysplastic	11.3	0.4
Unclassifiable	9.9	9.3

There is apparent a strong tendency for manic-depressives to be pyknic in physique and for schizophrenics to be leptosome or athletic. Dysplasia is most likely to be associated with schizophrenia.

American investigations carried on by Wertheimer and Hesketh (1926) and by Burchard (1936) substantiated the general trend of the Kretschmer results. There is one factor in all this work, however, that is very difficult to control, namely, the *age* of the subjects. Schizophrenia is characteristically a mental disease of youth. The average manic-depressive is about ten years older than the average schizophrenic. Since most people become heavier as they grow older, it is natural that a group of people in their thirties should appear more pyknic than a group in their twenties. Garvey (1933), who matched his manic-depressive and schizophrenic patients by age, found almost complete overlapping in physical measurements for the two groups. Burchard (1936) found that at all ages there was some difference in body index between manic-depressives and schizophrenes, but it was much less pronounced than when age was not controlled. We are left then in some doubt as to the relative importance of constitutional and age factors in the physical differences that undoubtedly exist between the two abnormal groups.

Eysenck (1947, p. 85) has pointed out some other sources of confusion in the evidence and called attention to the fact that various subgroups of schizophrenics differ from one another in physique almost as much as schizophrenics differ from manic-depressives. His own work, reported in the same volume, showed that anxious, inhibited *neurotics* tended to be leptosomic, whereas hysterical, impulsive neurotics were closer to the pyknic end of the distribution. Schizophrenics did not differ from manic-depressives except with regard to chest *depth*, the front-to-back measurement. This is an interesting suggestion which has not yet been corroborated by other research.

If any general conclusions are to be drawn, work on abnormal cases must of course be supplemented by work on persons within the normal personality range. Klineberg, Asch, and Block (1934) selected from a large group of male college students a group of 56 whose physical measurements combined into a Pignet Index [3] classified them as "pure" pyknics and 59 who could be called "pure" leptosomes. They gave them a number of psychological tests of intelligence, special abilities, and emotional adjustment. The two groups, which differed so sharply in physique, gave almost identical distributions for all the psychological traits. They were not differentiated mentally in any way.

Most psychologists had decided that the relationship between constitutional type and temperament was of no particular importance, within the normal range, at least, when Sheldon *et al.* (1940, 1942, 1949) came out with an important new method and some challenging results. Sheldon's technique is to rate accurately the degree to which an individual shows each of three main *components* of physique and each of three main components of temperament. To shift the method from *types* to *components* may not seem to involve a very important change, but it serves to distribute people along a sort of three-way continuum instead of forcing them into a small number of classes. The physical components were chosen after careful inspection of 4,000 photographs of nude males taken under carefully controlled conditions. The ratings can now be made with complete objectivity from measurements of five different regions of the body in these photographs. Sheldon *et al.* (1940) furnish norms to which these measurements can be referred.

The *temperament* components were chosen after an analysis of correlations between ratings of separate traits made on the basis of a series of twenty interviews with each individual. There appeared to be three and only three clusters of these basic traits. The standard procedure for getting the temperament ratings now that the scales have been drawn up is to rate the individual for each separate trait on each scale, and then get the composite rating for each of the three, using the norms given in the Sheldon and Stevens book (1942). The three components of physique and their temperamental counterparts are as follows:

PHYSIQUE	TEMPERAMENT
Endomorphy—predominance of soft roundness in the body	*Viscerotonia*—predominance of relaxation and friendly, pleasure-loving traits
Mesomorphy—predominance of muscle, bone, and connective tissue	*Somatotonia*—predominance of vigorous, physical activity, adventurousness, and dominance
Ectomorphy—predominance of linearity and fragility	*Cerebrotonia*—predominance of intellectual, introverted trends

[3] Pignet Index = Height − (weight + chest circumference).

Each individual is rated from 1 to 7 on each of the three components and thus assigned a three-number combination. A great many such combinations are possible. Thus a 6 1 2 is slightly fatter and more massive than a 5 2 2, since the figures representing the first component differ by one step. A 3 2 5 and a 1 3 5 are both predominantly ectomorphic, but the latter is more muscular than the former.

In the third volume (Sheldon, 1949), devoted primarily to biographical studies of 200 delinquent boys, Sheldon sets up a third set of related dimensions each of which represents a pathological *deficiency* in one of the three basic components. He uses the suffix "-penia" to characterize these negative traits: cerebropenia, visceropenia, and somatopenia. Their importance in the whole system as now formulated is that they are the *psychiatric* variables underlying different abnormalities. For example, the person with a high degree of cerebropenia might be expected to show delinquent or manic-depressive tendencies, since he would *lack* the control and inhibition that ordinarily keep such tendencies in check. The somatopenic individual, on the other hand, would be susceptible to hebephrenia, because he lacked the drive and energy necessary to carry on a normal life. The typical visceropenic would be a paranoid because of his lack of the soft, relaxed qualities.

The crucial question with regard to these three *sets* of variables is the extent to which they are related to one another. So far as normal individuals are concerned, Sheldon and Stevens (1942) present two sorts of evidence. The first consists of some unusually high correlations between temperament and physique ratings for 200 young males. They are as follows:

Viscerotonia vs. endomorphy	$r = .79$
Somatotonia vs. mesomorphy	$r = .82$
Cerebrotonia vs. ectomorphy	$r = .83$

The second kind of evidence, upon which the authors place more weight, comes from case studies of individuals, each of whom was rated for adjustment and normality. These studies seem to indicate that there is a much larger proportion of good adjustment and satisfactory achievement in cases where the somatotype and temperament agree than in cases where they differ markedly. In other words, if you are a 4 2 5 and are satisfied to be an easy-going intellectual, you will probably get along all right. If you insist on trying to be an athlete or an Arctic explorer, maladjustment is the inevitable outcome.

Validation of the hypotheses with regard to psychiatric conditions was attempted at Elgin State Hospital and reported by Wittman *et al.* (1948) and by Sheldon (1949). Wittman rated the case histories of 167 male patients on three main types of abnormal reaction which it was thought would correspond to the three "-penias" described above—affective (manic-depressive), paranoid, and heboid (hebephrenic) reactions. Sheldon, working independently, somatotyped the subjects and made a temperament rating for each based on his behavior in the somatotyping situation. The correlations are as shown in Tables 50 and 51. It is the *negative* correlations that have the most direct bearing on the hypotheses being tested, since *lack* of the component is assumed to be at the root of the difficulty. In general, they support the theory, although there are a number of exceptions. Patients with affective psychoses (manic-depressive) do seem to lack ectomorphy and cerebrotonia. Hebephrenics do seem to lack mesomorphy and somatotonia. The paranoid component does not, however, show the expected negative relationship to endomorphy and viscerotonia. Sheldon feels that some modification of the original scheme is necessary, but that on the whole it is substantiated by the correlations.

TABLE 50.

Correlations Between Psychiatric Reaction Type Ratings and Somatotype
(Wittman, Sheldon, and Katz, 1948)

	AFFECTIVE	PARANOID	HEBOID
Endomorphy	.509	—.060	—.302
Mesomorphy	.468	.536	—.612
Ectomorphy	—.638	—.283	.542

TABLE 51.

*Correlations Between Psychiatric Reaction Type Ratings
and Temperament Ratings*
(Wittman, Sheldon, and Katz, 1948)

	AFFECTIVE	PARANOID	HEBOID
Viscerotonia	.733	.197	—.565
Somatotonia	.165	.688	—.456
Cerebrotonia	—.705	—.554	.808

To what extent can we accept the reported correlations in all these studies as evidence for the postulated close relationship between physique and temperament? In the psychiatric study by Wittman *et al.* (1948) care was taken to evaluate physique and diagnostic type *independently*, and the correlations were computed by a third worker who had seen neither the patients nor the case histories. Thus these correlations are probably free from the effects of initial bias. But this cannot be said for the evaluations of normal subjects. The psychologists who rated them on temperamental qualities were very familiar with the system of classifying physiques. It is almost an axiom in applied psychology that raters tend to see in people what they are prepared to see. Sheldon and Stevens point out that all possible precautions were taken to guard against this error. Temperament ratings were made before any physical measurements were taken. However, they admit that an investigator who has learned to think of physiques in such terms as these inevitably becomes aware of the somatotype as he talks with the subject. They state that their knowledge of the error they were likely to make constituted a defense against it. They "looked for it suspiciously behind every bush in the psychological garden."

When we examine studies by other workers using the Sheldon variables, we find that significant correlations (though often much lower than those Sheldon reported) have usually been obtained when any sort of *ratings* were used as personality measures (Seltzer *et al.* 1948; Glueck and Glueck, 1950; Hanley, 1951; R. N. Sanford, 1953; Child, 1950). But when either psychological tests or objective measurements of characteristic psychological reactions have been used, few if any significant correlations have appeared (Child and Sheldon, 1941; Fiske, 1944; H. C. Smith, 1949; Janoff *et al.*, 1950). The one apparent exception to this rule, Coffin's study (1944) in which fairly high correlations were reported between values, as measured by the Allport-Vernon scale, and physique ratings, cannot be given much weight, since in this case the somatotype figures were based on self-ratings, not measurements, and the same self-concepts could have affected both these ratings and the answers to the Allport-Vernon questions. Thus after all the work that has been done so far in constitutional psychology as defined by Sheldon, the evidence for the validity of the basic premises is still lacking. Most psychologists who have examined all the evidence are inclined to think that there is at least a limited relationship between introverted characteristics and tall-thin body build, but it is hardly possible to say more than this. To attempt to judge personality from physical appearance may involve one in serious errors.

The idea has been gaining ground among research workers in various places that another set of dimensions, somewhat different from the Kretschmer-Sheldon system, might help to show up the important relationships more clearly. There has always been controversy among constitutional typologists as to whether there are really three main types or only two. The correlations between separate measurements or separate temperamental traits shown in Sheldon's tables raise this same question. They show that his three components are not actually *independent* of one another. The fact that endomorphy, mesomorphy, and ectomorphy correlate *negatively* with one another does not prove that they are independent. Independence produces zero, not negative *r*'s. The question naturally arises: "Would it not be possible to describe these same relationships in terms of two independent dimensions rather than three which are correlated?" [4]

Ekman (1951) has suggested a simple workable scheme for reducing the Sheldon system to two dimensions. If we think of extreme ectomorphy as simply the *absence* of either endomorphic or mesomorphic trends, we can describe an individual physique by means of two digits rather than three. By specifying only a person's endomorphy and mesomorphy ratings, we give all the information which Sheldon's three-digit label contains.

Rather than to remodel the Sheldon system, others have preferred to start out with measurements of individuals and attempt to establish the basic dimensions by factor analysis. A number of such studies have been carried out in England, the largest of them based on measurements obtained from 2,400 RAF men (Burt, 1947). All of the studies agree remarkably well in locating one general factor of *body size* that accounts for about 50 per cent of the variance in the measurements, and a second bi-polar *shape* factor representing length vs. breadth. Various smaller factors, such as limb length vs. trunk length or bony breadth vs. fatty breadth, can also be distinguished, but their effects on the correlations between measurements are not very great. Eysenck (1947) has presented some evidence that body size is negatively related to general personality weakness, whereas the length vs. breadth dimension correlates significantly with introversion-extroversion. All correlations are too low to be of much value in diagnostic work. There have been a number of other factor analyses of physical measurements, but no common pattern emerges from them. It is interesting that both Sills (1950) and Heath (1952) obtained factors that seem to correspond to the two dimensions Ekman has proposed. Sills came out with separate factors for endomorphy and mesomorphy, both showing fairly high negative correlations with ectomorphy. Heath's two second-order factors seemed to represent the growth of fatty tissue and the de-

---

[4] Lubin (1950) has shown that some of the combinations of correlations between Sheldon's temperamental traits are not just an inefficient way of describing the relationship but downright *impossible*. If we use accepted partial correlation methods and try to evaluate the relationship between two of these traits with the third held constant, we come out with an *r* larger than 1.00. Thus Lubin concludes that there must be computational errors in Sheldon's table.

velopment of bones. Howells (1952), who based his factor analysis on correlations between persons rather than between measurements, came out with a factor he calls *mass*, which is perhaps identifiable with the *body-size* factor discussed above, and two others that seemed to represent top-heaviness vs. bottom-heaviness and trunk-face development vs. limb development. It is probably useless to seek for a common structure in these studies based on different kinds of subjects and different specific measurements. The last word on dimensions of physique has not yet been said.

The time may be ripe for someone to incorporate all the information we now have in some classification of physiques that will enable us to make a clearer analysis of the constitutional basis of personality. It is conceivable that a system could be worked out for evaluating size, length vs. breadth, and the relative contributions of fat and muscle. Enough work has been done to suggest that these three characteristics may be related, at least in some degree, to personality traits. Just how close the relationship is and how it comes into existence are questions that we cannot at present answer.

SUMMARY

It has been conclusively demonstrated that all the relationships between anatomical characteristics, such as height, body shape, and head size, and intelligence, although *positive*, are so low as to be of no practical value whatever in judging people. Growth studies have demonstrated that physiological or anatomical age is unrelated to mental age. Physical handicaps, such as adenoids, dental caries, and malnutrition, apparently do not lower children's intelligence, and correcting them does not make the children brighter. Similarly, illness does not depress intelligence-test scores. With the exception of diseases such as encephalitis, which attack the central nervous system itself, and extreme sensory handicaps, such as total deafness, which decrease greatly the amount of stimulation the individual receives from the outside world, there is very little connection between physical conditions of any sort and intelligence.

The research on the relationships of physiological factors, such as blood composition, allergies, basal metabolism, electroencephalograms, and autonomic functioning, to intelligence and personality traits has been suggestive but not conclusive.

Work on the relationship of total body type to psychological variables has tended to show that short-thick physiques predominate among manic-depressive patients and tall-thin physiques among schizophrenics. Since, however, there is a difference in the age at which these two types of psychosis manifest themselves, at least some of the difference in weight can be accounted for on this basis. Sheldon has worked out a very exact method of rating physiques on each of three components and thus obtaining a more accurate index of body type than has been available heretofore. Whether these indices are related to temperament is still a doubtful issue. When temperament is *rated* by constitutional psychologists, the relationship appears to be fairly close. When personality tests have been used, correlations so far have not been very high. Some relationship of both physique and temperament ratings to psychiatric diagnosis has been demonstrated. Factor analysis has identified a general body-size factor in addition to the length vs. breadth factor around which most of the constitutional research has centered.

CHAPTER 17

The Influence of the Environment
On Individual Psychological Traits

THE NATURE OF THE PROBLEM

MANY AND HEATED have been the arguments as to whether it is heredity or environment, nature or nurture, that makes men what they are. It is an issue on which almost everybody seems to have a strong opinion. Pastore (1949b) has suggested, on the basis of an analysis of the writings of 24 psychologists and sociologists, that hereditarian and environmentalist attitudes are tied in with generally conservative or generally liberal views on a variety of other issues. Environmentalists tend to be optimistic about human nature and like to think that under favorable circumstances any individual is almost infinitely improvable. Hereditarians tend to be pessimistic about the prospect that changed conditions will make much difference in the particular individuals with whom we are surrounded here and now and to stress the importance of producing better human material.

The time has come, however, for all of us to break away if we can from what we like to think and examine the evidence from a neutral position. If we say heredity *or* environment, nature *versus* nurture, we have already misstated the question. With the exception of a few simple physical characteristics, such as eye color, that depend upon genetic endowment alone, all human traits in which we are interested are produced through an interaction of heredity and environmental influences. From plant and animal research there has come abundant evidence of the same sort of interaction. In corn, for instance, the outer tissue of the grain, the *pericarp*, shows variations in color. A certain dominant gene is known to produce red pericarp. This does not happen, however, unless the kernels are exposed to sunlight while they are maturing. If the husk were not removed at the proper time in the ear's development, we would never know that the genetic potentialities for red coloring were there. Canaries sing in their characteristic fashion because of the way their throats and nervous systems are built. But when Metfessel (1940) exposed these birds in their soundproof cages to vibrato tones of a certain frequency, the sounds they learned to make resembled this pitch more than the one that is natural to the species. Birds put into cages with one another became more *alike* in their songs than were those reared alone. Thus a type of behavior that without question has an hereditary basis has been shown to be susceptible to considerable modification as systematic changes in the environment are made.

Still another example from animal research is the work which has been done on hoarding behavior in rats (Morgan, 1947). This seems to be a spontaneously occurring type of behavior that does not have to be learned. Adult rats placed in a situation where food pellets are available will hoard from five to twenty pellets a day in their home cages, eating only one or two. But there are a number of changes in environmental conditions that affect this behavior. Hoarding is increased by low temperatures, food deprivation, and frustration. It is decreased by placing lights in the home cage. Rats prefer the dark. Again we see that though the general pattern of behavior is determined by heredity, it is quite sensitive to environmental changes.

It is the sort of questions that Metfessel asked of his canaries and Morgan of his rats that we need to be concerned about with human beings. The most usable knowledge we can have with regard to *any* psychological characteristic is not the relative proportions of heredity and environment in its make-up, but how amenable it is to change, and under what circumstances we can expect changes to occur. One of the commonest misconceptions here is the idea that only the innate characteristics are fixed and unchangeable, and that environmentally produced traits are modifiable at will. Neither part of the generalization is true. Hereditary tendencies can often be strikingly modified. Environmentally produced traits are often so firmly fixed that it is impossible to shake them. We all know of persons with hereditary susceptibility to tuberculosis who have built up strong vigorous bodies in which the disease never gets a foothold. On the other hand, much work with college entrance tests has shown us that a freshman who is unusually weak in vocabulary will probably carry some degree of verbal disability throughout his adult years, even if it is plain that the deficiency grew out of an educational handicap during childhood rather than out of any innate lack of verbal intelligence. When our task is to decide whether a given individual belongs in college, whether a young man has enough mechanical aptitude to make good in an army training program for mechanics, or whether a person's interests are like those of scientists or of business men, we need not consider the heredity-environment issue at all. We have evidence as to the *permanence* of the traits in question, and that is all we need. We have come to realize that *all* traits, however they originate, are somehow built into the individual's nervous system. Since human beings show a considerable capacity for learning, most of these traits are subject to modification, but *both* heredity and previous experience set limits to its nature and amount. It is true that for long-range social planning over many generations we need to know as much as possible about the hereditary bases of important variables such as intelligence and emotional stability. There are a few practical problems such as those relating to the adoption of children for which direct information about the effects of heredity can be useful. But specific data about the development of children in good foster homes has met this need fairly well.

Loevinger (1943) has shown that the attempt which a number of psychologists have made to determine what *proportion* of the variance in some trait, intelligence for example, is due to heredity rests on unsatisfactory mathematical foundations. It is best that we classify this problem with the unanswerable questions and turn our attention to those for which answers are attainable. In this chapter we shall consider primarily the evidence that bears on two broad questions: (1) *How much* difference can we expect a change of environment to make in the kinds of traits that have interested psychologists, particularly intelligence and personality characteristics? (2) *Which* environmental conditions are the ones that really count most heavily in psychological development? In the following chapter we shall bring together research findings that show that hereditary differences underlie the manifold individual differences we observe in people. There is no incompatibility in these bodies of knowledge, no conflict between the conclusions. The heredity-environment *controversy* is an artifact.

Several types of investigation have contributed to our knowledge of environmental effects. The first and by far the most meaningful kind of evidence has come from the careful study of identical twins reared in different kinds of environments. Unfortunately, such cases are rare and not always available for complete investigation when they do occur, so that it has been necessary to devise other methods to supplement this one. In the second main type of research, groups are compared that, *on the average,* have the same hereditary potentialities but that differ in the kind of environmental influences to which they have been exposed. The studies of foster children come under this heading. In the third kind of study, a group is measured *before and after* being subjected to a certain kind of environmental influence. The change in this group is compared with the change in a control group initially equated with it not on the basis of any hereditary potentialities but simply on initial scores for the traits to be measured. The effects of schooling, nutrition, and various other things have been explored in this way. Besides the results of these three types of study designed to evaluate environmental effects directly, we now have at our disposal a considerable body of information growing out of work on other problems—race and social-class differences, follow-up studies of the feeble-minded, evaluations of educational procedures—which can be scrutinized for evidence on the general problem of the nature of environmental effects.

In discussing the question with which this chapter is concerned, however, it is more convenient to organize the material around the type of *persons* who have been used as subjects than to organize it around specific type of research design. We turn first to the work on identical twins.

IDENTICAL TWIN STUDIES

In order to appreciate the crucial importance of the research in which identical twins have been used as subjects, we must remember that a pair of such twins presents us with the *only* kind of opportunity we ever have to study two individuals whose hereditary makeup is exactly the same. Persons with the same parents or the same ancestors do *not* necessarily have the same heredity. Each singly born child gets only half the genes of each parent. The combinations thus produced may be such as to develop *hereditary* characteristics quite different from those shown by either parent. Thus differences between parents and children or brothers and sisters do not prove anything about the effects of environment. But differences between identical twins do, since in genetic make-up such individuals are exactly alike.

Identical or *monozygotic* twins are produced from a single fertilized ovum that separates into two parts at the time of the first cell division. The two individuals have the same assortment of genes. They may or may not be encased in the same protective membrane or chorion, so that birth records are not decisive in making a diagnosis as to whether they are truly monozygotic. What is usually done is to check a number of physical traits known to be determined by heredity, such as finger prints, hand and sole prints, hair texture, skin texture, and eye color. Since the probability that all these characteristics would be alike in two persons with

different genetic make-up is equal to the *product* of the separate probabilities, the error in such a diagnosis is negligible, and it can be made no
matter how old the subjects are.

Several types of research have utilized twin subjects. We shall postpone
until the next chapter the consideration of the studies that have compared
the degree of resemblance in *monozygotic* twin pairs with the degree of
resemblance in *dizygotic* or two-egg pairs. The latter are the so-called
fraternal twins, who are no more alike in heredity than are ordinary
siblings. Such studies are most useful for demonstrating the importance
of heredity rather than of the environmental influences with which we
are concerned here. The research we shall examine now deals with cases
in which identical twins were separated while they were children and reared
in different homes. These constitute a natural controlled experiment on
the effects of environmental differences. Careful study of such cases should
tell us something about *how much* difference environment makes in various
things, and *what features* of the environment are important.

TABLE 52.

Differences Between Twins
(Newman, Freeman, and Holzinger, 1937, pp. 724, 344,
as brought together by Woodworth, 1941, p. 19)

	FRATERNALS	IDENTICALS REARED TOGETHER	IDENTICALS REARED APART
Stature	4.4 cm	1.7 cm	1.8 cm
Weight	10.0 lb.	4.1 lb.	9.9 lb.
Binet IQ	9.9 points	5.9 points	8.2 points

Newman, Freeman, and Holzinger (1937) made thorough, complete
case studies of nineteen pairs of identical twins reared apart. The average
difference they found, compared with the average differences in identical
twins reared together and fraternal twins, are shown in Table 52, and the
correlation between twin pairs are shown in Table 53. If we look only at
these averages, we come out with the conclusion that environmental differences do not have much effect on intelligence. As would be expected
on the basis of their hereditary similarity, identicals are more alike in
everything than are fraternals. Differences between them are smaller;
correlations between them are larger. At first glance it looks as though
the pairs reared apart showed more difference in Binet IQ than they did in
height. For these subjects, the correlation for Binet IQ, .767, was con-

TABLE 53.

Correlations Between Twins *

(*Ibid.* pp. 97, 347)

	FRATERNALS	IDENTICALS REARED TOGETHER	IDENTICALS REARED APART
Stature	.645	.932	(.969)
Weight	.631	.917	(.886)
Binet IQ	.631	.881	(.767)

* Correlations not in parentheses corrected for age, and last figure corrected for range. (See Woodworth, 1941, p. 19.)

siderably lower than the *r*'s for either height or weight. But Woodworth (1941) in his analysis of the results has pointed out a factor the authors themselves seem to have overlooked—the error of measurement that is always involved in intelligence testing. The average variation in score when the same individuals are tested twice is about 5 IQ points. It would appear then that the average pair of identical twins reared together is almost as similar as are the two scores of a single person tested twice, and that those reared apart show a difference not very much greater. After allowing for chance errors, Woodworth estimates that the average IQ difference for identical twins reared apart is about 6 points. This can be compared with the average difference for identicals reared together, which is 3 points, and with the average difference for unrelated children from the same community paired at random, which is 15 points. What we can conclude from the figures is that environmental differences do operate to produce IQ differences in persons with exactly the same hereditary potentialities, but that differences thus produced are not nearly as large as those we find among children whose heredity is *not* alike.

Material assembled from the detailed case studies is more illuminating than the averages, particularly when we attempt to determine what it is about the environment that makes a difference in intellectual development. Table 54 contains Woodworth's summary of the evidence for the nineteen pairs, along with three other pairs that have been reported separately. It can be seen that in some individual cases the IQ differences are large, much larger than the average differences. It seemed natural to the investigators to ask themselves whether there was any evidence that the difference between the environments in which the two twins were reared was larger for these pairs than for the others. In order to get an answer to this question, they had five judges rate the social and educational quality of the

TABLE 54.

Some Data from Identical Twins Reared Apart *

(Newman, Freeman and Holzinger, 1937; Muller, 1925; Gardner and Newman, 1940; Saudek, 1934. Data brought together by Woodworth, 1941, p. 23)

CASE NUMBER	SEX	AGE AT SEPARATION	AGE AT TESTING	ENVIRONMENTAL DIFFERENCES			IQ DIFFERENCE
				1. IN YEARS OF SCHOOLING	2. IN ESTIMATED EDUCATIONAL ADVANTAGES	3. IN ESTIMATED SOCIAL ADVANTAGES	
11	f	18 mo.	35	14	37	25	24
2	f	18 mo.	27	15	32	14	12
18	m	1 yr.	27	4	28	31	19
4	f	5 mo.	29	4	22	15	17
12	f	18 mo.	29	5	19	13	7
1	f	18 mo.	19	1	15	27	12
17	m	2 yr.	14	0	15	15	10
8	f	3 mo.	15	1	14	32	15
3	m	2 mo.	23	1	12	15	—2
14	f	6 mo.	39	0	12	15	—1
5	f	14 mo.	38	1	11	26	4
13	m	1 mo.	19	0	11	13	1
10	f	1 yr.	12	1	10	15	5
15	m	1 yr.	26	2	9	7	1
7	m	1 mo.	13	0	9	27	—1
19	f	6 yr.	41	0	9	14	—9
16	f	2 yr.	11	0	8	12	2
6	f	3 yr.	59	0	7	10	8
9	m	1 mo.	19	0	7	14	6
Muller	f	1 mo.	30	9	?	?	—1
Gardner & Newman ..	f	1 mo.	19	0	2	?	—3
Saudek	m	1 mo.	20	0	?	?	—4

* The estimated differences in educational and social advantages are in "points" with a maximum possible of 50. From the case material each of five judges rated the environmental differences between every pair of twins on a scale of 10 points, and the figure given in the table is the sum of these five ratings. A minus sign before an IQ difference means that the twin who received the higher rating for educational advantages obtained the lower IQ.

environment for each person and estimate on a ten-point scale the amount of difference there was for each pair. Table 54 shows that educational factors are related to IQ differences. On the average, the IQ of the better-educated twin is 6 points higher than the other, a difference that is statistically significant. For the six pairs shown in Table 54 for which there is a *marked* difference in formal schooling, defined as four years or more, the average difference is 13 IQ points in favor of the better-educated twin. There is a correlation of .79 between the ratings for educational difference and the IQ differences. This analysis proves rather conclusively that educational influences can produce IQ differences in persons having the same heredity, but that it is the *large* rather than the minor environmental discrepancies that are important. The largest difference of all, listed first in Table 54, occurred in the case of a pair of girls, one of them reared in the backwoods with only two years of regular schooling, the other reared in a good farming community and given a college education. It is to be noted that the 24-point difference in IQ for this pair is still far less than the extreme differences we encounter in the population as a whole. We cannot explain the difference between the moron with an IQ of 50 and the gifted child scoring 180 in terms of educational influences alone.

The evidence assembled by Newman, Freeman, and Holzinger with regard to the effects of environment in producing *personality* differences in separated identical twins was less clear. The inadequacy of personality tests available in the 1930's limited the analysis. The case studies produced several examples of marked differences in superficial personality traits. The pair cited in the last paragraph was an instance of this. The college-educated schoolteacher was well-groomed and polished in her manners, whereas the backwoods girl was "all business without social charm or concern about how she impressed others." The authors had the impression, however, that there were basic temperamental traits in which the members of each pair of twins resembled each other in spite of environmental differences. In this sort of basic trait, for instance, one young man from Tennessee, who was brought up in the mountains without benefit of much formal schooling and who had engaged in some illegal activity, was identical with his brother, a high-school graduate who was a business man in a small town. Both were individualistic and stubborn; it was the way in which the traits were expressed that differed. Further evidence for some hereditary determination of basic temperamental characteristics will be presented in the next chapter.

The conclusions that can be drawn from the research on separated identical twins are: (1) Marked educational differences can produce substantial differences in measured intelligence; and (2) Intellectual differences in the population as a whole are too large to be accounted for in terms of environmental differences alone. Results would seem to justify a moderate optimism with regard to the social usefulness of a good educational system. It is quite possible that the intelligence level of the population as a whole could be moderately increased. What we are not justified in assuming is that dull individuals can be brought up to the level of the bright ones by some form of education.

Before turning our attention to other kinds of research, another sort of twin study should be briefly mentioned. Child psychologists have used the method of *co-twin control* to study maturation and learning. In such studies, one member of a twin pair is given specific training in a skill, such as climbing or manipulation of materials, and the other is left to develop at his own rate or given training at a later age. In general, such studies have shown that the simple skills develop by the appropriate ages whether training is given in them or not (Hilgard, 1933; Strayer, 1930; Gesell and Thompson, 1941). More complex functions, such as skating, jumping, or swimming, show more of a training effect than do the simple reactions (McGraw, 1935). These studies have little direct bearing on the question with which we are principally concerned, however, since they do not give any evidence as to whether differences stemming from variations in training during infancy and early childhood can account for the relatively *permanent* differences we encounter in adults. In all these studies, the control twin had every opportunity to practice the skills involved in the experiment after the experimental period was over—and they were skills practically all normal children do practice a great deal. The environmental difference during the few days or weeks that the experiment lasted could hardly have been expected to have a great effect on the subjects' ultimate development. In fact, if there were a possibility of such effects, it would hardly be ethical to carry out such studies. These experiments have taught us more about maturation, as it occurs naturally in everyone, than they have about individual differences.

One co-twin study involved a much more drastic and prolonged difference between the way in which members of the pairs were treated. As a part of the study by Schmidt (1946), reported in detail in a previous chapter, nine pairs of twins in the feeble-minded group were sent to separate schools. In each case the twin whose IQ was originally higher was assigned to the regular training program, whereas the lower one was placed in the special classes for the enriched school experience described in the monograph. Schmidt reports that the average IQ increased from 54 to 92 in the nine experimental twins during the three-year period. The controls dropped slightly, from 61 to 59. Case studies show in a colorful way how much difference the new experience made in the lives of those who participated in it. Unfortunately, in addition to the statistical criticisms that have cast doubt on the whole Schmidt study, there is another serious question that arises with regard to this part of it in particular. If these twin pairs were identical, as the author states that they were, how could they have been as different both in IQ and in other psychological traits as she describes them to have been when the experiment began? It has been a universal finding that identical twins in the same home are more alike than this. If we can trust the reported figures, the fact that the twin who was initially lower in each case turned out to be much higher after the special training would be a fact of considerable importance, even if the pairs were not monozygotic. But can we trust them? For the present it seems wise to suspend judgment on this study until we see what others set up in the same way will show.

RESEARCH ON FOSTER CHILDREN

Because identical twins, especially those separated in infancy, are comparatively rare, it has seemed desirable to get supplementary data on the influence of the environment from other types of experiment. A number of excellent studies have been made of what happens to children adopted into good homes, but there are certain difficulties inherent in such research that make the interpretation of what they mean uncertain. If one could plan a simple "before-and-after" experiment in which a number of children were tested, then placed in good homes, then tested again after various lengths of time, the problem would be readily soluble. The trouble with such a simple idea is that all work in child psychology emphasizes the importance of the development that takes place during the *very earliest* years, whereas all work in mental testing has shown us that an IQ that is reliable (in the sense of showing a high correlation with a retest some time later) and valid (in the sense of showing a high correlation with another test of intelligence or with school achievement) cannot be obtained for an infant. Even for children of two, three, and four, IQ's are not very satisfactory predictors of later mental ability. Therefore various compromise methods have had to be devised for the study of the effects of foster-home placement. The most satisfactory one of these is to make an *estimate* on the basis of known facts about the children's parents as to the *average* IQ to be expected from a *group* under ordinary circumstances. It is then possible to test them after residence in good foster homes to find out whether or not their intellectual development has exceeded the estimates. Fairly sound estimates of the IQ in a group of children can be made from information about mother's or father's IQ, father's occupation, mother's or father's education, home ratings, and various other data. To predict the IQ of an *individual* by such methods would of course be highly unsound, but the averages of *groups* at different socio-economic and educational levels in the population are known. (See Chapter 12.)

The factor of selective placement must always be considered when the results are interpreted. Child-placing agencies usually make an attempt to fit a child to the home. This tends to produce a small but consistent correlation between the children's intelligence and the intellectual quality of the foster home, a correlation that is *not* the result of the good environment but of the fact that child and home are matched to start with. For instance, illegitimate children may have brilliant fathers even if their mothers are not very bright. If a child of such a match is placed in a cultured, well-educated family, an observer, comparing his IQ with his real mother's, is likely to be tremendously impressed with the influence of a good environment. What the observer is not so likely to realize is that the child's brightness may be inherited from his intelligent father. The home may have nourished it rather than created it. In most of the large-scale investigations, there has been a good deal of discussion of the possible effects of selective placement on the results.

One of the first important studies was an attempt to find out simply how *successful* adopted children are. The New York State Charities Aid Association (Theis, 1924) undertook to check up on 910 persons more than eighteen years of age whom the agency had placed in adopted homes during childhood. They used a simple judgment of "capable" for persons who were managing their own affairs successfully, and attempted to relate the success or lack of success to factors on which the case records gave them information. The most important finding was that 77 per cent of the subjects could be described as capable. Only 10 per cent were delinquent or vicious. Popular notions that adopted children are likely to turn out badly were thus shown to be without foundation. There was a slightly higher percentage of capable individuals coming from the group whose *own* families were good, but the majority of those whose own families were inferior also turned out well. Differences in economic level of the foster home were not related to success of the children, but differences in kind of care were. This study made a real and very practical contribution to the literature on adopted children.

In 1928, the National Society for the Study of Education published two important studies of foster children, one conducted by Freeman, Holzinger, and Mitchell (1928) at the University of Chicago, the other by Burks (1928) at Stanford. The Chicago group tested 401 adopted children and their foster parents and analyzed the results in various ways, trying to sort out the effects of environment from those of heredity alone. In one analysis, the correlation between the IQ's of *foster* siblings was .37. Since the correlation between IQ's of *real* siblings living in their own homes is usually in the neighborhood of .50 and the correlation between IQ's of unrelated children is .oo, the value obtained represents an intermediate amount of relationship, and would seem to show that just living in the same environment, though it does not make children as much alike as individuals in the same family, does to a limited extent make for similarity in their mental development. It was also found that there was a tendency for children adopted into the better homes to obtain the higher IQ's. The 114 children placed in good homes averaged 106.8; the 186 children placed in average homes averaged 96.4; the 101 children placed in relatively poor homes averaged 88.9. The correlation between cultural level and IQ was .48. Intelligence seemed to be related to the *age* at which the child was placed for adoption. Those who were young when adopted scored higher on the average than those who were older. Much of the significance of the comparisons between children adopted into homes of different economic and cultural levels hinges on the question of the extent to which selective placement could have operated in the group. If any attempt was made by the child-placing agencies to give superior children to superior foster parents, it would not, of course, be at all surprising that this group should get better-than-average scores when tested. The authors of the report considered the possibility, but they felt that the effect of what selection there was was negligible. The failure to show any clear evidence on this point, however, leaves the interpretation of the results somewhat doubtful so far as differences in types of home are concerned.

Burks (1928), in California, compared a group of adopted children placed within the first year of life with a control group of "own" children matched with the adopted children for age and sex, and living in homes matched with the foster homes for locality and occupational level. From the information available about their real parents, she estimated the average IQ of the foster children's group at about 100. When they were tested at ages five to fourteen, their average IQ actually turned out to be 107.4. The mean IQ of the control children, however, was 115.1. The most reasonable conclusion is that a superior home can produce a moderate increase in a child's tested intelligence, but can not bring him to the level of individuals who have *both* superior heredity and superior environment on their side. Burks also computed correlations between IQ and various home characteristics, for both foster children and own children. For the foster children, these ranged from a low of .09 with father's IQ to a high of .29 with the rating of the home for cultural advantages. For the own children, all except the correlation with income were in the neighborhood of .50. It would seem that while there is a slight tendency for the intellectual level of adopted children to correspond to that of the home in which they are reared, it is not nearly so close a relationship as that which holds for children in their own homes.

The study by Leahy (1935) in Minnesota was similar in design to the Burks study, but even more carefully planned. Matched foster-child and control groups, 194 in each, were compared. Foster children were all illegitimate, all placed for adoption at six months or younger, and all from five to fourteen years old when tested. Leahy found evidence that there had been a certain amount of selective placement even with children adopted when so young. The social agency, knowing the real mother's education, took this into consideration when placing the child. The mean IQ of the group was 110, the same as that of the control children, and there was the same tendency in both groups for children in homes of higher occupational level to get higher scores. However, this was less pronounced in the case of the foster children, who ranged from an average of 108 in unskilled labor homes to 113 in professional homes, as compared with a range of 102 to 119 for the own children. It would seem that the correspondence of child's IQ to father's occupation is less evident in the case of the foster children; and selective placement, since it undoubtedly exists, might conceivably account for what there is. Correlations of child's IQ with total home rating, based on occupation, economic condition, parental education, and material, social, and cultural level, were .23 for the foster children, and .53 for the own children. By this method also, a slight relationship between environmental advantages and child's mental level was indicated, but again we must remember that selective placement works in this direction.

These three major studies agree in their findings that the intelligence of adopted children averages somewhat higher than that of children in homes of the educational level from which they come. They are also in essential agreement with the findings of the identical-twin research studies in which marked educational differences were shown to produce moderate IQ differences. That hereditary factors are still important determiners is suggested by a study by Lawrence (1931) in England in which the correlation between child's IQ and *own* father's occupational level was shown to be as high for children living in an orphanage, who had never lived with their own families at all, as for children in their own homes. A middle-of-the-road conclusion would seem to fit all this evidence best. Change to a good environment will probably lead to some improvement in an underprivileged child's IQ, but too much change in him should not be expected.

The principal challenge to this conclusion came from a group of studies carried on over a period of years at the University of Iowa. Results up to 1940 were summarized in a paper by Skeels (1940). Several different kinds of evidence were presented, leading to the conclusion that the environment wields a much larger influence than has been ordinarily attributed to it. In one study, children from very inferior homes were tested at the time of their entrance into an orphanage and the results classified by *age* of entrance. The figures show that the older the children were when they entered the orphanage, the lower their IQ's were. For children entering at the age of four, for instance, the average IQ was 92.6. For those who entered at twelve, it was only 81.6. This was taken to mean that continued residence in an inferior home has a progressive depressing effect on the IQ. It fits in with the results on age differences in isolated groups like the canal-boat and mountain children. In another study, 65 children from inferior homes were tested before and after foster-home placement. There was a consistent shift upward. The mean IQ of three-year-olds before placement was 98.5. A year later, upon reëxamination, it was 104.2. One should note, however, that this difference is small.

The most important studies were those made of children placed in infancy (Skodak, 1939). As has been explained, valid intelligence test results cannot be obtained on infants. Consequently no tests previous to placement were possible. The first test was given, in each case, at the time the final papers were made out to legalize the adoption. The ages of the 180 children when the test was given ranged from one and a half to six, with a mean of two. A second test was given each of them a little over two years later. The mean IQ of the group at the time of the first test was 116. At the time of the second test it was 111.5. The distribution showed a predominance of superior children, with fewer cases in the dull-normal range than are customarily found. The crucial question is of course related to the thing that could not be measured, that is, the intelligence of the children to start with. The authors present evidence that in occupational and educational level the true parents were definitely below average, so that below-average intelligence would have been predicted for the group of children as a whole. By the same criteria, the adopting parents were above the average of the population. Furthermore, children placed in the most superior adoptive homes turned out higher on the average than those placed in the less superior environments.

A follow-up study ten years later (Skodak and Skeels, 1949) corroborated the conclusions. For the 100 children out of the original 180 who could be located, the mean IQ was 107 on the 1916 Stanford-Binet Test, 117 on the 1937 revision. (The question as to which was the better measure to use here arose from the fact that on the one hand it seemed better to use the same test that was given at the beginning of the study, but on the other hand, the 1937 revision which came into use after the study began probably furnishes a better estimate of intellectual level, particularly in adolescents.) Whichever figure we take, it is clear that this group of adopted children still scored above the general average. Their average of 107 was 20 points higher than the average score that had been made by their true mothers when tested years before.

In connection with these various Iowa studies, a good many "family correlations" have been computed. Skodak and Skeels in the paper just discussed report practically zero correlations between child's IQ and education of the foster parent. The correlation of child's IQ with either the educational level or the IQ of the *true* parent seems to increase as the children get older. At the time of the second test, the mother-child correlation for IQ was .28. At the time of the fourth test it was .44. This seems to show that children tend to approximate the intelligence of their true parents more closely as they grow up, whether they are living with them or not. Skodak (1950) ran some correlations on pairs of children in the same homes. For 41 pairs in which two adopted children lived in the same foster home, a surprisingly high *r* was obtained, .65. For 22 pairs consisting of one adopted and one own child in the same home, the correlation was .21. The author's conclusion is that adopted children in the same home come to resemble each other in intelligence as much as ordinary siblings do. (Sibling correlations usually turn out to be about .5.)

It is difficult to extract any evidence about causes from correlations. They can only be suggestive of hypotheses. When we put together the bits of evidence summarized in the two previous paragraphs, the figures with regard to the *level* of intelligence reached by the foster children point to the importance of environmental influence, whereas the *correlations* suggest that the differences between individuals rest on an hereditary basis. The correlation between the IQ's of foster siblings could arise from selective placement rather than from the standardizing effect of the home environment. We can fit these facts in with findings from other types of research and say that the effect of improving the environment is to raise the level of the whole group involved but not to make the individuals in it any more *alike*.

The most controversial of these Iowa reports have been those on the children of feeble-minded mothers. We have already discussed in a previous chapter the study of thirteen such children who made marked gains, averaging 27.5 IQ points, under the loving care of moron girls in an institution for the feeble-minded. In a later report, Skeels and Harms (1948) show that groups of subjects selected from the total group on the basis of (*a*) the fact that their true mother's IQ's had been under 75, or (*b*) the fact that their true father's occupational level was known to be very low, or (*c*) both these factors in combination, all averaged well above 100 when tested at the age of five. They stress the fact that an inferior social history does not seem to be as much of a handicap as one would expect it to be when favorable opportunities are given for intellectual development.

Criticisms that have been made of these Iowa studies by other psychologists have centered more around the conclusions and implications that have been presented than around the figures themselves. The IQ's of 105 to 117 that have been reported in the various studies are not a great deal higher than those which previous workers obtained for adopted children. All have agreed that adopted children average somewhat higher than the population as a whole. There is also some question as to whether the true parents of many of the children were as inferior as the investigators thought they were. The number of grades the mothers had completed in school was about as high as the average for the population at large. Furthermore, only 56 per cent of the fathers were located; it is possible that there were a fairly large number of superior individuals in the total group. (The study by Skeels and Harms cited above does show, however, that even when fathers are clearly inferior in occupational level, children can turn out to be above average.) Finally there is evidence in the reports that the ever-present selective placement factor did operate. There was a correlation of .30 between the education of true and foster parents. It looks as though placement workers consciously or unconsciously took a child's family background into consideration in finding a suitable adoptive home for him.

On the whole, then, all these studies of foster children support our previous conclusions from research based on identical twins. Children do improve in IQ when stimulated by a marked improvement in educational environment. The improvement to be anticipated in any one case is, however, moderate. Nothing but disappointment can result from statements that lead foster parents to expect miraculous changes. Woodworth (1941, p. 68) stresses the point that these studies can be interpreted as showing us, not that hereditary factors have no effect on intelligence, but rather that the hereditary limits in many cases are higher than we had thought they were. "If a child, from whatever parentage, develops superior intelligence, we know for certain that his heredity was good enough to make that achievement possible. We have simply been misjudging his heredity. The low economic and cultural level of his parents has misled us."

THE EFFECTS OF NURSERY-SCHOOL EXPERIENCE ON INTELLIGENCE

Another series of reports that have come from the child-study laboratories of the University of Iowa have been concerned with the effect of nursery-school attendance on children's IQ's. A good summary of this work up to 1940 was given by Wellman (1940). Since then, criticisms and counter-criticisms have appeared from time to time in various journals, so that it is now possible to make some judgment as to the meaning of the results and decide what conclusions are warranted.

Interpretation of nursery-school findings is complicated by the presence of special selective factors. Up till the present time it has been true that most such schools are organized for the children of the well-to-do and of the poor. Children from social classes in between do not attend. Most of the nursery schools in college and university departments of psychology and child study charge a fairly high fee and enroll chiefly the children of professors and other professional men in the community. Nursery schools in settlement houses or community centers, on the other hand, are for the benefit of low-income families in which the mother finds it necessary to leave her family in order to earn a living.

The Iowa investigators report results from both types of school. The work in the University of Iowa Nursery School involved first the comparison of IQ changes made from fall to spring, while school was in session, with those from spring to fall when it was not. The average gain in the first year was 6.6 IQ points. After a small loss from spring to fall, those who continued in preschool made a further gain of 3.8 points the second year. For those who attended for a third year, there was very little further gain. There seemed to be a "diminishing-returns" factor in the situation. Paired groups of preschool and non-preschool children, matched for age and IQ, were also compared. The preschool group gained 7.0 points, and the non-preschool lost 3.9 points; the difference was statistically significant. A little evidence was presented that the advantage the preschool experience had given the children was maintained even up to the time of college entrance. In matched groups of 29 "grown-up" children, the ones who had attended preschool made an average percentile of 88 on the American Council of Education Test given at the time of college entrance, whereas the non-preschool group averaged 78. Since this difference is not statistically significant, however, it fails to prove the point.

The other major Iowa project was the establishment of a nursery school in an orphanage. Subjects here were from underprivileged families, definitely below average in intellectual promise. The preschool itself was a novel and interesting activity superimposed upon a monotonous dead level of routine. An attempt was made to divide all children of preschool age into two matched groups, so that one could be given nursery-school experience and the other held as a control. The fact that children were constantly entering or leaving the orphanage, however, made it impossible to keep the groups matched very precisely during the three years that the experiment ran. Of the many publications by the investigators and their critics, the most dependable analysis of just what the study did show is to be found in the papers by Wellman and Pegram (1944) and by McNemar (1945). Wellman stresses the fact that the control group, lacking nursery-school experience, tended to *lose* significantly in IQ. The preschool's effect was to counteract such losses and produce small gains instead. A certain minimal amount of exposure to the stimulating influences seemed to be required, since the figures showed no difference between the preschool group and the controls for less than 400 days of residence while the experiment was in progress, or for less than 50 per cent attendance at preschool. McNemar's critical analysis confirms Wellman's conclusion with regard to gains during preschool and the relationship of gains to amount of attendance, but throws doubt on the conclusion that in the non-preschool group, losses were the rule. He shows that all of the apparent average loss is produced by eight extreme cases not typical of the whole group.

As has been said, the Iowa studies started a flood of criticism. The specific points made by critics center around two principal issues. In the first place, the statistical methods used have often been inadequate or misleading. There has been too much selecting for discussion of exceptional cases in which an IQ change of perhaps 30 to 40 points has occurred, in an experiment where the *average* change has been very moderate. The effects of the regression factor discussed in previous chapters were not always taken into consideration when changes in groups with low IQ's on the first test were compared with changes in groups with high IQ's. IQ's based on different intelligence tests, particularly the Kuhlmann-Binet and the Stanford-Binet, have been used interchangeably, although they are not exactly comparable statistically. In the second place, there has been a rather general failure to get similar results elsewhere. Of nine reports from various parts of the country cited in the *Thirty-ninth Yearbook* (from which most of the summary reports we have cited were taken), only the one from Merrill-Palmer school showed significant gains, and it contained statistical errors similar to those for which the Iowa people have been criticized. A study reported by Page (1940) shows quite conclusively that attendance at nursery school in one place at least did not give the children higher IQ's than their non-preschool siblings at a *later* time, when they were all in the elementary grades.

It is worth noting, however, that most of the reported studies are from nursery schools of the *first* type outlined above, in which the children are from well-to-do homes. The fact that the gains Wellman reported in the orphanage study stood up even under McNemar's searching analysis suggests that we may be dealing in this case with a different psychological situation. Nursery-school attendance coming as a tremendous enrichment of a drab, stultifying environment may have an effect that is much more drastic than the same experience added to the generally favorable situation that a good home provides. We need more research to clarify this point. To lump all nursery schools for all kinds of children together is perhaps to obscure the most interesting features of the problem. The evidence cited in Chapter 11 for some sort of perceptual defect in Negro subjects of low educational level may fit in here. Nursery school may give such individuals something they need for their full development.

More recently there has been considerable interest in the effects of "institutionalism" or "hospitalism" on development, especially in early infancy. Spitz (1945-46) and Fischer (1952) have described cases of extreme developmental retardation which they interpret as a consequence of lack of "mothering," or the absence of a close emotional relationship to another human being. The absence of quantitative data and control groups makes this material difficult to interpret, but it may at least justify the hypothesis that a less extreme degree of neglect may constitute a developmental handicap that prevents a child from actualizing his hereditary potentialities, and that an experience like nursery school which is stimulating both intellectually and emotionally may help to counteract this deficiency in deprived children.

EFFECTS OF PRACTICE ON INDIVIDUAL DIFFERENCES

At the same time that some psychologists were concerning themselves with the effects of certain aspects of the individual's general environment on his mental characteristics, others were tackling another sort of problem which is more closely related to learning experiments. What happens with regard to variability or the differences between individuals in a group of subjects who go through a series of practice trials on some specific skill? There is no question here about the *average* change. Everybody improves markedly between the first trial and the last. But does practice involve a *leveling* or a *diversifying* trend? Are subjects more like each other after they have had this common experience, or does it serve to make latent differences between them more evident?

It can be seen that this question has important practical implications with regard to aptitude testing, industrial training programs, and education. If there is a tendency for all subjects to approach the same level of competence when adequate training has been given, then there is little point in developing elaborate testing programs to select persons for such training. In general, society is interested more in trained skills than in undeveloped talents, and thus it becomes especially important to identify the factors that account for differences in these finished products.

As in so many other areas of research, psychologists who initiated research on this question hoped to be able to obtain a general answer applicable to all kinds of material, persons, and situations. The typical design of an experiment was as follows:

1. A fairly large group of subjects would be given an initial test on one or more measurable skills. A measure of central tendency and of variability would be computed.
2. An interval would intervene during which all subjects would be given equal amounts of practice in the given skill.
3. A final test equivalent in every way to the initial one would be given. Central tendency and variability would again be determined.

Early experiments planned in this way came out with conflicting results. In some, variability was shown to increase with practice; in others, it was shown to decrease. More careful scrutiny of the methods used explained most of these discrepancies. Anastasi (1934) in the introduction to the report on her carefully planned study analyzes the reasons for many of the discrepant findings. In the first place, measures of *absolute* variability, usually the standard deviation, and of *relative* variability lead to different results. (The most common index of relative variability is the coefficient of variation, usually abbreviated CV, defined as $\dfrac{100 \text{ SD}}{M}$. Dividing by the mean makes an adjustment for the general level of performance.) As we have previously shown, the making of a fraction or ratio is not a legitimate numerical operation for most types of psychological-test scores, so that the results of studies in which relative variability was used are meaningless.

Secondly, Anastasi shows that it makes a difference whether the time taken to complete a task or the number of units completed in a standard length of time constitutes the measure of proficiency. With regard to this difference it seems more reasonable to use amount scores, since they bear more resemblance to real-life situations. Time is a constant for all of us. It is the amount we accomplish in each twenty-four-hour period that varies. Thirdly, experiments give different results depending upon whether the practice during stage 2 is measured in number of practice trials or in time spent on the activity. Here again it seems more reasonable to use time spent as our measure of amount of practice, since this is the way the learning of real-life skills is usually organized—six hours a day in school, an hour a day at the piano, twenty hours a week on the football field.

With terms defined in this way, the evidence tends to show that individual differences *increase* with practice. Table 55, taken from Anastasi's study, is a good example of these trends. Results are shown for four different tests given to four different groups of about 120 college students. It can be seen that the groups as a whole show considerable improvement, but that differences between individuals, as shown by the standard deviations, are larger at the end than at the beginning.

TABLE 55.

Averages and Standard Deviations of Scores
on First and Last Trials
(Anastasi, 1934)

	FIRST TRIAL		LAST TRIAL	
	MEAN	S D	MEAN	S D
Cancellation	40.63	6.78	59.60	7.88
Symbol-Digit	41.15	7.58	70.07	9.98
Vocabulary	39.06	6.84	59.28	8.87
Hidden Words	43.58	6.94	69.28	11.44

The development of more complex ways of designing an experiment, using analysis of variance methods, has made it possible for more recent workers to analyze more precisely what happens to individual differences during a series of practice trials. Owens (1942a, b, c) gave his subjects, fifteen junior high school boys, a number of motor-skills tests.[1] He compared the variance associated with differences between *individuals* in the

[1] Good experimental design made it possible to obtain from a relatively small number of cases dependable information as to the statistical significance of different factors.

early trials, numbers 2, 3, and 4, with that in later trials, numbers 6, 7, and 8. The individual differences were slightly greater on the later trials, but the difference was not statistically significant. A large part of the variability at all stages, 82 to 85 per cent, was determined by individual differences rather than by practice differences. Garrett (1940) came out with a different conclusion. His subjects were college students doing tasks of an intellectual rather than a motor nature. He found that variability remained constant within the groups as the experiment progressed, and that practice was more significant than individual differences in its effect on total variability. The differences between everybody's averages from trial to trial was greater than the differences between persons on any one trial. Hamilton (1943), who allowed groups of fifth-grade children to practice three different paper-and-pencil tasks, found that the proportion of the total variance that could be attributed to practice varied with the task and with the stage of proficiency that had been reached. In early trials, practice differences overshadowed individual differences. In later stages where improvement was slower, individual differences played a somewhat larger role.

The effect of these studies taken together has been to show us that like so many other broad general questions, this one about whether individual differences increase or decrease with practice cannot be answered once and for all. What we get in any given situation seems to depend on the homogeneity or heterogeneity of the group, the nature of the task, the length of the training period, and perhaps a number of other things. Tilton (1936) called attention to the importance of differential *forgetting* after an experiment is over as a source of individual differences. He summarized figures from thirty-nine sources, which seemed to show a general tendency for standard deviations to increase, showing that differences between individuals are still greater after a fallow period than they were at the time practice trials ended. Burns (1937) stressed the importance of motivation in the subjects of the experiment, and Ewert (1934) reported one study in which under high motivation, variability increased with practice. In view of the complexity of the question, it seems best that practice effects be considered under the general heading of *sources of variability* and that we investigate their nature and extent for each specific trait in which we are interested rather than take them for granted.

There are two special questions in this area, however, that are important in a practical way to those who are using tests for selection purposes. To what extent do the subjects in an experiment maintain their relative positions of superiority or inferiority in their group as practice progresses?

Unless there is a fair amount of correlation between initial and final scores, the use of skills tests of any sort to select workers to be trained would seem to be unjustified. There would be no point in hiring the people who score highest on a motor-coördination test, if the lower-scoring applicants are just as likely to get high scores after a period of training. Related to this is the question of identifying factors upon which *ultimate* proficiency rests. It is trained skills that count in the end, not aptitudes.

In general, a good foundation for personnel testing has been demonstrated in many reports showing positive correlations between initial and final scores in a variety of learning experiments. Those who are superior at the beginning maintain that superiority even during a period when all subjects are improving. Kincaid (1925) brought together the results of a number of early studies, and showed that the majority of the correlations between scores for first and last trials were above .60. In Anastasi's (1934) study, the initial-final correlations were as follows:

Cancellation	.67
Symbol-Digit	.30
Vocabulary	.51
Hidden Words	.82

It would seem then that we are quite safe in placing our bets on subjects who are initially high. However, the variation in reported correlations is also interesting. Hertzman (1939) focused attention on the way in which coefficients vary from group to group and from task to task. The most interesting fact he pointed out is that in cases where the practice period consists of a *short* series of trials, the correlations are higher than where it involves a *long* series. This suggests what some other research has pointed out more explicitly that over an extended practice period, a subject's performance changes qualitatively as well as quantitatively, and that by developing different methods of work he may change his position in the group to a significant extent.

Brief mention should be made of one question that has often been asked but cannot be adequately answered because of technical difficulties. It is the question as to who *gains* or improves most during practice in some sort of skill, the initially low individual or the one initially high? Many correlations have been computed between variable 1, *gain* scores obtained by subtracting the initial from the final score, and variable 2, the initial scores themselves. Taken at face value, such correlations seem to indicate that the poorer beginners improve more than better beginners, since the vast majority of the correlations are *negative*. They cannot, however, be taken at their face value. The double dose of chance errors in gain scores, the fact that most tests have too low a *ceiling* to permit unlimited improvement in the better performers, and the unequal difficulty of test items, so that a gain of one point means something different at different levels of performance—all these things make gain scores very tricky to work with and put us on guard against conclusions based on them.

The best series of studies on the whole problem of factors that affect ultimate proficiency in learned tasks was carried out by Woodrow (1938a, b, c, d; 1939a, b; 1940). Some of the results have already been discussed in Chapter 4. The general procedure was to give a group of students a large number of practice periods on a variety of different tests. In addition, tests of intelligence and special aptitudes were administered at the beginning and at the end of the series of practice trials. Then the figures were analyzed by a variety of methods to ascertain what the essential relationships were. These analyses show rather conclusively that it is not the *fast* learners who are highest at the end. It is rather the ones who *go on improving* for a long time who come out ahead. *Rate* of learning depends to some extent on the amount of practice the individual has had with similar material before the experiment began. The more previous practice he has had, the slower his progress will appear to be, since he enters the experiment at a later stage of the learning process, and learning curves always tend to show steeper climbs in early than in later stages. Therefore, to predict a person's ultimate score on the basis of the rate at which he improves during early stages of his training is not feasible. Final attainment depends to some extent on something that cannot be measured at the beginning, namely, the length of time over which improvement will continue. (This does not negate the fact discussed above—that correlations between initial and final scores are uniformly positive. We can predict a person's final score to a partial degree by looking at his initial score. The point is that such predictions are by no means perfect, and that a measurement of rate of learning at the beginning does not add anything to their accuracy.)

As has been mentioned in Chapter 4, Woodrow found that rate of learning was not correlated with the intelligence we measure by our tests. He considered also another hypothesis—that there is some general learning ability, not the same as the trait our intelligence tests measure, which affects the efficiency of all learning. This too turned out to be untenable. Gains were specific. The individual who improved most rapidly on one type of skill might be slow or only average on another.

One of the most interesting of Woodrow's findings was that the *correlations* between tests were different after practice than they were before, and that factor analysis produced a different pattern of loadings. This result suggests that subjects must accomplish the tasks after practice by methods that are different from those they used at the beginning. This often-neglected factor of *work methods* as a source of individual differences in manifest ability and accomplishment has been emphasized also by Sargent (1942) and R. H. Seashore (1939). What seems to occur during a series of practice trials is that subjects stumble upon specific changes in their methods of doing a task which make more efficient performance possible. Most of us have had such experiences in connection with one or another special learning problem. The pianist working on a difficult sonata discovers that a change in the position of his hands makes it possible to execute a phrase smoothly and rapidly. A golf player learns to keep his eye on the ball instead of on the spot in the distance where he wants it to go. Woodrow's changes in factor pattern fit in with common knowledge that learning is not simply a quantitative improvement in the rate at which the same thing is done, but a qualitative change in the psychological factors lying back of what is done.

Such results would suggest that we ought to investigate specifically the effects of *training* rather than practice alone on individual differences. It might be that by demonstrating to all members of a group the work methods that the best performers hit upon for themselves we could reduce the differences between individuals and raise the average level more than we do in most of our learning experiments. In practical situations, of course, music teachers, coaches, and efficiency engineers do this constantly. The fact that they do not succeed in bringing all their trainees up to the level of the highest ones shows that work methods are not the *only* factor involved in individual differences. But we need more research on *training* as contrasted with *practice* in order to determine how important a source of variability they are.

MISCELLANEOUS EVIDENCE ON ENVIRONMENTAL EFFECTS

In addition to the types of study we have been considering, designed especially to analyze the effects of new factors introduced into an individual's environment on his intelligence or other mental characteristics, there are a number of other kinds of research that are often interpreted as evidence for environmental influences. Many of these studies have been reported in previous sections of this book in connection with other problems.

There is, first of all, the fact that children's IQ's are positively correlated with socio-economic indices, and especially with parents' education. The meaning of this sort of evidence is far from clear. The fact that the correlations increase as the children grow older (Bayley, 1954) might indicate that longer exposure to the kind of environment furnished by the home produces more and more of the mental characteristics that are typical for such environments. But the fact that this happens in cases where the children do not grow up in their own homes (Skodak and Skeels, 1949) casts considerable doubt on this interpretation.

Studies of the relationship of intelligence to education generally show that individuals with more schooling achieve higher test scores. The fact that there are intellectual differences related to differences in amount of formal education even in subjects who initially tested alike, as Lorge (1945) showed, indicates that schooling does make a difference. Other studies such as those of S. Smith (1942) in Hawaii, Wheeler (1942) in East Tennessee, and Finch (1946) in Minnesota indicate that when there has been a considerable upward shift in the educational opportunities available in a region, the IQ level of the school population goes up accordingly. Tuddenham's (1948) finding that World War II men were considerably higher than World War I men on Army Alpha shows the same trend.

We have considered the evidence for *handicapping* effects of inadequate environments in some detail in the chapters on race and social-class differences. It seemed reasonable to conclude that at least part of the difference between privileged and non-privileged groups in the population reflects the retarding influence of poor environment on mental development.

Finally, the studies showing that many individuals originally labeled feeble-minded or mentally defective become able to function as normal citizens in the community after receiving the right kind of education constitute important testimony to the value of providing stimulating environments. Whether such persons were actually feeble-minded or pseudo-feeble-minded, the school and the subsequent work experience it made possible changed them in favorable ways.

What none of the kinds of evidence discussed in this chapter proves is that *all* mental differences between individuals arise from environmental differences *alone*. If they did, it is unlikely that we would ever have a brilliant writer coming from the slums or a president from a log cabin in the backwoods. Such occurrences are only dramatic instances of what we find in every frequency distribution—that for a group coming from a standardized environment, whether its level is low or high, we obtain a wide range of individual scores. The more we have studied the effects of various aspects of environment on individuals, the more apparent it has become that persons will *differ* even when their environments are alike. We turn in the next chapter to the evidence that there is an hereditary basis for such differences.

SUMMARY

Modern research workers have largely given up the attempt to determine the proportion of the variance of any trait attributable to hereditary and environmental influences and are concentrating instead on discovering how human characteristics can be changed in desirable ways. Study of identical twins raised in different homes has shown that environment, particularly its educational aspects, can have a measurable effect on intelligence. Studies of foster children have corroborated this conclusion. Adopted children tend to score, as a group, somewhat higher than children from low social levels who remain in their own homes.

Nursery schools have produced some improvement in the intelligence level of orphanage children, whose previous environment was unusually sterile, but seem to have had little effect on the mental development of children from good homes.

Studies designed to show the effect of a series of practice trials on individual differences in some specific skill have shown that such effects vary with many features of the learning situation, so that the question is not answerable in general terms. There is enough correlation between initial and final scores to justify aptitude testing and prediction of final scores, but such predictions are only moderately accurate. Unpredictable individual differences in work methods show up during the course of learning, and some subjects continue to improve for a much longer time than others.

In all these kinds of research, there is evidence that environmental influences, whether they are as broad and general as schooling, or as narrow and well-defined as a series of ten practice trials in a dart-throwing experiment, affect the central tendency of the group being studied more than they do its variability. They produce *improvement* but not *uniformity*.

CHAPTER 18

The Hereditary Basis of Individual Differences

INTRODUCTION

IT HAS BEEN emphasized in the preceding chapter that there is no longer any scientific justification for the heredity-environment controversy. Its perpetuation in our time reflects attitudes rather than evidence. Each individual constitutes a pattern of hereditary potentialities developed to a greater or lesser extent under the impact of various environmental influences. We have considered what some of these influences and their characteristic effects are. Now let us turn to the evidence that there are such things as hereditary differences in psychological traits. The facts reported in the previous chapter, collected and organized to show how environment changes people, still leave a place for the hereditary differences we are considering here. The twin studies indicate that even when they have been reared in different homes, identical twins are much more *similar* in their mental abilities than are fraternal twins or ordinary siblings. Even the largest IQ difference reported, in the case of the twins with the great discrepancy in education, is not nearly as large as the extreme differences we find among unrelated persons. The persistent tendency for foster children to resemble their real parents more than they resemble their foster parents also fits in with the idea that hereditary differences are not eradicated by environmental influences. The learning experiments show that differences tend to persist even after long periods of standardized practice. Finally, the fact that in the most underprivileged groups, individuals of the highest level of mental ability are constantly turning up is most easily explained in terms of genetic differences. As has been indicated in previous chapters, we must be cautious in our conclusions as to the meaning of below-average scores that various underprivileged groups tend to make on intelligence tests—Southern Negroes, rural school children, unskilled laborers. But it is difficult to account in purely environmental terms for the *brilliant* Southern Negroes, farm children, and unskilled workers whom we have all encountered. The fact is that no matter how uniformly good or poor the environment of a group is, when we measure mental traits we obtain a *distribution* of individuals. Although this of course proves nothing about heredity, it does constitute a framework around which evidence about genetic differences can be organized.

BASIC IDEAS AND CONCEPTS

Men have discussed heredity for centuries, but it was not until the rise of the young science of genetics that they had more than a vague idea of how it operates. The discovery that inherited characteristics were controlled by minute particles called *genes* which make up the chromosomes each individual receives from his parents and passes on intact to his children has introduced clarity and order into a field where there was much confusion. Knowing that the person receives only half the chromosomes of each parent enables us to explain the *differences* between children in the same family as well as their likenesses. Knowing that there are *recessive* as well as dominant genes accounts for the fact that traits not showing up in either parent can appear in the offspring. Knowing that the only hereditary characteristics are those whose potentialities for development are present in the single cell at the moment of conception has enabled us to see that some *innate* characteristics present at birth are results of prenatal conditions rather than of heredity, and that some conditions that do not develop until years later may still be genetically determined.

One of the greatest contributions that genetics has made to differential psychology is to give us a general idea of what kinds of characteristics can and cannot be inherited. Structural or anatomical characteristics are determined to a large extent by genes, and any psychological trait that is directly related to differences in structure can thus have a hereditary basis. Athletic ability could be "inherited" in the sense that the kind of bone and muscle structure on which it depends could be determined by the genes. Musical ability could be "inherited" since it requires a certain kind of ear for its optimum development. Besides these traits which depend upon structure, it is conceivable that some tendencies and predispositions depend upon chemical processes which the genes may initiate. Such processes are terrifically complex and may require years of patient experimental work before biochemists and physiologists understand them completely, but psychologists can go ahead with their research independently if they have reasonable grounds for assuming such chemical predispositions. Most of the work on inherited personality or temperamental characteristics depends upon such an assumption.

As a matter of history, most of the work psychologists have done on the influence of heredity has centered around the *intelligence* problem. Either or both of the lines of thinking set forth above is plausible when applied to our thinking about intelligence. It is quite conceivable that either structural differences in brain cells or chemical differences in brain metabolism have something to do with the intelligence differences we identify by means of our tests.

Remembering always that it is only structures, predispositions, or chemical susceptibilities than can be determined by genes enables us to recognize at once that there are a great many things that cannot possibly be inherited. In the human individual, complex patterns of *behavior* are always learned. Law-breaking and criminal activities are not determined by heredity, though it is conceivable that a psychopathic personality might be. Beliefs and attitudes are learned, though there might be hereditary differences in temperament making some more congenial for an individual than others. Diseases, both physical and mental, are acquired, and the more we know about their causation the more we shall be able to protect those persons who have inherited special susceptibilities to certain kinds of stress. A man gets his frugality, his Presbyterianism, his passion for stamp-collecting, and his liberal political views from his parents by precept and example, not by physical inheritance.

Although it is the genes that control all hereditary characteristics, they exercise their influence in different ways. One important distinction is the one that is being made between the two kinds for which Fuller (1954) has used the terms *major genes* and *polygenes*. The distinction has to do with what is commonly referred to as single-factor and multi-factor inheritance. The major gene is one which by itself determines some character. If it is of the dominant type, a person who receives it from one of his parents will develop the trait. If it is of the recessive type, transmission from both parents is necessary in order that the trait may develop. Examples of this type of inheritance are the blood groups and Huntington's chorea, a serious degenerative disease of young adulthood. The action of major genes is modified to some extent by that of various accessory genes. Not all those who have a dominant gene for brown eyes develop eyes of exactly the same color.

Polygenes represent the extreme of this tendency for the effects of different genes to combine. For a large number of human characteristics, including those that have most social significance, no *single* gene can be identified. Many separate genes combine to produce the precise physical size and shape that an individual eventually shows. It seems likely that the hereditary basis of intelligence, special talents, and some basic qualities of temperament is this sort of multi-factor inheritance. At least one rare variety of feeble-mindedness, phenylpyruvic amentia, is known to be determined by a single pair of recessive genes, but in general, single-factor control of non-pathological characteristics is the exception rather than the rule. For most traits we can assume that the greater the number of genes helping to produce the characteristic, the more of it the person will show.

It may be, however, that in order for a trait to show up at all, the number of genetic determiners must reach a certain threshold level. Thus a personality disorder might never appear, although a person was carrying a number of genes for it, if the number was just below a certain minimum. It is conceivable, even quite probable, that many persons genetically are *almost* epileptic without ever having seizures, and that others are *almost* schizophrenic without ever experiencing a psychotic breakdown. It is in the cases of such persons who are near the genetic threshold for illness that environmental influences may count most heavily in determining whether or not symptoms develop. As presented here, this concept of gene thresholds is a hypothetical construct. We shall examine the actual evidence on the problem of mental illness in a later section of the chapter.

One other distinction that has been of some importance in the thinking people have done about heredity should be considered before we approach the research evidence. We can conceive of heredity as producing constitutions that differ in their general level of strength or weakness. If this were the case, the person who had inherited a strong constitution would show high resistance to all sorts of diseases and efficient defenses against many kinds of unfavorable circumstances. The person at the weak end of the continuum would be unable to withstand any sort of attack or strain. Or, instead of postulating some general strength, we can think in terms of specific susceptibilities to specific kinds of things, and hereditary defenses that operate within limited ranges. Traditionally, it has been the idea of general constitutional strength or weakness that has been most influential in men's thinking. Fears of vague hereditary "taints" are still common. Scientific work has brought the idea of specific susceptibilities into the foreground. In this area, as in connection with the controversy over general intelligence versus independent mental abilities, it is quite possible that the truth lies somewhere between the two extreme positions. A certain level of general constitutional strength and a certain pattern of specific vulnerabilities and defenses could both be included in a man's genetic inheritance.

To accept the idea of a hereditary basis for abilities, temperament, and susceptibility to mental disease does not mean pessimism if we remember that hereditary abilities can be cultivated and improved, and hereditary weaknesses can be overcome. Every human individual must live out his life within limits set by circumstances. His period of history, his social group, his childhood training, his finances, and the inexorable time limitations to which we are all subject keep him from developing in all directions. Hereditary limitations are no more frustrating than the others. As Kallman is continually pointing out, the more knowledge we acquire as to how the inherited constitutional defenses carry out their work, the better we shall be able to assist and promote such processes by medical means. Here as elsewhere knowledge is power. Let us turn now to the evidence.

ANIMAL EXPERIMENTS

That heredity sets limits to mental development is accepted by many people with so little question that it comes as a shock to realize that there was no real proof of the fact until recently. Watson caused a considerable stir when he stated that if he were given a healthy average child to train from birth on, he would guarantee to make of him anything that anyone desired. This was a possible hypothesis, even if it was sensational, until the animal-breeding experiments showed that some kind of mental ability *could be inherited*. Breeding experiments on rats have been carried on by Tryon (1942) at the University of California and by Heron (1935) at the University of Minnesota. The learning behavior that has been most widely investigated in rats is maze-running, and animals have been shown to differ widely. The plan of both these experiments was to select in the F-1 generation the animals who made the best and the worst maze scores. By breeding good maze-runners with each other and poor maze-runners with each other, groups of offspring were produced that differed to some extent in this ability. The process was continued generation after generation, environmental factors being kept as uniform as possible for all the animals. Each generation the groups drew farther apart, until by the F-8 in the Tryon experiment (see Figure 50) there was almost no overlapping and the poorest individual in the "bright" group was as good as the best individual in the "dull" group. Maze-running ability had been shown to depend on something that could be inherited.

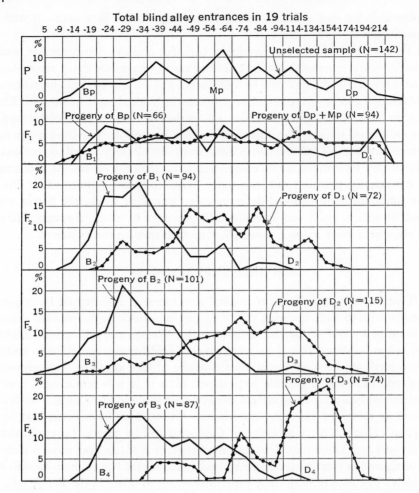

FIGURE 50. Differences between groups of "maze-bright" and "maze-dull" rats in successive generations. (Reproduced by permission of the publishers from *Comparative psychology*, Revised Edition, edited by F. A. Moss. Copyright, by Prentice-Hall, Inc., 1934, 1942.)

Other workers have bred strains of animals differing markedly in what might be called *temperamental* or *motivational* characteristics. Rundquist (1933) after twelve generations of selective breeding obtained groups of *active* and *inactive* rats. Active males averaged 123,000 revolutions of a revolving drum during a fifteen-day experimental period, whereas inactive males averaged only 6,000. C. S. Hall (1934, 1936, 1937) produced strains of rats differing in *emotionality*, and Hall and Klein (1942) showed that

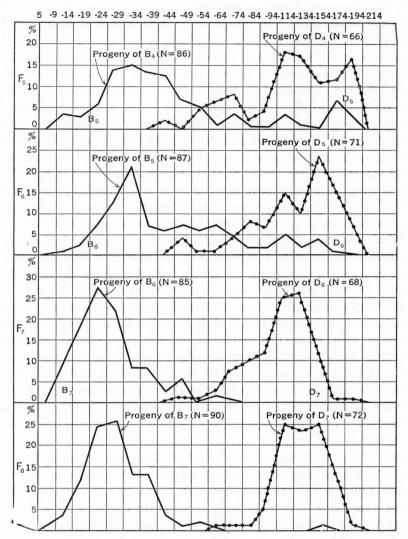

FIGURE 50 (continued). Differences between groups of "maze-bright" and "maze-dull" rats in successive generations.

aggressiveness was a part of the complex of traits that was being inherited in the non-emotional, fearless strain.

At the time Tryon and Heron first approached their work on "maze-bright" and "maze-dull" rats, many psychologists saw these characteristics as analogous to human intelligence. Trying these "bright" and "dull" rats out on other sorts of learning problems demonstrated that this interpretation was unwarranted. The "bright" rats were not good at everything, but simply at maze-running. The best evidence as to what the differences between the strains really means comes from a study by Searle (1949). He obtained 30 measurements for ten rats of each strain. Rats from each group showed a characteristic *pattern* of high and low scores, quite different for the two groups. The "dull" group did as well as the bright on many learning tasks that did not involve mazes. In general the "maze-bright" animals were "characteristically food-driven, economical of distance, low in motivation to escape from water, and timid in response to open spaces," whereas "dulls" were "relatively disinterested in food, average or better in water motivation, and timid of mechanical apparatus features." The striking thing about these differences is that they seem to be of a temperamental or motivational rather than of a cognitive nature.

Work with dogs has also emphasized the importance of inherited differences in temperament. It is possible to look upon pure-bred dogs as subjects in a natural experiment on inherited characteristics. Stockard *et al.* (1941) showed that basset hounds differ from German shepherd and Saluki dogs in their reactions to conditioning experiments as well as in the activity and alertness evident in their behavior. Scott (1953) and Fuller and Scott (1954) have reported on experiments conducted at the Jackson Memorial Laboratory. Different breeds of dogs differ in many motivational characteristics, such as aggressiveness, timidity, and sensitivity to noise. Three kinds of learning situation that were used as "tests" of their abilities—leash-control training, discrimination training, and spatial orientation—showed clearly that some breeds excelled in one sort of thing, others in another. There was practically no correlation between scores on the different "tests." Furthermore, when measurements were made at different stages of the learning process it was apparent that methods of attack on a new situation differed from breed to breed. It was characteristic of beagles, for example, to make many errors at the beginning, to make very rapid progress at the second stage, and to come out with variable, nonrigid habits at the end.

Two conclusions which may be important for our thinking about human heredity emerge from this animal research. One is that *patterns* of characteristics, some high and some low, rather than different levels of general ability, show up in these inbred strains. The other is that it is with regard to temperamental differences that there is clearest evidence for genetic determination. These conclusions are of particular interest, since they point in a direction opposite to the orientation that has characterized most of the work done on problems of heredity with human subjects. A large part of our effort has been directed toward an attempt to show that general intelligence is a hereditary trait, and we have amassed very little evidence on special aptitudes or types of learning. Furthermore, it seems to have been assumed by many workers that though ability may be inherited, personality is entirely the result of environmental variables, such as cultural influences and treatment during infancy. It might be well for us to reconsider these often unstated assumptions in the light of the animal results.

FAMILY RESEMBLANCES IN INTELLIGENCE

The facts that constitute the evidence for heredity most obvious and convincing to the man on the street are the least convincing to the scientist. Resemblances between members of the same family can mean many things. However, since there have been many studies in which family resemblances were systematically explored, they can legitimately be used to supplement more conclusive types of evidence. The trouble is, of course, that in the family we have a mixture of hereditary and environmental influences which it is impossible to disentangle.

Students in the social sciences do not get far before they encounter the Jukes and the Kallikaks. The Jukes were a New York family traced through seven generations, of pauperism, feeble-mindedness, crime, vice, and disease. The "Kallikaks" consisted of two families starting at the time of the American Revolution from the union of Martin Kallikak with two different women. The descendants of the feeble-minded girl's illegitimate son included a large number of feeble-minded and degenerate individuals. The descendants of Martin Kallikak and his lawful wife were predominately normal, self-respecting citizens. Both these studies were widely quoted for a long time as evidence for the serious effects of bad heredity through many generations. Of recent years, however, critics have pointed out that such a conclusion is not justified in view of the fact that the degenerate parents furnished for their children very unfavorable environments in which to develop excellent human qualities. It is impossible for us to say whether the genes or the environments constituted the greater handicap.

Other workers have studied *correlations* between members of families and have set up various hypotheses as to what these might mean. Although members of a family do not have the *same* heredity, they are genetically considerably more alike than persons chosen at random from the general population. If in a fairly large number of family groups, we can get an estimate of the amount of intra-group resemblance that heredity alone would account for, then we can consider deviations from this trend as evidence of the effects of environment. The following hypotheses have been tried by one or more investigators:

1. If environment is an important factor in the production of intellectual traits, then correlation coefficients between siblings should be *lower* for these traits than for physical characteristics like eye color, height, and head measurements which are thought to be almost entirely hereditary.
2. If environment is an important factor, correlations between like-sexed siblings should be higher than those between different-sexed siblings, since the environment is more closely similar for two boys or for two girls than it is for a boy and a girl in the family.
3. If environment is an important factor, correlations between siblings should be higher than correlations between parents and children since the fact that they belong to the same generation would operate to make the siblings' environment more similar.
4. If environment is an important factor, correlations between mothers and children should be higher than those between fathers and children since the mother is more closely associated with the children during their early formative years.

Scattered evidence has been cited both for and against each of these hypotheses. So far as the first is concerned, practically all investigators agree that the intra-family correlations for intelligence-test scores are of a magnitude comparable to those for structural physical traits. They center around .50 for both kinds of characteristics. Thus they furnish no evidence that intelligence is more dependent upon environmental influences than eye color or height is. The most thoroughgoing tests of the other three hypotheses are available in the work of Conrad and Jones (1940), who gave 997 individuals in 269 family groups the Army Alpha examination. None of the hypotheses outlined finds any support in their results. No clear trend with regard to like-sexed vs. different-sexed or mother-children vs. father-children correlations was apparent. The correlation between siblings was exactly the same as the correlation between parents and children: .49. The only conclusion we can draw is that if differences in environment have a pronounced effect on differences in mental ability, we cannot demonstrate that they have by methods of this sort. Jones and Conrad show that correlations such as those they obtained *can be* accounted for on the basis of heredity alone. That they *are* actually based on genetic similarity must be established in some other way.

TWIN STUDIES

We have explained in the previous chapter why it is that work on identical twins produces the soundest evidence we have that environmental influences affect measured intelligence. The best evidence we have on the hereditary basis of human psychological traits also comes from twin studies. The use that is made of twin subjects differs according to which questions we are asking. As we have seen in the previous chapter, the best way to evaluate the effects of environment is to hold heredity constant. This can be done where two monozygotic twins, known to be exactly alike in their genetic possibilities, are separated and exposed to different environmental stimulation. The best way to evaluate the influence of *heredity* is to take subjects who have experienced the *same* environment but who are known to differ in genetic endowment and compare them with a group in which *both* heredity and environment are the same. This is commonly done by comparing the amount of difference between identical twin pairs with the amount of difference between fraternal twins or between siblings.

Two words that figure prominently in reports on such research are *concordance* and *discordance*. Twin pairs are said to be concordant if they both show a certain characteristic. They are discordant if one shows it and the other does not. In general, whenever it can be shown that the percentage of concordant pairs is much higher among identical than among fraternal twins, there is a sound basis for concluding that the trait in question has a genetic origin. There are some qualifications and difficulties that arise in connection with this type of research, but we will postpone consideration of them until we have examined the important findings.

As was shown in Table 52 in the previous chapter, IQ differences between identical twins are smaller than are IQ differences between fraternal twins. When they are reared together, identical twins tend to get scores on intelligence tests that are almost as similar as the scores one person gets when he is tested twice. Furthermore, the fact that the resemblances in IQ are as striking as the resemblances in height and weight suggests that intelligence may be as much dependent on the genes as these physical characteristics are. (This is not a contradiction of what has been said in the previous chapter about environmental, especially educational, influences, since we know that environment can modify hereditary potentialities.) As has been indicated, all the work with foster children, family relationships, and the feeble-minded has supported the plausibility of the conclusion that intelligence differences in human beings are based at least in part on genetic differences.

So far as special abilities and talents are concerned, there is very little real evidence, but what there is corroborates the findings for general intelligence. Brody (1937) found that the correlations between scores on the Minnesota Spatial Relations Test (a test of mechanical aptitude) were .28 for fraternal twins and .69 for identical twins. McNemar (1933) found correlations averaging about .43 for fraternal twins and .79 for identical twins on motor-skills tests.

A large-scale study of the part heredity plays in some important psychological characteristics is in progress at the New York State Psychiatric Institute under the direction of Kallman (1950). The method is to start with a group of persons characterized by a certain diagnosis and then to locate and check up on their blood relatives. While much information has been accumulated about family members who show all degrees of relationship to the index cases, it is the figures for the twins that are most meaningful. Table 56 summarizes the concordance rates for monozygotic and dizygotic twins from the principal research studies that have been reported by Kallman and his associates.

TABLE 56.

Concordance Rates in Monozygotic and Dizygotic Twins Summarized from Kallman Studies
(Hurst, 1952)

	N	MONOZYGOTIC % CONCORDANT	N	DIZYGOTIC % CONCORDANT
Schizophrenia	268	86.2	685	14.5
Manic-Depressive	23	95.7	52	26.3
Senile Psychosis	33	42.8	75	8.0
Involutional Psychosis	29	60.9	67	6.0
Homosexuality	40	100	45	11.5

The results for schizophrenia are most striking because of the large number of cases on which they are based. According to these figures, if one of a pair of identical twins has the disease, eighty-six times out of a hundred the other twin has it also. The other fourteen who are not frankly schizophrenic are found to have schizoid personalities. Family comparisons for lesser degrees of relationship show much smaller percentages of agreement. As shown in Table 56 only 14.5 per cent of the fraternal twin pairs are concordant. Siblings of schizophrenics show about this same rate, as do children of one schizophrenic parent. Where both parents are schizophrenic, however, about 65 per cent of the children develop the condition. The genetic mechanism Kallman believes to be involved here is the inheritance by way of a single recessive gene producing a predisposition to schizophrenia. Along with this, however, some kind of constitutional defense system is inherited, and this seems to depend upon many genes. Thus the resistance to schizophrenia also varies from person to person. It is the evidence for the importance of these natural defense processes that keeps Kallman from taking a pessimistic view with regard to the disease. If we could learn what this defense process is like, we ought to be able to duplicate it, or at least strengthen it in persons whose family history shows them to be susceptible.

The results for manic-depressive psychosis also show far higher concordance rates for monozygotic than for dizygotic twins. Kallman thinks that the figures for this disease suggest the operation of a dominant gene whose action is somewhat irregular. The number of cases reported so far is not sufficient to warrant a definite statement. One minor fact of some interest in these studies, since it seems to show that the two mental diseases are quite different in their genetic origin, is that among monozygotic twin pairs there was not a single instance where one twin was schizophrenic, the other manic-depressive.

The evidence summarized in Table 56 with regard to the senile psychoses comes from a much larger study of senescent twin pairs. All twins obtainable in New York state who were sixty or over at the time the research began are being studied in a variety of ways. In 1951, 2,500 such pairs had been observed for six years (Kallman, Feingold, and Bondy, 1951). Longevity figures show that the life span is more similar for monozygotic than for dizygotic pairs. This adds to the evidence that longevity itself may have a hereditary basis. Physical similarities in the monozygotic pairs are pronounced even to an advanced age. Twins stay about the same size, develop wrinkles in the same places, and lose about the same amount of hair. Intellectual capacities are more similar for the identical than for the fraternal pairs, just as former studies have shown them to be in childhood and early youth. This suggests that the amount of deterioration in intelligence that comes with old age may depend upon the genes.

Kallman's study of male homosexuals was less successful than the others because of the difficulty in locating such subjects and getting their cooperation (Kallman, 1952). The findings do point in the same direction, since in cases where a subject was monozygotic the other twin always had a record of at least a moderate amount of homosexual activity. Kallman was convinced from what the men said that this complete concordance did not represent mutual influence. The practices were developed independently and often far apart, according to their reports. What Kallman thinks is inherited in these cases is some weakness, perhaps based on opposing sex genes, which might be one cause of the failure to develop mature sex behavior. Much more evidence is needed before any more precise theory can be formulated.

Slater's research in England corroborates Kallman's conclusions with regard to schizophrenia (Slater, 1953). The concordance rate for 67 monozygotic twin pairs was 76 per cent; for 224 dizygotic pairs, 14 per cent.

Another English study is of particular interest because it suggests an heredity basis for *neurotic* trends in the personality. These are usually explained entirely in terms of experiences that the person has undergone. Eysenck and Prell (1951) searched the birth records of five boroughs in south London for the names of all like-sex twins born during the period 1935-37. Out of 130 such pairs they located 68 and made careful tests to determine whether the pairs were of the one-egg or two-egg variety. They then administered the battery of tests by means of which the "neuroticism" factor is being measured in their research. (See Chapter 7.) The correlation between identical twins for neuroticism was .85. For fraternal twins the corresponding figure was .22. This constitutes just about the same amount and kind of evidence that neuroticism depends to some degree on heredity as that intelligence is genetically determined.

It is possible to criticize many of the studies of psychiatric variables on various counts, as Pastore (1940a) has shown. Diagnosis may be faulty. Selection may be biased to some extent if all twins are not located. Reports do not always show whether bias in the judgments made by experimenters was completely ruled out by keeping judges in ignorance of the group to which each subject belonged. However, the large number of cases on which the better-substantiated conclusions are based, the magnitude of the differences between concordance rates for one-egg and two-egg pairs, and the fact that evidence from England corroborates that from the United States make one hesitate to try to explain away all of these findings on the basis of technical criticisms that can be made of any one study or any one method.

One question that always arises in interpreting differences between identical and fraternal twin pairs has to do with whether the environmental factors that count most heavily in psychological developments are really equally similar for the two kinds of twins. As emphasis is placed on emotional rather than physical aspects of the environment, this becomes a factor of considerable potential importance. In many areas, such as intelligence, special abilities, and personality, there is a possibility that identical twins tend to be more alike than fraternals at least partly because they have lived through more nearly identical experiences. As one examines Kallman's figures for the major psychoses, however, it seems very improbable that the difference in concordance rates could have been produced entirely in this way. Psychogenic explanations of schizophrenia postulate an emotional trauma of such severity that it does not seem possible that only one of two fraternal twins would suffer it from his family. Even if some of the evidence for heredity reported from the type of twin study that compares monozygotic and dizygotic pair differences can be explained away when we examine environmental influences closely, it seems unlikely that all of it can be disposed of in this way.

Twin studies also involve biases which would lead us to *under*estimate the importance of genetic determiners. Price (1950) has called attention to two types of *prenatal* environmental influence that act differentially upon monozygotic twins. These may eventually produce behavioral differences between the two individuals which we will attribute to post-natal causes such as education and training. *Lateral inversions* are common in identical twin pairs. In such cases each twin is a mirror image of the other. If one is right-handed, the other is left-handed, and other characteristics follow the same pattern. We do not know enough about these cases to know whether there is a possibility of some impairment of cerebral dominance in one twin that would tend to hamper him in his development. Price is inclined to stress more strongly his second point having to do with a factor that affects monozygotic pairs developing in a single chorion or membrane. Since in such cases the two individuals share the same circulatory system, there is a real possibility that a temporary imbalance may create a deficiency in oxygen supply or moisture for one twin at a crucial developmental stage. This could handicap him permanently, if only to a slight degree. In such a pair, differences that we measure years later in intelligence, neuroticism, or general vitality would be wrongly attributed to the external environment, and our conclusions about its influence would thus be in error.

The whole field of research on human heredity is beset with difficulties. Its importance, however, justifies the expenditure of large amounts of money and research ingenuity, and the study of twins is by far the most promising approach.

POPULATION TRENDS

As we have explained earlier, decisions about individuals and attitudes of pessimism or optimism about the future possibilities of any one person do not depend upon our conclusions with regard to heredity and environment. If a trait is *modifiable*, and a good share of all human psychological traits are, improvement can be brought about through learning. When we understand anyone's weaknesses or special susceptibilities we can often counteract the effects of these and prevent difficulties from occurring. So far as the *individual* is concerned, the progress of knowledge about both environmental and hereditary determiners of psychological traits fits in with a moderately hopeful outlook.

The significance of the work on heredity, as many workers see it, is its implications for the future of the total population of our West European society. If the progress of science leads to a steady increase in a segment of the population somewhat lacking in intelligence and stability, the generations to come will face serious problems.

This possibility occurred to psychologists when they became aware of the sizable differences in average IQ between the various social classes. (See Chapter 12.) Social statistics consistently show that the so-called lower classes have more children per family than the middle and upper classes do. A differential of this sort could lead to a considerable drop in average intelligence in the course of a few generations.

A number of attempts have been made to predict from the figures just how great this decline is likely to be. Thomson (1946), on the basis of data from the Isle of Wight, presented the figures found in Table 57 which illustrate clearly the way in which such predictions are made. Thomson showed, as have a number of others in Great Britain and the United States, that if we use a weighted average of the IQ level in families of different sizes as an indicator of what the IQ level will be in the next generation, we come out with a predicted drop of about 2 IQ points per generation. In correlation terms, studies with various groups of school children consistently give negative r's from —.16 to —.26 between intelligence and number of children in the family (Lorimer, 1952). In the Thomson study it was —.25.

The new material that has been contributed toward our thinking on this problem in the years since World War II has served to make the problem more puzzling than it was before. There have been several studies in which the same test has been given to school children in the same area after an

TABLE 57.

Data from the Isle of Wight Leading to a Prediction of a Decline in the Intelligence Level from One Generation to the Next

(Thomson, 1946)

(a) NUMBER OF FAMILIES	(b) NUMBER IN FAMILY	(c) AVERAGE IQ	(d) PRODUCT OF a x c	(e) NUMBER OF CHILDREN	(f) PRODUCT OF c x e
115	1	106.2	12,213.0	115	12,213.0
212	2	105.4	22,344.8	424	44,689.6
185	3	102.3	18,925.5	555	56,776.5
152	4	101.5	15,428.0	608	61,712.0
127	5	99.6	12,649.2	635	63,246.0
103	6	96.5	9,939.5	618	59,637.0
88	7	93.8	8,254.4	616	57,780.8
102	8	95.8	9,771.6	816	78,172.8
1,084			109,526.0 Mean = 101.04		434,227.7 Mean = 98.98

interval of from seven to fifteen years. The largest and most complete of these is reported in *The Trend of Scottish Intelligence* (Scottish Council, 1949) but the same kind of findings are reported by R. B. Cattell (1950a). Instead of the expected decrease in average IQ, these retest studies show a slight but significant increase. In the Scottish study it was about 2 points for the fifteen-year period.

This unexpected gain can be interpreted in various ways. As yet there is no general agreement as to what it means. Writers who prefer to explain all intelligence differentials as much as possible on the basis of difference in environment and education tend to discount the significance of the negative *r*'s between intelligence and family size. If these mean simply that the opportunity for intellectual development is on the average somewhat lower in large families, they of course tell us nothing about genetic potentialities. Nisbet (1953) has assembled some correlational evidence that at least part of the negative *r* between intelligence and family size can be explained on this basis. Writers who are impressed with the importance of hereditary determiners of intellectual ability can explain away the increase over a period of time, arguing that it is simply an increase in *test score* and that this may reflect nothing more than the growing familiarity of school children with tests of this type. Anastasi (1954) and Lorimer (1952) point out various other possible interpretations of the facts obtained. P. E. Vernon (1951) has decided that intelligence tests cannot be validly used in such investigations.

One factor that may be of some eugenic importance is that it has been found at the lower end of the intelligence distribution that the reproduction rate falls off markedly. It has been known for some time that idiots and imbeciles seldom have children. Most of the idiots and imbeciles of each new generation come from normal or moron families. A follow-up study by Reed *et al.* (1954), in which family data are being obtained on individuals who were inmates of the institution for the feeble-minded in Faribault, Minnesota during the period from 1911 to 1918, is interesting in this connection. The average IQ for the subjects in the original group was 38. For these institutionalized cases the reproduction rate is of course negligible. The new data that Reed *et al.* are reporting show that the *siblings* of these cases, whose average was probably dull but not feeble-minded, also have failed to attain the reproduction rate necessary for replacement. The figures suggest the possibility that unfavorable genes like those making for mental deficiency tend to eliminate themselves.

The whole problem is terrifically complex. It seems unlikely that any simple statement can be made to describe dysgenic or eugenic population trends now in operation. At the present time, a realization that a problem of this sort exists and an attitude of receptiveness to whatever kinds of new evidence we may be able to obtain in connection with it would seem to be indicated. The natural resource that it is most important for us to conserve is human quality.

SUMMARY

The rapidly growing science of genetics has shown us how to think about heredity as a basis of human differences. Anatomical and biochemical characteristics are under genetic control. Any kind of psychological potentialities or predispositions that are thought to have a structural or a chemical basis thus can be assumed to be inherited. Learning and experience determine what becomes of such hereditary potentialities. Some traits depend upon a single gene; more of them arise from the combination of a large number of genes.

Animal experiments have demonstrated that psychological traits can be inherited. Differences in motivation and temperament, and differences in the pattern of learning abilities which may depend upon such motivation, have been the most striking findings in the selective breeding experiments.

The study of family resemblances is not very conclusive for understanding heredity, since differences as well as likenesses within the same family depend upon genes. In general, correlations for intelligence are as high as for physical traits.

The twin studies most crucial for the demonstration of the effects of heredity are those in which concordance and discordance rates are compared for identical and fraternal twins. The most striking findings have been in the medical and psychiatric fields. Identical twins are much more similar than are fraternals with regard to several mental diseases and length of life. The evidence is less clear for homosexuality.

Work on heredity has led to a considerable interest in eugenics and the effort to identify and check dysgenic trends in our population. Predictions that the average intelligence level will decline because of the negative correlation between IQ and family size have not been borne out when testing programs were repeated in communities where tests had previously been given. Improvements in education may be covering up a decline in hereditary potentialities, or there may be biological trends that tend to eliminate genes making for mental deficiency from the population. Evidence is insufficient to enable us to decide among the explanations that have been proposed.

CHAPTER 19

Toward A Science of Human Differences: Achievements and Challenges

IT IS APPARENT as one reviews the considerable body of research cited in the successive chapters of this book that millions of man hours have already gone into the task of creating a science of individual differences. What have they produced in the way of generalizations and principles? In this ocean of data what icebergs can be discerned from their outlines on the surface of the water?

METHODS OF ATTACK ON RESEARCH PROBLEMS

Perhaps the principal accomplishment has been the working out of a variety of methods by means of which human individuality can be investigated. No longer need we base our conclusions entirely on philosophical reasoning, clinical observation, or personal experience. If we have an idea about any sort of difference between individuals—what it means, from what source it arises, how stable it is from time to time—we can turn to the reports of psychologists who have worked on such problems for suggestions as to how to proceed. Each research worker can start where his predecessor on that particular road stopped. Undoubtedly, in a field where so much activity is going on, the methods of the future will not be exactly *like* the methods of the present, but they will be in some way an outgrowth of them.

The basic methodological cornerstone in differential psychology has been the idea of *measuring* the individual by comparing him with a group. The realization that it was possible to develop systems of *measurement* by using the average for a group as the reference point and a number representing the variability of the group as the unit of measurement, obvious as it seems to this test-wise generation, constituted the most decisive forward step. Once it was taken, progress in many directions quickly followed. Binet's first intelligence scale, with mental-age norms determined by the testing of ten children at each age level, seems very inadequate from a statistical standpoint today. But to have realized that intelligence could be measured in this manner was an intellectual achievement that made all the later intelligence tests possible. Ways of measuring special abilities, interests, attitudes, and personality traits all rest on this central idea of using data from a group to fix a scale along which individuals can be measured.

Another methodological foundation of what we know and hope to know about individual differences is *correlation*, or the exploration of relationships. This too is something that was recognized by the first workers in this field, Binet, Spearman, Stern, and others, and has been taken for granted ever since. We orient ourselves and discover what a new measurement of any human characteristic is showing us about the persons to whom it is applied by correlating the scores with other scores or measurements obtained from the same persons. This basic idea has been elaborated in many complex ways. On the one hand we have the vast literature about test validity, resting on correlations between tests and all sorts of criteria. On the other hand we have the even vaster literature of factor analysis, resting on the correlations of test scores with each other. Little by little we have shifted from simple concrete questions like "Is this test valid?" to the larger questions, "What are the basic dimensions on which human beings differ and how can they best be measured?"

As a result of all this body of work, we take as a matter of course some high correlations (such as those consistently obtained between different verbal intelligence tests), some moderate correlations (such as those between intelligence tests and school criteria), and some correlations that have again and again turned out to be very low (such as those between physical measurements and abilities). The challenging problem for present-day research workers is to unravel the meanings of these low correlations from the complex fabric in which they appear. Two approaches seem to be most promising.

One is to examine carefully the mathematical characteristics of the relationship about which information is being sought and determine whether it may perhaps be *curvilinear* rather than linear. It is quite conceivable that a minimum of some ability or talent may be absolutely necessary for success in some field, and yet that more of the same ability may be no advantage at all. Characteristics of what we call an "ear for music" seem to work in this way. One must have a good sense of pitch in order to sing or play an instrument. Below a certain level, pitch discrimination is correlated with success in music. Above that level it is not. In a group composed of persons all of whom show adequate pitch discrimination, it is other aspects of ability and personality that correlate with achievement. The scatter plots for such relationships look like Figure 51 or Figure 52. In Figure 51 the two variables show a fairly close relationship throughout the lower half of their range of scores but none at all from there on up. In Figure 52 the two variables show a positive correlation in the lowest third of the range of scores, a zero relationship in the middle third, and a negative rela-

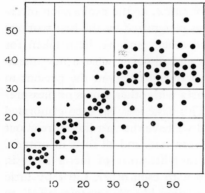

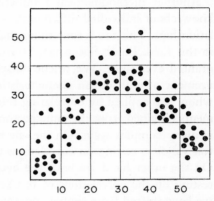

FIGURE 51. Scatter plot illustrating one type of curvilinear relationship.

FIGURE 52. Scatter plot illustrating a second type of curvilinear relationship.

tionship in the highest third. Methods are available for computing correlation coefficients that take this curvilinearity into consideration, but if they are to be used, there must be a fairly large number of cases in the sample on which research is being done. There is a real possibility that in many areas where low correlations have been consistently reported curvilinear relationships may exist, since the effect of curvilinearity is to make coefficients computed by the ordinary correlation formulas turn out to be low. One of the tasks we face, then, is to obtain some large samples and check up on this possibility in some important areas. An example of a kind of problem for which this might be useful is the relationship of special aptitudes to job success.

Another way of throwing light on the meaning of low correlations is what might be called the phenomenological or clinical method. What shows up as a low correlation in a group may represent a very close relationship for some individuals in the group, none at all for others. When we know something about what the trait in question *means* to the person in question we can understand why the figures turn out as they do. The work of Barker *et al.* (1953) on somatopsychological problems, mentioned in Chapter 16, is a good example of this method. Physical characteristics of all sorts—size, shape, coloring—are evaluated differently by different individuals. What one person sees as an asset appears to another to be a liability. Standard correlation methods cover up these very interesting personal idiosyncrasies.

A low but statistically significant correlation consistently obtained in a variety of samples is a challenge to research. If it were zero, we could abandon the hypothesis underlying it. If it were high, we could assume that the important factors had been brought out. As differential psychology now stands, there are many of these puzzling correlations which might be clarified if we were to test the relationship for curvilinearity, or to examine the "phenomenal field" of each subject. Probably more precise methods of analysis will eventually be developed. The point here is that progress now depends not on repeatedly investigating and reporting correlations of the same magnitude for the same pairs of variables, but on devising some way to analyze such relationships to make them more meaningful.

The third large family of methods that is now at the disposal of research workers includes ways that have been developed for making inferences about populations from limited samples. This is perhaps the most basic problem in statistics, involved in all the other special problems with which research workers in different fields are concerned. For differential psychologists it has been a tremendous advantage to be able to determine whether an obtained result is statistically significant—to know for example that there is only a small probability that the groups from which two means come are samples from the same population. It has enabled us to focus our attention on important human differences and ignore the slight ones, to resolve conflicts between investigators over the meaning of research data, and to make good decisions about the number of subjects we need to use in any projected study. The statistics of sampling distributions has made a *general* science of human differences possible.

Along with the mathematical developments underlying the concepts of sampling distributions and statistical significance have come important advances in our understanding of the concrete practical steps that must be taken to obtain a sample of persons who will really represent the population from which they are drawn. The mathematical reasoning is based on *random* sampling which can easily be used for drawing cards from a deck or balls from an urn, but which is often impractical when one wishes to test human beings. Out of experience with public opinion polling, market research, and test standardization have come a number of practical techniques for drawing samples to which the mathematical formulas can legitimately be applied.

As psychologists have become more sophisticated about sampling they have begun to realize that it is not just the choice of *subjects* in an experiment to which sampling principles must be applied. Brunswik (1947) has pointed out that we must make sure that the situations with which we are confronting our subjects also constitute an adequate sample of such situations. This is a difficult thing to do, and probably some new sampling principles will need to be worked out. How shall we obtain a sample of tests for a factor analysis which are truly representative of mental abilities as a whole? How shall we guarantee that the raters who give us our basic data for a personality study are representative of all possible judges of personality? Unanswerable as such questions are at present, even to consider them tends to broaden the scope of our work.

During the half-century during which our standard techniques of mental measurement, correlation, and sampling were being developed and applied to the study of human individuality, many errors have been made and corrected, many obstacles recognized and surmounted. We now know a great deal about number systems and are immediately suspicious of conclusions based on data in which interval scales have been handled like ratio scales. We know some of the tricks that can be played on the unwary investigator by gain scores, achievement quotients, and the like. We know how unreliability in the measuring instrument affects group differences and correlations. We know that tests labeled "intelligence" cannot be used interchangeably, and that scores on a personality inventory do not always mean what they appear to mean. It is easy to criticize and feel superior to the psychologists of the past who have fallen into these traps. What we should remember is that it is their work that has shown us where the serious pitfalls are and thus enabled us to avoid them.

In summing up the progress that has been made in studying psychological differences between persons, the least that can be said is that usable methods of attack on such problems have been formulated. Can we go any farther than this? Are there general principles or ideas that can serve as organizers for the mass of detailed data produced by the research studies? Such general principles or concepts should be of value to persons working in all areas of human relations. It seems worth while to try to state them even though there is as yet no complete agreement as to what they are.

SOME EMERGING CONCEPTS

Dimension

The first of these concepts which is proving to be widely applicable in the study of individual differences is that of *dimension*. It has been used in various chapters of this book when we were discussing the investigations of intelligence, personality, and physical characteristics, especially the conclusions based on factor analysis. Measuring scales can be thought of as *axes*, and a person's score can be represented by a distance along one of these reference lines.

Superficially it might seem that "dimension" is simply a new name for characteristics that at various periods have been called faculties, types, or traits. Often descriptions phrased in these earlier terms can easily be translated into the dimensional phraseology. But the newer way of putting the facts does have some advantages over the older. For one thing, it is a *neutral* system that does not commit us to any one kind of evaluation of human individuals. The name of a trait almost always carries some evaluation along with it. Since we think of it as something contained in or possessed by the person, we naturally make automatic judgments about superiority and inferiority when we use the label. To shift from the discussion of traits like intelligence to that of dimensions like V, N, and S involves an attempt to maintain an objective, non-judgmental attitude toward the data.

Furthermore, dimensional statements do not carry the connotation of finality or certainty that statements in terms of type or trait do. A person either has a trait or he has not. He belongs to one type or to another. It is difficult to combine or reconcile two proposed typologies. One must choose between them. Dimensional analysis permits us to view the same data from different points in space, so to speak—to try out different theories about what the basic directions are and see how they fit. Thus bodies of data obtained in the service of different theories can often be combined. We have seen examples of such combinations in the gradual rapprochement of the English and American theories about the components of intelligence (see Chapter 4), and in Eysenck's demonstration that the results of his factor analysis of social attitudes did not disagree fundamentally with Ferguson's formulations (see Chapter 8). Dimensions are tentative, relative concepts. They can be moved around and modified more readily than faculties, types or traits can.

The dimensions we are now using in our descriptions of abilities and personality have been made apparent to us in two ways. The first and earliest method was to take some common concept already being applied to individuals and try to refine it and make its meaning more precise. "Intelligence" and "adjustment" are examples of such qualities. Psychologists worked out tests to measure as well as they could what they thought was intelligence. Experience showed that different tests did not give identical results when applied to the same group of individuals—that the characteristic was more complex than they had assumed at the beginning. Experience showed also that not everything the layman includes in his idea of intelligence was being picked up by the tests designed to measure it—that test intelligence was a somewhat narrower characteristic than intelligence as observed in life situations. Similarly, "adjustment" as measured by the various inventories psychologists worked out proved to be both more complex and more limited than the general characteristic the term refers to in common speech. To be accurate, psychologists should really put quotation marks around such words as "intelligence," "adjustment," and "mechanical aptitude" when they use them to refer to characteristics measured by tests, since they refer to dimensions specified in definite ways rather than to broad unanalyzed qualities. The kind of research that has led to the specifying and pinning down of these elusive concepts that have been used for centuries to describe human individuality has been summarized in the chapters on intelligence, personality, and other characteristics in Part II. So far as these things are concerned, differential psychology is simply an extension of previous knowledge.

As indicated earlier, another method has been increasingly coming into use for the identification of basic dimensions. Instead of starting with what people think some important trait is and with the word they have used to stand for it, we can start with a correlation matrix representing known relationships between scores on various tests. We can deliberately postpone any effort to specify what each test is measuring until we have applied factor-analytic techniques to this correlation matrix and laid bare its essential structure. We then can use these *factors*, which did not exist in anybody's mind prior to the analysis, as dimensions around which we organize our thinking about individuals. The development of high-speed electronic computers has made these techniques increasingly feasible. The results so far have been encouraging. The advantage over previous methods of attack is that factor analysis frees the psychologist to some extent from the set that traditional ways of describing human beings have imposed upon him. The freedom is far from absolute, because his choice of variables to be correlated and the names he gives factors when the mathematical work is completed still are determined by what previous thinkers have said. But he is at least ready for something new if he happens to encounter it.

As has been shown in Part II, much of the recent work within each of the broad areas represented by the chapter headings consists of factor-analytic studies. What we are beginning to suspect now is that the broad areas themselves have been wrongly separated. We know that if we discuss intelligence in one chapter and vocational aptitudes in another, it is purely for the sake of convenience and not because the two kinds of dimension are completely independent of one another. The S factor that repeatedly shows up in factor analyses of intelligence-test materials is the same thing as the judgment of spatial relationships that has been measured for years by mechanical aptitude tests. It was a historical accident that produced any separation between these areas in the first place. Psychologists working in schools and colleges were most aware of aspects of intelligence. Psychologists working in guidance centers and personnel offices were most aware of vocational aptitudes.

A more surprising development that is becoming increasingly evident in our time is what looks like an obliteration of the distinction between abilities and emotional-motivational characteristics. Over most of its short history as a science and its long history as a branch of philosophy, psychology has assumed that cognitive and conative characteristics are independent of one another. The behavior of an individual was thought to depend upon what he *could* do and what he *wished* to do. The preceding pages have furnished many examples of traits or dimensions that are defined in both cognitive and conative terms. Perhaps the clearest signposts pointing in this direction are the results reported in the chapter on individual differences in perception. Psychology textbooks of the future may be organized in terms of basic variables only dimly sensed at the present stage of research.

Hierarchy

Along with the identification of dimensions along which human individuality can be measured has come the realization that the dimensions themselves must be organized in some manner if the whole system is to be manageable. Factor analysts working with intelligence-test materials now think in terms of twenty or thirty separate factors rather than the six or eight Thurstone first envisaged. Cattell finds a dozen or more personality factors, Guilford twenty or more interest factors. What are we to do with this embarrassing abundance of "basic" traits?

The most reasonable solution is one that the British factor analysts have been advocating for some time. Let us think of these characteristics as a hierarchy. Such a way of thinking about intelligence and about personality has already been set forth in some detail in Chapters 4 and 7. Some of the dimensions we have identified are broader and more general in their scope than others. What Spearman called "g" is one example; what Eysenck calls "neuroticism" is another. A person can be described in terms of five measurements or in terms of fifty. Which system we choose will depend upon the purpose we wish the measurements to serve. In connection with many types of research project, all we need to know about the subjects is their general level of intelligence and emotional stability. But the army personnel officer who wishes to assign each man to the job he can do best needs to know more specific things about new recruits. A hierarchical scheme takes care of both kinds of need.

Pattern

With even a limited number of dimensions along which human characteristics can be measured, it becomes possible to account for much individuality without postulating any traits that are unique or peculiar to one person alone. Suppose we assume, for example, that there are ten dimensions for each of which seven degrees of the characteristic can be distinguished. The number of types of individual this state of affairs would produce is something over 56,000!

Psychologists have for some time been applying in various special areas the notion that *traits* are common to all, but *patterns* of traits constitute individuality. Counselors interpreting test results to their clients have used profiles. Factor analysts have discovered different patterns of mental abilities in persons of identical IQ levels. Williams has called our attention to individual patterns of metabolic activity. Both Kuder and Strong have stressed patterns of interests. Hathaway and Meehl (1951) have developed the system for interpretation of scores on the Minnesota Multiphasic Personality Inventory around patterns of subscores and have developed a workable coding system for describing such patterns.

In general, patterns of measurements have been used more in practical counseling and clinical situations than they have in research. We need more complex statistical methods than those we have used in the past if we are to investigate the problems that this kind of thinking raises. How are we to decide, for example, whether the patterns of metabolic activity Williams has pointed out have any relationship to patterns of scores on the MMPI or the Kuder Preference Record? Cronbach (1949b) has been exploring methods of approach to such problems as this, but it may be a

considerable time before completely adequate methods of analysis are available and psychologists really learn to think in terms of patterns instead of
in terms of single traits taken one at a time.

APPLICATIONS AND PRACTICAL ISSUES

Facts, principles, and techniques that come out of the study of individual differences can be applied immediately to human enterprises. Among
the most important of such applications have been those made in our
schools. Teachers have probably always been aware that marked individual differences exist. Psychological research has enabled them to give
concrete form to some of these differences and to cope with them more
adequately.

From the time that Binet placed the first intelligence test at the disposal
of the Paris public schools, teachers and administrators have been using
tests of this type to help them make decisions about the general level of
difficulty at which each child can most successfully operate. As vocational
aptitude tests and tests based on factor analysis have been made available,
forward-looking teachers have been trying to take into consideration the
pattern as well as the level of each student's abilities. Important issues in
education center around this point. We have now abundant evidence, most
of it summarized in Chapter 4, that it is only the verbal and reasoning
abilities that are related significantly to school achievement, even in
present-day American schools which have broken away from traditional
curricula. Some educational theorists would say that the teacher's task is
to capitalize on these verbal and reasoning abilities and cultivate them, and
that the other kinds of teaching that enter into the broad characteristic we
call intelligence are irrelevant so far as the school is concerned. Other
theorists argue that this relationship between achievement and the verbal
and reasoning factors is a vestige of our bookish academic past. They insist
that there are many avenues to learning and that the school must explore
these other possibilities in order to be fair to its students whose profile of
abilities has its peak in the space, visualization, or perception section.
Meanwhile many boys and girls who know nothing of the theoretical controversy are forced by compulsory education laws to spend unhappy years
in a situation to which it is impossible for them to adapt themselves very
successfully. For a people who have committed themselves to a vast program of public education, knowledge about the nature of intelligence is a
necessity, not a luxury.

The second type of activity in which knowledge of individual differences is being extensively applied is counseling. Because of the great diversity of opportunities and possibilities in our complex society, it is required of each person that he make good decisions about what he wishes to do with his own life. The measurement along defined dimensions of mental characteristics known to be of some importance in various fields of work has already served us well in this connection. It is standard practice in vocational counseling agencies to give a battery of tests and combine the results into a profile, making apparent the pattern of the person's abilities and interests.

The principal difficulties that counselors and clients face in making use of this method center around a problem discussed earlier in this chapter—the interpretation of *low* correlations. The best available tests of vocational aptitudes have only moderate correlations with criteria of occupational success. In order to give clients who seek counseling more dependable information, it will be necessary to develop a body of knowledge about basic abilities and personality traits that goes far beyond reports of validity coefficients of .45 or .39 for the tests being used. The need for research analyzing the psychological meaning of low correlations is urgent here. If a relationship with success is curvilinear, as it may well be for various kinds of talent, it would be extremely useful to know about it. There may be some definite points where the curvature of the regression lines represented by some of our test-validity coefficients changes abruptly. There could easily be a situation, for example, where persons scoring low on a clerical aptitude test almost always failed at clerical jobs, but excellent workers scored no higher than mediocre ones. The other approach to low correlations, that of finding out the *attitudes* of different individuals to the facts represented by the measurements, is also directly relevant to counseling where attitudes are all-important. We have noted earlier that one of the reasons why measures of dexterity and reaction time show low correlations with criteria of success as drivers of motor vehicles might be that individuals react to deficiencies in various ways. Some slow reactors may exercise particular care to drive a little more slowly and take more precautions than the average driver. Others, interpreting slow reaction time as a defect, may constantly practice speeding themselves up in an attempt to overcome it. The first type of person would tend to rank high, the second type low, on the criterion "freedom from accidents." The correlation might be near zero although there is a genuine relationship between the two variables in each individual case. Once we understand what some of these intervening variables between test and criterion are, counseling can be made more meaningful by discussing the attitudes themselves. Thus with counseling as with educational programs, there is real need for further research.

The third type of situation in which the findings of differential psychologists are being applied is in selection programs. There are a great many of these programs—in industry, in the Civil Service, in all branches of the military service. In some cases, the responsible person simply selects a battery of tests from those which have been published and tries them out in a particular situation. In other cases, as in the Army Air Force program, an elaborate battery of new tests is constructed for a special purpose. In terms of the basic concepts we have been discussing, the questions such a selection program raises at the beginning are, "What dimensions would appear to be useful?" and "At what level in the hierarchy will it be most profitable to work?" It often turns out that there is room for a considerable difference of opinion about these matters. For example, in military selection programs, most of the American psychologists in responsible positions were of the opinion that it would be desirable to measure as many narrowly-defined special abilities as possible and to weight the scores in a way that would give the maximum predictive value to the composite. British psychologists preferred to work as much as possible with measurements high in the hierarchy—to measure primarily "g" and the cluster of abilities that depend upon schooling—and then simply to allocate to each branch of the services equal numbers of men who were adequate or superior in this all-round way (Vernon and Parry, 1949). Published reports would seem to indicate that both systems worked reasonably well. Again we are confronted with the need for further research. When we must make such a choice between alternatives, we have as yet no sound basis for deciding whether to measure abilities as broad and general as possible or as narrow and specialized as possible.

The fourth purpose that we might expect knowledge about individual differences to serve is that of guiding the progress of our whole society in desirable directions. Each year in our national Congress and in the legislatures of forty-eight different states, laws are passed which are based on some assumptions or hypotheses about differences between groups and individuals. Immigration laws reflect the ideas legislators have about race and nationality differences. Compulsory education laws probably reflect general public attitudes about the educability of individuals. In addition to the new crop of laws that it harvests, each year reaps the fruits of thousands of policy decisions in which some conception of the meaning of individuality has been involved. A housing administrator assumes that esthetic considerations have no place in a slum clearance project for the benefit of "lower"-class residents. A school board member assumes that good teaching will bring all pupils up to a fairly high level of proficiency in reading, writing, and arithmetic. A mother assumes that because her son is interested in sketching he must have an important talent for art.

Even with the limited knowledge we now have about differential psychology we can plainly see that some of the assumptions people are making are wrong. The total effect of a number of laws and policy decisions based on wrong premises is of course to produce a society that does not fit the individuals in it as well as it might. This leads to a certain amount of maladjustment and frustration that could be avoided. Furthermore, it seems probable that the positive values that could emerge in a society where each individual's unique contribution to the common good was utilized and rewarded are not being realized.

We need to know more, and the knowledge we have needs to be disseminated more widely. The research problems that still have the most work to be done on them are those relating to the interaction of basic hereditary differences with the effects of education and experience. If we are willing to give up the hopeless arguments about heredity and environment and settle down to a program of studying specific ways of influencing specific characteristics and patterns of characteristics, we may develop a much sounder basis than we now have for intelligent social decisions. If it could be shown, for example, that children with a considerable number of schizophrenic relatives and ancestors (the type of subjects in which Kallman has been interested) show at an early age a certain pattern of metabolic characteristics (the type of phenomenon in which Williams has been interested) we *might* be able to prevent the disease by compensating for known deficiencies before they produce the psychosis.

Most of our efforts so far have been directed to the problem of the effects of environmental deprivation or enrichment on the *level* of intelligence, the traditional nature-nurture problem. We know little or nothing about the effects of life experiences and environmental situations on the *patterns* of traits which constitute individuality. Longitudinal studies can be expected to provide us with much useful information. Such tests as the Primary Mental Abilities Tests for children of different age levels now make it possible for us to collect relevant data. There is no reason why these problems should not be attacked by means of controlled experiments set up to study the effects of specified kinds of learning situations on patterns of abilities, interests, or personality traits. The evidence Strong has presented (see Chapter 8) would suggest that in adults patterns of interests are highly resistant to change. This may or may not be true for earlier age levels or for other dimensions of variation in personality. There is much to be investigated here.

THE BASIC VALUES

In all our talk of problems and methods, of hypotheses and levels of significance, it is important that we do not lose sight of our basic aim, the welfare of concrete human individuals. It is sometimes hard to see that science means this. One of the effects of the tragedy and destruction that our century has witnessed has been to make us very critical of the world scientific progress has given us. There are many who insist that the civilization we have developed no longer fits man, that its destructive potentialities are beyond his control, its complexities beyond his comprehension, its uncertainties deeply frustrating to his longing for order and peace. In the face of these difficulties, prominent writers and thinkers of our time are advocating a return to a simpler, more congenial world. They would base their ideas of the nature and needs of man upon the authoritative writings of the past, the intuitive wisdom of the world's great authors, philosophers, and religious leaders.

Psychologists as a group are committed to a conviction that the cure for the ill effects of an incomplete science is a more complete science. If our knowledge of the physical world has far outrun our knowledge of man himself, then the solution is to obtain, as rapidly as possible, the information that will enable us to direct our own energies toward constructive ends as effectively as we have harnessed the power in stream and atom. Inherent in the whole program of scientific research is a faith that it is better to *know*. And since man is not separate from but a part of the universe, there is ample justification for the belief that laws governing his behavior, individually and in groups, can be discovered. When we adopt this viewpoint we are forced to realize that we can expect no certainty to lean back upon for a long time to come. We must learn to proceed upon the basis of tentative judgments. We must develop the flexibility that will permit us to change our convictions and our procedures with respect to human problems as new evidence becomes available.

The unique contribution the differential psychologist makes to this ongoing scientific enterprise is his constant insistence that the "proper study of mankind" is not only "man" but "men." It is not that he denies human similarities. In fact, inherent in most of his procedures is the hypotheses that basically all men are alike, measurable along the same dimensions, differing in amount and pattern of characteristics rather than in quality. But in the last analysis "mankind" is an abstraction. It is individual boys and girls, men and women, that our schools, our factories, and our political institutions are designed to serve. If they are to do this adequately, we must see that they adapt themselves to a considerable range of variation in individuals. Chairs must be of different sizes; some assignments must be harder and longer than others. Recognition must be given to many kinds of work and self-expression.

Psychologists here join forces with persons in other professions who are emphasizing the importance of individuality. The work of Williams on individual differences in body chemistry has been mentioned several times in previous pages. He has made a convincing plea for research undertakings in which individuals can be studied from many points of view simultaneously—biochemical, medical, psychological. Perhaps some day we shall have a science of human individuality which will cut across the boundaries of all these separate disciplines. Out of this scientific work can come an attitude deeper than tolerance, a realization of the most basic human right of all—the individual's right to be what he is.

Bibliography

ABERNETHY, E. M. 1925. Correlations in physical and mental growth. *J. educ. Psychol.*, **16**, 458-466, 539-546.

ADAMS, C. W. 1946. The age at which scientists do their best work. *Isis*, **36**, 166-169.

ADKINS, D. C., and LYERLY, S. B. 1952. *Factor analysis of reasoning tests*. Chapel Hill, University of North Carolina Press.

ADORNO, T. W., FRENKEL-BRUNSWIK, E., LEVINSON, D. J., and SANFORD, R. N. 1950. *The authoritarian personality*. New York: Harper.

ALBERT, K., HOCH, P., and WAELSCH, H. 1951. Glutamic acid and mental deficiency. *J. nerv. ment. Dis.*, **114**, 471-491.

ALEXANDER, H. B. 1922. A comparison of the ranks of American states in Army Alpha and in social-economic status. *Sch. and Soc.*, **16**, 388-392.

ALEXANDER, W. P. 1935. Intelligence, concrete and abstract. *Brit. J. Psychol.*, *Monogr. Suppl.*, No. 19.

ALLPORT, G. W., and ODBERT, H. S. 1936. Trait-names, a psycholexical study. *Psychol. Monogr.*, **47**, No. 1.

ALLPORT, G. W., and VERNON, P. E. A test for personal values. *J. Abnorm. soc. Psychol.*, 1931, **26**, 231-248.

————, and LINDZEY, G. 1951. *Study of values (Rev. Ed.)*. Boston: Houghton.

ALPER, T. G., and BORING, E. G. 1944. Intelligence test scores of Northern and Southern white and Negro recruits in 1918. *J. abnorm. soc. Psychol.*, **39**, 471-474.

ALTUS, W. D. 1948. A college achiever and non-achiever scale for the Minnesota Multiphasic Personality Inventory. *J. appl. Psychol.*, **32**, 385-397.

American Psychological Association, 1954. Technical recommendations for psychological tests and diagnostic techniques. Supplement to *Psychol. Bull.*, **51**, No. 2.

ANASTASI, A. 1934. Practice and variability: a study in psychological method. *Psychol. Monogr.*, **45**, No. 5.

————. 1948. The nature of psychological traits. *Psychol. Rev.*, **55**, 127-138.

————. 1954. Tested intelligence and family size. *Eugen. Quart.*, **1**, 155-160.

————, and D'ANGELO, R. Y. 1952. A comparison of Negro and white preschool children in language development and Goodenough Draw-a-Man I.Q. *J. genet. Psychol.*, **81**, 147-165.

ANDERSON, J. E. 1940. The prediction of terminal intelligence from infant and preschool tests. *Yearb. nat. Soc. Stud. Educ.*, **39** (I), 385-403.

———. 1952. The relation of attitude to adjustment. *Education*, **73**, 210-218.

ANDERSON, O. D. 1930. An experimental study of observational attitudes. *Amer. J. Psychol.*, **42**, 345-369.

ANDREW, D. M., and PATERSON, D. G. 1946. *Minnesota Clerical Test: manual.* New York: Psychological Corporation.

ANGYAL, A. F. 1948. The diagnosis of neurotic traits by means of a new perceptual test. *J. Psychol.*, **25**, 105-135.

Army Air Forces, Staff, Psychological Section. 1945. Psychological activities in the training command. *Psychol. Bull.*, **42**, 37-54.

ARSENIAN, S. 1945. Bi-lingualism in the post-war world. *Psychol. Bull.*, **42**, 65-86.

ASCH, S. E. 1936. A study of change in mental organization. *Arch. Psychol.*, No. 195.

———, and WITKIN, H. A. 1948. Studies in space orientation: I. Perception of the upright with displaced visual fields. *J. exp. Psychol.*, **38**, 325-337.

ASHER, E. J. 1935. The inadequacy of current intelligence tests for testing Kentucky mountain children. *J. genet. Psychol.*, **46**, 480-486.

AULD, F., Jr. 1952. Influence of social class on personality test responses. *Psychol. Bull.*, **49**, 318-332.

AXLINE, V. M. 1949. Mental deficiency—symptom or disease? *J. consult. Psychol.*, **13**, 313-327.

AYRES, L. P. 1909-10. The effect of physical defects on school progress. *Psychol. Clin.*, **3**, 71-77.

BAILEY, H. K. 1949. A study of the correlations between the group mental tests, the Stanford-Binet, and the Progressive Achievement Test used in the Colorado Springs elementary school. *J. educ. Res.*, **43**, 93-100.

BALINSKY, B. 1941. An analysis of the mental factors of various age groups from nine to sixty. *Genet. Psychol. Monogr.*, **23**, 191-234.

BALL, R. S. 1938. The predictability of occupational level from intelligence. *J. consult Psychol.*, **2**, 184-186.

BALLER, W. R. 1936. A study of the present social status of a group of adults who, when they were in the elementary schools, were classified mentally deficient. *Genet. Psychol. Monogr.*, **18**, 165-244.

BALYEAT, R. M. 1929. The general health and mental activity of allergic children. *Amer. J. Dis. Child.*, **37**, 1193-1197.

BARKER, R. G. 1953. *Adjustment to physical handicap and illness: a survey of the social psychology of physique and disability* (2d Ed.). New York: Social Science Research Council.

BARRETT, D. M. 1952. Differential value of Q and L scores on the ACE Psychological Examination for predicting achievement in college mathematics. *J. Psychol.*, **33**, 205-207.

BARRETT, H. O. 1950. Sex differences in art ability. *J. educ. Res.*, **43**, 391-393.

BARRON, F. 1952. Personality style and perceptual choice. *J. Pers.*, **20**, 385-401.

———. 1953. An ego-strength scale which predicts response to psychotherapy. *J. consult. Psychol.*, **17**, 327-333.

BARRON, F., and WELSH, G. S. 1952. Artistic perception as a possible factor in personality style: its measurement by a figure preference test. *J. Psychol.*, 33, 199-203.

BARTLETT, F. C. 1932. *Remembering*. Cambridge: Cambridge University Press.

BAYLEY, N. 1949. Consistency and variability in the growth of intelligence from birth to eighteen years. *J. genet. Psychol.*, 75, 165-196.

———. 1954. Some increasing parent-child similarities during the growth of children. *J. educ. Psychol.*, 45, 1-21.

———, and JONES, H. E. 1937. Environmental correlates of mental and motor development: a cumulative study from infancy to six years. *Child Developm.*, 8, 329-341.

BEACH, F. A. 1948. *Hormones and behavior*. New York: Hoeber.

BECHTOLDT, H. P. 1947. Factorial investigation of the perceptual speed factor. *Amer. Psychologist*, 2, 304-305.

BEIER, E. G., GORLOW, L., and STACEY, C. L. 1951. The fantasy life of the mental defective. *Amer. J. ment. Defic.*, 55, 582-589.

BELL, H. M. 1939. *The theory and practice of counseling*. Stanford: Stanford University Press.

BENEDICT, R., and WELTFISH, G. 1943. *Races of mankind*. New York: Public Affairs Comm.

BENNETT, G. K., and CRUIKSHANK, R. M. 1942. Sex differences in the understanding of mechanical problems. *J. appl. Psychol.*, 26, 121-127.

BENNETT, G. K., SEASHORE, H. G., and WESMAN, A. G. 1947. *Differential Aptitude Tests*. New York: Psychological Corporation.

BENTON, A. L. 1936. Influence of incentives upon intelligence test scores of school children. *J. genet. Psychol.*, 49, 494-497.

BENTZ, V. J. 1953. A test-retest experiment on the relationship between age and mental ability. *Amer. Psychologist*, 8, 319-320.

BERDIE, R. F. 1945. Range of interests. *J. appl. Psychol.*, 29, 268-281.

BERNHARDT, K. S., NORTHWAY, M. L., and TATHAM, C. M. 1948. The effect of added thiamine on intelligence and learning with identical twins. *Canad. J. Psychol.*, 2, 58-61.

BERNREUTER, R. G. 1933. The theory and construction of the personality inventory. *J. soc. Psychol.*, 4, 387-405.

BINET, A., and HENRI, V. 1895. La psychologie individuelle. *Année psychol.*, 2, 411-465.

BINGHAM, W. V. 1946. Inequalities of adult capacity. *Eugen. News*, 31, 41-43.

BIRREN, J. E., BICK, M. W., and FOX, C. 1948. Age changes in the light threshold of the dark adapted eye. *J. Geront.*, 3, 267-271.

BLAKE, R. R., and RAMSEY, G. V. (Eds.). 1951. *Perception: an approach to personality*. New York: Ronald.

BLOCK, Jack, and BLOCK, Jeanne. 1951. An investigation of the relationship between intolerance of ambiguity and ethnocentrism. *J. Pers.*, 19, 303-311.

BLUM, G. S. 1949. A study of the psychoanalytic theory of psychosexual development. *Genet. psychol. Monogr.*, 39, 3-99.

———. 1953. *Psychoanalytic theories of personality*. New York: McGraw.

BLUM, G. S., and MILLER, D. R. 1952. Exploring the psychoanalytic theory of the "oral character." *J. Pers.*, **20**, 287-304.

BOAS, F. 1911. *Abstract of the report on changes in bodily form of descendants of immigrants*. Washington: Government Printing Office.

BOGER, J. H. 1952. An experimental study of the effects of perceptual training on group IQ test scores. *J. educ. Res.*, **46**, 43-52.

BOICE, M. L., TINKER, M. A., and PATERSON, D. G. 1948. Color vision and age. *Amer. J. Psychol.*, **61**, 520-526.

BOLTON, T. L. 1892. The growth of memory in schoolchildren. *Amer. J. Psychol.*, **4**, 362-380.

BORDIN, E. S. 1943. A theory of vocational interests as dynamic phenomena. *Educ. psychol. Measmt.*, **3**, 49-65.

——, and WILSON, E. H. 1953. Change of interest as a function of shift in curricular orientation. *Educ. psychol. Measmt.*, **13**, 297-307.

BORING, E. G. 1923. Intelligence as the tests test it. *New Republic*, **35**, 35-37.

BOROW, H. 1945. A psychometric study of non-intellectual factors in college achievement. Ph.D. Thesis, Pennsylvania State College.

BOTZUM, W. A. 1951. A factorial study of the reasoning and closure factors. *Psychometrika*, **16**, 361-386.

BOUSFIELD, M. B. 1932. The intelligence and school achievement of Negro children. *J. Negro Educ.*, **1**, 388-395.

BOYD, G. F. 1952. The levels of aspiration of white and Negro children in a non-segregated elementary school. *J. soc. Psychol.*, **36**, 191-196.

BOYD, W. C. 1950. *Genetics and the races of men*. Boston: Little, Brown.

BRAND, H., BENOIT, E. P., and ORNSTEIN, G. N. 1953. Rigidity and feeblemindedness: an examination of the Kounin-Lewin theory. *J. clin. Psychol.*, **9**, 375-378.

BRIGHAM, C. C. 1923. *A study of American intelligence*. Princeton: Princeton University Press.

——. 1930. Intelligence tests of immigrant groups. *Psychol. Rev.*, **37**, 158-165.

BRILL, M. 1936. Studies of Jewish and non-Jewish intelligence. *J. educ. Psychol.*, **27**, 331-352.

BRODY, D. 1937. Twin resemblances in mechanical ability, with reference to the effects of practice on performance. *Child Developm.*, **8**, 207-216.

BROWN, A. W. 1940. The development and standardization of the Chicago Non-Verbal Examination, Part II. *J. appl. Psychol.*, **24**, 122-129.

BROWN, C. W., and GHISELLI, E. E. 1952. The relationship between the predictive power of aptitude tests for trainability and for job proficiency. *J. appl. Psychol.*, **36**, 370-372.

BROWN, F. 1944. An experimental and critical study of the intelligence of Negro and white kindergarten children. *J. genet. Psychol.*, **65**, 161-175.

BRUCE, M. 1940. Factors affecting intelligence test performance of whites and Negroes in the rural South. *Arch. Psychol.*, No. 252.

BRUNSWIK, E. 1947. *Systematic and representative design of psychological experiments*. Berkeley: University of California Press.

BUHLER, C., BUHLER, K., and LEFEVER, D. W. Copyright 1949. *Development of the Basic Rorschach Scores with manual of directions.* Berkeley: University of California Press.

BURCHARD, E. M. L. 1936. Physique and psychosis: an analysis of the postulated relationship between bodily constitution and mental disease syndrome. *Comp. Psychol. Monogr.,* **13,** No. 1.

BURKS, B. S. 1928. The relative influence of nature upon mental development. *Yearb. nat. Soc. Stud. Educ.,* **27** (I), 219-316.

———, JENSEN, D. W., and TERMAN, L. M. 1930. *Genetic studies of genius,* Vol. III. The promise of youth; follow-up studies of a thousand gifted children. Stanford: Stanford University Press.

BURNS, Z. H. 1937. Practice, variability, and motivation. *J. educ. Res.,* **30,** 403-420.

BUROS, O. K. (Ed.). 1953. *The fourth mental measurements yearbook.* Highland Park, N. J.: The Gryphon Press.

BURT, C. L. 1939. The factorial analysis of emotional traits. *Char. and Pers.,* **7,** 238-254, 285-299.

———, 1940. *The factors of the mind.* London: University of London Press.

———. 1947. Factor analysis and physical types. *Psychometrika,* **12,** 171-188.

———. 1949. The structure of the mind: a review of the results of factor analysis. *Brit. J. educ. Psychol.,* **19,** 100-111, 176-199.

BUSBY, C. 1932. *Comparisons of achievement of pupils by schools and grades based on New Stanford Achievement Tests, 1931-32.* Richmond, Va.: Department of Research, Richmond Public Schools.

BUXTON, C. E., and HUMPHREYS, L. G. 1935. The effect of practice upon intercorrelations in motor skills. *Science,* **81,** 441-442.

CAMPBELL, A. A., and HILGARD, E. R. 1936. Individual differences in ease of conditioning. *J. exp. Psychol.,* **19,** 561-571.

CANADY, H. G. 1936. The effect of "Rapport" on the IQ. *J. Negro Educ.,* **5,** 209-219.

CANTOR, G. N., and STACEY, C. L. 1951. Manipulative dexterity in mental defectives. *Amer. J. ment. Defic.,* **56,** 401-410.

CARROLL, J. B. 1941. A factor analysis of verbal abilities. *Psychometrika,* **6,** 279-308.

CARTER, H. D. 1940. The development of vocational attitudes. *J. consult. Psychol.,* **4,** 185-191.

CASTLE, C. S. 1913. A statistical study of eminent women. *Arch. Psychol.,* No. 27.

CATTELL, A. K. S., CATTELL, R. B., and RHYMER, R. M. 1947. P-technique demonstrated in determining psycho-physiological source traits in a normal individual. *Psychometrika,* **12,** 267-288.

CATTELL, J. McK. 1890. Mental tests and measurements. *Mind,* **15,** 373-380.

———. 1903. A statistical study of eminent men. *Pop. Sci. Mon.,* **62,** 359-377.

———. 1915. Families of American men of science. I. *Pop. Sci. Mon.,* **86,** 504-515.

———. 1917a. Families of American men of science. II. *Sci. Mon.,* **4,** 248-262.

CATTELL, J. McK. 1917b. Families of American men of science. III. *Sci. Mon.*, **5**, 368-377.

————, and CATTELL, J. 1933. *American men of Science* (5th Ed.). New York: Science Press.

CATTELL, J. McK., and FARRAND, L. 1896. Physical and mental measurements of the students of Columbia University. *Psychol. Rev.*, **3**, 618-648.

CATTELL, R. B. 1944. *A culture-free test: manual of directions.* New York: Psychological Corporation.

————. 1946. *The description and measurement of personality.* Yonkers, N. Y.: World Book.

————. 1947. Confirmation and clarification of the primary personality factors. *Psychometrika*, **12**, 197-220.

————. 1948a. Primary personality factors in the realm of objective tests. *J. Pers.*, **16**, 459-487.

————. 1948b. The primary personality factors in women compared with those in men. *Brit. J. Psychol., Statist. Sect.*, **1**, 114-130.

————. 1950a. The fate of national intelligence; test of a thirteen-year prediction. *Eugen. Rev.*, **42**, 136-148.

————. 1950b. *An introduction to personality study.* London: Hutchinson.

————. 1950c. The main personality factors in questionnaire self-estimate material. *J. soc. Psychol.*, **31**, 3-38.

————. 1950d. *Personality: a systematic, theoretical and factual study.* New York: McGraw.

————, and GRUEN, W. 1953. The personality factor structure of 11-year-old children in terms of behavior rating data. *J. clin. Psychol.*, **9**, 256-266.

————. 1954. Primary personality factors in the questionnaire medium for children from eleven to fourteen years old. *Educ. psychol. Measmt.*, **14**, 50-89.

CATTELL, R. B., and LUBORSKY, L. B. 1950. P-technique demonstrated as a new clinical method for determining personality and symptom structure. *J. gen. Psychol.*, **42**, 3-24.

CATTELL, R. B., and SAUNDERS, D. R. 1950. Inter-relation and matching of personality factors from behavior rating, questionnaire, and objective test data. *J. soc. Psychol.*, **31**, 243-260.

————, and STICE, G. 1950. *The sixteen personality factor questionnaire.* Champaign, Ill.: Inst. Pers. Abil. Testing.

CAVAN, R. S., BURGESS, E. W., HAVIGHURST, R. J., and GOLDHAMER, H. 1949. *Personal adjustment in old age.* Chicago: Science Research Associates.

CAVINS, L. V. 1928. *Survey of education in West Virginia,* Vol. II. State Board of Education, West Virginia.

CENTERS, R. 1949. *Psychology of social classes.* Princeton: Princeton University Press.

————. 1950. Social class identifications of American youth. *J. Pers.*, **18**, 290-302.

————. 1951. Toward an articulation of two approaches to social class phenomena: II. The Index of Status Characteristics and class identification. *Int. J. Opin. Att. Res.*, **5**, 159-178.

CHAPANIS, A. 1950. Relationships between age, visual acuity, and color vision. *Hum. Biol.*, 22, 1-33.

——, and WILLIAMS, W. C. 1945. Results of a mental survey with the Kuhlmann-Anderson Intelligence Tests in Williamson County, Tennessee. *J. genet. Psychol.*, 67, 27-55.

CHARLES, D. C. 1953. Ability and accomplishment of persons earlier judged mentally deficient. *Genet. Psychol. Monogr.*, 47, 3-71.

CHAUNCEY, H. 1952. The use of the Selective Service College Qualification Test in the deferment of college students. *Science*, 116, 73-79.

CHEN, T. L., and CHOW, H. H. 1948. A factor study of a test battery at different educational levels. *J. genet. Psychol.*, 73, 187-199.

CHESROW, E. J., WOSIKA, P. H., and REINITZ, A. H. 1949. A psychometric evaluation of aged white males. *Geriatrics*, 4, 169-177.

CHILD, I. L. 1950. The relation of somatotype to self-ratings on Sheldon's temperamental traits. *J. Pers.*, 18, 440-453.

——, and SHELDON, W. H. 1941. The correlation between components of physique and scores on certain psychological tests. *Char. and Pers.*, 10, 23-34.

CHIPMAN, C. E. 1946. Psychological variation within a homogeneous psychometric group. *Amer. J. ment. Defic.*, 51, 195-205.

CHOBAT, R., SPADAVECCHIA, R., DE SANCTIS, R. M. 1939. Intelligence rating and emotional pattern of allergic children. *Amer. J. Dis. Child.*, 57, 831-837 (*Psych. Abst.*, 1939, 4032.)

CHRISTIAN, A. M., and PATERSON, D. G. 1936. Growth of vocabulary in later maturity. *J. Psychol.*, 1, 167-169.

CHRISTIE, R., and JAHODA, M. 1954. *Studies in the scope and method of The Authoritarian Personality*. Glencoe, Ill.: The Free Press.

CLARK, R. E. 1949. Psychoses, income, and occupational prestige. *Amer. J. Socio.*, 54, 433-440.

CLARK, W. W. 1923. *Educational status of Los Angeles Negro children*. Department of Psychology and Educational Research, Los Angeles City Schools.

CLARKE, D. P. 1941. Stanford-Binet Scale L response patterns in matched racial groups. *J. Negro Educ.*, 10, 230-238.

COFFIN, T. E. 1944. A three-component theory of leadership. *J. abnorm. soc. Psychol.*, 39, 63-83.

CONRAD, H. S., and JONES, H. E. 1940. A second study of familial resemblances in intelligence, environmental and genetic implications of parent-child and sibling correlations in the total sample. *Yearb. nat. Soc. Stud. Educ.*, 39, (II), 97-141.

COOK, W. W. 1947. Individual trait differences in public schools with implications for school organization and curriculum development. *Teach. Coll. J.*, 19, 56-59, 67-70.

COPPINGER, N. W., and AMMONS, R. B. 1952. The Full-Range Picture Vocabulary Test: VIII. A normative study of Negro children. *J. clin. Psychol.*, 8, 136-140.

CORSINI, R. J., and FASSETT, K. K. 1953. Intelligence and aging. *J. genet. Psychol.*, 83, 249-264.

CORTER, H. M. 1952. Factor analysis of some reasoning tests. *Psychol. Monogr.*, 66, No. 8, 1-31.

COTTLE, W. C. 1950. A factorial study of the Multiphasic, Strong, Kuder, and Bell inventories using a population of adult males. *Psychometrika*, 15, 25-47.

COUNTS, G. S. 1925. Social status of occupations. *Sch. Rev.*, 33, 16-27.

COX, C. M. 1926. *Genetic studies of genius:* Vol. II. *The early mental traits of three hundred geniuses.* Stanford: Stanford University Press.

CRAWFORD, A. B., and BURNHAM, P. S. 1946. *Forecasting college achievement.* New Haven: Yale University Press.

CRISSY, W. J. E., and DANIEL, W. J. 1939. Vocational interest factors in women. *J. appl. Psychol.*, 23, 488-494.

CRONBACH, L. J. 1949a. *Essentials of psychological testing.* New York: Harper.

———. 1949b. "Pattern tabulation": a statistical method for analysis of limited patterns of scores with particular reference to the Rorschach test. *Educ. psychol. Measmt.*, 9, 149-172.

———. 1950. Studies of the group Rorschach in relation to success in the college of the University of Chicago. *J. educ. Psychol.*, 41, 65-82.

CURTIS, H. A. 1949. A study of the relative effects of age and of test difficulty upon factor patterns. *Genet. Psychol. Monogr.*, 40, 99-148.

DANA, R. H. 1954. Personality orientation: an organizational focus for current research. *J. Psychol.*, 37, 139-150.

DARLEY, J. G. 1937. Tested maladjustment related to clinically diagnosed maladjustment. *J. appl. Psychol.*, 21, 632-642.

DAVIDSON, H. H., and KRUGLOV, Lorraine. 1952. Personality characteristics of the institutionalized aged. *J. consult. Psychol.*, 16, 5-12.

DAVIDSON, K. S., GIBBY, R. G., McNEIL, E. B., SEGAL, S. J., and SILVERMAN, H. 1950. A preliminary study of Negro and white differences on Form I of the Wechsler-Bellevue Scale. *J. consult. Psychol.*, 14, 489-492.

DAVIS, A. 1943. Child training and social class. In R. G. Barker, J. S. Kounin, and H. F. Wright. *Child behavior and development.* New York: McGraw. Ch. 34.

———, GARDNER, B. B., and GARDNER, M. B. 1941. *Deep south.* Chicago: University of Chicago Press.

DAWSON, S., and CONN, J. C. M. 1926. Effect of encephalitis lethargica on the intelligence of children. *Arch. Dis. Child.*, 1, 357-368.

DEARBORN, W. F. 1949. The student's background in relation to school success. In W. T. Donahue, C. H. Coombs, and R. M. W. Travers, *The measurement of student adjustment and achievement.* Ann Arbor: University of Michigan Press. Pp. 191-200.

DECROLY, O., and DEGAND, J. 1910. La mesure de l'intelligence chez les enfants normeaux d'après les tests de Mm. Binet et Simon. *Arch. Psychol.*, Genève, 9, 81-108.

DEEG, M. E., and PATERSON, D. G. 1947. Changes in social status of occupations. *Occupations*, 25, 205-208.

DEGARDIN, E. 1949. Étude critique des échelles de motricité. *Travail hum.*, **12**, 215-244.

DENNIS, W. 1942. The performance of Hopi children on the Goodenough Draw-a-Man test. *J. comp. Psychol.*, **34**, 341-348.

DE SILVA, H. R. 1938. Age and highway accidents. *Sci. Mon.*, **47**, 536-545.

DE STEPHENS, W. P. 1953. Are criminals morons? *J. soc. Psychol.*, **38**, 187-199.

DODGE, A. F. 1935. Occupational ability patterns. *Teach. Coll. Contrib. to Educ.*, No. 658.

DOLL, E. A. 1946. The feeble-minded child. In L. Carmichael (Ed.), *Manual of child psychology*. New York: Wiley. Ch. 17.

――――. 1953a. *The measurement of social competence: a manual for the Vineland Social Maturity Scale*. Minneapolis: Educational Test Bureau.

――――. 1953b. Mental deficiency vs. neurophrenia. *Amer. J. ment. Defic.*, **57**, 477-480.

DONAHUE, W. T., COOMBS, C. H., and TRAVERS, R. W. M. 1949. *The measurement of student adjustment and achievement*. Ann Arbor: University of Michigan Press.

DOPPELT, J. E. 1950. The organization of mental abilities in the age range 13 to 17. *Teach. Coll. Contrib. to Educ.*, No. 962.

――――, and WESMAN, A. G. 1952. The Differential Aptitude Tests as predictors of achievement test scores. *J. educ. Psychol.*, **43**, 210-217.

DOWNEY, J. E. 1923. *The will-temperament and its testing*. Yonkers, N. Y.: World Book.

DUBLIN, L. I. 1942. Longevity in retrospect and prospect. In E. V. Cowdry (Ed.), *Problems of ageing*. Baltimore: Williams and Wilkins. Ch. 6.

DVORAK, B. J. 1935. *Differential occupational ability patterns*. Minneapolis: University of Minnesota Press.

EAGLESON, O. W. 1937. Comparative studies of white and Negro subjects in learning to discriminate visual magnitude. *J. Psychol.*, **4**, 167-197.

EBBINGHAUS, H. 1897. Über eine neue Methode zur Prüfung geistiger Fähigkeiten und ihre Anwendung bei Schulkindern. *Z. angewand. Psychol.*, **13**, 401-459.

EDGERTON, H. A., and BRITT, S. H. 1944. Sex differences in the Science Talent Test. *Science*, **100**, 192-193.

――――. 1947. Technical aspects of the Fourth Annual Science Talent Search. *Educ. psychol. Measmt.*, **7**, 3-21.

――――, and NORMAN, R. D. 1948. Later achievements of male contestants in the First Annual Science Talent Search. *Amer. Scientist.*, **36**, 403-414.

Educational Test Service. 1952. *A summary of statistics on the Selective Service College Qualification Test of December 13, 1951, April 24, 1952, and May 22, 1952.*

Educational Testing Service Developments. 1953. 2, No. 1.

EELS, K., DAVIS, A., HAVIGHURST, R. J., HERRICK, V. E., and TYLER, R. 1951. *Intelligence and cultural differences*. Chicago: University of Chicago Press.

EKMAN, G. 1951. On the number and definition of dimensions in Kretschmer's and Sheldon's constitutional systems. In *Essays in psychology dedicated to David Katz*. Uppsala: Almquist and Wiksells.

ELLIS, H. A. 1904. *A study of British genius*. London: Hurst.

ELLSON, D. G., FULLER, P. R., and URMSTON, R. 1950. The influence of glutamic acid on test performance. *Science*, 112, 248-249.

EMBREE, R. B. 1948. The status of college students in terms of IQ's determined during childhood. *Amer. Psychologist*, 3, 259.

ERIKSON, E. H. 1951. Sex differences in the play configurations of preadolescents. *Amer. J. Orthopsychiat.*, 21, 667-692.

EWERT, H. 1934. The effect of practice on individual differences when studied with measurements weighted for difficulty. *J. gen. Psychol.*, 10, 249-285.

EYSENCK, H. J. 1947. *Dimensions of personality*. London: Routledge and Kegan Paul.

———. 1951. Primary social attitudes and the "social insight" test. *Brit. J. Psychol., Gen. Sect.*, 42, 114-122.

———. 1952. *The scientific study of personality*. London: Routledge and Kegan Paul.

———. 1953a. Primary social attitudes: a comparison of attitude patterns in England, Germany, and Sweden. *J. abnorm. soc. Psychol.*, 48, 563-568.

———. 1953b. *The structure of human personality*. London: Methuen.

———, and PRELL, D. B. 1951. The inheritance of neuroticism: an experimental study. *J. ment. Sci.*, 97, 441-465.

FERGUSON, G. O. 1916. The psychology of the Negro. *Arch. Psychol.*, No. 36.

FERGUSON, L. W. 1944. A revision of the Primary Social Attitude Scales. *J. Psychol.*, 17, 229-241.

———, HUMPHREYS, L. G., and STRONG, F. W. 1941. A factorial analysis of interests and values. *J. educ. Psychol.*, 32, 197-204.

FERNBERGER, S. W. 1948. Persistence of stereotypes concerning sex differences. *J. abnorm. soc. Psychol.*, 43, 97-101.

FINCH, F. H. 1935. The permanence of vocational interests. *Psychol. Bull.*, 32, 682.

———. 1946. Enrollment increases and changes in the mental level of the high school population. *Appl. Psychol. Monogr.*, No. 10.

FISCHER, L. K. 1952. Hospitalism in six-month-old infants. *Amer. J. Orthopsychiat.*, 22, 522-533.

FISHER, J. 1951. The memory process and certain psychosocial attitudes with special reference to the Law of Prägnanz: I. Study of nonverbal content. *J. Pers.*, 19, 406-420.

FISHER, M. B., and BIRREN, J. E. 1947. Age and strength. *J. appl. Psychol.*, 31, 490-497.

FISKE, D. W. 1944. A study of relationships to somatotype. *J. appl. Psychol.*, 28, 504-519.

———. 1949. Consistency of the factorial structures of personality ratings from different sources. *J. abnorm. soc. Psychol.*, 44, 329-344.

FJELD, H. A. 1934. The limits of learning ability in Rhesus monkeys. *Genet. Psychol. Monogr.*, 15, 369-537.

FLEISHMAN, E. A. 1953. Testing for psychomotor abilities by means of apparatus tests. *Psychol. Bull.*, 50, 241-262.

FORD, C. F., and TYLER, L. E. 1952. A factor analysis of Terman and Miles' M-F Test. *J. appl. Psychol.*, 36, 251-253.

FOULDS, G. A., and RAVEN, J. C. 1948a. Intellectual ability and occupational grade. *Occup. Psychol., Lond.*, 22, 197-203.

———, and RAVEN, J. C. 1948b. Normal changes in the mental abilities of adults as age advances. *J. ment. Sci.*, 94, 133-142.

FOX, C., and BIRREN, J. E. 1950. The differential decline of subtest scores of the Wechsler-Bellevue Intelligence Scale in 60-69-year-old individuals. *J. genet. Psychol.*, 77, 313-317.

FRANCK, K., and ROSEN, E. 1949. A projective test of masculinity-femininity. *J. consult. Psychol.*, 13, 247-256.

FRANKLIN, J. C. 1945. Discriminative value and patterns of the Wechsler-Bellevue Scales in the examination of delinquent Negro boys. *Educ. psychol. Measmt.*, 5, 71-85.

FRANZBLAU, R. N. 1935. Race differences in mental and physical traits studied in different environments. *Arch. Psychol.*, No. 177.

FREDERICSEN, N., and MELVILLE, S. D. 1954. Differential predictability in the use of test scores. *Educ. psychol. Measmt.*, 14, 647-656.

FREEMAN, F. N., HOLZINGER, K. J., and MITCHELL, B. C. 1928. The influence of environment on the intelligence, school achievement, and conduct of foster children. *Yearb. nat. Soc. Stud. Educ.*, 27 (I), 101-217.

FRENCH, J. W. 1940a. Individual differences in paramecium. *J. comp. Psychol.*, 30, 451-456.

———. 1940b. Trial and error learning in paramecium. *J. exp. Psychol.*, 26, 609-613.

———. 1951. The description of aptitude and achievement tests in terms of rotated factors. *Psychomet. Monogr.*, No. 5. Chicago: University of Chicago Press.

———. 1953. *The description of personality measurements in terms of rotated factors.* Educational Testing Service. Princeton, N. J.

FRENKEL-BRUNSWIK, E. 1954. Further explorations by a contributor to "The Authoritarian Personality." In R. Christie and M. Johoda (Eds.), *Studies in the scope and method of "The Authoritarian Personality."* Glencoe, Ill.: The Free Press. Pp. 226-275.

FRYER, D. 1931. *The measurement of interests in relation to human adjustment.* New York: Holt.

FULLER, J. L. 1954. *Nature and nurture: a modern synthesis.* New York: Doubleday.

———, and SCOTT, J. P. 1954. Heredity and learning ability in infrahuman mammals. *Eugen. Quart.*, 1, 28-43.

FURFEY, P. H. 1928. The relation between socio-economic status and intelligence of young infants as measured by the Linfert-Hierholzer scale. *Ped. Sem. and J. genet. Psychol.*, 35, 478-480.

GADSON, E. J. 1951. Glutamic acid and mental deficiency—a review. *Amer. J. ment. Defic.*, 55, 521-528.

GALTON, F. 1883. *Inquiries into human faculty and its development.* London: Macmillan. P. 387.

GALTON, F. 1952. *Hereditary genius* (New Ed.). New York: Horizon.

GARDNER, R. 1953. Cognitive styles in categorizing behavior. *J. Pers.*, 22, 214-233.

GARFIEL, E. 1923. The measurement of motor ability. *Arch. Psychol.*, 9, No. 62.

GARRETT, H. E. 1938. Differentiable mental traits. *Psychol. Rec.*, 2, 259-298.

———. 1940. Variability in learning under massed and spaced practice. *J. exp. Psychol.*, 26, 547-567.

———. 1945a. Comparison of Negro and white recruits on the Army tests given in 1917-1918. *Amer. J. Psychol.*, 58, 480-495.

———. 1945b. "Facts" and "interpretations" regarding race differences. *Science*, 101, 404-406.

———. 1945c. A note on the intelligence scores of Negroes and whites in 1918. *J. abnorm. soc. Psychol.*, 40, 344-346.

———. 1945d. Psychological differences as among races. *Science*, 101, 16-17.

———. 1946. A developmental theory of intelligence. *Amer. Psychologist*, 1, 372-378.

———, BRYAN, A. I., and PERL, R. E. 1935. The age factor in mental organization. *Arch. Psychol.*, No. 176.

GARRETT, H. E., and KELLOGG, W. N. 1928. The relation of physical constitution to general intelligence, social intelligence, and emotional stability. *J. exp. Psychol.*, 11, 113-129.

GARRETT, H. F. 1949. A review and interpretation of investigations of factors related to scholastic success in colleges of arts and science and teachers colleges. *J. exp. Educ.*, 18, 91-138.

GARTH, T. R. 1925. A review of racial psychology. *Psychol. Bull.*, 22, 343-364.

GARVEY, C. R. 1933. Comparative body build of manic-depressive and schizophrenic patients. *Psychol. Bull.*, 30, 567-568.

GATES, A. I. 1924. The nature and educational significance of physical status and of mental, physiological, social, and emotional maturity. *J.. educ. Psychol.*, 15, 329-358.

GAW, F. 1925. A study of performance tests. *Brit. J. Psychol.*, 15, 374-392.

GEIER, F. M., LEVIN, M., and TOLMAN, E. C. 1941. Individual differences in emotionality, hypothesis formation, vicarious trial and error, and visual discrimination learning in rats. *Comp. Psychol. Monogr.*, 17, No. 3.

GESELL, A., and THOMPSON, H. 1941. Twins T and C from infancy to adolescence: a biogenetic study of individual differences by the method of co-twin control. *Genet. Psychol. Monogr.*, 24, 3-122.

GHISELLI, E. E. 1949. The validity of commonly employed occupational tests. *Univ. Calif. Publ. in Psychol.*, 5, 253-288.

———, and BROWN, C. W. 1951. Validity of aptitude tests for predicting trainability of workers. *Personnel Psychol.*, 4, 243-260.

GIBSON, J. J. 1941. A critical review of the concept of set in contemporary experimental psychology. *Psychol. Bull.*, 38, 781-817.

GILBERT, G. M. 1942. Sex differences in musical aptitude and training. *J. gen. Psychol.*, 26, 19-33.

GILBERT, J. A. 1897. Researches upon children and college students. *Iowa Univ. Stud. Psychol.*, 1, 1-39.

GILBERT, J. G. 1941. Memory loss in senescence. *J. abnorm. soc. Psychol.*, **36**, 73-86.

GIST, N. P., and CLARK, C. D. 1938. Intelligence as a selective factor in rural-urban migrations. *Amer. J. Sociol.*, **44**, 36-58.

GLUECK, S., and GLUECK, E. 1950. *Unraveling juvenile delinquency.* New York: Commonwealth Fund.

GOLDMAN-EISLER, F. 1951. The problem of "orality" and of its origin in early childhood. *J. ment. Sci.*, **97**, 765-782.

GOLDSTEIN, H. 1935. The biochemical variability of the individual in relation to personality and intelligence. *J. exp. Psychol.*, **18**, 348-371.

GOLDSTEIN, K., and SCHEERER, M. 1941. Abstract and concrete behavior. *Psychol. Monogr.*, **53**, No. 2.

GOODENOUGH, F. L. 1926. Racial differences in the intelligence of school children. *J. exp. Psychol.*, **9**, 388-397.

———. 1927. The consistency of sex differences in mental traits of various ages. *Psychol. Rev.*, **34**, 440-462.

———. 1936. The measurement of mental functions in primitive groups. *Amer. Anthrop.*, **38**, 1-11.

———. 1949. *Mental Testing.* New York: Rinehart.

GOODMAN, C. H. 1943a. Factorial analysis of Thurstone's seven primary mental abilities. *Psychometrika*, **8**, 121-129.

———. 1943b. A factorial analysis of Thurstone's sixteen primary mental abilities tests. *Psychometrika*, **8**, 141-151.

GORDON, H. 1923. *Mental and scholastic tests among retarded children.* Educ. Pamphlet No. 44. London: Board of Education.

GOUGH, H. G. 1948a. A new dimension of status: I. Development of a personality scale. *Amer. sociol. Rev.*, **13**, 401-409.

———. 1948b. A new dimension of status: II. Relationship of the St scale to other variables. *Amer. sociol. Rev.*, **13**, 534-537.

———. 1949a. Factors relating to the academic achievement of high school students. *J. educ. Psychol.*, **40**, 65-78.

———. 1949b. A new dimension of status: III. Discrepancies between the St scale and "objective" status. *Amer. sociol. Rev.*, **14**, 275-281.

———. 1953. What determines the academic achievement of high school students. *J. educ. Res.*, **46**, 321-331.

GOULD, B. A. 1869. Investigations in the military anthropological statistics of American soldiers. *Sanitary Memoirs, II, Statistics.* New York: *U. S. San. Comm.*

GUERTIN, W. H. 1950. Differential characteristics of the pseudo-feebleminded. *Amer. J. ment. Defic.*, **54**, 394-398.

GUETZKOW, H., and BROZEK, J. 1946. Intellectual functions with restricted intakes of B-complex vitamins. *Amer. J. Psychol.*, **59**, 358-381.

GUILFORD, J. P. 1947. The discovery of aptitude and achievement variables. *Science*, **106**, 279-282.

———. 1948. Factor analysis in a test-development program. *Psychol. Rev.*, **55**, 79-94.

———. 1950. Creativity. *Amer. Psychologist*, **5**, 444-454.

GUILFORD, J. P., CHRISTENSEN, P. R., BOND, N. A., and SUTTON, M. A. 1954. A factor analysis study of human interests. *Psychol. Monogr.*, **68**, No. 4.

GUILFORD, J. P., CHRISTENSEN, P. R., KETTNER, N. W., GREEN, R. F., and HERTZKA, A. F. 1954. A factor analytic study of Navy reasoning tests with the Air Force Air Crew Classification Battery. *Educ. psychol. Measmt.*, **14**, 301-325.

GUILFORD, J. P., and GUILFORD, R. B. 1936. Personality factors S, E, and M, and their measurement. *J. Psychol.*, **2**, 109-127.

———. 1939a. Personality factors D, R, T, and A. *J. abnorm. soc. Psychol.*, **34**, 21-36.

———. 1939b. Personality factors N and GD. *J. abnorm. soc. Psychol.*, **34**, 239-248.

GUILFORD, J. P., SHNEIDMAN, E., and ZIMMERMAN, W. S. 1948. *The Guilford-Shneidman-Zimmerman Interest Survey*. Beverly Hills, Calif.: Sheridan Supply Co.

GUILFORD, J. P., WILSON, R. C., and CHRISTENSEN, P. R. 1952. *A factor analytic study of creative thinking: II. Administration of tests and analysis of results*. U. SC Reports from Psychol. Lab., No. 8.

GUILFORD, J. P., and ZIMMERMAN, W. S. 1949. *The Guilford-Zimmerman Temperament survey*. Beverly Hills, Calif.: Sheridan Supply Co.

HALL, C. S. 1934. Emotional behavior in the rat: I. Defecation and urination as measures of individual differences in emotionality. *J. comp. Psychol.*, **18**, 385-403.

———. 1936. Emotional behavior in the rat: II. The relationship between need and emotionality. *J. comp. Psychol.*, **22**, 61-68.

———. 1937. Emotional behavior in the rat: IV. The relationship between emotionality and stereotyping of behavior. *J. comp. Psychol.*, **24**, 369-375.

———. 1951. Individual differences. In C. P. Stone, *Comparative psychology* (3rd Ed.). New York: Prentice-Hall.

———, and KLEIN, S. J. 1942. Individual differences in aggressiveness in rats. *J. comp. Psychol.*, **33**, 371-383.

HALL, G. S. 1905. The Negro in Africa and America. *Ped. Sem.*, **12**, 350-368.

HALL, J., and JONES, D. C. 1950. Social grading of occupations. *Brit. J. Sociol.*, **1**, 31-55.

HALSTEAD, W. C. 1947. *Brain and intelligence*. Chicago: University of Chicago Press.

———. 1951. Biological intelligence. *J. Pers.*, **20**, 118-130.

HAMILTON, M. E. 1943. The contribution of practice differences to group variability. *Arch. Psychol.*, No. 278.

HAMMER, E. F. 1954. Comparison of the performances of Negro children and adolescents on two tests of intelligence, one an emergency scale. *J. genet. Psychol.*, **84**, 85-93.

HANES, B. 1953. Perceptual learning and age. *J. consult. Psychol.*, **17**, 222-224.

HANFMANN, E. 1941. A study of personal patterns in an intellectual performance. *Char. and Pers.*, **9**, 315-325.

HANLEY, C. 1951. Physique and reputation of junior high school boys. *Child Develpm.*, **22**, 247-260.

HARRELL, R. F. 1943. Effect of added thiamin on learning. *Teach. Coll. Contrib. to Educ.*, No. 877.

———. 1947. Further effects of added thiamin on learning and other processes. *Teach. Coll. Contrib. to Educ.*, No. 928.

HARRELL, T. W., and HARRELL, M. S. 1945. Army general classification test scores for civilian occupations. *Educ. psychol. Measmt.*, 5, 229-239.

HARRIS, D. B. 1950. Behavior ratings of post-polio cases. *J. consult. Psychol.*, 14, 381-385.

HARTSHORNE, H., and MAY, M. A. 1928. *Studies in deceit.* New York: Macmillan. P. 306.

———, and MALLER, J. B. 1929. *Studies in service and self control.* New York: Macmillan.

HARTSHORNE, H., MAY, M. A., and SHUTTLEWORTH, F. K. 1930. *Studies in the organization of character.* New York: Macmillan.

HATHAWAY, S. R., and MEEHL, P. E. 1951. *An atlas for the clinical use of the MMPI.* Minneapolis: University of Minnesota Press.

HAVIGHURST, R. J. 1952. Social class and basic personality structure. *Social soc. Res.*, 36, 355-363.

———, and BREESE, F. H. 1947. Relation between ability and social status in a midwestern community: III. Primary mental abilities. *J. educ. Psychol.*, 38, 241-247.

HAVIGHURST, R. J., GUNTHER, M. K., and PRATT, I. E. 1946. Environment and the Draw-a-Man Test. *J. abnorm. soc. Psychol.*, 41, 50-63.

HAVIGHURST, R. J., and JANKE, L. L. 1944. Relations between ability and social status in a midwestern community: I. Ten-year-old children. *J. educ. Psychol.*, 35, 357-368.

HAVIGHURST, R. J., and TABA, H. 1949. *Adolescent character and personality.* New York: Wiley.

HEATH, H. 1952. A factor analysis of women's measurements taken for garment and pattern construction. *Psychometrika*, 17, 87-100.

HEBB, D. O. 1949. *The organization of behavior.* New York: Wiley.

HEGGE, T. G. 1944. The occupational status of higher-grade mental defectives in the present emergency. *Amer. J. ment. Defic.*, 49, 86-98.

HEIDBREDER, E. 1926. Intelligence and the height-weight ratio. *J. appl. Psychol.*, 10, 52-62.

HEILMAN, J. D. 1933. Sex differences in intellectual abilities. *J. educ. Psychol.*, 24, 47-62.

HEMPEL, W. E., and FLEISHMAN, E. A. 1955. A factor analysis of physical proficiency and manipulative skill. *J. appl. Psychol.*, 39, 12-16.

HENRY, C. E., and KNOTT, J. R. 1941. A note on the relationship between "personality" and the alpha rhythm of the electroencephalogram. *J. exp. Psychol.*, 28, 362-366.

HERON, W. T. 1935. The inheritance of maze learning ability in rats. *J. comp. Psychol.*, 19, 77-89.

HERSKOVITS, M. J. 1928. *The American Negro.* New York: Knopf.

HERTZ, M. R. 1952. The Rorschach: thirty years after. In D. Brower and L. E. Abt, *Progress in clinical psychology*. New York: Grune and Stratton. Vol. I, Sect. 1, Ch. 8.

HERTZMAN, M. 1939. Specificity of correlations between initial and final abilities in learning. *Psychol. Rev.*, 46, 163-175.

HERZBERG, F., and BOUTON, A. 1954. A further study of the stability of the Kuder Preference Record. *Educ. psychol. Measmt.*, 14, 90-100, 326-331.

HERZBERG, F., and LEPKIN, M. 1954. A study of sex differences on the Primary Mental Abilities Test. *Educ. psychol. Measmt.*, 14, 687-689.

HESTON, J. C., and CANNELL, C. F. 1941. A note on the relation between age and performance of adult subjects on four familiar psychometric tests. *J. appl. Psychol.*, 25, 415-419.

HIERONYMUS, A. N. 1951. A study of social class motivation: relationships between anxiety for education and certain socio-economic and intellectual variables. *J. educ. Psychol.*, 42, 193-205.

HILDEN, A. H. 1949. A longitudinal study of intellectual development. *J. Psychol.*, 28, 187-214.

HILDRETH, G. 1950. Individual differences. From W. S. Monroe, *Encyclopedia of educational research*. (Rev. Ed.) New York: Macmillan.

HILDRETH, G. H., BIXLER, H. H., *et al.* 1948. *Metropolitan Achievement Tests: manual for interpreting*. Yonkers, N. Y.: World Book.

HILGARD, J. R. 1933. The effect of early and delayed practice on memory and motor performances studied by the method of co-twin control. *Genet. Psychol. Monogr.*, 14, 493-567.

HILL, A. 1948. Does special education result in improved intelligence for the slow learner? *J. except. Child.*, 14, 207-213; 224.

HIMMELWEIT, H. T., HALSEY, A. H., and OPPENHEIM, A. N. 1952. The views of adolescents on some aspects of the social class structure. *Brit. J. Sociol.*, 3, 148-172.

HIMMELWEIT, H. T., and PETRIE, A. 1951. The measurement of personality in children. *Brit. J. educ. Psychol.*, 21, 9-29.

HINTON, R. T., Jr. 1936. The role of the basal metabolic rate in the intelligence of ninety grade school students. *J. educ. Psychol.*, 27, 546-550.

———. 1939. A further study on the role of the basal metabolic rate in the intelligence of children. *J. educ. Psychol.*, 30, 309-314.

HIRSCH, N. D. M. 1927. Cephalic index of American-born children of three foreign groups. *Amer. J. phys. Anthrop.*, 10, 79-90.

———. 1928. An experimental study of the East Kentucky mountaineers: a study in heredity and environment. *Genet. Psychol. Monogr.*, 3, 183-244.

HOBSON, J. R. 1947. Sex differences in Primary Mental Abilities. *J. educ. Res.*, 41, 126-132.

HOFSTAETTER, P. R. 1954. The changing composition of "intelligence": a study in T-technique. *J. genet. Psychol.*, 85, 159-162.

HOLBROOK, S. F. 1953. A study of the development of motor abilities between the ages of four and twelve, using a modification of the Oseretsky Scale. *Dissertation Abstr.*, 13, 875.

HOLLINGSHEAD, A. 1949. *Elmtown's Youth*. New York: Wiley.

HOLLINGWORTH, L. S. 1922. Differential action upon the sexes of forces which tend to segregate the feeble-minded. *J. abnorm. Psychol.*, **17**, 35-37.

———. 1940. Intelligence as an element in personality. *Yearb. nat. Soc. Stud. Educ.*, **39** (I), 271-275.

———. 1942. *Children above 180 IQ.* Yonkers, N. Y. World Book.

HOLTZMAN, W. H., and BROWN, W. F. 1953. Study habits and attitudes in the prediction of academic success. *Amer. Psychologist*, **8**, 369.

HOLZMAN, P. S. 1954. The relation of assimilative tendencies in visual, auditory, and kinesthetic time-error to cognitive attitudes of leveling and sharpening. *J. Pers.*, **22**, 375-394.

———, and KLEIN, G. S. 1954. Cognitive system-principles of leveling and sharpening: individual differences in visual time-error assimilation effects. *J. Psychol.*, **37**, 105-122.

HONZIK, M. P. 1938. The constancy of mental test performance during the preschool period. *J. genet. Psychol.*, **52**, 285-302.

———. 1951. Sex differences in the occurrence of materials in the play constructions of preadolescents. *Child Develpm.*, **22**, 15-35.

———, MACFARLANE, J. W., and ALLEN, L. 1948. The stability of mental test performance between two and eighteen years. *J. exp. Educ.*, **17**, 309-324.

HOWELLS, W. W. 1952. A factorial study of constitutional type. *Amer. J. phys. Anthrop.*, **10**, 91-118.

HULL, C. L. 1928. *Aptitude testing.* Yonkers, N. Y. World Book. Pp. 131-138.

HUMPHREYS, L. G., BUXTON, C. E., and TAYLOR, H. R. 1936. Steadiness and rifle marksmanship. *J. appl. Psychol.*, **20**, 680-688.

HURST, L. A. 1952. Research in genetics and psychiatry: New York State Psychiatric Institute. *Eugen. News*, **37**, 86-9.

HUSEN, T. 1951. The influence of schooling upon IQ. *Theoria*, **17**, 61-88.

———. 1953. The stability of intelligence test scores. *Acta Psychol.*, **9**, 53-81.

IRWIN, O. C. 1948. Infant speech: the effect of family occupational status and of age on the use of sound types. *J. Speech Hearing Disorders*, **13**, 224-226, 320-323.

JACOBSON, W. E. 1945. First impressions of classmates. *J. appl. Psychol.*, **29**, 142-55.

JAENSCH, E. R. 1938. *Der Gegentypus.* Leipzig: Barth.

JAMES, W. 1927. Great men and their environment. In *The will to believe and other essays in popular philosophy.* New York: Longmans. Pp. 216-254.

JAMIESON, E., and SANDIFORD, P. 1928. The mental capacity of Southern Ontario Indians. *J. educ. Psychol.*, **19**, 313-328, 536-551.

JANKE, L. L., and HAVIGHURST, R. J. 1945. Relations between ability and social status in a midwestern community: II. Sixteen-year-old boys and girls. *J. educ. Pyschol.*, **36**, 499-509.

JANOFF, I. Z., BECK, L. H., and CHILD, I. L. 1950. The relation of somatotype to reaction time, resistance to pain, and expressive movement. *J. Pers.*, **18**, 454-460.

JASTROW, J. 1891. Some anthropometric and psychologic tests on college students—a preliminary survey. *Amer. J. Psychol.*, **4**, 420-428.

JENKINS, J. G. 1946. Validity for what? *J. consult. Psychol.*, **10**, 93-98.

JENKINS, M. D. 1948. The upper limit of ability among American Negroes. *Sci. Mon.*, **66**, 399-401.

JEPSEN, V. L. 1951. Scholastic proficiency and vocational success. *Educ. psychol. Measmt.*, **11**, 616-628.

JOHNSON, D. M. 1948. Applications of the standard-score IQ to social statistics. *J. soc. Psychol.*, **27**, 217-227.

JOHNSON, W. B., and TERMAN, L. M. 1940. Some highlights in the literature of psychological sex differences published since 1920. *J. Psychol.*, **9**, 327-336.

JOLLES, I. 1947. The diagnostic implications of Rorschach's test in case studies of mental defectives. *Genet. Psychol. Monogr.*, **36**, 89-198.

JONES, A. W. 1941. *Life, liberty, and property.* Philadelphia, New York: Lippincott.

JONES, H. E., and CONRAD, H. S., 1933. The growth and decline of intelligence. *Genet. Psychol. Monogr.*, **13**, 223-298.

———, and BLANCHARD, M. B. 1932. Environmental handicap in mental test performance. *Univ. Calif. Publ. in Psychol.*, **5**, No. 3, 63-99.

JONES, L. V. 1949. A factor analysis of the Stanford-Binet at four age levels. *Psychometrika*, **14**, 299-331.

JONES, M. C., and BAYLEY, N. 1950. Physical maturing among boys as related to behavior. *J. educ. Psychol.*, **41**, 129-148.

JUDD, C. H. (Ed.). 1936. *Education as cultivation of the higher mental processes.* New York: Macmillan.

KALLMAN, F. J. 1950. The genetics of psychoses. *Amer. J. hum. Genet.*, **2**, 385-390.

———. 1952. Twin and sibship study of overt male homosexuality. *Amer. J. hum. Genet.*, **4**, 136-146.

———. 1953. *Heredity in health and mental disorder; principles of psychiatric genetics in the light of comparative twin studies.* New York: Norton.

———, FEINGOLD, L., and BONDY, E. 1951. Comparative adaptational, social, and psychometric data on the life histories of senescent twin pairs. *Amer. J. hum. Genet.*, **3**, 65-73.

KAY, H. 1951. Learning of a serial task by different age groups. *Quart. J. exp. Psychol.*, **3**, 166-183.

KEMPF, G. A., and COLLINS, S. D. 1929. A study of the relation between mental and physical status of children in two counties of Illinois. *U. S. Pub. Reports*, **44**, 1743-1784.

KENNEDY, R. J. R. 1948. *The social adjustment of morons in a Connecticut city.* Hartford, Conn.: Mansfield-Southbury Training Schols, Social Service Department.

KEPHART, N. C. 1939. The effect of a highly specialized program upon the IQ in high-grade mentally deficient boys. *Proc. Amer. Ass. Ment. Defic.*, **63**, 216-221.

———, and STRAUSS, A. A. 1940. A clinical factor influencing variations in the IQ. *Amer. J. Orthopsychiat.*, **10**, 343-350.

KEYS, A., *et al.* 1950. *The biology of human starvation.* Minneapolis: University of Minnesota Press.

KIMBALL, B. 1952. The sentence completion technique in a study of scholastic under-achievement. *J. consult. Psychol.*, **16**, 353-358.

KINCAID, M. A. 1925. A study of individual differences in learning. *Psychol. Rev.*, **32**, 34-53.

KINSEY, A. C., POMEROY, W. B., and MARTIN, C. E. 1948. *Sexual behavior in the human male.* Philadelphia: Saunders.

———, and GEBHARD, P. H. 1953. *Sexual behavior in the human female.* Philadelphia: Saunders.

KIRK, B. A. 1952. Test vs. academic performance in malfunctioning students. *J. consult. Psychol.*, **16**, 213-216.

KIRK, S. A. 1948. An evaluation of the study by Bernadine C. Schmidt entitled: "Changes in personal, social, and intellectual behavior of children originally classified as feebleminded." *Psychol. Bull.*, **45**, 321-333.

KLEIN, G. S. 1951. The personal world through perception. In R. R. Blake and G. V. Ramsey (Eds.), *Perception: an approach to personality.* New York: Ronald. Ch. 12.

———, and SCHLESINGER, H. J. 1949. Where is the perceiver in perceptual theory? *J. Pers.*, **18**, 32-47.

———. 1951. Perceptual attitudes toward instability: I. Prediction of apparent movement responses from Rorschach responses. *J. Pers.*, **19**, 289-302.

KLINEBERG, O. 1928. An experimental study of speed and other factors in "racial" differences. *Arch. Psychol.*, No. 93.

———. 1931. A study of psychological differences between "racial" and national groups in Europe. *Arch. Psychol.*, No. 132.

———. 1935. *Negro intelligence and selective migration.* New York: Columbia University Press.

———. 1938. The intelligence of migrants. *Amer. sociol. Rev.*, **3**, 218-224.

———, ASCH, S. E., and BLOCK, H. 1934. An experimental study of constitutional types. *Genet. Psychol. Monogr.*, **16**, 140-221.

KLOPFER, W. 1946. Personality patterns of old age. *Rorschach Res. Exch.*, **10**, 145-166.

KLUGMAN, S. F. 1944. The effect of money incentive versus praise upon the reliability and obtained scores of the Revised Stanford-Binet Test. *J. gen. Psychol.*, **30**, 255-269.

KNOTT, J. R., FRIEDMAN, H., and BARDSLEY, R. 1942. Some electroencephalographic correlates of intelligence in eight-year- and twelve-year-old children. *J. exp. Psychol.*, **30**, 380-391.

KOCH, A. M. 1935. The limits of learning ability in Cebus monkeys. *Genet. Psychol. Monogr.*, **17**, 164-234.

KOUNIN, J. S. 1943. Intellectual development and rigidity. In R. G. Barker, J. S. Kounin, and H. F. Wright, *Child behavior and development.* New York: McGraw. Ch. 11.

KRAEPELIN, E. 1895. Der psychologische Versuch in der Psychiatrie. *Psychol. Arbeiten*, **1**, 1-91.

KRECH, D., and CALVIN, A. 1953. Levels of perceptual organization and cognition. *J. abnorm. soc. Psychol.*, **48**, 394-400.

Kreezer, G. L. 1940. The relation of intelligence level and the electroencephalogram. *Yearb. nat. Soc. Stud. Educ.*, 39 (I), 130-133.

———, and Smith, F. W. 1950. The relation of the alpha rhythm of the electroencephalogram and intelligence level in the non-differentiated familial type of mental deficiency. *J. Psychol.*, 29, 47-51.

Kretschmer, E. 1925. *Physique and character.* New York: Harcourt.

———. 1931. *The psychology of men of genius.* New York: Harcourt.

Kuder, G. F. 1951. *Examiner manual for the Kuder Preference Record-Vocational-Form C.* Chicago: Science Research Associates.

Kuhlen, R. G. 1940. Social change: a neglected factor in psychological studies of the life span. *Sch. and Soc.*, 52, 14-16.

———. 1945. Age differences in personality during adult years. *Psychol. Bull.*, 42, 333-358.

Kuhlmann, F. 1921. The results of repeated mental reëxaminations of 639 feebleminded over a period of ten years. *J. appl. Psychol.*, 5, 195-224.

Lacey, J. I. 1950. Individual differences in somatic response patterns. *J. comp. physiol. Psychol.*, 43, 338-350.

———, and Van Lehn, R. 1952. Differential emphasis in somatic response to stress. *Psychosom. Med.*, 14, 71-81.

Lambeth, M., and Lanier, L. H. 1933. Race differences in speed of reaction. *J. genet. Psychol.*, 42, 255-297.

Lange-Eichbaum, W. 1931. *The problem of genius.* London: Kegan Paul.

Larson, L. A. 1941. A factor analysis of motor ability variables and tests, with tests for college men. *Res. Quart. Amer. Ass. Hlth. Phys. Educ.*, 12, 499-517.

Lawrence, E. M. 1931. An investigation into the relation between intelligence and inheritance. *Brit. J. Psychol., Monogr. Suppl.*, No. 16.

Leahy, A. M. 1935. Nature-nurture and intelligence. *Genet. Psychol. Monogr.*, 17, 235-308.

Learned, W. S., and Wood, B. D. 1938. *The student and his knowledge.* New York: Carnegie Foundation for the Advancement of Teaching.

Lee, E. S. 1951. Negro intelligence and selective migration: a Philadelphia test of the Klineberg hypothesis. *Amer. sociol. Rev.*, 16, 227-233.

Lehman, H. C. 1942. The creative years: oil paintings, etchings, and architectural works. *Psychol. Rev.*, 49, 19-42.

———. 1953. *Age and achievement.* Princeton: Princeton University Press.

———. 1954. Men's creative production rate at different ages and in different countries. *Sci. Mon.*, 78, 321-326.

Levine, P. R., and Wallen, R. 1954. Adolescent vocational interests and later occupation. *J. appl. Psychol.*, 38, 428-431.

Levy, D. M. 1929. A method of integrating physical and psychiatric examination: with special studies of body interest, overprotection, response to growth, and sex differences. *Amer. J. Psychiat.*, 9, 121-194.

———. 1932. Body interest in children and hypochondriasis. *Amer. J. Psychiat.*, 12, 295-315.

LEVY, D. M. 1953. Psychosomatic studies of some aspects of maternal behavior. In C. Kluckhohn and H. A. Murray, *Personality* (2nd Ed.). New York: Knopf. Ch. 6.

LEWIS, W. D. 1941. A comparative study of the personalities, interests, and home backgrounds of gifted children of superior and inferior educational achievement. *J. genet. Psychol.*, **59**, 207-218.

——. 1945. Sex distribution of intelligence among inferior and superior children. *J. genet. Psychol.*, **67**, 67-75.

LICHTE, W. H. 1952. Shape constancy: dependence upon angle of rotation; individual differences. *J. exp. Psychol.*, **43**, 49-57.

LINDQUIST, E. F. 1948. *Iowa Tests of Educational Development: General Manual*. Chicago: Science Research Associates. (1st Ed., 1942.)

LIVESAY, T. M. 1944. Relation of economic status to "intelligence" and to the racial derivation of high school seniors in Hawaii. *Amer. J. Psychol.*, **57**, 77-82.

LOEVINGER, J. 1940. Intelligence as related to socio-economic factors. *Yearb. nat. Soc. Stud. Educ.*, **39** (I), 159-210.

——. 1943. On the proportional contributions of differences in nature and in nurture to differences in intelligence. *Psychol. Bull.*, **40**, 725-756.

LOMBROSO, C. 1896. *The man of genius*. London: Scott.

LONGSTAFF, H. P. 1948. Fakability of the Strong Interest Blank and the Kuder Preference Record. *J. appl. Psychol.*, **32**, 360-369.

LORGE, I. 1936. The influence of the test upon the nature of mental decline as a function of age. *J. educ. Psychol.*, **27**, 100-110.

——. 1945. Schooling makes a difference. *Teach. Coll. Rec.*, **46**, 483-492.

——. 1949. Trends in the measurement of achievement. In W. T. Donahue, C. H. Coombs, and R. W. M. Travers, *The measurement of student adjustment and achievement*. Ann Arbor: University of Michigan Press. Pp. 85-96.

LORIMER, F. 1952. Trends in capacity for intelligence. *Eugen. News*, **37**, 17-24.

LOVELL, C. 1945. A study of the factor structure of thirteen personality variables. *Educ. psychol. Measmt.*, **5**, 335-350.

LOWENFELD, V. 1945. Tests for visual and haptical aptitudes. *Amer. J. Psychol.*, **58**, 100-111.

LUBIN, A. 1950. A note on Sheldon's table of correlations between temperamental traits. *Brit. J. Psychol.*, *Statist. Sect.*, **3**, 186-189.

LURIE, L. A. 1938. Endocrinology and the understanding and treatment of the exceptional child. *J. Amer. Med. Ass.*, **110**, 1531-1536.

LYND, R. S., and LYND, H. M. 1929. *Middletown*. New York: Harcourt.

——. 1937. *Middletown in transition*. New York: Harcourt.

McANDREW, M. B. 1943. An experimental investigation of young children's ideas of causality. *Stud. Psychol. Psychiat. Cathol. Univ. Amer.*, **6**, No. 2.

McCLELLAND, D., ATKINSON, J. W., CLARK, R. A., and LOWELL, E. L. 1953. *The achievement motive*. New York: Appleton-Century-Crofts.

McCONNELL, J. W. 1942. *The evolution of social classes*. Washington: American Council on Public Affairs.

McConnell, T. R. 1940. A study of the extent of measurement of differential objectives of instruction. *J. educ. Res.*, **33**, 662-670.

McCulloch, T. L. 1947. Reformulation of the problem of mental deficiency. *Amer. J. ment. Defic.*, **52**, 130-136.

McGraw, M. B. 1935. *Growth: a study of Johnny and Jimmy.* New York: Appleton-Century.

McGurk, F. C. 1953. On white and Negro test performance and socio-economic factors. *J. abnorm. soc. Psychol.*, **48**, 448-450.

Machover, S. 1943. Cultural and racial variations in patterns of intellect. *Teach. Coll. Contrib. to Educ.*, No. 875.

McIntosh, W. J. 1949. Follow-up study of one thousand non-academic boys. *J. except. Child.*, **15**, 166-170.

McNemar, Q. 1933. Twin resemblances in motor skills, and the effect of practice thereon. *J. genet. Psychol.*, **42**, 70-99.

———. 1942. *The revision of the Stanford-Binet scale.* New York: Houghton.

———. 1945. Note on Wellman's reanalysis of IQ changes of orphanage pre-school children. *J. genet. Psychol.*, **67**, 215-219.

———, and Terman, L. M. 1936. Sex differences in variational tendency. *Genet. Psychol. Monogr.*, **18**, 1-65.

McPherson, M. W. 1948. A survey of experimental studies of learning in individuals who achieve subnormal ratings on standardized psychometric measures. *Amer. J. ment. Defic.*, **52**, 232-254.

Magaret, A., and Thompson, C. W. 1950. Differential test responses of normal, superior, and mentally defective subjects. *J. abnorm. soc. Psychol.*, **45**, 163-167.

Maller, J. B. 1934. General and specific factors in character. *J. soc. Psychol.*, **5**, 97-102.

———, and Zubin, J. 1932. The effect of motivation upon intelligence test scores. *J. genet. Psychol.*, **41**, 136-151.

Mallinson, G. G., and Crumrine, W. M. 1952. An investigation of the stability of interests of high school students. *J. educ. Res.*, **45**, 369-383.

Mallory, J. N. 1922. A study of the relation of some physical defects to achievement in the elementary school. *George Peabody Coll. for Tchrs. Contrib. to Educ.*, No. 9.

Malzberg, B. 1935. A statistical study of age in relation to mental disease. *Ment. Hyg.*, **19**, 449-476.

Martin, H. G. 1945. The construction of the Guilford-Martin inventory of factors G-A-M-I-N. *J. appl. Psychol.*, **29**, 298-300.

Mauldin, W. P. 1940. Selective migration from small towns. *Amer. sociol. Rev.*, **5**, 748-758.

Mayo, M. J. 1913. The mental capacity of the American Negro. *Arch. Psychol.*, No. 28.

Mead, M. 1935. *Sex and temperament in three primitive societies.* New York: Morrow.

———. 1949. *Male and female.* New York: Morrow.

Meehl, P. E. 1954. *Clinical vs. statistical prediction.* Minneapolis: University of Minnesota Press.

MEILI, R. 1946. L'Analyse de l'intelligence. *Archives de Psychologie*, 31, 1-64.

——. 1949. Sur la nature de facteurs d'intelligence. *Acta Psychol.*, 6, 40-58.

METFESSEL, M. 1940. Relationships of heredity and environment in behavior. *J. Psychol.*, 10, 177-198.

MICHAEL, W. B. 1949. Factor analysis of tests and criteria: a comparative study of two AAF pilot populations. *Psychol. Monogr.*, 63, No. 3.

——. 1954. A suggested research approach to the identification of psychological processes associated with spatial-visualization factors. *Educ. psychol. Measmt.*, 14, 401-406.

MILES, C. C. 1935. Sex in social psychology. In C. Murchison (Ed.), *Handbook of social psychology*. Worcester, Mass.: Clark University Press. Ch. 16.

——. 1954. Gifted children. In *Manual of child psychology*. New York: Wiley.

——, and MILES, W. R. 1932. The correlation of intelligence scores and chronological age from early to late maturity. *Amer. J. Psychol.*, 44, 44-78.

MILES, C. C., and WOLFE, L. S. 1936. Childhood physical and mental health records of historical geniuses. *Psychol. Monogr.*, 47, 390-400.

MILES, W. R. 1933. Age and human ability. *Psychol. Rev.*, 40, 99-123.

——. 1942. Psychological aspect of ageing. In E. V. Cowdry (Ed.), *Problems of ageing*. Baltimore: Williams and Wilkins. Ch. 28.

MILNER, E. 1949. Effects of sex role and social status on the early adolescent personality. *Genet. Psychol. Monogr.*, 40, 231-325.

MONROE, W. S. 1950. *Encyclopedia of Educational Research* (Rev. Ed.). New York: Macmillan.

MONTAGU, M. F. A. 1945. Intelligence of northern Negroes and southern whites in the first World War. *Amer. J. Psychol.*, 58, 161-188.

MOORE, J. E. 1941. A comparison of Negro and white children on speed of reaction on an eye-hand coördination test. *J. genet. Psychol.*, 59, 225-228.

MORGAN, C. T. 1947. The hoarding instinct. *Psychol. Rev.*, 54, 335-341.

MOSIER, M. F., and KUDER, G. F. 1949. Personal preference differences among occupational groups. *J. appl. Psychol.*, 33, 231-239.

MOURSY, E. M. 1952. The hierarchical organization of cognitive levels. *Brit. J. Psychol., Statist. Sect.*, 5, 151-180.

MUENCH, G. A. 1944. A follow-up of mental defectives after eighteen years. *J. abnorm. soc. Psychol.*, 39, 407-418.

MULLEN, F. A. 1952. Mentally retarded youth find jobs. *Personnel Guid. J.*, 31, 20-25.

MUNROE, Ruth L. 1945. Prediction of the adjustment and academic performance of college students by a modification of the Rorschach method. *Applied Psychol. Monogr.*, No. 7. Stanford: Stanford University Press.

MÜNSTERBERG, H. 1891. Zur Individualpsychologie. *Centralblatt für Nervenheilkunde und Psychiatrie*, 14, 196-198.

MURDOCK, K., and SULLIVAN, L. R. 1923. A contribution to the study of mental and physical measurements in normal children. *Amer. Phys. Educ. Rev.*, 28, 209-215; 276-280; 328-330.

Muscio, B. 1922. Motor capacity with special reference to vocational guidance. *Brit. J. Psychol.*, 13, 157-184.

Myers, C. S. 1947. A new analysis of intelligence. *Occup. Psychol., Lond.*, 21, 17-23.

Myers, R. C. 1952. Biographical factors and academic achievement: an experimental investigation. *Educ. psychol. Measmt.*, 12, 415-426.

Naccarati, S. 1921. The morphologic aspect of intelligence. *Arch. Psychol.*, No. 45.

Neidt, C. O., and Merrill, W. R. 1951. Relative effectiveness of two types of response to items of a scale on attitudes toward education. *J. educ. Psychol.*, 42, 432-436.

Newland, T. E., and Lawrence, W. C. 1953. Chicago Non-Verbal Examination results on an East Tennessee Negro population. *J. clin. Psychol.*, 9, 44-46.

Newman, H. H., Freeman, F. N. and Holzinger, K. J. 1937. *Twins: a study of heredity and environment.* Chicago: University of Chicago Press.

Nisbet, J. D. 1953. *Family environment.* Occasional Papers on Eugenics, No. 8. London: Cassell.

Occupational Analysis Division, War Manpower Commission. 1945. Factor analysis of occupational aptitude tests. *Educ. psychol. Measmt.*, 5, 147-155.

O'Connor, N. 1952. The prediction of psychological stability and anxiety-aggressiveness from a battery of tests administered to a group of high-grade male mental defectives. *J. gen. Psychol.*, 46, 3-17.

———. 1953. The occupational success of feeble-minded adolescents. *Occup. Psychol., Lond.*, 27, 157-163.

Odum, H. W. 1910. *Social and mental traits of the Negro.* New York: Columbia University Press.

Oehrn, A. 1889. *Experimentelle Studien zur Individualpsychologie.* Dorpater Dissertation. (Also published in *Psychol. Arbeiten*, 1895, 1, 92-152.)

Olander, H. T., Van Wagenen, M. J., and Bishop, H. M. 1949. Predicting arithmetic achievement. *J. educ. Res.*, 43, 66-73.

Oseretsky Tests of Motor Proficiency, by N. Oseretsky. 1947. *J. consult. Psychol.*, 11, 157.

O'Shea, H. E., Elsom, K. O'S., and Higbe, R. V. 1942. Studies of the B vitamins in the human subject; mental changes in experimental deficiency. *Amer. J. Med. Sci.*, 203, 388-397.

Otis, A. S. 1939. *Otis Quick-Scoring Mental Ability Tests. Manual of Directions for Alpha Test.* Yonkers, N. Y.: World Book.

Owens, W. A. Jr. 1942a. Intra-individual difference versus inter-individual differences in motor skills. *Educ. psychol. Measmt.*, 2, 299-314.

———. 1942b. A new technic in studying the effects of practice upon individual differences. *J. exp. Psychol.*, 30, 180-183.

———. 1942c. A note on the effects of practice upon trait differences in motor skills. *J. educ. Psychol.*, 33, 144-147.

Owens, W. A. 1953. Age and mental abilities: a longitudinal study. *Genet. Psychol. Monogr.*, 48, 3-54.

OWENS, W. A., and JOHNSON, W. C. 1949. Some measured personality traits of college underachievers. *J. educ. Psychol.*, **40**, 41-46.

PAGE, J. D. 1940. The effect of nursery-school attendance upon subsequent I.Q. *J. Psychol.*, **10**, 221-230.

PASCAL, G. R. 1951. Psychological deficit as a function of stress and constitution. *J. Pers.*, **20**, 175-187.

PASTORE, N. 1949a. The genetics of schizophrenia. *Psychol. Bull.*, **46**, 285-302.

———. 1949b. *The nature-nurture controversy.* New York: King's Crown Press, Columbia University.

PATERSON, D. G. 1930. *Physique and intellect.* New York: Century.

———, ELLIOTT, R. M., ANDERSON, L. D., TOOPS, H. A., and HEIDBREDER, E. 1930. *Minnesota mechanical ability tests.* Minneapolis: University of Minnesota Press.

PEARSON, G. H. J. 1928. Effect of age in vibratory sensibility. *Arch. Neurol. Psychiat.*, Chicago, **20**, 482-496.

PEMBERTON, C. L. 1952a. The closure factors related to other cognitive processes. *Psychometrika*, **17**, 267-288.

———. 1952b. The closure factors related to temperament. *J. Pers.*, **21**, 159-175.

PERRIN, F. A. C. 1921. An experimental study of motor ability. *J. exp. Psychol.*, **4**, 24-56.

PETERSON, J. 1925. *Early conceptions and tests of intelligence.* Yonkers, N. Y.: World Book.

———, and LANIER, L. H. 1929. Studies in the comparative abilities of whites and Negroes. *Ment. Meas. Monogr.*, No. 5.

———, and WALKER, H. M. 1925. Comparisons of white and Negro children in certain ingenuity and speed tests. *J. comp. Psychol.*, **5**, 271-283.

PHILLIPS, B. A. 1912. Retardation in the elementary schools of Philadelphia. *Psychol. Clin.*, **6**, 79-90.

PHILLIPS, E. L. 1950. Intellectual and personality factors associated with social class attitudes among junior high school children. *J. genet. Psychol.*, **77**, 61-72.

———, BERMAN, I. R., and HANSON, H. B. 1948. Intelligence and personality factors associated with poliomyelitis among school age children. *Monogr. Soc. Res. Child. Devlpm.*, **12** (2).

PIAGET, Jean. 1947. *The psychology of intelligence.* New York: Harcourt.

PICKFORD, R. W. 1951. *Individual differences in colour vision.* London: Routledge and Kegan Paul.

PINTNER, R. 1928. A mental survey of the deaf. *J. educ. Psychol.*, **19**, 145-151.

———. 1931. *Intelligence testing.* New York: Holt. Ch. 20.

PORTER, W. T. 1895. The physical basis of precocity and dullness. *Trans. Acad. St. Louis*, **6**, 161-181.

PORTEUS, S. D. 1918. The measurement of intelligence: 653 children examined by the Binet and Porteus tests. *J. educ. Psychol.*, **9**, 13-31.

———, and BERRY, R. J. A. 1920. Intelligence and social valuation, a practical method for the diagnosis of mental deficiency and other forms of social inefficiency. *Vineland Tr. Sch. Res. Publ.*, No. 20.

PRADOS, M., and FRIED, E. 1947. Personality structure in the older age groups. *J. clin. Psychol.*, **3**, 113-120.

PRESSEY, S. L. 1949. Educational acceleration. *Ohio State Univ. Bureau of Educ. Res. Monogr.*, No. 31.

PRICE, B. 1931. A perceptual test for comparing the performance of age groups: preliminary report. *Psychol. Bull.*, **28**, 584-585.

————. 1950. Primary biases in twin studies: a review of prenatal and natal difference-producing factors in monozygotic pairs. *Amer. J. hum. Genet.*, **2**, 293-352.

PRYOR, J. W. 1905. *Development of the bones of the hand.* Bulletin of the State College of Kentucky.

————. 1906. *Ossification of epiphyses of the hand.* Bulletin of the State College of Kentucky.

————. 1908. *The chronology and order of ossification of the bones of the human carpus.* Bulletin of the State College of Kentucky.

RABBAN, M. 1950. Sex-role identification in young children in two diverse social groups. *Genet. Psychol. Monogr.*, **42**, 81-158.

RAZRAN, G. H. S. 1933. Conditional responses in animals other than dogs. *Psychol. Bull.*, **30**, 261-324.

REDLICH, F. C., HOLLINGSHEAD, A. B., ROBERTS, B. H., ROBINSON, H. A., FREEDMAN, L. Z., and MYERS, J. K. 1953. Social structure and psychiatric disorders. *Amer. J. Psychiat.*, **109**, 729-734.

REED, S. C., REED, E. W., and PALM, J. D. 1954. Fertility and intelligence among families of the mentally deficient. *Eugen. Quart.*, **1**, 44-52.

REID, J. W. 1951. Stability of measured Kuder interests in young adults. *J. educ. Res.*, **45**, 307-312.

Reports of the Cambridge anthropological expedition to the Torres Straits. 1901 and 1903. Vol. II, Cambridge (Eng.).

RHODES, A. 1937. A comparative study of motor abilities of Negroes and whites. *Child Develpm.*, **8**, 369-371.

RIBBLE, M. A. 1943. *The rights of infants.* New York: Columbia University Press.

RIESS, B. F., and DE CILLIS, O. E., 1940. Personality difference in allergic and non-allergic children. *J. abnorm. soc. Psychol.*, **35**, 104-113.

RIMOLDI, H. J. A. 1948. Study of some factors related to intelligence. *Psychometrika*, **13**, 27-46.

————. 1951. The central intellective factor. *Psychometrika*, **16**, 75-101.

ROBINSON, M. L., and MEENES, M. 1947. The relationship between test intelligence of third grade Negro children and the occupations of their parents. *J. Negro Educ.*, **16**, 136-141.

ROE, A. 1951a. A psychological study of eminent biologists. *Psychol. Monogr.*, **65**, No. 14, 1-68.

————. 1951b. A psychological study of physical scientists. *Genet. Psychol. Monogr.*, **43**, 121-235.

————. 1953. A psychological study of eminent psychologists and anthropologists, and a comparison with biological and physical scientists. *Psychol. Monogr.*, **67**, No. 2, 1-55.

Roff, M. 1952. A factorial study of tests in the perceptual area. *Psychometric Monogr.*, No. 8.

Rogers, M. C. 1922. Adenoids and diseased tonsils, their effect on general intelligence. *Arch. Psychol.*, No. 50.

Rogerson, C. H. 1943. Psychological factors in asthma. *Brit. Med. J.*, 1, 406-407.

Rosenberg, N. 1953. Stability and maturation of Kuder interest patterns during high school. *Educ. psychol. Measmt.*, 13, 449-458.

Rosenzweig, S. 1945. The picture-association method and its application in a study of reactions to frustration. *J. Pets.*, 14, 3-23.

Rotch, T. M. 1910. Roentgen-ray methods applied to the grading of early life. *Amer. Phys. Educ. Rev.*, 15, 396-420.

Ruch, F. L. 1934. The differentiative effects of age upon human learning. *J. gen. Psychol.*, 11, 261-286.

Rundquist, E. A. 1933. Inheritance of spontaneous activity in rats. *J. comp. Psychol.*, 16, 415-438.

Sackett, E. B. 1932. The Negro schools of the Canal Zone. *J. Negro Educ.*, 1, 347-353.

Sandström, C. I. 1953. Sex differences in localization and orientation. *Acta Psychol.*, 9, 82-96.

Sandwick, R. L. 1920. Correlation of physical health and mental efficiency. *J. educ. Res.*, 1, 199-203.

Sanford, G. A. 1940. Selective migration in a rural Alabama community. *Amer. sociol. Rev.*, 5, 759-766.

Sanford, R. N. 1953. Physical and physiological correlates of personality structure. In C. Kluckhohn and H. A. Murray, *Personality* (2nd Ed.). New York: Knopf. Ch. 5.

Sarason, S. B. 1953. *Psychological problems in mental deficiency* (2nd Ed.). New York: Harper.

Sarbin, T. R. 1943. A contribution to the study of actuarial and individual methods of prediction. *Amer. J. Sociol.*, 48, 593-602.

———, and Berdlie, R. F. 1940. Relation of measured interests to the Allport-Vernon Study of Values. *J. appl. Psychol.*, 24, 287-269.

Sargent, S. S. 1952. How shall we study individual differences? *Psychol. Rev.*, 49, 170-181.

Saul, L. G., Davis, H., and Davis, P. A. 1949. Psychologic correlations with the electroencephalogram. *Psychosom. Med.*, 11, 361-376.

Schaie, K. W., Rosenthal, F., and Perlman, R. M. 1953. Differential mental deterioration of factorially "pure" functions in later maturity. *J. Geront.*, 8, 191-196.

Scheerer, M., Rothmann, E., and Goldstein, K. 1945. A case of "Idiot Savant": an experimental study of personality organization. *Psychol. Monogr.*, 58, No. 4.

Scheinfeld, A. 1944. *Women and men.* New York: Harcourt.

Schiele, D. C., and Brozek, J. 1948. "Experimental Neurosis" resulting from semistarvation in man. *Psychosom. Med.*, 10, 31-50.

SCHLESINGER, H. J. 1954. Cognitive attitudes in relation to susceptibility to interference. *J. Pers.*, **22**, 345-374.

SCHMIDT, B. 1946. Changes in the personal, social, and intellectual behavior of children originally classified as feeble-minded. *Psychol. Monogr.*, **60**, No. 5.

SCHNEIDLER, G. G., and PATERSON, D. G. 1942. Sex differences in clerical aptitude. *J. educ. Psychol.*, **33**, 303-309.

SCHULMAN, M. J., and HAVIGHURST, R. J. 1947. Relations between ability and social status in a midwestern community: IV, size of vocabulary. *J. educ. Psychol.*, **38**, 437-442.

SCOTT, J. P. 1953. New directions in the genetic study of personality and intelligence. *Eugen. News*, **38**, 97-101.

Scottish Council for Research in Education. 1939. *The intelligence of a representative group of Scottish children.* London: University of London Press.

Scottish Council for Research in Education. 1949. *The trend of Scottish intelligence.* London: University of London Press.

SEARLE, L. V. 1949. The organization of hereditary maze-brightness and maze-dullness. *Genet. Psychol. Monogr.*, **39**, 279-325.

SEARS, P. S. 1951. Doll play aggression in normal young children: Influence of sex, age, sibling status, father's absence. *Psychol. Monogr.*, **65**, No. 6.

SEARS, R. R. 1943. *Survey of objective studies of psychoanalytic concepts.* New York: Social Science Research Council.

———, PINTLER, M. H., and SEARS, P. S. 1946. Effect of father separation on preschool children's doll play aggression. *Child Develpm.*, **17**, 219-243.

SEASHORE, H. G. 1955. Methods of expressing test scores. *Psychol. Corp. Test Service Bulletin*, No. 48.

SEASHORE, R. H. 1930. Individual differences in motor skills. *J. gen. Psychol.*, **3**, 38-66.

———. 1939. Work methods: an often neglected factor underlying individual differences. *Psychol. Rev.*, **46**, 123-141.

———. 1940. An experimental analysis of fine motor skills. *Amer. J. Psychol.*, **53**, 86-98.

———, and ADAMS, R. 1933. The measurement of steadiness. *Science*, **78**, 285-287.

SEDER, M. A. 1940. The vocational interests of professional women. *J. appl. Psychol.*, **24**, 130-143, 265-272.

SELTZER, C. C., WELLS, F. L., and McTERNAN, E. B. 1948. A relationship between Sheldonian somatotype and psychotype. *J. Pers.*, **16**, 431-436.

SEWARD, G. H. 1945. Cultural conflict and the feminine role. *J. soc. Psychol.*, **22**, 177-194.

SHAGASS, C. 1946. An attempt to correlate the occipital alpha frequency of the electroencephalogram with performance on a mental ability test. *J. exp. Psychol.*, **36**, 88-92.

SHAKOW, D., and GOLDMAN, R. 1938. The effect of age on the Stanford-Binet vocabulary scores of adults. *J. educ. Psychol.*, **29**, 241-256.

SHARP, S. E. 1899. Individual psychology: a study in psychological method. *Amer. J. Psychol.*, 10, 329-391.

SHAW, D. G. 1949. A study of the relationships between Thurstone Primary Mental Abilities and high school achievement. *J. educ. Psychol.*, 40, 239-249.

SHEEHAN, M. R. 1938. A study of individual consistency in phenomenal constancy. *Arch. Psychol.*, 31, No. 222.

SHELDON, W. H. 1927. Morphologic types and mental ability. *J. Pers. Res.*, 5, 447-451.

———. 1949. *Varieties of delinquent youth.* New York: Harper.

———, and STEVENS, S. S. 1942. *The varieties of temperament.* New York: Harper.

———, and TUCKER, W. B. 1940. *The varieties of human physique.* New York: Harper.

SHEPARD, E. L. 1942. Measurements of certain nonverbal abilities of urban and rural children. *J. educ. Psychol.*, 33, 458-462.

SHEPLER, B. F. 1951. A comparison of masculinity-femininity measures. *J. consult. Psychol.*, 15, 484-486.

SHERMAN, M., and KEY, C. B. 1932. The intelligence of isolated mountain children. *Child Develpm.*, 3, 279-290.

SHERRIFFS, A. C., and JARRETT, R. F. 1953. Sex differences in attitudes about sex differences. *J. Psychol.*, 35, 161-168.

SHIMBERG, M. E. 1929. An investigation into the validity of norms with special reference to urban and rural groups. *Arch. Psychol.*, No. 104.

SHOCK, N. W. 1952. Aging and psychological adjustment. *Rev. educ. Res.*, 22, 439-458.

———, and JONES, H. E. 1939. The relationship between basal physiological functions and intelligence in adolescents. *Psychol. Bull.*, 36, 642-643.

SIBLEY, E. 1942. Some demographic clues to stratification. *Amer. sociol. Rev.*, 7, 322-330.

SILLS, F. D. 1950. A factor analysis of somatotypes and of their relationship to achievement in motor skills. *Res. Quart. Amer. Ass. Hlth. Phys. Educ.*, 21, 424-437.

SIMON, L. M., and LEVITT, E. A. 1950. The relation between Wechsler-Bellevue IQ scores and occupational area. *Occupations*, 29, 23-25.

SIMONSON, E., and BROZEK, J. 1952. Flicker fusion frequency: background and applications. *Physiol. Rev.*, 32, 349-378.

SIMRALL, D. 1947. Intelligence and the ability to learn. *J. Psychol.*, 23, 27-43.

SIPPRELLE, C. 1954. An empirical test of Pascal's formula. *J. Pers.*, 23, 195-206.

SIRKIN, M. 1929. The relation between intelligence, age, and home environment of elementary-school pupils. *Sch. and Soc.*, 30, 304-308.

SKEELS, H. M. 1940. Some Iowa studies of the mental growth of children in relation to differentials of the environment: a summary. *Yearb. nat. Soc. stud. Educ.*, 39 (II), 281-308.

———. 1942. A study of the effects of differential stimulation on mentally retarded children: a follow-up report. *Amer. J. ment. Defic.*, 46, 340-350.

———, and DYE, H. B. 1939. A study of the effects of differential stimulation on mentally retarded children. *Proc. Amer. Ass. ment. Defic.*, 44, 114-136.

SKEELS, H. M., and HARMS, I. 1948. Children with inferior social histories; their mental development in adoptive homes. *J. genet. Psychol.*, 72, 283-294.

SKODAK, M. 1939. Children in foster homes: a study of mental development. *Univ. Iowa Child Welf.*, 16, No. 1.

———. 1950. Mental growth of adopted children in the same family. *J. genet. Psychol.*, 77, 3-9.

———, and SKEELS, H. M. 1949. A final follow-up study of one hundred adopted children. *J. genet. Psychol.*, 75, 85-125.

SLATER, E. 1953. *Psychotic and neurotic illnesses in twins.* London: H. M. Stationery Office (Med. Res. Counc., Spec. Rep. Ser., No. 278).

SLOAN, W. 1947. Mental deficiency as a symptom of personality disturbance. *Amer. J. ment. Defic.*, 52, 31-36.

———. 1951. Motor proficiency and intelligence. *Amer. J. ment. Defic.*, 55, 394-406.

———, and HARMAN, H. H. 1947. Constancy of IQ in mental defectives. *J. genet. Psychol.*, 71, 177-185.

SLOAN, W., and RASKIN, A. 1952. A study of certain concepts in high grade mental defectives. *Amer. J. ment. Defic.*, 56, 638-642.

SMILLIE, W. G., and SPENCER, C. R. 1926. Mental retardation in school children infested with hookworms. *J. educ. Psychol.*, 17, 314-321.

SMITH, A. J. 1950. Menstruation and industrial efficiency. *J. appl. Psychol.*, 34, 1-5.

SMITH, G. J. W., and KLEIN, G. S. 1953. Cognitive controls in serial behavior patterns. *J. Pers.*, 22, 188-213.

SMITH, H. A. 1949. The relationship between intelligence and the learning which results from the use of educational sound motion pictures. *J. educ. Res.*, 43, 241-249.

SMITH, H. C. 1949. Psychometric checks on hypotheses derived from Sheldon's work on physique and temperament. *J. Pers.*, 17, 310-320.

SMITH, S. 1939. Age and sex differences in children's opinions concerning sex differences. *J. genet. Psychol.*, 54, 17-25.

———. 1942. Language and non-verbal test performance of racial groups in Honolulu before and after a 14-year interval. *J. gen. Psychol.*, 26, 51-93.

SOLLENBERGER, R. T. 1940. Some relationships between the urinary excretion of male hormone by maturing boys and their expressed interests and attitudes. *J. Psychol.*, 9, 179-189.

SORENSON, H. 1933. *Adult abilities in extension classes.* Minneapolis: University of Minnesota Press.

SPEARMAN, C. E. 1927. *The abilities of man.* New York: Macmillan.

SPIER, L. 1929. Growth of Japanese children born in America and in Japan. *Wash. State Univ. Publ. In Anthrop.*, 3, No. 1., 1-301.

SPITZ, R. A. 1945-46. Hospitalism. In *The psychoanalytic study of the child.* New York: International Universities Press. Vols. I and II.

SPITZER, H. F., et al. 1947. *Iowa Every-Pupil Tests of Basic Skills: Manual.* Boston: Houghton.

SPRANGER, E. 1928. *Types of men* (trans. by P. J. W. Pigors). Halle: Niemeyer.

STALNAKER, E., and ROLLER, R. D., Jr. 1927. A study of one hundred non-promoted children. *J. educ. Res.*, 16, 265-270.

STALNAKER, J. M. 1948. Identification of the best Southern Negro high school seniors. *Sci. Mon.*, 67, 237-239.

STEAD, W. H. 1942. *The occupational research program of the United States Employment Service*. Chicago: Public Adm. Serv.

———, SHARTLE, C. L., OTIS, J. L., et al. 1940. *Occupational counseling techniques*. New York: American Book.

STEINBERG, A. 1952. The relation of vocational preference to emotional adjustment. *Educ. psychol. Measmt.*, 12, 96-104.

STEPHENSON, W. 1953. *The study of behavior: Q-technique and its methodology*. Chicago: University of Chicago Press.

STERLING, E. B., and BELL, E. 1930. Hearing of school children as measured by the audiometer and as related to school work. *U. S. Pub. Hlth. Reports*, 45, 1117-1130.

STERN, W. 1900. *Über Psychologie der individuellen Differenzen (Ideen zur einer "Differenziellen Psychologie")*. Leipzig: Barth. P. 146.

STEVENS, S. S. 1951. Mathematics, measurement, and psychophysics. In S. S. Stevens (Ed.), *Handbook of experimental psychology*. New York: Wiley.

STEWART, Naomi. 1947. AGCT scores of Army personnel grouped by occupation. *Occupations*, 26, 5-41.

STOCKARD, C. R., ANDERSON, O. D., and JAMES, W. T. 1941. *Genetic and endocrine basis for differences in form and behavior*. Philadelphia: Wistar Institute Press.

STOLZ, H. R., and STOLZ, L. M. 1944. Adolescent problems related to somatic variations. *Yearb. nat. Soc. Stud. Educ.*, 43 (1).

STONE, C. P., and BARKER, R. G. 1939. The attitudes and interests of pre-menarcheal and postmenarcheal girls. *J. genet. Psychol.*, 54, 27-71.

STORDAHL, K. E. 1954. Permanence of Strong Vocational Interest scores. *J. appl. Psychol.*, 38, 423-427.

STRAYER, L. C. 1930. Language and growth: the relative efficacy of early and deferred vocabulary training, studied by the method of co-twin control. *Genet. Psychol. Monogr.*, 8, 209-319.

STRONG, E. K., Jr. 1943. *Vocational interests of men and women*. Stanford: Stanford University Press.

———. 1951a. Interest scores while in college of occupations engaged in 20 years later. *Educ. psychol. Measmt.*, 11, 335-348.

———. 1951b. Permanence of interest scores over 22 years. *J. appl. Psychol.*, 35, 89-91.

———. 1952a. Nineteen-year follow-up of engineer interests. *J. appl., Psychol.*, 36, 65-74.

———. 1952b. Twenty-year follow-up of medical interests. In L. L. Thurstone (Ed.), *Applications of psychology*. New York: Harper. Pp. 111-130.

SUPER, D. E. 1940. The ACE Psychological Examination and special abilities. *J. Psychol.*, 9, 221-226.

———. 1942. *The dynamics of vocational adjustment*. New York: Harper.

———. 1949. *Appraising vocational fitness*. New York: Harper.

SUPER, D. E., and ROPER, S. 1941. An objective technique for testing vocational interests. *J. appl. Psychol.*, 25, 487-498.

SWARD, K. 1945. Age and mental ability in superior men. *Amer. J. Psychol.*, 58, 443-479.

SWEENEY, E. J. 1953. *Sex differences in problem solving.* Stanford: Department of Psychology, Stanford Univ. Tech. Report 1, Dec. 1.

SWINEFORD, F. 1949. General, verbal, and spatial bi-factors after three years. *J. educ. Psychol.*, 40, 353-360.

SYMONDS, P. M. 1931. *Diagnosing personality and conduct.* Century Psychology Series. New York: Appleton-Century-Crofts.

SZAFRAN, J. 1951. Changes with age and with exclusion of vision in performance at an aiming task. *Quart. J. exp. Psychol.*, 3, 111-118.

TANSER, H. A. 1939. *The settlement of Negroes in Kent County, Ontario.* Chatham, Ontario: Shephard Publ. Co.

TAYLOR, K. von F. 1942. The reliability and permanence of vocational interests. *J. exp. Educ.*, 11, 81-87.

——, and CARTER, H. D. 1942. Retest consistency of vocational interest patterns of high school girls. *J. consult. Psychol.*, 6, 95-101.

TERMAN, L. M. 1954. Scientists and nonscientists in a group of 800 gifted men. *Psychol. Monogr.*, 68, No. 7.

——, et al. 1925. *Genetic studies of genius:* Vol. I., *Mental and physical traits of a thousand gifted children.* Stanford: Stanford University Press.

TERMAN, L. M., and MERRILL, M. A. 1937. *Measuring intelligence.* Boston, New York: Houghton.

TERMAN, L. M., and MILES, C. C. 1936. *Sex and personality: studies in masculinity and femininity.* New York: McGraw.

TERMAN, L. M., and ODEN, M. 1940. The significance of deviates: II. Status of the California gifted group at the end of sixteen years. *Yearb. nat. Soc. Educ.*, 39 (I), 67-74.

——. 1940. The significance of deviates: III. Correlates of adult achievement in the California gifted group. *Yearb. nat. Soc. Stud. Educ.*, 39 (I), 74-89.

——. 1947. *The gifted child grows up.* Stanford: Stanford University Press.

TERMAN, L. M., and TYLER, L. E. 1954. Psychological sex differences. In L. Carmichael (Ed.), *Manual of child psychology* (2nd Ed.). New York: Wiley.

TERRY, R. A. 1953. Autonomic balance and temperament. *J. comp. physiol. Psychol.*, 46, 454-460.

THEIS, S. V. 1924. *How foster children turn out.* New York, State Charities Aid Association.

THOMPSON, C. W. 1951. Decline in limit of performance among adult morons. *Amer. J. Psychol.*, 64, 203-215.

THOMPSON, L. 1951. Perception patterns in three Indian tribes. *Psychiatry*, 14, 255-263.

THOMSON, G. 1946. The trend of national intelligence. *Eugen. Rev.*, 38, 9-18.

THORNDIKE, E. L., BREGMAN, E. O., LORGE, I., METCALF, Z. F., ROBINSON, E. E., and WOODYARD, E. 1934. *Prediction of vocational success.* New York, Commonwealth Fund.

THORNDIKE, E. L., BREGMAN, E. O., TILTON, J. W., and WOODYARD, E. 1928. *Adult learning*. New York: Macmillan.

THORNDIKE, R. L. 1948a. An evaluation of the adult intellectual status of Terman's gifted children. *J. genet. Psychol.*, **72**, 17-27.

———. 1948b. Growth of intelligence during adolescence. *J. genet. Psychol.*, **72**, 11-15.

———, and GALLUP, G. H. 1944. Verbal intelligence of the American adult. *J. gen. Psychol.*, **30**, 75-85.

THOULESS, R. H. 1932. Individual differences in phenomenal regression. *Brit. J. Psychol.*, **22**, 216-241.

———. 1933. A racial difference in perception. *J. soc. Psychol.*, **4**, 330-339.

———. 1951. Individual differences in perception and their significance in psychology. In *Essays in psychology dedicated to David Katz*. Uppsala: Almquist and Wiksells.

THURSTONE, L. L. 1938. *Primary mental abilities*. Psychometr. Monogr. No. 1. Chicago: University Chicago Press.

———. 1944a. *A factorial study of perception*. Chicago: University of Chicago Press.

———. 1944b. Second-order factors. *Psychometrika*, **9**, 71-100.

———. 1946. Theories of intelligence. *Sci. Mon.*, **62**, Sup. 5, 101-112.

———. 1949. *Mechanical aptitude: III. Analysis of group tests*. University of Chicago Psychometric Laboratory Report, No. 55.

———. 1950a. *Creative talent*. University of Chicago, Psychometric Laboratory Reports, No. 61.

———. 1950b. *Thurstone Temperament Schedule*. Chicago: Science Research Associates.

———. 1951a. *An analysis of mechanical aptitude*. Chicago: University of Chicago Psychometric Laboratory Reports, No. 62.

———. 1951b. The dimensions of temperament. *Psychometrika*, **16**, 11-20.

———. 1951c. Experimental tests of temperament. In *Essays in psychology dedicated to David Katz*. Uppsala: Almquist and Wiksells. Pp. 248-262.

———. 1953. *The development of objective measures of temperament*. Chapel Hill, N. C.: Psychometric Laboratory Report No. 1.

———, and THURSTONE, T. G. 1941. *Factorial studies of intelligence*. Psychometr. Monogr. No. 2. Chicago: University of Chicago Press.

THURSTONE, T. G. 1941. Primary mental abilities of children. *Educ. Psychol. Measmt.*, **1**, 105-116.

TILTON, J. W. 1936. The effect of forgetting upon individual differences. *Psychol. Monogr.*, **47**, No. 2, 173-185.

———. 1949. Intelligence test scores as indicative of ability to learn. *Educ. Psychol. Measmt.*, **9**, 291-296.

———. 1953. The intercorrelations between measures of school learning. *J. Psychol.*, **35**, 169-179.

TIZARD, J., O'CONNOR, N., and CRAWFORD, J. M. 1950. The abilities of adult high-grade male defectives. *J. ment. Sci.*, **96**, 889-907.

TOMLINSON, H. 1944. Differences between preschool Negro children and their older siblings on the Stanford-Binet scales. *J. Negro Educ.*, **13**, 474-479.

Toops, H. A. 1926. Returns from follow-up letters to questionnaires. *J. appl. Psychol.*, **10**, 92-101.

Travers, R. M. W. 1949. Significant research on the prediction of academic success. In W. T. Donahue, C. H. Coombs, and R. M. W. Travers, *The measurement of student adjustment and achievement*. Ann Arbor: University of Michigan Press. Pp. 147-190.

Travis, L. E., and Gottlober, A. 1936. Do brain waves have individuality? *Science*, **84**, 532-533.

———. 1937. How consistent are an individual's brain potentials from day to day? *Science*, **85**, 223-224.

Traxler, A. E., and McCall, W. C. 1941. Some data on the Kuder Preference Record. *Educ. psychol. Measmt.*, **1**, 253-268.

Triggs, F. O. 1944a. A further comparison of interest measurement by the Kuder Preference Record and the Strong Vocational Interest Blank for Men. *J. educ. Res.*, **37**, 538-544.

———. 1944b. A further comparison of interest measurement by the Kuder Preference Record and the Strong Vocational Interest Blank for Women. *J. educ. Res.*, **38**, 193-200.

Trinkaus, W. K. 1954. The permanence of vocational interests of college freshmen. *Educ. Psychol. Measmt.*, **14**, 641-646.

Trout, D. M. 1949. Academic achievement in relation to subsequent success in life. In W. T. Donahue, C. H. Coombs, and R. M. W. Travers, *The measurement of student adjustment and achievement*. Ann Arbor: University of Michigan Press. Pp. 201-217.

Tryon, R. C. 1942. Individual differences. In F. A. Moss (Ed.), *Comparative psychology* (Rev. Ed.). New York: Prentice-Hall. Ch. 13.

Tuddenham, R. D. 1948. Soldier intelligence in World Wars I and II. *Amer. Psychologist*, **3**, 54-56.

———. 1951. Studies in reputation: III. Correlates of popularity among elementary school children. *J. educ. Psychol.*, **42**, 257-276.

———. 1952. Studies in reputation: I. Sex and grade differences in school children's evaluations of their peers. *Psychol. Monogr.*, **66**, No. 1.

Tyler, L. E. 1941. The measured interests of adolescent girls. *J. educ. Psychol.*, **32**, 561-572.

———. 1953. Changes in children's scores on Primary Mental Abilities Tests over a three-year period. *Amer. Psychologist*, **8**, 448-449.

———. 1955. The development of "vocational interests": I. The organization of likes and dislikes in ten-year-old children. *J. genet. Psychol.*, **86**, 33-44.

Tyler, R. W. 1936. The relation between recall and the higher mental processes. In C. H. Judd (Ed.), *Education as cultivation of the higher mental processes*. New York: Macmillan.

Tylor, E. B. 1881. *Anthropology*. New York: D. Appleton and Co.

UNESCO. 1952. *What is Race?*

Vernon, M. D. 1952. *A further study of visual perception*. Cambridge: Cambridge University Press.

Vernon, P. E. 1938. *The assessment of psychological qualities by verbal methods*. London: H. M. S. O.

Vernon, P. E. 1948. Changes in abilities from 14 to 20 years. *Advanc. Sci.*, **5**, 138.

——. 1950. *The structure of human abilities.* London: Methuen.

——. 1951. Recent investigations of intelligence and its measurement. *Eugen. Rev.*, **43**, 125-137.

——. 1953. *Personality tests and assessments.* London: Methuen.

——, and Parry, J. B. 1949. *Personnel selection in the British forces.* London: University of London Press.

Vincent, D. F. 1952. The linear relationship between age and score of adults in intelligence tests. *Occup. Psychol., Lond.*, **26**, 243-249.

Walter, L. M., and Marzolf, S. S. 1951. The relation of sex, age, and school achievement to levels of aspiration. *J. educ. Psychol.*, **42**, 285-292.

Walter, W. G. 1953. *The living brain.* New York: Norton.

Warner, W. L., Havighurst, R. J., and Loeb, M. B. 1944. *Who shall be educated?* New York: Harper.

Warner, W. L., and Lunt, P. S. 1941. *The social life of the modern community.* New Haven: Yale University Press.

Warner, W. L., Meeker, M., and Eells, K. 1949. *Social class in America.* Chicago: Science Research Associates.

Webb, E. 1915. Character and intelligence. *Brit. J. Psychol., Monogr. Suppl.*, **1**, 3.

Webster, J. C., Himes, H. W., and Lichtenstein, M. 1950. San Diego County Fair Hearing Survey. *J. Acoust. Soc. Amer.*, **22**, 473-483.

Wechsler, D. 1941. *The measurement of adult intelligence.* Baltimore: Williams and Wilkins.

——. 1950a. Intellectual development and psychological maturity. *Child Developm.*, **21**, 45-50.

——. 1950b. *The measurement of adult intelligence.* Baltimore: Williams and Wilkins.

——. 1952. *The range of human capacities.* Baltimore: Williams and Wilkins.

Weisenburg, T., Roe, A., and McBride, K. E. 1936. *Adult intelligence.* New York: Commonwealth Fund.

Welch, M. K. 1949. The ranking of occupations on the basis of social status. *Occupations*, **27**, 237-241.

Welford, A. T. 1951. *Skill and age.* London: Oxford University Press.

Wellman, B. L. 1940. Iowa studies on the effects of schooling. *Yearb. nat. Soc. Stud. Educ.*, **39** (II), 377-399.

——, Case, I. M., Mengert, I. G., and Bradbury, E. 1931. Speech sounds of young children. *Univ. Iowa Stud. Child. Welf.*, **5**, No. 2.

——, and Pegram, E. L. 1944. Binet IQ changes of orphanage pre-school children. *J. genet. Psychol.*, **65**, 239-263.

Wells, F. L., Williams, R., and Fowler, P. 1938. One hundred superior men. *J. appl. Psychol.*, **22**, 367-384.

Wembridge, E. R. 1931. *Life among the lowbrows.* New York: Houghton.

Wenger, M. A. 1941. The measurement of individual differences in autonomic balance. *Psychosom. Med.*, **3**, 427-434.

——. 1942. The stability of measurement of autonomic balance. *Psychosom. Med.*, **4**, 94-95.

WENGER, M. A. 1947. Preliminary study of the significance of measures of autonomic balance. *Psychosom. Med.*, **9**, 301-309.

———. 1948. Studies of autonomic balance in Army Air Forces personnel. *Comp. Psychol. Monogr.*, **19** (101), 1-111.

WERTHEIMER, F. I., and HESKETH, F. E. 1926. The significance of the physical constitution in mental disease. *Medicine*, **5**, 375-463.

WEST, J. 1945. *Plainville, U. S. A.* New York: Columbia University Press.

WESTENBERGER, E. J. 1927. A study of the influence of physical defects upon intelligence and achievement. *Cath. Univ. of Amer. Educ. Res. Bull.*, **2**, No. 9, 1-53.

WESTON, H. C. 1948. The effect of age and illumination upon visual performance with close sights. *Brit. J. Ophthal.*, 645-653.

WHEELER, L. R. 1942. A comparative study of the intelligence of East Tennessee mountain children. *J. educ. Psychol.*, **33**, 321-334.

WHITNEY, E. A., and CARON, R. E. 1947. A brief analysis of recent statistics on mental deficiency. *Amer. J. ment. Defic.*, **51**, 713-720.

WILLIAMS, H. D. 1933. A survey of predelinquent children in ten middle western cities. *J. juv. Res.*, **17**, 163-174.

WILLIAMS, R. J. 1946. *The human frontier.* New York: Harcourt.

———. 1951. Introduction, general discussion and tentative conclusions. *Univ. of Texas Biochemical Inst. Stud.* IV, May 1, pp. 7-21.

———. 1953. *Free and unequal.* Austin: University of Texas Press.

WILSON, F. T. 1953. Some special ability test scores of gifted children. *J. genet. Psychol.*, **82**, 59-68.

WISSLER, C. 1901. The correlation of mental and physical traits. *Psychol. Monogr.*, **3**, No. 6.

WITKIN, H. A., LEWIS, H. B., HERTZMAN, M., MACHOVER, K., MEISSNER, P. B., and WAPNER, S. 1954. *Personality through perception.* New York: Harper.

WITTMAN, P., SHELDON, W. H., and KATZ, C. J. 1948. A study of the relationship between constitutional variations and fundamental psychotic behavior reactions. *J. nerv. ment. Dis.*, **108**, 470-476.

WITTY, P. A. 1930. Study of one hundred gifted children. *Univ. Kans. Bull. Educ.*

———. 1940. A genetic study of fifty gifted children. *Yearb. nat. Soc. Stud. Educ.*, **39** (II), 401-408.

———, and LEHMAN, H. C. 1929. Nervous instability and genius: poetry and fiction. *J. abnorm. soc. Psychol.*, **24**, 77-90.

———. 1930. Nervous instability and genius: some conflicting opinions. *J. abnorm. soc. Psychol.*, **24**, 486-497.

WOLFF, C. 1947. The form and dermatoglyphics of the hands of 115 difficult and high-grade boys. *Brit. J. med. Psychol.*, **21**, 38-49.

WOODROW, H. 1938a. The effect of practice on groups of different initial ability. *J. educ. Psychol.*, **29**, 268-278.

———. 1938b. The effect of practice on test intercorrelations. *J. educ. Psychol.*, **29**, 561-572.

———. 1938c. The relation between abilities and improvement with practice. *J. educ. Psychol.*, **29**, 215-230.

WOODROW, H. 1939. Factors in improvement with practice. *J. Psychol.*, **7**, 55-70.

———. 1939a. The application of factor analysis to problems of practice. *J. gen. Psychol.*, **21**, 457-460.

———. 1939b. The relation of verbal ability to improvement with practice in verbal tests. *J. educ. Psychol.*, **30**, 179-186.

———. 1940. Interrelations of measures of learning. *J. Psychol.*, **10**, 49-73.

———. 1946. The ability to learn. *Psychol. Rev.*, **53**, 147-158.

WOODWORTH, R. S. 1910. Racial differences in mental traits. *Science, N. S.*, **31**, 171-186.

———. 1938. *Experimental psychology.* New York: Holt. P. 889.

———. 1941. *Heredity and environment.* New York: Social Science Research Council Bulletin 47.

WOOLLEY, H. T. 1910. A review of the recent literature on the psychology of sex. *Psychol. Bull.*, **7**, 335-342.

WORBOIS, G. M. 1951. Predicting long-range performance of substation operators. *J. appl. Psychol.*, **35**, 15-19.

WRENN, C. G. 1949. Potential research talent in the sciences based on intelligence quotients of Ph.D.'s. *Educ. Rec.*, **30**, 5-22.

YANNET, H., and LIEBERMAN, R. 1944. The Rh factor in the etiology of mental deficiency. *Amer. J. ment. Defic.*, **49**, 133-137.

YELA, M. 1949. Application of the concept of simple structure to Alexander's data. *Psychometrika*, **14**, 121-135.

YERKES, R. M. (Ed.). 1921. *Psychological examining in the U. S. Army.* Memoirs of National Academy of Science, Vol. 15.

YOUNG, F. A. 1948. The projection of after-images and Emmert's Law. *J. gen. Psychol.*, **39**, 161-166.

ZIMMERMAN, F. T., and BURGEMEISTER, B. B. 1951. Permanency of glutamic acid treatment. A.M.A. *Arch. Neurol. Psychiat., Chicago*, **65**, 291-298.

———, and PUTNAM, T. J. 1948. The ceiling effect of glutamic acid upon intelligence in children and in adolescents. *Amer. J. Psychiat.*, **104**, 593-599.

Index